THE NAVAL INSTITUTE GUIDE TO THE Soviet Navy

FIFTH EDITION

THE NAVAL INSTITUTE GUIDE TO THE Soviet Navy

Norman Polmar

Naval Institute Press
Annapolis, Maryland

Library of Congress Cataloging-in-Publication Data

Polmar, Norman.
    The Naval Institute guide to the Soviet Navy / Norman Polmar.—
5th ed.
      p. cm.
    Rev. ed. of: Guide to the Soviet Navy.
    Includes bibliographical references and indexes.
    ISBN 0-87021-241-9
    1. Soviet Union. Voenno-Morskoĭ Flot. I. Polmar, Norman. Guide
to the Soviet Navy. II. United States Naval Institute. III. Title.
IV. Title: Guide to the Soviet Navy.
VA573.P598 1991
359′.00947—dc20
                                                 90-41568
                                                 CIP

9 8 7 6 5 4 3 2
First printing

For Morton and Beth Frome
with appreciation and affection

Eternal peace lasts only until the next war.

—Old Russian Proverb

Contents

Preface

I cannot forecast to you the action of Russia. It is a riddle wrapped in a mystery inside an enigma; but perhaps there is a key. That key is Russian national interest.

British Prime Minister Winston Churchill gave this apt description of the Russian psyche on 1 October 1939, a month after World War II had erupted in Europe.[1] A half century later—despite the *glasnost,* or "openness," of General Secretary and Executive President Mikhail Gorbachev—there are still many unknowns about the Soviet Union, especially its military institutions. Moreover, as this fifth edition of the *Guide to the Soviet Navy* went to press the political and economic changes occurring in the Soviet Union and Eastern Bloc nations make attempts to understand current Soviet military and naval plans and procurement programs a virtual impossibility.

The rapidly changing Soviet political, economic, and military scene of the past few years accelerated into a revolution during August 1991. It was a "revolution" by reason of ending, with unquestioned decisiveness, the right-wing, conservative movement in the Soviet Union that was based on the power and threat of the military, police (MVD), and security apparatus (KGB).

Beginning in the late 1980s there were major reductions in the strength of the Soviet armed forces and cutbacks in weapons procurement. This situation will certainly be accelerated by the failure of the three-day coup attempt. Before August 1991 the Soviet space and strategic missile programs and naval forces were continuing to be funded at high levels, especially relative to the cutbacks in the other military services. How much this situation will change in the near future was unknown when this edition went to press. (Some of the immediate effects of the abortive coup are discussed, albeit briefly, in the Addenda.)

Significantly, in his speech to the Russian Republic's assembly on the day of his return to Moscow, 21 August, President Mikhail Gorbachev praised the Navy for its loyalty to the government. And, in Leningrad, the senior naval commander gave unqualified support to the city government in resisting the coup.

The amount of largess that this loyalty will give to the Navy is unknown. But the loyalty of the Navy's leadership, the size and complexity of the shipbuilding industry, the very long lead time required to construct warships, and the long borders and ocean interests of the Soviet Union—and many of the republics—will all be factors in future decision making by Gorbachev and his successors.

Several facts, however, are evident: First, at least into 1991, the rate of production of Soviet submarines and warships continued unabated. Indeed, in 1990 the Soviets launched ten submarines—six nuclear and four diesel-electric—more than in any year during the 1980s.[2] (In 1989 Soviet yards launched nine submarines—five nuclear-propelled and four diesel-electric units. While this was only one submarine more than was launched in 1988, the 1989 launchings had a surface displacement of some 65,000 tons, a greater tonnage in submarines than any year since 1980.) By the end of 1991, production of cruisers had ceased, although other warship construction was ongoing, with new ship classes being introduced.

A high level of effort is continuing in the impressive aircraft carrier, destroyer, frigate, and small combatant construction programs (the last including surface effect ship, air cushion vehicle, and hydrofoil projects). Another area of naval growth has been the transfer of large numbers of tactical strike and fighter aircraft from the Air Forces to the Navy.

Thus, while production of weapons and platforms for the Ground Forces, Air Forces, and even Air Defense Forces has declined precipitously, the resources allocated to the Navy, strategic missiles, and space activities appear to continue without reduction.

Second, there is a massive effort underway to dispose of older surface combatants and submarines through scrapping; for example, all of the SVERDLOV-class cruisers are gone as well as many older destroyers, and scores of submarines (some of which had been laid up in reserve) were towed away for scrap in 1989 and 1990. These disposals are saving maintenance and support costs, and are freeing up personnel for release from active service or for manning new construction ships. Also, by scrapping many ships and submarines overseas, the Soviets are able to earn much needed hard currency.

Third, at-sea naval operations have been reduced, again saving funds. This cutback, however, will have the effect of reducing training periods, a critical factor for the Soviet Navy, whose enlisted ranks are entirely composed of conscripts.

Despite the advent of aircraft carriers and large surface combatants in the Soviet Navy, the submarine remains the capital ship of that fleet. The U.S. Director of Naval Intelligence, Rear Admiral Thomas A. Brooks, has described the expected Soviet submarine force of the mid-1990s in this manner:

The picture we are left with is one of a substantially shrunken Soviet submarine force. The implication in many people's minds is that Soviet submarine capability will shrink in direct proportion. This is greatly misleading; I would suggest perhaps even dangerously misleading. The Soviets are, indeed, reducing the size of their submarine force. . . . they continue a submarine construction and modernization program which will leave the Soviet submarine force of the mid-1990s, albeit a much smaller force, a significantly more capable force.[3]

As predicted in the previous edition of *Guide to the Soviet Navy*, the continued top-level support of naval and merchant fleets in the Soviet Union could be expected to continue, even if the current Kremlin leadership did not fully understand the significance of maritime power as did their predecessors—Brezhnev, Khrushchev, and Stalin. But the evidence is that Mikhail Gorbachev and his colleagues in the Soviet leadership have learned this or at least are not willing to risk destroying the fleet that has been created during the past three decades.

I am again in debt to many individuals for their assistance in the research and writing of this book, especially: A.D. Baker III, the U.S. editor of *Combat Fleets of the World;* Captain Patrick Bryan, Royal Navy, and Captain Martin MacPhearson, Royal Navy, of the Ministry of Defence; Jeffrey Bray, naval analyst; Robert Bockman and Kenneth Carter of Public Affairs, Office of the Secretary of Defense; Rear Admiral Thomas A. Brooks, USN, former U.S. Director of Naval Intelligence, and his principal deputy, Captain William Manthorpe, USN (Ret.); Dr. Thomas Cochran and Dr. Stan Norris of the Natural Resources Defense Council; Lieutenant Joseph DiRenzo III, USCG; Kenneth Ebata, leading Japanese military journalist; Russell Egnor and Patricia Toombs of the U.S. Navy Office of Information; John Englehardt, naval engineer and submarine analyst; Rear Admiral Yohei Kondoh, Japanese Maritime Self-Defense Force (Ret.); Edward L. Korb, editor of *The World's Missile Systems* (General Dynamics/Pomona); Jean Labayle Couhat, formerly editor of *Flottes de Combat,* and his successor, Bernard Prézelin; Rear Admiral Kalus-Dieter Laudien, Federal German Navy, Commander, NATO Standing Naval Force Atlantic; Lieutenant Commander Jurrien Noot, Royal Netherlands Navy, on the staff of the NATO Atlantic Command; K.J. Moore, submarine analyst; Raymond Robinson, former intelligence analyst and student of Soviet naval development; Rear Admiral Steven Tichelman, Royal Netherlands Navy, defense attaché in Washington; Dr. Milan Vego, naval analyst and author; Dr. Don Walsh, oceanography expert; Jack Wamsley, Soviet analyst; Captain Gordon A.S.C. Wilson, Royal Navy, head of Defence Studies (Royal Navy); Commander Hans Joachim Witthauer and Lieutenant Commander Hans Joachim du Roi, Federal German Navy, of the staff of NATO Standing Naval Force Atlantic and the FGN intelligence staff, respectively; and Stan Zimmerman, editor of *Navy News.*

Several Soviet naval officers have also been most helpful in providing material for this edition, specifically Vice Admiral I.V. Kasatonov, First Deputy Commander in Chief of the Northern Fleet; and Captains 1st Rank N.N. Ilyashenko and V.I. Akulov, and Captain 2nd Rank V.V. Nikitin of the naval attaché office, Washington, D.C.

Khoji Ishiwata, formerly editor of *Ships of the World,* and Leo Van Ginderen have been of invaluable help in providing illustrations for this volume, as has the Japanese Maritime Self-Defense Force, the Royal Navy, the Navy of the Federal Republic of Germany, and the U.S. Navy. I have again benefited from the drawings and keen observations of Michael J. Dodgson, who did several of the major ship drawings in this edition, and William Clipson, who executed the submarine drawings and maps in this volume.

The aircraft drawings were provided through the courtesy of Messrs. William Green and Gordon Swanborough of Pilot Press, Ltd.

Several members of the staff of the U.S. Naval Institute were particularly helpful in making this edition a reality: Patty Maddocks, Linda Cullen, and Mary Beth Straight of the photographic library; Deborah Farrell, the book's production editor; Susan Artigiani of the marketing department staff; and, especially, Fred Rainbow, editor in chief of the Naval Institute *Proceedings.* Mr. Rainbow and his staff and Dr. Scott C. Truver of Techmatics Inc., have continued to provide essential support and encouragement to this project.

This book is updated and published at three-year intervals. The compilation of information and photographs for the next edition begins almost immediately. Material for the next edition should be sent to the undersigned in care of the U.S. Naval Institute, Annapolis, Maryland 21402.

NORMAN POLMAR

1. Sir Winston Churchill, *The Gathering Storm* (Boston: Houghton Mifflin, 1948), p. 449.
2. Those ten submarines were: 1 Delta IV strategic missile submarine (SSBN), 2 Oscar II cruise missile submarines (SSGN), 1 Akula attack submarine (SSN), 1 Sierra attack submarine (SSN), 1 Victor III attack submarine (SSN), and 4 Kilo-class attack submarines (SS), one for foreign transfer.
3. Rear Adm. Thomas A. Brooks, USN, Director of Naval Intelligence, presentation at U.S. Naval Institute seminar "ASW: The Navy's Top Warfighting Priority?" Arlington, Va., 27 Feb. 1990.

THE NAVAL INSTITUTE GUIDE TO THE Soviet Navy

CHAPTER 1

State of the Fleet

The aircraft carrier ADMIRAL KUZNETSOV (ex-TBILISI) is the largest warship yet completed in the Soviet Union and the largest built by any nation since World War II except for U.S. aircraft carriers. She is first of a series of large ships that will operate conventional, high-performance aircraft. The ADMIRAL KUZNETSOV is shown here in the Black Sea during her November 1989 sea trials and initial flight operations. (Sovfoto)

The Soviet Navy continues to increase in quality while declining slightly in absolute numbers of warships. These changes in the Navy occur as the Soviet Union undergoes the most drastic political and economic changes since the Revolution and Civil War some 70 years ago. In this environment, rapid changes are occurring in all of the Soviet armed forces.

Related to these changes, General Secretary Mikhail Gorbachev, who took office in March 1985, has undertaken an intensive campaign to achieve nuclear and conventional arms reductions by both the Soviet Union and United States.[1] At the 27th Communist Party conference in March 1986, Gorbachev announced a major shift in Soviet military posture to a defensive orientation with forces to be limited to "reasonable sufficiency." The term "reasonable sufficiency" was defined in *Pravda*, the daily newspaper of the Communist Party, as "a structure of a state's armed forces which is enough to repulse any possible aggression, but which is inadequate for the conduct of offensive actions." Speeches, articles, and other pronouncements by Soviet officials followed, supporting Gorbachev's views, with some proposing total, worldwide nuclear disarmament by the year 2000.

This campaign for disarmament is part of Secretary Gorbachev's *perestroika*, or "restructuring," of the Soviet Union. Its primary purpose is to revitalize the stagnated Soviet economy and raise the level of Soviet technology to enable the nation to compete in the world marketplace.

As a part of *perestroika*, Secretary Gorbachev announced in January 1989 that over the next two years the Soviet Union would reduce defense spending by 14.2 percent, with a reduction of 19.5 percent in weapons production. By the end of 1990 the strength of the Soviet armed forces was reduced by approximately 1 million men and women from the more than 5 million on active service when Mr. Gorbachev took office in 1985; the Navy's share of the cut was reported at 14,000 men. Subsequently, a reduction to about 3 million men has been announced.

1. Gorbachev holds the positions of General Secretary of the Politburo of the Central Committee of the Communist Party, and Chairman of the Presidium of the Supreme Soviet (often called the state President). It is the former position by which he is generally referred to by Soviet military officers. In 1990 he became the "executive president" of the Soviet Union.

Further, in a recent statement, General of the Army M.A. Moiseyev, the Chief of the Soviet General Staff, said that the Navy and "rear services" or logistics organization are specifically exempted from planned reductions.

When this edition of *Guide to the Soviet Navy* went to press the naval arms reductions undertaken by the Soviet Union included more than 50 surface ships and submarines stricken from the Pacific Fleet alone in the period 1984–1988. But the ships stricken were older units—Romeo submarines, and SKORYY, Kotlin, and Kanin destroyers; the at-sea time of naval ships and flight time of naval aircraft were also reduced. During the same time period the Pacific Fleet received modern Akula attack submarines, another KIEV-class aircraft carrier, and SOVREMENNYY and UDALOY destroyers. According to the Director of U.S. Naval Intelligence, "While it is true the Soviet Navy is undergoing a major reduction in the size of its fleet, the real situation is not a reduction in capability but, as Soviet Navy Deputy Commander in Chief Admiral [I.M.] Kapitanets described it, a reduction in quantity balanced by an improvement in quality."[2]

Soviet naval shipbuilding programs continue unabated at approximately the same rates as the 1980s. A third large aircraft carrier, for example, was laid down in the fall of 1988. The construction of several classes of advanced submarines, cruisers, and destroyers continues, while ballistic missile submarines retired under strategic arms agreements are being converted to other roles. At the same time, the Navy continues the development of several advanced naval weapons, sensors, and platforms: Wing-In-Ground (WIG) effect vehicles, Air Cushion Vehicles (ACV), Surface Effect Ships (SES), Surveillance Towed-Array Sonar System (SURTASS), and improved reconnaissance satellites.

Some Western observers have attempted to compare the Gorbachev reductions with those instigated by Georgi Malenkov and Nikita Khrushchev after the death of the Soviet dictator Josef Stalin in March 1953. Within days of Stalin's death, stop-work orders went out to shipyards to cancel the construction of large numbers of cruisers, destroyers, and submarines. During the next few years—from 1955 to 1960—the Soviet armed forces were reduced from 5.75 million men to 3.7 million.[3] But during that period of severe personnel cutbacks, there was an acceleration in the development of the Soviet space program, nuclear-propelled submarines, guided and ballistic missiles, and several other advanced weapons.

The cutbacks of the late 1950s were opposed by many traditionalist officers, and Khrushchev made major changes in the nation's military leadership. As part of those changes, in mid-1955, Admiral S.G. Gorshkov was ordered to Moscow as deputy head of the Navy, and in January 1956 he became Commander in Chief (CinC) of the Soviet Navy (a post that he held until December 1985—almost 30 years).

Similarly, within a few months of becoming General Secretary, Gorbachev initiated major changes in the leadership of the armed forces (as well as in the ruling politburo and the heads of the important commissions of the Central Committee of the Communist Party). Admiral of the Fleet V.N. Chernavin became CinC in December 1985.[4] Admiral Chernavin and the other Gorbachev appointees to the senior military ranks have fully accepted *perestroika* and the defense cutbacks:

What makes this acceptable to the Soviet military leadership is the realization that such an investment is necessary to improve and strengthen its national industrial and technological base if the Soviet Union is to compete with the West either economically or militarily

in the next century. In the short run *perestroika* is meant to improve the Soviet civil economy and industry but in the long run it will also improve Soviet defense capabilities.[5]

This acceptance is not, however, absolute in the opinion of some Western observers. Dr. Robert Conquest, distinguished political historian, has written: "By and large, both the army [armed forces] and KGB have been under effective party control for the past thirty years. Crisis conditions are likely to change that. . . . The army and KGB are both bodies with an *esprit de corps* and a *raison d'être* not as yet much affected by the way in which the party proper is losing its grip."[6]

The Communist Party may, in reality, be "losing its grip" as evidenced by the independent political movements in Poland and the Baltic Republics, the violence in the minority regions of Central Asia, and the lack of improvement in the traditional problems in the Soviet supply of food and consumer goods. The armed forces may also be in a state of internal turmoil because of Gorbachev's troop reductions and recriminations over the army's poor performance in Afghanistan and the failure of air defenses to stop a civilian light aircraft from flying from West Germany to land in Red Square.

The Soviet Navy's leadership has already described the fleet that it sees in the 21st century as it benefits from *perestroika*. In the official volume *The Navy: Its Role, Prospects for Development, and Employment*, the Navy argues for a high-technology force that will be able to carry out the future missions that are "vitally important to the state."[7] The book, with a foreword written by Admiral Gorshkov before his death in 1988, provides a picture of what the fleet could look like in the 21st century if the Navy is properly funded.

The submarine remains the capital ship of the Soviet Navy. This was reaffirmed by Admiral Chernavin (a nuclear submariner) when he told an American audience, "We considered both nuclear and diesel submarines, along with naval aircraft, to be the main forces of our fleet."[8] He noted that the main purpose of surface ships and of naval aircraft is "to support and cover the fleet's forces . . . first of all submarines on their routes and their emergence from base. . . ."

During the 1980s the four Soviet submarine construction yards annually launched up to nine submarines—five nuclear and four diesel-electric—demonstrating that submarine construction had not suffered under the massive defense cutbacks.[9] During 1990 the shipyards launched ten submarines: one Delta IV SSBN, two Oscar II SSGNs, two Akula SSNs, one Victor III SSN, and four Kilo diesel-electric submarines (some of which may have been intended for foreign transfer). A slowdown in building ballistic missile submarines could permit the construction of a larger number of SSN/SSGN designs. (Also, three of the submarine yards have a titanium construction capability.)

In *The Navy*, prospects for future submarine designs include operating depths of 6,560 feet (2,000 m), near-term speeds of 50 to 60 knots with eventual speeds of 100 knots; decreased submarine signatures; and improved sensors and weapons, the latter including 200- to 300-knot torpedoes with laser guidance.

---

2. Rear Adm. Thomas A. Brooks, USN, statement before the Armed Services Committee, House of Representatives, 7 March 1991, p. 18.

3. Another million men were cut from the armed forces between 1960 and 1965, reducing them to 2.6 million men. In addition, there were some 400,000 frontier (NKGB) and internal security (MVD) troops on active duty.

4. Chernavin had served as both Chief of the Main Naval Staff and First Deputy CinC of the Navy from December 1981 to December 1985; see *Guide to the Soviet Navy*, 4th ed., pp. 505–507.

5. Rear Adm. Thomas A. Brooks, USN, Statement before the Armed Services Committee, House of Representatives, 22 February 1989, p. 2.

6. Dr. Robert Conquest, "The Soviet Armed Forces and the KGB in the Forthcoming Crisis," in *Vulnerabilities of the Soviet Empire* (New York: International Security Council, June 1988), pp. 11–12; based on a paper presented at the ISC conference in Geneva, Switzerland, 13 September 1987.

7. Rear Adm. N.P. V'yunenko, Capt. 1st Rank B.N. Makeyev, and Capt. 1st Rank V.D. Skugarev, *The Navy: Its Role, Prospects for Development, and Employment* (Moscow: Military Publishing House, 1988).

8. "Chernavin Responds" [Interview], U.S. Naval Institute *Proceedings* (February 1989), p. 76.

9. There are in reality five submarine yards—Admiralty and Sudomekh in Leningrad, Severodvinsk in the north, Gor'kiy inland, and Komsomol'sk in the Far East; the first two are administratively joined as the United Admiralty Association (see chapter 31).

Aircraft carriers and surface combatants will also have a major role in the Soviet fleet of the 21st century, taking advantage of advanced weapons, sensors, and propulsion technology.

In the last decade of the 20th century the Soviet Navy already has leadership in several important areas of naval warfare, among them:

- mine warfare
- anti-ship missiles
- nuclear/chemical warfare
- short-range amphibious assault

In addition, there are major Soviet efforts under way in the areas of submarine warfare and ocean surveillance, and unquestioned leadership in these two vital areas of naval warfare could shift to the Soviets by the end of this century.

With respect to submarine warfare, the massive Soviet submarine effort is clearly "closing the gap" between U.S. and Soviet undersea warfare capabilities. Although two decades ago the quality of U.S. submarines was above comparison with Soviet undersea craft, the planned U.S. SEAWOLF (SSN 21) class is expected to be only five to ten years—*at most*—ahead of Soviet submarines in quieting and acoustic detection capabilities when completed in the mid-1990s. In most other criteria Soviet submarines *are already* superior to those of the U.S. Navy (see chapter 12). The U.S. Navy has been periodically surprised by Soviet submarine developments in such areas as anechoic coatings, speed and depth capabilities, torpedoes, and submarine-launched missiles. The ability of the U.S. Navy to retain leadership in the important areas of submarine quieting and acoustic detection will depend upon astute leadership within the Navy and support by the Congress.

In the area of ocean surveillance the U.S. Navy probably has a superior peacetime and crisis capability. This is due primarily to the seafloor Sound Surveillance System (SOSUS) and the new series of T-AGOS ships with SURTASS. Both SOSUS and SURTASS, however, are highly vulnerable during conflict. Other surveillance systems are more difficult to compare; the Soviets certainly lead in the important category of surveillance satellites and the use of passive intelligence collection ships (see chapter 6). Related to satellite surveillance, the Soviet Union has an operational Anti-Satellite (ASAT) system that can threaten U.S. satellite surveillance. The current U.S. ability to destroy Soviet reconnaissance satellites is severely limited.

(The U.S. Navy continues to have unquestioned leadership in several important areas of naval warfare, especially aircraft carrier operations, anti-air warfare, and probably anti-submarine warfare, although the last maybe rapidly dissipating in view of recent Soviet submarine developments.)

The course that Secretary General Gorbachev's *perestroika* is taking is still not clear, not even within the Soviet hierarchy. Major political, economic, and social changes are occurring within the Soviet Union and the heretofore Soviet-controlled Eastern Bloc countries. Those changes will affect the Soviet defense establishment, including the Navy. Regardless of the changes and restructuring that do occur, in the past 25 years the Navy and the other maritime activities of the Soviet Union have demonstrated their importance to the state. Undoubtedly, the USSR will continue to be a major maritime power, one that in crisis or war can challenge the use of the seas by the United States and its allies.

Regardless of the enhancements in the Soviet economy and technology-industrial base that are achieved through *perestroika* and Gorbachev's reforms, the Soviet Union's military forces will continue to suffer many of the problems now experienced. These include personnel training and quality control in the industrial sectors. The training problems are being exacerbated by the increasing Central Asian and Transcaucasian populations, which have limited technical backgrounds and problems with the Russian language. Quality control is a major concern throughout the Soviet society, although the situation in the military services appears to be better than in the rest of society. For example, the Chairman of the U.S. Joint Chiefs of Staff, Admiral William Crowe, after visiting a Soviet Victor III–class submarine, remarked that the "important parts of that submarine were of good quality."[10]

ORDER OF BATTLE

The estimated 1991 Soviet naval order of battle is shown in the accompanying Table 1-1. Such estimates are precarious because of the dramatic changes taking place in the Soviet Union. Certain ships listed in Soviet sources as being operational have not gotten under way in several years; other ships that are in fact operational can be expected to be laid up or scrapped in the near future. The submarines listed as older types (indicated by asterisks) are expected to be stricken by the mid-1990s.

Similarly, direct comparisons of the Soviet and U.S. fleets are difficult and have limited meaning because the ships differ in size,

10. Adm. William Crowe, USN, discussion with author, Washington, D.C., 28 July 1989. Adm. Crowe is a submariner.

Eight Soviet Whiskey-class submarines are shown being barged from a Soviet Baltic port to the breakers. Scores of Soviet submarines have been discarded in the past couple of years—all of 1950s' and early 1960s' vintage. Soviet shipyards, however, continue to produce large numbers of modern nuclear and conventionally propelled submarines. (Royal Danish Navy)

TABLE 1-1. SOVIET NAVAL ORDER OF BATTLE, 1991

	Soviet Navy	U.S. Navy + Coast Guard
Submarines—nuclear	(~210)	(124)
Ballistic missile submarines		34
SSBN Typhoon class	6	
SSBN Delta classes	42	
SSBN Yankee classes	14	
SSBN Hotel III*	1	
Attack submarines		87
SSGN types (land-attack)	2	
SSGN types (anti-ship)	22	
SSGN types (anti-ship)*	27	
SSN types	56	
SSN types*	35	
Special purpose submarines	4	3[a]
Submarines—non-nuclear	(~100)	(1)
Ballistic missile submarines		
SSB Golf II*	2	
Attack submarines		
SS types	70	
SS types*	few	
SSG Juliett class*	14	
Special purpose submarines	12	1[b]
Total submarines	(~310)	(125)
Aircraft carriers	5	13
Helicopter Carriers	2	13
Battleships	—	2
Missile Cruisers	31	45
Missile Destroyers	40	51[c]
ASW Frigates (Krivak class)	38	109 + 12
Light frigates	140	—
Frigates (Riga class)*	28	—
Missile corvettes	72	6 + 13[d]
ASW/patrol corvettes	90	—
Missile/patrol/torpedo craft	115	—
Minelayers	3	—
Fleet/ocean/coastal minesweepers	205	23
Amphibious ships	75	66[e]

[a] Two former SSBNs employed as transport submarines and the nuclear-propelled research submarine NR-1.
[b] Deep-diving research submarine DOLPHIN (AGSS 555).
[c] Includes all SPRUANCE (DD 963)-class ships, all of which have Harpoon anti-ship missiles and have or are being fitted with Tomahawk cruise missiles.
[d] The U.S. Navy ships are the PEGASUS (PHM 1)-class hydrofoil missile craft.
[e] Four ships are modified and employed as fleet/area flagships.

configuration, and purpose, and because the missions and tactics of the navies are different. Still, with these qualifications, comparisons can be instructive.

The Soviet data for frigates and smaller ships include those units operated by the KGB Maritime Border Troops. U.S. Coast Guard cutters of the HAMILTON (WHEC 715) and BEAR (WMEC 901) classes are included in the U.S. totals, as these ships are being fitted with first-line weapon and sensor systems; they are listed as frigates and corvettes, respectively. Smaller Coast Guard cutters are not included because, in comparison to the KGB ships, they have very limited combat capabilities. Not included in the Soviet totals are the KGB-operated armed icebreakers, ocean-going tugs, and minesweepers, which are generally comparable to U.S. Coast Guard cutters, except that the Soviet units are more heavily armed than their U.S. counterparts.

U.S. Navy tabulations include Naval Reserve Force (NRF) ships, which are operated by composite active-reserve crews.

The U.S. Navy's 13 LHA/LHD/LPH-type amphibious ships are listed as helicopter carriers. The two Soviet ships in this category are the MOSKVA and LENINGRAD, which are combination helicopter-guided missile cruisers.

The bow of the aircraft carrier ADMIRAL KUZNETSOV (formerly TBILISI and before that LEONID BREZHNEV). This photo clearly shows the ski ramp forward, with hatches open for three of the 12 vertical launchers for the SS-N-19 anti-ship missile. Also visible is the starboard jet blast defector, in the retracted position. A Ka-32 Helix-D search-and-rescue helicopter is in the foreground.

CHAPTER 2

Glossary of Terms

A quiet, high-speed Akula-class submarine broaches in Arctic waters. Her role is similar to that of U.S. attack submarines—anti-submarine and anti-surface operations, and cruise missile strikes. This 1988 photograph is believed to show the first unit built at the Severodvinsk shipyard. (Royal Norwegian Air Force)

These are mostly U.S. and NATO terms. In general, the use of U.S. ship designation symbols is avoided in this volume except for submarines because of the major differences in U.S. and Soviet ship designs and roles.

AA	Anti-Aircraft
AA-( )	NATO designation for Soviet Air-to-Air missile
AAW	Anti-Air Warfare
ACV	Air Cushion Vehicle
ACW	Anti-Carrier Warfare
AEW	Airborne Early Warning
AGI	Intelligence collection ship
AGSS	Auxiliary submarine (diesel)
AGSSN	Auxiliary submarine (nuclear)
AS-( )	NATO designation for Soviet Air-to-Surface missile
ASAT	Anti-Satellite
ASUW	Anti-Surface Warfare
ASW	Anti-Submarine Warfare
CBW	Chemical-Biological Warfare
CinC	Commander in Chief
displacement	in metric tons (2,200 lbs/1,000 kg)
DP	Dual-Purpose (for use against surface and air targets)
draft	maximum draft of hull at full load
DWT	Deadweight Tons (cargo-carrying capacity)

ECM	Electronic Countermeasures
ehp	equivalent horsepower
ELINT	Electronic Intelligence
EROSAT	ELINT Ocean Reconnaissance Satellite
EW	Electronic Warfare
FCS	Fire Control System
full load	ship displacement complete and ready for sea in all respects, including all fuels, munitions, and provisions as well as aircraft; given in metric tons (2,200 lbs/1,000 kg)
GFCS	Gunfire Control System
hp	horsepower
IGE	In-Ground Effect (hover)
kgst	kilograms static thrust
lbst	pounds static thrust
length	length overall
light	ship displacement without crew, fuel, munitions, or provisions, and without aircraft; given in metric tons (2,200 lbs/ 1,000 kg)
MAD	Magnetic Anomaly Detector
MaRV	Maneuvering Re-entry Vehicle
MIRV	Multiple Independently targeted Re-entry Vehicle
MOD	Ministry of Defense
MPA	Main Political Administration of the Army and Navy
NATO	North Atlantic Treaty Organization
n.mile	nautical mile (1.15 statute miles)
OGE	Out-of-Ground Effect (hover)
OTH	Over-The-Horizon (targeting)
RORSAT	Radar Ocean Reconnaissance Satellite
RV	Re-entry Vehicle
SA-N-( )	NATO designation for Soviet Surface-to-Air Naval missile

SES	Surface Effect Ship
shp	shaft horsepower
SIGINT	Signals Intelligence
SLBM	Submarine-Launched Ballistic Missile
SLCM	Submarine-Launched Cruise Missile
SNA	Soviet Naval Aviation
SOSS	Soviet Ocean Surveillance System (U.S. term)
SP	Self-Propelled (artillery)
SRF	Strategic Rocket Forces
SS	torpedo attack submarine (diesel)
SSB	ballistic missile submarine (diesel)
SSBN	ballistic missile submarine (nuclear)
SSC-N-( )	NATO designation for Soviet Surface-to-Surface Coastal defense Naval missile
SSG	guided (cruise) missile submarine (diesel)
SSGN	guided (cruise) missile submarine (nuclear)
SSN	torpedo attack submarine (nuclear)
SS-N-( )	NATO designation for Soviet Surface-to-Surface Naval missile
SSQ	communications submarine (diesel)
SSQN	communications submarine (nuclear)
SSR	radar picket submarine (diesel)
SST	target-training submarine (diesel)
standard	ship displacement complete and ready for sea with all munitions, provisions, and aircraft but without fuels; measured in metric tons (2,200 lbs/1,000 kg)
STOL	Short Take-Off and Landing (aircraft)
SUW-N-( )	NATO designation for Soviet Surface-to-Underwater Naval missile
3-D	three-dimensional (radar)
VDL	Video Data Link
VDS	Variable Depth Sonar
VSTOL	Vertical/Short Take-Off and Landing (aircraft)
VTOL	Vertical Take-Off and Landing (aircraft)

CHAPTER 3

Ship Classifications

The Soviet Navy designates the TASHKENT, shown here in heavy seas in the Pacific, as a large anti-submarine ship (BPK). She has no exact contemporary in Western navies although there are similarities to certain U.S. Navy guided missile cruisers (CGN). A Ka-25 Hormone-A ASW helicopter sits on her fantail. (U.S. Navy)

The general arrangement of ships in this volume is by generic type based on the U.S. Navy's ship classification scheme (e.g., cruisers, destroyers, frigates). Because of the major differences in U.S. and Soviet warship designs and roles, this volume does not use U.S. Navy ship-type designations (CG, CGN, DD, DDG, etc.). However, the similarity of submarine types does make it feasible to use U.S. submarine designations, such as SS, SSN, SSG, and SSGN.

During the post–World War II period the Western intelligence services developed two principal schemes for identifying Soviet naval ships:

(1) Submarines were assigned code-letter designations; generally the phonetic words are used for the letters, as Alfa, Bravo, Charlie, and Delta. Major variations within the class are indicated by roman numerals, such as Charlie I and Charlie II. The principal exception to this scheme is the Western use of the Soviet term Typhoon (*Tayfun*).

There has been no order in the assignment of the submarine code letters, the first having been Whiskey. Because of the massive Soviet submarine construction effort, by 1985 no letters remained available for assignment (even with one Soviet "name" being used for the Typhoon class). The current NATO designation scheme for submarines is discussed in chapter 12.

(2) Surface warships have been given K-series code names from the mid-1950s onward, such as Kara, Kresta, Kynda. Again, Roman numerals indicate principal class variants, as Kresta I and Kresta II. Since the late 1960s most new Soviet surface combatant classes have been generally identified by their Soviet names, such as KIEV, KIROV, UDALOY, and SOVREMENNYY. Lesser Soviet naval ships have been assigned names according to where they were built or first observed, such as the landing ships of the Polnocny class, which were constructed at the Polnocny shipyard in Poland.

The Soviet Navy's designations for its ships are listed below, in table 3-1. In addition to these designations, the Soviets use a "ship rank" (*rang korablya*) classification scheme based on the ship's purpose, firepower, displacement, and crew size. The seniority of the ships' commanding officers, the status of their crews, and their logistic support are based on this ranking. There are four ranks:

1st Rank: nuclear-powered submarines, ASW cruisers (i.e., ADMIRAL KUZNETSOV, KIEV, MOSKVA), guided missile cruisers.

2nd Rank: large and medium diesel submarines, large guided missile and ASW ships, destroyers.

3rd Rank: small ASW ships, escort ships, medium amphibious warfare ships, ocean minesweepers, missile craft.

4th Rank: ASW patrol boats, motor torpedo boats, gunboats, landing craft, coastal and harbor minesweepers.

Under Soviet naval regulations, first- and second-rank ships hoist the naval jack simultaneously with the naval ensign when not under way; the third- and fourth-rank ships do not fly the naval jack.

TABLE 3-1.　SOVIET SHIP TYPE CLASSIFICATIONS

	Russian Terminology	English Translation		Russian Terminology	English Translation
AK	Artilleriyskiy Kater	Artillery Cutter (craft)	OS	Opitnoye Sudno	Experimental Vessel
AK	Avionosfnyy Kreyser	Aircraft Carrying Cruiser	PB	Plavuchaya Baza	Floating Base
AKVP	Amfibiynyy Kater na Vozdushnoy Podushke	Air Cushion Amphibious Craft	PKA	Protivolodochnyy Kater	Anti-Submarine Cutter (craft)
AKVPR	Amfibiynyy Kater na Vozdushnoy Podushke, Rechnoy	Air Cushion Amphibious Craft	PKR	Protivolodochnyy Kreyser	Anti-Submarine Cruiser
			PL	Podvodnaya Lodka	Submarine
			PLA	Podvodnaya Lodka Atomnaya	Submarine (nuclear)
BDK	Bol´shoy Desantnyy Korabl´	Large Landing Ship	PLARB	Podvodnaya Lodka Atomnaya Raketnaya Ballisticheskaya	Ballistic Missile Submarine (nuclear)
BPK	Bol´shoy Protivolodochnyy Korabl´	Large Anti-Submarine Ship	PLARK	Podvodnaya Lodka Atomnaya Raketnaya Krylataya	Cruise Missile Submarine (nuclear)
BRK	Bol´shoy Raketnyy Korabl´	Large Missile Ship	PLRB	Podvodnaya Lodka Raketnaya Ballisticheskaya	Ballistic Missile Submarine
BT	Bazovyy Tral´shchik	Base Minesweeper			
BTK	Bol´shoy Torpednyy Kater	Large Torpedo Cutter (craft)	PLRK	Podvodnaya Lodka Raketnaya Krylataya	Cruise Missile Submarine
DK	Desantnyy Korabl´	Landing Ship			
DKA	Desantnyy Kater	Landing Cutter (craft)	PM	Plavuchaya Masterskaya	Floating Workshop
DKVP	Desantnyy Korabl´ na Vozdushnoy Podushke	Air Cushion Landing Ship	PSKR	Pogranichniy Storozhevoy Korabl´	Border Guard Ship
DS	Desantoye Sudno	Landing Vessel	PZHK	Pozharnyy Kater	Firefighting Cutter (craft)
EM	Eskadrennyy Minonosets	Destroyer	PZHS	Pozharnoye Sudno	Firefighting Vessel
ENS	Elektrostanttsiye Nalivatel´noye Sudno	Electric Power Station Vessel	RKA	Raketnyy Kater	Missile Cutter (craft)
			RKR	Raketnyy Kreyser	Missile Cruiser
EHOS	Ekspeditsionnoye Okeanograficheskoye Sudno	Expeditionary Oceanographic Vessel	RT	Reydovoy [or Rechnyy] Tral´shchik	Roadstead Minesweeper
GKS	Gidroakusticheskoye Kontrol´noye Sudno	Hydroacoustic Monitoring Vessel	SB	Spasatel´nyy Buksir	Salvage Tug
GP	Gidrograficheskiy Pribrezhnyy Bot	Inshore Survey Craft	SBR	Sudno Bol´shogo Razmagnichivanya	Large Degaussing Vessel
GS	Gidrograficheskoye Sudno	Hydrographic Vessel	SKA	Storozhevoy Kater	Patrol Cutter (craft)
KIL	Kilektor	Lift Ship	SDK	Srednyy Desantnyy Korabl´	Medium Landing Ship
KR	Kreyser	Cruiser			
KRZ	Korabl´ Razvedyvatel´nyy	Intelligence Ship	SKR	Storozhevoy Korabl´	Guard Ship
KS	Kabel´noye Sudno	Cable Vessel	SR	Sudno Razmagnichivanya	Degaussing Vessel
KSV	Korabl´ Svyazey	Communications Ship	SS	Spasatel´noye Sudno	Salvage Vessel
KT	Kontrol´naya Tsel´	Controlled Target	SSV	Sudno Svyazyy	Communications Vessel
KT	Kater Tral´shchik	Minesweeping Cutter (craft)	TAKR	Takticheskoye Avianosnyy Kreyser	Tactical Aircraft Carrying Cruiser
KVN	Korabl´ Vozdushnogo Nablyudeniya	Radar Surveillance Ship			
LDK	Ledokol	Icebreaker	TKA	Torpednyy Kater	Torpedo Cutter (craft)
MB	Morskoy Buksir	Seagoing Tug	US	Uchebnoye Sudno	Training Vessel
MPK	Malyy Protivolodochnyy Korabl´	Small Anti-Submarine Ship	VM	Vspomagetel´noye Sudno	Auxiliary Vessel
MRK	Malyy Raketnyy Korabl´	Small Missile Ship	VT	Vspomagetel´nyy Tral´shchik	Auxiliary Minesweeper
MT	Morskoy Tral´shchik	Seagoing Minesweeper	VT	Voyennyy Tanker	Military Tanker
			VTR	Voyennyy Transport	Military Transport
MVT	Morskoy Vodnyy Tanker	Seagoing Water Tanker	ZM	Zaggraditel´ Minnyy	Minelayer

CHAPTER 4

Command and Organization

The VSTOL carrier ADMIRAL GORSHKOV (ex-BAKU) under way in the Northern Fleet. This ship, the ADMIRAL KUZNETSOV, and the KIROV-class cruisers have special facilities for supporting area commanders. The elevator aft of the massive island structure is partially lowered, with four Ka-25 Hormone and Ka-27 Helix helicopters as well as two canvas-covered Yak-38 Forgers visible on deck.

The Soviet Union has the world's largest military establishment (with an estimated 4.2 million men under arms) and the world's largest military-industrial base in terms of production capability.[1]

The armed forces of the Soviet Union consist of five military services plus supporting services that are under the Ministry of Defense plus the border guards of the Committee for State Security (*Komitet Gosudarstvennoi Bezopasnosti*—KGB) and the interior troops of the Ministry of Internal Affairs (*Ministerstvo Vnutrennikh Del*—MVD). The five military services, listed in their normal order of precedence, are:

Strategic Rocket Forces
Air Defense Forces[2]
Ground Forces
Air Forces
Navy

The term *Army and Navy* is still widely used by the Soviet leadership to indicate all of the armed forces. For example, the military political directorate is called the Main Political Administration of the Army and Navy (MPA). However, on an administrative and practical

1. The 4.2 million strength compares to over 5 million in 1985, with a reduction to about 3 million planned. Some Soviet defense intellectuals have argued for deeper cuts, perhaps to as few as 2 million.
2. Generally known by the designation *Voyska* PVO for *Voyska Protivovozdushnoy Oborony*.

basis, the current defense establishment has five separate military services in addition to several supporting services (see figure 4-1).

The Soviet defense establishment is organized for both functional and geographic combat operations. Two of the five military services within the defense establishment are functionally structured—the Strategic Rocket Forces and the Air Defense Forces. The three other military services—the Ground Forces, Air Forces, and Navy—are structured primarily for geographic operations in three strategic theaters, five regional theaters, and three oceanic theaters (see below).

Overall direction of the Soviet armed forces is vested through a series of committees and other agencies in three men: the President, Mikhail Gorbachev; the Minister of Defense, Marshal of the Soviet Union Dmitri Yazov; and the Chief of the General Staff, General of the Army M.A. Moiseyev. In addition, Marshal of the Soviet Union S.F. Akhromeyev, former Chief of the General Staff, serves as personal military advisor to Gorbachev and has considerable influence in Soviet military decisions.[3] (In 1990–91 there were rumors that the Commander in Chief of the Soviet Navy, V.N. Chernavin, might similarly be assigned as a special advisor to Gorbachev; if this were to happen, he would probably be replaced as CinC of the Navy by Admiral of the Fleet I.M. Kapitanets, the First Deputy CinC.)

THE HIGH COMMAND

Communist Party control of the armed forces is exercised through the Defense Council (*Sovyet Oborony*). The Defense Council is the highest Soviet military-economic-political planning and decision-making body, responsible for preparing the country for war. The Defense Council controls the defense budget and makes the decisions to develop and deploy each major weapon system and major warship class. The appointments of senior military officers and organizational changes must be approved by the council.

Chaired by the President (Gorbachev), the council consists of selected members of the politburo, including the Chairman for the Committee for State Security (KGB), and the heads of the Ministry of Defense, Council of Ministers, GOSPLAN (the national economic planning agency), and the Chief of the General Staff.[4]

The Minister of Defense and the Chief of the General Staff are traditionally the only military officers who are members of the Defense Council. There is a likelihood that Marshal Akhromeyev, the previous Chief of the General Staff, who now serves as military advisor to Gorbachev, is also a member of the council.

In wartime the Defense Council would become the State Committee of Defense (*Gosudarstvenny Komitet Oborony*—GKO), essentially a war cabinet to oversee all aspects of the nation at war, including strategic leadership. At that time the General Secretary would assume the function of Supreme Commander in Chief of the Armed Forces. When it became the State Committee of Defense, others would probably join the Defense Council, including the Commander in Chief of Warsaw Pact Forces and the party secretary for the defense industry.[5]

The Soviet armed forces have both an administrative and an operational chain of command. The senior peacetime body of the armed forces is the Main Military Council (*Glavnyy Voyennikh Sovyet*), or the Collegium of the Ministry of Defense (*Kollegiya Ministerstva Oborony*), which is responsible to the Defense Council for military strategy and operations, including training and readiness. The Minister of Defense heads this council. The members of the council include the 14 deputy ministers of defense—5 military service chiefs, 6 heads of defense agencies, and 3 other senior

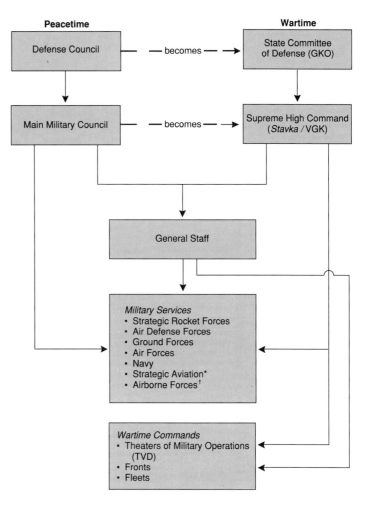

*There are five air armies composed of strategic bombers and strike aircraft; these air armies are administratively part of the Air Forces, and operationally they are directly under the General Staff

†Airborne units are administratively part of the Ground Forces, and operationally they are directly under the General Staff.

Figure 4 - 1.   Soviet High Command

defense officials (see figure 4-2). In wartime this council would become the Headquarters of the Supreme High Command, or *Stavka*, which would exercise direct operational control of the Soviet armed forces, either through the General Staff or directly through the various theater and front commanders.[6]

The General Staff is the executive agency for the Main Military Council in peacetime and for the wartime *Stavka*. It is charged with basic military planning for all of the services. Together the *Stavka* and the General Staff form the Supreme High Command (*Verkhovnoye Glavnoye Kommandovaniye*—VGK).

The Soviet General Staff was formally established in 1935 and was changed to its present form in 1942. Although Josef Stalin took personal direction of many aspects of the Soviet war direction, the General Staff provided considerable and generally effective leadership. The head of German intelligence on the Eastern Front in World War II wrote: "With the Russians, as I was always at some pains to stress, we were dealing with strategic and political brains of high caliber and cunning."[7]

The Soviet General Staff differs significantly from the U.S. Joint Chiefs of Staff (JCS) in two respects. The JCS is composed of a

3. Akhromeyev has been a key participant in the relationship between the U.S. and Soviet defense establishments and has visited the United States on several occasions. He served as Chief of the General Staff from 1984 to December 1988.

4. The KGB is also responsible for operating and protecting the communications systems of the Soviet state and political leadership, and for safeguarding nuclear warheads in transit to and at storage facilities.

5. The party secretary for the defense industry is also the Chief of the Military Industrial Commission, or VPK (*Voyenno Promyshlenaya Kommisiya*).

6. *Stavka* was a tsarist term. Stalin established the first *Stavka* of the Soviet regime when the Germans invaded Russia in June 1941. During World War II the *Stavka* consisted of about 20 general officers. (At the end of the tsarist regime in 1917 there were about 250 senior officers and officials in the *Stavka*.)

7. Maj.-Gen. Reinhard Gehlen, German Army, *The Service* (New York: World Publishing, 1972), pp. 61–62. Gehlen was Chief, Foreign Armies East (intelligence) on the German General Staff.

chairman, vice chairman, and the heads of the four U.S. military services and has a working staff of officers drawn from the various services, generally individuals with no specialized staff training who are assigned for about two years at a time. In contrast, the Soviet General Staff is a professional planning staff, which consists mostly of "army" officers, with the key positions held only by officers who have graduated from the two-year course at the Voroshilov General Staff Academy, the highest professional military school in the nation. These are professional staff officers, who may spend their entire senior career on the General Staff or other major Soviet planning bodies. As representatives of the Soviet military viewpoint, they do not have to divide their loyalties between the staff and their parent service as do their American counterparts (who will usually return to their respective services for subsequent assignments).

Although the Soviet General Staff is dominated by Ground Forces (army) officers, since 1972 a senior naval officer has been assigned as a deputy chief, serving as the principal naval liaison to the staff. Several other naval officers hold lesser positions on the General Staff.

MINISTRY OF DEFENSE

The direct control and administration of the armed forces on a daily basis in peacetime is the responsibility of the Ministry of Defense (MOD). The Minister of Defense exercises his duties through the 3 first deputy ministers and 11 deputy ministers.

The first deputies are the Chief of the General Staff, the Commander in Chief of Warsaw Pact Forces, and a first deputy for general affairs. Five of the deputies are the heads of the five armed services: the commanders in chief of the Strategic Rocket Forces, Air Defense Forces, Ground Forces, Air Forces, and Navy. The other deputies are responsible for Civil Defense, Personnel, Main

Inspectorate, Rear Services, Armaments, and Construction and Billeting of Troops. The Warsaw Pact was abolished 1 July 1991.

In peacetime the MOD administers military activities through groups of forces (located in Eastern Europe), 15 military districts within the Soviet Union, 4 naval fleets, and 1 naval flotilla. In 1990, however, Soviet troops were being withdrawn from all of the Eastern Bloc nations, and their new organization structure was not clear.

History. The progenitor of the current Ministry of Defense was the Commissariat for Military Affairs, organized in late 1917 during the Bolshevik Revolution. By early 1918 it was divided into separate commissariats for the Army and Navy. In 1923, however, the two bodies were again unified into a Commissariat of Military and Naval Affairs to direct all Soviet military activities. In 1934 this body was reorganized into a unified Commissariat of Defense (combining the Army and Navy), but Josef Stalin, as part of his buildup of a major fleet, in 1937 established the separate Commissariat of the Navy.

After the war, in 1946, the two services were unified again, in the Commissariat for the Armed Forces. The Navy again had a brief period of independence, but upon Stalin's death in March 1953 the current, unified Ministry of Defense was established.

During the next few years the other services and most other components of the current MOD were established in their current form. The Air Forces became a separate service in 1946; the National Air Defense Forces—at the time known as PVO-*Strany*—gained the status of a separate service in 1948 and was reorganized as the Air Defense Forces about 1980, incorporating the air defense troops of the Ground Forces; and the Strategic Rocket Forces became a separate service in December 1959.

The first Minister of Defense under the 1953 reorganization was Marshal Nikolai Bulganin, a political officer with very limited military experience, who had served as head of the armed forces from

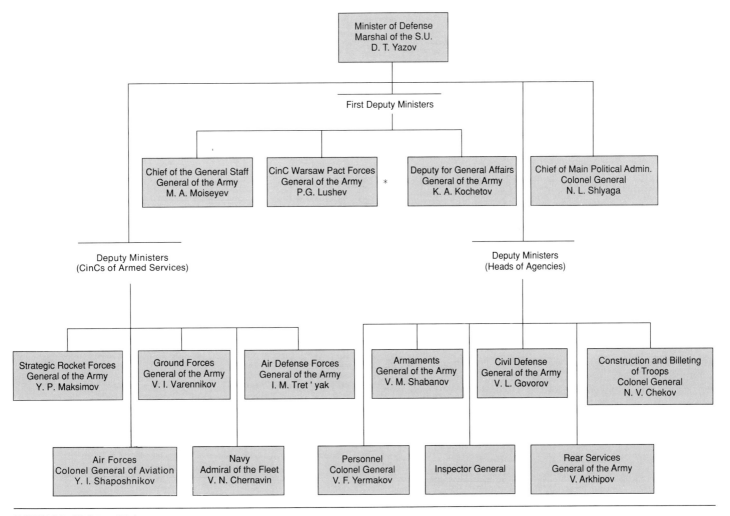

FIGURE 4-2 Ministry of Defense

* Position abolished in 1991; see page 445.

1947 to 1950. Bulganin was succeeded in 1955 by Marshal Georgi Zhukov, the leading Soviet military hero of World War II. Zhukov was the successful architect of the defenses of Leningrad and Moscow, and of the Battle of Stalingrad (now Volgograd); the latter battle is considered the turning point in the 1941–1945 war against Germany. Zhukov, the first professional soldier to head the Soviet defense establishment, was immensely popular in the Soviet Union. As Minister of Defense he was the first soldier to hold full membership in the ruling presidium (as the politburo was then called). Still, in 1957 the Soviet political leadership under Nikita Khrushchev ousted Zhukov from office because of fears that he was gaining too much power.

His place was taken by another professional soldier, Marshal Radion Malinovsky, who had been closely associated with Khrushchev in the Ukraine region during World War II. Malinovsky died in 1967 and the top defense post was given to still another professional soldier, Marshal Andrei Grechko. He too was given membership in the politburo, but only with candidate (non-voting) status. After Grechko's death in 1976 the position of Minister of Defense went to Dmitri Ustinov, already a full member of the politburo and the head of the defense industry.

Ustinov, a civilian ordnance specialist and industrial administrator, had been head of armament production in the Soviet Union since June 1941 and afterwards held a succession of senior positions in the defense industry and economic planning. Ustinov held the rank of engineer–colonel general before being appointed Minister of Defense in April 1976, when he was awarded the rank of General of the Army. Later that year the rank of Marshal of the Soviet Union was conferred upon him. He was a candidate member of the politburo from 1966 to 1976, and a full member from 1976 until his death in 1984.

Marshal of the Soviet Union S.L. Sokolov, a professional army officer, was appointed to succeed Ustinov upon the latter's death in December 1984. The following year he was named a candidate member of the politburo. Sokolov, age 73, was the oldest man ever appointed to the top defense position, a reflection of the unsettled leadership situation (at the time General Secretary Konstantin Chernenko, himself 73, was in failing health; he died in March 1985). Thus, Sokolov was an interim appointment pending the advent of a new government.

Mikhail Gorbachev became General Secretary in March 1985 (age 54) and rapidly began changing the political and military leadership of the USSR. General of the Army Yazov, formerly the Deputy Minister of Defense for Personnel, was appointed Minister of Defense in June 1987. Subsequently there were further changes in key military posts throughout the armed forces. He is considered a Gorbachev protégé and in 1990 was promoted to Marshal of the Soviet Union, the first officer to receive that rank under the Gorbachev regime.

As noted above, a senior admiral has served as a deputy chief of the General Staff since 1972. Additionally, Admiral A.I. Sorokin has served as First Deputy Chief of the Main Political Administration (MPA) during the 1980s. Admiral Sorokin has served in the MPA since 1976 as one of several lesser deputy chiefs. (The chief of the MPA is an army colonel general.)

Also in 1981, Admiral of the Fleet G.M. Yegorov stepped down as Chief of the Main Naval Staff, a most important position that he had occupied since 1977. He then became chairman of the Central Committee of DOSAAF (voluntary society for cooperation with the army, aviation, and fleet), the national paramilitary training organization. Most Western analysts believe that his move was a demotion, resulting from the grounding of a Soviet submarine in Swedish waters in November 1981. The DOSAAF position has probably not been held before by a naval officer and thus may have given the Navy added prestige and influence.

Several other admirals hold major non-Navy positions, among them Admiral A.I. Rassokho, Chief of the Main Directorate of Navigation and Oceanography within MOD; and Admiral N.I. Khovrin, Deputy Commander in Chief for Warsaw Pact naval forces.

THEATERS OF OPERATIONS

In wartime the Soviets envision the conduct of military operations on the basis of three strategic theaters and several subordinate theaters of operations, or TVDs (*Teatrii Voyennykh Deystviy*).

The three strategic theaters are permanent, regional high commands intended to provide wartime control over air, ground, and sea forces in their sectors. The headquarters of the strategic theaters have commanders assigned and are partially staffed. This organization facilitates the Soviets conducting a war on multiple fronts. The three strategic theaters and their subordinate TVDs and naval components are:

Western (covering Western Europe, Scandanavia, the Mediterranean, North Africa, Arctic-Atlantic)
TVDs: Western, Northwestern, Southwestern; Fleets: Northern, Black Sea; Mediterranean
Southern (covering the Middle East, Afghanistan, Pakistan, India, Indian Ocean)
TVD: Southern; Flotilla: Caspian Sea; *Eskadra*: Indian Ocean
Far Eastern (covering the Far East, Southeast Asia, Pacific)
TVD: Far East; Fleet: Pacific

During the 1980s it was assumed in the West that for most combat operations the Soviet Navy's four fleets would be subordinated to the strategic theater commands. As a conflict developed, additional TVDs could be activated within the strategic theaters to direct specific operations; these could include TVDs for extended naval campaigns in the Arctic, Atlantic, and Pacific oceans. However, the Soviet newspaper *Izvestiya* on 22 February 1990 published a detailed organization chart of the Soviet armed forces. The Strategic Rocket Forces *and* the Navy were outside of the "operational-strategic and operational formations," indicating that in wartime those services would operate under the direct control of the Supreme High Command (*Stavka*) and not be subordinate to the strategic theaters.

The Soviets do not normally have commanders and staffs assigned to the TVDs but would form these staffs from the groups of forces, major border military districts, and MOD.

History. The concept of the TVD—i.e., an intermediate level between the *Stavka* and the fronts (army groups)—was used briefly and ineffectively early in the war against Germany. More significantly, in March 1945 a theater command was established in the Far East in preparation for Soviet entry into the war against Japan.[8] This High Command of Soviet Forces in the Far East was "invested with broad authority for direction of combat operation" and had "a relatively autonomous character." The distance from Moscow to the new war zone and the limitations that distance put on communications led to the formation of this TVD, which directed three ground fronts, three air armies, the Pacific Fleet, and the Amur Flotilla in the war against the Japanese. Soviet experience with the theater command concept was limited. The success of the admittedly brief but complex and large-area campaign in the Far East has provided Soviet military leaders with a model for future theater command structures.

The first of the current strategic theaters to be established was apparently the Far Eastern command, in 1979.

MILITARY DISTRICTS

The Soviet Union is divided into 15 administration regions called Military Districts (MD).[9] These MDs control subordinate military activities and units within their region including bases, training institutions, and recruitment and mobilization agencies.

---

8. In February 1945 at the conference of Allied leaders in Yalta in the Soviet Crimea, the USSR agreed to enter the war against Japan three months after the end of the war in Europe, i.e., in early August 1945.

9. There were 16 Military Districts until 1 September 1989, when the Ural MD was abolished and merged into the Volga MD to form the Volga-Ural district.

Admiral N.G. Kuznetsov (U.S. Army)

Admiral S.G. Gorshkov (U.S. Navy)

Admiral V.N. Chernavin (Sovfoto)

The MD commander is responsible for overseeing draftee registration and induction, mobilization planning, civil defense, and paramilitary and reserve training.

NAVY (Voyenno-Morskoy Flot)

The Soviet Navy is an administrative organization (as are the other military services) as well as an operational command organization for forces afloat and related land-based aviation and marine units.

The senior naval officer is both a deputy minister of defense and Commander in Chief (CinC) of the Navy and thus the equivalent of both the U.S. Secretary of the Navy and Chief of Naval Operations, respectively. The Soviet CinC directs operations afloat and ashore primarily through four fleet commands plus the flotilla command on the inland Caspian Sea. (There is evidence that the daily operational control of the later Soviet strategic missile submarines is vested in the Soviet General Staff, as is control of the Soviet strategic aviation and Soviet airborne forces.)

The current CinC of the Soviet Navy is Admiral of the Fleet V.N. Chernavin, who was appointed to the dual positions of deputy minister and naval CinC in December 1985. His immediate predecessor was Admiral of the Fleet of the Soviet Union S.G. Gorshkov, who had served in that position for almost 30 years—from January 1956 until he was relieved by Chernavin. Gorshkov's tenure had spanned that of 13 U.S. Secretaries of the Navy and 9 Chiefs of Naval Operations.[10]

Chernavin's subsequent appointment to command of the Soviet Navy became probable when he became a first deputy CinC in early 1982 and was promoted from admiral to Admiral of the Fleet the following year. At the time of his appointment as Navy CinC Chernavin was 57 years of age.

Admiral Chernavin served as Chief of the Main Naval Staff and First Deputy CinC for a little less than four years. Before that Chernavin had command of the important Northern Fleet, holding that position from July 1977 until early 1982. Previously Chernavin held mainly submarine positions, having received the Hero of the Soviet Union award for participating in the trip of a November-class SSN to the North Pole in 1965.

History. The Navy traces its roots to Tsar Peter I (1672–1725), who sought to westernize Russia after he became tsar under a regency at age ten. In 1702, Peter established Russia's first naval force, on Lake Ladoga where Sweden maintained a naval squadron. His 18 small boats—pulled by oars, with a single sail, and manned by 400 soldiers—attacked a Swedish squadron on 20 June. This victory and others that followed marked the beginning of the Russian Navy as well as Peter's successful drive to the Gulf of Finland and the Baltic beyond. By the time of his death, Peter had established Russia as the dominant Baltic naval power. One British military historian has written, "The Russian navy was possibly the proudest of Peter's creations . . . ."[11]

The Russian Navy survived under various titles and organizational concepts as a separate ministry for more than two centuries.

Under the Communist regime a separate People's Commissariat (ministry) for the Navy had existed briefly in 1918, and then from December 1937 through World War II. In February 1946, when the decisions were being made to initiate a major fleet building program, the Navy was integrated into the People's Commissariat for the Armed Forces, whose title was changed on 15 March of that year to Ministry for the Armed Forces. Four years later, in February 1950, this unified ministry was divided into a War Ministry and a Navy Ministry, again placing the Navy high command in a position of parity with the Army. Finally, the supra-level MOD was established in 1953, with the Navy once again becoming a subordinate service.

The basic organization of the Soviet Navy is shown in figure 4-3. The headquarters is a highly centralized organization with several deputy CinCs supporting the CinC. Current operations and long-range planning are the province of the Main Naval Staff, which in some respects is comparable to the U.S. Office of the Chief of Naval Operations.

The other deputy CinCs appear to have specific responsibilities and supporting organizations, but not all have been publicly identified. The Soviet Navy does not appear to have deputy CinCs for warfare areas or "platforms," like the U.S. Navy's assistant (formerly deputy) chiefs of naval operations for air, surface, and submarine matters. Rather, the principal deputy commanders in the Soviet Navy are:

    combat training
    naval educational institutions
    rear services (logistics)
    shipbuilding and armaments

10. The longest-serving U.S. Chief of Naval Operations since that position was established in 1915 has been Admiral Arleigh Burke, who served as CNO from August 1955 to August 1961.

11. Christopher Duffy's excellent *Russia's Military Way to the West*, subtitled "Origins and Nature of Russian Military Power, 1700–1825" (London: Routledge & Kegan Paul, 1981), p. 36.

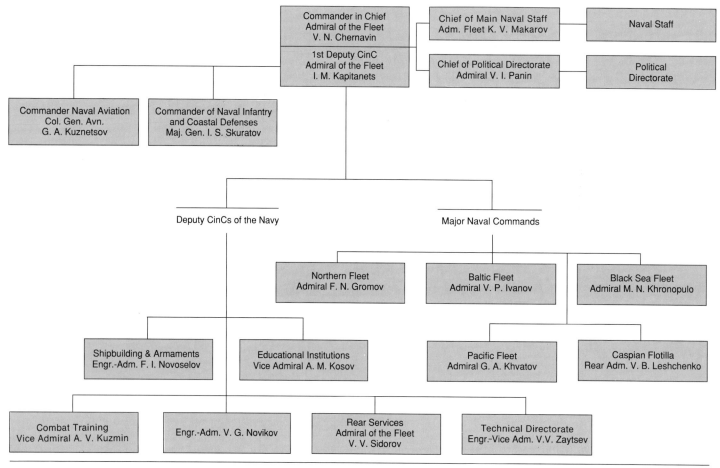

Figure 4-3.   Navy Organization

Although technically not a deputy CinC, the head of the Navy's political administration has the stature of one. This post has been held since 1987 by Admiral V.I. Panin. Other senior officers within Soviet naval headquarters include:

Commander of Naval Aviation
Commander of Naval Infantry and Coastal Defense
Chief Naval Air Defense
Chief of Hydrographic Services
Chief of Auxiliary Fleet and Salvage–Sea Rescue Service
Chief of Firefighting Service
Chief of Inventions Bureau
Chief of Personnel Directorate

The officers now holding these posts are listed in appendix A.

Naval Headquarters directs fleet operations through four fleet commanders (see chapter 5) except that a forward-deployed squadron (*eskadra*) appears to be under the direct operational control of Navy Headquarters. And, as noted above, strategic missile submarines are under the operational control of the General Staff.

The Military Council of the Navy consists of the CinC, the First Deputy CinC, the Chief of the Main Naval Staff, the Chief of the Political Directorate, and possibly some of the other deputy CinCs. The council appears to be an advisory body to the CinC, providing a senior forum for discussions of major policy issues, especially those that transcend political and specialized areas.

SPETSNAZ FORCES

The Soviet Union maintains a large force of special warfare forces, known by the Soviet acronym *Spetsnaz* (for *Voiska Spetsialnogo*

Naznacheniia). These forces are controlled by the Main Intelligence Directorate (GRU) of the Soviet General Staff.

The *Spetsnaz* forces conduct reconnaissance and special warfare missions in "peacetime" as well as in war. Peacetime operations, such as the assassination of Afghanistan's president in December 1979, are under the direction of the KGB.

There are *Spetsnaz* brigades of some 900 to 1,300 officers and men assigned to each of the four groups of forces in Europe as well as to several of the major military districts. There are also four naval *Spetsnaz* brigades that are assigned to the four fleets (see chapter 9). According to a former Soviet intelligence officer, there are a total of 20 *Spetsnaz* brigades plus 41 separate companies.[12] Thus, total strength of *Spetsnaz* forces could be on the order of 30,000 troops within the Soviet armed forces (which total almost five million men and women in the five military services).

KGB MARITIME BORDER TROOPS

The KGB Maritime Border Troops protect Soviet maritime borders against penetration by foreign agents or paramilitary forces and prevent Soviet citizens from leaving by water without proper authorization. The troops operate patrol ships and craft in most if not all of the nine border districts. Details of the Maritime Border Troops and descriptions of the ships and craft are provided in chapter 26.

12. Viktor Suvorov [pseud.], *Inside Soviet Military Intelligence* (New York: Macmillan, 1984), p. 173.

CHAPTER 5

Fleets and Flotillas

The Soviet Mediterranean *eskadra* and the U.S. Sixth Fleet are now the object of arms limitation talks as the Soviet Union and United States seek to reduce operating costs and potential military confrontation. Here the guided missile destoyer OTLICHNYY of the SOVREMENNYY class refuels from the civilian tanker MARSHAL BIRYUZOV; there is a Krivak-class frigate in the background. (U.S. Navy, Lt. P.J. Azzolina)

The current Soviet naval organization consists of four fleets and one flotilla: the Northern Fleet, Baltic Fleet, Black Sea Fleet, Pacific Fleet, and the Caspian Sea Flotilla. The Caspian Flotilla is the only survivor of the 12 lake, sea, and river flotillas that existed in the Soviet Navy during World War II. In peacetime the fleets are administrative as well as tactical organizations.

Each fleet and the Caspian Flotilla has a headquarters that is generally similar in organization to that of Naval Headquarters (see figure 5-1). Each fleet has its own naval aviation, naval infantry, coastal defense, and special warfare (*Spetsnaz*) components. The fleets' warships are organized into brigades and divisions. When ships are formed into a specific grouping or task force, they are designated an *eskadra*, literally a squadron. This grouping is a semi-independent command, as the Fifth *Eskadra* in the Mediterranean with control of its operations vested in Naval Headquarters in Moscow and not in the fleet headquarters. The Soviet naval forces in the Indian Ocean and Persian Gulf, assigned from the Pacific Fleet, form a similar *eskadra*.

NORTHERN FLEET

The Red Banner Northern Fleet is the largest of the three European fleets and in several respects is the most important.[1] Based mainly in the Kola Peninsula and White Sea areas, the Northern Fleet has more direct access to the Atlantic than do the Baltic and Black Sea fleets and is thus responsible for wartime operations in the Atlantic and Arctic regions. In addition, the Northern Fleet normally provides submarines for operations in the Mediterranean Sea because the Montreux Convention of 1936 imposes restrictions on submarine transits between the Black Sea and the Mediterranean.

Russia's longest and most inhospitable coast is in the Arctic region. The waters are largely icebound in the winter except for a 70-mile (112-m) stretch of the Kola Peninsula, which includes the major ports of Pechenga and Murmansk. The region is subjected to long winter nights; in the Murmansk area the sun does not rise above the horizon from mid-November to mid-January.

1. The Order of Red Banner has been awarded to various Soviet units and activities for exemplary service in wartime. The Baltic Fleet was cited for its role in the Revolution of 1917 and all four fleets and the Caspian Flotilla were cited for the Great Patriotic War (1941–1945). The Baltic Fleet is formally referred to as the Twice-Honored Red Banner Baltic Fleet.

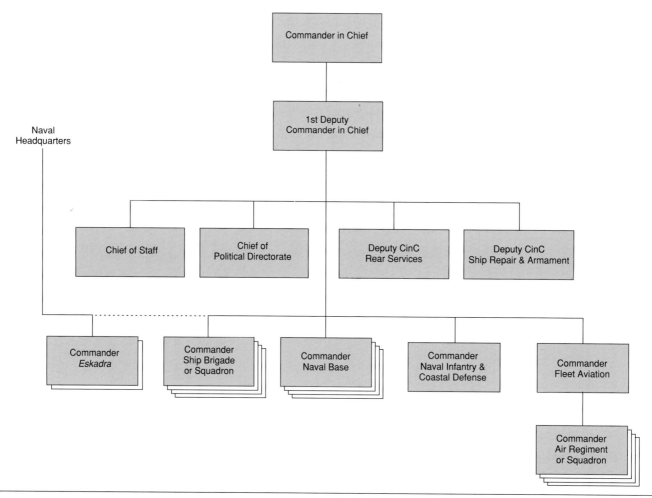

Figure 5-1.   Soviet Fleet Organization

History. At the beginning of the reign of Peter I, the father of modern Russia as well as the Russian Navy, the northern region was the country's only access to the sea. Although Peter soon undertook campaigns to gain access to the Baltic and Black seas, the Arctic coast remained vital to Russian trade. During World War I the ports on the northern coast provided the route for Allied aid to the tsarist regime, and then for the landings of U.S. and British troops during the Civil War (1917–1920).

The first major Soviet naval units to be assigned to the region were the patrol ships SMERCH and URAGAN, and the submarines DEKABRIST (D-1) and NARODOVOLETS (D-2), which transited the newly completed Baltic–White Sea Canal from Kronshtadt to Murmansk in the summer of 1933. This was the start of the Northern Naval Flotilla. Reinforcements of ships and submarines followed, and in September 1935 a flight of MBR-2 flying boats was transferred to the Kola Gulf to begin naval air operations in the northern area.

The flotilla was reorganized as the Northern Fleet on 11 May 1937. At the start of the Great Patriotic War in June 1941, the fleet had 15 submarines, 8 destroyers, 7 patrol ships, and numerous lesser craft, plus 116 naval aircraft. It was thus the smallest of the four fleets when the Soviet Union entered World War II. (Those naval forces in the White Sea area were organized as the White Sea Flotilla in August 1941.) The Northern Fleet participated in extensive combat operations against German naval forces off northern Norway and Finland. The Arctic operating area was important to the United States and Britain for convoys carrying war material to the Soviet Union.

In the initial postwar period the Northern Fleet was considered of secondary importance to the fleets in the Baltic and Black seas. This situation changed in the late 1950s when, under Admiral Gorshkov's direction, the naval forces that would operate in the Atlantic during war were shifted to the Northern Fleet where they would have more direct access to the open sea.

Today the Northern Fleet has two of the KIEV-class VSTOL carriers, an estimated 47 percent of the Soviet Navy's submarines, some 27 percent of the surface warships (frigates and larger units), about 25 percent of the naval aircraft, and about 20 percent of the naval personnel. The Pacific Fleet is slightly larger than the Northern Fleet in all categories except submarines. The Northern and Pacific fleets share all of the Navy's nuclear submarines and ballistic missile submarines. When this edition went to press the large aircraft carrier ADMIRAL KUZNETSOV (ex-TBILISI) had recently arrived in the Northern Fleet.

Beyond operations in the Atlantic, the Northern Fleet probably has the responsibility for amphibious operations, should they be undertaken, against Norway, Iceland, and the North Sea approaches to the Danish Straits. Periodically, amphibious ships from the Northern Fleet have entered the Baltic for multi-fleet amphibious exercises.

Admiral F.N. Gromov has been CinC of the Northern Fleet since 1988. He previously served as First Deputy CinC of the Northern Fleet. His predecessor in the Northern Fleet, Admiral I.M. Kapitanets, had held the position for three years; he is now the First Deputy CinC of the Soviet Navy.

Northern Fleet headquarters is located at Severomorsk, just north of the large port of Murmansk on the Kola Peninsula.

BALTIC FLEET

The Twice-Honored Red Banner Baltic Fleet is the smallest of the four Soviet fleets. It was the principal Russian naval force for most of the period from the time of Peter I until early in the tenure of Admiral Gorshkov as CinC of the Soviet Navy. Because the Baltic

A Delta IV strategic missile submarine with two periscopes, Pert Spring ECM antenna, and Snoop Tray radar masts raised. The Deltas and other Soviet SSBNs are assigned to the Northern and Pacific fleets, where they can operate in "bastions," or havens, protected from Western anti-submarine forces and have access to the open sea. (Royal Navy)

Fleet's access to the open ocean is through waters controlled by NATO navies (the waters of Denmark, Norway, and West Germany), Admiral Gorshkov directed a redeployment of naval forces. As a result, those air, surface, and submarine forces with wartime assignments in the Atlantic were shifted to the Northern Fleet.

The Soviet naval forces in the Baltic are intended almost exclusively for operations in that area. The major exceptions are those ships undergoing trials and training in the huge Leningrad shipbuilding complex and training facilities. Thus, the principal missions of the Baltic Fleet in wartime appear to be supporting army operations, and conducting landing and other naval operations to gain control of the Danish Straits. Amphibious operations and certain other Soviet naval activities would be supported in the past by the East German and Polish navies. At the same time, Soviet naval and land-based air forces would seek to deny use of the Baltic to the NATO navies.

In 1980 and again in 1981 a task group of Soviet, East German, and Polish ships passed out of the Baltic through the Danish Straits and conducted exercises in the North Sea. These exercises have continued as non-Soviet Warsaw Pact naval missions have extended beyond the Baltic. This move may have been partially political, a counter to the long-established NATO multi-national naval maneuvers in the Atlantic and the recent extension of West German naval operational areas to the North Sea.

The Baltic is of major importance to the Soviet Union as a commercial shipping route from the western Russian industrial region to European and world ports. In addition, Leningrad is the transshipment point for the express container route from Japan across the Soviet Union by train and then by ship to Atlantic nations. From a military viewpoint the Baltic forms the northern flank of the Central Front, while the Soviet shipyards on the Baltic are vital to the Soviet fleet in a prolonged conflict.

Much of the northern Baltic, including the Gulf of Finland, where Leningrad is located; the Gulf of Riga; and the Gulf of Bothnia, are frozen during the winter. Low clouds in the autumn and winter months limit air operations in the region.

History. Russian influence in the Baltic area dates to 1703, when Peter I established a city in the marshes of the Neva River where it enters the Gulf of Finland. Naming this city St. Petersburg and making it the capital of Russia, he sought to bring Western influence to the country and envisioned St. Petersburg as a "window on the West." (The city's German-sounding name was changed to Petrograd in 1914, on the eve of World War I, and subsequently to Leningrad after Lenin's death in 1924.) In 1721 forces under Peter, relying heavily on assistance from British and other foreign naval specialists, defeated the Swedes in a series of battles in the Gulf of Finland. These victories established Russia as a Baltic power and as a principal European state.

Russian activity and interests in the region grew rapidly under Peter's successors. The Baltic was a major theater of combat between German and Russian naval forces in World War I. During the Bolshevik (Communist) Revolution that erupted in October 1917 against the Kerensky government, sailors from the Baltic Fleet were in the forefront of the revolutionaries. The crew of the cruiser AVRORA, moored in the Neva River, refused orders to get under way and fired blank rounds to signal the start of the Bolshevik assault on the Winter Palace (Hermitage), site of the government that had replaced the tsarist regime in Russia.

Although sailors had helped spark the Revolution in 1917, by 1921 many were disillusioned with Lenin's form of dictatorship. In February they rioted in the city and seized control of the island naval base of Kronshtadt, on Kotlin Island in the Gulf of Finland. The gulf was frozen over and the island was taken by Bolshevik forces after a series of bloody assaults across the ice. The Baltic in 1918–1920 was also the scene of extensive British naval operations against the Communists, including highly successful torpedo-boat attacks against anchored Russian battleships.

Between the two world wars Leningrad became the industrial and training center of the Soviet Navy. In June 1941, at the outbreak of conflict, the Baltic Fleet was the largest of the Soviet naval forces, consisting of 2 battleships, 4 cruisers, 21 destroyers, 65 submarines, and numerous lesser craft, supported by 656 naval aircraft. German naval forces almost immediately gained control of the Baltic as German armies pushed north and east from Poland, eventually encircling Leningrad (and being stopped almost within sight of Moscow). Pro-German Finland assisted in the war against the Soviet Union.

The Germans laid anti-submarine minefields and nets across the entrance to the Gulf of Finland to stop Soviet submarines from operating in the Baltic. These measures, plus German naval forces and the winter ice, limited the effectiveness of the Baltic Fleet. During the three-year siege of Leningrad the large-caliber guns of the battleships and cruisers trapped in the port were used to provide fire support for Soviet ground forces.

After the war Leningrad's shipyards and other naval facilities were rebuilt having had high priority as part of Stalin's fleet rehabilitation program.

Today the Baltic Fleet consists primarily of combat forces intended for wartime control of the area, amphibious assaults against West German or Danish positions, the support of Soviet ground operations, or the control of vital waterways. (The Danish island of Bornholm is considered a prime target of Soviet amphibious assault). The Baltic Fleet is currently assigned 12 percent of the Soviet Navy's submarines, 18 percent of its surface warships (frigate and larger), 16 percent of its aircraft, and about 19 percent of its personnel.

The operational submarines normally assigned to the Baltic Fleet are all diesel-electric craft. The nuclear submarines constructed at the Leningrad yards are transported via inland waterways to the Severodvinsk yard in the Arctic for completion and trials.

During September–October 1976 six Golf II ballistic missile submarines (SSBs) were shifted from the Northern Fleet to the Baltic to provide a sea-based theater nuclear strike capability; each carried three SS-N-5 missiles. Those submarines were in the process of being withdrawn from the Baltic when this volume went to press. In 1982 at least four diesel-propelled Juliett cruise missile submarines (SSGs), each armed with four SS-N-3 Shaddock missiles, shifted from the Northern Fleet to the Baltic. These boats replaced older Shaddock missile submarines of the Whiskey class.

Although the Baltic Fleet is intended principally for Baltic operations, its diesel-electric attack submarines do conduct periodic training patrols in the North Sea and in waters off the western approaches of Great Britain.

The Red Banner Leningrad Naval Base is the nation's largest naval complex, with a number of major schools and other training facilities (see chapter 10) as well as several large shipyards (see chapter 31). Leningrad also has the Central Naval Museum (housed in the imposing stock exchange building of the tsarist era) and the Central Naval Library, with its collection of about one million volumes. Headquarters for the naval base is in the historic Admiralty building, whose distinctive gold-coated spire dominates the skyline of the lower Neva River. The Leningrad Naval Base is commanded by Vice Admiral V.Y. Selivanov.

The Baltic Fleet is under the command of Admiral V.P. Ivanov, who succeeded Admiral K.V. Makarov in 1985. Makarov subsequently was named to the important position of Chief of the Main Naval Staff in 1986. (Makarov's predecessor was Admiral I.M. Kapitanets, who went on to the command of the Northern Fleet and then became First Deputy CinC of the Navy, demonstrating the importance of the Baltic command.)

The fleet's headquarters is located at Baltiysk (formerly Pillau) near the Lithuanian port of Kaliningrad (formerly Königsberg).

BLACK SEA FLEET

The Red Banner Black Sea Fleet is responsible for operations in the Black Sea and, more significantly, it provides surface warships and aircraft for operations in the Mediterranean Sea as the Fifth *Eskadra*. The Black Sea Fleet, however, does not provide submarines for Mediterranean operations. (As previously noted, the submarines for the Mediterranean are provided by the Northern Fleet.)

Because of the significance of Black Sea–Mediterranean operations, the Black Sea Fleet has a greater proportion of large warships than the Baltic Fleet, although—unlike the Baltic Fleet's operational area—the Black Sea is essentially a "Soviet lake," with Turkey the only potentially hostile nation bordering the sea.

Black Sea ports are second only to those of the Baltic in handling Soviet maritime imports and exports. As in the Baltic, there are

major shipyards located along the Black Sea coast. Despite its relatively southern location, some Black Sea ports, including the leading port of Odessa, are frozen for about six weeks of the year as is the smaller Sea of Azov, which is immediately north of the Black Sea. Still, the Black Sea climate is the best in the Soviet Union, with many resorts located along the coast, several for naval personnel. Good flying weather is a major reason why the Navy's air training center is located at Saki in the Crimea.

History. Russian naval activities on the Black Sea can be traced to 1783, when ships from the Sea of Azov visited the village of Akhtiar (renamed Sevastopol the following year). Subsequent Russian interest in the area led to a series of wars with Turkey during the late 18th and 19th centuries, with British and French naval forces at times being allied with those of Turkey. The Russians were highly innovative in tactics and weapons during their battles with the Turks, introducing rifled shells among other developments. During this period shipbuilding became a major activity along the Black Sea coast, especially at Nikolayev on the Yuzhnnyy Bug River, a short distance from the sea.

At the start of this century, many sailors of the Black Sea Fleet, like their comrades in the Baltic, were consumed by revolutionary fervor. In the abortive revolt of 1905 there was a much-publicized mutiny on board the battleship POTEMKIN, an event made immortal in Sergei Eisenstein's classic film of 1925.[2] During the Russian revolution of 1917 and the subsequent Civil War, the British and French landed troops on the Black Sea coast to support the anti-Red forces in the area. After the success of the Communists and the withdrawal of foreign fleets, the remnants of the Black Sea Fleet fled to North Africa, where they were interned.

In May 1920 the newly established Bolshevik regime organized the Naval Forces of the Black Sea and Sea of Azov. These forces were redesignated as the Black Sea Fleet on 11 January 1935. During the 1930s the Black Sea region regained its importance in the shipbuilding and maritime industries. At the outbreak of the Great Patriotic War in June 1941, the Black Sea Fleet was the nation's second largest, with 1 battleship, 6 cruisers, 3 destroyer leaders, 14 destroyers, 47 submarines, and 625 land-based aircraft.

During the early stages of the German invasion of the Soviet Union in 1941, German troops assaulted the Ukraine. German land-based aircraft were the primary threat to the Soviet ships supporting the Red Army. The Germans pushed through the Ukraine and along the Black Sea coast, finally being stopped at Novorossiysk late in 1942. During the German offensive the ports and shipyards along the Black Sea were devastated.

The surviving Soviet ships and naval aircraft then supported the Soviet counteroffensive. Several naval flotillas were established in the Black Sea area by the Soviet high command during the war, among them the Azov and Danube flotillas. Both flotillas saw extensive combat under the command of then–Rear Admiral Gorshkov. Also, L.I. Brezhnev, General Secretary of the Communist Party from 1964 until his death in 1982, saw action with the Black Sea Fleet as a political officer during an amphibious landing by the 18th Army.

After the war the shipyards in the Black Sea region were rapidly rehabilitated to help rebuild the Soviet fleet. The formation of NATO in 1949 and the fact that Turkey and Greece successfully resisted Communist takeover efforts seemed to deny the Black Sea Fleet easy access to the Mediterranean through the Turkish Straits. Still, in 1958 the Soviets deployed naval forces into the Mediterranean. These were submarines that in 1960 were based, with a tender, at Vlore (Valona), Albania. The following year, as a result of the Sino-Soviet dispute, the Soviets were forced to abandon Vlore, leaving behind two Whiskey-class submarines that had been seized by the Albanians. The loss of this base pointed up the limitation of Soviet naval logistics, and Soviet combatant forces were not again deployed on a sustained basis to the Mediterranean until 1964.

2. More properly the KNIAZ POTEMKIN TAVRICHESKI. After the mutiny she was renamed the PANTELEIMON and from May 1917 the BORETZ ZA SVOBODU.

From that time onward Soviet naval forces have operated continuously in the Mediterranean, with surface ships and aircraft coming from the Black Sea Fleet and submarines from the Northern Fleet (see chapter 7). By the early 1970s the Soviets had an average daily strength of 50 or more naval units in the Mediterranean. This force, designated as the Fifth *Eskadra*, reached a peak strength of some 73 surface ships and 23 submarines during the October 1973 confrontation with the United States in the Yom Kippur war in the Middle East.[3] Efforts to obtain support bases for the Soviet Mediterranean squadron centered on Egypt (until the Soviets were ejected in 1973) and continue in Syria. Air bases are available to the Soviets in Libya as well as Syria.

The typical composition of the Fifth *Eskadra*'s 50 or more naval units during the 1980s was:

- 7 torpedo attack submarines
- 2 cruise missile attack submarines
- 12 cruisers, destroyers, and frigates
- 1 to 3 minesweepers
- 1 to 3 amphibious ships
- approx. 25 auxiliary ships, including survey, research, and intelligence collection ships

By the late 1980s, apparently as part of the reduction in fleet operating tempo, the Mediterranean squadron was reduced to an average of 30- to 40-odd ships: 6 to 10 large surface combatants, 5 to 7 attack submarines, with the remainder small combatants, amphibious ships, and auxiliary ships.

Soviet combat operations in the Black and Mediterranean seas would be supported by land-based aircraft from bases in the Crimea, with forward deployments possible into Libya and Syria. In addition, cruiser-helicopter-carriers of the MOSKVA class are based in the Black Sea and operate regularly in the Mediterranean as do the KIEV-class aircraft carriers when they are in the Black Sea area. The Black Sea Fleet also has the largest cruiser-destroyer force of any of the Soviet fleets.

In total, the Black Sea Fleet has 26 percent of the Navy's major combatants (frigates and above) but only 7 percent of the Navy's submarines with no nuclear or ballistic missile units. The Black Sea Fleet has 28 percent of the Navy's aircraft—which includes a large number of transport and training aircraft—and 19 percent of the Navy's personnel.

The Black Sea Fleet is commanded by Admiral M.N. Khronopulo, who took command in mid-1985. Before that, from December 1981, he was the fleet's first deputy commander. Khronopulo replaced Admiral A.M. Kalinin, who had only been appointed to the command of the Black Sea Fleet in June 1983. The removal of a fleet CinC after only two years was highly unusual; Kalinin was retired. (He had commanded the two Soviet destroyers that visited the port of Boston in 1975.)

The fleet headquarters is located at Sevastopol.

CASPIAN SEA FLOTILLA

The Red Banner Caspian Sea Flotilla is primarily a small patrol force operating on the world's largest inland sea, which is shared with Iran.

The Caspian Flotilla currently operates 4 Riga-class frigates, 1 light frigate, 5 patrol combatants, 22 lesser patrol craft, 11 minesweepers, 13 Polnocny-class LSMs, and several auxiliary ships. No aircraft are assigned to the flotilla. Total personnel strength is about 4,000 officers and enlisted men.

The Caspian Sea Flotilla is commanded by Rear Admiral V.B. Leshchenko, who has his headquarters at Baku.

Although naval activity on the Caspian is limited, there is considerable shipping with most of the cargo being oil and grain. Offshore oil wells in the Caspian contribute significantly to the Soviet Union's petroleum production.

History. Under Peter I Russian forces fortified portions of the Caspian coast and built a fleet that gained the ports of Baku and Derbend by treaty. Subsequently Baku was lost, only to be recaptured from Persia in 1816. Later treaties gave the Russians the exclusive right to have warships on the sea, although Persia continued to hold the southern coast and Iran continues to operate patrol boats in this area.

Russian and Soviet naval operations on the Caspian continued with the construction of a canal from the Black Sea permitting the rapid transfer of ships up to destroyer size between the two bodies of water.

PACIFIC FLEET

The largest of the four Soviet fleets and the one with the largest operating area is the Red Banner Pacific Fleet. Whereas in war the three European fleets would oppose the United States and NATO forces, the Pacific Fleet would oppose the People's Republic of China as well as the United States and its allies (South Korea, Japan, and possibly other nations, depending upon the wartime scenario).

The peacetime responsibilities of the Pacific Fleet include operations throughout the Pacific, and the fleet provides most of the ships that deploy to the Indian Ocean.

There has been a significant buildup of the Pacific Fleet during the past few years because of the unsettled political situation in Southeast Asia, the Soviet invasion of Afghanistan in 1979, the turmoil in the Persian Gulf region, and the continued unrest along the eastern coast of Africa. The principal mission of the Pacific Fleet, of course, is defending the Soviet Siberian coast, second only to the Arctic coast in length. But the fleet also has offensive missions: it has a large submarine force, supported by two of the four KIEV-class VSTOL carriers and a large number of other surface combatants, and it has the largest amphibious lift capability of the four fleets, including two IVAN ROGOV-class ships.

In general, the Soviet Pacific coast provides more direct access than European coasts to the open oceans. The major port complex of Vladivostok opens into the Sea of Japan with four major straits giving egress into the Pacific. The Soviets control one exit (Kuril Strait), and another separates Japan and the Russian-held island of Sakhalin (La Perouse), while the two other exits are controlled by Japan (Tsugaru Strait) and Japan and South Korea (Korea Strait). Their blockade by the West is unlikely except in the most extreme circumstances because of the dependence of Japan and Korea on maritime trade. The second major naval port in the Far East is Petropavlovsk on the coast of desolate Kamchatka. Most of the Pacific Fleet's nuclear-propelled submarines are based there, with direct access to the Pacific Ocean.

The Soviet Siberian coast has several ports vital to Soviet trade. These ports move cargo to and from European Russia (reducing the load on the severely limited trans-Siberian railway). They facilitate the economic and politically lucrative trade with the Third World nations of western South America, Southeast Asia, India, the Middle East, and eastern Africa.

History. Russians reached the Pacific coast of Siberia in significant numbers in the mid-seventeenth century. The towns of Anadyr' and Okhotsk were founded in 1649. The area grew in importance at a rapid pace, largely because of trade with China and then with Japan. Commodore Matthew Calbraith Perry, commander of the U.S. Navy's East India Squadron, forced the economic opening of Japan in 1853–1854 to preempt a Russian squadron in the area and prevent the tsar's officers from reaping the benefits of a treaty with Japan.

The Russian Okhotsk Flotilla was formed in 1731, then reorganized and renamed the Siberian Naval Flotilla in 1856. In addition

---

3. The Soviet force consisted of 5 cruisers, 14 destroyers, 6 escort ships, 2 Nanuchka-class missile ships, 8 amphibious ships, 38 intelligence collection and auxiliary ships, and about 23 submarines. Most if not all of these surface ships were from the Black Sea Fleet; all of the submarines were from the Northern Fleet. At the time the U.S. Sixth Fleet in the Mediterranean had some 60 ships, but that force's three aircraft carriers provided a superior surface striking force.

to the flotilla, the 1st Pacific Squadron was established. At the start of the 1904–1905 war with Japan, the Russian Navy had 7 of its 15 modern battleships based at Port Arthur (the Japanese Navy had six modern battleships then in commission).

The Russo-Japanese War of 1904–1905 was a disaster for the Pacific Squadron as well as for a large reinforcing fleet sent by the Russians from the Baltic and Black seas. The Japanese triumph at the Battle of Tsushima on 27 May 1905 destroyed Russian naval power in the Pacific and established Japan as a world power. After the war the Russian Navy in the Far East consisted of the weakened Siberian and Amur flotillas. After the Revolution of 1917 Japanese and American troops landed at Vladivostok to support anti-Communist forces and help remove a Czech army in central Russia that the Allies wished to transport to the European theater.

The Japanese left Siberia in 1922, after which the Soviets formed the Vladivostok ship detachment and the Amur Naval Flotilla in the Far East. These organizations were disbanded in 1926, with the ships and craft being assigned to the border guards and the new Far Eastern Naval Flotilla. The naval units were organized as the Naval Forces of the Far East in April 1932, and on 11 January 1935, as Soviet forces in the area increased, the title Pacific Fleet was assigned.

Pacific Fleet aircraft were involved in the fighting with Japan in Manchuria in the late 1930s. Russian naval ships moved troops and material and evacuated wounded. When the Great Patriotic War began in Europe in June 1941 the Pacific Fleet consisted of 14 destroyers, 91 submarines, numerous lesser craft, and some 500 aircraft. These units were essentially idle during the war with 147,000 men from the fleet being sent to fight as ground troops in the European theater.

When the Soviet Union attacked Japan in August 1945, the Pacific Fleet had 2 cruisers, 13 destroyers, 78 submarines, plus other ships and craft, and 1,549 aircraft. During operations against Manchuria and Korea in the final days of the war, the fleet attacked Japanese shipping and supported ground operations with air attacks and logistic support. Several amphibious landings, largely unopposed, were made at ports along the coast of Korea, Sakhalin, and the Kuril Islands. Some were undertaken in conjunction with parachute landings.

In January 1947 the Pacific Fleet was divided into the Fifth Fleet (headquartered at Vladivostok) and the Seventh Fleet (headquartered at Sovetskaya Gavan'). They were reunited into a single Pacific Fleet in 1953.

Significant long-range operations of the Pacific Fleet began in 1959 when a SVERDLOV-class cruiser and two destroyers visited Djakarta, Indonesia. This was the harbinger of extensive Soviet naval assistance to the Sukarno government in Indonesia. Soviet naval operations expanded in the Pacific during the 1960s and spread into the Indian Ocean, with major ship and missile transfers to the Indian Navy contributing to that force's startling success against Pakistan in the 1971 war between the two nations.

The Soviet Pacific Fleet observed the U.S. naval and air operations in the Vietnam War with great interest. Soviet intelligence collection ships (AGIs) periodically operated in the Gulf of Tonkin, with one AGI usually on station off Guam to observe the U.S. Polaris submarine base and detect B-52 bomber missions taking off from the island. Warnings of raids against Communist forces in Vietnam were broadcast moments after the planes took off. Soviet naval ship visits to Communist Vietnam began in March 1979, calling at the northern port of Haiphong and the southern ports of Da Nang and Cam Ranh Bay. Bear-D reconnaissance aircraft began flights from Da Nang in April 1972, flying missions over the South China Sea including flights over U.S. naval ships. Reportedly, the Soviets also began improvements to facilities at Kompong Som in Cambodia.

During the 1970s the Pacific Fleet began receiving first-line units at about the same time as the Soviet European fleets. This was highlighted by the transfer of the MINSK, the second of the KIEV-class aircraft carriers, to the Pacific in June 1979. The carrier was accompanied by the IVAN ROGOV, the largest amphibious ship in the Soviet Navy. Four guided missile cruisers (one Kresta I, one Kresta II, and two Karas) plus several lesser surface warships and submarines also joined the Pacific Fleet from 1978 to 1980.

Another KIEV-class carrier, the NOVOROSSIYSK, transferred to the Pacific Fleet in 1984, followed in 1985 by the nuclear-propelled battle cruiser FRUNZE, the second ship of the KIROV class. The buildup and modernization of the Pacific Fleet is continuing.

In addition to the two VSTOL carriers, the Pacific Fleet boasts

A Tarantul III missile corvette and an Osa II missile craft in the Baltic. Small combatants are important for Soviet sea control operations in coastal waters and adjacent seas. The 76.2-mm gun mounting and four SS-N-22 anti-ship missiles in the Tarantul III are similar to weapons in larger surface combatants. (West German Navy)

one-third of the Soviet submarine force (including 23 of the 62 modern strategic missile submarines), 28 percent of the major surface warships (frigate and larger), and the largest of the fleet air arms with 32 percent of the total naval aircraft. Some 16 percent of the Navy's manpower is assigned to the fleet, including the largest contingent of Naval Infantry (marines).

Admiral G.A. Khvatov commands the Pacific Fleet, having taken the command in January 1987. Previously he was the fleet's Chief of Staff. Khvatov's predecessor as fleet commander was Admiral of the Fleet V.V. Sidorov, who held the position from 1981 to 1987. He is now the Deputy CinC of the Navy for Rear Services.

Fleet headquarters are at Vladivostok.

A Kiev-class VSTOL carrier is silhouetted in the Mediterranean as seen across the deck of a Sovremennyy-class destroyer. Modern ships such as these are found in all four of the Soviet fleets.

Submarines are major players in essentially all Soviet naval missions. The 1990s will see continued production of advanced Soviet submarines—such as this Northern Fleet Akula-class SSN—and probably the debut of the next generation of submarines from Soviet shipyards by the end of the decade. (Royal Navy)

CHAPTER 6

Missions and Tactics

Aviation—both land-based and ship-based—is very important for Soviet naval operations. Here a Tu-20 Bear-D, a long-range surveillance and missile guidance aircraft, is looked over by a U.S. Navy F-14A Tomcat fighter. Despite the extensive use of satellites for these roles, the venerable Bear is still an important component of Soviet naval operations. (U.S. Navy)

Soviet naval missions have evolved continuously since World War II. The current missions—according to the Soviet volume *The Navy: Its Role, Prospects for Development, and Employment*—"include those of vital importance to the state."[1] Three missions are listed (with specific activities added by the author of this volume):

- Repulse enemy aerospace attack
    - anti-strategic missile submarine (SSBN)
    - anti-carrier
    - anti-submarine-launched cruise missile
- Neutralization of enemy military-economic potential
    - strategic attack (with submarine-launched ballistic and cruise missiles)
    - anti-Sea Lines Of Communications (SLOC)
- Destruction of groupings of enemy armed forces
    - local sea supremacy
    - support of ground troops
    - protection of Soviet strategic missile and attack submarines

To a significant degree these are traditional missions of the Soviet Navy that have been revised and articulated in different terms more acceptable to the contemporary Soviet leadership. Since World War II there have been several changes in the principal missions of the Soviet Navy. Immediately after the war Josef Stalin gave high priority to rebuilding the fleet (see chapter 11); he envisioned a large, balanced force that could undertake a number of offensive as well as defensive missions. In part Stalin's fleet begun in the late 1940s was an updated repeat of the large fleet he had begun a decade earlier.

1. Rear Adm. N.P. V'yunenko, Capt. 1st Rank B.N. Makeyev, and Capt. 1st Rank V.D. Skugarev, *The Navy: Its Role, Prospects for Development, and Employment* (Moscow: Military Publishing House, 1988), USN trans. pp. 27–32.

The postwar evolution of primary Soviet naval missions appears to have been:

early 1950s	Fleet in Being
	Coastal Defense/Anti-Amphibious*
1950s	Anti-Carrier*
1960s	Anti-Western Sea Lanes*
	Anti-Polaris*
	Strategic Strike
1960s–1970s	Forward Deployments for Political Considerations
1980s	Force Projection—Support to Third World Conflicts and Confrontations
	National Aerospace Defense

* indicates "defense of the homeland" missions

At the same time that Soviet naval missions are being clarified to fit with the new Gorbachev defense posture, there are major improvements being made to capabilities in virtually all naval combat areas—anti-surface, anti-submarine, and anti-air warfare, plus theater/tactical nuclear and chemical operations, mine warfare, and intelligence collection.

MISSIONS

Repulse of an enemy aerospace attack or defense of the homeland from Western naval forces is considered the primary Soviet naval mission. This mission has led to a tactical style that tends to pervade all naval missions. Although the Navy has gone through a series of radical changes in organization and leadership as well as some changes in mission, the consistency of tactical style in the Soviet Navy is remarkable.

It would appear in 1990—as it did more than 60 years earlier—that the basic tactical concept of the Soviet Navy is to attack any hostile ship attempting to approach within striking range of the Soviet landmass or sensitive sea-air space. The concepts of concentration of force and of all-arms strike developed during the post-Revolution decade also remain in force today. These concepts, of course, have been transmuted very considerably, so that the attack may now be mounted far from the Soviet coast and the target may now be a U.S. strategic missile submarine rather than a hostile battleship approaching the coast. However, conceptual similarities and their theoretical consequences remain.

Profound differences between Soviet and Western naval "styles" have important analytical consequences. Soviet warships with characteristics somewhat similar to Western types often have very different roles and should not be counted as analogous to those Western ships. Perhaps the most significant point here is that the fundamental Soviet mission has been, and remains, the defense of the homeland, with the perimeter of that defense continuously expanding.

The naval targets for these operations are U.S., British, and French ballistic missile submarines (SSBNs); U.S. aircraft carriers; and U.S. submarines and surface ships armed with the Tomahawk Land-Attack Missile (TLAM). Thus, Anti-Submarine Warfare (ASW) is of major importance to the Soviet Navy. Also included, however, is the defense against cruise missiles themselves, with indications that the Soviets believe that warships can defend the shore from cruise missiles as well as from naval forces.

Neutralization of enemy military-economic potential consists primarily of strategic attack with submarine-launched ballistic missiles and cruise missiles. Included in this mission are strategic missile submarines that serve in the roles of deterrence, preemptive strike, warfighting, and strategic reserve, depending upon the scenario of the crisis or conflict.

The large number of SSBNs in the Soviet fleet, their relatively high survivability, their large weapons payload, and missile ranges that permit them to strike targets in the United States from Soviet home waters or from under the Arctic ice pack, make these forces highly attractive to Soviet planners. About one-third of the Soviet Union's strategic warheads are now in submarine ballistic missiles; that number, however, is expected to be reduced to about 20 per-

cent of the strategic warheads in the late 1990s because of the extensive Soviet deployment of mobile ICBMs.

It is not clear how much submarine-launched cruise missiles will count in considerations of future Soviet strategic forces. The SS-N-21 can be fired from the torpedo tubes of several submarine classes as well as from the especially configured Yankee Notch SSGN; the larger SS-N-24 missile is now carried in a single converted Yankee SSGN, but additional submarines to launch that missile are probably under construction.

Also included under this mission are attacks on Allied SLOCs, especially U.S. merchant shipping that would carry tanks, munitions, and other sinews of war across the Atlantic and Pacific for a campaign against the USSR. Merchant ships would be targets for the older Soviet attack submarines, including the Echo II and Juliett cruise missile craft (SSGN/SSG). However, the anti-SLOC mission will also be assigned to the non-nuclear submarines of the Foxtrot, Tango, and Kilo classes. These submarines would be particularly effective in shallow areas, such as the Caribbean–Gulf of Mexico and Western European waters. In addition to torpedoes and anti-ship missiles, the submarines could be employed effectively as minelayers.

The Soviet interest in interdicting Western SLOCs has a high priority on the basis of articles published in the January and February 1990 issues of the Soviet naval journal *Morskoy Sbornik* under the byline of Admiral Chernavin. His name on this detailed and lengthy exposition of "The Struggle for the Sea Lanes of Communication: Lessons of War and the Modern Era" is a clear indication of emphasis on this role for the Soviet Navy.

Chernavin observes:

> Maritime shipping became an important factor that determines the capacity of NATO countries to maintain economic and military potential at a high level. . . . Hence in our view arises the need to once again return to the problem of warfare on sea lanes of communication.

After drawing on historical data on the effectiveness of anti-shipping efforts in both World Wars, Chernavin further observes that experience

> keenly revealed the need to develop submarines with improved characteristics. This once again confirmed the irrefutable fact that the state that manages to approach the beginning of a war with the best combat equipment will have an advantage. It is difficult to set up mass production of modern types of submarines during war.

While stressing the importance of submarines in the anti-SLOC campaign, Chernavin also stresses the importance of mines, of marines and other strike forces in the opening stages of a war to capture or close certain ports, and direct attacks on ports and shipyards (that could replace lost merchant tonnage). Chernavin acknowledges, however, that such attacks "inevitably" result in nuclear exchanges.

Although interpretations of Chernavin's articles in *Morskoy Sbornik* may differ, his emphasis on attacking merchant shipping/SLOCs is highly significant.

Destruction of groupings of enemy armed forces would be accomplished by Soviet naval air, surface, and submarine forces. Included under this mission are both amphibious forces (to provide support of Soviet ground forces) and specialized anti-submarine forces. The importance of ASW—for attacking Western SSBNs as well as for protecting Soviet undersea craft—has been constantly stressed by Soviet naval leaders and has been used as the rationale for the development of the MOSKVA and KIEV classes of aviation ships and for several classes of surface combatants.

Attacks against Western surface ships would also be made by missile-carrying aircraft of Soviet strategic aviation (see chapter 8).

The Soviet approach to ASW is required, in part, because of geography. Soviet attack submarines must reach the open seas through straits or "choke points" where they could be vulnerable to interdiction. But there is also a historical precedent. Admiral S.G. Gorshkov, Commander in Chief of the Soviet Navy from 1956 to 1985, has written of the U-boat campaign in the Atlantic during World War II: "Despite the exceptional threat to submarines by ASW forces, the German naval command did not conduct a single operation or other specially organized combat actions directed at destroying these forces, which doubtlessly reduced the intensity of the [German U-boat] communications battle."[2] And, one of the main reasons why the U-boats did not achieve victory "was that the submarines did not receive support from other forces, and above all from the Air Force, which would have been able both to carry out the reconnaissance for the submarines and destroy ASW forces."[3]

While some Western analysts contend that such statements are hyperbole, a ruse to gain more support for surface warships and naval aviation, internal Soviet naval documents show otherwise. And, the use of such forces to destroy or distract an enemy's ASW forces certainly is logical. Finally, the indications that the Soviets place SSBNs in "havens" or "bastions" in the Arctic and Sea of Okhotsk, where they can be more easily defended by land-based aircraft and are less vulnerable to Allied surface and air attacks, further support Admiral Gorshkov's contentions.

There appears to be no strain of Soviet naval thought, on either the mission or the tactical level, parallel to Western concepts of sea control. On the mission level, the Soviet Navy under Gorshkov rejected the theories of Rear Admiral Alfred Thayer Mahan, which form the basis of U.S. naval thought (although Mahan is more often quoted by U.S. naval officers who have not actually read him). Admiral Gorshkov wrote, "The Mahan theory of 'control of the sea,' considered indisputable, according to which only a general engagement of major line forces could lead to victory . . . did not at all take into account not only the near-future prospects, but even the notable trends in the development of naval technology."[4]

Rather, Gorshkov preferred a Russian naval strategist and historian, Rear Admiral V.A. Belli, who wrote:

> To achieve superiority of forces over the enemy in the main sector and to pin him down in the secondary sectors at the time of the operation means to achieve *control of the sea* in a theater or a sector of a theater, i.e., to create such a situation that the enemy will be paralyzed or constrained in his operations, or weakened and thereby hampered from interfering with our execution of a given operation.[5] [Gorshkov's emphasis]

In reality, Mahan's concepts had little practical application to the Soviet Union during the 1920s and 1930s because of the lack of capital ships and their maritime activities were limited. From the 1950s the availability of radar, effective radio (and then satellite) communications, long-range aircraft, advanced submarines, guided missiles, and even nuclear weapons for the war at sea made Mahan's concepts even more questionable. Coupled with geographic considerations and other factors, modern technology has given Mahan little if any relevance to the Soviet Navy of the modern era. Indeed, in his January-February 1990 articles on SLOC interdiction (*Morskoy Sbornik*), Admiral Chernavin called on the historical experience of World War II to demonstrate that

> The theory of the "eternal principles" of war at sea proclaimed by Admiral A. Mahan, the apologist of imperialist sea power, who advocated the creation of overwhelming material superiority over enemy navies and who asserted that an advantage in ships-of-the-line

has decisive significance for success in war at sea, also turned out to be untenable.

On the tactical level of sea control, the Soviets certainly wish to protect their own coastal shipping and their ocean-going units from Western naval attack. But in general the Soviets appear to view the sea in wartime as a jungle, with all or most warships subject to rapid destruction. Recent decisions to build relatively large and expensive surface combatants as well as aircraft carriers may lead to reconsideration of this tactical issue.

Indeed, the development of these ships fits more with a new Soviet naval mission, first espoused during the 1960s when Soviet naval forces began regular, and in some cases sustained, deployments in noncontiguous seas—the Mediterranean and Caribbean seas, the Indian Ocean, and the western Pacific. These are mainly missions to show political presence and project force in the Third World. To quote Admiral Gorshkov, again, speaking of forward operations in peacetime:

> Friendly visits by Soviet seamen offer the opportunity to the peoples of the countries visited to see for themselves the creativity of socialist principles in our country, the genuine parity of the peoples of the Soviet Union and their high cultural level. In our ships they see the achievements of Soviet science, technology and industry. Soviet mariners, from rating to admiral, bring to the peoples of other countries the truth about our socialist country, our Soviet ideology and culture and our Soviet way of life.[6]

The Soviet Union, with approximate strategic and conventional weapons parity with the United States, during the Brezhnev era began seeking to gain advances in the Third World, and as Oliver Cromwell remarked, "A man-of-war is the best ambassador." Now the Soviets have gone a step beyond that sending sailors as ambassadors. In a less-publicized exposition on naval cruises, Admiral Gorshkov was more pointed:

> Further growth in the power of our navy will be characterized by an intensification of its international mission. While appearing within our armed forces as an imposing factor in regard to restraining imperialist aggression and ventures, at the same time the Soviet Navy is a consolidator of international relations.[7]

For several years the Soviet Union has used proxy troops in Africa, the Middle East, and Southeast Asia, armed with Soviet weapons and sometimes directed by Soviet advisors. Soviet merchant ships and, to a more limited degree, naval ships have supported these activities. The Soviet Navy has used amphibious ships to move Third World troops in the Middle East, while warships steaming offshore have provided political support as well as collected intelligence for allies.

The Soviet naval and merchant fleets now being built permit—in Western terms—"force projection" into the Third World. According to Gorshkov, "The Soviet navy, in the policy of our Party and state, acts as a factor for stabilizing the situation in different areas of the world, promoting the strengthening of peace and friendship between the peoples and restraining the aggressive strivings of the imperialist states."[8]

TACTICS

Soviet naval missions require the destruction of enemy warships attempting to enter defensive and operational areas. This, in turn, requires a combination of (1) reconnaissance and surveillance to detect the intruder, (2) command and control to bring superior forces to attack at the proper time and location, and (3) effective strikes against the target ship or group of ships. These elements have been well developed by the Soviet Navy.

2. Adm. Gorshkov, *Red Star Rising at Sea* (Annapolis, Md.: Naval Institute Press, 1974), p. 100. This is a compilation of translations of the 11 articles authored by Admiral Gorshkov that originally appeared in *Morskoy Sbornik* [Naval Digest] in 1972–1973. These unprecedented articles by the serving head of a navy were reprinted in the Naval Institute *Proceedings* during 1974. The articles were revised and reprinted in book form, again under Gorshkov's byline, as *Morskaya Moshch Gosudarstva* [The Sea Power of the State] (Moscow: Voenizdat, 1976), and in English by the Naval Institute Press in 1979.

3. Ibid., p. 103.

4. Ibid., p. 40.

5. Ibid., p. 71. Rear Adm. Belli, at the time a captain 2nd rank, made the statement in his synopses-theses, "Theoretical Principles of Conducting Operations" at the Soviet Naval Academy [i.e., Soviet naval war college], 1938.

6. Adm. Gorshkov, *The Sea Power of the State* (Annapolis, Md.: Naval Institute Press, 1979), p. 252.

7. Adm. Gorshkov, "Naval Cruises Play Role in Training, International Relations," *Bloknot Agitatora* (no. 8, April 1973), pp. 3–6.

8. Adm. Gorshkov, *The Sea Power of the State*, p. 277.

History. The evolution of contemporary Soviet doctrine and tactics dates from the problems faced immediately after the Revolution and Civil War. The new socialist state had neither the capital ships nor the industrial base to build an effective fleet. At the same time, threats from the sea were a major concern, as Britain, France, Japan, and the United States had used their navies to support anti-Bolshevik forces during the Russian Civil War.

Soviet naval forces were only gradually built up, and then in the context of a military program that emphasized ground and air forces. Once Soviet industrialization had begun in earnest, it was far easier to build light craft and then small warships. Although former tsarist officers continued to call for a battle fleet as a prerequisite for effective naval defense, a "young school" (*molodaia shkola*) of Soviet naval theorists attempted to turn this weakness into a tactical strength by a combination of limiting the naval mission and at the same time enforcing combined-arms operations.

The debate was considerable. V.I. Zov, the naval commissar from 1924 to 1926, personally criticized members of the "old school." In an address at the Naval Academy (i.e., war college) in early 1925, Zof declared:

> You speak of aircraft carriers and of the construction of new types of ships . . . while at the same time completely ignoring the economic situation of our country and the corresponding conditions of our technical means—and completely ignoring the fact that perhaps tomorrow or the day after we will be called on to fight. And with what shall we fight? We will fight with those ships and personnel that we have already.[9]

Thus, the concept of sea control in the Western sense was largely abandoned. In its place came pure coastal defense, with the advantages to be gained by tight coordination of the forces that could be afforded: coastal guns, land-based aircraft, light craft, and mines. Submarines and offshore pickets—designated *Storozhevoy Korabl'* (SKR) or "guard ship" by the Soviets—were, it appears, seen primarily as a means of detecting enemy ships entering the guarded area.

Josef Stalin, however, in the late 1920s decided to build a conventional, blue-water surface fleet (see chapter 11). By that time a heavy industry base was being built up in Russia. The Soviet support of the Republicans in the Spanish Civil War of 1936–1938 and the limited campaign against Japan in 1937 demonstrated the need for major naval forces to support Soviet foreign policy.

World War II halted Stalin's fleet building program, but he sought to promote it again after the war.

It is remarkable in retrospect that there appears to have been no development of tactics for blue-water operations, even with the few large ships available. For example, the Soviets spent little if any effort in developing anti-submarine tactics for the screening of large ships, even when the SVERDLOV-class cruisers appeared in the early 1950s. The destroyers built in that period were primarily armed for and exercised in the anti-ship role, not ASW (or for that matter, even for air defense).

Similarly, not until the *Okean* exercises of 1975 did the Soviets demonstrate major interest in escorting ocean-going convoys and amphibious groups. Previous naval escort activities appear to have been oriented either to coastal operations or to simulating Western tactics.

Before World War II the Soviets employed submarines, guard ships, and land-based aircraft to detect intruders in Soviet territorial areas. They reported detection and track information to a central commander ashore who could maintain a plot of the combat area and coordinate the attack. This type of command and control led directly to the present Soviet command structure and the Soviet Ocean Surveillance System (SOSS) that seeks to make available to a fleet commander a full picture of the potential battle area. (SOSS—a Western term—is discussed below.)

An important concept in centralized targeting by Soviet forces is the "circle of uncertainty." Target data are generally fleeting: an enemy ship or force is reported at a specific point for a brief period. Its movement after that may be random and may well be unknown. In this situation there is an expanding circle of uncertainty around the original datum in which the target may be found. The longer the delay in reaching the target area, the larger the circle and the more difficult the subsequent search and reacquisition.

The Soviets have often emphasized high speed in their attack platforms and missiles precisely because of this problem. There is a great difference in the circle of uncertainty for a Mach 2 missile compared to a Mach 0.8 cruise missile at, for example, 200 miles (320 km), and the need for the high speed (with all its design penalties) testifies to continued reliance on centralized targeting and an attempt to avoid the need for mid-course guidance, which may be difficult or impossible in a combat environment.

Rigid, centralized tactical control has several advantages. First, in the early Soviet period it enhanced political control of military units, which for many years appeared to come before military effectiveness in priority. Second, a central commander could, at least in theory, make the most effective use of the available weapons. Initially small attack craft, submarines, and land-based aircraft were the main striking force of the Soviet Navy; individually they would not be effective against an enemy's capital ships, but under centralized control their potential effectiveness was enhanced considerably. Centralized control also permitted a reduction in the search and targeting requirements for the individual units (radar, sonar), so that more units could be procured for a given cost.

Soviet naval tactics, in contrast with traditional Western tactics, have thus become statistical in character—or to use the Soviet term, "scientific." The combination of centrally collected intelligence and centrally controlled attack forces continues as the basis of Soviet naval practice, although a trend toward decentralization has become apparent in the past few years. In virtually every tactical context, the attack is delivered simultaneously, often along several different axes in an effort to overwhelm the defenses of the target ship or group of ships.

Also, the strike is delivered at almost maximum weapon range. Increases in stand-off weapon range and speed permit attacks to be made sooner than would be possible if the attacking ships or aircraft had to close with the target; moreover, these increases facilitate strikes by more ships or aircraft within a given area.

The longer weapon range also contributes to another key Soviet tactical concept, that of surprise, or, in Admiral Gorshkov's words, "the battle for the first salvo." This is a favorite topic of Soviet tactical discussions. One Soviet military writer has used this definition:

> Surprise is one of the most important principles of military art. This principle consists in choosing the time, means and methods of combat actions allowing to deliver a surprise blow at the enemy and thus to a certain extent to paralyse his will to resist. Surprise gives the possibility to achieve maximum result with the minimum spending of manpower, equipment and time.[10]

Addressing this concept, Admiral Gorshkov wrote:

> the battle for the first salvo—is taking on a special meaning in naval battle under present-day conditions (conditions including the possible employment of combat means of colossal power [nuclear weapons]). Delay in the employment of weapons in a naval battle or operation inevitably will be fraught with the most serious and even fatal consequences, regardless of where the fleet is located, at sea or in port.[11]

Citing Western analysis to explain or justify Soviet beliefs—a common ploy in Soviet writing—one text notes that the combat potential of a force can be increased two and one-half times if it attains surprise. At the same time, a Soviet naval officer has cited Western naval specialists as believing that "under present-day con-

9. V.I. Zof, "The International Situation and the Missions for the Naval Defense of the U.S.S.R.," *Morskoy Sbornik* (May 1925), p. 16.

10. Col. B. Frolov, Ph.D. Candidate of Sciences (History), "Surprise," *Soviet Military Review* (no. 9, 1980), pp. 27–29.

11. Adm. Gorshkov, *Red Star Rising*, pp. 131–132.

ditions the probability of attaining surprise in the first operations by time, axis, and location has *increased considerably in comparison with the past.*"[12] [emphasis added]

The combat concepts of (1) centralized control, (2) comprehensive intelligence and reconnaissance, (3) increasing weapon ranges, and (4) surprise are applicable to almost all phases of Soviet naval tactics. These include anti-surface, anti-submarine, and anti-air warfare as well as missile strikes against hostile territory.

ANTI-SUBMARINE WARFARE

The Soviets employ air, surface, submarine, and possible space-based activities for ASW.[13] The various ASW platforms, weapons, and sensors are discussed elsewhere in this volume. Of particular concern to Western naval planners is the increasing potential of Soviet space-based systems for ASW as well as for anti-surface operations. The Director of U.S. Naval Intelligence predicts that in the near future, "We can also expect the Soviets to expand their manned program, building at least one large space station, which supports military missions, including ASW and ASAT [Anti-Satellite]."[14]

There are two aspects of space-based ASW. The first is to deny Western submarines the use of satellites and space for their navigation and communications. The U.S. Chief of Naval Operations has observed, "Although some thought was given to their vulnerability to jamming, nuclear EMP [Electromagnetic Pulse], laser destructors, or anti-satellite devices, the view was that in peacetime the [U.S.] systems were safe and that in wartime we would not need them for very long."[15] The Soviet ability to interfere with U.S. use of satellites puts the potential for U.S. submarines to carry out their missions.

Second is the actual detection of submarines by space-based devices. The advantages of such concepts are obvious because of their rapid search rate and other factors.[16] Little has been said in public by U.S. officials on the subject of space-based ASW. Reportedly, the U.S. intelligence community has been in agreement that the Soviets have carried out experiments in detecting submerged submarines with side-looking Synthetic Aperture Radar (SAR) on board *Salyut* manned spacecraft as well as from various types of aircraft. The radar is apparently used in efforts to detect surface "signatures" of submerged submarines.

According to Soviet statements, the *Kosmos* 1500 satellite launched in 1983 had radar image–processing capabilities and could transmit real-time images to more than 500 Soviet ships and ground stations. The radar is said to be able to detect or measure sea surface winds, surface effects of naturally occurring internal waves, surface oil slicks, and ice.

The Soviets have written extensively about the potential of space-based submarine detection. One scientist stated:

> It is now becoming clear that, because of satellites, we can know not only the surface patterns of phenomena in the ocean, but also the volumetric, deep picture. Internal waves occur very extensively in the ocean. Their manifestations at the surface can be registered from aboard satellites, and it is possible to judge what is occurring in the upper layer of several hundred meters, which is most important for us.[17]

A trio of Soviet destroyers in the North Atlantic maneuver in an anti-submarine exercise. The Soviet Navy uses multiple platforms in many tactics to take advantage of multiple and at times diverse sensors and weapons. (U.S. Navy, PH2 D. Beech)

Soviet naval officers have also commented on this subject. Citing "materials published in the open press" as a means of avoiding the security issue, one officer stated that SAR "seems especially promising to American specialists for space-based detection of comparatively small (with respect to underwater relief elements) objects in the ocean depths, above all, submerged submarines."[18] Although acknowledging "a host of problems are being noted in the way of practical realization of this possibility," the author, a doctor of technical sciences, believes that those problems could be surmounted.

Americans are not unaware of such developments. In 1985, for example, the U.S. Chief of Naval Operations said that scientific observations from an American space shuttle (orbital) flight the year before had perhaps revealed some submarine locations. A Navy oceanographer on the flight "found some fantastically important new phenomology [sic] that will be vital to us in trying to understand the ocean depths," the admiral explained.[19] While not releasing details of the observations, which were called "incredibly important to us," a Navy spokesman implied that "internal waves"—left by a submarine's underwater transit—were involved. There are also indications that developments in synthetic aperture radar fitted in aircraft and satellites could contribute to submarine detection.[20] The Soviets are known to be working on projects in both internal wave detection and synthetic aperture radar.

Two principal categories of sensors are considered in submarine detection: acoustic and non-acoustic.

Acoustic. Western ASW is overwhelmingly based on passive acoustic detection (i.e., sonars). Advances in acoustic detection are becoming increasingly more difficult as submarines grow quieter and the oceans become nosier with the background sounds of offshore oil drilling, coastal fishing, shipping, and other activities. Moreover, environmental prediction techniques are telling submariners (as well as ASW forces) more about ocean conditions, making it easier for them to hide in their operating environment.

Also, Soviet ASW forces have long emphasized active acoustic detection. This is effective against submarines regardless of how quiet they might be; however, this technique reveals the presence and possibly the location of the "pinging" ship or submarine. Still,

12. Capt. 1st Rank A. Aristov, "Surprise-Factor Effect on the Success of Combat Actions at Sea," *Morskoy Sbornik* (no. 1, 1985), pp. 16–23.

13. A detailed discussion of contemporary ASW methods is found in Donald C. Daniel, "Antisubmarine Warfare in the Nuclear Age," *Orbis* (Fall 1984), pp. 527–552.

14. Rear Adm. Thomas A. Brooks, USN, Director of Naval Intelligence, statement before the Armed Services Committee, House of Representatives, 22 February 1989.

15. Adm. Carlisle A.H. Trost, USN, speech before the National Security Industrial Association, 20 May 1987.

16. See Capt. William D. O'Neil, USNR, "Winning the ASW Technology Race," U.S. Naval Institute *Proceedings* (October 1988), pp. 86–88, 91.

17. B. Nelepo, Member, Ukrainian Academy of Sciences, *Izvestia* (29 July 1981).

18. Capt. 1st Rank A. Partala, "Possibilities of Space-based Radar Detection of Submarines," *Morskoy Sbornik* (no. 8, 1985), p. 89.

19. "Shuttle Flight Yields Data on Hiding Subs," *The Washington Post*, 22 March 1985, and "'Transparent' oceans are more opaque," *The Washington Times*, 22 March 1985.

20. Edgar Ulsamer, "Penetrating the Sea Sanctuary," *Air Force Magazine*, September 1984, p. 29. Such reports were officially denied by the U.S. Department of Defense, e.g., Walter Andrews, "Soviet ability to target subs is denied," *The Washington Times*, 17 August 1984.

in many scenarios, especially in shallow water, active sonar may be the key to detection. (It is possible to deploy a remote active sonar system to work in conjunction with a passive platform, or a remote sound generator to allow a passive sonar to detect echoes.)

Future advances in acoustic detection will also be based on computer technology, and here the West is far ahead of the Soviet Union. As a result of computer research, and of buying and stealing computer technology from the West, Soviet advances in this field are expected. But at some point even computer advances will become subject to the diminishing returns of acoustic detection.

Known Soviet sonars—including seafloor acoustic systems akin to the U.S. SOSUS—are listed in chapter 29.

Non-acoustic. While the Soviets have a large investment in acoustic submarine detection, they have also undertaken intensive research in several areas of non-acoustic submarine detection. These include:

- *surface signature detection* to sense the disturbance on the ocean surface caused by a passing submarine
- *wake detection* to sense the turbulent wake, internal wave wake, or contaminant wake (chemical or radioactive)
- *magnetic/electric field detection* to sense the submarine or the subsurface disturbances caused by the craft's passage

Non-acoustic sensors have been deployed on Soviet ships; however, they are not considered by U.S. officials to be threatening to Western submarines at this time due to their low search rates and sensor/environment limitations.

Some authorities believe that if a breakthrough in non-acoustic detection is forthcoming, the breadth of the Soviet research effort would give them the advantage. There are some who would suggest that the Soviets are close to a breakthrough in ASW. Professor James McConnell, of the U.S. Navy–sponsored Center for Naval Analyses, has written a noteworthy paper on this subject based on Soviet writings.[21] In particular, McConnell cited writings that claimed the Soviets would achieve an effective anti-submarine capability by the late 1980s; "Experience indicates that the Soviets do not normally discuss the capabilities for an option until the arrival of the doctrinal/planning period in which the capabilities are to be put into operation. (Perhaps that is because only then do personnel have a 'need to know.')"[22] Professor McConnell does not, in his unclassified writings, indicate the specific means by which the Soviets could achieve a high non-acoustic detection rate, but it is known that Soviet efforts in this field are significant.

McConnell has also addressed the subject of striking at submarines once they are detected at long range. In particular, he calls attention to the shelved submarine-launched SS-NX-13 ballistic missile as potentially having ASW application, although other weapons could be candidates (see the Anti-Surface Warfare discussion, below).

Regardless of the specific means by which the Soviets would hunt Western SSBNs, to do so is important for them. Increasing concern on SSBN vulnerability in 1984 led the U.S. Congress to secretly vote $10 million for the Central Intelligence Agency to determine how susceptible U.S. strategic missile submarines are to Soviet ASW forces. And, following a review of Soviet submarine developments in 1989 by a blue-ribbon panel that included several of the senior U.S. submarine experts, the chairman of the Armed Services Committee of the House of Representatives, Les Aspin, stated:

> Their [Soviet] subs are not quieter than ours, but they are now quiet enough that classic detection methods are becoming obsolete. And the fact that we have quieter subs simply holds out the certainty that Russian subs will become much quieter still in the years to come.
>
> This development could bring about a sea change in sea warfare—

and not one to our benefit. Soviet hunter subs may now gain a substantial lead over U.S. sub hunters. We depend on the seas to reach other countries, to transport supplies for our troops, and to maintain our carrier task forces. If they are now to be seriously threatened by enemy subs, our entire military strategy and logistics system is in jeopardy.

Traditional Soviet ASW has developed along similar tactical lines as anti-surface tactics. At least into the 1970s most ASW forces were organized into brigades controlled by commanders ashore. In search-and-attack operations, all of the ships defending an area would transmit their sonar data to a shore-based computer that would assign them attack courses and speeds, thus determining the appropriate point for attack. Then the computers went to sea in a cruiser or destroyer, designated *Bol'shoy Protivolodochnyy Korabl'* (BPK), or large anti-submarine ship. BPKs thus became command ships for ASW groups.

The development of the MOSKVA-class helicopter carriers in the 1960s was in line with these ASW tactics. The carriers would bring many units (helicopters) into an area to attack a U.S. Polaris submarine initially detected by long-range, surface ship sonar or possibly by other means. This concept was abandoned, and the MOSKVA class was halted at two ships, because of the increasing range of Polaris missiles and the large number of U.S. missile submarines, and because the MOSKVA probably was not performing as well as expected.

Nevertheless, the two MOSKVAs and their Hormone-A anti-submarine helicopters did give the Soviet fleet its first experience with ship-based aircraft while taking to sea a significant ASW capability. The experience with the MOSKVAs was essential to the development of the subsequent KIEV-class aircraft carriers.

Also in 1967, the first Kresta I missile cruiser went to sea, carrying a single Hormone-B helicopter for missile targeting. This was the first Soviet surface combatant (other than the helicopter ship MOSKVA) to have a full helicopter support capability. The ship design was altered to that of an ASW ship with the Kresta II, which appeared in 1970. This ship carries a Hormone-A ASW helicopter and SS-N-14 ASW missiles in place of anti-ship missiles, demonstrating a significant advance in Soviet ASW doctrine for surface forces.

The Soviets have shown considerable interest in helicopter ASW. They have operated helicopters in this role from ashore as well as afloat as their principal means of attacking submarines at "medium" ranges, i.e., 30–40 n.miles (55–74 km). The Soviet enthusiasm for helicopters can be seen in the Mi-14 Haze, developed specifically for land-based ASW operations, and in the multiple helicopter capacities of the newer surface combatants KIROV and UDALOY. Writing on ASW tactics, a Soviet specialist explained the enthusiasm:

> The participation of helicopters in the search for submarines . . . not only widens the field of "visibility" of the warship carrying it but also substantially increases the ship's capability for conducting protracted tracking of a detected enemy. [Also] it increases the reliability of the employment of ASW weapons. And if it presents no great problem to a submarine to avoid a surface ship, the situation changes radically when a shipborne helicopter comes into the picture. Having a significantly greater speed than a submarine, [the helicopter] puts the submarine in a far more difficult situation.[23]

Systematic airborne ASW tactics were developed in the late 1960s as new ASW aircraft became operational, beginning with the Il-38 May. The tactics were analogous with air anti-ship tactics: the land-based ASW aircraft would fly out to a datum, release sonobuoys to reacquire and localize the target, and then attack. Limitations in the technique included the short range of Soviet sonobuoys, meaning that aircraft could rarely reacquire the target. Nor could the Il-38 carry enough weapons to achieve the "saturation" effect of surface ships firing anti-submarine rockets or releasing depth-charge patterns.

21. James M. McConnell, "A Possible Change in Soviet Views on the Prospects for Anti-Submarine Warfare" (Alexandria, Va.: Center for Naval Analyses, January 1985). This was reprinted as "New Soviet Methods for Antisubmarine Warfare?" *Naval War College Review* (July–August 1985), pp. 16–27.

22. McConnell, "A Possible Change in Soviet Views," p. 8.

23. Capt. 1st Rank N. Vo'yunenko, Doctor of Naval Science, "Concerning Some Trends in the Development of Naval Tactics," *Morskoy Sbornik* (no. 10, October 1975), pp. 21–26.

The later and larger land-based, Tu-142 Bear-F ASW aircraft may have been developed to overcome this limitation. The turbo-prop bomber carries large numbers of sonobuoys to acquire and hold contact on a submarine and also carries a large weapons payload.

Whereas the U.S. Navy considers its nuclear-powered attack submarines (SSN) primarily as anti-submarine platforms, the first Soviet SSN class (November) was not developed for the anti-submarine role. The high-performance Alfa SSN, developed shortly afterwards, may have been originally intended as an anti-submarine craft; however, the Victor and later classes of attack submarines (completed from 1967 onward) are generally considered to be primarily ASW craft in the Western sense, i.e., for trailing enemy submarines and possibly serving in anti-submarine barriers. The Soviets also use diesel-electric attack submarines in this role.

Soviet attack submarines have been observed working with surface forces, apparently in the ASW role. While the U.S. Navy has put forward the concept of employing the high-speed Los Angeles (SSN 688)-class submarines in direct support of surface task forces, the Soviets have envisioned their SSNs in this role for a longer period. The SSN, in coordination with surface ASW ships or aircraft, is a deep, relatively quiet sonar platform. Once a target submarine is detected, the SSN could itself attack or—after communicating with other "killer" forces—withdraw from danger during the ensuing surface or air attack.

A related factor in Soviet submarine ASW is the use of submarines to support other submarines. For example, as a Soviet submarine attempts to transit a U.S. ASW barrier, a U.S. submarine might be unaware that a second, quieter Soviet submarine is in turn trailing the first, masking its own noise signature, waiting for the American craft to attack the transitor, thus revealing its presence and location.

The concept of "breakout," or breaking through U.S. anti-submarine barriers, is very important in Soviet strategy. All three Soviet ASW platforms—aircraft, surface ships, and submarines—can be employed to help submarines break through NATO ASW barriers as well as to defend against Western strategic missile submarines. With the advent of the Delta-class SSBN in 1972, which could strike targets in the United States from Soviet home waters, a new operational capability evolved. Soviet missile submarines from the Northern Fleet would no longer have to transit narrow, and hence potentially dangerous, passages into the Atlantic. Instead, "sanctuaries" could be established in home waters where the missile submarines defended by a combination of surface ships, submarines, and land-based aircraft would be safe from American SSNs.

From a political viewpoint, this role of protecting SSBN sanctuaries may have justified the Kiev-class aircraft carriers. The ships, along with the BPK-series of cruisers and destroyers, supported by land-based aircraft, provide an increasing open-ocean ASW capability. However, without the seafloor surveillance system (SOSUS) available to the United States, at least in the early phases of a war, and without the sensor and computer capabilities available in the West, Soviet ASW is generally thought by the U.S. Navy's leadership to be many years behind Western ASW, although many specialists in the field now question that evaluation.

Anti-submarine warfare is of continuing—and increasing—importance to the Soviet Union. Western strategic missile submarines pose a potent threat to the Soviet homeland. In addition, the Soviets seek to protect their own SSBNs, which are believed to form the primary component of the Soviet strategic missile reserve. Finally, as the Soviets use the seas for long-range political and commercial activities, they must defend their own surface forces from Western and Third World submarines.

ANTI-SURFACE WARFARE

The Soviets have exercised forces in the Anti-Surface Warfare (ASUW) role with land-based strike aircraft flying coordinated, multi-plane anti-ship missile strikes.

Before the strikes there are extensive reconnaissance and intelligence collection efforts. As sufficient data on the target ships is received at the appropriate headquarters, the strike aircraft are launched toward the predetermined datum, under centralized control. The aircraft generally fly high enough for the lead plane to acquire the target with its own missile-control radar, although missiles that can lock-on after launch reduce this requirement. All aircraft in the wave then lock their missiles onto the target. The aircraft—possibly coming from several directions, either simultaneously or in series, and even from different bases—will generally launch their missiles together in an effort to overwhelm defenses.

While naval aircraft are primarily employed in the anti-ship role, during exercises strategic strike aircraft have also participated in this role (see chapter 8).

Surface and submarine missile attacks are coordinated with the strike aircraft when possible. Tactics of the surface force are analogous to those of the strike aircraft. Attacks are controlled either from a headquarters ashore or from a command ship. This is especially true of small combatants—missile and torpedo boats—that are merely attack platforms acting with external targeting data under the directions of a central commander.

There are obvious problems in coordinating air, surface, and submarine attacks. However, improved communications and longer-range and higher-speed missiles do facilitate such coordination. Again, in exercises the Soviets have attempted to synthesize such tactics. In the anti-carrier phases of the *Okean* 1970 exercises the Soviets sent aircraft against simulated U.S. carriers in the waters between Iceland and Britain, while simultaneously in the Far East naval strike aircraft flew against simulated U.S. carriers in the Western Pacific.

In the context of the first salvo concept, these exercises, in pitting their warships against U.S. and Allied task forces, provide the Soviets the opportunity for updated targeting. Shortly before the planned strike, the accompanying Soviet ship or "tattletale" moves away from the target ships. This maneuver prevents the distraction of incoming Soviet missiles from their real targets. Also, the departing tattletale can participate in the missile strike (this probably accounts for the rear-firing missiles that were fitted in the modified Kashin and Kildin destroyers classes).

Multi-platform ASUW tactics are receiving new attention in the Soviet Navy as new surface warship classes emphasizing the anti-ship role are joining the fleet. The Kynda (1962) and Kresta I (1967) classes had a principal armament of anti-ship missiles; they were followed by several cruiser and destroyer classes whose weapons were heavily oriented toward ASW. But three major surface-ship classes have now emerged with heavy anti-ship armament: the destroyer Sovremennyy (1981), the cruiser Slava (1983), and the nuclear-propelled battle cruiser Kirov (1980). However, it should be taken into account that destroyer and ASW cruiser classes built in the 1960s and 1970s have the SA-N-1 and SA-N-3 surface-to-air launchers, both of which can be used against surface targets according to Soviet statements. (It should be noted that the Kiev and Kuznetsov [ex-Tbilisi] classes also have anti-ship missiles.)

With respect to submarines in the anti-shipping role, at least through the 1950s Soviet submarines acting in the coastal defense role were closely controlled by headquarters ashore. This was a continuation of prewar Soviet practices. In a related matter, the Soviets appear to have developed the "flying torpedo"—underwater-launched anti-ship missiles—to give these submarines greater stand-off range against intruders. Note that these submarines are best employed with off-board sensors and centralized control to coordinate missile strikes. Recent developments, especially the SS-N-19 missiles fired from the large Oscar-class SSGN, significantly increase Soviet capabilities because of the submarine's high submerged speed, the long range of its missiles, and the large number of missiles in this class (24 compared to 8 in the Echo II and Charlie classes).

(The older, surface-launched SS-N-3/12 submarine missiles originally were developed from the land-attack SS-N-3c, intended for strategic attack against the United States. When the SS-N-3/12 missiles are used in the anti-ship role, the submarine must remain on the surface for many minutes after launching to send target data updates while the missile is in flight.)

A final consideration in ASUW is the possible use of land-based ballistic missiles against enemy ships. Soviet coastal defense forces have surface-to-surface cruise missiles for use against ships in the coastal defensive zones, possibly out to a couple of hundred miles (see chapter 9). Obviously, ballistic missiles have long offered the advantages of longer range and shorter flight time; but initially a ballistic missile could not be guided toward a moving target after being launched, and the time delay from target acquisition to missile arrival at the datum could be considerable—enough to permit the target ship to escape, especially if the mode of surveillance could not provide an exact location. The limited accuracy of the early ballistic missile would further reduce possible effectiveness.

There is ample evidence, however, that at least from the early 1960s, when the classic work of Marshal V.D. Sokolovskiy, *Military Strategy*, was published, the Soviets have been considering the use of land-based ballistic missiles against surface ships *and against submarines*.[24] For example, in a then-classified article published in October 1961, Admiral V.A. Kasatonov, later the First Deputy CinC of the Soviet Navy (1964–1972), wrote:

> The essence of the problem is to create effective means for the distant destruction of submarines from the air which will make it possible to employ for their destruction the most effective modern means of destruction—missiles with nuclear charges launched from submarines, aircraft, and ships and possibly also from shore launching mounts.[25]

By the late 1960s the Soviet Navy was developing a submarine-launched ballistic missile, the SS-NX-13, apparently for use against surface ships. (This weapon was developed but not deployed; see chapter 28.)

Relatively recent developments in ballistic missile technology, especially the Multiple Independently targeted Re-entry Vehicle (MIRV) and the Maneuvering Re-entry Vehicle (MaRV), coupled with improvements in ocean reconnaissance and high-speed communications, have offered new opportunities for the use of ballistic missiles against naval forces at sea. While Soviet professional writings of late have not discussed this subject, there are other indications of continued Soviet interest. For example, on 2 April 1982 the Soviets fired six SS-20 intermediate-range ballistic missiles into the Barents Sea. These firings are believed to have been related to a naval exercise in the same general area.

Available technology offers the potential for land- and ship-launched ballistic missiles to be used against surface forces. In particular, multiple, maneuvering, and homing warheads for ballistic missiles, plus the ability to re-target the "bus," or warhead dispenser, while in flight will increase the threat to Western naval forces.

ANTI-AIR WARFARE

Anti-Air Warfare (AAW) is a major concern of the Soviet Navy, both for air defense of ships and submarines, and for the defense of land areas of the USSR against Western strike aircraft and land-attack cruise missiles. The potential role of naval forces in providing cruise missile defense for the Soviet homeland has been confirmed by a senior Soviet flag officer.[26] In 1982 Rear Admiral

S.P. Teglev was appointed Chief of Naval Air Defense at naval headquarters.

The development of anti-air warfare in the Soviet Navy has differed significantly from that of the U.S. Navy. American concepts of fleet air defense evolved in the Pacific during World War II, from the use of carrier-based fighters and massive shipboard anti-aircraft gun batteries. By the end of the war the U.S. Navy was developing radar pickets and surface-to-air missiles to combat the Japanese *kamikaze* threat.

In marked contrast, the Soviet fleet's coastal operations from 1941 to 1945 were almost always under the protection of land-based fighter aircraft. With a large land-based naval fighter force, limited long-range operations, and lack of modern technology, there was essentially no advanced AAW development in the Soviet Navy during the first postwar decade.

The situation changed in the 1950s with the revolution in Soviet military affairs. The missile and related developments of the national air defense force, along with the loss of the Navy's fighter arm, led to the accelerated development of ship-based air defenses. Beginning with the new missile ships that went to sea in the early 1960s, the Soviets armed several classes with the SA-N-1 Goa surface-to-air missile. This missile was adopted from the ground-based SA-3, a low- to medium-altitude weapon. The trend at the time was to adopt army missiles and other weapons for naval use; the SA-N-1 was followed by the SA-N-2, converted from the ground-launched SA-2, and the SA-N-4 from the SA-8.

Similarly, ground-based radars and fire-control systems were modified for shipboard use. (In some cases they were unsuccessful; although the SA-2 was one of the most important Soviet missiles, used extensively in Vietnam and the Middle East conflicts, the naval SA-N-2 was fitted to only one ship, the DZERZHINSKIY, and it was a failure.)

These missiles supplemented the anti-aircraft and dual-purpose guns in Soviet warships. Without ship-based aircraft the Soviets were unable to achieve the defense-in-depth of U.S. naval forces. Still, shipboard AAW received significant emphasis, as indicated by Soviet leadership in developing close-in, rapid-fire guns and, with the SA-N-9, missiles for defense against attacking cruise mis-

24. Marshal of the Soviet Union V.D. Sokolovskiy, *Voyennaya Strategiya* [Military Strategy] (Moscow: Voyenizdat, 1962). The book was revised and republished in 1963 and 1967. Sokolovskiy was Chief of the Soviet General Staff from 1953 to 1960. A comparative analysis of the three editions was published in Harriet Fast Scott, *Soviet Military Strategy* (London: Macdonald and Jane's, 1968).

25. Adm. V.A. Kasatonov, "On the Problem of the Navy and Methods for Resolving Them," noted by Capt. Harlan Ullman, USN, "The Counter-Polaris Task" in Michael MccGwire et al., eds., *Soviet Naval Policy: Objectives and Constraints* (New York: Praeger, 1975), pp. 585–600.

26. Interview with Vice Adm. I.V. Kasatonov, First Deputy CinC Northern Fleet, Norfolk, Va., 24 July 1989.

Soviet surface ships are designed to be closed up to operate in chemical and biological environments. Here Vice Admiral I.V. Kasatonov, First Deputy CinC of the Northern Fleet, poses at a periscope on the bridge of the cruiser MARSHAL USTINOV. (Soviet Navy)

siles. Another significant event was the introduction of vertical launchers for AAW with the SA-N-6, with the attendant advantages of firing rate, flexibility, and protection that conventional, single- and twin-arm launchers do not have. The Soviets are also developing submarine-launched air defense missiles.

The availability of the KIEV-class Vertical/Short Take-Off and Landing (VSTOL) carriers from 1975 onward has not resulted in a real ship-based fighter capability. The ships' Yak-38 Forgers, however, do provide an intercept capability against maritime patrol aircraft like the U.S. P-3 Orion, British Nimrod, and French Atlantic. This could be a highly significant capability in some scenarios. Also, the British experience with the Harrier VSTOL in the Falklands conflict indicates that the KIEV-class ships, with the Forger or the next-generation Yak-41 VSTOL aircraft, could have significant capabilities against Third World air forces.

Most authorities believe Soviet naval air defense unquestionably lags behind that of the United States in view of U.S. carrier-based fighters and radar aircraft (i.e., the Navy E-2 Hawkeye as well as the Air Force E-3 AWACS, which have operated with naval task forces). Soviet shipboard radars, missiles, and guns, as well as such tactical concepts as target data exchange among ships, are improving. And, an airborne early-warning aircraft is reported under development for the larger aircraft carriers. That aircraft is expected to be the Airborne Early Warning (AEW) version of the An-74 Madcap.

There is one area of AAW in which the Soviets are unquestionably ahead of the West—nuclear-armed missiles. Western intelligence believes that the SA-N-3 and probably the SA-N-1 and SA-N-6 in some ships can carry nuclear warheads. This would enhance air defense against large-scale air strikes. (While analyses have indicated that a nuclear AAW capability would enhance U.S. force survivability, relatively few U.S. ships are fitted to fire the outdated Terrier-BTN nuclear missile, the only such weapon available to Western navies, and it is being discarded.[27])

The Soviets are increasingly aware of the need for effective AAW, and it is expected to have an increasing role in providing air defense coverage of the Soviet Union against aircraft/cruise-missile attack from seaward sectors.

At the same time, Soviet high-priority ASW operations will be extended because of the threat from U.S. land-attack cruise missiles (i.e., Tomahawk TLAM) that can be carried by all current U.S. attack submarines.

NUCLEAR AND CHEMICAL WARFARE

Discussions of Soviet tactics must include theater/tactical nuclear weapons and chemical weapons, both of which appear to be fully integrated into all levels of Soviet naval forces and planning.[28] The Soviet Navy is armed with a variety of nuclear weapons and regularly conducts offensive and defensive exercises. While there is less public information concerning the potential use of chemical weapons by the Soviet Navy, the massive chemical-warfare capability of the Ground Forces, the apparent use of Soviet-made chemical and

Soviet sailors exercise chemical-biological protective gear on board ship. The Soviet Navy appears to be better trained and prepared to fight in chemical-biological-nuclear environments than are Western navies.

toxin weapons in Afghanistan, Kampuchea (Cambodia), Laos, Yemen, and possibly the Iraq-Iran War, and the Soviet Navy's extensive nuclear and chemical defense training all point to a significant capability in this field as well. (There is also considerable Soviet activity in research for biological warfare.)

The Soviet armed forces began developing their nuclear doctrine in the mid-1950s, after the death of Stalin. Previously, Stalin had believed that the geographic expanse and manpower reserves of the Soviet Union would more than compensate for Western superiority in nuclear weapons. Although he gave high priority to the development of such weapons, Stalin prevented military leaders from realistically considering how to use them or even how to defend against them. This new examination of nuclear issues was labeled a "revolution" by the Soviets.

The initial Soviet nuclear doctrine postulated that any war with the West would rapidly escalate to a strategic nuclear exchange. This concept was quite in line with Khrushchev's defense policies, which sought to reduce large (expensive) conventional forces in favor of a minimal strategic force, primarily ICBMs, and "unconventional" efforts against the West—for example, wars of national liberation and foreign trade.

In the post-Khrushchev era, this attitude has been modified considerably. Writing in *Krasnaya Zvezda*, the daily newspaper of the Ministry of Defense, a Soviet general officer in 1976 warned that a conventional conflict in Europe "carries with it the constant danger of being escalated into a nuclear war."[29] This appears to be the central theme of contemporary Soviet views on theater/tactical nuclear weapons; the officer's article claims that (1) war in Europe is the principal factor in Soviet non-strategic planning, and that (2) there is a distinct danger of conventional conflict escalating to nuclear conflict. But the same article also implies that should a NATO conflict reach a nuclear phase, it need not necessarily reach an all-out, intercontinental nuclear exchange between the Soviet Union and the United States.

An American analysis of Soviet military writings in this field concludes:

> One of the striking aspects of Soviet military literature is the heavy emphasis given to nuclear war fighting and the minute detail with which certain of its combat aspects are addressed. This is particularly true in those writings dealing with the ground-air campaign in the continental land theater, but it also carries over into the Soviet naval professional literature. The net impression is that the Soviet military has faced up to the reality of nuclear warfare, focused on it in their military schools and academies, and at least worked out the

27. Previously the U.S. Navy also had a nuclear version of the ship-launched Talos surface-to-air weapon, which was in service from 1958 to 1978. The nuclear version of the Terrier-BTN missile (Beam-riding, Terrier, Nuclear) entered service in 1962. It is an obsolescent weapon. A nuclear version of the Navy's Standard SM-2 missile had been considered but not approved for development.

28. There has been minimal discussion in the United States on the subjects of nuclear and chemical war at sea on either an official or unofficial basis. One of the few published articles on this subject by a U.S. naval officer is Capt. Linton F. Brooks, USN, "Tactical Nuclear Weapons: The Forgotten Facet of Naval Weapons," U.S. Naval Institute *Proceedings* (January 1980), pp. 28–33. This article draws heavily on research of the BDM Corporation, published in part as "The Soviet Navy Declaratory Doctrine for Theater Nuclear Warfare" (Washington, D.C.: Defense Nuclear Agency, 30 September 1977). Also see Lt. Comdr. T. Wood Parker, USN, "Theater Nuclear Warfare and the U.S. Navy," *Naval War College Review* (January–February 1982), pp. 3–16, and Raymond A. Robinson and Norman Polmar, "Defending Against 'the Poor Man's A-Bomb,'" U.S. Naval Institute *Proceedings* (February 1989), pp. 100–103.

29. "The Soviet Navy Declaratory Doctrine," p. 10.

theory of how it should be fought and won. There is abundant evidence that the Soviets have designed and structured their forces in accordance with their theoretical writings, given the impression that these writings have rationalized concepts that were later incorporated into doctrine.[30]

This attitude is reflected in the Soviet Navy by the relatively large number and variety of tactical nuclear weapons in the fleet.[31] These include "offensive" anti-ship weapons and "defensive" anti-aircraft and anti-submarine weapons, apparently deployed in ships ranging in size from the Nanuchka and Tarantul classes of missile corvettes to the large KUZNETSOV (ex-TBILISI)-class aircraft carriers. Tactical nuclear weapons of various types are also carried in Soviet attack/cruise missile submarines and aircraft.

Nuclear weapons appear to offer two major offensive advantages over conventional weapons in war at sea. First, whereas multiple hits with conventional weapons would probably be required to sink a cruiser or an aircraft carrier, the same task could be performed by a single nuclear weapon, of even small size. Second, a defense against nuclear weapons would require a 100-percent effectiveness, since a single missile penetrating the defenses (leaker) could destroy the target.

A lesser factor is the number of anti-ship weapons that a ship could carry. Basic Soviet military policies dictate that some nuclear weapons will be carried. Any mix of nuclear and conventional would limit the launching ship to firing only conventional weapons in a conventional exchange; but all weapons—conventional as well as nuclear—could be used in a nuclear exchange.

From the Soviet perspective, the use of nuclear weapons in the AAW role would deter concentrated U.S. air attacks against ships, while in ASW operations, a nuclear weapon could compensate for the target submarine's area of uncertainty or the limited effectiveness of conventional weapons. Another consideration is the potential use of high-altitude bursts of nuclear weapons to create Electromagnetic Pulse (EMP) effects that could seriously degrade the electronic and optical systems of ships and aircraft over large ocean areas. Underwater nuclear bursts could similarly reduce sonar effectiveness, creating a condition known as "blue out." Soviet writings demonstrate a familiarity with all of these aspects of nuclear engagement.

Soviet naval readiness for nuclear warfare also includes significant defensive measures. The design of Soviet warships incorporates Chemical-Biological-Radiological (CBR) defensive measures. Warships, even the small Osa missile craft, have protective "citadels," areas that can be sealed to provide a safe, controlled atmosphere, with overpressure to keep out contaminants. Naval ships also have periscopes and other equipment for conning from sealed bridges, CBR washdown devices, and additional features to facilitate survival in a nuclear or chemical environment.[32] Observations of Soviet ships also indicate some hardening features, such as protection of radar wave guides (cables) from blast damage and the EMP effects of nuclear explosions. However, such protective features are not universal in Soviet warships.

A third area of Soviet nuclear preparedness is training and fleet exercises. Soviet naval personnel carry out CBR defense training on a regular basis, and nuclear defensive and offensive maneuvers are a regular part of fleet exercises.

Thus, Soviet naval weapons, warship configurations, and training and exercises point to a major capability for fighting a theater/tactical nuclear conflict at sea. It must be noted, however, that all known Soviet writings on this subject accept that nuclear weapons would first be used on land before they were released for use at sea.

Almost all of the nuclear defensive features point to a chemical warfare capability as well. Again, the munitions and protective

measures of the Soviet Ground Forces have a considerable chemical capabiity. An official U.S. government evaluation states:

> The USSR is better prepared to conduct operations in a chemical environment than any other force in the world. Soldiers receive extensive chemical defense training. Most combat vehicles are equipped with a chemical protective system and a chemical detection alarm system. Chemical defense troops with specialized detection and decontamination equipment are found throughout the ground forces. . . .
> The Soviet Union continues to test, produce, and stockpile chemical weapons. The Soviets have developed the doctrine, plans, personnel and equipment to support their use of chemical weapons.[33]

An earlier U.S. Department of Defense publication had noted: "In Soviet military doctrine, toxic chemicals are associated primarily with theater warfare. The basic principle is to achieve surprise by using massive quantities of chemical agents against unprotected troops or against equipment or on terrain to deny its use."[34]

Chemical munitions can inflict considerably more casualties per weapon than can conventional, high-explosive munitions. This means that chemical weapons offer the opportunity of very high effectiveness per hit without escalation to the threshold of nuclear weapons. It is safe to say that the Soviet Navy is prepared for the use of theater/tactical nuclear weapons and chemical weapons, while the U.S. Navy's surface forces are highly vulnerable to their use.

ELECTRONIC WARFARE

The Soviet Navy's own reliance on "real-time" transmission of reconnaissance and targeting data; the Soviet need for effective Command, Control, and Communications (C³); and the comprehensive Soviet understanding of the potential vulnerabilities of U.S. military C³ activities have led to a heavy emphasis on Electronic Warfare (EW). The Soviet term for offensive and defensive EW, *radioelectronnaya bor'ba* (Radio Electronic Combat, or REC), covers the detection of hostile electronic transmissions, as noted above, but also the neutralization or destruction of the electronic threat and the protection of Soviet systems.

Offensive EW includes jamming and spoofing as well as destroying hostile communications centers and radars using a variety of systems from Soviet shore- air-, surface-, land-, and possibly submarine-based systems. One U.S. Navy communications security specialist has speculated that the Soviet Golf and Hotel submarines converted to special communications craft (SSQ/SSQN)

> may have a REC mission in addition to, if not in place of, their postulated C³ function. What could be more perfect than a jamming/ deception platform that you would probably not detect until it started transmitting? Even then, given the confusion that even a partially successful IFF [Identification Friend or Foe] spoofing, pulse jamming, deceptive repeating or intrusion incident generates, the submarine would probably remain undetected, especially if the source could not be seen on radar.[35]

Several Soviet publications have stressed the need to strike Western C³ installations at the onset of a conflict. Although public Soviet discussion in this area of naval warfare is limited, an official U.S. Army evaluation of Soviet REC estimates that the goal of this activity is to destroy or disrupt at least 50 percent of an enemy's command, control, and weapon-direction systems by either jamming or disruptive fires.[36] In addition to missile and gunfire (and the

30. Ibid., pp. 21–22.

31. See chapter 28 for a list of Soviet naval weapons believed to have nuclear warheads.

32. The only U.S. Navy surface warship configured to operate in a nuclear-chemical environment was the destroyer HERBERT J. THOMAS (DD 833), which was modified in 1963–1964 and discarded in 1974 (transferred to Taiwan).

33. Secretary of Defense Caspar Weinberger, *Soviet Military Power, 1985* (Washington, D.C.: Department of Defense, 1985), pp. 71–72. In June 1990 President Bush and President Gorbachev agreed to reduce U.S. and Soviet chemical weapon stockpiles.

34. Secretary of Defense Caspar W. Weinberger, *Soviet Military Power, 1981* (Washington, D.C.: Department of Defense, 1981), p. 38.

35. Lt. Comdr. Guy Thomas, USN, "Soviet Radio Electronic Combat and the U.S. Navy," *Naval War College Review* (July–August 1982), pp. 16–24. This is an excellent discussion of Soviet REC.

36. Department of the Army, *Soviet Army Operations* (Arlington, Va.: U.S. Army Intelligence and Threat Analysis Center, 1978), p. 5–81.

potential use of nuclear weapons in the EMP mode), Soviet techniques employed in offensive EW are: radar jamming by barrage and spot "noise," chaff, and decoys; electronic jamming of command guidance systems by pulse and simulation techniques; and radio communications noise jamming of AM and FM signals.

Numerous defensive EW techniques have also been noted that stress Communications Security (COMSEC) and Electronic Counter Countermeasures (ECCM). For example, although the Soviets must insure effective radio communications, to the extent possible radio operators will change power, modulation, and antenna direction along with frequency. In addition to command ships and communications submarines (SSQ/SSQN), Soviet naval communications achieve a high degree of survivability through redundant and hardened communications centers ashore. In the Soviet tradition, Naval Headquarters, the fleet command centers, and probably naval communications stations, all have fully equipped backup facilities.

Radar operators will similarly change frequency, power, polarization, and modulation to reduce vulnerability. And, of course, the Soviets stress Emission Control (EMCON) with all electronic and communications equipment. Finally, the Soviets employ anti-radar "camouflage" when possible by doing such things as creating false targets or blending into the terrain and background.

(The West has seen several examples of Soviet REC effectiveness, especially when the Soviets invaded Czechoslovakia in 1968 and when the Egyptians crossed the Suez Canal in the Yom Kippur War of 1973).

INTELLIGENCE AND SURVEILLANCE

Intelligence and surveillance are vital to successful military operations.[37] This is especially true for the Soviet military forces with their highly centralized control.

There are three separate and distinct Soviet agencies that collect intelligence for naval requirements. These are the KGB, the GRU (*Glavnoye Razbedyatel'noye Upravleniye*—Chief Directorate of the Intelligence of the Soviet General Staff), and the naval intelligence organization. The last consists of an intelligence directorate of the Main Naval Staff in Moscow and intelligence directorates within each of the four fleet headquarters. The four fleet directors support operating forces within their areas; operate intelligence collection ships (AGIs), aircraft, and other naval and civilian assets; and make the results of their intelligence gathering available to the Main Naval Staff as well as to the GRU.

Obviously there is duplication and overlap between the KGB, GRU, and naval intelligence activities. But this is not necessarily a shortcoming. Efficiency and cost-effectiveness have never been part of the Soviet attitude toward intelligence. More information is always better, and duplicative intelligence activities serve to check one another.

The general relationships and information flow for naval intelligence are shown in figure 6-1. In wartime there would be an additional reporting/direction route, for the headquarters of the theater of operations. Each fleet intelligence directorate (*razvedyatell'noye upravleniya*) has five divisions to carry out its functions (fig. 6-2). Note that the third division is charged with the naval *Spetsnaz*, or special operations, activities within the fleet area. These forces conduct covert actions and intelligence collection activities, similar to those of the U.S. Navy's SEALs (see chapter 9).

From an operational viewpoint, the Soviet Ocean Surveillance System (SOSS) is the principal means of keeping track of Soviet

37. Among the few useful articles on Soviet intelligence and surveillance are: Desmond Ball, "Soviet Signals Intelligence," *The International Countermeasures Handbook*, 12th ed. (Palo Alto, Calif.: EW Communications, 1987), pp. 73–89; C.F. Carnes, "Soviet Naval Intelligence Gathering Operations," Part 1, *Naval Forces* (no. 6, 1987), pp. 56–63; and Commo. Thomas A. Brooks, USN, "[Soviet] Intelligence Collection," U.S. Naval Institute *Proceedings* (December 1985), pp. 47–49. Also see Viktor Suvorov [pseud.], *Inside Soviet Military Intelligence* (New York: Macmillan, 1984). (Suvorov was a GRU officer from 1971 until he defected to the West in Vienna in 1977.)

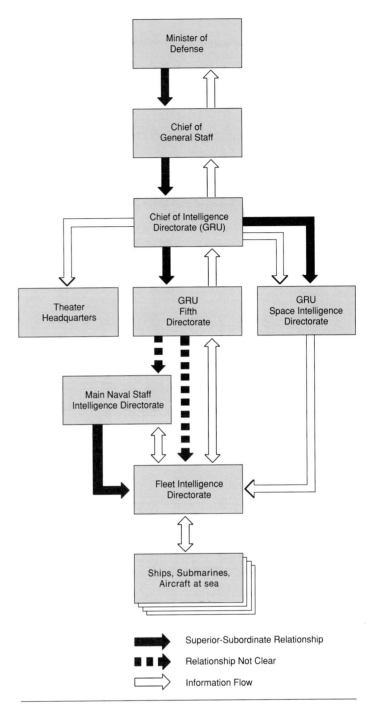

Figure 6-1. Intelligence Command Relationships

and foreign naval and air forces. It is fed by a variety of surveillance and reconnaissance activities, among them the Navy's operating forces (aircraft, surface ships, and submarines) and specialized collection activities. The principal contributors to SOSS are aircraft, radio intercept, satellites, surface ships, submarines, and "spies."

Aircraft. The Soviet Navy employs specially configured An-12 Cub, Il-18 Coot, Tu-16 Badger, and Tu-20 Bear aircraft for ocean reconnaissance and surveillance.

The most notable aircraft are the long-range, four-turboprop Bear-D aircraft, which conduct radar and Electronic Intelligence (ELINT) reconnaissance missions and have the ability to transmit radarscope data to missile-launching platforms through a video data link. Although the approximately 45 Bear-D aircraft in service would be highly vulnerable in wartime, their range (enhanced by in-flight refueling and overseas basing) makes them an invaluable component of SOSS during peacetime and crisis periods. Deploy-

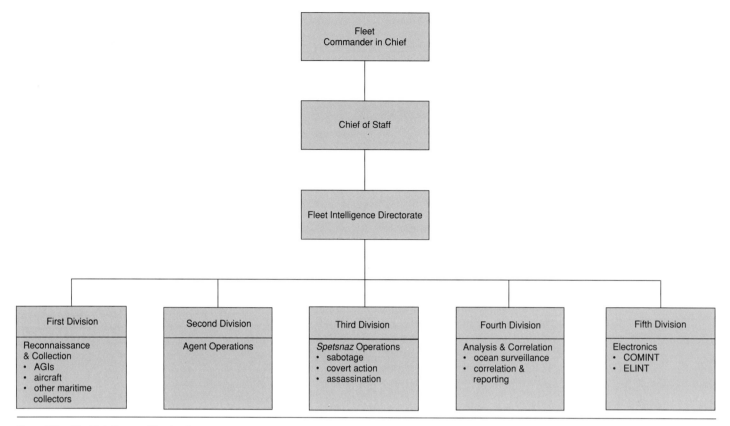

Figure 6-2.   Fleet Intelligence Directorate

ing to and from Cuba, these planes regularly fly along the U.S. Atlantic coast to conduct electronic surveillance.

The Tu-16 Badger flies in Soviet naval markings in several reconnaissance configurations, again using radar and ELINT collection systems. While lacking the Bear's range, the Badger can be refueled in flight and has a higher speed. (This reconnaissance aircraft is not the same as the Badger electronic countermeasures aircraft that supports strikes against surface forces.)

Reconnaissance-ELINT variants of the An-12 Cub and Il-18 Coot transports are also employed to seek out surface naval forces, mainly for the purpose of collecting data on electromagnetic emissions from Western ships.

Signals Intercept. The Soviets operated a network of land-based radio intercept stations before World War II for Signals Intercept (SIGINT). Beginning in the late 1940s, employing captured German technology, the Soviets built an elaborate High-Frequency/ Direction-Finding (HF/DF) network given the code name *Krug* (German for "ring" or "circle").

The original *Krug* system has been improved and enlarged. There are several hundred of these SIGINT systems installed along the land and sea borders of the Soviet Union, seeking to intercept transmissions from foreign land bases, ships, submarines, and aircraft. Several overseas HF/DF stations have also been established, notably in Egypt during the period of close cooperation between the armed forces of the two nations (1956 to 1973), Cuba, Syria, Vietnam, and South Yemen (Aden).[38] The massive Lourdes facility in Cuba is reported to be manned by 2,100 Soviet technicians.[39]

Satellites. The Soviets began testing satellites for ocean surveillance about 1968, with an operational system having been in use at least since 1974. The Soviets currently employ three types of satellites for ocean surveillance: (1) "ferreting," or ELINT Ocean Reconnaissance Satellites (EROSAT) vehicles, (2) Radar Ocean Reconnaissance Satellites (RORSAT), and (3) photographic satellites.

The ELINT satellites detect and "lock on" electronic signals emanating from ships, providing location and, possibly from radar signals, information on the type of ship; they cue in radar satellites to suspected naval targets.

The RORSAT vehicles use active radar to detect ships. This requires considerable electrical power, which is provided by nuclear reactors. When the service life of these *Kosmos*-series RORSATs is completed the section carrying the radioactive fuel is designed to be boosted into higher orbits—more than 550 miles (880 km)—where it will circle the earth for more than 500 years and then cause no danger when it does come down and burn up in the atmosphere. RORSATs normally orbit at a height of some 130 miles (208 km).[40] The reactor section weighs about one ton and carries some 100 pounds (45 kg) of enriched uranium (U-235).

Little is publicly known about the photographic satellites, which eject recoverable film packets over the Soviet Union.

Since early 1986 the Soviets have been carrying out an unprecedented period of experimentation in their ocean reconnaissance program. Both RORSAT and EROSAT satellites have exhibited variations in orbital planes, periods, and inclinations. A new generation of active RORSAT vehicles will employ improved nuclear-powered energy sources and will have both low-resolution (broad search area) and high-resolution (synthetic aperture) radars. These improvements will provide longer endurance, more reliable satellite operations over wider search areas, and provide more accurate targeting data for air- and sea-launched anti-ship cruise

38. There were also major signals intercept stations in Czechoslovakia, East Germany, Hungary, Mongolia, and Poland. Soviet intercept stations have been reported in Nicaragua, but in July 1989 Marshal of the Soviet Union S.F. Akhromeyev said that the total Soviet military personnel in Nicaragua totaled less than ten. It is unlikely that the system would be manned by civilians, unless they were KGB.

39. This is in addition to an estimated 2,800 Soviet military advisers in Cuba and a 2,800-man combat brigade. There are also a large number of Soviet civilian advisers/technicians in Cuba.

40. Two reactors have malfunctioned and plunged into the atmosphere: *Kosmos* 954 in January 1978, and *Kosmos* 1402 in February 1983. They scattered uranium fuel particles when they reentered the atmosphere.

missiles as well as possibly land-launched ballistic missiles employed against naval targets.[41]

Other types of ocean reconnaissance satellites have been referred to by U.S. officials, but no details have been released. In the 1990s Soviet reconnaissance devices should be able to detect all target ships at least once every day, regardless of their location and passive countermeasures. Satellites can already be used to target ships for anti-ship missiles, much the same as land-based Bear-D aircraft have been employed.

These and other satellites are in extensive use by the Soviet armed forces for tactical and strategic reconnaissance and surveillance. The Soviets made extensive use of reconnaissance satellites to keep track of wars and crises, such as the 1973 war in the Middle East (when four reconnaissance satellites were orbited during a 12-day period), during the Iranian and Afghan crises that began in 1979, and during the Falklands War and massive Israeli invasion of Lebanon, which both occurred in 1982.

Soviet reconnaissance satellites pose a particular threat to Western naval forces. In early statements about its Anti-Satellite (ASAT) program, U.S. Department of Defense officials stated that Soviet ocean surveillance satellites were the primary target of ASAT efforts: "The principal motivation for our ASAT program is to put us in a position to negate Soviet satellites that control Soviet weapon systems that could attack our fleet."[42]

The Soviet Navy also makes use of satellites for communications and navigation. One American observer has raised the issue of the Soviet employment of manned satellites for ocean reconnaissance/weapons control. This, he notes, could be the ultimate "force multiplier." In this context, the large Soviet investment in missile-range instrumentation ships and Space Event Support Ships (SESS)—some now under construction are nuclear propelled—is intended to serve as the "link" between future manned satellites and naval forces afloat and ashore.[43]

Surface Ships. More than 65 specialized "intelligence collectors," designated AGI by Western intelligence, are in Soviet naval service.[44] While often depicted in the Western press as disguised fishing trawlers, the AGIs are naval units, readily identified by their naval ensign and electronic antennas, and are manned by naval personnel. Several new classes entered service in the 1980s with a major AGI construction program under way. The larger units have an onboard processing as well as collection capability; these ships also have guns and/or anti-air missiles for self-defense.

These AGIs normally keep watch off the U.S. strategic submarine base at Holy Loch, Scotland, and off the southeastern coast of the United States—a position that permits surveillance of submarine bases at Charleston, South Carolina, and at Kings Bay, Georgia, and of the missile activity off Cape Canaveral, Florida. The AGIs also operate in important international waterways, such as the Strait of Gibraltar, the Sicilian Straits, and the Strait of Hormuz. And AGIs regularly keep watch on U.S. and other NATO exercises.

Soviet warships also conduct surveillance of Western forces. Those Soviet ships and AGIs engaged in close trailing operations are generally referred to as tattletales.

In addition to naval ships, SOSS can also be expected to make use of information obtained from the state-owned and centrally controlled merchant and fishing fleets and, especially, from the

large Soviet research fleets. The last consist of ships and aircraft engaged in academic oceanographic and polar research, which supports the nation's civilian and military space and atmospheric research programs.

Submarines. Submarines, because they are capable of visual, radar, acoustic, and ELINT collection, especially in areas where aircraft and surface ships cannot operate, make highly useful intelligence platforms. They are particularly effective in garnering acoustic data from other undersea craft as well as from surface ships.

In addition to observing Western naval exercises, Soviet submarines regularly conduct reconnaissance off Western ports. In November 1983 a Victor III–class SSN was apparently observing a U.S. escort ship employing a towed-array sonar some 470 n.miles (750 km) east of Charleston, South Carolina, when the submarine fouled the array and was disabled. (The submarine was towed to Cuba for repairs.)

Spies. Both the KGB and the GRU also employ agents as well as their own officials to gather information on Western naval movements and activities. They appear to do everything from placing agents in Western defense organizations to reading articles that discuss naval deployments, exercises, and port visits.

The information collected by the various components of SOSS are correlated at command centers in the four fleet headquarters and at Naval Headquarters in Moscow. These centers have hardened, highly survivable communications facilities with alternate facilities ready to serve as a backup, ensuring the rapid intake of intelligence

An Oscar II cruise missile submarine—armed with long-range anti-ship missiles—is a major consumer of tactical intelligence as her missiles permit her to engage targets far beyond her on-board sensors. Note the missile hatches along the sides covering the SS-N-19 missile tubes; her diving planes are recessed immediately forward of the hatches.

41. A comprehensive discussion of the potential use of land-launched and submarine-launched ballistic missiles against naval targets is Raymond A. Robinson, "Incoming Ballistic Missiles at Sea," U.S. Naval Institute *Proceedings* (June 1987), pp. 66–71.

42. Testimony of Dr. Seymour Zeiberg, Deputy Under Secretary of Defense (Research and Engineering) for strategic and space systems, before the Committee on Armed Services, House of Representatives, 27 March 1979.

43. See Commo. Thomas A. Brooks, USN, "The Ultimate Force Multiplier," U.S. Naval Institute *Proceedings* (July 1985), pp. 137–139.

44. The U.S. Navy discarded passive intelligence collection ships after the capture of the PUEBLO (AGER 2) by North Korea in 1968 and the Israeli attack on the LIBERTY (AGTR 5) during the 1973 Middle East war.

data and the rapid outflow of directions to fleet and tactical commanders. Although Soviet tactics are highly dependent upon communications, once hostilities start it is possible that Soviet forces may be less dependent on command direction than are Western naval forces because of the Soviets' relatively rigid doctrine and tactics.

In addition to these fixed facilities, the KIROV-class battle cruisers, possibly the fourth KIEV-class carrier (the ADMIRAL GORSHKOV, ex-BAKU), and the carrier ADMIRAL KUZNETSOV (ex-TBILISI) and several submarine tenders are fitted with sufficient C^3 systems to process and employ the products of SOSS.

Intelligence and surveillance are essential for Soviet naval forces to successfully carry out their missions.

The battle cruiser KIROV is a multi-mission ship, a distinct break from the Soviet warship designs that went to sea in the 1960s. The KIROV also has an impressive array of electronics as well as weapons. Here the hatch is open to the helicopter hangar. Successive ships of this class have upgraded weapon systems—both guns and missiles.

CHAPTER 7

Operations and Exercises

The reductions in Soviet naval operations did not affect the unprecedented visit by Soviet warships to the U.S. naval base of Norfolk, Virginia, in 1989. These are the cruiser MARSHAL USTINOV and the destroyer OTLICHNYY lying to off the U.S. Atlantic coast for paint touch up and other preparations for the visit. (U.S. Navy, PH3 W.M. Perry)

The reduction in Soviet naval operations and exercises that began in 1986 continues. The reduced operational tempo appears to reflect economic constraints on the Navy, with immediate savings being realized in fuels and other expendables. Although this permits ships to be maintained in port at a high state of readiness (for rapid transition to war), there is some reduction in operational training that can be only partially compensated for by shore-based simulators.

As the Soviets acquired more capable ships and aircraft in the 1970s and early 1980s there was a dramatic expansion of exercises and operations. In this period the availability of long-range naval forces fit with General Secretary L.I. Brezhnev's doctrine of expanding Soviet political-economic interests in the Third World. According to the U.S. Department of Defense:

> The Soviet Navy is the most visible element of the Soviet Union's forward military presence. The Navy has vastly increased its capabilities since the mid-1960s for the projection of power. Except for combat forces in Afghanistan, no other Soviet military asset has played as significant a role in Soviet policy toward the Third World. Soviet Naval forces can play roles of major significance in power projection in peacetime—with missions ranging from showing the flag to threatening strategic areas and waterways—in regional conflicts, as well as in the initial period of global hostilities.[1]

Into the early 1950s most of the Soviet Navy's surface warships and submarines were based in the Baltic. Exercises were conducted only in Soviet coastal waters while port visits by warships beyond eastern bloc nations were not carried out until after Josef Stalin's death in March 1953. The following year—in July 1954—the new cruiser ORDZHONIKIDZE and two destroyers visited Helsinki, and a month later the cruiser ADMIRAL USHAKOV and four destroyers paid a visit to Stockholm. The cruisers were of

1. Secretary of Defense Caspar Weinberger, *Soviet Military Power, 1985* (Washington, D.C.: Government Printing Office, April 1985), p. 115. A useful analysis of Soviet naval operations up to 1980 is Comdr. Bruce W. Watson, USN, *Red Navy at Sea: Soviet Naval Operations on the High Seas, 1956–1980* (Boulder, Colo.: Westview Press, 1982).

the large, graceful-looking SVERDLOV class. While Nikita Khrushchev would describe them as being suitable only to carry admirals on port visits, they were in fact very useful in that role. These ships were the mainstay of Soviet operations out of coastal areas for more than a decade.

Following these visits to neutral countries, in October 1955 the commander of the Baltic Fleet, Admiral A.G. Golovko, led the new cruisers SVERDLOV and ALEKSANDR SUVOROV and a quartet of destroyers to Portsmouth, England. This was the first visit of Soviet warships to a Western nation in the decade since the end of World War II. More significant politically, six months later, the cruiser ORDZHONIKIDZE accompanied by two destroyers, carried Soviet leaders Khrushchev and N.A. Bulganin to Portsmouth for a state visit.[2] (This was the last visit of a Soviet warship to England until June 1976 when a Kashin-class destroyer called at Portsmouth.)

When Khrushchev came to power in the mid-1950s the Northern Fleet, with headquarters at Severomorsk on the Kola Peninsula, had only a few surface ships and about 30 submarines—less than 10 percent of Soviet underwater strength at that time. During the Khrushchev-Gorshkov regime, the Northern Fleet's submarine arm was rapidly reinforced. For operations against the U.S. Navy or NATO forces, Soviet submarines could more easily transit the Greenland–Iceland–United Kingdom (GIUK) gaps to reach the Atlantic Ocean then they could through the Danish Straits.

Today, 175 submarines are assigned to the Northern Fleet, or almost one-half of the Soviet submarine inventory. Similarly, the Pacific Fleet, with more direct access to open seas, has been built up and now shares virtually all of the Soviet Navy's nuclear-propelled and ballistic missile submarines with the Northern Fleet. Further, the Pacific Fleet provides the surface ships, submarines, and aircraft for operations across the Pacific, in Southeast Asian waters, and in the Indian Ocean.

The Black Sea Fleet has also been augmented to provide the surface ships and naval aircraft for deployments into the Mediterranean. (The submarines assigned to the Mediterranean Eskadra are from the Northern Fleet.)

After Admiral S.G. Gorshkov took command of the Soviet Navy in early 1956 he admonished his admirals to emphasize at-sea training. By the 1960s Soviet ships and squadrons were ranging farther from their home ports than at any time since the Russo-Japanese War of 1904–1905.[3]

The periodic fleet training exercises not only sailed farther from Soviet territory but also, in time, became more complex. A joint command and staff exercise code named Sever—Russian for "north"—was held in the North Atlantic, Baltic, Norwegian, and Barents seas in July 1968. East German and Polish ships joined the Soviet units in the first major naval exercise of Warsaw Pact nations and the largest Soviet naval exercise to that time. Sever included "eastern" and "western" fleets simulating Soviet and NATO naval groups meeting in combat—plus convoy escort, anti-submarine, and amphibious operations, with land-based naval aircraft participating. On 16 July a simulated Western amphibious force, under a Polish naval officer, carried out landings in the Baltic. Polish troops came ashore first, followed first by Soviet naval infantry and then by East German troops. The following day another amphibious group, under Soviet command, conducted a larger landing on the Rybachiy Peninsula. Apparently only Soviet troops were brought ashore in this second, larger landing.

This was the harbinger of still larger and more complex exercises that would come in the 1970s and 1980s. Almost every year of the past decade has seen more Soviet ships at sea steaming farther from

the Soviet homeland and remaining at sea for longer periods of time. This extension of blue-water operations has brought about an increased use of the few available overseas ports and facilities and open-sea anchorages where Soviet ships cannot easily use foreign bases; it has also caused the development of the techniques and equipment needed for deploying ships at sea (such as afloat support of ships and underway replenishment). The issue of support was addressed by the First Deputy CinC of the Navy, Admiral N.I. Smirnov:

> One very serious problem facing us is the replenishment of our ships at sea. Our Navy has no bases of its own outside Soviet borders. This means that all resupply operations take place at sea. These must be timely, complete and cost-effective.[4]

The "peacetime" employment of Soviet naval forces on the world's oceans has been summed up by James Cable, a distinguished British political scientist, in an essay "Political Applications of Limited Naval Force":

> In time of peace, a superior warship on the spot can achieve results not obtainable in other ways and without regard to the purpose for which the ship was built. What counts is the existence of the Soviet Navy, not the original motives of its builders. To be precise, what counts is the existence of ocean-going surface warships . . . when the object is to threaten force rather than use it, and if you have to employ violence to do it at a level which will not provoke [nuclear] war.[5]

BALTIC SEA

The Soviet Navy has a large number of ships in the Baltic Sea that are primarily dedicated to (1) performing naval missions in the Baltic during a non-nuclear conflict, such as seizing the island of Bornholm and the Danish Straits, and supporting ground forces moving westward through Germany; (2) supporting naval training activities in the Leningrad area; and (3) sea trials for the products of the Baltic shipyards.

Cruisers and destroyers are normally the largest warships in the Baltic. As of early 1986 there were one each of the Kresta I, Kresta II, and Kynda classes there—the smallest cruiser force in any of the four Soviet fleets. Major warships built or overhauled at the Kaliningrad, Baltic, and Zhdanov shipyards carry out their sea trials in the Gulf of Riga and the Baltic.

Periodically there are major exercises in the Baltic that bring in ships from the other Soviet fleets. For example, during the Zapad (West) '81 exercise in September 1981 the VSTOL carrier KIEV and the helicopter carrier LENINGRAD operated in the Baltic, the first time such ships had entered that sea. The large amphibious ship IVAN ROGOV, which had recently returned from the Pacific, was also among the 60 Soviet naval units that participated in the exercise, the largest peacetime maneuvers ever held in the Baltic. During Zapad '81 Soviet amphibious ships and merchant ships landed some 6,000 marines (Naval Infantry) and ground troops along the coast, a short distance from the Polish border. The landings were conducted by the Baltic Fleet's Naval Infantry regiment and by components of the "Proletarian-Moscow-Minsk" Guards Motorized Rifle Division, stationed in Leningrad.

In addition to the IVAN ROGOV, the troops were carried in Alligator and Ropucha LSTs from the Northern and Black Sea fleets as well as the Baltic Fleet. The landings also demonstrated a variety of new equipment, including air-cushion landing vehicles, Mi-24 Hind helicopters, and T-72 tanks.

2. During this visit Lionel Crabb, a retired British naval diving expert, at the behest of the Secret Intelligence Service (MI6) dived into Portsmouth Harbor near the Soviet cruiser, apparently to examine her underwater hull form. His headless body was later found floating in the harbor.

3. In October 1904–May 1905 Russian squadrons from the Baltic and Black Sea fleets steamed 18,000 miles (28,800 km) to the Tsushima Strait, between Japan and Korea, where the Russian force was decisively defeated on 27 May 1905 by a Japanese fleet.

4. "Peristroika and the Soviet Navy," International Defense Review (no. 12, 1987), p. 1593. Excerpts from an interview in Krasnaya Zveda with Admiral of the Fleet N.I. Smirnov, First Deputy CinC of the Soviet Navy, 1974–1988.

5. This essay appeared in The Soviet Union in Europe and the Near East: Her Capabilities and Intentions, a report of a seminar sponsored jointly by Southampton University and the Royal United Services Institute, Milford-on-Sea, March 1970. Cable, who spent 20 years in the British diplomatic service, expanded these views in Gunboat Diplomacy (New York: Praeger Publishers, 1971).

This landing, near Baltiysk on the Lithuanian coast, was the site of several previous exercises, but because it was only 15 miles (24 km) from the Polish border and in view of the unrest in Poland at the time, it took on special significance. Official Soviet statements cited more than 100,000 troops participating in the Baltic coast exercise. *Zapad* '81 was observed by the Soviet Defense Minister and ministers from the other Warsaw Pact nations, Cuba, Mongolia, and Vietnam. However, no ships from other Warsaw Pact navies participated in the exercise.

The fall naval exercises in the Baltic have continued on a smaller basis. On 6–8 September 1988, for example, 32 warships and 26 naval aircraft manned by 2,500 officers and men carried out exercises in Soviet territorial waters.

BLACK SEA–MEDITERRANEAN SEA

The Russian and Soviet governments have long sought free access to the Mediterranean. During World War II, Winston Churchill had proposed such access, but this concept died in the Cold War era. Stalin subsequently feared to send warships into the Mediterranean because of the possibility of a confrontation with the U.S. Navy, which began postwar operations in the area in 1946. Stalin explained his sensitivity to British and U.S. interests in the Mediterranean when, in January 1948, he responded to proposals of Soviet support for the communist uprising in Greece:

> No, they have no prospect of success at all. What do you think, that Great Britain and the United States—the United States, the most powerful state in the world—will permit you to break their line of communications in the Mediterranean Sea! Nonsense. And we have no navy. The uprising in Greece must be stopped, and as quickly as possible.[6]

Probably the first sortie of Soviet warships into the Mediterranean after World War II occurred in May–June 1956 (three years after Stalin's death). The Black Sea Fleet commander, Admiral V.A. Kasatonov, led the new cruiser MIKHAIL KUTUZOV and two destroyers on a visit to Albanian and Yugoslav ports.

Soviet cruisers continued to make periodic visits into the Mediterranean. In particular, in October 1957 the cruiser ZHDANOV visited the Syrian port of Latakia which, coupled with Soviet arms transfers to Egypt that began the year before, marked the beginning of Soviet political-military interest in the Middle East.

More port visits to Albania and Yugoslavia followed, in part related to Soviet efforts to obtain naval bases in those communist states, thereby reducing the need to send ships through the Turkish Straits, which Soviet leaders feared could be easily closed in wartime. This became a major concern when Turkey joined the Western Alliance (NATO), formally tying Turkish defenses to the United States and Britain. A port was made available in Albania for Soviet ships from about 1958, and in 1961 several Whiskey-class submarines and a tender were briefly based in there (see chapter 34). However, deteriorating relations with Albania and Yugoslavia ended all hopes of a permanent naval presence in the Mediterranean.

In mid-1964 Soviet warships initiated a continual presence in the Mediterranean when a cruiser and two destroyers passed southward through the Turkish Straits. The move came shortly after President Johnson had advised the Turkish prime minister that if Turkish forces landed on trouble-plagued Cyprus, and the Soviet Union responded with military moves, Turkey could not count on the United States to come to its defense. This was a watershed in Turkish-American relations. Following this event, the Turkish foreign minister visited the Soviet Union for a week of discussions. Unquestionably, the passage of Soviet ships through the Turkish-controlled Dardanelles was discussed and restrictions were eased. Increased Soviet-Turkish economic relationships also followed.

Action in coastal waters: The Krivak I-class frigate BEZZAVETNYY bumps and grinds the U.S. cruiser YORKTOWN (CG 48) as a pair of U.S. warships steamed in Soviet coastal waters off the Crimean peninsula. In the foreground are the port AN/SLQ-32(V)3 electronic warfare installation on the YORKTOWN and the quad SS-N-14 ASW missile tubes on the BEZZAVETNYY. (U.S. Navy)

During 1964, the Soviets probably maintained an average of five naval ships in the Mediterranean. Thereafter, deployment into the Mediterranean continued at a gradually increasing rate, with an "intelligence collector"—a trawler-type ship especially modified for electronic spying—or a warship normally dogging the U.S. and British aircraft carriers in the area. Periodically, submarines and sometimes their support ships would also be sighted in what previously had been considered an "American lake." In 1966, for example, a Soviet submarine tender in company with surface warships and submarines visited Egyptian and Algerian ports.

MIDDLE EAST BUILDUP

Direct Soviet interests in the Middle East began in 1956 when the Soviet government undertook a massive sale of arms to Egypt, with Czechoslovakia serving as the "middle man" for the sale. Two SKORYY-class destroyers as well as torpedo boats were transferred to Egypt that year, and there was some exchange of Soviet and Egyptian naval personnel in conjunction with the sale. Coupled with occasional Soviet warship visits to Syrian and Egyptian ports, this led to significant interest in the Middle East by the Soviet Navy.

During the June 1967 Arab-Israeli conflict, a steady stream of Soviet ships passed through the Dardanelles, until there were about 70 Soviet ships in the Mediterranean. From 1967 until 1972, Soviet Badger reconnaissance aircraft, Mail ASW flying-boats, May patrol aircraft, and Cub ELINT aircraft were based in Egypt to support Soviet naval activities in the eastern Mediterranean.[7] (Many of

6. Milovan Djilas, *Conversations With Stalin* (New York: Harcourt, Brace & World, 1962), p. 182. A Yugoslav patriot, he had several meetings with Stalin during and after World War II.

7. Egypt expelled some 20,000 Soviet military advisors and air defense personnel in 1972.

The Soviets appeared to have "wall-to-wall" missile ships in the eastern Mediterranean during the 1973 Middle East crisis. From left are a Kara-class anti-submarine cruiser, a Kashin-class missile destroyer, and a Kynda-class anti-surface cruiser; the after bank of four SS-N-3b missile tubes on the cruiser ADMIRAL GOLOVKO are elevated to the launch position (when fired they will also be trained outboard). (U.S. Navy)

these planes had Egyptian markings but appear to have been flown only by Soviet crews.) Some Badgers were also sighted on runways in Libya, reportedly including the concrete strips at Wheelus, the former U.S. Air Force base that sprawls across the Libyan desert; and Blinder bombers were operating out of Iraqi airfields.

The Soviets again rapidly reinforced their naval forces in the Mediterranean during the Yom Kippur War in October–November 1973. Within a few days of the outbreak of hostilities, the Soviet *eskadra* began to receive additional ships, reaching a peak in early November of 5 cruisers, 14 frigates and destroyers, 6 escort ships, 2 Nanuchka-class missile corvettes, 8 amphibious ships, 38 intelligence and support ships, and 23 submarines, several of which were nuclear propelled. There were 88 anti-ship missiles in the Soviet force, exclusive of air-launched missiles that could be carried on Badger bombers flying from bases in the Crimea. This Soviet force of 96 ships confronted a U.S. Sixth Fleet that totaled some 60 ships.

The relative combat capabilities of the two fleets were difficult to compare. The Soviets had superiority in ship-to-ship missiles and submarines, while the U.S. Navy possessed considerable striking power in the fighters and attack planes on board the Sixth Fleet's three aircraft carriers. But a precedent had been established: the fall of 1973 was probably the first time that a Soviet naval force in a crisis area was larger—and significantly larger—than the U.S. naval force in the region. The U.S. Sixth Fleet commander at the time, Vice Admiral Daniel Murphy, reported:

> The U.S. Sixth Fleet and the Soviet Mediterranean Fleet were, in effect, sitting in a pond in close proximity and the stage of the hitherto unlikely "war at sea" scenario was set. This situation prevailed for several days. Both fleets were obviously in a high readiness posture for whatever might come next, although it appeared that neither fleet knew exactly what to expect.[8]

The Soviets maintain the large Fifth *Eskadra* in the Mediterranean, supported by naval aircraft flying from airfields in the Crimea, Syria, and Libya and, at times, from ships. While the Soviets were forced to abandon bases in Egypt in 1972, the current Soviet military presence in Syria includes use of the port of Tartus with naval air deployments to Tiyas airfield. A new logistic and docking facility with one fixed and two floating piers for Soviet ships was dedicated at Tartus in mid-1989. There are also communications and

8. Quoted in Admiral Elmo R. Zumwalt, Jr., USN(Ret), *On Watch* (New York: Quadrangle/The New York Times Book Co., 1976), p. 447.

logistic facilities ashore with more than 1,000 Soviet personnel assigned. A Soviet submarine tender and a small oiler and water carrier operate from Tartus, while May ASW aircraft and, at times, other naval aircraft periodically deploy from Tiyas.

The Soviet squadron and the Syrian Navy conducted a joint exercise in October–November 1988. Included was a port visit by the entire Soviet squadron to Tartus—the VSTOL carrier BAKU and ten other ships, the largest port concentration of Soviet ships ever in the Mediterranean.

Libya, which has received numerous Soviet aircraft and naval units including submarines, regularly allows Soviet naval aircraft to operate there. May ASW aircraft have also flown from a Libyan airfield.

During periods of regional conflict or tension, Soviet ships often enter friendly Mediterranean ports to deter hostile attacks. This has been true of Egyptian and Syrian ports during Arab-Israeli wars, and a Soviet submarine tender entered the Libyan port of Tripoli in February 1986 when it appeared that U.S. naval forces in the Mediterranean might strike Libya in response to President Muammar Qaddafi's support of terrorist activities.

THE OKEAN EXERCISES

Two years after the *Sever* exercise, the Soviet Navy alone conducted operation *Okean* (Ocean), the largest naval exercise to be held by any navy since World War II. *Okean* '70 was conducted during April and May 1970, with some 200 surface ships and submarines, plus several hundred land-based aircraft participating.

The exercises were conducted simultaneously in the Atlantic and Pacific regions, including the Barents, Norwegian, Baltic, Mediterranean, and Philippine seas, and the Sea of Japan. In the main operating areas the exercises followed the same sequence: (1) deployment of forces, (2) anti-submarine warfare, (3) anti-carrier warfare, and (4) amphibious landing. In the anti-carrier phase simulated air strikes were flown against Soviet task groups in the Atlantic and Pacific. The Badgers of Soviet Naval Aviation struck at the simulated U.S. carrier groups in the North Atlantic and North Pacific within a few minutes of each other. Although this was a preplanned schedule, the strike was a remarkable achievement in planning and execution. Surface missile ship and submarines also simulated attacks against the carrier groups.

Interestingly, there were several Soviet surface ships and submarines in the Indian Ocean during *Okean* '70, including a Kynda-class missile cruiser. However, the Soviets did not consider that area part of the exercise, nor the subsequent detachment of a task group to Cuba. (During the height of *Okean*, two pairs of naval Bear-D reconnaissance aircraft flew from a Northern Fleet base nonstop to Cuba. The first pair of Bear-Ds conducted reconnaissance of Soviet surface forces in the North Atlantic late on 21 April, the day before the simulated attacks against the Western carrier group.)

Okean '70 had several purposes. Marshal Andrei Grechko, then Minister of Defense, who observed the landings on Rybachiy Peninsula with other Soviet and Warsaw Pact officials, declared: "The *Okean* maneuvers were evidence of the increased naval might of our socialist state, an index of the fact that our Navy has become so great and so strong that it is capable of executing missions in defense of our state interests over the broad expanses of the World Ocean." For the Soviet Navy the *Okean* exercises were conducted "to test and make further improvements in the combat training level of our naval forces and in staff operational readiness." And, coming at the 100th anniversary of Lenin's birth, *Okean* also had a psychological purpose, demonstrating that the Soviet Navy was a full component of the communist system.

But most significant, *Okean*, along with a large exercise by Soviet Ground Forces, came at the end of the five-year defense-economic program. Thus, *Okean* was a "report" to the Soviet government and people of the capabilities of the Soviet Navy; it was intended to impress the political leadership that the huge investments in ships and aircraft had in fact benefited the Soviet Union.

Five years later, in April 1975, there was a similar multi-ocean exercise, dubbed *Vesna* by the Soviets and *Okean* '75 in the West. Again, there was a series of evolutions in the Atlantic and Pacific regions, involving some 200 naval ships and submarines, plus numerous aircraft. Major convoy defense exercises were conducted in the Barents Sea and Sea of Japan. These were possibly to evaluate Soviet convoy-defense as well as anti-convoy tactics. Several overseas bases were used by naval aircraft in April 1975, with Bear-D reconnaissance aircraft using an airfield in Guinea, May ASW aircraft and Cub recce/ELINT aircraft flying from Somalia, and Cubs using the airfield at Aden. (Bear-D aircraft also operated over the Indian Ocean, flying from bases in the Soviet Union.)

Significantly, the cruiser-helicopter ships MOSKVA and LENINGRAD, which had major roles five years earlier, were not at sea during the *Okean* '75 exercises.

After *Okean* '70 and '75 the Soviet Navy continued large-scale annual exercises as part of the regular training cycle for naval forces. The carrier KIEV joined in major exercises for the first time in 1976 as did other new ships. A major *Okean*-style exercise was expected to occur in the spring of 1980, as had happened at the conclusion of the previous Soviet five-year plans. During the year there were several small exercises, and there was a major Soviet naval presence in the Indian Ocean as well as in the Mediterranean. But there was no *Okean* '80.

The reasons may have been the potential danger of a superpower confrontation because of the high state of U.S. military readiness and related operations in the Indian Ocean due to the Iranian hostage situation and the fear of further antagonism of the West following the Soviet invasion of Afghanistan in 1979. However, one senior U.S. intelligence officer has noted that the Soviet Navy by that time had demonstrated its ability to conduct multi-ocean exercises, and that an *Okean* would not be worth the time and expense. More likely, *Okean* '80 did not occur for a combination of these reasons.

But the Soviet fleet was not idle. In July 1981 there was a large amphibious operation in the eastern Mediterranean, a joint Soviet-Syrian exercise in which 1,000 Soviet marines were landed. Also that summer, a combined Soviet–Polish–East German naval maneuver was held in the Baltic, and the massive, all-Soviet *Zapad* '81 landing was carried out that fall in the eastern Baltic. These maneuvers and exercises were particularly important because of their location and timing. They demonstrated that the combat training of the Soviet Navy had reached the point where it could respond directly to crises.

In 1983 there was another large-scale, multi-ocean series of exercises. Although smaller than those of *Okean* 1970 and 1975, this 1983 operation included more than 40 surface warships and a large number of submarines. There was the now-traditional emphasis on simulated anti-carrier strikes in defense of the Soviet homeland. But highly significant, there were also simulated attacks against convoys. These exercises included the highest ever level of participation by Soviet merchant ships—about 40 of them—as the Soviets apparently were practicing tactics for defending their own convoys against attacks by Western naval and air forces.

There were also extensive air operations in the 1983 exercise, with naval aircraft flying from Cuba, Ethiopia, Libya, Syria, and Vietnam as well as Soviet bases.

The following year there was an even larger series of fleet exercises. The spring 1984 operation was conducted primarily by the Soviet Navy's three European fleets. This time there were more than 140 surface ships, including the new nuclear-propelled battle cruiser KIROV, and over 40 submarines participating, along with a large number of naval and air force bombers that fanned far out over the Atlantic. There were simultaneous but less intensive exercises in the Pacific region.

The reasons for the large-scale 1983 and 1984 exercises are not fully clear. Again, the principal reason may well have been political. With the accession of Yuri Andropov to the head of the politburo in November 1982 and of Konstantin Chernenko to succeed him in February 1984, along with other changes in the Soviet political leadership, the Soviet Navy may have felt the need to impress the nation's leaders with the capabilities and importance of the Soviet fleet.

ATLANTIC AND CARIBBEAN SEA

The Soviet exercises in the Norwegian Sea slowly extended southward. Beginning in 1959 when Fidel Castro took control of Cuba and began negotiations with the Soviet Union for economic and military assistance, there has been intense Soviet interest in the Caribbean. Except for submarines, however, apparently no Soviet warships operated in the Caribbean during the 1960s. During the 1962 Cuban missile crisis several Soviet diesel-electric submarines operated in the Western Atlantic–Caribbean areas, all of which were located and identified by U.S. anti-submarine forces.

Then, in mid-June 1969, two diesel submarines, a nuclear-propelled attack submarine of the November class, and a submarine tender departed the White Sea base area, steamed around North Cape, and down into the Atlantic. Almost simultaneously, a surface force consisting of a Kynda-class missile cruiser, a missile frigate, and a missile destroyer passed through the Turkish Straits, transited the Mediterranean, and exited into the Atlantic. The submarine and surface groups rendezvoused off the Azores on 3 July, and after fueling from two Soviet tankers, steamed westward. The nine ships then entered the Caribbean and remained for almost a month of exercises and port visits. This is believed to have been the first visit of a Russian squadron to the Western Hemisphere since the American Civil War.

Almost a year later, in April 1970, during the height of the multi-ocean *Okean* naval exercises, a pair of Bear-D naval reconnaissance aircraft from the Northern Fleet flew to Cuba. Two additional pairs of Bear-D aircraft flew to Cuba during 1970, initiating the regular deployments of Bear-D and later Bear-F ASW aircraft into Cuba.

Also in April 1970, a Kresta-class missile cruiser and a destroyer broke away from the *Okean* exercises in the North Atlantic and steamed southwest, being joined en route by a nuclear-propelled cruise missile submarine, two diesel attack submarines, and a submarine tender. This force entered the Caribbean and conducted exercises and port calls during May.

In September 1970, a third Soviet squadron was en route to the Caribbean. It consisted of a missile cruiser, a missile destroyer, a submarine tender, oiler, and an LST. The landing ship carried two barges that subsequently were identified as submarine support barges. The LST entered Cienfuegos harbor to unload the barges and

Soviet visitors to the sunny Caribbean: a Kildin missile destroyer, a Kynda missile cruiser, and a Kashin missile destroyer are tied up in "Med moors" during a visit to Havana. There is a Ugra-class submarine tender in the background. Ship visits have had both political and military benefits for the Soviet Union. (Soviet Navy)

The cruiser MARSHAL USTINOV and the destroyer OTLICHNYY held open house for thousands of Americans at Norfolk in 1989. The ships were impressive as was the candor of their officers and the sincerity of their enlisted men. (Peter B. Mersky)

other equipment believed to be for servicing submarines. This visit brought a public warning from the Nixon administration that the Soviet Union "can be under no doubt that we would view the establishment of a strategic base in the Caribbean with the utmost seriousness." Two weeks later the submarine tender left Cienfuegos. The ship remained in Cuban waters, and on 15 October the tender entered the port of Mariel, 25 miles (40 km) west of Havana. The barges remained at Cienfuegos, and construction continued on various shore facilities for servicing naval forces.

Additional Soviet naval forces have visited the Caribbean, including a diesel-propelled ballistic missile submarine of the Golf class. However, no nuclear-propelled ballistic missile submarine is reported to have entered the area. In March–April 1984—as part of the 23rd Soviet naval deployment to the Caribbean—the helicopter carrier LENINGRAD and one of the new UDALOY-class ASW destroyers participated in the Caribbean operations, raising the deployments to a new level of capability. The LENINGRAD, the largest Soviet warship to ever operate in the Caribbean, conducted exercises in the area for seven weeks.

There were no Soviet naval deployments to Cuba in 1986–1987. These operations resumed in October–November 1988 when a UDALOY-class destroyer led a frigate, Tango-class submarine, and oiler into Cuban waters, the 27th such visit. (The commander of this task group was Vice Admiral I.V. Kasatonov, First Deputy CinC of the Northern Fleet; the following year he led a task group of the cruiser MARSHAL USTINOV, a destroyer, and an oiler on a port visit to Norfolk, Virginia, only the second Soviet warship visit to the United States since World War II.)[9] The 1988 deployment to Cuba, however, lasted only 30 days; normally such visits averaged 45 days. Subsequent visits have been even shorter.

These operations to the Caribbean demonstrate Soviet political interest in the region as well as support for the Castro regime. From

9. In May 1975 the Soviet Kanin-class destroyers BOIKIY and ZHGUCHY visited Boston on the 30th anniversary of the end of World War II in Europe.

a military perspective, they familiarize Soviet forces with the region and provide training for the Cuban Navy. In wartime, Soviet ships, submarines, and aircraft in the area could attack U.S. cargo ships carrying Army units from ports on the Gulf of Mexico to Europe.

WEST AFRICAN OPERATIONS

On the eastern side of the Atlantic, the Soviets have also been maintaining essentially a continuous patrol of warships off the central African coast since late 1970. The presence of Soviet warships in the Gulf of Guinea, and probably directly off the Ghanian coast, coincided with the release by the Accra government of two Soviet fishing craft impounded some months earlier. There appears to have been a direct relationship between the Soviet warships and the release of the fishing craft.

In the aftermath of a Portuguese-backed attack on Conakry, Guinea, in November 1970, the Soviet Navy appears to have begun a regular patrol of the area in support of Guinea, and Soviet naval aircraft have been operating from Guinea. Conakry was subsequently used as a refueling base by Soviet Bear reconnaissance aircraft (see chapter 8). Although access for Bear aircraft has been terminated, the Soviets continue to use the Conakry harbor on a routine basis.

Farther south, in Angola, a former Portuguese colony, a revolution in 1974 sparked a long-term revolution. The Soviets supported the MPLA organization in the conflict, with Cuban combat troops being flown in by Soviet planes, their arms being delivered by Soviet merchant ships. Despite covert American aid to another faction, the MPLA was successful in establishing a communist government for Angola. Angola became the next base for Soviet naval aircraft, an important factor after use of the Conakry airfield was denied in 1977.

The Soviets have continued to maintain a small naval squadron of some five to eight naval units off the west African coast. In addition to being in a position to support events in Angola, the force sits astride the oil route from the Arabian Sea to Western Europe.

The VSTOL carrier NOVOROSSIYSK refuels from a BORIS CHILIKIN-class oiler while under way in the Pacific. The Soviet deployment of aircraft carriers of the KIEV and ADMIRAL KUZNETSOV (ex-TBILISI) classes and underway replenishment have extended Soviet naval operating ranges and endurance. (U.S. Navy, JO2 V.R. Everts)

PACIFIC OCEAN

Today the Soviet Pacific Fleet is the largest of the four fleets, with significantly more ships and aircraft in most categories than the other fleets, and the largest number of naval personnel, including the only naval infantry division.[10] (The major exception is the Northern Fleet, which has considerably more submarines.) Admiral V.N. Chernavin, the CinC of the Soviet Navy, has explained the Soviet emphasis on Pacific naval forces:

> We proceed from the fact that the operative and combat preparation of the U.S. Navy and its allies in the Pacific zone, by its range and its tasks, goes beyond the bounds of the development of defensive operations. This forces us to show particular alertness and maintain the fleet at the necessary degree of preparedness.[11]

Soviet naval forces traveled far beyond the Far East area of Soviet Siberia and Communist China as early as 1959, when a SVERDLOV-class cruiser and two destroyers visited Djakarta. Subsequent political and naval discussions between the Soviet Union and Indonesia led to the transfer of a large number of warships and auxiliaries to the latter, among them a SVERDLOV-class light cruiser, fourteen Whiskey-class submarines, eight destroyers, eight escort ships, a dozen Komar missile boats, numerous torpedo and patrol craft, and support ships. Sukarno's later alignment with Communist China, and his dramatic fall from power in 1965, ended the close Soviet association with Indonesia. After that, Moscow began talks with the city-state of Singapore, apparently aimed at obtaining permission for Soviet warships to join Soviet merchantmen in using the British-built dry docks of that port.

In general, exercises and operations by the Soviet Pacific Fleet were limited in scope compared to those of the three European fleets. They were constrained mostly to the Sea of Japan and the Sea of Okhotsk. The first operation that was truly reactive to U.S.

activities occurred in January 1968, shortly after the North Koreans seized the U.S. intelligence ship PUEBLO (AGER 2). The Soviets sortied 16 ships—including intelligence ships and auxiliaries—into the Sea of Japan, maneuvering them between the Korean coast and the U.S. carrier group that had been dispatched to threaten the Koreans. The U.S. force was larger, including the nuclear-propelled aircraft carrier ENTERPRISE (CVAN 65). Veteran British foreign service officer James Cable observed:

> The Soviet ships could neither have prevented a nuclear strike against North Korea nor even have defended themselves. But it was a discrete, yet unmistakable indication of Soviet interest and concern in American reactions. . . . Indeed, in so far as it was intended to symbolize Soviet commitment to the defence of North Korea, it may have been a more effective threat than that posed by the greatly superior American fleet. It was also a striking instance of the occasional willingness of the Soviet Government to divert their ships to tasks which are both intrinsically risky and are likely to increase tension with the United States even at a moment of crisis.[12]

Less publicized Soviet naval operations in the Pacific, including the deployment of Yankee-class missile submarines to the eastern Pacific from about 1970, were followed by an open demonstration of Soviet naval capabilities in the Pacific phase of the *Okean* exercises of April–May 1970. A surface and submarine task force—led by a SVERDLOV-class cruiser—steamed south to the Philippine Sea, while there were extensive maneuvers, including long-range air strike operations.

In the fall of 1971 a Soviet task force sortied across the Pacific and passed through the Hawaiian Islands, coming within sight of Oahu. This force consisted of a Kresta I–class missile cruiser, two missile-armed destroyers, a nuclear-powered cruise missile submarine, two diesel-electric attack submarines, and a tanker.

Soviet naval operations in Southwest Asia expanded in the late 1970s when Soviet naval and air units began using the sprawling American-built air and harbor facilities at Cam Ranh Bay, Vietnam. Cam Ranh Bay became the center of the largest concentration of Soviet naval forces outside of the Soviet Union. There are seven

10. This does not include the three motorized rifle divisions transferred from the Soviet Ground Forces to the Navy in 1989–1990; they were redesignated "coastal defense" divisions.

11. "Chernavin Responds" [Interview], U.S. Naval Institute *Proceedings* (February 1989), p. 77.

12. James Cable, *Gunboat Diplomacy*, p. 142.

major piers at Cam Ranh Bay, one or two floating dry docks, and extensive shore facilities including ammunition and fuel storage, a communications center, and an intelligence/signals collection station.

Soviet naval strike, reconnaissance, and ASW aircraft operate from the base, which also has a squadron of protective fighter aircraft (see chapter 8). The base brings Badger and Backfire aircraft within unrefueled striking range of the important Indonesian straits as well as all of Indochina, Indonesia, the Philippines, and the southern coast of China.

These naval operations have been abetted by a continued flow of modern surface warships, submarines, and aircraft. In 1979 the second KIEV-class VSTOL carrier, the MINSK, was sent to the Far east, being followed in 1984 by her sister ship NOVOROSSIYSK. The second nuclear-propelled battle cruiser of the KIROV class, the FRUNZE, followed in late 1985 as the Pacific Fleet lagged only slightly behind the Northern Fleet in receiving modern surface warships. In June 1986 the NOVOROSSIYSK and FRUNZE, accompanied by two other cruisers, carried out exercises in the Sea of Japan, commencing the first periodic operations by paired capital ships. These exercises soon extended out into the Pacific Ocean.

The flow of warships from European shipyards to the Far East continues. In 1988, for example, the Pacific Fleet received the SOVREMENNYY-class destroyer STOYKIY, the UDALOY-class destroyer ADMIRAL TRIBUTS, a Krivak III–class frigate for the KGB Maritime Border Troops, two Vishnya-class intelligence ships, and a floating dry dock. (The only major naval units constructed in the Far East are submarines; see chapter 31.) While the Pacific Fleet was decreased by 57 naval units from 1984 to 1988, the overall capabilities of the fleet were enhanced by the newer combatants (and aircraft) entering service.

Into the 1990s the Soviets have continued to vie with China for influence in North Korea, especially in view of increasing North Korean contact with other nations (including South Korea). In 1975, North Korea permitted the Soviets to use the port of Najin on the northeast coast and in the early 1980s a second port, Chongjin, located farther south; by the end of 1985 Wonsan and Hungnam on the east coast and Nampo and Haeju on the west coast were added to the Soviet access list, being connected by rail to the Soviet Far East. That year Soviet warships began visiting North Korean ports. Thus, the Soviets had access to ports in northeast Asia outside of the entry "chokepoints" of the Sea of Japan.

Soviet military assistance to North Korea was stepped up in the 1980s to include newer tanks, missiles, and aircraft, with the Pyongyang government in 1985 agreeing to overflight rights for Soviet military aircraft from Vladivostok flying to the Yellow Sea and beyond. In May 1989, the CinC of the Pacific Fleet, Admiral G.A. Khvatov, led the carrier NOVOROSSIYSK and two destroyers into Wonsan harbor for a historic port visit.

Both General Secretary Brezhnev (in 1974) and General Secretary Gorbachev (in 1986) visited Vladivostok and called special attention to the Soviet Union as a Pacific power, indicating that the growth of Soviet naval forces and operations in the Pacific region would continue.

INDIAN OCEAN

The Indian Ocean became increasingly of interest to the Soviet Navy in the 1960s. This was in part because of the dependence of the West and Japan on Middle Eastern oil, much of which exits through the Strait of Hormuz into the Indian Ocean, and Soviet logistic support for the North Vietnamese that relied heavily upon merchant ships that sailed primarily from Baltic and Black Sea ports through the Suez Canal (and after June 1967 around Africa), and across the Indian Ocean to Haiphong.

The Soviet Union first gained major access into the Indian subcontinent when Soviet leaders helped mediate the Indian-Pakistani conflict in 1965. Because of Pakistan's links with both the United States and Communist China, India was a most desirable ally.

Soviet ships had occasionally visited Indian Ocean ports, especially Massawa (Ethiopia), on the Red Sea. Early in 1968, a SVERDLOV-class cruiser, two missile-armed destroyers, and an oiler visited ten ports in eight countries of the area. The significance of these cruises was indicated by the presence of Admiral Gorshkov when a missile destroyer visited Massawa, Ethiopia, in January 1967, and at Pacific Fleet visits to Bombay and Madras early in 1968. (Soviet forces had used bases in Somalia, but they were abandoned for political reasons.)

Admiral Gorshkov's visit to India in February 1968 marked the beginning of massive Soviet naval assistance to that country. Since then, the Soviet Union has transferred to the Indian Navy submarines—including a nuclear-propelled Charlie I–class SSGN—destroyers, missile boats, various other craft, and a submarine tender. Soviet technical assistance has enlarged the capabilities of the Indian east coast naval base at Viskhapatnam.

Soviet-Indian political relations reached a high point in August of 1971 with the signing of a Treaty of Friendship, Peace, and Cooperation. Among its various articles, the treaty provides that each nation

> undertakes to abstain from giving any assistance to any third party that engages in an armed conflict with the other party. In the event of either party being subjected to attack or threat thereof . . . [the countries] shall immediately enter into mutual consultation with a view of eliminating this threat and taking appropriate effective measures to ensure the peace and security of their countries.

Four months later, India invaded and overran East Pakistan; Soviet-provided missile boats sank several Pakistani naval and merchant ships and bombarded shore facilities.

In the aftermath of that conflict the nation of Bangladesh was established in what had been East Pakistan and the Soviets were quick to offer political and economic assistance. During the India-Pakistani War a number of merchant ships had been sunk in the harbors of Chittagong and Chalna, while the Pakistanis had laid mines off the former port.

The Soviet Navy was called upon to sweep the mines and salvage the sunken ships. Beginning in early April 1972, a total of 22 minesweepers, salvage ships, and support ships arrived in Bangladesh waters. The salvage operations took almost two years. While there were reports that the Soviets were stalling while seeking permanent use of port facilities, the delay was more likely due to the limitations of Soviet salvage gear. The mine clearance operation was easier and accomplished on a more realistic schedule. Both tasks provided valuable experience for the Soviet Navy.

Following the Bangladesh mine clearance, Soviet minesweepers and a support ship steamed for the Gulf of Suez, where in mid-July 1973, they rendezvoused with the helicopter carrier LENINGRAD, which had transited around Africa, coming from the Black Sea. On board the LENINGRAD were Mi-8 Hip helicopters configured for aerial minesweeping. This force then began a four-month minesweeping operation in the Straits of Gubal as part of the multination operation to open the Suez Canal. In this operation the Soviet force suffered from high winds, and one minesweeper was damaged in a mine explosion. (Simultaneously, a U.S. Navy helicopter minesweeping force was clearing the northern end of the canal in Operation Nimbus.)

More recently, in the mid-1984 mining of the Red Sea by a Libyan merchant ship—using Soviet-provided bottom mines—South Yemen apparently requested Soviet assistance in sweeping the Bab al Mandeb for suspected mines.[13] Yemen at the time had a single former Soviet T-58 minesweeper. Two Soviet minesweepers from the Black Sea Fleet transited the Suez Canal en route to South Yemen, followed shortly by a task force consisting of the helicopter ship LENINGRAD, a cruiser, and a destroyer. The minesweepers reportedly conducted sweep operations, but no observations of minesweeping helicopter flights from the LENINGRAD were publicly noted.

---

13. See Dr. Scott C. Truver, "Mines of August: An International Whodunit," U.S. Naval Institute *Proceedings*/Naval Review (May 1985), pp. 94–117.

During the Iran-Iraq war of the 1980s the Soviets operated warships in the Persian Gulf, in part to help protect merchant shipping (the Soviets had offered to reflag Kuwaiti tankers but were preempted by the United States; in the event, the Soviets did charter several of its own tankers to Kuwait during the war).[14]

On 6 May 1987 the Soviet freighter IVAN KOROTEEV was raked by machine-gun and rocket fire from Iranian speedboats but suffered little damage. On 17 May the Soviet tanker MARSHAL CHUYKOV, while under charter to Iran, struck a mine—believed to have been laid by Iranians—near the Kuwaiti port of Al-Ahmadi.

The Soviet response to these attacks was an increase of flights into Iranian air space—reportedly there were 50 penetrations the day of the IVAN KOROTEEV incident—and naval forces were deployed into the gulf. There were a number of challenges of Iranian craft by the Soviet ships. For example, in November 1987 an Iranian frigate approached a Soviet tanker and freighter being escorted by the SOVREMENNYY-class destroyer STOYKIY. The destroyer challenged the Iranian ship, which backed down. A few months later the commanding officer of the STOYKIY stated, "Tense situations are arising on practically every escort operation."

Under the command of Rear Admiral Valeriy Sergeev, the Soviets continuously deployed about a dozen ships to the area in the late 1980s. Most of the ships were kept anchored in the Gulf of Oman, entering the Persian Gulf for specific escort missions. A BELYAYEV VYTEGRALES–class communications ship as well as destroyers was available as force flagship. Up to three destroyer-type ships were usually present, plus heavily armed minesweepers, an Alligator-class LST, and various auxiliary ships. An Oskol-class repair ship from the Black Sea Fleet provided afloat maintenance; the other units rotated from the Black Sea and Pacific fleets.

Soviet installations have been established on the island of Socotra, just east of the Gulf of Aden and astride the southern entrance to the Red Sea and the Suez Canal. The island, belonging to the former British protectorate of Aden, once contained a British air base; subsequently Aden, part of communist South Yemen, has been opened to Soviet ships and aircraft, military and civilian.

A naval repair and replenishment facility has been established at Ethiopia's Dehalak Island in the Red Sea with Aden harbor and Socotra Island also being used as anchorages by Soviet naval ships.

---

14. An excellent summary of Soviet activities in the Persian Gulf area is provided in Norman Cigar, "The Soviet Navy in the Persian Gulf: Naval Diplomacy in a Combat Zone," *Naval War College Review* (Spring 1989), pp. 56–88.

At Dehalak there is a maintenance and fuel depot as well as an 8,500-ton floating dry dock operated by the Soviets. A submarine tender and other auxiliaries have also operated there.

Soviet reconnaissance aircraft regularly fly over the Indian Ocean from an airfield in Asmara in Ethiopia as well as from bases in the Soviet Union. Until about 1990 Soviet aircraft also flew reconnaissance missions over the Indian Ocean from the Aden international airport and the Al-Anad military airfield in South Yemen. Those flights apparently ceased about 1990 with the merger of North and South Yemen.

These bases at the southern end of the Suez Canal–Red Sea route place the Soviet Navy in an excellent position to interdict shipping through that vital waterway, and they are not far from the tanker routes between the Arabian Sea and western Europe and Japan.

In 1970, the government of Mauritius, a former British colony east of Madagascar, signed a treaty with the Soviet Union providing port facilities for Soviet fishing craft. Soviet warships soon were anchoring in Mauritius ports as well. During the *Okean* naval maneuvers in April 1970, a missile-armed cruiser and other Pacific Fleet warships made prolonged port visits there.

These bases and anchorages facilitate the Soviet deployment of naval forces in the Indian Ocean region. Soviet ships now operate regularly in the Indian Ocean, coming primarily from the Pacific Fleet. The Indian Ocean *Eskadra* now consists of 20 to 25 units—surface warships, submarines, amphibious, and auxiliary ships, periodically reinforced for exercises and during crises. These units were regularly deployed into the Persian Gulf in the 1980s during the Iraq-Iran conflict, both to demonstrate Soviet support for free navigation of that vital waterway and to "show the flag," demonstrating Soviet political-military presence in that important region.

Soviet naval presence in the Red Sea and Persian Gulf areas remained esssentially constant during the Desert Shield/Desert Storm operations in 1990–1991. Only a single major combatant (cruiser or destroyer), one amphibious ship, and about 15 support and intelligence collection ships were present in the region. Most of the ships operated from an afloat logistics base in the Gulf of Oman and from the Soviet naval base at Dehalak Island in Ethiopia.

The future trend in Soviet at-sea operations is unclear. Soviet ship days "out of (coastal) area" peaked in 1984–1985. After that, the Gorbachev-directed reductions in operation funds reduced ship days at sea. This trend is continuing as this edition went to press. At the same time, the increased size of Soviet naval ships, the availability of a major base facility in Vietnam, and other factors provide an enhanced at-sea capability.

CHAPTER 8

Naval Aviation

The VSTOL carrier KIEV in the Atlantic with a quartet of Yak-38 Forgers parked aft and a single Ka-25 Hormone forward. The flight deck markings—scarred by Forger landings and takeoffs—indicate VSTOL and helicopter operating areas. A pair of aircraft tow tractors are parked on the elevator aft of the island structure, and flight deck crewmen are assembled outboard of the island. (U.S. Navy)

The Soviet Navy's air arm is continuing to increase in numbers of aircraft and aviation ships while improving qualitatively. The Soviet Navy's interest in sea-based aviation is now personified by the two MOSKVA-class helicopter cruisers, the four KIEV-class ships capable of operating Vertical/Short Take-Off and Landing (VSTOL) aircraft, and the first full-deck carrier, ADMIRAL KUZNETSOV (ex-TBILISI), which initially went to sea in November 1989. At least two additional aircraft carriers are under construction.

During her initial sea trials in November 1989, the TBILISI began flight-deck trials of several Short Take-Off and Landing (STOL) aircraft. The first aircraft to make an arrested landing was an Su-27 Flanker air-intercept fighter flown by Viktor Pugachev, test pilot for the Sukhoi design bureau. The Su-27 (and other fixed-wing aircraft) subsequently took off using the ship's ski ramp without the aid of catapults. The second ship of the class, the VARYAG, and the larger UL'YANOVSK, also under construction, are expected to have catapults fitted.

In addition to the continued production of Tu-22M Backfire strike aircraft and Tu-142 Bear-F anti-submarine aircraft as well as lesser types for Soviet Naval Aviation, several new aircraft are being introduced. The high-performance MiG-29 Fulcrum and Su-27 Flanker fighters, and the Su-25 Frogfoot light attack aircraft have been introduced to STOL carrier operation.

The An-74 Madcap radar aircraft has been suggested for the new carrier air wings in addition to the helicopters that will be embarked. Also entering naval service is the MiG-27 Flogger for the land-based strike role. Perhaps the most surprising Soviet Naval Aviation activity of the past few years has been the development of a new flying boat, the Be-42 Albatross (initially designated TAG-D by NATO intelligence). Also in development is an improved VSTOL aircraft for the KIEV-class carriers. This aircraft, designated Yak-41, has experienced development problems. It is expected to replace the Yak-38 Forger fighter/attack aircraft now embarked in the four KIEVs. (These aircraft are described in chapter 27.)

With a current inventory of about 2,000 combat and support aircraft and almost 600 utility, cargo, and training aircraft, Soviet Naval Aviation (SNA), or *Aviatsiya Voyenno-Morskogo Flota* (AVMF), is the world's second largest naval air arm after that of the United States. The Soviet Navy flies more combat aircraft than the air forces of Britain, France, or Germany. (The current strength of SNA is shown in table 8-1.)

During most of the 1980s the strength of SNA increased at an average rate of some 30 aircraft per year. However, from the spring of 1989 through mid-1990 the Soviet Air Forces transferred some 275 first-line tactical aircraft to the Navy: 90 Su-24 Fencer strike aircraft, 100 Su-17 Fitter and 40 MiG-27 Flogger fighter-bomber aircraft, and 45 Frogfoot light attack aircraft. These transfers boosted SNA strength to more than 2,000 aircraft, and the shift of aircraft was continuing (see Addenda).

Some of these transfers have caused major concern among NATO defense leaders as they may represent a Soviet effort to avoid combat aircraft limitations of the Conventional Forces in Europe (CFE) treaty. Those U.S.-Soviet negotiations place limitations on land-based tactical aircraft in Europe but not on land-based naval aircraft, although this "loophole" was addressed in 1991 U.S.-Soviet talks.

Soviet naval air activity outside of Soviet coastal areas has declined since 1986 as have surface naval operations. The reduction in flight hours has the immediate impact of reducing costs for fuel and extends intervals between overhauls. Flights by SNA aircraft, however, continue from airfields at Cam Ranh Bay in Vietnam, Angola, Cuba, Libya, and Syria. These bases could put SNA strike and reconnaissance aircraft within tactical range of several important international waterways as well as regional seas and the Indian Ocean.

History. Russian naval officers had shown strong interest in aviation since the end of the 19th century. The Russians generally cite Captain 1st Rank Alexander Fyodorovich Mozhaisky as the first man to build a flying machine. The naval officer initially built kites and flying models of airplanes. Following private development, he completed this first aeroplane in 1882. (He retired from the Navy that year with the rank of rear admiral.)

Mozhaisky's plane had a 40-foot (12.2-m) wingspan with cloth covering and was powered by two light-weight, British-built steam engines. He mounted a 10-horsepower engine in the nose of the airplane to drive a "puller" propeller mounted in front of the plane and a 20-horsepower engine buried in the fuselage using chains to drive two propellers that rotated through slots cut in the wing. The plane weighed nearly a ton.

Piloted by a man named Golubev, Mozhaisky's aeroplane was launched from an inclined ramp and actually flew for a few feet, but its weight was too great for the available engine power. (Few details of the flight are available as there was no newspaper coverage and the official records were later lost.)

By the start of the 20th century there were several other airplane projects under way in Russia, with significant glider and balloon activity as well as efforts to build rotary-wing and conventional airplanes. But it was not until 25 July 1909 that the first practical airplane flight in Russia was recorded when a French-built Voisin biplane was flown at Odessa on the Black Sea. The following year Jacob M. Hackel, a Russian factory owner of German extraction, built a biplane along the lines of a Henry Farman design. Several other Russians followed Hackel, producing a large number of airplane designs, some quite innovative and successful. The government recognized the military potential of airplanes and in 1910 the Imperial Russian Flying Corps was established, with an Army Central Flying School at Gatchina Park, just south of St. Petersburg, and a Naval Flying School at Kronshtadt, in the Gulf of Finland, with training shifted during the winter months to Sevastopol on the Black Sea in the Crimea. The separate naval air arm would survive through World War I and remain a part of the Navy to the present.

The Navy contracted with the firm "Antoinette" for 1,200 rubles to manufacture an airplane and to train a pilot. The plane was delivered to Sevastopol in July 1910, and, after assembly, it was flown on 16 September by Lieutenant S.F. Dorozhinskiy. The following year there was an unsuccessful attempt to fly the aircraft with floats.

A naval air arm was established in 1912, and during World War I the Russian Navy flew a large number of aircraft with several floatplanes being based on board merchant ships. Soviet military and naval aviation were highly innovative before the Revolution of 1917 and the ensuing civil war—Russians experimented with helicopters, built the world's first four-engine aircraft, flew aircraft armed with recoilless cannon in addition to more conventional weapons, and pioneered in the field of aerial photography for military purposes.

After production halted during the civil war, the number of operational aircraft fell until by the early 1920s only a handful could be considered effective. Subsequently, the rebuilding of Red air forces received high priority; the naval air arm was rebuilt as part of the fleet programs of the 1930s. Late in that decade there was an effort to obtain plans and components for aircraft carriers in the United States, but that project did not come to fruition.

TABLE 8-1 SOVIET NAVAL AVIATION, 1990

Strike/Bomber Aircraft	(330)
Backfire-B/C	160
Badger-G	145
Blinder-A	25
Fighter/Fighter-Bomber Aircraft	(460)
Fulcrum, Flanker	few
Frogfoot	50
Fitter-C/D	170
Forger-A	80
Flogger	50
Fencer	100
Electronic and Reconnaissance Aircraft	(230)
Badger-D/E/F/H/J	130
Bear-D	45
Bear-J	few
Coot-A/B	14
Cub	few
Blinder-C	few
Hormone-B	25
Aerial Tankers	(50)
Badger-A	
Anti-Submarine Aircraft	(475)
Bear-F	65
Mail	90
May	45
Haze-A	100
Helix-A	75
Hormone-A	100
Transport/Training/Utility	(580)
Total Aircraft	2,150

When the Soviet Union entered World War II in June 1941—referred to by the Soviets as the Great Patriotic War—naval aviation was reported to have 1,445 aircraft, although they were mostly outdated types.[1] Soviet naval aircraft flew exclusively from land bases during the war.

According to Soviet sources, at the end of the war there were 1,495 aircraft assigned to the Pacific Fleet alone. This demonstrated the importance accorded to air support of naval operations. Most of the naval aircraft were of indigenous design and manufacture; however, 186 were the ubiquitous PBY/PBN Catalina flying boats, transferred to Russia in 1942–1943, followed by licensed Soviet production of several hundred aircraft.

The Soviet aircraft industry profited from the spoils of war as German technology, machinery, and aircraft engineers were brought to the Soviet Union. The unfinished German aircraft carrier GRAF ZEPPELIN was loaded with booty and taken in tow across the Baltic, destined for Leningrad, but she sank in rough seas. The fleet rebuilding Stalin initiated in the late 1940s was to include aircraft carriers, but none was laid down before the buildup was halted in 1953.

Even after the halt of Stalin's shipbuilding program in 1953, Nikita Khrushchev, his successor, wrote in his purported memoirs: "Aircraft carriers, of course, are the second most effective weapon in a modern navy (after submarines). I'll admit I felt a nagging desire to have some in our own navy, but we couldn't afford to build them. They were simply beyond our means."[2]

Rather, after World War II the Soviet naval air arm concentrated on land-based aircraft. Postwar Soviet Naval Aviation reached a peak strength of several thousand aircraft in the late 1950s, including large numbers of land-based strike aircraft supported by fighter aircraft, which could also be employed to protect naval installations from American carrier strikes. In the late 1950s SNA was stripped of its fighters, which were assigned to the national air defense force. This reduced the Navy to a nadir of about 750 aircraft, mostly light bombers, amphibious patrol planes, and reconnaissance aircraft.

By the late 1950s the Navy was being assigned land-based bomber aircraft armed with air-to-surface missiles for use against enemy ships. The first such weapon was designated AS-1 Kennel by Western intelligence. It was credited with being able to deliver a high-explosive warhead against surface ships or ground targets some 63 miles (100 km) from the launching bomber. The missiles were initially carried by Tu-4 Bull piston-engine bombers, the Soviet copy of the American B-29 Superfortress. Subsequently, the Kennel and other anti-ship missiles were carried by the Tu-16 Badger turbojet bomber.

In 1959–1960 the Soviet strategic air arm transferred most if not all of its missile-armed Badger medium bombers to the Navy for the anti-ship role. (The only missile-armed bombers retained by strategic aviation at the time were the long-range Bears.) By the mid-1960s SNA had some 400 Tu-16 Badger medium bombers and 100 older Il-28 Beagle light/torpedo bombers. The remaining 250 naval aircraft were patrol, ASW, transport, and utility aircraft, including some helicopters.

From the early 1960s SNA has increased steadily in quality and quantity. In the early 1960s the large, four-turboprop Tu-20 Bear entered Soviet naval service in the Bear-D variant. Some 300 Bears were produced during 1961–1962 for the Soviet Air Forces, all bombers, with the B/C carrying land-attack missiles. The naval Bear-D carried no weapons (except defensive guns) but was a long-range reconnaissance and missile targeting aircraft. Significantly, during the 1960s and 1970s the Bear production line was kept open only for the Navy; the Bear-F configured for ASW subsequently entered naval service in the early 1970s.

In the late 1960s, two other important naval aircraft entered service: the Ka-25 Hormone—an ASW helicopter in the A model and a missile-targeting helicopter in the B model—and the Il-38 May, a maritime patrol/ASW aircraft resembling the U.S. P-3 Orion. From 1974 on the Badgers were supplemented in the missile strike role by the new Tu-22M Backfire, a variable-wing, capable of Mach 1.9 at high altitude and Mach 0.9 at sea level.

The Navy was without any type of fighter aircraft for several years. In 1975 the Yak-38 Forger VSTOL fighter-attack plane entered naval air service. About 1976, SNA began acquiring Su-17 Fitter-C ground-attack fighters with the first unit established in the Baltic Fleet, followed a few years later by a Fitter-C unit in the Pacific Fleet. These planes are suited for the support of amphibious landings and attacks against small, surface combat craft.

Subsequently, in early 1986 the Su-24 Fencer-E maritime reconnaissance/strike aircraft was introduced to SNA. While given a fighter-series code name by NATO intelligence, the Fencer provides SNA with a medium-range aircraft for use against ships and naval targets ashore.

About 1988 a small number of MiG-27 Flogger strike fighters were transferred to SNA. It is not known whether these aircraft are to be replacement for the Fitter-C, or if they are for use in their own right. (There is also no indication that the Floggers will be adapted for carrier use.)

The acquisition of modified Fulcrum and Flanker fighters for carrier use will provide SNA with true fighter-interceptor aircraft. (These and the MiG-31 Foxbat are the most effective interceptors in Soviet service.) The adaptation of the Fulcrum and Flanker as well as the Frogfoot attack aircraft to carrier operations, including catapult launching and arrested landings, has been a severe challenge for the Soviet aviation community. Few land-based aircraft modified for carrier use have been fully successful.

In addition, carrier operations are difficult, and they are expensive in terms of operational accidents and pilot casualties. The operation of conventional fixed-wing aircraft from the ADMIRAL KUZNETSOV (ex-TBILISI) and later carriers is an arduous undertaking.

AIR OPERATIONS

The first significant flights by naval aircraft from bases outside of the Soviet bloc began in the 1960s when SNA aircraft began flying from airfields in Egypt, undertaking reconnaissance missions against the U.S. Sixth Fleet in the Mediterranean with Egyptian markings but Russian flight crews. At that time Soviet aircraft were also being transferred to Egypt.

By 1970 there were also reports of Badgers and possibly other naval aircraft being seen on Libyan airfields. The use of Egyptian airfields ceased in 1972, but SNA aircraft continue to make extensive use of bases in Libya and Syria for operations over the Mediterranean.

The first truly long-range flights by SNA began in 1963 when the Soviets began an intensive series of mid-ocean flights over U.S. aircraft carriers. Between 27 January and 22 February, Soviet planes flew over four U.S. carriers in both the Pacific and Atlantic oceans.[3] The aircraft were generally detected some 200 miles (320 km) from the U.S. ships, and they were "escorted" in by U.S. fighters. U.S. Navy officials stated that the flights were probably intended to "convince the Russian people that carriers were obsolescent," although it is difficult to believe that there was public interest in such activities. More likely these were surveillance and training flights, which have continued.

The first major overseas landings by SNA aircraft took place during the *Okean* multi-ocean exercises of April 1970, when a pair of Bear-D reconnaissance aircraft took off from the Kola Peninsula, flew around North Cape and down the Norwegian Sea, over Soviet ships operating in the Iceland-Faeroes gap, and then continued

---

1. During the war naval aircraft flew missions in support of maritime operations but also carried out other missions on a regular basis, directed by ground and area commanders. A few "strategic" missions were flown by the Navy, as on the night of 7–8 August 1941, when five Navy Il-4 bombers left a base in Estonia to make a token and ineffective raid on Berlin. (The British had flown the first air raids against the Berlin area in August 1940.)

2. Nikita Khrushchev, *Khrushchev Remembers; The Last Testament* (Boston: Little, Brown, 1974), p. 31.

3. These carriers were the KITTY HAWK (CVA 63) and PRINCETON (LPH 5) in the North Pacific (with Tu-16 Badgers); ENTERPRISE (CVAN 65) in the eastern Atlantic and FORRESTAL (CVA 59) southeast of the Azores (both with Tu-20 Bears). On 16 March 1963 four Bears overflew the CONSTELLATION (CVA 64) some 600 n.miles (1,100 km) southwest of Midway.

south to land in Cuba. This nonstop flight of more than 5,000 miles (8,000 km) marked the first time that Bear aircraft had landed outside of Soviet bloc countries. After a few days in Cuba the Bears returned to their home base. In late April another pair of Bear-D aircraft flew into Cuba, and a third pair made the flight in May 1970, establishing a regular pattern for such operations. There were an average of five such flights per year until 1981, normally with two Bears in each flight (with four aircraft making the trip in September 1972 and three in July of 1973).

In 1973, pairs of Bear aircraft began flying into Conakry, Guinea. On several occasions Bears in Cuba and Bears in Conakry appear to have carried out coordinated reconnaissance over the South and Central Atlantic. Soviet aircraft ceased flying out of Conakry in 1977, and the pattern changed as Bear-D flights began to use the airfield at Luanda, Angola. These flights crossed the Atlantic between Cuba and Angola.

From 1981 the presence of Bears in Cuba has been virtually continuous, with the aircraft using the San Antonio de los Banos military airfield since November of that year. Bear-F ASW aircraft joined the Bear-D flights to Cuba in 1983. These Bear flights provide long-range navigation training and are a familiarization for the aircraft crews. The Bears also conduct surveillance and Electronic Intelligence (ELINT) collection along the coast of North America, generally flying 200 to 250 miles (320 to 400 km) offshore.

Naval air operations over the Indian Ocean usually originate from bases in the Crimea and include flights over Iran. During the 1970s a major base complex was available to the Soviets at Berbera in Somalia, but they were soon evicted from that country and began using a base in Ethiopia instead. Naval aircraft then flew from South Yemen (formerly Aden). Soviet aircraft also operate from Madagascar.

In the Pacific, long-range flights from Far Eastern bases have been supplemented since 1974 by Bear operations from the former U.S. air bases at Da Nang and Cam Ranh Bay in Vietnam. From 1979 through the 1980s Bear-D/F aircraft flights were continuous, with those aircraft being followed to Vietnam by Badger strike and electronic aircraft, ASW aircraft, and, finally, fighters. During 1988 there were an average of some two dozen naval aircraft at Cam Ranh Bay at any given time—10 Badger strike aircraft, 6 reconnaissance/electronic Badgers, and 8 Bear-D/F aircraft. Also, since late 1984 the Soviet Air Forces has deployed a squadron of 14 MiG-23 Flogger-C fighters to Cam Ranh Bay to provide air defense and fighter escort. However, in late 1989 the Badgers returned to the Soviet Union as part of the cutback in naval activity in forward operating areas.

COMMAND, ORGANIZATION, AND STRENGTH

The overall commander of Soviet Naval Aviation, on the staff of the CinC of the Navy in Moscow, is currently Colonel-General of Aviation G.A. Kuznetsov, who took that post in mid-1982. A career naval aviator, he had commanded naval aviation in the Northern Fleet from 1966 to 1975, then served as the Chief of Staff of Naval Aviation from 1975. His rank, colonel-general, is approximately equivalent to that of full admiral.

Within each of the four fleets there is a naval air force commander with the rank of major or lieutenant general of aviation. The senior staff of SNA Headquarters in Moscow and of each fleet air force includes a first deputy, chief of staff, chief of the political department, and senior engineer.

The current SNA strength of about 2,160 aircraft represents a net increase of over 700 aircraft since 1980. An estimated 65,000 officers and enlisted men were assigned to SNA into 1989, representing 14 percent of the Navy's total personnel. Based on data provided by NATO intelligence, this was an increase of some 6,000 men and women during the past decade within an overall decline in Soviet naval personnel. The transfer of at least 275 fighter-type aircraft from the Soviet Air Forces in 1989–1990 has obviously increased this number. The demand for high-quality flight personnel to man the new aircraft and to maintain them has led a Soviet naval aviator to tell the author most or all SNA enlisted men must

be replaced by warrants, or *michmanii,* who are long-term, technically trained personnel (see chapter 10).

The composition of the various fleet air arms vary with geography and fleet missions. For example, anti-ship strike aircraft and patrol/ASW aircraft are assigned to all four fleets. The long-range Bear reconnaissance and ASW aircraft are found only in the Northern and Pacific fleets, where their great range provides large-area search capabilities.

Within the fleet air arms are regiments and squadrons, with the bomber regiments of some 28 to 30 aircraft believed to include three strike squadrons and a few Electronic Countermeasure (ECM) aircraft.

Two of the KIEV-class aircraft carriers are assigned to the Northern Fleet and two to the Pacific Fleets, bringing to their operating areas Forger VSTOL aircraft and Hormone or Helix helicopters. Both of the MOSKVA-class helicopter ships, with primarily Hormone-A ASW helicopters embarked, are in the Black Sea Fleet. Several classes of cruisers carry Hormone-A ASW helicopters or Hormone-B missile targeting helicopters, with some Hormone-C utility variants also being seen on board ship. The Hormone's successor, the Helix, was first seen at sea in 1981 on board the ASW destroyer UDALOY and then the VSTOL carrier NOVOROSSIYSK. The new ADMIRAL KUZNETSOV was transferred to the Northern Fleet in mid-1991.

The major SNA bases are believed to be located at:

Northern Fleet	Arkhangel'sk, Belusha-Guba, Murmansk, Pechenga, Severomorsk, and Olenegorsk.
Baltic Fleet	Baltysk, Bykov, Kaliningrad, and Riga.
Black Sea Fleet	Donuslav Lake, Gvardeyskoye, Nikolayev, and Oktyabryskoye.
Pacific Fleet	Alekseyevka, Vladivostok, Aleksandrovsk-Sakhalinsky, Petropavlovsk, and Korsakov.

In some instances these are base complexes; for example, four separate naval airfields are located at Petropavlovsk on barren Kamchatka peninsula, according to some reports. Also, there is a naval air research facility at Saki in the Crimea, where since at least 1979 there has been a mockup of a carrier flight deck used for developing carrier launch and recovery procedures and equipment. It is some 1,050 feet (320 m) in length and has arresting wires installed.

The Soviet Air Forces provides basic and technical training for naval aviation. The Levanskiy SNA school at the Nikolayev complex provides specialized naval air training.

NAVAL AIRCRAFT

Bomber/Strike Aircraft. SNA's anti-ship strike role developed in the 1950s to counter American aircraft carriers, which were, at the time, justified primarily for the nuclear strike mission against the Soviet Union. Called Anti-Carrier Warfare (ACW) by the U.S. Navy, anti-ship strike is a high-priority Soviet mission.

The principal aircraft employed in the anti-ship role are the Badger and, increasingly, the Backfire. There are some 135 Badger-G aircraft in SNA, each capable of carrying up to three AS-5 Kelt missiles or two of the newer AS-6 Kingfish missile (see chapter 28 for missile characteristics).

The Backfire has been in SNA service since late 1974; the latest aircraft of this type to enter service is the Backfire-C variant. This aircraft has been the subject of considerable controversy in the United States because of its possible use in the strategic attack role against North American targets. However, the fact that from the start of Backfire deliveries one-half of the planes have gone directly into SNA regiments and not the strategic air arm suggests that these are theater and not strategic strike aircraft. If they were intended for the strategic role, the strategic air arm would undoubtedly have been given more of the early Backfire production run to replace the outdated Bear and Mya-4 Bison long-range bombers.

The Backfire represents a particularly potent aircraft because of

A Backfire strike aircraft—accompanied by a NATO F-16 fighter—carrying a single AS-4 Kitchen anti-ship missile nested into the weapons bay. The principal anti-ship strike force of Soviet Naval Aviation remains land-based Backfire and Badger aircraft, apparently supplemented by Soviet Air Forces Bear-G missile-carrying aircraft.

its high speed, long range, and ability to carry two of the AS-4 or AS-5 missiles. In the anti-carrier role, Backfires flying from bases in the Kola Peninsula could attack ships in the North Atlantic through an arc intersecting Gibraltar and the coast of Labrador. Backfires from bases in the Crimea could reach throughout the Mediterranean. In the Pacific, Backfires from Petropavlovsk bases could reach the Philippine Sea and the westernmost Hawaiian Islands. Flying from Cam Ranh Bay, Backfires and Badgers can cover the entire Indonesian archipelago and the important Indonesian straits between the Pacific and Indian oceans.

There are some 160 Backfires in naval service. In 1988 the Northern Fleet became the last of the four fleet commands to receive Backfires when the Badger regiment at Olenegorsk, a base south of Murmansk used by the 36th Air Army (Air Forces) as well as the Navy, was upgraded to accommodate SNA Backfires. That was the first time that naval Backfires had been permanently based north of the Arctic Circle.

The Badgers and Backfires were designed for in-flight refueling. The refueling probes have been removed from the Backfires under a Soviet-U.S. agreement; they could, however, be refitted to the aircraft within a few hours.

Backfire production through the 1980s continued at the rate of about 30 aircraft per year, being allocated between the SNA and strategic air armies. The production rate has been cut back, but details were not available when this volume went to press.

A new high-performance bomber, given the NATO code name Blackjack, has entered service with Soviet strategic air armies. However, there is no indication that the aircraft will be assigned to SNA. Because of the large number of aircraft and different types now entering naval service, it is unlikely that the Blackjack will be assigned to SNA. Su-24 reconnaissance and strike aircraft are also flown by SNA.

Beyond the missile-armed strike aircraft, SNA still operates a small number of Tu-22 Blinder-A bombers that carry free-fall bombs. These aircraft would probably be used against ground targets in support of amphibious operations or to support ground forces in combat. About 25 remain and are expected to be discarded in the near future.

The Navy also flies 50 Badger-A tankers that can refuel other Badgers and more than 130 other Badgers configured for ELINT/ECM missions in support of strike aircraft (see below).

Fighter-Attack Aircraft. Six types of fighter aircraft are currently in SNA service: the high-performance MiG-29 Fulcrum and Su-27

Flanker all-weather fighters adapted for carrier operation; the Su-25 Frogfoot light-attack aircraft, also reconfigured for carrier use; the Yak-38 Forger VSTOL aircraft; and the land-based Su-17 Fitter-C/D and MiG-27 Flogger-D/K attack aircraft.

The Fulcrum and Flanker are among the best fighter-interceptors in the current Soviet inventory. The Forger is a limited-capability VSTOL aircraft that serves in the four KIEV-class ships. An estimated 80 of the Forger-A single-seat variants are in service plus a small number of the Forger-B two-seat variants. The Forger, which has lift-plus-cruise engines, is considered less efficient than the ship-based Harrier VSTOL attack aircraft, flown by the Britain's Royal Air Force and Fleet Air Arm, the U.S. Marine Corps, and the Spanish and Indian Navies. The Yak-41 is to replace the Forger.

The Fitter is a ground-attack aircraft with some 170 aircraft now in naval service. As noted above, these are probably intended to support amphibious landings and attacks against small, high-speed naval craft. Less is known about the configuration and role of the Floggers, with an estimated 50 aircraft in SNA service by 1990.

The Su-25 Frogfoot, a light attack aircraft, has been adapted for carrier operation. This aircraft, which saw extensive service in the Afghanistan conflict, is a limited, daylight-only aircraft. When this edition went to press only the two-seat Su-25UB trainer had flown aboard the carrier ADMIRAL KUZNETSOV.

Electronic/Reconnaissance Aircraft. Several specialized electronic and reconnaissance aircraft are flown by SNA. There are about 185 bomber-type aircraft now in service (Bear, Badger, and Blinder aircraft), at least 100 Su-24 Fencer-E multi-purpose aircraft, plus a few modified cargo-type aircraft (Cub and Coot). Also in service are Hormone-B helicopters for shipboard use in the over-the-horizon missile targeting role.

In many respects the most remarkable Soviet aircraft in service today is the giant Bear. This graceful-looking aircraft has large, swept-back wings and four turboprop engines turning contra-rotating propellers. The Bear-D has an unrefueled range of up to 9,000 miles (14,400 km) and is fitted for in-flight refueling! This aircraft, with a prominent under-fuselage radome (NATO designation Big Bulge) makes radar and electronic sweeps of ocean areas and can relay target information via Video Data Link (VDL) to missile-armed surface ships and submarines. The approximately 45 Bear-D aircraft are assigned to the Northern and Pacific fleets.

The Badger-D/E aircraft are employed in the photographic and electronic reconnaissance role. The Badgers in the recce (Recon-

The performance of the Yak-38 Forger aircraft is not impressive, while the follow-on Yak-41 VSTOL aircraft has encountered development problems. Still, the Forger provides a useful capacity for operations beyond the range of land-based tactical aircraft. The Forger initially flew

naissance) roles can be identified by camera ports or electronic pods under their wings and "blisters" or electronic domes on their fuselages.

The SNA also flies the Badger-H/J aircraft in the ECM role. The ECM mission calls for some aircraft to accompany the strike planes in close formation and others to stand off from the ships being attacked to jam or confuse defensive radars. These planes have powerful on-board radar jammers and can also drop chaff. (The built-in ECM capabilities of the Backfire appear to permit it to operate without the need for specialized jammer escort planes.)

A small number of Blinder-C aircraft may still be in use in the photo-electronic reconnaissance role.

The Cub-C variant of the An-12 transport aircraft has been configured for the ELINT role, as has the Coot-A variant of the Il-18 transport. The Cub-C, sometimes in civil Aeroflot markings, has periodically overflown U.S. naval forces. The Coot-A is a modification of the transport model of this aircraft and not a variant of the Il-38 May that was originally based on the Il-18.

Another naval reconnaissance and targeting aircraft is the Hormone-B helicopter. This ship-based aircraft, operational since 1967, is carried in several guided missile cruisers plus the KIEV-class carriers to provide over-the-horizon targeting for the SS-N-3 and SS-N-12 anti-ship missiles. Only about two dozen of these helicopters are in service. (A modification of the Big Bulge radar is fitted in this helicopter.)

When this edition went to press it was not known publicly if the larger Helix ship-based helicopter will be adopted for the reconnaissance and targeting role.

The An-74 Madcap variant of the An-72/74 Coaler transport configured for Airborne Early Warning (AEW) has been indicated as possibly intended for use on board later aircraft carriers. Soviet naval officers have expressed strong views on the importance of AEW aircraft to naval operations, based in part on the British experience in the 1982 war in the Falklands. One frequent Soviet writer, Captain 1st Rank B. Rodinov, noted that the analysis of combat in the Falklands indicated that the first of several steps "that must be taken to increase the effectiveness of weapons to defend aircraft carriers in striking forces and ship formations . . . [is] equipping carrier striking forces with long-range radar surveillance aircraft."[4] The size of this aircraft is a problem.

Maritime Patrol/Anti-Submarine Aircraft. At this time SNA flies an estimated 90 Be-12 Mail flying boats, 45 May aircraft, and 65 of the Bear-F variants in the maritime patrol/ASW role.

The Mail—dubbed *Chaika* ("seagull") by the Soviets—may soon be joined by a new flying boat aircraft, the Be-42 (having the

A senior officer takes the salute from an Il-38 May patrol aircraft unit. Soviet naval aviators compose a specialized branch of the Soviet Navy, much like the Naval Infantry. Naval aviators cannot hold shipboard billets or command at sea. (Soviet Navy)

design bureau designation A-40). The Mail as well as the land-based May has a limited effectiveness although both aircraft have demonstrated relative longevity in service.

The May, developed from the Il-18 commercial transport, first appeared in its naval configuration about 1970. Relatively few Mays were built in comparison with their U.S. Navy counterparts, the P-3 Orions, which continue in production (more than 700 Orions have been delivered to the U.S. and allied navies and air forces). From the available information it is not clear whether May production was limited because SNA was not satisfied with the plane or because a more capable ASW platform was being developed in the Bear-F. Some Western analysts have speculated that the May simply could not carry sufficient sonobuoys and torpedoes for the long-endurance ASW mission.

The Bear-F, an extensively updated variant of the venerable Tupolev design, remains in production more than three decades after the first flight of the first Bear prototype in the summer of 1954. Another naval Bear variant is the Bear-J, which is flown in small numbers by SNA as a strategic communications relay aircraft, similar to the U.S. Navy's TACAMO program.[5] These Bears have trailing wire antennas and probably Very-Low Frequency (VLF) relay systems. (The Air Forces' Bear-H, a strategic missile carrier,

---

4. Capt. 1st Rank B. Rodinov, Capt. 2nd Rank Ye. Nikitin, and N. Novichkov, "The Electronic War in the South Atlantic," *Morskoy Sbornik* (no. 1, 1983), p. 85.

5. TACAMO is an acronym for the expression Take Charge And Move Out. The U.S. Navy flies the E-6A Hermes and EC-130Q Hercules aircraft in this role.

from carriers only in the VTOL mode; however, since the early 1980s they have been observed making short-run takeoffs, as in this montage of flight operations from the carrier MINSK. (*Joint Services Recognition Journal*).

continues in production while the Bear-G is being converted from earlier Bear B/C bombers. The Bear-G carries the AS-4 missile.)

The An-12 Cub is being used as a test platform for ASW systems. Little has appeared in the Western press about this role of the plane.

Helicopters are employed extensively for ASW, the Hormone-A and new Ka-27 Helix-A being carried for that purpose in the MOSKVA and KIEV aviation ships, the UDALOY destroyers, and the KIROV, Kara, and Kresta II cruisers. About 100 Hormone-A helicopters, which first become operational about 1967, are in service as are 75 Helix-A models.

Also flown by SNA is the larger, land-based Mi-14 Haze, an amphibious derivative of the Mi-8 Hip transport helicopter. The Haze is too large for shipboard use, being unable to fit on the elevators of the MOSKVA and KIEV classes. Rather, it was developed to replace the out-dated Mi-4 Hound for shore-based ASW operations. Over 125 Hazes of all types have been delivered to the Soviet Navy plus others to several foreign air forces.

Minesweeping, Utility, and Training Aircraft. The Soviet Navy has adopted Hip helicopters for the minesweeping role, probably starting in the early 1970s. The helicopter carrier LENINGRAD carried a

The open hangar of the ADMIRAL ISAKOV shows the complex doors and angled ramp employed in hangaring the Ka-25 Hormone-A on board a Kresta II–class cruiser. The Kamov tandem-rotor design permits a more compact shipboard helicopter than those with tail rotors. The striped windsock, flight control station, and an RBU-1000 anti-submarine rocket launcher are visible. (Royal Navy)

The Tupolev-designed Bear has been in continuous production longer than any other combat aircraft in aviation history. This is a Tu-142 Bear-F Mod IV (NATO designation) with a magnetic detection antenna mounted on the tail fin and a sensor fairing under the tail gun mounting.

pair of these helicopters into the Red Sea in 1973–1974 for mine-sweeping operations at the southern end of the Suez Canal.

Subsequently, the Haze has been observed in the minesweeping role, that variant being designated Haze-B by NATO with at least 25 aircraft believed to be in naval service.

The Soviet Navy also flies several Mi-8 helicopters in the transport and utility role. The transport helicopters have been observed with Naval Infantry markings during amphibious exercises; the Mi-8 as well as Hormone-C and Helix-B/C helicopters have been seen on the IVAN ROGOV amphibious ship and several auxiliary ships.

In addition to the operational aircraft described above, SNA has some 580 transport, training, and utility aircraft. These service the fleets and Navy headquarters in Moscow and provide specialized naval aviation training, the last mostly in the Black Sea Fleet area.

STRATEGIC AVIATION

The Soviet Air Forces have a mission to support maritime operations with the most significant contribution being the strategic air arm (formerly designated *Aviatsiya Dalnovo Deistviya*, or Long-Range Aviation). In the early 1980s Soviet strategic aviation was reorganized into five air armies, directly subordinate to the Supreme High Command. (The armies are under the administrative control of the Air Forces.)

The bomber aircraft assigned to these air armies are estimated by Western intelligence as 21 Tu-160 Blackjack, 170 Backfire, and 160 Bear long-range aircraft; 290 Badger and Blinder medium-range aircraft; and some 400 Su-24 Fencer strike aircraft. All are capable of carrying nuclear weapons as well as conventional bombs and missiles.

Also assigned to these air armies to support the bomber aircraft are some 270 fighter escorts, 330 reconnaissance/electronic warfare aircraft, and a small number of tankers. The older Bear-A/B bombers flown by the Air Forces are being upgraded to the Bear-G configuration, carrying the AS-4 Kitchen missile for anti-ship attacks. Flying from Soviet bases in the Far East, their radius in the anti-ship role reaches out to the Hawaiian Islands. Other aircraft of the Air Forces have been observed in maritime exercises, including Blinder and Bear-E reconnaissance aircraft that have flown missions against Western naval task forces.

The aircraft of these five air armies provide a significant capability for over-ocean reconnaissance, in-flight refueling, minelaying, and anti-ship operations.

The Beriev design bureau's Be-42 Albatross took Western aviation experts by surprise. The largest flying boat now in service, the aircraft is shown here during its 1989 public debut at Moscow's Tushino airport. Boost engines for takeoff may be located in the massive dorsal structure, partially beneath the wing roots. (Detlev Grass courtesy Pilot Press)

CHAPTER 9

Naval Infantry, Coastal Missile-Artillery, and Spetsnaz Forces

The Soviet Union maintains a major force for amphibious operations in the several regional seas that surround the country. Here a Polnocny-A LSM and a Ropucha LST unload T-55 main battle tanks of Soviet Naval Infantry during a Pacific Fleet exercise. (Sovfoto, S. Kozlov)

The Soviet Navy's three special ground-combat arms are, like other components of the fleet, undergoing significant change, but those changes are less clear than with other aspects of Soviet maritime power. The Soviet Navy has three ground-combat arms: the Naval Infantry, which corresponds in many respects to the U.S. Marine Corps and Royal Marines; the Coastal Missile-Artillery Force, which helps to defend key points from seaborne assault; and *Spetsnaz* forces, which are somewhat akin to the U.S. Navy's SEALs and the Royal Marines' Special Boat Squadron. Each of the four Soviet fleets has components of all three combat arms assigned to support operations in their respective areas.

During the 1980s all three of these specialized combat arms increased in size: The Naval Infantry increased from an estimated 12,000 men in 1980 to about 18,000, while the Coastal Missile-Artillery has increased from some 8,000 to an estimated 14,000 in the same period. There have also been additions to the *Spetsnaz* forces, although details are lacking, and it is possible that some of the reported increases in the Naval Infantry were actually in the other forces.

However, in the late 1980s there was a precipitous reduction in the coastal defense forces, according to U.S. intelligence sources; the current Coastal Missile-Artillery Force is now believed to consist of only some 7,000 troops. At the same time, while official U.S. sources list Naval infantry strength at 18,000, in 1988 a Soviet official cited a marine force of only 12,600 men.[1] Then, in 1990–1991 four motorized rifle divisions of the Soviet Ground Forces (i.e., Army) were subordinated to Navy command. This transfer was apparently intended to circumvent CFE (Conventional Forces in Europe) multi-national agreements.

1. V.F. Petrovsky, Deputy Head of the USSR Delegation to the United Nations General Assembly, speech to the 43rd session of the General Assembly, New York City, 18 October 1988.

TABLE 9-1 SOVIET AMPHIBIOUS SHIPS

Class	Northern Fleet	Baltic Fleet	Black Sea Fleet	Caspian Flotilla	Pacific Fleet
IVAN ROGOV	—	1	—	—	2
Alligator	2	2	5	—	5
Ropucha	5	8	3	—	7
Polnocny/MP-4	5	10	6	15	5

Each of these divisions has 12,700 troops organized into three rifle, one tank, and one artillery regiment.

The Naval Infantry structure also changed significantly in the 1980s, with the forces assigned to the four fleets raised to higher organizational levels. The three European fleets (Northern, Baltic, Black Sea) now have marine brigades vice regiments, and the Pacific Fleet has a division vice brigade. At the same time, the Naval Infantry units received new weapons and vehicles, while the steady production of high-speed assault craft provides an improved assault capability. Within the range of these craft, they compensate for the relatively slow growth in the capabilities of the larger, long-range amphibious ships (see chapters 20 and 21). At the same time, a limited number of Wing-In-Ground (WIG) effect vehicles have been introduced for the amphibious assault role.

When viewed in the context of other on-going Soviet modernization programs (e.g., naval aviation, surface ships, and submarines) the current investment in amphibious assault forces is also substantial.

The assignment of Soviet amphibious ships, based on U.S. intelligence sources, is shown in table 9-1.

NAVAL INFANTRY

The primary mission of Naval Infantry (*Morskaya Pekhota*) is to gain control of territory adjacent to important straits and other waterways; this would be done through independent amphibious landings, or as the spearhead for combined marine-army operations, or in concert with airborne troops. The secondary mission is to defend naval bases and captured coastal territory.

The Soviet Naval Infantry currently has a strength estimated at 18,000 officers and enlisted men by the U.S. Defense Intelligence Agency.[2] This represents a limited growth over the past few years. The relatively small size of the Soviet marine force when compared to the U.S. Marine Corps, its distribution among the four Soviet fleets, and the limited capacity of Soviet amphibious ships tend to prevent the employment of the Soviet Naval Infantry in large-scale landings in the manner planned by the U.S. Marine Corps. The Soviet Navy's leadership has carefully stated that the Naval Infantry is not intended to be employed in the American style. For example, Vice Admiral K.A. Stalbo, Soviet naval historian and theorist, has written:

> The experience of our Navy in landing naval forces during the Great Patriotic War [1941–1945] attests to the fact that in those years the Soviet school of the art of the amphibious landing of troops was built up and was crystallized in the course of battle, having developed along its own paths, which differ considerably from the paths taken by the naval art of the foreign navies, primarily the U.S. Navy.[3]

History. Tsar Peter I on 16 November 1705 established the first Naval Infantry regiment for his newly created fleet on the Baltic. The regiment had a total of 45 officers and 1,320 soldiers, organized in two battalions of five companies each. The creation of the regiment is considered the birth date of the Russian marine force. One

of the first victories of the Russian marines came a year later when they captured the Swedish boat ESPERN in a boarding fight. And, beginning in 1707, the marines as well as large numbers of soldiers were used repeatedly in landings along the coasts of Finland and Sweden and on offshore islands in the Baltic during the latter stages of Peter's lengthy conflict with Sweden (1700–1721).

Peter reorganized his marine regiment in 1712 because of the confusion caused by the distribution of marines among the several Baltic squadrons. Instead the marines were formed into five marine battalions, each with an organization of 22 officers and 600 to 650 men—a total of more than 3,000 marines. Of the five battalions, three were to be carried in the Baltic sailing fleet, one was with the galley fleet, and one (Admiralty Battalion) guarded naval installations in St. Petersburg. The battalions were enlarged over time, with the Admiralty Battalion reaching an authorized strength of 881 officers and men.

These marines fought at sea and ashore, with a significant number being in the Russian fleets that periodically operated in the Mediterranean. They helped to capture the city of Navarino in 1770, the fortress of Beirut in 1773, and several islands in the Ionian Sea and the fortress of Corfu in 1798–1800. The number of marines in the fleet was rarely large, the exceptions being during the Crimean War (1853–1856) and the Russo-Japanese War (1904–1905) when sailors from immobilized or sunken ships were formed up to fight as naval infantry. In World War I a specially formed regiment of marines made several amphibious landings in the Baltic, with as many as 2,000 marines participating in some of the operations. Smaller landings were carried out in the Black Sea. Plans were under way to organize a marine division and then a corps, probably for assaults on the Turkish Straits, when the October Revolution erupted in 1917.

During the Revolution and the Civil War that followed, many Russian sailors served ashore, but they could hardly be considered as marines although they apparently participated in some river crossings and coastal operations while under fire. There do not appear to have been organized Soviet marine units from the Revolution until 1939, when the 1st Separate Naval Infantry Brigade was established in the Baltic Fleet and used in the war with Finland (1939–1940). By mid-1941, when the Soviet Union entered World War II, there were 25 individual naval rifle brigades and 12 naval artillery brigades.

As the war continued, a total of 40 brigades, 6 independent regiments, and several separate battalions of Naval Infantry were formed. They varied in composition, with most having organic artillery units and two of the Baltic Fleet's brigades having tank battalions. (These two brigades, the 2nd and 5th, fought as ground troops and were not used in landing operations.) When the war ended there were almost 500,000 sailors fighting ashore, some in what were called naval rifle units and some in army units, while the troops with the fleet were still called Naval Infantry. There were significant amphibious operations during the conflict. Approximately 100,000 naval infantrymen who remained under fleet and flotilla control were used to defend naval bases and islands as well as carry out amphibious landings with army troops.

The Soviet Navy conducted 114 amphibious landings during World War II, some quite small—essentially raids of platoon size. But four of the landings, two at Kerch-Feodosya and one at Novorossiysk on the Black Sea, and one at Moon Sound in the Baltic, each involved several thousand troops. According to Soviet sources, of the 114 landings, 61 were planned and organized in less than 24 hours! In all, the Navy landed some 330,000 troops during the war, soldiers as well as marines.[4] Most of the landings were short-range operations across straits, bays, and rivers, and several were made in coordination with parachute landings, especially those against the North Korean coast in August 1945.

Several important Soviet officials were associated with these amphibious operations during the war. Admiral S.G. Gorshkov directed landings in the Black Sea–Azov–Danube campaigns; Leonid Brezhnev, head of the Soviet government from 1964 to 1982,

---

2. The U.S. Marine Corps strength in 1991 is 201,500, comprising primarily three divisions and three aircraft wings. The next largest marine forces (generally including commando/special forces) are: Taiwan, 30,000; Vietnam, 27,000; South Korea, 25,000; and Thailand, 20,000. (Great Britain's Royal Marines number some 7,700.)

3. Rear Adm. K.A. Stalbo, "The Naval Art in the Landings of the Great Patriotic War," *Morskoy Sbornik* (no. 3, 1970), pp. 23–30. Subsequently promoted to vice admiral, Stalbo is a PhD (naval sciences), an honored scientist, and a state prize laureate.

4. Stalbo, ibid.

Aist-class air cushion landing craft unload marines and their vehicles onto the beach during an exercise on the Black Sea coast. The massive Soviet investment in amphibious air cushion vehicles and wing-in-ground effect machines has provided a substantial short-range assault capability. (Sovfoto, N. Malyshev)

was a political officer with the 18th Assault Army during landings on the Black Sea coast, where he suffered a minor wound; and Marshal V.F. Margelov, commander of Soviet airborne forces from 1954 to 1974, served in the Naval Infantry during the war. (Margelov changed the uniform of airborne troops to include the blue-striped tee shirt of the Navy as a symbol of the specialized nature of paratroopers, who could also "cross seas" for the assault.)

After the war the Naval Infantry was disbanded for almost two decades. However, Soviet observations of U.S. and British marines in the postwar period and the Soviets' own analyses of their requirements as naval operations expanded led to the decision to reinstitute a marine force. The Soviets publicly acknowledged the existence of Naval Infantry units on 24 July 1964, when, in conjunction with the traditional Navy Day, a front-page pictorial in the military newspaper *Krasnaya Zvezda* (Red Star) showed marines coming ashore in amphibious personnel carriers.

These newly formed units conducted amphibious maneuvers during joint operations with other Warsaw Pact forces. Naval Infantry—about 500 marines from the Baltic Fleet—participated in the Moscow parade on 7 November 1967 commemorating the October Revolution, the first time such a body had been seen on parade in Red Square since World War II.

Marine units were soon built up in the various fleets, until by the 1970s each of the fleets had a regiment of some 2,000 marines. By the early 1980s the Pacific Fleet was increased to a marine brigade. Subsequently, the European fleets' marines were increased to brigade size and the marines in the Pacific Fleet enlarged to a division. Under current Soviet doctrine, Naval Infantry units used to strike at hostile shores come ashore primarily from amphibious ships, mostly in amphibious personnel carriers supported by amphibious tanks. Troop-carrying helicopters and Air Cushion Vehicle (ACV) landing craft are also used, but the smaller ACVs can be carried in only a few naval and merchant ships, while the large Aist-class ACVs have a strike range of only a few hundred miles. The assault echelon consists of the most mobile landing forces, using amphibious tanks and amphibious personnel carriers. These are unloaded from amphibious ships directly into the water and then they "swim" ashore. As air cushion landing craft become increasingly available, they will be used to bring the assault echelon, including tanks, ashore faster than the amphibious tractors. The follow-up echelons are then landed by the beaching of amphibious ships if the beach conditions permit. If the water depth is insufficient, the follow-up echelons are brought ashore in landing craft.

During the past few years troop-carrying helicopters have begun to be employed in amphibious assault exercises. Some of these, of the Mi-8 Hip type, have been observed with Soviet Naval Aviation markings. It should be noted, however, that the three ships of the IVAN ROGOV class are the only Soviet amphibious ships with a

The Pomornik air cushion landing craft is impressive even at rest. This large high-speed craft can carry tanks and assault troops in amphibious operations out to several hundred miles from their bases. (West German Navy)

helicopter flight deck and hangar. But the availability of large ACV landing craft and, at least in limited numbers, the Orlan WIG amphibious vehicle, are rapidly changing the character of Soviet amphibious assault capabilities and tactics.

Most Soviet articles and manuals addressing amphibious tactics point out that naval gunfire support and close air support will be provided in landing operations. The Soviets have designated the SOVREMENNYY-class missile destroyers (each carrying two 100-mm twin gun mounts) and possibly the SLAVA-class missile cruisers (one 100-mm twin gun mount) for the gunfire support role.

The Baltic and Pacific fleets both have regiments of Fitter-C/D fighter/ground attack aircraft, highly suitable for providing close air support for amphibious landings within a few hundred miles of Soviet bases. These can be supplemented by the older Tu-16 Badger and Tu-22 Blinder bombers that can deliver "iron bombs" against coastal targets as well as the newer Su-24 Fencer and MiG-27 Flogger strike aircraft.

Mine countermeasure craft and special units to deal with obstacles in the beach approaches and on the beach are also considered in amphibious planning. Also, extensive command and control facilities are provided in some of the warships that will participate in the operation. Indeed, the Soviet Navy's leadership has stated that the modern amphibious assault is the most complex type of military operation.

Shortly after the Naval Infantry branch was reestablished, marine units began periodic deployments aboard amphibious ships. There have been troop-carrying "amphibs" in the Mediterranean periodically since the mid-1960s. The first amphibious ship deployment to the Indian Ocean (from the Pacific Fleet) took place in 1968, and subsequently, beginning in 1970, amphibious ships with marines on board have been observed on deployments off the western coast of Africa (Angola). These periodic amphibious landings in the fleet areas have been supplemented by larger landings in the *Okean* '70 and '75 exercises, as well as by a landing by Naval Infantry on the coast of Syria and the practice amphibious assault near the Polish border (*Zapad* '81), both in 1981 (see chapter 7).

In most exercises the initial assault by marines is followed by ground forces being landed from amphibious ships or merchant ships. Motorized rifle battalions have been seen in this role. Also, the Soviets appear to plan to use airborne troops from airborne divisions in coordination with amphibious forces.

COMMAND AND ORGANIZATION[5]

Naval Infantry and the Coastal Missile-Artillery Force appear to be jointly directed by Major General I.S. Skuratov, on the staff of the Commander in Chief of the Navy. His rank is relatively low compared to other branch and department chiefs at Naval Headquarters and indicates the direct subordination of these forces to their respective fleet commanders.

Soviet Naval Infantry is currently organized into three brigades and one division. There is one brigade with the Northern Fleet (based at Pechenga, near Murmansk)[6]; one brigade with the Baltic Fleet (at Baltiysk); one brigade with the Black Sea Fleet (at Kazachya Bukhta near Sevastopol); and a division composed of two regiments and supporting units with the Pacific Fleet (at Vladivostok).

A marine brigade has some 3,000 to 4,000 officers and enlisted men, the latter number reflecting the addition of one or two rifle battalions above the standard of triangular structure in Soviet combat units. These brigades are combined arms units, as shown in figure 9-1. There is also a tank battalion organic to each brigade as well as several weapons battalions and separate batteries. Command and support functions for the brigade are provided by several small companies.

5. The organization charts are based primarily on Lt. Col. Louis N. Buffardi, U.S. Army, *The Soviet Naval Infantry* (Washington, D.C.: Defense Intelligence Agency, April 1980), and *Soviet and NSWP [Non-Soviet Warsaw Pact] Amphibious Warfare* (Washington, D.C.: Defense Intelligence Agency, November 1984).

6. The Northern Fleet's marine unit has been identified as the Kirkenesskiy Brigade; during World War II it appears to have been the 63rd Red Banner Brigade of Naval Infantry. The later title was awarded to commemorate the battle against German forces at Kirkenes, Norway.

The Pacific Fleet's division has a strength of about 7,000 men, with each of its three regiments containing some 2,000 men. The division also has a tank and an artillery regiment, plus several support battalions (see figure 9-2).

The principal components of the brigades and regiments are (see fig. 9-1):

Infantry Battalions. Each of the infantry battalions has some 400 men, organized primarily into three infantry companies of about 100 men each (see figure 9-3). Each company has three platoons.

Transportation for the battalion is provided by 34 armored, amphibious assault vehicles of the BTR-60PB type.

Each battalion also has a mortar platoon, with three 82-mm or 120-mm mortars, and an anti-tank platoon with AT-3 Sagger or AT-5 Spigot guided missiles.

The BTR-60PB is an amphibious/armored personnel carrier. It is a wheeled vehicle with a loaded weight of 21,000 pounds and carries a crew of two, plus 12 troops. A turret with one 14.5-mm and one 7.62-mm machine gun is mounted, with some vehicles fitted to carry SA-7 Grail anti-aircraft missiles or AT-3 or AT-5 anti-tank missiles.[7]

Tank Battalion. The tank battalion has one medium tank company, with ten T-54/55 or, more likely, the newer T-72 tanks, and three light tank companies, each with ten of the amphibious PT-76 light tanks (see fig. 9-4).

The T-54 medium tank entered service in 1959, with the improved T-55 version operational from about 1961. The T-55 tank weighs 36 tons and has a 100-mm main gun with a crew of four. Diesel-powered, it can ford water 18 feet (5.5 m) deep with a snorkel that can be rapidly installed by the crew.

The T-72 is a main battle tank that entered service with the Soviet Ground Forces in 1976 and was probably introduced into the Naval Infantry shortly afterward. Weighing some 41 tons, the T-72 has a smooth-bore 125-mm cannon. The tank has automatic loading for the main gun, reducing the crew to three men.

PT-76 is a fully amphibious light tank that weighs 14 tons with a 76-mm gun fitted and a crew of three.

Howitzer Battalion. The brigade artillery components consist of self-propelled howitzer, rocket-launcher, and anti-tank battalions plus an air defense battery.

The recent addition of the 122-mm M-1974 self-propelled howitzer battalion represents a significant improvement in marine firepower. The battalion probably has three firing batteries, each with six guns, for a brigade total of 18 weapons.

7. SA for Surface-to-Air missiles and AT for Anti-Tank missiles are Western designations; all others used here are Soviet nomenclature.

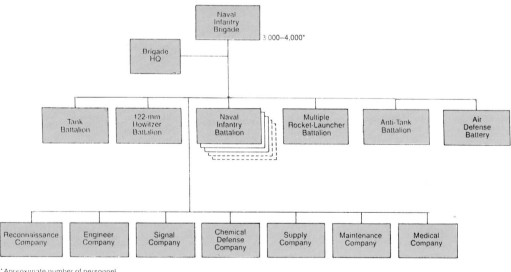

* Approximate number of personnel

FIGURE 9-1.   Naval Infantry Brigade

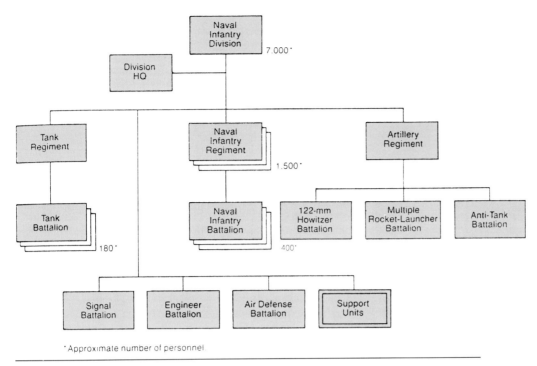

* Approximate number of personnel.

FIGURE 9-2.   Naval Infantry Division

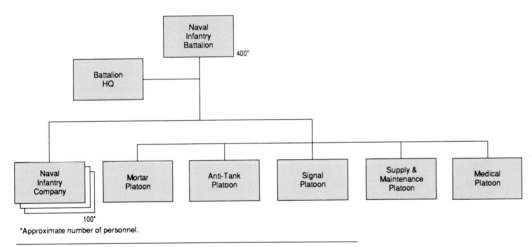

*Approximate number of personnel.

FIGURE 9-3.   Naval Infantry Battalion

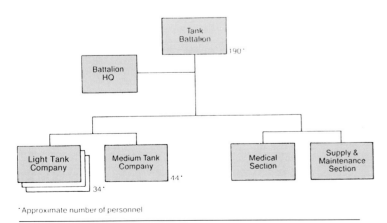

* Approximate number of personnel

FIGURE 9-4.   Naval Infantry Tank Battalion

T-54B main battle tank.

T-72 main battle tank.

PT-76 amphibious tank.

M1974 122-mm self-propelled gun.

The M-1974 gun is a 122-mm howitzer weighing 20 tons mounted on a light armored vehicle for high mobility. The firing range is estimated at nine miles. The gun crew is 4 or 5 men.

Rocket-Launcher Battalion. The rocket-launcher battalion has 18 BM-21 multiple rocket launchers, descendants of the infamous "Stalin's organ" of World War II.

The BM-21 is a truck-mounted, 40-tube, 122-mm rocket launcher. Range is about 22,500 yards (20 km) and manual reload time is ten minutes.

Air-Defense Battery. Anti-aircraft defense of the brigade is provided by this battery, consisting of one platoon armed with four ZSU-23-4 Shilka, self-propelled, quad 23-mm guns, and one platoon equipped with SA-9 Gaskin guided missiles on four BRDM-2 armored vehicles.

The ZSU-23-4 is a potent short-range anti-aircraft weapon, with integral fire control radar, mounted on a tank chassis. The rate of fire is about 200 rounds per minute per barrel. The SA-9 is carried and fired from a canister, four of which are mounted atop the BRDM-2. It is an infrared-homing missile, with a maximum range of some 8,800 yards (8 km). In addition to these vehicle weapons, there are several SA-7 Grail man-portable rocket launchers in Naval Infantry units.

Anti-Tank Battalion. This unit has 18 multiple-rail AT-3 Sagger or AT-5 guided missile systems mounted on BRDM-2 vehicles. There are also several SPG-9 73-mm recoilless rifles and AT-3 man-carried guided missiles in the brigade.

Reconnaissance Company. The brigade's reconnaissance company has three PT-76 light tanks and nine BRDM-2 reconnaissance vehicles.

The BRDM-2 is a wheeled amphibious personnel carrier weighing 15,400 pounds loaded, which carries four men and provides protection against small arms fire. Single 14.5-mm and 7.62-mm machine guns are mounted in a rotating turret.

Engineer Company. These troops are used primarily to clear underwater and land obstacles in the assault area. K-61 amphibious cargo vehicles are used by these engineers, but they also land by BTR-60P vehicles, helicopters, and high-speed boats in advance of the assault waves.

At the division level (see figure 9-2) there is a tank regiment, thought to contain three standard tank battalions; three infantry regiments, each with three rifle battalions; and an artillery regiment composed of several battalions. Details of this organization are not publicly available; for example, when there were separate regiments in the fleet they consisted of some 2,000 officers and men, but that number included a tank battalion (190 men) and two artillery batteries (totaling more than 100 men). The divisional regiments are smaller and some of the support units that were assigned to the regiments are now at the division level.

Similarly, the principal components of the division's artillery regiment have not been published. The division does have an air defense battalion with SA-8 Grecko surface-to-air missiles. This is a low-to-medium range missile, with the missile and associated radars mounted on a six-wheeled amphibious vehicle. The launcher itself consists of six missile rails (enclosed in the SA-8B version), with six reload missiles carried in the vehicle. The effective ceiling of the missile is between 150 and 20,000 feet (46 to 6,100 m).

PERSONNEL

The Naval Infantry has distinctive fatigue uniforms, consisting of black coveralls with blue-and-white-striped tee shirt visible at the open neck and a circular anchor insignia on the left sleeve. The marines also wear a black beret with an anchor insignia on the left side and a red star in front. The enlisted dress uniform is almost the same as for the rest of the Navy, with some differences in cut and color.

Military rather than naval ranks are used by the Naval Infantry (and Coastal Missile-Artillery Force). As noted above, the senior

BTR-60PB armored personnel carrier.

ZSU-23-4 quad 23-mm self-propelled gun.

officer is a major general (one star) with probably colonels commanding the brigades, a major general commanding the Pacific Fleet's division, and lieutenant colonels or majors commanding the battalions. Naval Infantry officers are graduates of higher military rather than higher naval schools, with a number of officers known to be graduates of the Baku Higher Combined Arms Command School.

Enlisted men are conscripted into the Naval Infantry for two years, the same as for the Soviet Ground Forces. Training for Naval Infantry personnel concentrates on amphibious landings, although most types of ground combat tactics are also taught.

Selected personnel receive parachute training. Other marines perform in the swimmer/underwater demolition roles, which also require specialized training. The relationship, however, of these specialized marines and *Spetsnaz* forces is not clear.

COASTAL MISSILE-ARTILLERY FORCE

The Soviet Navy's Coastal Missile-Artillery Force has received far less publicity than the Naval Infantry. There are believed to be only 7,000 men currently assigned to coastal defense, a significant reduction from the large increase in the early 1980s (reported going from a strength of about 8,000 men to 14,000).

A few years ago the Coastal Missile-Artillery Force was reported to consist of three missile battalions with the Northern Fleet, six battalions in the Baltic Fleet, and five battalions each in the Black Sea and Pacific fleets. It is not publicly known how the battalions are organized.

The missile battalions are believed to be armed with the SSC-1b Sepal anti-ship missile, with a range of at least 250 n.miles (460 km). This is a land-launched version of the SS-N-3 Shaddock missile. The 15 to 18 missiles in each Sepal battalion are carried on eight-wheeled, transporter-launcher vehicles. This provides a high degree of mobility, even over rough terrain, with road speeds up to 50 mph (80 km/h).

(The smaller Samlet anti-ship missile, previously used for coastal defense, has been phased out of Soviet service.)

Coastal defense guns are also used by the Coastal Missile-Artillery Force. The older weapons have been discarded. The more modern guns reported in service include the improved M-46 130-mm gun, with a range of approximately 22 miles (35 km), and SM-4-1 130-mm guns; both are towed weapons. There may also be a few anti-aircraft gun and missile units in the Coastal Missile-Artillery Force.

In addition, coastal defense exercises are periodically conducted by the Ground Forces. Again, motorized rifle battalions are most often cited in accounts of these coastal defense maneuvers, although there has been some mention in the Soviet press of mountain infantry battalions being employed in this role.

An SSC-X-4 (Soviet designation RK-55) became operational in 1986–1987 but apparently was not deployed. The missile was banned by the December 1987 treaty on Intermediate-range Nuclear Force (INF) missiles between the United States and the Soviet Union. It is not clear whether this would have been employed as a coastal defense weapon or a theater strike missile.

SPETSNAZ FORCES

Soviet *Spetsnaz* forces are an increasing concern for Western military planners.[8]

The *Spetsnaz* forces are somewhat similar to U.S. special operations forces, e.g., the Navy's SEALs and the Army's Green Berets. The Soviet troops are trained and equipped to carry out a number of sensitive missions: among them clandestine reconnaissance, sabotage or destruction of targets behind enemy lines, and assassination. A hierarchy of *Spetsnaz* targets in the event of a conflict with NATO has been postulated by one analyst as:

- seaborne nuclear delivery forces (missile submarines, aircraft carriers, naval bases, associated command and control facilities)
- command, control, communications, and intelligence activities (including SOSUS)
- political/military leaders
- other military targets
- reinforcements and resupply[9]

As noted in chapter 4, the *Spetsnaz* forces are controlled by the Main Intelligence Directorate (*Glavnoye Razvedyvatelnoye Upravlenie*—GRU) of the Soviet General Staff. Within each of the four fleets there is a naval *Spetsnaz* unit; official U.S. sources state that these are brigade-size units. This would place the strength of the naval *Spetsnaz* in each fleet at about 1,000 men, although some of these may be included in the fleet's Naval Infantry numbers. Some semi-official Western sources place total Soviet naval *Spetsnaz* strength at 2,000 men.

Each fleet brigade is estimated to consist of one or more battalions of combat swimmers and parachutists, a midget submarine group, plus a signals company and support units (see figure 9-5). The *Spetsnaz* "battalions," however, are probably not battalion size in the context of other military units.

During wartime, according to official U.S. statements:

Small 5–12 man teams would be transported to a target area by aircraft, submarine, or surface ship and would be inserted immediately prior to hostilities. Their training includes parachuting, scuba diving, demolition, sabotage, surveillance, and target selection, as well as languages.

Once deployed, naval associated *Spetsnaz* would conduct reconnaissance and tactical operations against a wide variety of naval targets, such as ship and submarine bases, airfields, command and intelligence centers, communication facilities, ports, and harbors, radar sites, and—of primary importance—nuclear weapons facilities.[10]

---

8. Recent analyses include Marc J. Berkowitz, "Soviet Naval Spetsnaz Forces," *Naval War College Review* (Spring 1988), pp. 5–21, and Col. Lynn Hansen, USAF (Ret.), *Soviet Naval Spetsnaz Operations on the Northern Flank: Implications for the Defense of Western Europe* (College Station, Texas: Center for Strategic Technology, 1984).

9. Berkowitz, p. 16.

10. Secretary of Defense Caspar Weinberger, *Soviet Military Power, 1985* (Washington, D.C.: Government Printing Office, 1985), p. 104.

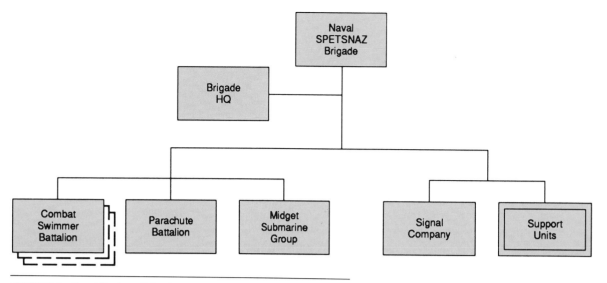

FIGURE 9-5. Naval *Spetsnaz* Brigade

The Nikolayev is a large, flexible amphibious assault ship. The Soviet Navy has only three of these ships, two in the Pacific Fleet and one in the Baltic Fleet. (Japanese Maritime Self-Defense Force)

CHAPTER 10

Personnel and Training

Submariners crowd the sail of a Soviet submarine, with one officer photographing the photographer taking this photo. Soviet submariners are among the elite of the Red fleet—they man the fleet's capital ships. Hatches open to reveal various masts, with a large electronic dome antenna visible just behind these crewmen; the windshield is raised. (Royal Navy)

Although Soviet naval manpower is declining slightly, the reductions appear to be minimal in comparison with overall cuts expected in Soviet military strength. At the same time, the qualitative demands on Soviet sailors for operatng new warships and aircraft appear to be major manpower problems.

The recent disposal of relatively large numbers of Soviet warships only marginally compensates for the larger crew size of the newer warships and the large shore establishments required to support them. At the same time, newer warships and aircraft are more complex, requiring higher levels of personnel skills. Indeed, some Soviet military officers have proposed an end to the traditional conscription of military personnel and the development of a professional, volunteer force, at least for the more technical services (i.e., Navy, Air Defense Forces, Strategic Rocket Forces, and Air Forces—but not the Ground

Forces). As an interim measure to overcome the shortages in long-term, skilled technical personnel, the Navy is increasing the number of long-term warrant personnel (*michman*) in warships (see below).

The Soviet Navy had more than 400,000 officers and enlisted men and women on active duty in 1990.[1] This was almost 190,000 fewer than in the U.S. Navy. In addition, the Soviet Navy had some 18,000 Naval Infantry (marines) and 8,000 Coastal Defense troops in active service, while the KGB Maritime Border Troops numbered some 23,000 (that last service akin to the U.S. Coast Guard).

Subsequently, in 1990–1991 the strength of the Soviet naval services increased with the transfer of several hundred aircraft from the Air Forces to the Navy, and of motorized rifle divisions from the Ground Forces to the cognizance of Naval Infantry. (See chapters 8 and 9, respectively.)

The following is an estimate of the breakdown of Soviet naval personnel in 1990 (percentages are rounded):

Afloat	160,000	(37%)
Naval Aviation	65,000	(15%)
Naval Infantry	18,000	(4%)[2]
Coastal Defense	7,000	(2%)
Training	45,000	(10%)
Shore Support	132,000	(31%)
Communications/Observation	5,000	(1%)

There had been a gradual increase in naval personnel during the 1970s and early 1980s as the overall strength of the Soviet fleet and naval air arm were increased. This followed a sharp reduction in naval personnel during the early 1970s, with Western intelligence reporting a Navy strength of 470,000 at the start of the decade but only 427,000 five years later (including Naval Infantry and Coastal Defense). The gradual increases to match the increasing numbers of new ships and aircraft peaked at about 455,000 in 1985, according to Western intelligence estimates.

Exact data on the current strength and status of the Soviet armed forces are difficult to obtain because of the great social revolution taking place. The efforts by the Baltic Republics (Estonia, Latvia, and Lithuania) as well as some of the minority republics (e.g., Georgia, Azerbaijan, and Armenia) to gain independence from the central Soviet government have led to large-scale draft evasion and desertions by men called to military service from those areas. Relatives of servicemen from those areas have visited naval and military bases to induce the servicemen to desert and return to their homes. Some of the republic governments have actively supported draft evasion and have even attempted to establish their own territorial armies as an alternative to Soviet military service.

MILITARY SERVICE

The Soviet Union's Law on Universal Military Service is the basis for naval service. This law, last revised in 1988, states that all male citizens of the Soviet Union must perform military service—two years for naval shore duty, aviation, Naval Infantry, and the other armed services, and three years for naval personnel assigned to ships and coastal logistic support units. (Before 1967 conscription was for three years with four years of service for shipboard duty.) However, in 1990–1991, in response to the social reforms in the Soviet Union, many additional categories of naval services were reduced to two years.

For men who have completed higher education (college) the requirement is for one year of military service (before 1989 it was two years in the Navy and 18 months in the other services). In 1989, however, the government decided to discharge all college graduates from military service, in part because of the need for their skills in civilian industry and agriculture. At the time the Minister of Defense, then-General of the Army Dmitri Yazov, complained that their discharge impaired the combat effectiveness of their units.

Conscription for all of the services takes place twice a year, in the spring and in the fall. Those conscripts who have a higher or secondary education, have taken certain training courses, and have passed specific tests before completing their military service, are commissioned as officers after one year or more of service and are transferred to the reserve. The twice-yearly influx of so many post-adolescent males—turning boys into men and civilians into soldiers and sailors—absorbs a large portion of the time and energy of the career military personnel, ashore and, in the Navy, afloat.

The Soviet manpower pool is based on the conscription of an 18-year-old population that has generally completed the Soviet Union's required ten-year secondary school system. (The Soviet Union provides free education at all levels, including institutions of higher learning, instruction in minority languages as well as Russian, coeducation at all levels, and a uniform course of study.) According to Soviet statements, over 90 percent of the men entering Soviet naval service have completed the ten-year education program.

Draft deferments are provided for family, medical, or educational reasons. Exemptions are more difficult to obtain, generally being given to men with a physical disability or a serious criminal record, to married men with two or more children, and to men who are the sole support of elderly parents or siblings. The extent to which deferments and exemptions are granted because a man's skills are needed in the civilian sector is not clear.

Under Soviet conscription there is a call-up twice a year, in May–June and in November–December, with about 450,000 men drafted for all of the armed services in each call-up. Conscription, reserve programs, and support activities for all of the armed services are directed by the 15 Military Districts that encompass all areas of the Soviet Union (see chapter 4).

Service in the Soviet Ground Forces (i.e., army) is extremely arduous and spartan. Despite the longer term of naval service and the possibly long cruises, the other services—especially the Navy—are often preferred. Those men with physical or psychological problems not sufficient to exempt them from military service are assigned to duties usually performed in Western navies by civilians, such as cargo handling and facility maintenance. This accounts in part for the large size of the Soviet Navy's shore establishment. The social revolution ongoing in the Soviet Union has caused the refusal of recruits from the Baltic republics and certain Asian areas to report for duty.

Enlisted men can be held beyond their official two- or three-year period for up to six months of additional service. Men who wish to reenlist are usually placed in the warrant (*michman*) program (see below).[3] Very few sailors are allowed to remain on active duty as enlisted men beyond their initial service, in part because of the requirement to take in large numbers of conscripts on a continuous basis. The number of men retained as petty officers has been estimated by some Western sources to be as low as 1 or 2 percent. These are generally men who do not have the qualifications to enter the *michman* program.

Men who have completed their obligatory service and certain individuals who have received exemptions are required to serve in the reserves up to age 50. All reservists are subject to periodic recalls to active duty for a total of up to two years of active service, the exact amount of time and the assignment being decided largely by the military district and varying with the category of reservist. There is evidence that the reserve program is hindered by resentment, both by the reservists who dislike the recalls and other requirements, and by active personnel who make only limited use of reservists who are recalled.

The military service law also provides for the voluntary service by women from age 19 to 40 who are trained in medical and other specialties. Very few serve in the Navy in technical roles. The use of women in the Soviet armed forces is limited also by the high percentage employed in the civilian sector as well as by the cultural and religious problems related to Asian and minority women working outside of their homes or villages.

1. All personnel figures unless otherwise indicated are as estimated by Western intelligence; changing methods of estimating may account for differences of as much as 10 to 15 percent over a period of time.
2. Soviet sources list the 1989 strength of Naval Infantry as 12,600; see chapter 9.
3. Adopted from the English term "midshipman." The British midshipman was originally a petty officer under the immediate command of the boatswain.

Most women in the Navy serve in support units, military hospitals, or communications units. Only a few have been seen on board naval ships. In 1978 several women sailors were observed in the helicopter carrier MOSKVA; an Italian journalist described them as "solid Russian girls in white uniform-dresses, certain are pretty, all at ease and treated with great gentility by the male crew, who evidently spoil them a little."[4]

Another problem related to military service is the decline in the birth rate of the Russian and Ukrainian portions of the Soviet population and hence the increase in the number of conscripts from Asian groups. By the year 2000 ethnic Russians will make up less than one-half of the USSR population. The Asians tend to lack upbringing in a technical environment and many speak Russian very poorly (and in some cases not at all). This problem is becoming more acute. A U.S. defense analyst has observed, "From the standpoint of socialization and education, however, those same young men who are least desirable from a narrowly military perspective are also those most in need of the socialization and vocational training offered by the military experience."[5] In 1980, 28 percent of the military conscripts came from the Central Asian and Transcaucasian regions; in 1988 the number had increased to 37 percent. The Soviets do not allow the need to use such people in the military to threaten combat effectiveness or the political stability of units. Specific minorities who lack language or technical competence, and certain other groups who may be politically questionable, do not serve in sensitive positions (communications, intelligence, nuclear weapons).

In the long view the Soviets can solve this minority problem by selective personnel assignments (an option not fully available to U.S. personnel managers), reduction of the number of legal deferments, extending naval service for all conscripts by six months as allowed under the existing law, or a change in the law affecting length of service. However, extreme care must be taken that any action to help the military manpower situation does not adversely affect the civilian sector, which has shortages in many technical disciplines.

Another problem facing the Soviet military services is the diversion of military personnel from their primary duties. For example, in the Baltic Fleet's submarine force, in 1987 submarine personnel stood 64 guard details at their bases and in 1988 it was 94. The number of garrison patrols also increased, from 201 to 228. Hundreds of work days were spent on civil economic projects, including helping with harvests. Reorganizations are under way to reduce the guard details levied on ships and to introduce technical security measures. Still, the diversion of ships' crews away from training and readiness is another problem confronting the Navy.[6]

PRE-SERVICE TRAINING

The reduction of required service in the 1967 law, coupled with the basic Soviet concept of political indoctrination for all citizens, has led to a comprehensive pre-military training program. Closely related are military sports and political activities.

There is military-patriotic training at all levels and in numerous aspects of Soviet life, often depicting the struggle between the Soviet Union and the Western world. Official Soviet literature is inundated with such statements as, "School children . . . must know the real danger which imperialism poses to mankind. The work done in a school by way of military-patriotic indoctrination

must prepare students in practical ways to overcome difficulties during times of possible severe trials."[7]

From this basis, the Soviet Union has developed an intensive program of pre-conscription military training. It begins at the pre-school level with cartoon comics depicting military heroes and continues throughout the required ten years of school and the year between the completion of public school and call-up into the armed forces. History books emphasize the importance of the military in Russian history, the children visit war memorials and military museums, and retired military persons visit schools for presentations and talks. There are part-time, voluntary, para-military training programs for children as young as age nine or ten.

Civil defense training begins in the second grade and continues throughout the educational career of most Soviet youth. (The Soviet civil defense program is under the direction of a senior military officer and is a part of the Ministry of Defense.) During the last two years of school, all male students in the 9th and 10th grades (normally ages 16 and 17) participate in a compulsory pre-military training program of 140 formal hours. Courses are given in military history, the wearing and care of uniforms, small arms (with live munitions, including hand grenades), and radio and radar operation. Field exercises of several days' duration are also conducted as part of the program.

In the year between leaving high school and being called into active service, the young men participate in a part-time military program with courses in driving, vehicle maintenance, and communications. Although training does not always prepare men for the branch of service they will enter, those who will go into the airborne forces are often given preliminary parachute training, prospective submariners may receive a submarine familiarization course, and those who are to go into Navy diving work participate in the following program:

> During their period of training at the Naval Club, the future divers learn a great deal and acquire many practical skills. They must be able to read drawings and schematics; draw sketches and measure underwater structures; and carry out rigging, assembly, repair, and construction work while submerged. They must possess a good knowledge of the principles for conducting photographic, movie-making, and television work, while submerged.[8]

These training programs are for young men in school, working in factories or on farms before induction. Soviet press statements indicate that one conscript in three has a technical specialty before entering active service.

The various pre-service para-military activities are conducted by the Little Octobrists (ages 6–9), Young Pioneers (ages 10–15), the *Komsomol* (Communist Youth League, ages 14 and up), and DOSAAF (Voluntary Society for Cooperation with the Army, Aviation, and Fleet, ages 14 and up). The programs are conducted through the military districts, with all groups participating in war games as a part of the yearly round of activities, obviously tailored to the members' age and level of training.

The Young Pioneers participate in *zarnitsa* or "summer lightning" games. Introduced in 1967, these games include familiarization with army weapons, including firing with dummy ammunition, CBR defense, first aid, drill, and reconnaissance tasks. DOSAAF trains young men and women in 75 military skills and related trades in thousands of schools, factories, and collective farms. There is a heavy emphasis on sports, among them parachuting and swimming.

The pre-military training programs vary in their degree of success, in part because of different attitudes and approaches within the separate military districts. With respect to civil defense, the general public attitude is not serious and there are major material deficiencies, in part because of general shortages and poor organization and management—traditional Russian problems. In the physical training programs the administrators tend to be overin-

---

4. Women served extensively in the Soviet army and air forces during World War II, with many seeing extensive combat. In the postwar period the Soviets have had several woman test pilots and the world's first woman cosmonaut/astronaut, Engineer-Col. Valentina Tereshkova, who flew 48 earth orbits in June 1963. No female naval aviators have been identified in the postwar period.

5. See Dr. Ellen Jones, "Soviet Military Manpower: Prospects in the 1980s," *Strategic Review* (Fall 1981), pp. 65–75; "Minorities in the Soviet Armed Forces" *Comparative Strategy* (vol. III, no. 4, 1982), pp. 285–318; and *Red Army and Society* (Boston, Mass.: Allen & Unwin, 1985).

6. Capt. 2nd Rank A. Pilipchuk [Baltic Fleet correspondent], "Percentage of Diversion," *Krasnaya Zvezda* (12 January 1989).

7. N.P. Aksenova, "On the Effectiveness of Military-Patriotic Indoctrination of School Children," *Sovetskaya Pedagogika* (February 1972), pp. 46–51.

8. Engineer-Capt. 1st Rank Ye. Shikanov, "Conquerors of the Depths," *Voennyie Znaniia* (February 1973), pp. 36–37.

dulgent and inconsistent, often approving young men for military service who should fail or are marginal in order to fulfill the program's pre-established norms.

With respect to actual pre-induction military training, there is a range of quality. There are reports of inadequately prepared instruction, overworked instructors, significant absenteeism, lack of equipment, and improper facilities. However, there is evidence of major efforts to upgrade the areas in which there are failings, and the overall programs must be considered successful in that they provide the draftee with some knowledge of the military before he enters active service. As periodically noted in the Soviet press, these pre-military programs do result in the average Soviet man being far different from his Western counterpart when he is called into active service at the age of 18.

From the viewpoint of military training, the most significant program is DOSAAF, which has several thousand units that provide pre-conscription training to some one-third of the young men entering the Soviet armed forces. Some aspects of DOSAAF activities are considered as only one step removed from active military service.

ENLISTED MEN

The Soviet Navy is a conscript navy, the sea-going sailors being called up for three years, and those who serve ashore conscripted for two years. Once on active duty, most conscripts will undergo an initial Navy training program that can vary from four or five weeks to as long as six months; some with previous DOSAAF or technical training may go directly to fleet assignments, and a few go directly into the *michman* program.

Each of the four fleets conducts its own basic training and assigns enlisted men. "Boot camp" of up to eight weeks is devoted mostly to close-order drill, small arms, regulations and traditions of the service, individual CBR defense, and, of course, the ubiquitous physical training and political indoctrination. Upon completion of this brief recruit training the conscript takes the formal military oath and becomes a full-fledged member of the Soviet Navy. At this point those sailors destined for menial or support jobs ashore—because of physical or political reliability problems or lack of aptitude—or who have previously acquired technical skills (from DOSAAF or other programs) go on to their permanent duty stations.

Those men slated for duty afloat or who require more technical schooling attend specialist training, which is normally of five or six months' duration. Men going to nuclear submarines receive nuclear crew training in addition to their specialty course. The fleet is confronted with a paradox: the reduction in naval service to three years reduced the time available for training, while the complexities of modern equipment and operations require that personnel be more highly qualified than previously. Two results are more intensive on-the-job training (OJT in the Western vernacular) and making more use of pre-service military training. During his active service the typical sailor will only work on one piece of equipment at one duty station, permitting the Navy to make maximum use of the time he is available.

While the level of vocational training in the Soviet Union is very high, the Soviet sailor is narrowly trained by U.S. standards although he is increasingly encouraged to expand his knowledge beyond his narrow specialty. Stability in the assignment of officers to ships and stations and the emphasis on specialist qualifications make up for this lack of versatility in the conscripts.

Conscripts begin naval service with the rank of seaman, or *matros* (see table 10-1). The majority of seamen can expect to be

Sailors stand around before falling into formation at a naval training base near Kiev. They carry the well-known 7.62-mm AK-47 assault rifle. The large turnover of enlisted men—who can be retained for only two or three years—is a major problem for the Soviet Navy. (Peter Hrycenko)

promoted one grade, to senior seaman, by the time they have completed their three years of service. A first-term seaman may be promoted to petty officer second class and possibly even first class if his billet calls for that rank and he can pass the qualification tests, or if he is able to attend additional specialized training. Billet availability seems to be the key factor. Although there is a procedure for enlisted men to extend service for two years and hence become eligible for first class or chief petty officer status, few take this option, preferring instead to remain in the Navy in the warrant rank if they can qualify or leaving the Navy and taking their technical knowledge to industry.

The first-term serviceman lives a spartan life compared to Western sailors; pay is low, food is simple, alcoholic beverages are forbidden, and there is little, or in some cases no, off-base liberty. However, an annual leave is given to visit home, and on base or aboard ship there is a variety of social and cultural activities. In general, naval life is less harsh and less demanding than that in the Ground Forces. The families of first-term servicemen have special privileges, such as having work found for their wives and being exempt from the tax on married citizens with few or no children. Family housing assistance and guarantees of post-service employment also help the serviceman. Of course, he may learn a technical skill while in the Navy that could be in great demand by the civilian economy when he leaves the service.

During his shipboard service the first-term sailor undergoes a year of training and specialist qualification. This training year is a carefully planned program in which the sailor becomes integrated first with his ship or unit, then with small formations, and, finally, with fleet exercises. While he was Commander in Chief of the Navy, Admiral S.G. Gorshkov stated:

> Our fleets conduct strenuous training the year round. In classrooms, on gunnery ranges and in simulators, on ships and in units (*chasti*), our seamen gain sound knowledge and the ability to handle machinery and systems and intricate weapons.
>
> Ocean cruises and distant voyages serve as the highest stage of this training.[9]

Combat training in the Soviet Navy is highly centralized and conducted in accordance with a detailed annual, monthly, weekly, and daily plan. The importance of combat training and of having continuity of training is evidenced by there being a Deputy CinC for

9. Adm. Gorshkov, "Ocean Cruises—School of Combat Training," in Rear Adm. N.I. Shablikov, et al., *Okean—Manevry Voyenno-Morskogo Flota SSR* [*Okean*—Maneuvers of the USSR Navy] (Moscow: Military Publishing House, 1970), p. 11.

TABLE 10-1.   ENLISTED RANKS

Naval Rank	Military Rank
Chief Petty Officer (*Glavnyy Starshina*)	Senior Sergeant
Petty Officer 1st Class (*Starshina Pervoy Stati*)	Sergeant
Petty Officer 2nd Class (*Starshina Vtoroy Stati*)	Corporal
Senior Seaman (*Starshiy Matros*)	Private 1st Class
Seaman (*Matros*)	Private

Submariners on this Echo II SSGN take advantage of the sunshine during a warm day in the Pacific while the submarine takes on supplies from a surface ship. Recreation opportunities for Soviet sailors are limited ashore as well as afloat. (U.S. Navy)

Combat Training, the post currently held by Vice Admiral A.A. Kuz'min (The Deputy CinC for Educational Institutions and the Chief of the Navy's Personnel Directorate are also vice admirals; see Appendix A.)

Shipboard training encompasses a wide range of activities. Because of the large number of draftees the Navy must accept twice a year, a very detailed plan is worked out for the training cycles of each type of ship. In the first phase the crew engages in both theoretical and practical training in classrooms and simulators ashore and aboard ships in port.

After review of the ship's squadron or division staffs, the ship moves to the second, at-sea training phase of the training cycle. This includes steaming exercises and live firings of all (conventional) weapons. Again, there is an examination at the end of the phase.

The third phase consists of small numbers of ships operating together, carrying out formation steaming and multi-ship exercises.

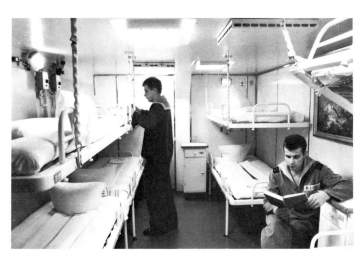

Enlisted berthing spaces in the carrier Novorossiysk are typical of those in newer Soviet warships. Small cabinets are provided for personal gear and clothing; the bunks do not have the under-mattress storage space found in U.S. ships. Modern Soviet warships have crew accommodations that are generally similar to those in West European warships. (Sovfoto)

After approval by higher command, the ships move into the fourth phase, with larger groupings of ships conducting exercises. The duration of the phases and the specific evolutions vary with the type of ship. Also, the phase can be determined by the percentage of new crewmen on board.

Specialist qualification, which is independent of rank, is awarded on the basis of examinations in a man's skill. A man who qualifies as a specialist receives extra pay, and his qualification may be withdrawn for disciplinary reasons. Enlisted specialist badges, which indicate 1st, 2nd, and 3rd class and master specialist, are worn on dress uniforms. (The experience required for the master specialist is too extensive for a first-term conscript to acquire.) The number of men in a crew who have specialist qualifications contribute to the standing of the ship or unit in the Navy-wide socialist competition.

Socialist competition within the Navy provides for the entire crew of a ship, unit, or base to strive for specialist qualification. This system of officially recognized rivalry originated in the civilian economy and is now an integral part of military training. It relies on moral incentives, honorary awards, and exhortations to stimulate servicemen and units to improve their skills, operational performance, discipline, and even political education. It involves meeting or exceeding "norms" in almost every facet of naval activity from the quality of food served in the messes to the accuracy of missile firings. (To some extent it is reminiscent of the intensive competition in the U.S. Navy for battle efficiency "E" awards in the 1920s and 1930s, when everything legally permissible was encouraged to gain a ship or aircraft squadron a coveted "E.")

During a competition the crew of the nuclear submarine 60 LET VELIKYO OKTYABR "analyzed the results of the previous training year and in endeavoring to reinforce the achieved successes, approved new socialist obligations."[10] The submarine crew's new socialist obligations included:

- Reducing by 15 percent the time required for bringing the equipment, weapons and the ship as a whole into a state of combat readiness.
- Seeing to it that 75 percent of the departments and services are outstanding.

10. "New Scope for the Socialist Competition/High Dependability for the Ocean Watch," *Krasnaya Zvezda* (23 November 1978), p. 1.

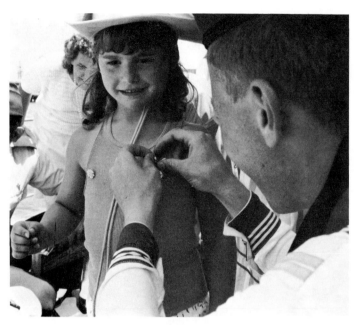

Sailors and girls are a natural combination. This Soviet sailor made a friend of a young miss during the visit of Soviet warships to Norfolk in 1989.

- Having each crew member become a class specialist, 20 percent of the sailors should have the qualifications of master, and 70 percent 1st and 2nd class. The number of 1st class missile troops and sonar operators should be increased by 50 percent.

The submariners' pledges for the following year included cultural and political promises as well as proposals for military achievement, including "to have a permanent amateur artistic collective and on the long voyages to systematically organize amateur artistic concerts," and "to constantly study the military, revolutionary and labor traditions of the Communist Party, the Soviet people and their Armed Forces, and the experience of political indoctrination."[11]

A report of the achievement of the Krivak-class frigate BODRYY, commended as the first ship in the fleet in the mid-1970s, cited that the crew "overfilled their Socialist commitments: 92 percent of their men have become class specialists, and one-third of them have mastered a related specialty. Aboard the ship eight out of ten men have been declared by their CO to be outstanding in combat and political training."[12]

There is a standard scoring scheme for socialist competition, the ships and units having high scores being rewarded and publicized, while "laggards" are exposed to public censure and pressure is brought to force them to improve. Failure to achieve "norms" can bring even stronger penalties. One ship—identified only as "X" in the Soviet military press—failed to fulfill certain commitments. The "defects" in the ship were examined and as a result during late 1980 the ship's commanding officer, V. Churikov (no rank was given) was relieved of his post and reassigned with a demotion, while officers (again no rank given although some were named) were made "answerable to the party."

Enlisted men who achieve outstanding individual ratings are rewarded with decorations, are publicized, and are given additional home leave. Petty officers and warrant officers whose sub-units have achieved excellent results may be promoted or given preference in admission to higher naval schools that would graduate them as commissioned officers. Another form of award for outstanding performance is to notify an enlisted man's former place of employment of his exemplary performance, a significant action because many sailors will return to their previous job when they

11. These "pledges" are highly publicized throughout the Navy and in national political publications.
12. "Large ASW Ship Bodryy Lauded," *Krasnaya Zvezda* (1 December 1974), p. 1.

leave the Navy. Departments, ships, and units that are cited by the fleet command as the year's best get to fly a special pennant or banner, and their officers can expect such an achievement to help advance their careers.

Since the rewards for success and penalties for failure are greatest for career warrant officers and commissioned officers, there is some falsification or exaggeration of achievements. The most serious competition is sometimes between officers and this can lead to friction and tension. Thus, the greatest positive results of socialist competition are probably at the individual and sub-unit level, where skills can be increased in return for direct and important personal benefits.

Again, only a few sailors remain on active duty in an enlisted status beyond the required conscription period (with extensions adding up to six months to the required two or three years being possible in some instances). Most sailors are discharged into the reserves, in which they serve up to age 50.

WARRANT RANKS

Warrant ranks (*michmanii*) have increasing importance in the modern Soviet fleet because of the advanced technology found in modern Soviet ships and naval aircraft. The three-year enlisted conscript can no longer maintain and operate this equipment, while the officer corps is being called upon for broader shipboard and ashore duties. The warrant system has become the model for Soviet consideration of a "professional" military force—volunteer, higher paid, long-term servicemen (and women). The major problem facing such an effort would be financial, with personnel costs increasing 5 to 8 times for such a force. These costs, which include improved housing and other benefits, are currently beyond Soviet economic resources.

The warrant rank, or *michman,* was first introduced in the Russian Navy in 1716 and was used almost continuously until 1917 as the initial officer grade, corresponding to 2nd lieutenant in the army. The Soviet government reintroduced the rank of *michman* in the Navy on 30 November 1940 as the highest rank for petty officers (*starshinii*).

The status of warrant rank in the Soviet armed forces (equal to *praporshchik* in the other military services) was changed to a separate category on 1 January 1972. The program is open to qualified enlisted men under age 35 as well as to qualified civilians. Most enlisted candidates have completed a term of service as a conscript, but some with sufficient prior training are recruited directly from "boot" camp to warrant military technical schools. After graduation from the schools they are promoted to the rank of *michman.* Some former servicemen who have returned to active duty from the reserves are also promoted to *michman.* Increasingly, however, warrants are being brought in from two-year civilian technical schools and colleges.

The reason for establishing warrant ranks at this level appears to have been the need for more career enlisted men, especially those with technical experience. Previously there was no formal program for training enlisted men after their first term of service. The importance and success of the *michman* program was indicated when in early 1981 the senior warrant rank (*starshi michman*) was established in the Navy, to be conferred on men who have served as warrants for five years or more, with at least one year in positions normally staffed by officers or senior warrants.

After their appointment, the *michmanii* attend specialized, generally technical schools for two to two-and-a-half years, after which they usually go to an operational unit for their commitment of five years of post-training service. Subsequent multi-year enlistments are then possible until retirement age is reached. A senior *michman* in the cruiser Azov, A. Sotnikov, was identified in 1990 as having served for 13 years in the same ship.

On board ship the *michmanii* are assigned to each division, normally as the deputies to junior officers with direct command authority over petty officers and seamen. The peacetime complements of three Soviet warships are shown below and are indicative of the high percentage of warrant ranks:

	SLAVA-class cruiser	SOVREMENNYY-class destroyer	Mike-type submarine
Officers	84	37	32
Warrants	75	43	21
Enlisted	370	290	15

When possible, on board ship and at naval bases the *michmanii* have a separate mess. Along with having a distinctive uniform, special privileges, and higher pay than enlisted men, the *michmanii* represent the most technically competent group within the Soviet Navy.

OFFICERS

Soviet naval officers belong to an elite group that enjoys numerous privileges and opportunities while having a key role in Soviet defense and political strategies. The principal sources for the approximately 2,000 officers who are commissioned in the Soviet Navy every year are:

Higher Naval Schools	85%
Civilian Higher Schools	5%
Technical Institutes	10%

However, many naval officers begin their "career" at the age of 15 or 16 when they enter the Nakhimov secondary school in Leningrad.[13] One of four schools originally established in 1944 for the sons of deceased naval officers, the three others were subsequently disestablished. From the mid-1960s the remaining Nakhimov school in Leningrad has served as an officer "prep" school for specially chosen young men, generally the sons, nephews, or other relatives of naval officers and Communist Party officials. These students are accepted at Nakhimov for the last two years of secondary school, as preparation for higher naval schools.

At the Nakhimov school the cadets receive academic, military, and political training. Upon graduation from the Nakhimov school the young men join graduates of other secondary schools and a select number of enlisted men in attending one of 11 higher naval schools, the equivalent of the U.S. Naval Academy.[14] (The Nakhimov graduates do not have to take the entrance examination required of other applicants.)

The 11 higher naval schools, their location, and areas of specialization are shown in table 10-2.

Of the five schools that educate surface line officers, the Frunze school in Leningrad is the most prestigious, tracing its heritage to naval cadet training that began in St. Petersburg in 1701.[15] Two of the higher naval schools are dedicated to line engineering, and one each to shore engineering, radio-electronics, submarine warfare, and political affairs. All of the schools have a five-year course of instruction except for the political school, which offers a four-year curriculum. These higher naval schools provide a highly specialized education, with the first two years devoted primarily to basic, naval-related subjects and undergraduate studies; the remaining

---

13. Vice Adm. Povel Stepanovich Nakhimov won a major victory over a Turkish fleet at Sinope in 1853; his name is also given to a higher naval school and to a guided missile cruiser.

14. There are approximately 140 higher military schools for all services in the Soviet Union that provide officer education for the armed forces; there are four such schools in the United States—the Naval, Military, Air Force, and Coast Guard academies. After World War II the U.S. Navy had, briefly, sought to establish additional naval academies.

15. In 1712 Tsar Peter I decreed that all sons of landowners enter national service—the youngest were sent to the German city of Reval to study seamanship, the middle group went to Holland for naval training, and the eldest marched directly into the army (to serve as a private soldier for a period before being promoted on the basis of merit). In 1715 the tsar moved the School of Mathematics and Navigation from Moscow to St. Petersburg, and filled its classrooms with sons from almost all of the noble families in Russia between the ages of 10 and 18. This school was soon known as the Naval Academy.

TABLE 10-2. HIGHER NAVAL SCHOOLS

School	Location	Specialization
Black Sea Higher Naval School *imeni* P.S. Nakhimov	Sevastopol	surface line
Caspian Higher Naval School *imeni* S.M. Kirov	Baku	surface line
Higher Naval Electronics School *imeni* A.S. Popov	Petrodvorets (near Leningrad)	radio-electronics
Higher Naval Engineering School *imeni* F.E. Dzerzhinskiy	Leningrad	engineering
Kiev Higher Naval Political School	Kiev	political
Higher Naval School *imeni* M.V. Frunze	Leningrad	surface line
Higher Naval Submarine School *imeni* Leninisky Komsomol	Leningrad	submarine warfare
Kaliningrad Higher Naval School	Kaliningrad	surface line
Leningrad Higher Naval Engineering School *imeni* V.I. Lenin	Pushkin (near Leningrad)	engineering
Pacific Higher Naval School *imeni* S.O. Makarov	Vladivostok	surface line
Sevastopol Higher Naval Engineering School	Sevastopol	engineering

---

three years emphasize areas of specialization, with the result that Soviet naval officers are more technically educated and more specialized than their Western counterparts. Most naval officers will spend their career in the specialized field in which they were instructed at the higher naval school.

Practical school training includes long-range cruises in warships and special training ships, with cadets receiving a "distant cruise" badge afterwards. Physical fitness is stressed at sea and ashore. An article describes the Popov Higher Naval Radio-Electronics School:

> At the school they have a fine sports palace with a swimming pool, open sports area, and a firing range. Almost all of the students have sports ratings. In the past five years alone they have prepared here more than 20 masters of sports and hundreds of first-class sportsmen. Many students have often become champions and prize-winners of the armed forces, Leningrad, RSFSR [Russian Soviet Federated Socialist Republic] and USSR.[16]

Motivation is also stressed during an officer's education. The following comment by a ship's political officer illustrates this attitude: "Motivation comes first, the technology can come later. . . . without motivation, technology is worthless." This motivation carries over to an officer's use of technology:

> There is, first of all, the ship commanding officer's personal responsibility to the Motherland and the people for his use of the latest weapons and equipment. However, the responsibility is not limited to his service duties of controlling the ship and weapons. This responsibility is also determined by his role in training and educating his subordinates, in inculcating in them a high sense of duty to their Motherland.[17]

Graduates of higher naval schools are awarded an "all-union" academic degree similar to the American baccalaureate and are commissioned as officers, in most instances as junior lieutenants. After graduation the new officers generally go directly to their duty stations. The opportunity to proceed immediately to advanced education is available only to exceptional graduates. More than half the Soviet naval officers, however, will receive postgraduate education at a later stage of their careers, with a significant number achieving a level roughly equivalent to a doctorate in the West.

The other major sources for Soviet naval officers are civilian higher schools (colleges) and technical institutes. These are generally four- and two-year establishments, respectively. There are

---

16. Capt. 1st Rank (Reserve) V. Nikolayev, "Named for A.S. Popov," *Voyennyye Znaniya* (no. 5, 1978), pp. 18–19.

17. Rear Adm. G. Kostev (Assistant Professor), "The Ship's CO," *Soviet Military Review* (no. 8, 1979), pp. 16–17.

reserve training programs at some of these schools, the instructional staff consisting of active service, reserve, and retired officers, and civilians. Upon commissioning, these officers are generally sent to sea and spend their initial four to six years in a specific shipboard department (see below). During this period the young officer seeks to attain qualification in his specialty area, and he will seek to move to assistant commander (department head). Most officers will move up within their specialist area. Failure to serve in an executive or command position does not limit promotion and upward career movement. For example, a navigation specialist can serve as a ship, division, brigade, and fleet navigator, being promoted even while serving in the same position if his performance merits it. This policy sometimes results in rank inversion and at times officers of superior rank will work for more-qualified juniors.

Soviet ships have up to seven "command" and four "staff" departments. The command departments, designated BCh for *Boevayie Chasti* and headed by assistant commanders of the ship, are BCh-1 navigation, BCh-2 missile and/or gunnery, BCh-3 mine and torpedo, BCh-4 operations, BCh-5 engineering, BCh-6 air, and BCh-7 command and control. The four staff departments are S.1-R electronics, S.1-Kh chemical, S.1-M medical, and S.1-S supply. An officer who goes on board ship will probably serve in the same department during his entire time in that ship, and when he goes to another ship he will usually be in the same department as well.

Most graduates of higher naval schools are assigned to cruisers, destroyers, and frigates; graduates of the Leninsky Komsomol submarine school go to submarines; graduates of the Dzerzhinskiy and Leningrad engineering schools are assigned to BCh-5 departments in surface ships and submarines. Some outstanding graduates are immediately assigned as department heads, executive officers, and after brief service and additional training even commanding officers of small combatants. These latter officers generally have an edge in subsequent promotion and major command assignments.

In the larger ships the outstanding heads of departments compete for the position of executive officer, with the BCh-1 generally having the edge. The commanding officer often selects, or at least approves, the selection of the executive officer (called assistant commander, or *starpom,* in the Soviet lexicon). By tradition, the executive officer of a ship usually becomes her commanding officer. The Soviet method of preparation of these officers for command consideration was described as follows:

> The commanding officer trains commanding officers. This rule . . . corresponds to the well-known principle in the Navy that the leader personally trains his subordinates. There is something else to be remembered also: it is a Navy tradition to pass command know-how along to one's successors. It is a truly happy commanding officer who turns his ship over to his senior assistant (Executive Officer). Needless to say, this is only possible when capable, promising officers are appointed (by the COs) as senior assistants and the commanding officers work hard and thoughtfully to prepare their replacements.[18]

There are also formal classes for prospective executive and commanding officers, but little has been published about these. Before he is formally selected an officer must undergo a series of practical examinations in various naval areas that are administered by the staff officers of the command to which the ship is attached. He must also pass an interview with the division or other senior commander. The examinations are rigorous, and some candidates fail. At least one officer with previous command experience is known to have failed the examination.

18. Capt. 1st Rank I. Gordeyev, "Who Is Training Our Replacements?" *Morskoy Sbornik* (no. 12, 1981), pp. 44–48. Also see Officer Ye. Chernov, "We Raise Commanding Officers," *Morskoy Sbornik* (no. 3, 1981), pp. 33–38. Capt. William Manthorpe, Jr., USN, has analyzed Soviet CO selection and training in "Attaining Command at Sea," *U.S. Naval Institute Proceedings* (November 1975), pp. 97–98. Several other meaningful articles on Soviet officer training have appeared in the *Proceedings* during the past few years, authored by Manthrope; Capt. James W. Kehoe, USN (Ret); and Dr. Robert C. Suggs. (Manthorpe became the principal Deputy Director of U.S. Naval Intelligence in 1989.)

Soviet officers crowd the bridge as U.S. and Soviet ships pass close aboard. Soviet naval officers are highly specialized but at the same time are trained to undertake combined operations.

After taking command of a ship an officer undergoes a lengthy process to qualify for "independent command." During this process the division commander or a "flag specialist" with previous command experience will frequently ride the ship and observe the newly appointed CO. The rider may countermand or modify orders, as he deems appropriate. Thus the new CO is taken through the annual evolution of exercises and training and sometimes makes operational deployments with a flag specialist on his bridge before he is fully certified for command at sea.

This practice is quite alien to Western navies, and Soviet naval officers themselves have differing views on the success of the program. According to one writer, "Senior commanders located aboard ships often actually interfere in command and control of the ship—by advice, prompting, or direct instruction. And they do so even when it is not always necessary. A commander's independence in such cases ends up being very, very relative."[19]

The Soviet Navy wishes its COs to be independent, but it is a limited independence: to execute the assigned mission in conformity with the operational plan. Further, the Soviet concept of initiative is, in the opinion of some Western observers, confined to being creative in carrying out the assigned mission in the face of changed circumstances and/or the absence of orders from superiors.

The commanders of major warships (frigates and larger) range from captain-lieutenants to captains 1st rank, with at least two strategic missile submarines being identified as having rear admirals as commanding officer. From the mid-1970s onward there have been several "deep" selections for commanding officer, with captain lieutenants serving as commanders of several Krivak ASW ships and Kashin guided missile destroyers. These officers have nine years or less of commissioned service and some are under 30 years of age. This is approximately two ranks lower than frigate and destroyer commanders in the U.S. Navy. (There has been a similar reduction of unit commander ages in the Soviet Ground Forces, where there are regimental commanders as young as 32 and division commanders only 38 years old.)

Although young officers given such major assignments may not gain the staff experience of their Western counterparts, the use of general and naval staffs by the Soviet Union alleviates the need for all officers to be rotated through as many positions ashore as their Western counterparts. This, in turn, allows the Soviet line officers more fleet experience. Recent articles in the Soviet press have referred to a captain 1st rank in the Pacific Fleet having held command for 14 years and a captain 2nd rank in the Black Sea Fleet who

19. Capt. 3rd Rank P. Ishchenko [correspondent], "A Commander's Independence: Who Is the Boss on the Ship?" *Krasnaya Zvezda* (1 December 1988), p. 2.

spent seven years as a commanding officer! (Both of these officers subsequently served as watch officers at naval headquarters in Moscow.)[20]

The fleet commanders in chief and ship and unit commanders have a major voice in officer promotion and assignment, much more so than their counterparts in the U.S. Navy. Advancement through captain 3rd rank is reported to be essentially automatic in the Soviet Navy. Selection for captain 2nd rank and above is apparently done by the Main Naval Staff. Those officers failing this selection generally remain on active duty until age 45.

Postgraduate education/training is generally a requirement for promotion to senior naval rank, and most officers are required to take competitive examinations for entry to advanced educational programs. Exceptions include outstanding graduates from higher naval schools, who are exempt from some portions of the examinations. The entrance examinations for a military academy may be taken up to three times.

Candidates for flag rank generally attend the Naval Academy in Leningrad, renamed in 1990 for the late Admiral Kuznetsov (formerly the Marshal Grechko Naval Academy).[21] This Leningrad institution, founded in 1828, is similar in concept to the U.S. Naval War College, but attendance confers more prestige and is more significant to an officer's career than is the American institution.[22] Line officers up to age 38 and engineering officers up to age 35 are accepted for resident graduate study, while officers are accepted for nonresident correspondence courses up to age 40.[23] Candidates are required to pass entrance examinations in specialized areas and a foreign language.

In addition to its advanced academic curriculum, the Naval Academy conducts studies and analyses for naval headquarters and helps to develop strategy and tactics for the Navy. Potential flag officers may also attend the prestigious Voroshilov General Staff Academy in Moscow, where broad strategic, economic, and policy issues are addressed. The Voroshilov school has a two-year course (compared to the one-year course at the similar U.S. National War College and the Industrial College of the Armed Forces).

The higher naval schools offer graduate courses, both in residence and by correspondence, with the length of courses varying from 12 to 18 months. Correspondence students are exempt from certain duties to permit time for study. There are some naval postgraduate institutions, in particular the Krylov engineering institution—a technical school that has no counterpart in the United States except perhaps the civilian Massachusetts Institute of Technology (MIT)—and the Naval Officers Technical School at Kronshtadt, near Leningrad. In addition, naval officers receive specialized advanced education and training at the numerous schools operated by other services.

The Soviet military academies and higher military schools are commanded by general or flag officers, with several other senior officers on their teaching staffs.

20. A. Gorokov, "Today Is USSR Navy Day: Ocean Watch," *Pravda* (31 July 1988), p. 2.

21. Renamed in September 1990, having previously been named in 1976 for Marshal Grechko, having previously been named the Order of Lenin Naval Academy. The Academy includes the Krylov Academy of Shipbuilding and Armaments. The Krylov school, the foremost naval engineering institution in the USSR, has periodically been separate and at times a part of the Naval Academy.

22. There are believed to be 18 military academies in the Soviet Union; there are nine approximately equivalent schools in the United States: the Naval, Air, Army, and National war colleges; the Industrial College of the Armed Forces; the Armed Forces Staff College; the Army and Air Force command and staff colleges; and the Naval Postgraduate School.

23. The current Soviet military school system has recently been criticized because of the age of graduates. According to Soviet data, the average age of persons receiving their doctorates in the United States is 32.5 years compared to 48 years in the USSR, but it exceeds 55 years in institutions of the Ministry of Defense and is 60 years or more for PhDs in military sciences. Similarly, the average age for candidates of sciences in MOD institutions is 47 while the average age in the USSR is 37. See Col. Ye. Zhuravlev, "The Military Scientist. What Should He Be Like?" *Krasnaya Zvezda* (1 March 1988), p. 2.

Those naval officers who fail promotion to the next higher rank may be retired. However, there is considerable flexibility in the system because officers can be promoted while in the same position. There are published retirement ages: active service for all junior officers currently lasts at least until they reach age 40; for captain 2nd and 3rd rank the retirement age is 45; for captain 1st rank age 50; for rear admiral and vice admiral age 55; and for admiral and admiral of the fleet age 60. There have been numerous exceptions; the most notable was Admiral Gorshkov, who retired as Commander in Chief of the Navy in December 1985, shortly before his 76th birthday. But earlier retirements are expected in the context of force reductions under General Secretary Gorbachev.

Upon retirement most officers are transferred to the reserves, where they serve up to ten years. These officers are subject to annual call-up, but this happens infrequently.

OFFICER RANKS

Line officers of the Soviet Navy have traditional naval ranks, with seven grades of commissioned rank below flag ranks compared to six in the U.S. Navy. This rank structure reflects the early German naval influence on the Russian Navy.

Exact comparisons with U.S. ranks are difficult. For example, a Soviet captain 1st rank has the broad sleeve stripe of a commodore or rear admiral (lower half) in Western navies yet still wears the shoulder insignia of a colonel, his nominal army equivalent. The issue is further complicated because the Soviet military services do not have a brigadier rank; their one-star military rank is major general.

History. The military rank of admiral was introduced into the Russian Navy by Peter the Great in 1699, and the grades of rear (*kontr*), vice (*vitse*), and full admiral have been in subsequent use with minor variations. (Although Peter held military and naval ranks, he was only a captain in the Russian Navy until his victory over the Swedish Army at Poltava in 1709. Only after that triumph—the first by Russian forces against a major European army—did he take the rank of rear admiral in the Navy and promote himself from colonel to lieutenant general in the Army. The tsar did not assume the rank of full admiral until after his victory over Sweden in 1721.)[24]

The admiral grades fell into disuse at the start of the Soviet regime. Position titles were used for senior naval officers until late 1935, when the ranks of flagman (flag officer) 1st and 2nd grade were introduced. "Admiral" was still not acceptable to the Communist regime; at that time, the term "general" was also avoided in the Red Army, but five army officers were named Marshal of the Soviet Union in 1935. The various grades of general and admiral were belatedly introduced in the Soviet armed forces on 7 May 1940, when seven Soviet naval officers were given admiral rank: N.G. Kuznetsov, the naval commissar, and I.S. Isakov and L.M. Galler, both at naval headquarters, were made admirals; the commanders of the Baltic and Pacific fleets became vice admirals; and the commanders of the Northern and Black Sea fleets became rear admirals. S.F. Zhavoronkov, head of naval aviation, became a lieutenant general (three stars) at the same time. Many more flag officers were appointed during the war. The senior political officers assigned to the armed forces were given general or admiral ranks in December 1942.

The rank of admiral of the fleet (*admiral flota*) was also introduced in the Soviet Union on 7 May 1940. It was abolished on 3 March 1955 with the introduction of the rank of Admiral of the Fleet of the Soviet Union but was reestablished on 28 April 1962 and corresponds to the military ranks of general of the army and marshal of an arm or service.

Admiral of the Fleet of the Soviet Union (*Admiral Flota Sovetskogo Soyuza*) is the highest rank of the Soviet Navy and corresponds to the rank of Marshal of the Soviet Union. It was introduced on 3 March 1955 and on that date was awarded to Isakov, the

24. Also on 21 September 1721, the Russian Senate offered Peter the titles of *the Great* and *Emperor*.

leading Soviet theorist of the 1930s, and Kuznetsov, who had directed Stalin's fleet buildups of the late 1930s and early 1950s. On 28 October 1967 it was awarded to Gorshkov, 12 years after he was named CinC of the Soviet Navy.

The grades of captain 1st, 2nd, and 3rd rank (*ranga*) existed in the Russian Navy from 1713 to 1732, again from 1751 to 1917, and in the Soviet Navy since 22 September 1935. Historically, these officers held the rank corresponding to the rank of the ship they commanded (*rang korablya*). Thus, a captain 2nd rank normally commanded a second-rank ship (see chapter 3 for current Soviet naval ship ranks).

The captain 1st rank wears the single broad sleeve stripe similar to commodores and rear admirals, but ranks with a colonel in Soviet military service. Before February 1943 that rank was considered a one-star grade, equivalent to brigadier general. That month the Soviet naval ranks were reorganized and shoulder board insignias were introduced in the armed forces after having for decades been regarded as a hateful symbol of the tsarist military forces. From that time major general has been a one-star rank, lieutenant general a two-star rank, colonel general a three-star rank, and general of the army and marshal a four-star rank, further complicating comparisons with Western military rank.

In the Soviet Navy the rear, vice, and full admirals have insignia similar to their Western contemporaries and in most instances hold comparable positions. The flag-rank issue also becomes confused because the Soviet Navy had at least four admirals of the fleet on active duty in 1990, a rank equivalent not now held by serving officers in Western navies. The admirals currently in this grade are Admirals Chernnavin, the CinC of the Navy; I.M. Kapitanets, the first deputy CinC; K.V. Makarov, chief of the Main Naval Staff, and V.V. Sidorov, deputy CinC of the Navy for Rear Services.

An approximate comparison of Soviet military and naval ranks with U.S. naval ranks is provided in table 10-3. The Northern and Pacific fleets have generally been commanded by admirals and the Baltic and Black Sea fleets by vice admirals (although when this edition went to press both were commanded by full admirals). In the U.S. Navy the area fleet commanders are admirals (Atlantic and Pacific fleets) and the numbered fleet commanders are vice admirals (Second, Third, Sixth, Seventh). Thus, it seems reasonable to equate a Soviet admiral with the U.S. flag officer wearing the same insignia.

Direct comparisons of lower officer ranks are also difficult. For example, the commanding officers of some Soviet warships hold a similar rank to their American counterparts. However, large cruisers of the Moskva, Slava, Kara, and Kresta II classes are commanded mostly by captains 2nd rank, while ships of their size in the U.S. Navy would have full captains in command.

Senior instructors of the Soviet Navy have their rank prefixed with the term *professor* (professor) and engineering officers have the prefix *inzhener* (engineer).

The specialized branches of the Soviet Navy—Naval Aviation, Naval Infantry (marines), Coastal Missile-Artillery Force, *Spetsnaz*, Medical Service, and Rear Services—have distinctive uniforms and military ranks, separate schools, and other institutional trappings. These services are fully integrated into naval organizations in the same manner, for example, as U.S. Navy medical personnel are assigned to the Marine Corps units, and the Fleet Marine Forces are components of the U.S. Atlantic and Pacific fleet commands.

POLITICAL ACTIVITIES

The military establishment is in many respects the most powerful segment of the Soviet society, with probably more influence on the society than the educational, agricultural, or even industrial sectors. Because of this, the military has always been carefully watched and controlled by the Communist Party. During the past few years, however, there is increasing evidence that the Party now believes that the military establishment has become fully integrated with respect to ideals and goals.

More than 90 percent of all naval officers are believed to be members of the Communist Party or Komsomol—probably a higher percentage than in the other armed services. For a naval officer membership in the Party is essential to obtain command or hold other important or sensitive positions.

History. As explained above, the Communist Party has exercised close control over the military establishment. Although sailors were in the forefront of the ill-fated revolution of 1906 as well as the Great October Revolution of 1917, by 1921 the Baltic Fleet sailors at Kronshtadt were demanding free elections by secret ballot, freedom of the press and speech, the abolition of Bolshevik control over land use, and a "true people's revolution." The discontent of the Baltic sailors led to riots among Leningrad workers. The Bolshevik leaders and Red Army officer candidates attacked the Kronshtadt naval base, connected to the mainland by ice. After 18 days the base fell and with savage brutality the Bolsheviks executed or sent to Siberia several thousand sailors and the workers who had allied with them. There followed a long period of distrust of the political reliability of the fleet.

The loyalty of former tsarist officers was also a problem for the new Communist regime. Because of the lack of command experience and technical knowledge among the Communists, the ex-tsarist officers had to be used in military units. The result was the assignment of military commissars (*voyenkomi*) to each ship and

TABLE 10-3.   OFFICER AND WARRANT RANKS

Soviet Navy	Soviet Military and Specialized Naval Branches	Approximate U.S. Navy Equivalent
Officer Ranks		
Admiral of the Fleet of the Soviet Union (*Admiral Flota Sovyetskoga Soyuza*)	Marshal of the Soviet Union	Fleet Admiral
(none)	Chief Marshal Chief Marshal of Aviation	
Admiral of the Fleet (*Admiral Flota*)	Marshal Marshal of Aviation General of the Army	
Admiral (*Admiral*)	Colonel General Colonel General of Aviation	Admiral
Vice Admiral (*Vitse Admiral*)	Lieutenant General Lieutenant General of Aviation	Vice Admiral
Rear Admiral (*Kontr Admiral*)	Major General Major General of Aviation	Rear Admiral
Captain 1st Rank (*Kapitan Pervogo Ranga*)	Colonel	Captain
Captain 2nd Rank (*Kapitan Vtorogo Ranga*)	Lieutenant Colonel	Commander
Capital 3rd Rank (*Kapitan Pervogo Ranga*)	Major	Lieutenant Commander
Captain Lieutenant (*Kapitan Leytenant*)	Captain	Lieutenant
Lieutenant (*Leytenant*)	Lieutenant	Ensign
Junior Lieutenant (*Mladshiy Leytenant*)	Junior Lieutenant	Ensign
Warrant Ranks		
Senior Warrant (*Starshi Michman*)	Senior Ensign	Warrant Officer or Chief Petty Officer
Warrant (*Michman*)	Ensign	Warrant Officer or Chief Petty Officer

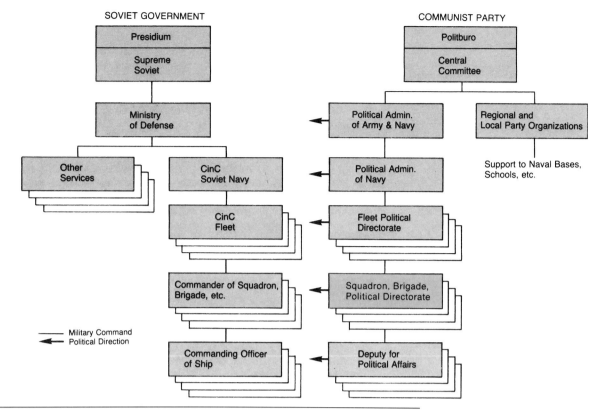

FIGURE 10-1. Naval Political Organization

unit to ensure that all orders by commanding officers were politically as well as militarily correct. At each subunit there were political instructors, or *politruks*, to indoctrinate soldiers and sailors in Party tenets. (Some former tsarist officers, especially I.S. Isakov and L.M. Galler, did serve in the senior positions of the Soviet Navy.)

In June 1924, the new head of the armed forces, M.V. Frunze, abolished the dual-command system in favor of "unity of command" (*yedinonachalye*), in which the commanding officer no longer needed to have all orders countersigned by the political officer. This scheme took several years to institute fully. In each unit, however, there was a political assistant to the commander, who was independent in virtually all respects.

The situation changed again in the late 1930s with Stalin's massive purges of the Soviet political and government leadership, which spread to the military establishment in 1937. Political commissars were reintroduced in June of that year, and "military councils" were established at all command levels, generally consisting of the commander, chief of staff, and political commissar. Decisions were made in the name of the council, with all three (or sometimes more) officers signing such orders—and sharing responsibility for them. In June 1940, as war approached, the concept of unity of command was again introduced, only to be abolished a year later when Germany invaded the Soviet Union and the dual-command system was reinstituted.

By the fall of 1942, when the German armies had been fought to a halt and Stalin was satisfied with the political reliability of most Soviet officers, he again ordered unity of command. But the October 1942 policy established an assistant commander for political affairs, in essence the system that continues today. These political officers were given military ranks in December 1942.

In general, there was distrust, if not actual hatred, for the political officers on the part of many naval officers. During World War II, Navy chief Kuznetsov discussed military matters with the chief political officer of the Navy, I.V. Rogov, "cautiously." Rogov was known as "Ivan the Terrible" in the fleet, his nickname a reference to the savage tsar of the 16th century who, partially mad, murdered his son. Another view of the Soviet Navy's political officers comes from a discussion of operations in the Baltic during the war:

It very frequently happened that when a Russian vessel was sunk the survivors, fearing their commissar, refused to be taken on board, and would not give up their resistance until the commissar had been shot. . . . This is how it was, for example, on 14 September 1943 when six survivors were sighted after a [Soviet] PT boat went down in the Baltic Sea. As the German boat approached, the commissar shot two of his people floating in the water, and the other three could not be taken aboard until after the commissar was shot dead.

When [the] large transport JOSEF STALIN, which had about 4,000 men on board, was stranded in the Gulf of Finland, the Russian survivors hanged their commissar.[25]

After the war the concept of one-man control continued with political officers serving as assistant or deputy commanders at every level of command. The current Soviet policy has been stated in the following words by the head of the Main Political Administration of the Army and Navy:

One essential condition for the establishment and maintenance of stable order in all units is strict observance of the Leninist principle of one-man command. In the Army and Navy it is more necessary than anywhere else to ensure the strictist unity of action of large masses of people, their subordination to the will of one man. As evidenced by the one-half century of the Soviet Armed Forces, one-man command is the most effective method of troop control, particularly in a combat situation. It ensures really efficient, centralised and reliable direction of operations, achievement of victory in war and the necessary level of fighting efficiency and combat readiness in peacetime.

One-man command plays an especially big role today, when the Army and Navy are armed with nuclear weapons and other up-to-date combat means.[26]

25. Capt. Erwin M. Rau, Federal German Navy, "Russia and the Baltic Sea: 1920–1970," *Naval War College Review* (September 1970), pp. 23–30.

26. Gen. of the Army A.A. Yepishev, *Some Aspects of Party-Political Work in the Soviet Armed Forces* (Moscow: Progress Publishers, 1975), pp. 197–198.

Political activities within the Soviet armed forces are directed by the Main Political Administration (MPA), established in its present structure in 1946. The MPA is also a department of the Central Committee of the Communist Party, making it responsible to the Party leadership outside of the military chain of command. Political staffs subordinate to the MPA were then established within each service. As indicated in figure 10-1, under the MPA each military service has a political directorate. The Chief of the Navy's Political Directorate is a senior flag officer, who is at the level of Deputy CinC of the Navy. (The late Soviet leader L.I. Brezhnev, as a civilian, was head of the Navy's political directorate in the early 1950s.) The Navy's Political Directorate, under Admiral V.I. Panin, supervises political officers assigned to the fleets and specialized branches of the Navy, and to all units, and ships.

The commanding officer of a ship or unit is personally responsible for his men's political attitudes and activities. Within each naval command (ashore and afloat) there is a political officer (*zampolit*) who serves as an assistant commander but additionally has his own chain of command up to the Navy's Political Directorate. The *zampolit*'s duties aboard ship are diverse: he directs the ideological indoctrination of the crew; monitors the political reliability of the officers and enlisted men; ensures that Party directives are carried out; enforces discipline; and acts as both "chaplain" and social worker for the crew. Under the direction of the commanding officer, he is responsible for the morale of the crew. A shipboard political officer holds formal sessions regularly for the enlisted men and meetings for officers conducted on a periodic basis. Beyond these meetings there are continual "agitation and propaganda" activities, described as:

> Agitation and propaganda work is designed to instil in the personnel profound conviction in communist ideals, Soviet patriotism, proletarian internationals, uncompromising hatred for the enemies of communism, to strengthen their ideological staunchness and resistance to bourgeois influence in whatever form. An uncompromising struggle is being daily waged against hostile ideology and the aggressive essence and schemes of imperialism is unmasked.
> The basic methods of agitation and propaganda work conducted in the Soviet Navy include:
> —printed agitation and propaganda through books, pamphlets, leaflets, magazines, and newspapers
> —oral agitation and propaganda through lectures, periodic reports, talks and consultations
> —poster agitation.[27]

Thus, the *zampolit* has a direct and integrated role in the operations and life of a ship. If a ship or unit performs well, the political officer will share credit with the commanding officer and his other assistants; if they do poorly, the political officer as well as the commanding officer will suffer. Also, according to a U.S. Navy evaluation, "In recent years . . . there has been a trend toward giving the political officer practical naval experience as a line officer prior to his entry into the political field."

The overlap of the naval and political areas reflects the current high degree of confidence of the Communist Party leaders in the reliability and loyalty of the armed forces. This is to be expected after more than 70 years of Communist rule and achievements. The last significant challenge to Party control over the military came in the early 1950s when Marshal Zhukov attempted to limit the influence of political officers over military decision making. However, since the unsettled period that followed Stalin's death in 1953 and the resulting "revolution" in military affairs, the political-military situation has settled down, and the political officers are generally considered a part of the service "team." This has resulted in significant "cross-fertilization" between the line and political officers, with some political officers eventually being given ship commands. Despite this integration of the *zampolit* into the "regular navy," the political officer retains his separate and direct line of communication to his political superiors up to the MPA and the Party leadership.

The Navy's political officers are trained at the Kiev Higher Naval Political School, one of several similar schools set up in 1967 for the different services. The four-year curriculum at the Kiev school stresses the political aspects of the armed forces, with emphasis on agitation and education in the fleet. Some naval line training is provided, but the newly commissioned political officers clearly do not have the same level of training as do graduates of the ten other higher naval schools. After service in the fleet and ashore, senior political officers receive graduate-level instruction at the Lenin Military Political Academy in Moscow.

The relationship between the professional naval officer and the Party's other means of control over the military—the Committee for State Security (KGB)—is less than cordial. The KGB, as noted in chapter 4, includes the Maritime Border Troops, whose maritime units are responsible for the security of the Soviet Union's long coastlines. There are other special KGB troops that deal with the Navy, such as those responsible for the security of nuclear weapons.

The KGB is charged with counterespionage against internal and foreign enemies. Officers of the Third Directorate of the KGB, which is responsible for counterintelligence within the armed forces, are assigned to all branches of the armed forces; they generally wear standard military uniforms but are readily known as KGB officers and report only through the KGB chain-of-command. In the Navy, uniformed KGB officers may be assigned to large surface ships. Covert KGB officers are assigned throughout the Navy and they operate a network of "informers."

Within naval units and ships the KGB officers recruit men to report directly to them. According to one KGB defector, a former captain assigned to a motorized rifle regiment in East Germany, he was instructed that "when recruiting informers, you must not only convince them but also compel them to work for us. The KGB has enough power for that."[28] And, he added:

> The KGB had the rights and the power needed. If it was an officer [wanted as an informer], then his career could be threatened (without KGB approval no officer can be sent to a military academy or get promotion). With regular [enlisted] servicemen it was even simpler; they could just be dismissed from the army. Any Soviet citizen's life, too, could be threatened; he could be barred from an institute or from work in any undertaking, or be forbidden to travel abroad.[29]

While the political officers are considered part of the Navy contributing to the performance of ships and units, the KGB officers can only be regarded with distrust and resentment. Another Soviet writer has given a description of the power possessed by a KGB officer—referred to as *Molchi-Molchi* ("Keep your mouth shut"):

> The head of the special department is terror—invisible, without color or scent—but the terror is felt by the soldier's every nerve cell. Young officers, somewhat drunk, would call Molchi-Molchi the Tsar's Eye, and add: "The scoundrel is sitting there, smiling, but what he's got in his skull, only the devil knows."
> These words meant that for the young officers Molchi-Molchi was neither a comrade, nor an officer, in the full meaning of the word. He was a foreign body. He was watching our thoughts and did not trust us, in accordance with his position, did not trust that all of us, soldiers and officers, would defend our country, if the need arose. And he had more power than anybody else, and to resist him equaled suicide.[30]

Despite the unity of the Communist Party and the armed forces in their goals, there is still some political unrest. Indeed, there is some evidence of this throughout the Soviet Union, mostly related to the privileges of Party leaders at all levels and to the nation's continued economic problems. On rare occasions this political un-

27. Adm. V.M. Grishanov, ed., *Man and Sea Warfare* (Moscow: Progress Publishers, 1978), p. 30.

28. Aleksei Myagkov, *Inside the KGB* (New York: Ballantine Books, 1981), p. 82.

29. Ibid.

30. Vladimir Rybakov, *Tiski: Armeyskiye Ocherki* [Vices: Army Sketches] (Frankfurt am Main: Possev Verlag, 1985), pp. 23–24.

rest surfaces. Probably the most dramatic example of the post-Stalin period occurred at the Baltic port of Riga on the night of 7–8 November 1975, when the crewmen of the Krivak-class frigate STOROZHEVOY mutinied. Led by the political officer, Captain 3rd Rank V.M. Sablin, several members of the crew took possession of the ship and took her to sea, hoping to reach neutral Sweden.

The Soviet naval high command learned of the mutiny, and aircraft as well as surface ships were dispatched to recapture or to sink the STOROZHEVOY. After several air attacks, the ship was recaptured. *Zampolit* Sablin was executed by firing squad in Moscow following his trial before the Military Division of the Supreme Court of the Soviet Union, as were several enlisted men. Another officer was sentenced to 15 years in a labor camp. After a conspicuous cruise in the Baltic just outside of Swedish territorial waters, as if to demonstrate the loyalty of the ship, the STOROZHEVOY was transferred to the Pacific Fleet.[31]

No other overt instances of unrest in the Soviet Navy in the recent past are known. Indeed, the opposite attitude appears to be common among the Navy's officers, who are increasingly part of the elite of the Soviet Union. A postscript to the STOROZHEVOY mutiny comes from a Swedish military officer:

> Those who think this shows weakness are a little stupid. There is not a point of weakness. This demonstrates a will and a skill in making decisions. It shows the Russians are strong enough to do what is necessary.[32]

On board ships and in other units the commanding officer is directly responsible for conducting the competition on a day-to-day basis. In organizing, publicizing, and running the competition he is assisted primarily by his political officer and, to a lesser degree, by Communist Party and Komsomol members aboard his ship. There is a standard scoring scheme for socialist competition: ships and units having high scores are rewarded and publicized, while "laggards" are exposed to public censure and pressure is brought to force them to improve.

PAY AND BENEFITS

There are two basic types of compensation paid to Soviet naval personnel: minimal pay to conscripts and a relatively high pay to career servicemen, most of whom are warrant officers and commissioned officers.

The lowest ranking conscript, the seaman (*matros*) receives 7 rubles 80 kopecks per month; a senior seaman (*starshii matros*), 8 rubles 80 kopecks.[33] Depending upon their assignment, they can receive between 10 rubles 30 kopecks and 11 rubles 30 kopecks per month basic allowance. An additional supplement is paid for specialist qualification, 2 rubles 50 kopecks for second class and 5 rubles if the sailor qualifies as a specialist first class. Petty officers and some senior seamen earn 13 to 25 rubles per month plus specialist pay if they are in certain specified billets.

In addition, an additional 30 percent of the basic allowance is paid for sea duty. Thus, a conscript who becomes head of a subunit aboard ship could earn as much as 35 to 40 rubles per month, still much less than the average Soviet worker in industry. Further, the additional money does not appear to compensate for the added responsibility and work of being head of a subunit.

31. There has been little authoritative writing about the STOROZHEVOY mutiny in the West. Probably the best work is the thesis by Lt. Gregory D. Young, USN, "Mutiny on STOROZHEVOY: A Case Study of Dissent in the Soviet Navy" (Monterey, Calif.: Naval Postgraduate School, March 1982). Recent Soviet writings on the mutiny include Nikolay Cherkashin, "The Last Parade," *Komsomolskaya Pravda* (1 March 1990) and S. Bystrov, "The Sablin Case," *Krasnaya Zvezda* (3 March 1990).

32. Quoted in Bernard D. Nossiter, "Soviet Mutiny Ended Swiftly," *The Washington Post* (7 June 1976), p. 18.

33. The official exchange rate is approximately 1 ruble = $1.65; however, such comparisons have little meaning. For example, a person living in the Washington, D.C., area would require some $40,000 to 50,000 per year to live at the same level as a person in Moscow could for 12,000 to 15,000 rubles.

TABLE 10-4. APPROXIMATE OFFICER PAY SCALE (Monthly Rate)

Rank	Basic Pay	Rank Pay
Lieutenant	120–150 rubles	120 rubles
Senior Lieutenant	↑	130 rubles
Captain Lieutenant		140 rubles
Captain 3rd Rank		150 rubles
Captain 2nd Rank	↓	160 rubles
Captain 1st Rank	190–300 rubles	180 rubles

Sailors are provided with food, uniforms, and full medical care. Free recreation and cultural activities are provided, often interrelated and stressing political themes. Specific recreation activities stressed in the Navy include choir singing, bands, do-it-yourself hobbies such as painting and handicrafts, and amateur acting. Discussions and reading are encouraged, with ship and station libraries stocked especially with books "dealing with political subjects, books on military history, the memoirs by outstanding military leaders, literature on the navies and armies of capitalist countries as well as books of fiction are all popular with Soviet navymen. While at sea during a prolonged cruise the men particularly appreciate magazines, satirical and comic publications."[34]

The sailor who is promoted to warrant rank can earn some 200 to 240 rubles per month, well above the income of the average Soviet worker.

Pay for commissioned officers is comparatively high and a major incentive for a naval career. Officer pay is based on commissioned status, rank, and length of service, with substantial supplements for sea duty, submarine duty, assignment to remote areas (Northern and Pacific fleet regions), and education. The most significant component of this pay package is position pay. The approximate officer pay scale is shown in table 10-4. The basic pay for an officer is related to his having professional status with a degree in engineering; the rank pay is referred to as "star pay," a reference to his shoulder board insignia.

Within the variations of basic pay, the more important the position held the higher the basic pay. The combined basic and rank pay are increased for longevity at the rate of 5 percent for each five years up to 30 percent. Submariners receive a bonus of 15 percent and duty in nuclear-propelled submarines earns an additional 20 percent; sea duty in surface ships and submarines adds 30 percent. The special rates for service in the Arctic or Pacific regions vary with the location—about 15 percent more for duty in Vladivostok, up to 50 percent more for assignment in Murmansk, and 100 percent more in Petropavlovsk.

Despite having to pay significant taxes and dues to the Communist Party (if a member), an officer's pay is significant by Soviet standards. Captains and flag officers earn from 500 to 2,000 rubles per month and have considerable non-monetary benefits, as befits the elite of a society.

Although officers (as well as enlisted personnel) in remote areas receive increased payments, there are other difficulties. For example, many wives work and comparatively few jobs are available in those areas. In the Northern Fleet, for example, more than 50 percent of the wives do not work; 24 percent give the reason as the lack of available positions. Sometimes a wife is refused employment because as a serviceman's spouse, she is a "temporary resident." About one-third of the women surveyed in the Northern Fleet have college educations.

Housing and medical service are provided free to all servicemen. Every year an officer receives one free round trip to any location in the Soviet Union, and if he uses one of the Navy's rest resorts, primarily along the Black Sea coast, his wife and children travel free. Upon being discharged from active military service, servicemen are entitled to housing on a priority basis, with those disabled while in military service receiving the highest priorities.

Although regulations prescribe housing standards for servicemen, in some cases they are known to be substandard, especially for conscripts. (However, the same situation exists in the U.S. armed forces.)

34. Grishanov, p. 174.

TABLE 10-5.   OFFICER CAREER ASSIGNMENTS

Years of Service	Rank	Typical Assignments
19 to 25	Captain 1st Rank	Military Academy of the General Staff (student)
		Brigade Command (small combatants)
		Division Command (cruisers/destroyers)
		Fleet Navigator
		CO strategic missile submarine
		CO ADMIRAL KUZNETSOV (aircraft carrier)
		CO KIEV (aircraft carrier)
14 to 21	Captain 2nd Rank	Naval Academy (student)
		Higher Naval School (instructor)
		Division Command (small combatants)
		CO KIEV (aircraft carrier)
		CO MOSKVA (helicopter carrier)
		CO Kara/Kresta/Kynda/SLAVA (cruiser)
		CO destroyer
		CO large landing ship
9 to 16	Captain 3rd Rank	Postgraduate Studies
		CO Kara/Kresta (cruiser)
		CO submarine tender
		CO destroyer
		CO Krivak (frigate)
		CO large landing ship
		CO large minesweeper
		XO surface combatant
		Department Head of surface combatant
5 to 12	Captain Lieutenant	CO Krivak (frigate)
		CO minesweeper
		CO small missile combat
		XO destroyer
		XO frigate
		Department Head of submarine
2 to 8	Senior Lieutenant	CO small combatant
		XO small combatant
0 to 5	Lieutenant	XO small combatant
0 to 2	Junior Lieutenant	sea duty

The daily food ration in the Soviet Navy is stipulated at providing 3,000 to 4,000 calories, with the highest allocation going to nuclear submarine crews. There are reportedly 40 special diets for Soviet servicemen, especially developed for men in arctic and tropical climates (on board ship or ashore), aviators, submariners, and so on. The quality of food is reported to vary widely, with limited variety and few fresh vegetables and meat reported in the Soviet press. In part as a supplement, military cafes, post exchanges, and mobile stores at many bases provide "luxury" food items such as fresh fruit and vegetables in addition to staples.

These benefits are supplemented by certain social services in the Soviet Union. A childless wife of a sailor or warrant officer is exempt from paying the income tax levied on other childless workers. If there are children they must be provided day care or kindergarten places, a benefit worth about 400 rubles per year. Special efforts are made to find housing and work for wives and to help integrate them in new surroundings when the Navy moves families to base areas or home ports if the sailor is assigned to a ship. And when the conscript leaves the Navy, efforts are made to ensure that he is employed. Also, upon discharge or retirement, a serviceman is entitled to interest-free loans up to 3,000 rubles for individual housing construction (to be repaid beginning the fifth year after construction is completed) and is authorized to enter a higher or secondary specialized educational institution on a non-competitive basis.

(Parents, wives, and children of servicemen who are killed or die as a result of wounds acquired in performance of duty who are unable to work are paid lump-sum allowances.)

Still, embezzlement, poor quality, poor service, and poor management reduce the value of many of the benefits and services intended for conscripts. But because the Soviet armed forces have a high priority in the Soviet society, major efforts are under way to remedy these problems. These problems reflect the overall conditions of the Soviet state.

The non-monetary benefits—including housing, goods, and services—have in the past been much better for officers. Naval officers are normally given 30 days of paid leave per year; senior officers and those who are assigned to remote areas or perform arduous duty receive 45 days per year. Special arrangements facilitate their travel, and recreation and vacation centers are available for them, including villas for senior officers on the Black Sea coast, the Soviet "Riviera." However, the current political-economic turmoil of the country has affected officers. A recent survey of 1,800 officers and 250 warrants, 300 of their wives, and 150 cadets revealed the deteriorating situation.

Ninety-one percent of those polled said their pay, given current inflation and shortages, does not correspond to their work, especially for younger officers. A typical response read: "To be discharged—this is now my main goal. I have not yet written a request, since there is no where to go with the family. But it is suffocating to serve on such a situation. For 12 to 14 hours of work per day, and for 10 or 12 daily duty details per month, they pay 260 rubles. I cannot buy clothes for my wife. It is shameful. I cannot help my parents, who are on pension."[35]

Housing is worst of all. At some bases, up to one-half or more of the officers do not have apartments. Another acute problem is wives of military personnel finding work. These situations are exacerbated by the large numbers of troops being brought back to the Soviet Union from Eastern Bloc countries.

35. S. Taranov, "How are Officers Living," *Izvestiya* (21 Oct 1989), p. 2.

CHAPTER 11

Fleet Development

The post-World War II development of the Soviet Navy has spawned a force of large, sophisticated warships. Although Western warships are superior in several respects, the actual reasons for certain features in Soviet ships may not be fully understood and hence their capabilities not adequately evaluated.

Arms and equipment are the physical basis for development of the military art, which has a substantial influence on the conduct of combat actions and the war as a whole. The appearance of new, effective kinds of weapons and technical equipment increases the combat effectiveness of armed forces, opens up opportunities for accomplishing more difficult tactical, operational, and strategic missions, and thus entails a change in methods and forms of warfare. This is especially noticeable in [the] development of naval forces.[1]

Thus spokesmen for the Soviet Navy explain the importance of weapons—including surface warships and submarines—to improved capabilities in combat. The Soviet Navy is entering what may be considered the fifth stage of fleet development of the post–World War II era. Into the 1980s—under the Brezhnev-Gorshkov regime—the Soviet Union undertook an intensive *offensive* naval development and construction effort.

Under the regime of General Secretary Mikhail Gorbachev the rate of naval development may be slowing; however, this situation is not completely clear. For example, the construction of aircraft carriers, destroyers, and submarines appears to be continuing at approximately the same rate as the 1980s. The U.S. Director of Naval Intelligence has made the following appraisal:

1. Rear Adm. N.P. V'yunenko, Capt. 1st Rank B.N. Makeyev, Capt. 1st Rank V.D. Skugarev, *The Navy: Its Role, Prospects for Development, and Employment* (Moscow: Military Publishing House, 1988), USN trans., p. 59.

Despite the USSR's escalating economic and social problems, the Soviet Navy had a year of growth in 1989 of which any navy could be proud. Indeed, in terms of the new construction of high-quality, high-technology submarines, surface ships and aircraft, as well as the further development and modernization of new weapons/electronic systems and shipyards, this was an outstanding year for Soviet naval power. It is true the Soviets are scrapping older, obsolescent units at an unprecedented rate. Yet . . . the new Soviet carriers (which are some of the most high tech and costly items in the Soviet naval construction program) become cost effective if you trim the fleet of its older units and progress to a more balanced mix within the Navy.[2]

With respect to surface ship developments, Admiral Brooks also noted: "While such programs would appear to be prime candidates for cancellation if more substantial diversion of resources from the defense sector were required to sustain *perestroika*, construction of surface ships, to date, remains high with no indication of imminent reduction."

PHASE I—THE STALIN PERIOD

The massive fleet building program initiated by Stalin after World War II was intended to provide a fleet to secure the seas adjacent to the Soviet Union, to prevent an amphibious assault against Soviet territory, and to support possible moves by the Red Army into bordering states. But in addition, Stalin was resurrecting the concept of a massive, ocean-going fleet that he had initiated in the 1930s.

After the war, as soon as the major shipyards could resume work, the unfinished hulls of the prewar and wartime programs were rushed to completion. These programs were principally the light cruisers of the CHAPAYEV class and various destroyers, submarines, and lesser craft; however, the unfinished hulls of the battleships and battle cruisers laid down in 1938–1940 were scrapped.

Simultaneous with the rejuvenation of the shipyards, the various ship design bureaus were rehabilitated and plans were prepared for a new generation of Soviet warships. These would become the first phase of the postwar development of the Soviet fleet. These postwar ships would be based largely on existing designs, with some updating from captured German drawings, equipment, and ships, plus the assistance of former German technicians used by the

2. Rear Adm. Thomas A. Brooks, USN, testimony before the Armed Services Committee, House of Representatives, 14 March 1990.

The massive cutbacks in naval construction following Stalin's death in March 1953 left this unfinished SVERDLOV-class cruiser, probably at the Marti (now Admiralty) yard in Leningrad, to be towed to the breakers. Alongside is the Belgium-built merchant ship STANISLAVSKY.

Soviets. By the late 1940s the keels for the first of these new designs were being laid down.

Professor Michael MccGwire, a former British intelligence officer, has asserted that under Stalin's direction a 20-year shipbuilding plan was developed. Although the credible data are limited, MccGwire has postulated the number of ships that were to have been completed by the late 1960s. His estimates and data, derived from an analysis of public statements, published naval annuals, and Soviet shipway capacity, are shown in table 11-1.[3]

Although MccGwire's numbers were speculative, they were indicative of the potential Soviet shipbuilding capability and of Stalin's plans to acquire a massive battle fleet. For the next several years MccGwire's numbers were studied attentively by naval officers and analysts in the West.

Stalin's program would have produced a massive albeit highly conventional fleet. The Soviets began building the first postwar capital ships to be laid down by any nation—the STALINGRAD-class battle cruisers. These ships were to displace some 38,000 to 40,000

3. MccGwire has written extensively on this subject. The accompanying table is adapted from "Soviet Naval Procurement," *The Soviet Union in Europe and the Near East: Her Capabilities and Intentions* (London: Royal United Services Institution, 1970), pp. 74–87, and discussions by the author with MccGwire.

TABLE 11-1.   POSTULATED SOVIET SHIPBUILDING PROGRAM, 1946–1965

Ship Type	Preliminary Period Complete 1945–1951	Intermediate Period Complete 1952–1957	Final Period Complete 1958–1965
Aircraft carriers			4 ships
Battle cruisers			12 STALINGRAD class
Heavy cruisers	complete KIROV class		
Light cruisers		24 SVERDLOV class	
Destroyers	complete OGNEVOI class	80 SKORYY class	40 Kruplin class**
		12 Tallinn class*	40 Kashin class*
		36 Kotlin class*	
Escort/guard ships	3 Bird class	24 Kola class*	48 Ritya class**
		72 Riga class*	(?) Petya/Mirka classes*
Submarines			
large		36 Zulu class*	144 Foxtrot class*
medium	complete SHCH IV class	336 Whiskey class*	576 Romeo class*
small	continue M V class		96 Quebec class*
nuclear-propelled		1 prototype	55 production units
Totals			4 aircraft carriers
		24 light cruisers	12 battle cruisers
		128 destroyers	80 destroyers
		96 escort/guard ships	48+ escort ships
		373 submarines	871 submarines

* NATO/U.S. code name.
** Code name derived by Michael MccGwire.

The graceful SVERDLOV-class cruisers came to represent Soviet warship designs of the immediate postwar period. They were impressive ships but lacked the advanced weapons and sensors found in contemporary U.S. and European warships. This is the ALEKSANDR SUVOROV in the Philippine Sea. (U.S. Navy)

tons full load, carrying a primary armament of 12-inch (304-mm) guns. Subsequently, the design was revised to provide surface-to-surface missile launchers (retaining some 12-inch guns). The lead ship probably was started at the Nikolayev south shipyard on the Black Sea in early 1949.

Several of the CHAPAYEV-class light cruisers begun before the war were completed, as were many lesser ships of the wartime building programs. At the same time, the new cruiser, destroyer, and submarine classes were initiated. Two years later, in July 1951 when Vice Admiral N.G. Kuznetsov was reappointed to head the Navy, he told the fleet's senior officers that the future of the Navy was bright and that in the near future the Soviet Union would construct aircraft carriers.

Of more concern to Western military planners in the immediate postwar period was the specter of some 1,200 Soviet submarines that could be operational by the late 1960s if the Soviets could attain the German building rates of World War II.[4] The medium-range Whiskey had been designed before the war ended, but plans were modified to take advantage of German wartime developments. The ocean-going Zulu demonstrated more German influence, with several features adopted from the highly advanced Type XXI U-boat. The Zulu's successor, the Foxtrot (operational from 1957), was even further developed and became widely used by the Soviet Navy as well as by several Third World navies.

The follow-on medium-range Soviet submarine, the Romeo (operational from 1957), also incorporated German technology, while the smaller Quebec, a coastal submarine, was to have a closed-cycle power plant to permit the use of diesel engines underwater to charge batteries without the need to raise a snorkel breathing tube. This concept also had considerable German influence although the Soviets had begun work on closed-cycle submarine propulsion in the 1930s.[5]

In the event, Stalin's death in March 1953 brought this ambitious shipbuilding program to an almost complete halt. Within days, stop-work orders were sent out to some yards, and several major revisions were made in the shipbuilding program during the 1953–1955 period. The battle cruiser STALINGRAD was about 60 percent

complete in 1953; the ship is believed to have been launched and expended in missile tests. While five of the CHAPAYEV-class cruisers, which had been started before the war, were completed, only 14 of the planned 24 light cruisers of the SVERDLOV class were finished. Significantly, large numbers of the destroyers and submarines were completed, although not all that were planned. The proposed aircraft carriers were never started.

Of great significance for the future Soviet fleet, Stalin's ambitious program did provide the industrial and design base for building a large navy.

PHASE II—THE KHRUSHCHEV PERIOD

Khrushchev and his colleagues who inherited the mantle of Stalin moved rapidly to cut back the naval rebuilding effort.[6] There was little opposition to the reductions. Early in his tenure as First Secretary and hence head of the ruling politburo, Khrushchev reassigned several of the recently rebuilt and new shipbuilding facilities to construct merchant ships instead of warships.

He then directed the Navy to seek more innovative weapons in place of large surface warships—low-cost, high-firepower ships that could counter Western naval forces. Khrushchev would later write quite candidly how he wanted to build large ships: "I'll admit I felt a nagging desire to have some [aircraft carriers] in our own navy, but we couldn't afford to build them. They were simply beyond our means. Besides, with a strong submarine force, we felt able to sink the American carriers if it came to war. In other words, submarines represented an effective defensive capability as well as reliable means of launching a missile counterattack."[7]

Admiral Kuznetsov continued to demand the construction of a large, conventional surface fleet and argued against Khrushchev's position. Finally, Kuznetsov was fired; Khrushchev appointed Admiral S.G. Gorshkov as Deputy Commander in Chief of the Navy in mid-1955, and he officially succeeded Kuznetsov as CinC in January 1956.[8] Khrushchev directed Gorshkov to scrap the fleet's battleships and cruisers and to build instead a fleet of smaller, missile-armed ships and submarines that could defend the Soviet Union against Western naval-amphibious attacks. Of particular concern to the Soviet leadership were the American aircraft carriers, which could launch nuclear-armed strike aircraft against the Soviet Union.

---

4. A comprehensive analysis of this Soviet submarine program—larger than the German World War II effort—is described in Norman Polmar and Lt. Comdr. Jurrien Noot, RNethN, *Submarines of the Russian and Soviet Navies* (Annapolis, Md.: Naval Institute Press, 1991).

5. After World War II the U.S. and British navies investigated closed-cycle diesel plants based on the German Walter concept. The British built two experimental submarines with this propulsion system, HM/Submarines EXPLORER and EXCALIBUR. The only U.S. craft built with such a closed-cycle (non-nuclear) system was the midget submarine X-1.

6. See "The Navy" in Nikita Khrushchev, *Khrushchev Remembers—The Last Testament* (Boston: Little, Brown, 1974), pp. 19–34.

7. Ibid, p. 31.

8. Kuznetsov had a heart attack in May 1955 and was confined to bed.

During the Khrushchev era the development of anti-ship missiles launched by surface ships, aircraft, and submarines was emphasized. This is an SS-N-1 Scrubber on a Krupnyy-class destroyer, shadowing the U.S. aircraft carrier SARATOGA (CVA 60). Although of severely limited capability, the SS-N-1 was a first step in the Soviet development of effective anti-ship missiles. (U.S. Navy)

The Soviet Union led the world in the development of submarine-launched ballistic missiles. The early weapons were launched from the surface. After the hatches opened a lift would raise the missile—held by a collar—to the launch position above the sail. This is a Golf I with an SS-N-4 missile in the launch position; all Western submarine-launched ballistic missiles have featured underwater launch.

The Soviets described this period as a "revolution" in military affairs as nuclear weapons and other advanced technologies belatedly became a subject of discussion by the Soviet military leadership. Within the next few years Admiral Gorshkov disposed of the outdated battleships and older cruisers and initiated or accelerated the advanced weapon programs. Soviet shipyards produced swarms of the Komar and then Osa missile boats armed with the short-range SS-N-2 Styx missile, and several destroyers were completed with the 100–n.mile (185–km) SS-N-1 Scrubber/Strela anti-ship missile. The Kennel surface-to-surface missile was developed for use in larger ships, but it was unsuccessful and evolved into the AS-1 air-to-surface weapon.

The more capable SS-N-3 Shaddock missile was subsequently developed, originally for submarine use in the strategic, land-attack role (and possibly for surface launch in the land-attack configuration). The Shaddock went to sea in the anti-ship version in 1962 in the Kynda-class missile cruisers. Labelled a rocket cruiser (*raketnyy kreyser*) by the Soviets, the Kynda demonstrated the progress made by Admiral Gorshkov in "selling" new surface ships to the Soviet leadership. Preparations were also put forward for building a still larger Shaddock missile cruiser.

During this phase of fleet development the Soviet Navy put to sea a strategic strike force. At first diesel-electric submarines were armed with nuclear torpedoes to strike American coastal cities. More significant, and more practical, the Soviets used captured German technology to develop both guided (cruise) and ballistic missiles for launching from submarines against land targets. The SS-N-3 Shaddock cruise missile was surface-launched, with a land-attack range of more than 400 n.miles (735 km), carrying a nuclear warhead.

Initially Whiskey-class submarines were converted to fire the Shaddock—first the single-cylinder type, then the twin-cylinder type, and finally the "long-bin" configuration, which had four tubes fitted in an enlarged conning tower. Some Western sources reported that 72 of the Whiskey long-bin conversions were planned (only seven were actually completed as were seven of the earlier conversions). Subsequently, new construction Shaddock submarines were begun—the diesel Juliett (SSG) and nuclear Echo I/II (SSGN) classes.

Almost simultaneously the Soviets developed submarine-launched ballistic missiles. Tests were undertaken with Army-developed ballistic missiles of the Komet series. The first submarine-launched ballistic missile to become operational was the Navy version of the Army's Scud-A missile (given the Soviet designation R-11FM). A surface-launched weapon, it had a range of some 80 n.miles (150 km). Several Zulu-class diesel submarines were converted to carry two of these missiles, followed by the new-construction diesel Golf (SSB) and nuclear Hotel (SSBN) classes that carried the improved SS-N-4 missile with a range of 300 n.miles (550 km).

Thus, the Soviets simultaneously built both diesel and nuclear submarines for the cruise- and ballistic-missile roles. Further, the SSGN and SSBN designs were developed at the same time as the first Soviet nuclear submarine design, the torpedo-armed November class. This large and multiple-design nuclear submarine program demonstrated (1) early Soviet belief in the effectiveness of nuclear submarines, (2) the decision to put large numbers of missile-armed submarines to sea as rapidly as possible, (3) the desire to use all available submarine shipyard capacity, and (4) possibly the limited availability of nuclear reactor plants. The size of the Soviet nuclear submarine program can also be seen when by 1970 the Soviet Union surpassed the United States in numbers of these submarines.

Although the capabilities of the Sark ballistic missile in the Soviet SSB/SSBNs were severely limited, especially when compared to the U.S. Polaris that would follow shortly, the Soviet Navy had in fact deployed a submarine-launched ballistic missile before the United States. This strategic submarine effort of the Soviet Navy was stopped short of its apparent goals. The establishment of the Strategic Rocket Forces (SRF) as a separate service in December 1959 caused a cutback, or quite probably termination, of the SSB/SSBN programs. Only 8 Hotel SSBNs were completed along with 23 of the Golf SSBs, and plans for more advanced ballistic missile submarines were shelved.[9]

Under both tsars and commissars, Russia has demonstrated a major interest in submarines. Although the Soviets failed in this period to build the 1,200 submarines that U.S. intelligence estimated could be built by the late 1960s, a large number of undersea crafts were produced. The medium-range Whiskey-class diesel boats were mass-produced at four yards, and when the last was completed in 1957 a total of 236 units had been built; 90 had been launched in a single year, an ominous indication of Soviet industrial potential a decade after World War II had ended.

While the Whiskey program was under way the larger Zulu diesel attack boat and the Quebec coastal submarine were being built, albeit in smaller numbers. The Quebec's closed-cycle diesel plant was not successful, with several accidents occurring; the submarines were modified to operate as conventional diesel-electric craft and served into the 1970s. Counting some older boats of wartime design, this massive submarine effort provided a peak strength of some 475 submarines by 1958, after which there was a decline as the older craft were retired at a faster rate than new ones were constructed.

By the mid-1950s the construction of nuclear-propelled submarines had begun. But even before the first unit was completed (in 1958), development of the Alfa SSN was initiated in this period. This technically advanced undersea craft was begun by the late 1950s. The Alfa's revolutionary design includes an advanced reactor plant with lead-bismuth used as a heat-exchange medium (in lieu of pressurized water) and a titanium pressure hull (instead of steel); these resulted in the Alfa being the fastest and one of the deepest diving combat submarine yet built by any navy.

9. Components for an additional Golf SSB were transferred to Communist China and assembled there.

There are three possible explanations for the development of the Alfa. First, the Alfa may have been intended as a high-speed "interceptor," to dart out from base upon warning of an enemy warship approaching the coast. Second, the American press of the time estimated—incorrectly—that the U.S. submarine SKIPJACK (SSN 585), launched in 1958, would have a top speed of 45 knots. Third, the Alfa was the result of a Soviet multi-track approach to the development of nuclear propulsion. If this last theory is correct, one development track produced the pressurized-water reactor used in the Hotel, Echo, and November classes, while a separate program track led to the lead-bismuth reactor of the Alfa.[10]

Both the Stalin period and this initial Khrushchev period saw efforts to develop an ocean-going offensive fleet. While some would argue that "defense of the homeland" was the primary Soviet naval mission of these periods (see chapter 6), even if correct the highest mission priority is not always the priority for a navy's ship construction. Further, the submarines being produced with land-attack missiles were certainly offensive weapons.

PHASE III—REACTING TO U.S. THREATS

The late 1950s saw a concentration of Soviet naval efforts on the anti-carrier mission as the U.S. Navy deployed nuclear strike aircraft aboard carriers in the Mediterranean and western Pacific. With the loss of the strategic land-attack mission the cruise-missile submarines of the Whiskey, Juliett, and Echo I/II classes were shifted to the anti-ship role and rearmed with the SS-N-3a version of the Shaddock. Both the Juliett and Echo II classes continued in construction several years after the cancellation of the Golf (SSB) and Hotel (SSBN) programs. The Julietts and Echo IIs were provided with the Front Door/Front Piece radars for missile guidance and video data links to receive targeting data from long-range Bear-D reconnaissance/targeting aircraft.

Air-to-surface missiles were also being developed for the anti-carrier role; bombers were transferred from the Air Forces to the Navy, to be armed with these weapons for the anti-carrier role (see chapter 8). There may also have been some initial interest in this period in developing sea-launched ballistic missiles for the anti-ship role, and there was some discussion in the Soviet literature of employing land-based ICBMs in this role.

But Khrushchev's plan to reduce the size of the Soviet Union's conventional military forces in favor of a nuclear striking force (operated by the SRF) and to "fight" the West in the Third World fell apart when John F. Kennedy became president of the United States in January 1961. Kennedy, elected in a campaign that publicized a "missile gap" because of the Soviet Sputnik and missile test successes, began a buildup of U.S. strategic and conventional military forces. He accelerated the development of the Polaris submarine-launched ballistic missile and the Minuteman ICBM,

10. A similar two-track effort had been initiated in the United States, but the liquid-metal project was cancelled after technical problems developed although the project offered the promise of higher reactor power. This plant, using liquid sodium as the heat-exchange medium, was operational from 1957–1958 in the USS SEAWOLF (SSN 575); a land-based prototype was also built at West Milton, New York.

The first Soviet nuclear-propelled submarine design, the November, followed the USS NAUTILUS (SSN 571) by four years; but the Soviets soon outpaced the United States in nuclear submarine numbers and in several aspects of submarine technology. This November SSN suffered an engineering casualty in the eastern Atlantic in 1970 and, after her crew was removed, sank; she was the first loss of a Soviet nuclear-propelled submarine.

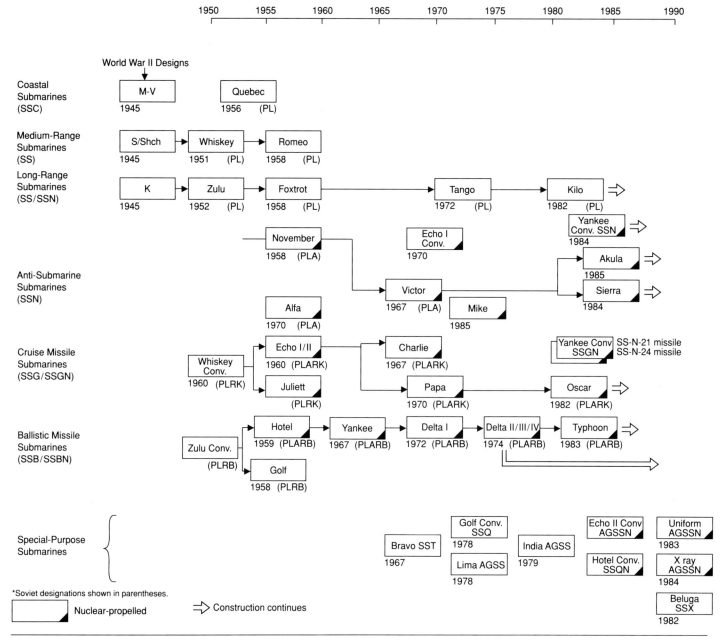

FIGURE 11-1. Submarine Development

giving them the highest possible priorities; increased the number of naval ships in commission; and built up forces to fight Soviet-sponsored insurgents in the Third World.

The U.S. strategic buildup was most rapid. This situation created consternation in the Kremlin and led to major reconsiderations in Soviet defense planning. The recently decided Soviet defense policies emphasizing ICBMs were found wanting, as was Soviet missile development, which was encountering technical problems. Several revisions in defense planning were initiated, and in a move to overcome shortfalls in the ICBM program, Khrushchev ordered medium-range missiles and nuclear-capable bombers to be secretly based in Cuba. The ensuing Cuban missile crisis of October 1962 demonstrated that (1) the United States was willing to use conventional military force against the Soviets in the Western Hemisphere, (2) the U.S. strategic offensive weapons could overwhelm those of the Soviet Union, and (3) the Soviet Navy was unable to support an overseas adventure.

Even while the Soviet missiles and bombers were still being withdrawn from Cuba, Deputy Foreign Minister V.V. Kuznetsov told an American official, "We will live up to this agreement, but we will never be caught like that again." Soviet military programs were accelerated, long-range plans were revised, and in March 1963 there was a top-level realignment of the country's economic management—just three months after a long-planned reorganization had occurred. A new Supreme Economic Council was set up, headed by Dmitri Ustinov, long-time head of armament production. This appointment gave military planning clear priority in the national economy after Khrushchev's earlier attempts at a more balanced approach. Within the defense establishment, in the aftermath of Cuba a new chief of the Soviet General Staff was named in early 1963, and there were indications that Khrushchev, age 71, might soon step down. (He was forced to do so in October 1964.)

The events of 1961–1963 had considerable effect on the Soviet Navy. The significance of the Navy within the armed forces was enhanced, for naval forces could help to counter the U.S. Navy's Polaris submarines, could help to redress the "missile gap" that had in fact existed in favor of the United States, and might make future incursions into the Third World more successful.

With respect to shipbuilding programs, the construction of Kynda-class missile cruisers was halted after only four units were built; plans for a larger Shaddock-armed ship for the anti-carrier role were abandoned. The anti-carrier effort would be left mainly to aircraft and submarines armed with cruise missiles. The Kyndas were replaced on the building ways at the Zhdanov shipyard in Leningrad by the interim Kresta I class, which has one-fourth of the Kynda's missile load; however, the Kresta I has improved anti-aircraft and helicopter capabilities. After only four of these ships were built the matured Kresta II design appeared. The Kresta II is an anti-submarine ship, with long-range ASW missiles (SS-N-14) replacing the Shaddock anti-ship missiles.

At the same time as the Kresta program, the Nikolayev south yard in the Black Sea area was producing the MOSKVA-class hermaphrodite missile cruiser–ASW helicopter carriers. These ships, the first true aviation ships to be built in the Soviet Union, were intended to counter the U.S. Polaris submarines in regional seas adjacent to the Soviet Union. The MOSKVA was completed in 1967 and her sister ship LENINGRAD was finished the following year. They were incapable of coping with the Polaris submarines, for by that time the U.S. Navy had 41 strategic missile submarines, at least half of which were always at sea. Also, the Polaris A-3 missile, which became operational in 1964, had a range of 2,500 n.miles (4,600 km), reducing the potential effectiveness of the MOSKVA with her short-range ASW helicopters. At the time the MOSKVA program halted, the Navy was planning a larger, more capable aircraft carrier.

The Kresta II and contemporary Kara ASW ships could effectively serve as command ships for ASW forces seeking to protect Soviet submarines from Western anti-submarine forces, especially U.S. nuclear attack submarines. The pro-submarine mission seems to have been the rationale for several major Soviet programs of this period. It should be noted that although specialized anti-ship weapons such as the SS-N-2 Styx and SS-N-3 Shaddock were not fitted in these ships, the SA-N-1 and later SA-N-3 surface-to-air systems, however, did have an anti-ship capability.

And, the Soviets continued to produce large numbers of submarines. The production of earlier types—nuclear and diesel—continued. Three major classes of nuclear submarines were begun in the early 1960s, the second generation of such craft. The Echo I/II cruise-missile submarines, which were required to launch their Shaddock missiles from the surface, were followed into service by the more-advanced Charlie-class SSGN. The initial Charlie I is armed with eight short-range (30-n.mile/55-km) SS-N-7 cruise missiles, but these can be fired while the submarine remains completely submerged; the subsequent Charlie II has the longer-range (60-n.mile/110-km) SS-N-9 missiles. This class, however, has not been completely successful.

The contemporary Victor torpedo-attack submarine (SSN) was a superior craft, believed to have been developed specifically for the anti-submarine role, as have essentially all U.S. Navy SSNs. With a maximum speed of some 33 knots, the Victor was the world's fastest operational submarine when it entered service in 1968. The improved (albeit slower) Victor II/III classes followed.

The third new submarine type of the period was the Yankee strategic missile submarine. As noted above, Soviet SSBN devel-

opment slowed, or was possibly halted completely with the defense decisions of 1959, with the last of the Golf/Hotel submarines being completed in 1962. Following the initiation of the U.S. strategic buildup, the Cuban missile fiasco, and problems in Soviet ICBM development, the Soviet SSBN program was given new life. The immediate result was a new submarine design closely resembling the U.S. Polaris submarines, to which NATO assigned the confusing code name Yankee. Armed with 16 missiles in two rows of internal tubes aft of the sail structure, the design of the Yankee shows evidence of having been hastily completed and ordered into construction with the highest priorities. Production was undertaken at two yards, Severodvinsk in the Arctic followed by Komsomol'sk in the Far East.

The first Yankee SSBN was completed in 1967, the year that the 41st and last U.S. Polaris/Poseidon submarine was completed. Yankee production reached a peak of ten units in 1970, after which it slowed as the yards prepared for the follow-up on the Delta SSBN. The later undersea craft, which began to enter service in 1972, was the world's largest submarine built up to that time.

More significant than the size, the Delta SSBN carried a very long-range missile, initially the SS-N-8 with a range of more than 4,000 n.miles (7,360 km). This meant that Delta submarines could remain in Soviet coastal waters of the Barents Sea and Sea of Okhotsk while targeting virtually the entire United States. This capability would invalidate Western ASW concepts that called for intercepting Soviet SSBNs (as well as attack submarines) as they transited from base or patrol areas to missile-launching positions.

Additional torpedo-attack and cruise-missile submarine classes were begun during the early 1960s, continuing the Soviet policy of not only building large numbers of submarines, but also developing multiple classes. The Papa of this period is a one-of-a-kind cruise-missile submarine, larger and faster than the Charlie SSGN, like the contemporary Alfa SSN incorporating technically advanced materials and propulsion plant. (The planned missile for the Papa was not successful.)

Diesel submarine construction was also continued in Soviet yards. The U.S. Navy had abandoned the construction of diesel combat submarines in the late 1950s. The Soviets apparently believed that diesel submarines could undertake some missions as effectively, or more so, as nuclear submarines. It has also been suggested that Soviet industry simply could not produce the number of reactor plants needed for an all-nuclear undersea force.

The long-range Foxtrot diesel submarines have been followed by the further improved Tango-class SS (operational in 1972); construction of this class has now been followed by the Kilo class, the first of which entered service in 1982. Also built in this period were the four Bravo-class submarines, which are specialized target-training craft (SST). These serve both as targets for ASW forces and to train submariners, while having some combat capability. (The Soviets continued to build specialized support and research submarines in significant numbers, with two of the most unusual being the pair of India-class rescue and salvage submarines completed in 1979–1980, which carry rescue/salvage submersibles and can support saturation diving operations.)

The Soviet Navy looked at several designs for putting naval aviation to sea during the Khrushchev-Gorshkov period. This is a model of a pre-MOSKVA concept showing a lengthened Kresta I-class cruiser with a large flight deck aft (with hangar below). This model was on display at the Central Naval Museum in Leningrad.

The LENINGRAD (left) and her sister ship MOSKVA were examples of highly innovative Soviet warship design. Although not successful in their intended anti-SSBN role, they did begin the familiarization of the Soviet Navy with operating aircraft at sea. (French Navy)

Thus, the Soviet Navy continued to emphasize submarine construction. Their production rate slowed in the late 1950s as the nuclear programs were instituted, and again in the late 1960s as the shipyards geared up to produce the second-generation nuclear submarines. Only seven submarines were completed in 1971: five Yankee SSBNs, one Charlie SSGN, and one Victor SSN. This was the smallest number of submarines built in any year since 1945. (The previous year—in 1970—an estimated 18 submarines were completed, all but one of which were nuclear powered.)

During this third phase of postwar Soviet naval development, the Naval Infantry (marines) was reactivated in the Soviet Navy (see chapter 9). Construction was begun of specialized ships to carry and land these troops—the Polnocny LSMs at the shipyard by that name in Gdansk, Poland, and the Alligator LST at Kaliningrad in the Soviet Union.

Finally, sustained deployments were beginning in the Mediterranean Sea and the Indian Ocean, and the periodic visits of warships to the Gulf of Mexico–Caribbean area and to African ports created new requirements for at-sea replenishment ships. Previously, almost all fuel and supplies transferred to Soviet warships on the high seas came from merchant ships; however, starting with the fuel-munitions ship BORIS CHILIKIN (completed in 1971) the Soviets have increasingly employed specialized underway replenishment (UNREP) ships, an often overlooked but vital component of fleet development. The six CHILIKIN-class ships were followed by the single large BEREZINA, comparable in some respects to the U.S. Navy's AOE/AOR ships.

PHASE IV—THE MODERN SOVIET FLEET

In 1970, after observing a major Soviet military exercise, Party Chairman L.I. Brezhnev declared, "No question of any importance in the world can be solved without our participation, without taking into account our economic and military might." Whereas Stalin had avoided involvement in the Third World, and Khrushchev's "adventurism" had too often failed, Brezhnev seemed determined that the Soviet Union would have an active role in the Third World. The Soviet Union supported emerging and established socialist states and carried out other Soviet goals in the Third World, including efforts to counter Western influence and activity.

Algeria, Angola, Cuba, Egypt, El Salvador, Ethiopia, Iraq, North Korea, Libya, Nicaragua, Somalia, Syria, Vietnam, and both North and South Yemen all became recipients of Soviet attention in the 1970s and 1980s. In some cases Soviet combat troops have been present (as in Cuba and, until 1972, in Egypt); more often, surrogate troops (especially Cubans but often with East German, Vietnamese, or Soviet advisors), have been used, and Soviet merchant ships carrying weapons and supplies are always in evidence.

Increasingly, Soviet naval ships have also been present. Admiral Gorshkov, when he was CinC of the Navy, had strongly supported this role (see chapter 7). By 1970, when Brezhnev made the statement cited above, decisions had already been made to construct still another generation of Soviet warships—including the

first aircraft carriers to be built by the Soviet regime and the first nuclear-propelled surface warships.

By late 1971 the U.S. reconnaissance satellites overflying the Soviet Union brought back evidence of an aircraft carrier under construction at the Nikolayev south yard, where the MOSKVA and her sister ship LENINGRAD were constructed. The following December the ship was launched, revealing the largest warship yet built in the Soviet Union. Named KIEV, the 43,000-ton ship is a true aircraft carrier, with an angled flight deck and a large starboard island structure. But there the similarity to Western aircraft carriers ends.

The KIEV is fitted with heavy batteries of anti-aircraft, anti-submarine, and anti-surface weapons, plus Gatling-type, rapid-fire guns for close-in defense against cruise missiles. The anti-ship weapons are the SS-N-12, an improved version of the Shaddock with a range of some 300 n.miles (550 km).[11] Also, the KIEV lacks the catapults and arresting wires of Western carriers that permit the operation of conventional aircraft. Instead, the KIEV carries an air group of some 35 Yak-38 Forger VSTOL aircraft and Ka-25 Hormone/Ka-27 Helix helicopters. The Forger, a transonic fighter-attack aircraft, was the second VSTOL combat aircraft to go to sea, the first having been the Anglo-American Harrier.

The decision to build the KIEV and her sister carriers seems to have been taken at the politburo level about 1965. The decision would have been made at the highest level of government because of the allocations of industrial facilities, materials, and people needed for those ships. A major factor in these decisions was the mission for the carriers. The fact that the KIEV is limited to a relatively small number of aircraft, of inferior types when compared to U.S. carrier aircraft, strongly indicates that the KIEV and her sister ships were not intended to counter Western carriers.

Rather, two other roles appear probable: First, the Soviet "pro-submarine" mission of supporting and protecting Soviet submarines, especially SSBNs, has been cited by Western analysts as an obvious rationale for the ship. Looked at in isolation, this thesis has some validity. However, the subsequent construction of larger aircraft carriers, the anti-ship weapons mounted in the KIEV, and the lack of a fixed-wing ASW aircraft for the KIEV reduce the credibility of the pro-submarine role.

A second and more likely rationale for the KIEV-class carriers is the increasing Soviet activity in the Third World. By the late 1960s the U.S. Department of Defense had announced the decision to reduce the American carrier force to 12 ships, and the Royal Navy as well as other NATO fleets were giving up their conventional aircraft carriers. At the same time, the number of airfields available to the United States in the Third World was declining. As a result, one or more KIEV-type ships in the right place at the right time could have considerable influence in crisis or combat situations.

Shortly after the lines of the KIEV became visible in satellite

---

11. The KIEV was the first aircraft carrier of any nation to be provided with significant anti-ship weapons since the U.S. carriers LEXINGTON (CV 2) and SARATOGA (CV 3) beached their 8-inch (203-mm) guns in 1940–1941.

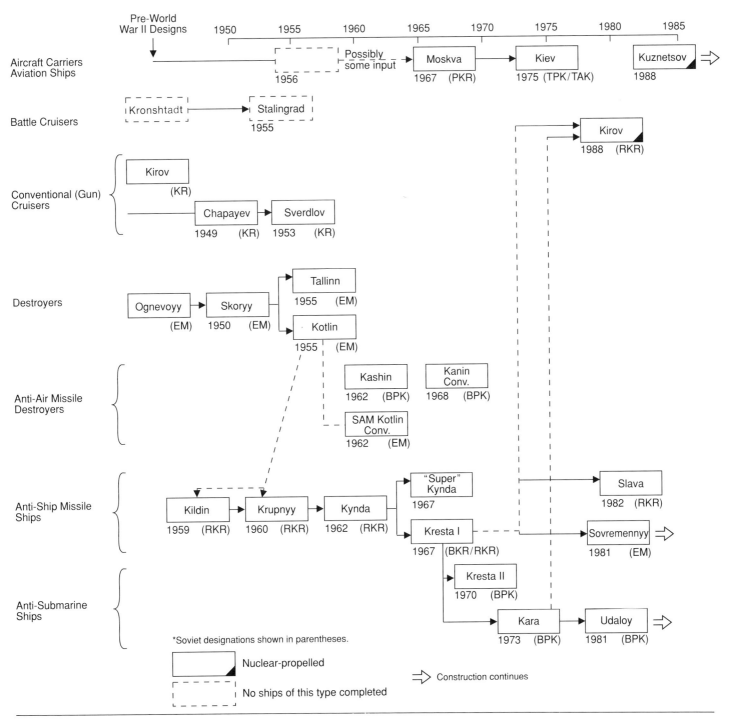

FIGURE 11-2. **Major Warship Development**

photography, there were indications that another large warship was being built at the Baltic shipyard in Leningrad. Although the Baltic yard had not constructed warships since the SVERDLOV program, the yard was building the nuclear-propelled icebreakers of the ARKTIKA class. The new Baltic ship was the KIROV, a nuclear-powered missile cruiser. Displacing 28,000 tons, the KIROV is the largest warship except for aircraft carriers to be built by any nation since World War II. Preliminary design studies of a nuclear-propelled battle cruiser may have been undertaken as early as 1963 with the first ship laid down in 1973.

Here again, the KIROV demonstrates a highly innovative design. The ship has vertical-launch anti-aircraft (SA-N-6) and anti-ship (SS-N-19) missiles, the latter giving the KIROV, like KIEV-class carriers, a stand-off strike weapon. In addition, the KIROV carries anti-submarine and close-in defense weapons, as well as several helicopters.

The role of the KIROV has also perplexed Western naval analysts. Most suggest that the KIROV class is intended to serve in a surface action group—that is, with cruisers and destroyers—or as a

principal carrier escort ship. Also, the KIROV and other ships of the class could be effectively employed as the core of surface action groups operating in Third World areas where the ability of the United States to project tactical air power from carriers or land bases is limited.

The VSTOL carrier KIEV has been followed from the Nikolayev south shipyard by three sister ships. Even as the fourth unit was being built, the graving dock where construction took place was being lengthened and components were being assembled in the yard for a larger aircraft carrier. The new ship was laid down shortly after the fourth KIEV was launched in 1982. Although initially estimated by Western intelligence to be nuclear propelled, even before the ship began trials it was obvious that she had conventional oil-fired boilers turning her steam turbines.

Named ADMIRAL KUZNETSOV (ex-TBILISI), this carrier is now the largest naval ship to be built in the Soviet Union; she was launched in December 1985, almost simultaneously with Admiral Gorshkov's retirement after his unprecedented three decades as CinC of a major fleet. In announcing the new carrier's launching,

U.S. officials revealed that a second ship of the class had been started. Further, several types of high-performance, land-based aircraft were observed at the Saki naval airfield in the Crimea being evaluated for carrier use (see chapters 8 and 27). A third, larger aircraft carrier, the UL'YANOVSK (for Lenin's birthplace), is being built at Nikolayev; she appears to have nuclear propulsion and to displace some 10,000 tons more than the KUZNETSOV class.

Simultaneous with these capital ships, the Soviets initiated three advanced cruiser-destroyer classes: the anti-ship missile cruiser SLAVA; the anti-ship missile destroyer SOVREMENNYY; and the anti-submarine destroyer UDALOY. With four yards engaged in building these three cruiser-destroyer classes and the KIROV, this is the largest surface combatant effort undertaken in the Soviet Union since the Stalin era.

In this fourth phase of postwar fleet development the Soviet Navy continued an intensive submarine construction program. In the 1980s seven different combat submarine designs entered Soviet service:

SSBN	Typhoon
SSBN	Delta IV
SSGN	Oscar I/II
SSN	Mike
SSN	Akula
SSN	Sierra
SS	Kilo

Also, two special research submarines were completed, and Yankee-class SSBNs were removed from the strategic-missile role with several converted to torpedo-attack (SSN) and cruise-missile (SSGN) submarines.

The Typhoon was the largest undersea craft yet built by any nation (some 25,000 tons submerged displacement[12]) and also showed a highly innovative design. Party Chairman Brezhnev revealed to President Ford at their meeting in Vladivostok November 1974 that the Soviet Union was building a giant strategic missile-submarine, the *Tyfun*. Brezhnev claimed the new SSBN was a response to the U.S. Trident program. The Soviets continued to build the Delta SSBNs; the Delta IV class was still larger than its predecessor and carried a new missile.

Similarly, the Oscar SSGN, displacing about 16,000 tons submerged, is more than twice the size of the U.S. LOS ANGELES (SSN 688)-class attack submarines. The Oscar presents a new level of threat to Western naval planners, being armed with 24 SS-N-19 anti-ship missiles, or three times the number of missiles carried by the earlier Echo II and Charlie SSGN classes. Further, the SS-N-19 combines the best features of the Echo II missiles (long range) and the Charlie missiles (underwater launch).

12. Western intelligence sources list the submerged displacement of the Typhoon SSBN as approximately 25,000 metric tons. However, Western and Soviet engineers have provided the author with calculations indicating a surface displacement of about 30,000 tons and submerged displacement of up to 40,000 tons!

In addition to innovative ships, the Soviets have produced the advanced weapon systems for those ships. Here sailors work on one of the forward 30-mm Gatling guns on the cruiser SLAVA. At left are RBU-6000 ASW rocket launchers, at top and bottom SS-N-12 missile launchers. (U.S. Navy, Lt. Comdr. Lyle Gordon)

The simultaneous development of the Mike, Sierra, and Akula SSN designs once more indicates the depth of Soviet submarine development capabilities. During the late 1980s Soviet yards launched four or five nuclear and four diesel submarines per year (with three of the latter intended for foreign transfer).

As this edition went to press, diesel-attack submarines of the Kilo diesel-attack submarine class were being produced at three shipyards. This indicates that a large number of these craft will probably be built for both Soviet and foreign use. Among the several submarine enigmas from a Western viewpoint is the Beluga, which may be the harbinger of a Soviet Air Independent Propulsion (AIP) submarine plant.

A final submarine type of particular interest in this period is the conversion of three Golf diesel ballistic-missile submarines and at least one Hotel nuclear submarine to special communications configurations (SSQ/SSQN). These submarines appear to be intended to serve as emergency command ships or communications relay ships for fleet or area commanders.

In this fourth phase of Soviet fleet development the building of amphibious and auxiliary ships has slowed considerably. Construction of over-the-beach LST and LSM classes continued into the 1970s, and in 1978 the first of three IVAN ROGOV-class ships was completed. The ROGOV is a highly capable amphibious ship, the first Soviet unit with a docking well for carrying air cushion vehicles and the first Soviet "amphib" with a helicopter landing area and hangar. Coupled with the continued Soviet merchant ship construction, these "amphibs" provide a steady increase in the ability of the

The Oscar II is the world's largest "attack submarine," being armed with 533-mm and 650-mm torpedoes as well as 24 long-range SS-N-19 anti-ship missiles. Note the lower position of her forward limber (flood) holes caused by the positioning of the six missile hatches on each side; a few anechoic tiles are missing from the sail and after hull reflecting adhesion problems.

Soviet Union to move troops and equipment by sea and to mount amphibious assaults. A new LST class has been reported under construction in Poland, but only three of the ROGOV-class ships were built.

The construction of specialized naval replenishment ships ceased after the one BEREZINA. A few additional tankers have been taken into the Navy from the merchant shipbuilding program, but the Soviet Navy still lacks effective Underway Replenishment (UNREP) ships on the scale of the U.S. Navy or even the Royal Navy. The compensating factor are the very large, flexible, and state-controlled Soviet merchant and fishing fleets.

One other naval program is significant in this period, the extensive Soviet work in advanced technology hull forms. The Soviet Union has the world's largest fleet of civilian and military hydrofoils and Air Cushion Vehicles (ACV). The latter include a major program of ACV landing craft with the production of large numbers of several designs. These craft can transport tanks, other combat vehicles, and troops at high speeds for ranges of several hundred miles, a short-range assault capability that is without equal among other amphibious forces.

A related development has been Soviet work with Wing-In-Ground (WIG) effect vehicles, called an *ekranoplan* in Russian. These craft resemble flying boats that travel over the water in the ground effect created by their own wings and hulls. A large WIG observed in the Caspian Sea in the 1970s was estimated to be an *ekranoplan*. That craft, with turbojet engines mounted in the wing roots, was estimated to weigh several hundred tons and was dubbed the "Caspian Sea monster." Its reported speed was 300 knots at a cruise altitude of 20–25 feet (6–8 m).

Subsequently, an amphibious assault WIG, known as Orlan by Western intelligence, entered limited series production and at least a prototype of a missile-attack vehicle, the Utka, has been developed (see chapter 22).

PHASE V—FLEET FOR THE 21ST CENTURY

The future of Soviet fleet development, like other aspects of the Soviet defense establishment, is not clear. In the book *The Navy: Its Role, Prospects for Development, and Employment*, Soviet Navy spokesmen have put forth an ambitious program for the Soviet Navy (see chapter 1). Regardless of whether or not General Secretary Gorbachev accepts the program outlined in *The Navy*, Soviet concern over the long-term technological competition with the West makes it unlikely that budgetary cuts will be made in naval research and development. According to a U.S. Navy evaluation:

A major goal of Gorbachev's economic reform policies is to use larger investments in RDT&E [Research, Development, Test & Evaluation] to develop technology more quickly and efficiently and improve the production base that could pay significant economic and military dividends by the turn of the century. This would be made easier by the large-scale modernization of Soviet defense industries in the 1970s, which has already put in place most of the equipment needed to produce weapon systems scheduled for deployment through the early 1990s.[13]

Taking a broader view, a U.S. Department of Defense appraisal states:

Economic reform and industrial modernization are unlikely to affect military production in the near term. Military industry is well situated through huge previous investments to produce the current generation of weapon systems. During the 12th Five-Year Plan (1986–1990), military industry has been assured continued growth. With the high priority accorded the industrial modernization program, there could be increased competition between the military and civil sectors for resources and materials. To date, however, there is no indication that the industrial modernization program has been at the expense of the military industry's growth.[14]

13. Rear Adm. Thomas A. Brooks, USN, testimony before the Armed Services Committee, House of Representatives, 22 February 1989.
14. Secretary of Defense Frank C. Carlucci, *Soviet Military Power, 1988* (Washington, D.C.: Government Printing Office, 1988), pp. 34–35.

When this edition of *Guide to the Soviet Navy* went to press there was little evidence of a cutback in naval ship construction. Indeed, the only specific example that could be cited was cancellation of the fifth KIROV-class battle cruiser. To be sure, there were major reductions being made in naval force levels with the accelerated retirement of SVERDLOV-class cruisers and older destroyers and submarines (nuclear as well as conventional). But three areas of defense-related investment/production continued at a steady level into the 1990s—space systems, strategic missiles, and naval forces.

INSTITUTIONAL FACTORS[15]

Friedrich Engels, who with Karl Marx wrote the *Communist Manifesto* (1847), the blueprint for the later Bolshevik movement in Russia, addressed the relationship of warships to the countries that produce them: "A modern warship is not merely a product of major industry, but at the same time is a sample of it."[16] The modern warships and other systems of the Soviet Navy are the product of numerous institutional factors of the Soviet Union. These include:

National Leadership. Traditionally the leadership of the Soviet Union has been very stable by Western standards. In the postwar period major military and industrial decisions have been vested mainly in the First Secretary (later General Secretary) of the Communist Party and the politburo. In 1989 Mikhail Gorbachev established the position of Executive President, superseding the senior state and party posts.

During the long period of Stalin's leadership (1921–1953) there were innumerable occasions when he personally made design and procurement decisions. Admiral Kuznetsov wrote, "Without Stalin no one ventured to decide the large questions concerning the navy."[17] British historian Albert Seaton analyzed Stalin's decision making:

Soviet writers are agreed that Stalin took a personal and directing role in the development of army equipment. Indeed, according to [Marshal G.K.] Zhukov, no single pattern of armament could be adopted or discarded without Stalin's approval.[18]

For the subsequent Khrushchev period (1955–1964) we have the late Party chairman's own words to describe his decision making. After learning that the United States was placing ICBMs in underground silos, he took action:

I summoned the people responsible and said, "Now look what's happened! The Americans have begun to dig the ballistic missile shafts which I proposed a long time ago. Let's get started on this program right away."[19]

Khrushchev continued, describing how he personally inquired about digging techniques and equipment, and how he was "proud of my role in originating the idea and later seeing [that] the conversion [to underground ICBM silos] was begun."

Decision making by senior Soviets with respect to specific weapons continued in the Brezhnev era. It acquired a different aspect after 1965 when Dmitri Ustinov was made a candidate member of the politburo. His background in armament development and then

15. This section is in part adapted from the author's report "Factors That Have Influenced the Soviet Navy—Potential Lessons for Aegis Shipbuilding" (30 April 1981), prepared for the U.S. Navy's Aegis shipbuilding project manager. Also see Arthur J. Alexander, *Decision-Making in Soviet Weapons Procurement* (London: International Institute for Strategic Studies, 1978; Adelphi Papers no. 147 and 148); Alexander Boyd, *The Soviet Air Force* (London: Macdonald and Jane's, 1977); and Colonel Oleg Penkovskiy, *The Penkovskiy Papers* (New York: Doubleday, 1965).
16. F. Engels, *Izbrannyye Voyennyye Proizvedeniye* [Selected Military Works] (Moscow: Voyenizdat, 1957), p. 17.
17. Adm. Kuznetsov, "On the Eve," *Oktyabr'* (no. 9, 1965), pp. 158–189; also see (no. 8, 1965), pp. 161–202 and (no. 11, 1965), pp. 134–137.
18. Albert Seaton, *Stalin as Military Commander* (New York: Praeger, 1976), pp. 87–89.
19. Khrushchev, p. 49.

his becoming a full politburo member and Minister of Defense in 1976 implied that defense policy and hardware could be discussed more freely in the politburo, without the need to call in outside experts.

Decision making at the politburo level coupled with the stability of the leadership of the Soviet Union tend to ensure that policy and hardware decisions by national leaders will be carried out. In the post-Khrushchev period there appears to have been less "interference" with naval programs from a technical viewpoint. This was probably due in large part to the relationship of Brezhnev, the late Prime Minister Kosygin, and politburo member Romanov with the Navy's leadership. Still, the increasing forward operations of the Navy and the related political implications probably make naval activities a periodic subject of politburo discussions.

The stability of Soviet leadership—military as well as political—has been impressive by Western standards. Brezhnev served as head of the Party from 1964 until his death in 1982, Ustinov as Minister of Defense from 1976 to 1984, and Marshal of the Soviet Union N.V. Ogarkov as Chief of the General Staff from 1977 to 1984. Admiral Gorshkov was CinC of the Navy from 1956 to 1985. The Navy's chief engineer—in charge of shipbuilding and armaments—was Engineer-Admiral P.G. Kotov from 1966 (before which he was the deputy) until the late 1980s.

This degree of longevity suggests that projects that win top-level approval will be pursued. But also, those projects that are rejected by the leadership must wait long periods before a change in administration will provide another opportunity.

Long-Range Planning. The Soviet Union has longer range planning in the defense and industrial sectors than Western nations. The entire Soviet economy is based on long-term, integrated planning. Whereas the United States has a five-year defense plan that is "extended" annually to add the "next" year, the Soviet five-year plan is for a finite period. Thus, while American leaders can repeatedly postpone difficult decisions or projects until the "later" years of the five-year program, the Soviet scheme provides for a specific period and end-of-plan accounting process.

In addition, the Soviet planning cycle is tied in with all aspects of society, including the military services and other defense agencies. Hence, a long-range naval construction effort would be linked to steel production, transportation, coal matters, commercial shipbuilding, and so on.

Employment Policies. Full employment is a basic goal of the Soviet state. The Soviet constitution guarantees the right to work. Thus, in the eyes of the Soviet leadership, the admission of unemployment would indicate the failure of this guarantee. Accordingly, once a factory or product line is established it is difficult to close it down without major political implications. This may, in part, explain the continued production of outdated and even obsolete hardware. The Tupolev-designed Bear aircraft is an example of the very long Soviet production runs, the plane having been in production, albeit with updates, since the mid-1950s— longer than any other combat aircraft in history.

There is also significant worker stability because Soviet citizens are generally not permitted to change jobs in critical industries without authorization, and factories and bases in remote areas are able to pay higher wages than those in more desirable regions.

Copying Technology. The Soviets have traditionally copied Western technology—by whatever means available. This began during the reign of Tsar Peter I and continues today. There are several classic examples of the Soviets doing this, from allies and enemies alike.

At the end of World War II the Soviets carted off much of Eastern Europe's surviving industrial facilities as well as German technology, scientists, and technicians. In the same manner, American equipment was copied, including radars on U.S. ships transferred to the Soviet Navy and the U.S. B-29 heavy bombers that, after bombing raids against Japan, landed in Siberia and were interned.

The Soviets continue to seek Western technology by overt and covert means. The covert activities by the KGB and GRU seek information on virtually all Western military and industrial activities. Both agencies have established regular "legal" collection networks through various attachés in Western countries and through extensive spy networks that attempt to penetrate Western military services, industry, and even government bureaus. The results of these efforts regularly appear in Soviet military systems. The Soviets are thus able to take advantage of Western developments while saving Soviet industrial and research resources that would have otherwise been invested in those areas.

Overt collection methods include the outright purchase of material and the vast amounts of information on technology published in the Western press and professional journals. In the naval-maritime area, the Soviets have purchased numerous merchant and fishing ships from the West as well as marine engines, computers, and electronics. Both the GRU and the KGB use traditional as well as high-tech means to garner Western secrets.

Production Rates. The Soviets have always stressed quantities of military equipment. Despite the ravages of war from 1941 to 1945, by the end of the conflict some 40,000 aircraft per year were being produced in the Soviet Union. About 80 percent of those were single-engine fighter and ground-attack aircraft, mostly of wooden construction. It was still a major achievement when one considers the manpower problems, shortages of materials, the severe weather conditions, and the fact that most of the plants producing aircraft and engines had been removed from European Russia and reestablished in the Urals early in the war.

After the war there were significant shifts in the types and numbers of aircraft produced, but the level of effort remained high. For example, in 1950 the Soviet aircraft industry produced about 4,000 MiG-15 turbojet fighters, 1,000 turbojet bombers, and several hundred Tu-4 Bull (B-29) four-engine piston bombers, plus a number of other aircraft. While these totalled significantly less than the number of aircraft produced five years earlier, the effort was probably similar in terms of man-hours and resources required.

This relatively high production rate continues for most types of weapons. For example, during the 1980s the Soviet Union produced more of the following types of weapons than combined U.S. and European NATO production: tanks, other armored vehicles, artillery of all types (100-mm or greater), fighter and attack aircraft, and military helicopters.

The United States and its NATO allies (combined) did produce more major surface warships than has the USSR (frigates and larger), but in the 1980s the Soviets outproduced the West in general purpose submarines (SSN/SSGN/SS/SSG) as well as ballistic missile submarines (SSBN/SSB).

The submarine building rate is particularly significant. In 1955 Soviet shipyards launched an estimated 81 submarines at the peak of the Stalin production effort; in 1989 Soviet yards launched only nine submarines, five of them nuclear-propelled. Of the 1955 launchings, 62 were of the Whiskey class with a 1,050-ton standard displacement. These were diesel-electric craft, armed only with torpedoes. The 1989 submarines included a Typhoon SSBN with a standard displacement of perhaps 18,500 tons, the rough equivalent of 17½ Whiskey-class submarines, and a Delta IV SSBN of about 10,800 tons standard displacement, equal in tonnage to more than ten Whiskeys. This displacement ratio provides a very rough approximation of the resources involved. Also, beyond being larger, the newer submarines have mostly nuclear propulsion, more complex electronics, and more advanced weapons than the earlier submarines, demonstrating the continuation of great effort in this category of industrial endeavor.

Another consideration in Soviet shipbuilding through the 1980s was the extensive use of Polish and, to a lesser extent, other Eastern European shipyards to provide amphibious, auxiliary, and merchant ships. This provided the Soviet shipbuilding industry with a high degree of flexibility while allowing them to concentrate to the degree desired on warship programs.

Table 11-2 shows the estimated Soviet and U.S. production of sea-launched ballistic (SLBM) and cruise (SLCM) missiles for the past few years.

TABLE 11-2. NAVAL MISSILE PRODUCTION

	1987		1988		1989	
	USSR	US	USSR	US	USSR	US
SLBM	100	0	100	0	100	21
SLCM > 600 km	200	170	200	260	200	420
SLCM < 600 km	1,100	570	1,100	380	1,100	180

Quantity versus Quality. The Soviet Union has historically been a land of quantity versus quality. Numbers are important and, indeed, are the means by which much of the Soviet military-industrial complex is graded. A given factory or industry is generally rated on the basis of numbers of units produced; quality is a secondary consideration. The grades thus given become the basis for promotions, pay increases, bonuses, and special privileges.

This numbers mentality results in the Soviet Union having more equipment of certain types than can be used by the active military establishment. This provides equipment for the reserves as well as ready equipment to replace combat losses and for foreign transfer. As an example, after the 1973 war in the Middle East the Soviet Union was able to provide rapidly several thousand tanks to Egypt and Syria to replace their losses, and was able to do the same for Iraq in the early 1980s to replace losses in the Iraq-Iran conflict.

This approach to producing large numbers of units has also led to the practice of replacing rather than repairing damaged equipment and platforms at the unit or organizational level. This, in turn, reduces the maintenance requirements in Soviet units, always a problem with the short-term draftees that compose the vast majority of the Soviet armed forces. At the same time, this emphasis on the production of "things" that can be easily counted, such as tanks and aircraft, sometimes leads to component short-falls, that is, "things" that cannot be as easily counted and are thus shorted in favor of producing more of what can be counted against "norms" and quotas.

During the 1980s, however, there was increasing evidence that the quality of certain Soviet weapon systems was clearly approaching that of the West or, at the least, being able to counter Western weapons. For example, in the 1980s Soviet tank armor (including reactive) was able to defeat probably *all* Western anti-tank missiles. Similarly, the quieting of the Akula-class SSN approached the noise levels of contemporary U.S. nuclear submarines with the prediction put forth by some analysts that the next-generation Soviet SSN could equal or surpass the quieting of the USS SEAWOLF (SSN 21), scheduled to enter service in the mid-1990s.

Component Similarity. Soviet design agencies and industry seek to provide similar components for successive generations of systems and platforms. Components appear to change only for specific reasons, such as product improvement or availability because of production-line changes. Accordingly, some components and systems have a long service life over successive classes of platforms.

There are obvious advantages to this scheme in terms of production costs, maintenance, spares, training, and personnel assignment. However, when there are limited production facilities or other problems with widely used components, there are bottlenecks. This appears to be the current situation with respect to integrated circuits; too many Soviet military (and possibly civil) systems are in need of advanced circuitry and too few production facilities are available.

Component Availability. Related to the issue of component similarity is the limited selection of components available, at least by Western standards. A design bureau cannot simply look through catalogues or phone up component producers to obtain minor but critical components for new systems. The Soviet industrial system limits the numbers and variety of equipment produced; relatively few components or systems are developed "on speculation"—that is, developed because they may be used or even needed.

As a result, new systems tend to make use of existing components, or for prototype systems the laboratory or factory may produce the components on an individual basis. While this is highly inefficient by Western standards, it may be the only way in which a Soviet producer can obtain a key component within required time constraints.

Innovation. The Soviet military-industrial environment simultaneously encourages and retards innovation. It encourages innovation because the various design bureaus, with one or more specializing in the development of different weapons and platforms, are continually producing new designs. These may or may not be put into production, but that is irrelevant to the purpose of these bureaus.

For all of the reasons cited above, however, innovation in the weapons and platforms being produced is difficult, and hence it is avoided when possible. This is acceptable to the armed forces because of manpower limitations on using and supporting new and more complex equipment. This is not to imply that innovation is opposed in principle—rather, that change must contribute to force or unit effectiveness and at not too great a cost. To quote the plaque that was alleged to have been in Admiral Gorshkov's office, "Better is the Enemy of Good Enough."

Soviet versus U.S. Defense Research and Acquisition. These factors have led to a current Soviet research and acquisition process that is in many respects quite different from that of the West. While the defense organizations of the Soviet Union and United States are quite different, there are some similarities in their military research and acquisition process. The similarities have been identified as a research base of developing technologies; senior management review and decision of major systems during specific phases of development; rigorous testing during all phases of development; and comparative periods for full-scale weapon development in both countries.

The differences, however, appear to be more significant:

(1) The Soviet Union has a single, top-level weapons development oversight agency, the Military Industrial Commission (VPK), that combines certain functions of various agencies of the U.S. Department of Defense, the Congress, and private industry.

(2) Approval for major weapons systems in the Soviet Union is made by the politburo (if appropriate) and by a joint decree of the Central Committee and the Council of Ministers. These are the only top-level approvals required in the Soviet Union whereas there are several major approvals in the United States, including the various milestones of the Defense Systems Acquisition Review Council (DSARC) of the Department of Defense, and less formal reviews by the Office of Management and Budget (OMB) and several Congressional committees, with major systems being considered by the entire House and Senate.

(3) Once a program is approved by the joint decree, appropriate resources are allocated within the Soviet military and industrial communities. Within the United States each program is "revisited" annually because of Congressional approval requirements.

(4) A major segment of Soviet industry is dedicated to defense programs, which programs unquestionably enjoy top priority. In the United States defense contractors compete for business under market conditions that are highly restrictive and, in some respects, retard innovation.

(5) The senior people involved in the Soviet research and acquisition process remain in the same position for long periods. The American system provides for frequent changes in defense and industry management.

MAINTENANCE AND SUPPORT

The maintenance and support of equipment in the fleet have been traditional problems for the Soviet Navy, in part because of the Soviet economic practice of producing "units" rather than spare parts, problems with workmanship and quality control, and personnel limitations.

The West's estimates of the success of the Soviet Navy in maintaining and supporting military equipment vary considerably. Undoubtedly some of the more critical comments are based on the appearance of some Soviet ships. Flaking paint and rust stains are sometimes used as the criteria for such judgments; another criterion sometimes used is the time at sea of individual Soviet ships compared with American units as well as the Soviet practice of towing ships to or from deployment areas. Observing appearances and operating modes may not be an entirely accurate means of measuring actual maintenance levels and the resulting readiness.

For example, the Soviet Navy seems to place less emphasis on the appearance of their ships—except during port visits—than does the U.S. Navy. Rather, the Soviet emphasis seems to be on keeping the equipment working. This has been a traditional attitude. For example, Rear Admiral Kemp Tolley, when assistant naval attaché in Moscow during World War II, recorded the following in his diary about the Soviet crews that brought former U.S. and British naval ships around North Cape to Soviet Arctic ports:

> Our people found the Russian sailorman can be a complex fellow. By nature slovenly, they kept their ordnance, engineering, and most mechanical equipment clean, plentifully greased and operative. Not energetic, they were physically capable of great hardship. They were "heavy handed" in operating, maintenance and repairing of equipment; wasteful of spare parts, tools and supplies. Mechanical sense was crude, jumping to conclusions child-like that they knew-it-all, to the hazard of the inanimate gear they were working on.[20]

This attitude coupled with the conservative design of their equipment—built with the level of technical competence of the sailor in mind—indicates that the equipment the Soviets have in their ships is kept in working order. (Officers and warrants perform

most of the technical maintenance tasks on board ship, a necessity because of the short term that enlisted men serve in the Navy; see chapter 10). At the same time, the operating mode of the Soviet fleet tends to conserve equipment and other resources whenever possible. In 1982 the U.S. Chief of Naval Operations told a Congressional committee:

> The Soviet concept of material readiness stresses conservation of resources by limiting the use of military equipment in peacetime. They apparently believe that limited use is the best way to ensure that equipment will be ready on short notice during a crisis. That is one reason the Soviets normally keep a smaller percentage of their forces deployed than we do, and why Soviet deployed forces generally maintain lower operational tempos.[21]

Still, the Soviet Navy suffers from the general maintenance and support problems that plague all aspects of Soviet society. Throughout the society there are too often examples of poor workmanship, insufficient quality control, shortages of parts, and lack of personnel competence or incentives to do the job properly. The only mitigation is that within the Soviet society the armed forces have the highest priorities for men and material (after certain party-related activities), and during the past two decades the Navy has received the "cream" of those resources.

Thus, for at least the near-term the Soviet Navy appears capable of maintaining and supporting the fleet that has been developed since World War II.

20. Rear Adm. Kemp Tolley, USN (Ret), *Caviar and Commissars* (Annapolis, Md.: Naval Institute Press, 1983), p. 170.

21. Adm. Thomas B. Hayward, USN, testimony before the Armed Services Committee, Senate, 25 February 1982.

The crash crew of the carrier ADMIRAL KUZNETSOV (ex-TBILISI) crosses the carrier's flight deck during the ship's November 1989 trials in the Black Sea. The Sky Watch fixed-array radar and Cake Stand TACAN are visible on the island structure; a Ka-27 Helix helicopter is at left. (Sovfoto, A. Kremko)

CHAPTER 12

Submarines

The Typhoon SSBN is the world's largest
submarine and seems to personify several
characteristics of the Soviet submarine
program: the Typhoon is large, innovative,
and represents considerable capability.
However, construction has halted with six
of these units, designed by Sergey
Nikitovich Kovolev, having been completed.
(Royal Navy)

The submarine remains the capital ship of the Soviet Navy and the Soviet Union has the world's largest submarine force. The exact number of Soviet submarines is not publicly known in the West and probably not known exactly by Western intelligence in view of the accelerated scrapping of older submarines, both from the active fleet and reserve units (the latter including some 75 Whiskey-class submarines).

The current number of active submarines is on the order of 310 of which about 200 are nuclear propelled and 110 have diesel-electric propulsion (see table 12-1). This is a decline of some 60 submarines during the past few years. Again, precise data is lacking. Still, the Soviet submarine force is the world's largest and more than twice the size of the U.S. submarine force.

Regardless of the exact number of submarines in Soviet service, the quantity is impressive. Before the recent cutbacks Soviet submarines represented more than 40 percent of the world's 900-plus operational submarines. The number of submarines in service may decline further as all surviving first generation nuclear-propelled submarines of the Hotel, Echo, and November classes are retired except for those Echo II units rearmed with the SS-N-12 anti-ship cruise missile.

Accordingly, a submarine force of perhaps 275–300 submarines appears more likely during the 1990s. This force could be even smaller as under possible options of the Strategic Arms Reduction Talks (START) between the United States and Soviet Union the number of modern Soviet ballistic missile submarines (SSBN) may be reduced from the current 62 to perhaps as few as 20 to 30 units. If such a decrease is forthcoming, it could free up SSBNs for other roles, especially cruise missile carriers, and free shipways for the construction of more nuclear torpedo-attack and cruise missile submarines (SSN/SSGN). A smaller Soviet SSBN force would consist of Typhoon and Delta III/IV units, and possibly a new class, i.e., all completed since 1975.

Construction continues on five classes of "attack" submarines. The current building rate (1990 launchings) is ten submarines per year—two of the Oscar II–class SSGNs, one each of the Akula, Sierra, and Victor III SSNs, and four Kilo-class boats (including one for foreign transfer) plus a single Delta IV. Although it is not known if this rate will continue, it is significant to note that more submarines were built during Gorbachev's first five years in office than in the previous five-year period (see Addenda).

Thus, the current submarine construction effort could maintain a force of 250 submarines, assuming a 25-year service life. Although smaller, the performance, quieting, and survivability of this force is increasing. For example, the Oscar SSGN now being built mounts 24 anti-ship missiles with a submerged launch capability; the Soviets are now retiring Echo II submarines with eight anti-ship missiles that are surface launched and far less capable.

The Soviet submarine design bureaus are undoubtedly at work on the next generation units, which may go to sea before the end of the 1990s. Their characteristics will include higher speeds (up to 50 knots), deep operating depths (on the order of 3,300 feet/1,000 m), and improved quieting, although all designs may not possess all attributes.

The United States had long accepted Soviet superiority in submarine numbers in return for qualitative superiority, especially with respect to submarine acoustic quieting and passive acoustic detection. From the appearance of the Akula, Sierra, and Oscar in the mid-1980s, U.S. Navy officials have expressed concern over improved Soviet submarine technology. The Akula exhibited sound levels not expected until the early 1990s. These Soviet submarine developments led the U.S. Chief of Naval Operations, Admiral Carlisle A.H. Trost (1986–1990), to declare that ASW was his number one war-fighting priority.

In reality, the Soviet completion of the first Alfa-class submarine in 1969—a titanium-hull, high-speed, highly automated, and relatively quiet submarine—demonstrated the Soviet competence in producing high-performance undersea craft. (The first Alfa encountered severe engineering problems and never became operational; the second unit entered the fleet in 1979.) Several other Soviet submarine developments have caused concern for Western analysts and engineers even if not the U.S. Navy's leadership. These developments have included anechoic coatings, submerged-launch

TABLE 12-1.   SOVIET SUBMARINE FORCE, EARLY 1990

Type	Class	Active	Comm.*	Notes
Modern Strategic Missile Submarines				
SSBN	Delta IV	6	1985	in production
SSBN	Typhoon	6	1983	world's largest submarine
SSBN	Delta III	14	1975	
SSBN	Delta II	4	1974	
SSBN	Delta I	18	1972	
SSBN	Yankee II	1		converted Yankee I
SSBN	Yankee I	13	1967	being retired from strategic role
Older Strategic Missile Submarines				
SSBN	Hotel III	1		conversion; missile test platform
SSB	Golf II	2	1958	diesel-electric; being retired from service
Modern Attack–Cruise Missile Submarines				
SSGN	Yankee	1		SS-N-24 missiles; converted SSBN
SSGN	Yankee-Notch	2		SS-N-21 missiles; converted SSBN
SSGN	Oscar I/II	6	1982	in production
SSGN	Papa	1	1971	test platform
SSN	Akula	6	1986	in production
SSN	Sierra I/II	3	1984	in production
SSN	Victor III	25	1978	in production
SSN	Victor II	7	1972	
SSN	Alfa	5	1969	
SSN/SSNX	Yankee	16	1967	converted SSBN; some may not be operational
SSN	Victor I	16	1967	
Older Attack–Cruise Missile Submarines				
SSGN	Charlie II	6	1973	
SSGN	Charlie I	10	1967	
SSGN	Echo II	~26(?)	1962	some units being retired
SSN	Hotel II	~5(?)	1961	former SSBN; being retired
SSN	Echo I	~3(?)	1960	converted SSGN; being retired
SSN	November	few	1958	being retired
Modern Diesel-Electric Attack Submarines				
SS	Kilo	19	1982	in production
SS	Tango	~15(?)	1972	
SS	Foxtrot	~40(?)	1958	some being retired; additional units in reserve
Older Diesel-Electric Attack-Cruise Missile Submarines				
SSG	Juliett	14(?)	1961	being retired
SS	Whiskey	few(?)	1951	being retired
Research/Experimental/Special Purpose Submarines				
SSX	Beluga	1	1982	probably advanced propulsion system
SSQN	Hotel	1		converted SSBN; communications configuration
SSQ	Golf	3		converted SSB; communications configuration
AGSSN	Echo II	1		converted SSGN; probably transport
AGSSN	Xray	1	1984	small research submarine
AGSSN	Uniform	2	1983	special missions
AGSS	India	2	1979	rescue and salvage submarine
AGSS	Lima	1	1978	research submarine
SST	Bravo	4	1967	target and training submarine
AGSS	Zulu IV	3	1952	converted SS
miscellaneous		several		
	Totals	~200	nuclear propelled	
		~110	diesel-electric propelled	

* Original completion/commissioning of first submarine of type or class.

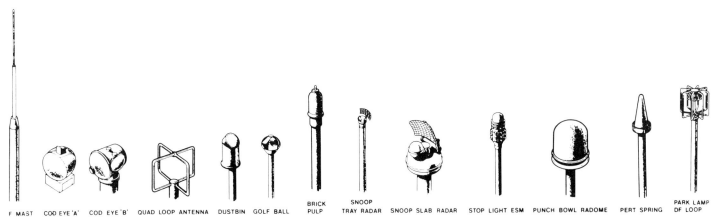

F MAST COD EYE 'A' COD EYE 'B' QUAD LOOP ANTENNA DUSTBIN GOLF BALL BRICK PULP SNOOP TRAY RADAR SNOOP SLAB RADAR STOP LIGHT ESM PUNCH BOWL RADOME PERT SPRING PARK LAMP DF LOOP

Submarine masts

cruise missiles, large-diameter torpedoes, survivability features, and, most recently, submarine quieting.

As noted in the previous edition of *Guide to the Soviet Navy*, the Soviets have *not* depended on the theft or commercial acquisition of Western technology for their submarine development. According to Melvyn R. Paisley, at the time U.S. Assistant Secretary of the Navy for research,

> The Soviet submarine technological advances for quieting, strengthened double hulls, higher speed, higher reserve buoyance [sic], and deeper operations are advances which are by and large not stolen or bought from the United States. Some technologies, [classified deletion], are Soviet design decisions which are different from our decisions. Other technologies, [deleted], are the result of Soviet engineered high power density material and high strength hull material. The Soviets are ahead of the U.S. in these technologies.[1]

This statement of Soviet innovation is valid despite the transfer of multi-axis propeller milling machinery and related computer programs by Norwegian and Japanese commercial firms. At the time the Akula-class submarine was observed to have significantly lower-than-expected noise levels, several Western government officials and analysts blamed those illegal technology sales as the cause of the Soviet advances. More likely—even if the equipment is now being used to produce submarine propellers—the Akula is the result of Soviet-developed submarine propulsion technology, since the first Akula had gone to sea before foreign-produced propellers could be incorporated into her design. (The Soviets were, obviously, informed of how vulnerable their submarines were to Western acoustic detection by U.S. Navy communications specialists John Walker and Jerry Whitworth, who spied against the U.S. Navy for the Soviets; at the time he became a spy for the Soviet Union in 1968, Walker was assigned to the operations center of the U.S. Atlantic Fleet's submarine force.)

Beyond these improvements in performance and quieting, Soviet submarines have long employed anechoic coatings to absorb acoustic energy to reduce the active sonar effectiveness of Allied submarines and acoustic homing torpedoes. There are some indications that the Soviets may employ compliant coatings and possibly polymers to further reduce internal noises as well as to absorb external acoustic energy. And, Soviet submarines are more survivable than their Western counterparts because of their higher reserve buoyancy (up to 40 percent compared to 10 to 15 percent in U.S. submarines), double-hull configurations (except for the single-hull Xray research submarine), and internal compartmentation. The Soviets have also pioneered in the development of anti-ship missiles launched from submarines and large-diameter torpedoes (see chapter 28). Of major concern to Western planners has been the Type 65 (650-mm/25.5-in) torpedo with wake-homing guidance. A single hit with this weapon, even with a conventional, high-explosive warhead, could probably sink or immobilize any Western surface warship or submarine except for a battleship or large air-

craft carrier. A properly placed, "under-the-keel" explosion of this weapon could inflict severe damage even on the largest Western warships. Most if not all Soviet combat submarines normally embark nuclear as well as conventional torpedoes. All Soviet submarines can carry mines in place of torpedoes.

The major shortfalls in the Soviet submarine force appear to be in personnel and quality control. (Training, especially of the three-year conscripts, is recognized as a major problem, even within the Soviet Navy. See chapter 10.)

These problems have contributed to some and possibly all four publicly acknowledged Soviet submarine losses since World War II: a November SSN in 1970, a Charlie SSGN in 1983, a Yankee SSBN in 1986, and the single Mike SSN in 1989.[2] In addition, one or more diesel-electric submarines may have been lost in Soviet coastal waters and, possibly, a Hotel-class SSBN; see individual class listings for details.

One other area of Soviet submarine development requires mention—Air Independent Propulsion (AIP) systems. Beginning at least in the late 1930s, the Soviets have demonstrated a major interest in closed-cycle/air-independent propulsion for submarines. In the post–World War II period this was abetted by captured German technology and technicians, with emphasis on the Krieslauf and Walter plants. Several submarines appear to have been built with (or at least intended for) such closed-cycle propulsion plants, including the enigmatic "Whale" (Project 617) and the Quebec class (Project 615).

The latest manifestation of the continuing Soviet interest in AIP submarines appears to be the Beluga, so far a one-of-a-kind, non-nuclear submarine. The various Western AIP concepts give promise of long-duration, relatively high submerged speeds for non-nuclear submarines. The success of the Beluga plant coupled with the Soviet expansion of non-nuclear submarine production (i.e., the Kilo class) to three shipyards offers the specter of a large number of high-performance, relatively low-cost submarines being produced. Such craft could be highly effective in European (and possibly U.S.) coastal waters.

Through the late 1980s Soviet shipyards produced an average of four nuclear-propelled submarines and four diesel-electric submarines per year, with up to three of the latter (Kilo class) being transferred to other nations. The newer submarines are quieter than their predecessors and have more advanced weapon and sensor systems.

At least six submarine classes are believed to be currently in production (see table 12-1): one strategic missile design (SSBN), one anti-ship cruise missile design (SSGN), and four torpedo-attack (SSN/SS), although the last are capable of launching the SS-N-21 land-attack cruise missile. A new SSGN class, to carry the large, SS-N-24 land-attack cruise missile, may also be under construction, as well as possibly a new SSBN design.

---

1. Melvyn R. Paisley, Assistant Secretary of the Navy (Research, Engineering, and Systems), testimony before Appropriations Committee, House of Representatives, 2 April 1985.

2. The U.S. Navy has lost four submarines since World War II: the Co-CHINO (SS 345) in 1949, STICKLEBACK (SS 415) in 1958, THRESHER (SSN 593) in 1963, and SCORPION (SSN 589) in 1968. Both navies have suffered several major, non-loss submarine casualties.

In addition, former Yankee-class strategic missile submarines are being converted to other configurations.

The current construction rate would provide the Soviet Navy with a minimum force of 120 nuclear-propelled and 120 non-nuclear submarines in the year 2015 (i.e., with a 25-year service life). However, in 1989 the number of launchings of nuclear units increased, indicating that a larger submarine force is more likely, perhaps on the order of 150 or more nuclear and 100 to 120 non-nuclear submarines.

(In comparison, the U.S. Navy in late 1990 had 33 SSBNs, 92 SSN/SSGNs, and one research submarine—one nuclear and one diesel-electric—a total of 127 submarines. By the year 2000 there will probably be on the order of 18 SSBNs and 65 SSN/SSGNs in active U.S. service.)

In addition to the submarines listed below, until the late 1980s the Soviet Navy had some 75 submarines laid up in reserve, mostly of the Foxtrot and Whiskey classes. These have been discarded.

Classes: The completion dates indicated for submarine classes are for all units of the class (including stricken or lost units).

Classification: Soviet submarine designations are listed in chapter 3. Because U.S. and Soviet submarines have somewhat similar configurations and missions, U.S. submarine type designations are used in this chapter (e.g., SS, SSN, SSGN).

Nevertheless, it should be noted that there are two significantly different types of cruise missile submarines (SSG/SSGN) in Soviet service: those configured to carry the SS-N-21 and SS-N-24 land-attack missiles (Yankee, Yankee-Notch, Akula, etc.) and those employing the SS-N-3/7/9/12 anti-ship cruise missiles (Juliett, Echo II, Charlie I/II). While the SS-N-3 Shaddock missile was originally designed for the land-attack role, like the U.S. Regulus, those weapons currently in the fleet are all assumed to be anti-ship variants.

Names: Soviet submarines have been assigned letter designations by U.S.-NATO intelligence. Phonetic words are generally used for these letters, as Alfa for *A* and Bravo for *B*. The letter *U* (Uniform) has been used twice, initially for the Victor II-class SSGN and then for a nuclear-propelled special missions submarine. The exceptions to this scheme were the Whale (1950s) and Typhoon (1980s), the latter name being based on the Soviet term *tayfun*.

The assignment of the code name Yankee to the Soviet SSBN class has caused confusion with the public. At times the U.S. Department of Defense has used the term *Russian Yankee*.

By 1985 all 26 letters of the alphabet had been exhausted and U.S.-NATO intelligence derived a new alphabetical series, beginning with *Akula* (Russian for "shark") and Beluga.

A modified Victor I-class SSN of the Northern Fleet running with her sail awash. Despite the heavy Soviet investment in naval aviation and surface ship programs, the submarine remains the capital ship of the Soviet Navy. There are additional sensor-like devices adjacent to the bow diving planes. (Royal Navy)

BALLISTIC MISSILE SUBMARINES

Delta IV

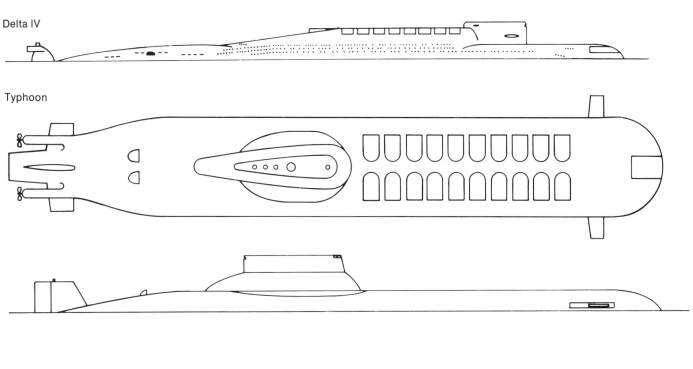

Typhoon

Delta III

Delta II

Delta I

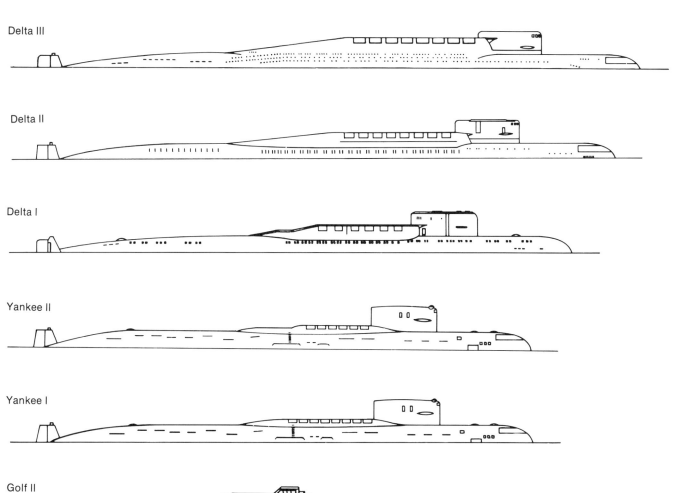

Yankee II

Yankee I

Golf II

6+ BALLISTIC MISSILE SUBMARINES: DELTA IV CLASS

Number	Builders	Launched	Completed
1 unit	Shipyard 402 (Severodvinsk)	Feb 1984	1985
1 unit	Shipyard 402 (Severodvinsk)	1984	1986
1 unit	Shipyard 402 (Severodvinsk)	1986	1987
1 unit	Shipyard 402 (Severodvinsk)	1987	1988
1 unit	Shipyard 402 (Severodvinsk)	1988	1989
1 unit	Shipyard 402 (Severodvinsk)	1989	1989
1 unit	Shipyard 402 (Severodvinsk)	1990	Building
. . . units	Shipyard 402 (Severodvinsk)		Building

Displacement:	10,800 tons surfaced
	13,550 tons submerged
Length:	537 ft 11 in (164.0 m) overall
Beam:	39 ft 4 in (12.0 m)
Draft:	28 ft 6 1/2 in (8.7 m)
Propulsion:	2 steam turbines; 45,000 shp; 2 shafts (7-bladed propellers)
Reactors:	2 pressurized-water type
Speed:	
	24 knots submerged
Depth:	probably 1,970 ft (600 m)
Complement:	approx. 120
Missiles:	16 SS-N-23 SLBM[3]
Torpedo tubes:	6 21-in (533-mm) or 25.5-in (650-mm) bow
Torpedoes:	
Radar:	Snoop Tray surface search
Sonar:	low-frequency active
	passive array
EW systems:	radar warning

This is a significantly enlarged version of the Delta/Yankee design, with a major increase in missile size. One or more additional units are under construction.

Design: Double-hull configuration. The Delta IV was designed for under-ice operation.

Electronics: All Delta classes and the Typhoon SSBNs are believed to be fitted with the Cod Eye radiometric sextant, Pert Spring satellite communications antenna, and a towed Very Low Frequency (VLF) antenna buoy.

3. SLBM = Submarine-Launched Ballistic Missile.

The Delta IV, which put to sea later than the Typhoon SSBN, survives that larger submarine in production at the Severodvinsk shipyard. The small fins near the stern of this Delta IV are vortex eliminators.

Engineering: These submarines, like all Soviet SSBNs, have twin propeller shafts. All Western SSBNs have single-shaft propulsion plants.

Operational: All active Delta IV SSBNs are assigned to the Northern Fleet. The deployment of the Delta IV on patrol was delayed several years, apparently because of difficulties in development of the SS-N-23 missile.

A Delta IV under way, showing the aperture atop her upper rudder for a towed array sonar; most Delta IVs appear to have a projection just aft of the missile tubes on the slanted casing that may be a housing for a communications cable or towed buoy, or a camera for viewing such devices released from the adjacent hatch. (Royal Navy)

6 BALLISTIC MISSILE SUBMARINES: TYPHOON CLASS (PROJECT 941)

Number	Builders	Launched	Completed
1 unit	Shipyard 402 (Severodvinsk)	Sep 1980	1983
1 unit	Shipyard 402 (Severodvinsk)	Sep 1982	1984
1 unit	Shipyard 402 (Severodvinsk)	Dec 1983	1985
1 unit	Shipyard 402 (Severodvinsk)	late 1984	1986
1 unit	Shipyard 402 (Severodvinsk)	late 1986	1988
1 unit	Shipyard 402 (Severodvinsk)	1989	1990

Displacement:	18,500 tons surfaced (see notes)
	25,000 tons submerged
Length:	560 ft 11 in (171.0 m) overall
Beam:	78 ft 9 in (24.0 m)
Draft:	41 ft (12.5 m)
Propulsion:	2 steam turbines; 45,000–80,000 shp; 2 shafts (7-bladed propellers)
Reactors:	2 pressurized-water type (see notes)
Speed:	
	25+ knots submerged
Depth:	
Complement:	approx. 150
Missiles:	20 SS-N-20 SLBM
Torpedo tubes:	6 21-in (533-mm) or 25.5-in (650-mm) bow
Torpedoes:	
Radar:	Snoop Pair surface search
Sonar:	low-frequency active
	passive array
EW systems:	radar warning

The Typhoon is the world's largest submarine. The lead unit was laid down in 1975; she underwent extensive sea trials beginning in June 1981. Western intelligence sources expected seven or eight units to be constructed; however, construction has halted with six units.

Design: The displacements listed above are those released by the U.S. Navy. Independent analysis by U.S. and foreign naval engineers indicates a more probable displacement of some 30,000 tons surfaced and 40,000 tons submerged.

The Typhoon has a unique configuration, unlike any other SSBN. There are apparently two large, Delta-type pressure hulls encased in a large outer (i.e., "double") hull casing with the missile tubes between the two large hulls, forward of a separate control compartment, also between the two hulls. The Typhoon was designed for under-ice operation.

Engineering: The configuration of the Typhoon propulsion plant is not publicly known; two reactor plants are probable, producing an aggregate of 330 to 360 mW of power.

Missiles: The lead ship launched two SS-N-20 missiles within a 15-second interval in October 1982.

Operational: All Typhoon SSBNs are assigned to the Northern Fleet.

Name: Western Intelligence assigned the code name Typhoon based on General Secretary L.I. Brezhnev's comment in 1974 that the Soviet Union was constructing a strategic missile submarine called the *tayfun*.

The massive sail structure of a Typhoon SSBN may house equipment for functions beyond controlling the giant undersea craft and launching SLBMs. (1990, Royal Navy)

Stern aspect of a Typhoon SSBN. Although the submarine has twin internal pressure hulls, there are centerline hatches. The small, white rectangular markings on the stern are salvage fittings, for blowing air into ballast tanks of a sunken submarine. (1990, Royal Navy)

A Typhoon SSBN under way at high speed. The two rows of SS-N-20 are forward of the massive sail structure. The bow-mounted diving planes, fitted far forward on the hull, are retracted in this view. Note also the height of the single tail fin-rudder. (1990, Royal Navy)

The Typhoon is the largest undersea vehicle ever to be constructed. Her unusual configuration with missile tubes forward and a massive sail structure are evident here. Not visible are her two parallel pressure hulls housed within the broad outer hull, with the missile tubes between the pressure hulls. (Royal Navy)

14 BALLISTIC MISSILE SUBMARINES: DELTA III CLASS

Number	Builders	Completed
2 units	Shipyard 402 (Severodvinsk)	1975
4 units	Shipyard 402 (Severodvinsk)	1976
2 units	Shipyard 402 (Severodvinsk)	1977
2 units	Shipyard 402 (Severodvinsk)	1978
3 units	Shipyard 402 (Severodvinsk)	1979–1981
1 unit	Shipyard 402 (Severodvinsk)	1982

Displacement:	10,600 tons surfaced
	13,250 tons submerged
Length:	510 ft (155.5 m) overall
Beam:	39 ft 4 in (12.0 m)
Draft:	28 ft 2 1/2 (8.6 m)
Propulsion:	2 steam turbines; 45,000 shp; 2 shafts (5-bladed propellers)
Reactors:	2 pressurized-water type

Speed:	
	24 knots submerged
Depth:	probably 1,970 ft (600 m)
Complement:	approx. 120
Missiles:	16 SS-N-18 SLBM
Torpedo tubes:	6 21-in (533-mm) bow
Torpedoes:	18
Radar:	Snoop Tray surface search
Sonar:	low-frequency active
	passive array
EW systems:	radar warning

A further improvement of the Yankee/Delta configuration, with an increased battery of SS-N-18 missiles.

Design: Double-hull configuration.

Names: One unit is named 60 LET VELIKYO OKTYABR.

Operational: Six Delta IIIs are assigned to the Northern Fleet and eight to the Pacific Fleet.

The Delta III introduced Multiple Independently targeted Re-entry Vehicles (MIRV) to the warheads of Soviet submarine missiles. This Delta III has open limber holes; they can be closed to reduce noise and decrease drag when the submarine is submerged and running quiet. This unit has been refitted with a towed-array sonar (aperture on rudder).

A Delta III photographed from the starboard quarter revealing the long "turtle back" over the submarine's 16 ballistic missile tubes. The Delta classes evolved from the Yankee-class SSBN.

4 BALLISTIC MISSILE SUBMARINES: DELTA II CLASS

Number	Builders	Completed
4 units	Shipyard 402 (Severodvinsk)	1974–1975

Displacement:	10,550 tons surfaced
	13,250 tons submerged
Length:	510 ft (155.5 m) overall
Beam:	39 ft 4 in (12.0 m)
Draft:	28 ft 2 1/2 in (8.6 m)
Propulsion:	2 steam turbines; 45,000 shp; 2 shafts (5-bladed propellers)
Reactors:	2 pressurized-water type
Speed:	
	24 knots submerged
Depth:	probably 1,970 ft (600 m)
Complement:	approx. 120
Missiles:	16 SS-N-8 SLBM
Torpedo tubes:	6 21-in (533-mm) bow
Torpedoes:	18
Radar:	Snoop Tray surface search
Sonar:	low-frequency active
	passive array
EW systems:	radar warning

The Delta II was an interim improvement of the basic Delta I SSBN design, carrying more missiles of the same type fitted in the Delta I.

Design: Double-hull configuration.

Operational: All four Delta II SSBNs are assigned to the Northern Fleet.

An interim Delta II-class SSBN on the surface, apparently during torpedo firing trials, with a Shelon-class torpedo retriever at right.

Delta II-class SSBN

18 BALLISTIC MISSILE SUBMARINES: DELTA I CLASS

Number	Builders	Completed
1 unit		1972
4 units		1973
6 units	Shipyard 402 (Severodvinsk)	1974
2 units	Shipyard 199 (Komsomol'sk)[4]	1975
2 units		1976
3 units		1977

Displacement:	9,000 tons surfaced
	11,750 tons submerged
Length:	459 ft 2 in (140.0 m) overall
Beam:	39 ft 4 in (12.0 m)
Draft:	28 ft 1 in (8.6 m)
Propulsion:	2 steam turbines; approx. 45,000 shp; 2 shafts (5-bladed propellers)
Reactors:	2 pressurized-water type
Speed:	_____
	25 knots submerged
Depth:	probably 1,970 ft (600 m)
Complement:	approx. 120
Missiles:	12 SS-N-8 SLBM
Torpedo tubes:	6 21-in (533-mm) bow
Torpedoes:	18
Radar:	Snoop Tray surface search
Sonar:	low-frequency active
	passive array
EW systems:	radar warning

Stern view of a Delta I at high speed; several anechoic tiles are missing on the port side, aft. Several masts and a periscope are raised. (1990, Royal Navy)

The Delta I is an enlargement of the Yankee SSBN design. When the first Delta I went to sea she was the world's largest submarine with the longest-range SLBM.

This was the last SSBN design to be constructed at Komsomol'sk in the Far East; the Amur River is too shallow for the launching of larger submarines.

Design: Double-hull configuration.

Operational: Nine Delta I SSBNs are assigned to the Northern Fleet and nine to the Pacific Fleet.

4. Nuclear-propelled submarines built at Komsomol'sk are generally completed at Petrovka.

The Delta I SSBN has a stepped "turtle back" aft of the raised outer hull to accommodate the submarine's 12 missile tubes. A Pert Spring antenna is partially raised and a periscope is almost fully extended.

14 BALLISTIC MISSILE SUBMARINES: YANKEE I/II CLASSES (PROJECT 667)

Number	Builders	Completed
6 units 5 units 2 units 1 unit	Shipyard 402 (Severodvinsk) Shipyard 199 (Komsomol'sk)	1967–1974

Displacement:	7,900 tons surfaced 9,600 tons submerged, except Yankee II approx. 10,000 tons
Length:	426 ft 5 in (130.0 m) overall
Beam:	39 ft 4 in (12.0 m)
Draft:	28 ft 2 1/2 in (8.6 m)
Propulsion:	2 steam turbines; 45,000 shp; 2 shafts (5-bladed propellers)
Reactors:	2 pressurized-water type
Speed:	
	27 knots submerged
Depth:	probably 1,970 ft (600 m)
Complement:	approx. 120
Missiles:	Yankee I 16 SS-N-16 SLBM Yankee II 12 SS-N-17 SLBM
Torpedo tubes:	6 21-in (533-mm) bow
Torpedoes:	18
Radar:	Snoop Tray surface search
Sonar:	low-frequency active passive array
EW systems:	Brick Group

The Yankee was the Soviet Navy's first "modern" SSBN design, i.e., similar to contemporary Western SSBN designs. One of the surviving SSBNs is a Yankee II; the other units remaining in an SSBN configuration are Yankee I submarines.

The SSBNs are now believed to be employed in the theater strike role, replacing the Golf SSB/Hotel SSBN classes and land-based missiles.

Design of the Yankee began in the late 1950s, but apparently work slowed or has halted completely with the reorganization of Soviet strategic forces in 1959–1960. Work on the project resumed in the early 1960s. The first submarine, probably named LENINETS, was launched in 1966 and formally placed in commission on 30 May 1967, according to Soviet press reports.

Double-hull configuration.

Class: Thirty-four submarines of this design were completed between 1967 and 1974: 1 has been lost (see below); at least 3 converted to carry land-attack cruise missiles (SSGN), and at least 2 converted to attack submarines (SSN); the status of the other 14 units is not clear (see page 117). As of late 1989, probaby 14 remain in the SLBM configuration (Yankee I/II) and 16 have had their SLBM capability deleted and now rate as SSN/SSNX. Some of the latter (SSNX) are being reconfigured to attack, minelaying, or other configurations.

Conversions: Yankee II—One unit was modified to carry the SS-N-17 SLBM (note that the number of launch tubes was reduced from 16 to 12). Submerged displacement increased to about 10,000 tons.

Yankee SSN—As newer SSBNs were completed the oldest Yankee SSBNs have had their SS-N-6 SLBM tubes disabled and certain missile-related equipment removed in accord with the U.S.-Soviet SALT agreements. Some of these submarines have been modified to serve as attack submarines, the first of which completed alterations and entered service as an SSN in 1984.

Yankee SSGN—One Yankee SSBN has been converted into a test platform for the SS-N-24 land-attack cruise missile. This submarine was extensively rebuilt, with an enlarged amidships section inserted carrying angled vertical-launch tubes for 12 SS-N-24 missiles. This unit was "relaunched" in December 1982 and commenced SS-N-24 missile tests in 1985.

Yankee-Notch SSGN—At least two Yankee SSBNs have been converted to carry the SS-N-21 (Submarine-Launched Cruise Missile; SLCM). Although nominally considered a torpedo-tube-

A Yankee SSBN surfaced and in trouble after suffering a missile propellant explosion while operating submerged in the western Atlantic. This photograph shows the damage caused by the missile explosion. The snorkel air intake is raised at the after end of the sail (probably to help ventilate the boat), the diving planes are in the vertical position; and the rescue buoy, forward hatch, and salvage fittings (rectangular markings) are clearly visible on the bow. (1986, U.S. Navy)

Yankee I SSBN with a number of masts and scopes raised. A small sonar "window" is visible at the front of the sail. (Royal Navy)

launched weapon, the Yankee-Notch SSGN is fitted with an estimated 40 missile launch tubes (in addition to bow torpedo tubes).
Unlike the SSGN/SS-N-24 conversion, the Yankee-Notch retains
the standard SSBN appearance amidships with a raised casing over
the now-defunct SS-N-8 missile tubes. Additional conversions
have been reported.

Design: The basic arrangement of the Yankee is similar to the
U.S. Polaris–class submarines of the GEORGE WASHINGTON
(SSBN 598) class, first completed in 1960. The Soviet submarines
have a double-hull configuration.

Electronics: These SSBNs are fitted with the Code Eye radiometric sextant and Pert Spring satellite communications antenna.

Operational: When this edition went to press the Yankee I
SSBNs were divided between the Northern and Pacific fleets; the
single Yankee II was assigned to the Northern Fleet.

A Yankee SSBN suffered a missile propellant explosion while
operating submerged some 600 miles (965 km) east of Bermuda in
October 1986. The submarine was able to surface; most of the crew
was removed and she was taken in tow by a merchant ship, but
progressive flooding forced her abandonment and she sank on 6
October. The Soviet government has announced that three men
were killed in the missile explosion; others were apparently injured.

The sail of a modified Yankee SSBN showing a "wedge" fitted at the
forward base of the sail and the sail hatch opened to reveal the Cod
Eye–B celestial sight. Several recessed masts and antennas can be
seen in the top of the sail.

The single Yankee II SSBN has been modified to carry 12 of the SS-N-17 solid-propellant missiles and is the only submarine armed with that
weapon. The Yankee II can be distinguished from other Yankees by the higher "turtle back" and slope of the fairing alongside the sail
structure.

A Yankee I SSBN with her sail-mounted diving planes at a slight down angle. These submarines are based on the U.S. Polaris SSBN design
of the late 1950s. The U.S. Navy constructed 41 Polaris submarines; Yankee production totaled 34 units and served as the basis for an
additional 40-plus Delta variants.

1 BALLISTIC MISSILE SUBMARINE: HOTEL III CLASS (PROJECT 658)

Number	Builders	Converted
1 unit	Shipyard 402 (Severodvinsk)	1969–1970

Displacement:	5,500 tons surfaced
	6,400 tons submerged
Length:	426 ft 5 in (130.0 m) overall
Beam:	29 ft 6 in (9.0 m)
Draft:	23 ft (7.0 m)
Propulsion:	2 steam turbines; approx. 35,000 shp; 2 shafts (6-bladed propellers)
Reactors:	2 pressurized-water type
Speed:	20 knots surfaced
	25 knots submerged
Depth:	
Complement:	approx. 80
Missiles:	6 SS-N-8 SLBM
Torpedo tubes:	6 21-in (533-mm) M-57 bow
	2 15.75-in (400-mm) stern
Torpedoes:	
Radar:	Snoop Tray surface search
Sonar:	medium-frequency active passive array
EW systems:	Stop Light

A Hotel II SSBN at sea. There are no unclassified photos of the one-of-a-kind Hotel III available. All other Hotels have been retired from the ballistic missile role under the SALT agreement between the United States and USSR. (Royal Navy)

The Hotel was the world's first nuclear-propelled ballistic missile submarine (SSBN) to be constructed, slightly predating the U.S. Polaris submarines. A single unit remains in service in a missile configuration, as a test ship for the SS-N-8 SLBM for the Delta SSBN class. One other serves as a communication ship (SSQN); a few other units served in an attack role (SSN) after having their missile tubes disabled.

Class: Eight Hotel-class SSBNs were completed in 1959–1962. The construction of the Hotel SSBN class was abruptly halted because of the Soviet defense program changes of 1959–1960, which essentially terminated SSBN development in favor of the land-based missiles of the Strategic Rocket Forces.

Some Western intelligence reports indicate that a ninth Hotel was built; that submarine, if she in fact existed, was probably an accidental loss in the early 1960s.

Conversions: One Hotel II was converted in 1969–1970 to a test ship for the SS-N-8 SLBM for the Delta-class SSBN and redesignated Hotel III by the Western intelligence community. The submarine was lengthened and displacement increased (see above); her sail structure was enlarged to accommodate the missile tubes.

Design: Double-hull configuration.

Operational: The single Hotel III SSBN is assigned to the Northern Fleet.

2 BALLISTIC MISSILE SUBMARINES: GOLF II CLASS (PROJECT 629)

Number	Builders	Completed
2 units	Shipyard 402 (Severodvinsk) Shipyard 199 (Komsomol'sk)	1958–1962

Displacement:	2,300 tons surfaced
	2,700 tons submerged
Length:	328 ft (100.0 m) overall
Beam:	27 ft 11 in (8.5 m)
Draft:	21 ft 8 in (6.6 m)
Propulsion:	3 diesel engines; 6,000 bhp
	3 electric motors; 5,300 shp
	3 shafts
Speed:	17 knots surfaced
	12 knots submerged
Range:	9,000 n.miles on snorkel at 5 knots
Depth:	
Complement:	approx. 80
Missiles:	3 SS-N-5 SLBM
Torpedo tubes:	10 21-in (533-mm) 6 bow + 4 stern
Torpedoes:	
Radar:	Snoop Tray
Sonar:	Herkules medium-frequency
	Feniks (passive)
EW systems:	radar warning

The Golf was the world's first submarine built specifically to launch ballistic missiles. Twenty-three were built for Soviet service with components and sections for one additional submarine delivered to China for assembly. That submarine served as a test platform for Chinese SLBM development.

As of early 1990 a reported two Golf II-class SSBs remained in active Soviet service operating in the Far East in the theater strike role. Six submarines assigned to the Baltic Fleet in 1976 were withdrawn in 1989–1990, according to Soviet statements, and are being scrapped. In addition, at least three Golfs have been converted to a communications role (SSQ).

Class: One Golf I was lost at sea with her entire crew in the North Pacific in April 1968. Portions of that submarine were raised in July 1974 by the U.S. Central Intelligence Agency, which employed the built-for-the-purpose lift ship HUGHES GLOMAR EXPLORER (later given the U.S. Navy designation AG 192).

Three submarines were scrapped in the Golf I configuration; subsequently, 14 Golf II/IV/V units have been discarded.

Conversions: Golf II—One unit was completed and 12 units were modified to the Golf II configuration to fire the submerged-launched SS-N-5 SLBM.

Golf III—Single unit converted in the early 1970s to test ship for SS-N-8 SLBM. Lengthened approx. 33 ft (10 m) and fitted with six missile launch tubes. Stricken.

Golf IV—Single Golf I converted to test ship for SS-N-6 SLBM; subsequently stricken. Fitted with six missile tubes. Lengthened approx. 60 ft (18.3 m). Stricken.

Golf V—Single Golf II converted to a test ship for SS-N-20 SLBM; subsequently stricken. Fitted with single missile tube. Stricken.

SSQ—Three Golf I units converted in the 1970s to serve as communications ships (SSQ). Fitted with extensive communications gear, including buoys and masts; conning tower structure enlarged and after torpedo tubes probably deleted. Pert Spring satellite communications antenna installed. (One Hotel nuclear-propelled missile submarine has been similarly converted to an SSQN configuration.)

Design: Double-hull configuration.

Operational: In the late 1970s all surviving Golfs were deployed to the Baltic and Far East as theater strike platforms. These were the first ballistic missile submarines to be assigned to the Baltic Fleet. Through the late 1980s the Baltic units transited, one at a time, to the Northern Fleet for periodic overhaul and missile test firings.

A Golf II SSB. There are three square hatches that hinge to port fitted atop the elongated sail structure (see page 000 for a view of a missile in the raised launching position). Two submarines of the Golf-class were reported to be in service when this edition went to press. (1988)

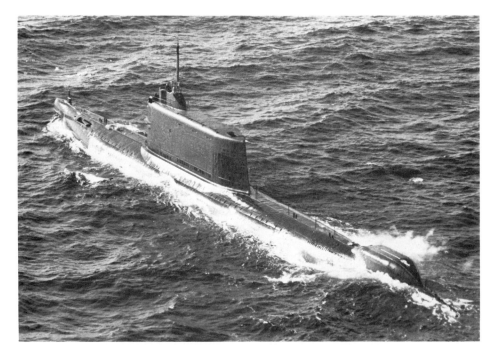

A Golf II SSB fitted with a housing for a towed communications buoy at the after end of her deck. The large communications mast alongside the sail is raised; it folds down onto the deck when not in use. The Soviet Union was the only nation to produce diesel-electric ballistic missile submarines in the Golf and Zulu classes. (Royal Navy)

GUIDED/CRUISE MISSILE SUBMARINES

Oscar I

Charlie II

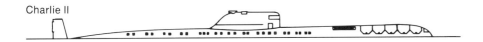

Papa

Charlie I

Echo II

Juliett

GUIDED MISSILE SUBMARINES: LAND-ATTACK CRUISE MISSILE DESIGN (?)

A new guided/cruise missile submarine was reported to be under construction in 1990 to carry the SS-N-24 strategic cruise missile. The submarine will probably be of Yankee/Delta SSBN dimensions with Severodvinsk or Komsomol'sk the probable building yard.

2+ GUIDED MISSILE SUBMARINE (SSGN): YANKEE-NOTCH

Number	Builders	Converted
1 unit		1967–1983
1 unit		Converting
. . . units (?)		

Displacement:	7,900 tons surfaced
	11,500 tons submerged
Length:	459 ft 2 in (140.0 m) overall
Beam:	39 ft 4 in (12.0 m)
Draft:	
Propulsion:	2 steam turbines; 45,000 shp; 2 shafts (5-bladed propellers)
Reactors:	2 pressurized-water type
Speed:	
	approx. 25 knots submerged
Depth:	probably 1,970 ft (600 m)
Complement:	approx. 120
Missiles:	approx. 40 launch tubes for SS-N-21 land-attack SLCM[5]
Torpedo tubes:	6 21-in (533-mm) bow
Torpedoes:	18
Radar:	Snoop Tray surface search
Sonar:	low-frequency active
	passive array
EW systems:	Brick Group

5. SLCM = Sea-Launched Cruise Missile.

The lengthened and extensively modified sail of the Yankee Notch SSGN. The Pert Spring antenna—the most forward mast visible here—is fitted on the starboard side of the sail. (1990, Royal Navy)

At least two Yankee SSBNs have been converted to carry the SS-N-21 SLCM; additional conversions are reported to be under way.

Class: Thirty-four submarines of this design were constructed; see Yankee SSBN listing.

Conversion: During conversion a new amidships section containing an estimated 20 to 40 launch tubes for cruise missiles replaced the 16 SS-N-8 SLBM tubes. The sail structure was lengthened by about 9¾ ft (3 m).

Design: Double-hull configuration.

Designation: Because the SS-N-21 missile is launched from a 21-inch torpedo tube, the NATO designation for this submarine is SSN vice SSGN. The SSGN designation is more appropriate because of the submarine's primary mission and special configuration.

Electronics: Fitted with the Code Eye radiometric sextant and Pert Spring satellite communications antenna.

One Yankee SSBN has been converted into a test platform for the SS-N-24 land-attack cruise missile. This submarine was extensively rebuilt, with an enlarged midships section inserted carrying angled vertical-launch tubes for 12 SS-N-24 missiles, i.e., six on each side.

This unit was "relaunched" in December 1982 and commenced SS-N-24 missile tests in 1985.

Class: Thirty-four submarines of this design were constructed. See Yankee SSBN listing (above).

Design: Double-hull configuration.

The Yankee Notch SSGN has an extensively modified sail structure and amidships hull section, where the SS-N-6 SLBM tubes and hatches have been replaced by launch tubes for the torpedo-size SS-N-21 missile. Note the various patterns of limber holes. (1990, Royal Navy)

1 GUIDED MISSILE SUBMARINE: CONVERTED YANKEE CLASS

Number	Builders	Converted
1 unit		1982–1985

Displacement:	7,900 tons surfaced
	13,650 tons submerged
Length:	501 ft 10 in (153.0 m) overall
Beam:	49 ft–52 ft 6 in (15–16.0 m)
Draft:	29 ft 6 in (9.0 m)
Propulsion:	2 steam turbines; 45,000 shp; 2 shafts (5-bladed propellers)
Reactors:	2 pressurized-water type
Speed:	
	23 knots submerged
Depth:	probably 1,970 ft (600 m)
Complement:	approx. 120
Missiles:	12 SS-N-24 land-attack SLCM
Torpedo tubes:	6 21-in (533-mm) bow
Torpedoes:	18
Radar:	Snoop Tray surface search
Sonar:	low-frequency active
	passive array
EW systems:	Brick Group

This is an artist's concept of a converted Yankee-class SSBN extensively rebuilt to test the SS-N-24 land-attack cruise missile. An enlarged amidships section with 12 tubes for the SS-N-24 replaced the 16 tubes for the SS-N-6 ballistic missile. There are land- and air-launched variants of the SS-N-24. (U.S. Department of Defense)

6+ GUIDED MISSILE SUBMARINES: OSCAR I/II CLASSES

Number	Builders	Launched		Completed
1 unit	Shipyard 402 (Severodvinsk)	Apr	1980	1982
1 unit	Shipyard 402 (Severodvinsk)	Dec	1982	1983
1 unit	Shipyard 402 (Severodvinsk)		1984	1985
1 unit	Shipyard 402 (Severodvinsk)		1988	1989
1 unit	Shipyard 402 (Severodvinsk)		1990	1991
1 unit	Shipyard 402 (Severodvinsk)		1990	1991
. . . units	Shipyard 402 (Severodvinsk)	Building		

Displacement:	Oscar I <u>11,500 tons surfaced</u>
	14,500 tons submerged
	Oscar II <u>13,000 tons surfaced</u>
	16,000 tons submerged
Length:	Oscar I 479 ft (146.0 m) overall
	Oscar II 512 ft (156.0 m) overall
Beam:	59 ft (18.0 m)
Draft:	32 ft 10 in (10.0 m)
Propulsion:	2 steam turbines; approx. 90,000 shp; 2 shafts (7-bladed propeller)
Reactors:	2 pressurized-water type
Speed:	
	Oscar I 33 knots submerged
	Oscar II 30+ knots submerged
Depth:	
Complement:	
Missiles:	SS-N-15 ASW
	SS-N-16 ASW
	24 SS-N-19 anti-ship SLCM
Torpedo tubes:	6 21-in (533-mm) or 25.5-in (650-mm) bow
Torpedoes:	24 (torpedoes and SS-N-15/16 missiles)
Radar:	Snoop Tray surface search
Sonar:	Shark Gill low-frequency active
	medium-frequency active
	passive array
EW systems:	radar warning

This view of an Oscar II SSGN shows the six hatches on either side of the craft's amidships section that cover the 24 SS-N-19 anti-ship missile launch tubes. The elongated sail is a feature familiar to earlier Soviet SSGNs; there is a fitting atop the upper rudder for a towed communications antenna.

This is the largest submarine to be built by any nation except for the Soviet Typhoon SSBN and the U.S. Trident SSBN. The lead unit was laid down in 1978. After two units were built to the Oscar I configuration, the modified Oscar II entered production.

Design: Double-hull configuration. The missile tubes are fitted between the pressure and outer hulls, 12 per side, angled upward at about 40° from the vertical; six rectangular hatches along each side cover pairs of missiles. The space between the hulls amidships (i.e., at the missile tubes) is almost 11½ feet (about 3.5 m).

Electronics: Fitted with the Punch Bowl antenna for receiving satellite targeting data; also fitted with Pert Spring satellite communications receiver.

Operational: An Oscar II transferred to the Pacific Fleet in September 1990, the first of this class to go to the Far East.

An Oscar I SSGN at high speed on the surface reveals the anechoic tiles found on most Soviet combat submarines. Several tiles are missing, a result of adhesive problems. Note that they cover the sail as well as the hull. The port-side bow diving plane is partially visible in this view.

The sail of an Oscar I SSGN shows the elongated form found in most Soviet cruise missile submarines. A single periscope is raised in this photo; all other masts and antennas are retracted. The bulge covers an antenna. No Soviet cruise missile–attack submarines have sail-mounted diving planes except the converted Yankee type.

6 GUIDED MISSILE SUBMARINES: CHARLIE II CLASS

Number	Builders	Completed
1 unit	Krasnoye Sormovo (Gor'kiy)[6]	1973
1 unit	Krasnoye Sormovo (Gor'kiy)	1974
1 unit	Krasnoye Sormovo (Gor'kiy)	1977
1 unit	Krasnoye Sormovo (Gor'kiy)	1979
1 unit	Krasnoye Sormovo (Gor'kiy)	1980–1981
1 unit	Krasnoye Sormovo (Gor'kiy)	1982

Displacement:	4,500 tons surfaced
	5,400 tons submerged
Length:	337 ft 10 in (103.0 m) overall
Beam:	32 ft 10 in (10.0 m)
Draft:	26 ft 3 in (8.0 m)
Propulsion:	2 steam turbines; approx. 30,000 shp; 1 shaft (5-bladed propeller)
Reactors:	1 pressurized-water type
Speed:	
	24 knots submerged
Depth:	probably 1,970 ft (600 m)
Complement:	approx. 100
Missiles:	8 SS-N-9 anti-ship SLCM
	SS-N-15 ASW
Torpedo tubes:	6 21-in (533-mm) bow
Torpedoes:	
Radar:	Snoop Tray surface search
Sonar:	low-frequency active
	passive array
EW systems:	Brick Pulp
	Brick Split

These submarines are similar to the Charlie I SSGN, with an improved missile capability. The slow, long-term production rate reflects the poor performance of these submarines; construction may have been drawn out to keep the Gor'kiy shipways occupied pending start-up of the Sierra SSN production.

Design: Double-hull configuration. They are 29½ ft (9 m) longer than the Charlie I, the additional length being added between the forward missile tubes and sail.

Electronics: The forward portion of the sail structure contains a sonar installation for targeting surface ships while the submarine operates at periscope depth.

6. Nuclear-propelled submarines built at Gor'kiy are completed at Severodvinsk.

This Charlie II SSGN has a "collar" fitted to the forward edge of the sail structure. This device—found in most if not all surviving Charlies—improves the flow of water over the hull. The Charlie was one of the poorest Soviet submarine designs and the only nuclear-propelled combat submarine with a single reactor except for the Mike SSN.

1 GUIDED MISSILE SUBMARINE: PAPA CLASS (PROJECT 661)

Number	Builders	Completed
1 unit	Shipyard 402 (Severodvinsk)	1971

Displacement:	6,400 tons surfaced
	8,000 tons submerged
Length:	357 ft 6 in (109.0 m) overall
Beam:	40 ft (12.2 m)
Draft:	31 ft 2 in (9.5 m)
Propulsion:	2 steam turbines; approx. 60,000–80,000 shp; 2 shafts (5-bladed propellers)
Reactors:	2 pressurized-water type
Speed:	
	42 knots submerged (see notes)
Depth:	1,310 ft (400 m)
Complement:	approx. 85
Missiles:	10 anti-ship SLCM (see notes)
	SS-N-15 ASW
Torpedo tubes:	6 21-in (533-mm) bow
Torpedoes:	
Radar:	Snoop Tray surface search
Sonar:	low-frequency active
	passive array
EW systems:	radar warning

The Papa was a prototype and test bed for an advanced SSGN design. In the event, none of the planned follow-on submarines of this type were constructed. Launched in 1968.

Design: The Papa has a titanium hull although she is not a deep-diving craft. Double-hull configuration. She has a large, spherical bow sonar installation; there is a small sail structure.

Electronics: Fitted with Pert Spring satellite communications receiver.

Engineering: U.S. Navy officials have officially credited the Papa with a speed of 39 knots. She is believed to have attained 42 knots on trials.

Missiles: The Papa was intended to carry a new anti-ship missile named Amethyst, which apparently did not become operational. Western intelligence credits the Papa with being able to carry the

SS-N-9 anti-ship missile although there is no public evidence that she has fired that missile.

Operational: This submarine has seen little active service; she

has undergone extensive overhauls. Assigned to the Northern Fleet. She will be stricken in the near future.

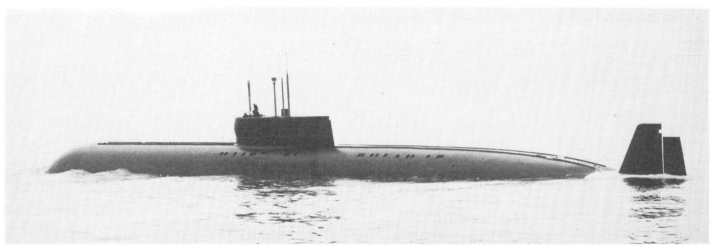

Papa SSGN showing the distinctive rudder configuration.

The Papa shows long, clean lines, with a "notched" upper rudder. There are relatively few limber holes, which end just forward of the sail structure to permit placement of five hatches on each side for what may have been planned for a large cruise missile—the Amethyst—that appears not to have become operational, or the SS-N-7 anti-ship missile.

10 GUIDED MISSILE SUBMARINES: CHARLIE I CLASS (PROJECT 670)

Number	Builders	Completed
10 units	Krasnoye Sormovo (Gor'kiy)	1967–1973

Displacement:	4,000 tons surfaced
	5,000 tons submerged
Length:	308 ft 4 in (94.0 m) overall
Beam:	32 ft 10 in (10.0 m)
Draft:	26 ft 3 in (8.0 m)
Propulsion:	2 steam turbines; approx. 30,000 shp; 1 shaft (5-bladed propeller)
Reactors:	1 pressurized-water type
Speed:	
	24 knots submerged
Depth:	1,970 ft (600 m)
Complement:	approx. 100
Missiles:	8 SS-N-7 anti-ship SLCM
	SS-N-15 ASW
Torpedo tubes:	6 21-in (533-mm) bow
Torpedoes:	12 (torpedoes and SS-N-15 missiles)
Radar:	Snoop Tray surface search
Sonar:	low-frequency active
	passive array
EW systems:	Brick Pulp
	Brick Split

The Charlie-class SSGN was among the least successful Soviet submarine designs and one of the few with a single nuclear reactor. The Charlie introduced the submerged-launch, anti-ship missile to the world's navies.

The Charlie I design was succeeded at Gor'kiy by the similar Charlie II, featuring an improved anti-ship missile capability.

Class: Of the 12 Charlie I-class submarines, one unit was accidentally lost in 1983 (see Operational below); another Charlie I was leased to India in January 1988, the first nuclear-propelled submarine to be transferred to another country by the building nation. That unit was given over to an Indian crew at Vladivostok. She was returned to Soviet custody in 1990.

Design: Double-hull configuration.

Operational: A Charlie I sank off Kamchatka in June 1983 while leaving harbor; 16 crewmen were lost. That unit was salvaged from a depth of 165 feet (50 m) but was not returned to service.

She was subsequently employed at Petropavolsk as a dockside trainer.

A Charlie I SSGN with her sail fitted with a "collar" forward and modified aft, probably to accommodate a towed communications buoy. (1988, Japanese Maritime Self-Defense Force)

26 (?) GUIDED MISSILE SUBMARINES: ECHO II CLASS (PROJECT 675)

Number	Builders	Completed
26 (?) units	Shipyard 402 (Severodvinsk) Shipyard 199 (Komsomol'sk)	1962–1967

Displacement:	5,000 tons surfaced 6,000 tons submerged
Length:	377 ft 2 in (115.0 m) overall
Beam:	29 ft 6 in (9.0 m)
Draft:	24 ft 7 in (7.5 m)
Propulsion:	2 steam turbines; approx. 35,000 shp; 2 shafts (4-bladed propellers)
Reactors:	2 pressurized-water type
Speed:	20 knots surfaced 23 knots submerged
Depth:	
Complement:	approx. 90
Missiles:	8 SS-N-3a anti-ship SLCM or 8 SS-N-12 anti-ship SLCM
Torpedo tubes:	6 21-in (533-mm) bow 4 15.75-in (400-mm) stern
Torpedoes:	
Radar:	Snoop Tray surface search Front Door/Front Piece missile guidance
Sonar:	Feniks low-frequency active passive array
EW systems:	radar warning

This was the ultimate SS-N-3 Shaddock-armed missile submarine design, combining the advantages of nuclear propulsion with a large missile battery (i.e., eight missiles vice six in the Echo I SSGN and four in the Juliett SSG).

Class: Twenty-nine units were completed from 1962 to 1967.

As of mid-1989 there were 26 units reported in active service; one unit has been converted (see below) and at least two units discarded. Additional units are expected to be discarded in the early 1990s with only those rearmed with the SS-N-12 missile being retained for a few more years.

Conversions: One Echo II SSGN has been converted to a special-purpose configuration. She may be employed as a special transport for swimmers or *Spetsnaz* forces. Her missile tubes were removed.

Design: Double-hull configuration.

Electronics: Fitted with the Drambuie Video Data Link (VDL) for missile guidance; submarines carrying the SS-N-12 missile are fitted with the Punch Bowl antenna for receiving satellite targeting data.

Engineering: An Echo II suffered an engineering casualty off Bear Island in the Barents Sea on 26 June 1989. An investigating commission found that the submarine had suffered microscopic

This view of an Echo II SSGN clearly shows the paired Shaddock missile tubes; the open spaces permit the exhaust to escape as the surface-launched missiles are fired. The safety tracks for personnel working topside are also visible.

The Echo II SSGN was the ultimate submarine for surface-launched cruise missiles, the end of a series of undersea craft built by the Soviet and U.S. navies for the SS-N-3/12 and Regulus I/II missiles, respectively. The front end of the Echo II sail rotates to reveal the Front Door/Front Piece radars; see chapter 29. (Courtesy *Ships of the World*)

cracks in a welded joint in a pipeline of the primary reactor coolant system. This discovery contributed to the decision to accelerate taking the first-generation nuclear submarines out of service.

(The submarine returned to her home port on the Kola Peninsula on 28 June; she traveled part of the way on the surface using diesel engines and the remainder under tow.)

Missiles: From 1975–1976 onward several Echo II SSGNs have been rearmed with the SS-N-12 Sandbox anti-ship missile in place of the SS-N-3. Reportedly, up to ten submarines were rearmed by the mid-1980s. The modified submarines have a bulge on either side of the sail and at the forward end of the missile tubes alongside the sail.

Names: One Echo II may have been named DEKABRIST.

An Echo II SSGN showing the Front Door/Front Piece targeting radar in the stowed position. There is a windshield, cockpit, and various periscopes and masts aft of the radar. (1990, Royal Navy)

14 GUIDED MISSILE SUBMARINES: JULIETT CLASS

Number	Builders	Completed
14 units	Krasnoye Sormovo (Gor'kiy)	1961–1967

Displacement:	3,000 tons surfaced
	3,750 tons submerged
Length:	284 ft 5½ in (86.7 m) waterline
	295 ft 2 in (90.0 m) overall
Beam:	32 ft 10 in (10.0 m)
Draft:	23 ft (7.0 m)
Propulsion:	2 diesel engines; 7,000 bhp
	2 electric motors; 5,000 shp
	2 shafts
Speed:	16 knots surfaced
	14 knots submerged
Range:	9,000 n.miles on snorkel at 7 knots
Depth:	1,310 ft (400 m)
Complement:	approx. 80
Missiles:	4 SS-N-3a Shaddock anti-ship SLCMs, except at least one unit rearmed with SS-N-12 anti-ship SLCM
Torpedo tubes:	6 21-in (533-mm) bow
	4 15.75-in (400-mm) stern
Torpedoes:	
Radar:	Front Door/Front Piece missile targeting
	Snoop Slab surface search
Sonar:	Tamir-5L medium-frequency
	Feniks (passive)
EW systems:	Stop Light

These submarines, armed with anti-ship cruise missiles, were constructed in parallel with the nuclear-propelled Echo I/II classes, with production of the Juliett continuing after building of the nuclear units had ceased.

Class: All 16 units were in service until 1984–1985. As of mid-1989 an estimated 14 units remained in service.

Design: Double-hull configuration. The submarine's configuration is not optimized for either surface or submerged speed.

Electronics: The Front Door/Front Piece radar is built into the forward edge of the conning tower; it rotates 180° to expose the antennas for missile guidance. The unit(s) modified for the SS-N-12 missile has the Punch Bowl receiver for satellite targeting data.

Missiles: The SS-N-3 and SS-N-12 missiles are surface launched.

A Juliett SSG with the after pair of SS-N-3a Shaddock tubes in the raised position. (U.S. Navy)

The Juliett SSGs were extensively used by the Soviet Navy through the 1980s despite their limited attack capability and the availability of nuclear-propelled submarines. The Front Door/Front Piece radar housed in the forward rotating end of the sail is visible in this view; the "heel" at the end of the sail is the snorkel exhaust.

A Victor III SSN at high speed on the surface. Forward of the sail is a large canister with two circular hatches at the forward end, apparently a system for test-launching missiles or torpedoes. A variety of masts and periscopes are raised. (1990, Royal Navy)

ATTACK SUBMARINES

Akula

Sierra

Yankee SSN conversion

Alfa

Victor III

Victor II

Victor I

Echo I

Hotel

Attack Submarines (*continued*)

Kilo

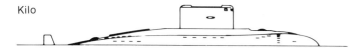

Tango

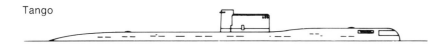

Foxtrot

A modified Victor I-class SSN in the Barents Sea showing the forward diving planes rigged out; what appear to be sensors are fitted just above the planes, on the face of the sail, and on a projection from the top of the sail; several masts and periscopes raised; note the raised windshield of the "cockpit." (1989, Royal Navy)

The size of the Victor III–class towed sonar array pod can be seen from the swimmer at the base of the upper rudder-pod pylon. The craft's propellers are visible at far left. (1983, U.S. Navy)

6 + ATTACK SUBMARINES: AKULA CLASS

Number	Builders	Launched	Completed
1 unit	Shipyard 199 (Komsomol'sk)	July 1984	
1 unit	Shipyard 199 (Komsomol'sk)		
1 unit	Shipyard 199 (Komsomol'sk)	1987	1986—
1 unit	Shipyard 402 (Severodvinsk)	1988	
1 unit	Shipyard 199 (Komsomol'sk)	1989	
1 unit	Shipyard 199 (Komsomol'sk)	1990	1991
. . . units	Shipyard 402 (Severodvinsk)		Building

Displacement:	7,500 tons surfaced
	10,000 tons submerged
Length:	370 ft 6 in (113.0 m) overall
Beam:	42 ft 8 in (13.0 m)
Draft:	32 ft 10 in (10.0 m)
Propulsion:	2 steam turbines; 1 shaft (7-bladed propeller)
Reactors:	2 pressurized-water type
Speed:	
	35+ knots submerged
Missiles:	SS-N-15 ASW
	SS-N-16 ASW
	SS-N-21 land-attack SLCM
Torpedo tubes:	6 21-in (533-mm) and 25.5-in (650-mm) bow
Torpedoes:	
Radar:	Snoop Pair surface search
Sonar:	low-frequency active
	passive array
	passive towed array (pod)
EW systems:	Amber Light
	Stop Light

The Akula is an extremely quiet attack–cruise missile submarine, going to sea about eight to ten years before Western intelligence estimated the Soviets could put a submarine to sea with as low sound levels. The craft may have been designed, in part, to serve as a launch platform for the SS-N-21 strategic cruise missile.

Design: Double-hull configuration.

Operational: The first two units served as test platforms for the SS-N-21 missile during the winter of 1987–1988.

3+ ATTACK SUBMARINES: SIERRA I/II CLASSES

Number	Builders	Completed
1 unit	Krasnoye Sormovo (Gor'kiy)	1984
1 unit	Krasnoye Sormovo (Gor'kiy)	1987
1 unit	Krasnoye Sormovo (Gor'kiy)	1990
. . . units	Krasnoye Sormovo (Gor'kiy)	Building

Displacement:	6,000 tons surfaced
	7,550 tons submerged
Length:	351 ft (107.0 m) overall (see notes)
Beam:	39 ft 4 in (12.0 m)
Draft:	
Propulsion:	2 steam turbines; 1 shaft (7-bladed propeller)
Reactors:	2 pressurized-water
Speed:	
	34–36 knots
Depth:	2,300 ft (700 m)
Complement:	
Missiles:	SS-N-15 ASW
	SS-N-16 ASW
	possibly SS-N-21 land-attack SLCM
Torpedo tubes:	2 21-in (533-mm) bow
	4 25.5-in (650-mm) bow
Torpedoes:	
Radar:	Snoop Pair surface search
Sonar:	Shark Gill low-frequency active
	passive array
	passive towed array (pod)
EW systems:	radar warning

The lead unit was launched in July 1983 and transported to Severodvinsk for completion (like other Gor'kiy-built nuclear submarines). Note the slow production rate.

Design: Double-hull configuration with titanium pressure hull. The operating depth may be greater than indicated above.

The third and later units are about 16 feet (5 m) longer and are referred to as the Sierra II class.

An Akula SSN in the Far East. These submarines—now being constructed at both the Komsomol'sk and Severodvinsk shipyards—introduced a new level of quieting to Soviet submarines, reducing the long-held U.S. Navy advantage in acoustic detection of submarines. The long sail structure may be related to the submarine's ability to launch SS-N-21 land-attack cruise missiles.

The Sierra SSN is a deep-diving, titanium-hulled submarine. In this respect, along with the ill-fated Mike SSN, the Sierra is a partial successor to the revolutionary Alfa design. Construction, however, continues at a relatively slow rate at the Gor'kiy shipyard. (1984, Royal Norwegian Air Force)

Sierra SSN sail (1984, RNorAF)

The prototype Sierra-class SSN in the Norwegian Sea (1984, RNorAF)

2+12 ATTACK SUBMARINES: CONVERTED YANKEE CLASS (PROJECT 667)

Number	Builders	Converted
1 unit	Shipyard 402 (Severodvinsk)	1984
1 unit	Shipyard 199 (Komsomol'sk)	1987
12 units		Status uncertain

Displacement:	7,900 tons surfaced
	9,600 tons submerged
Length:	approx. 426 ft 5 in (130.0 m) overall (see notes)
Beam:	39 ft 4 in (12.0 m)
Draft:	28 ft 2½ in (8.6 m)
Propulsion:	2 steam turbines; 45,000 shp; 2 shafts (5-bladed propellers)
Reactors:	2 pressurized-water type
Speed:	27 knots submerged
Depth:	probably 1,970 ft (600 m)
Complement:	approx. 120
Missiles:	SS-N-15 ASW (see notes)
Torpedo tubes:	6 21-in (533-mm) bow
Torpedoes:	18 (SS-N-15 + torpedoes)
Radar:	Snoop Tray surface search
Sonar:	low-frequency active
	passive towed array (pod)
EW systems:	Brick Group

The Yankee was the Soviet Navy's first "modern" SSBN design. Two or more units have been converted to an attack-submarine configuration.

Class: Thirty-four submarines of this design were constructed.

Conversion: Fourteen Yankee SSBNs have had their SLBM capability deleted and now rate as SSN/SSNX. The latter (SSNX) have not yet been altered and may be reconfigured to torpedo-attack, cruise-missile, minelaying, or some other configuration.

In the SSN role the submarines have been slightly lengthened with a modified bow fitted to accommodate a low-frequency active/passive sonar.

Design: Double-hull configuration.

5 ATTACK SUBMARINES: ALFA CLASS (PROJECT 705)

Number	Builders	Completed
5 units	Sudomekh (Leningrad)[7]	1979–1982
	Shipyard 402 (Severodvinsk)	

Displacement:	2,900 tons surfaced
	3,680 tons submerged
Length:	267 ft (81.4 m) overall
Beam:	31 ft 2 in (9.5 m)
Draft:	23 ft (7.0 m)
Propulsion:	2 steam turbines; approx. 45,000 shp; 2 shafts (5-bladed propeller)
Reactors:	2 lead-bismuth type
Speed:	43 knots submerged
Depth:	1,970–2,500 ft (600–760 m)
Complement:	25–45 (see notes)
Missiles:	SS-N-15 ASW
Torpedo tubes:	6 21-in (533-mm) bow
Torpedoes:	
Radar:	Snoop Tray surface search
Sonar:	low-frequency active
	passive array
EW systems:	Brick Pulp
	Brick Split

7. Nuclear-propelled submarines constructed at Admiralty and Sudomekh are completed at Severodvinsk.

The Alfa was a revolutionary submarine design of the mid-1950s. Although suffering severe development problems, the Alfa is the fastest submarine yet constructed by any nation and one of the deepest diving (the latter characteristic only exceeded by other Soviet submarines).

The lead submarine was probably launched on 22 April 1969, the birth date of V.I. Lenin. Beginning in 1969 that craft was engaged in lengthy trials in the Northern Fleet area; she suffered major engineering problems and was never fully operational. After extensive repairs, her hull was cut apart and beached in 1973–1974.

A second unit was decommissioned in the mid-1980s.

Class: Following the ill-fated prototype (built at Sudomekh), three additional units were built at Sudomekh and three at Severodvinsk, completed in 1979–1982.

Design: Double-hull configuration with a titanium pressure hull, the world's first submarine built of that material. The submarine's high-speed design (note the length-to-beam ratio) includes a streamlined sail that is "blended" into the hull.

The Alfa is fitted with a personnel rescue sphere provided for the escape of the crew in the event the submarine is disabled.

These submarine are highly automated; Western intelligence estimates that an Alfa crew is between 25 and 45 men. The former is probably more likely, with a very high percentage of officers and warrants, and few, if any, enlisted personnel.

An Alfa SSN with a periscope and two electronic masts raised; hatches cover mast and periscope openings to preserve the craft's streamlined surfaces. The escape hatch aft of the sail and markings for salvage fittings are evident. (Royal Navy)

An Alfa SSN on the Barents Sea. The sail is "blended" into the hull to enhance underwater performance. The limber hulls beneath the sail indicate the double-hulled configuration of the craft. Although the first Alfa suffered major engineering problems, a production run of six submarines followed. (U.S. Navy)

25+ ATTACK SUBMARINES: VICTOR III CLASS (PROJECT 671RTM)

Number	Builders	Completed
25+ units {	Admiralty (Leningrad) Shipyard 199 (Komsomol'sk)	} 1978—

Displacement:	4,900 tons surfaced
	6,000 tons submerged
Length:	347 ft 8 in (106.0 m) overall
Beam:	32 ft 10 in (10.0 m)
Draft:	23 ft (7.0 m)
Propulsion:	2 steam turbines; approx. 30,000 shp; 1 shaft (2 4-bladed propellers or 1 7-bladed propeller) + 2 pods (2-bladed propellers) (see notes)
Reactors:	2 pressurized-water type
Speed:	
	29 knots submerged
Depth:	1,970 ft (600 m)
Complement:	approx. 90
Missiles:	SS-N-15 ASW
	SS-N-16 ASW
	possibly SS-N-21 land-attack SLCM
Torpedo tubes:	4 25.5-in (650-mm) bow
	2 21-in (533-mm) bow
Torpedoes:	18 (SS-N-15/16/21 + torpedoes)
Radar:	Snoop Tray surface search
Sonar:	low-frequency active
	passive array
	towed array (pod)
EW systems:	radar warning

This is the ultimate variant of the Victor III design—significantly quieter than previous Soviet SSNs; the Victor III class is also fitted with an improved sonar suite. This is the largest Soviet submarine class with construction continuing at the rate of one unit per year when this edition went to press.

Design: Double-hull configuration.

Designation: The project number suffix RTM probably indicates *Raketnyy Modifikatsirovanny* (rocket-modified version).

Electronics: The Victor III was the first Soviet submarine to be fitted with a pod atop the upper rudder to house a passive towed-array sonar. This feature subsequently appeared on the Sierra, Yankee, and Akula SSNs.

Engineering: This class has approximately the self-generated sound levels of the US STURGEON (SSN 637) class; the later units of the Victor III class are quieter than the earlier ones. Most units have twin, contrarotating, four-bladed propellers fitted to the single shaft, oriented 22.5° apart and co-rotating. These are probably emergency "come home" propulsors.

Victor III–class SSN.

A Victor III showing the small sail typical of Soviet SSNs (with several anechoic tiles missing) and the towed array pod atop the rudder that was introduced with this class (see chapter 29).

7 ATTACK SUBMARINES: VICTOR II CLASS (PROJECT 671RT)

Number	Builder	Completed
3 units	Krasnoye Sormovo (Gor'kiy)	1972–1978
4 units	Admiralty (Leningrad)	

Displacement:	4,500 tons surfaced
	5,900 tons submerged
Length:	344 ft 7 in (102.0 m) overall
Beam:	32 ft 10 in (10.0 m)
Draft:	23 ft (7.0 m)
Propulsion:	2 steam turbines; approx. 30,000 shp; 1 shaft (5-bladed propeller) + 2 pods (2-bladed propellers) (see notes)
Reactors:	2 pressurized-water type
Speed:	
	approx. 30 knots submerged
Depth:	1,970 ft (600 m)
Complement:	approx. 80
Missiles:	SS-N-15 ASW
	SS-N-16 ASW
Torpedo tubes:	4 25.5-in (650-mm) bow
	2 21-in (533-mm) bow
Torpedoes:	
Radar:	Snoop Tray surface search
Sonar:	low-frequency active
	passive array
EW systems:	Brick Pulp
	Brick Split

An interim improvement over the Victor I, apparently enlarged to accommodate 25.5-in (650-mm) torpedo tubes plus reloads for the SS-N-16 missile. Gor'kiy was the lead yard for this design (later Victor classes were built at Admiralty and Komsomol'sk).

Class: This class was initially given the NATO code name Uniform; changed to Victor II when determined that the design was a variant of the original Victor, with the name Uniform subsequently being assigned to a later, one-of-a-kind submarine.

Design: Double-hull configuration.

Engineering: Some units may have eight-bladed propellers, as in the Victor III class.

The Victor II SSN head-on provides an impressive sight. The submarine has a search periscope and (thinner) attack periscope raised, with an antenna mast between them.

A Victor II in the Barents Sea. The "notched" upper rudder fin is visible at left; the submarine has some 16½ feet (5 m) added to the Victor I design, forward of the sail. Aft, over the engineering spaces, are an emergency marker buoy and the after escape hatch; there are another buoy and hatch forward. (U.S. Navy)

16 ATTACK SUBMARINES: VICTOR I CLASS (PROJECT 671)

Number	Builder	Completed
2 units	Admiralty (Leningrad)	1968
2 units	Admiralty (Leningrad)	1969
2 units	Admiralty (Leningrad)	1970
2 units	Admiralty (Leningrad)	1971
2 units	Admiralty (Leningrad)	1972
2 units	Admiralty (Leningrad)	1973
2 units	Admiralty (Leningrad)	1974
2 units	Admiralty (Leningrad)	1975

Displacement:	4,300 tons surfaced
	5,100 tons submerged
Length:	311 ft 7 in (95.0 m) overall
Beam:	32 ft 10 in (10.0 m)
Draft:	23 ft (7.0 m)
Propulsion:	2 steam turbines; approx. 30,000 shp; 1 shaft (5-bladed propeller) + 2 pods (2-bladed propellers)
Reactors:	2 pressurized-water type
Speed:	
	33 knots submerged
Depth:	1,970 ft (600 m)
Complement:	approx. 80
Missiles:	SS-N-15 ASW
Torpedo tubes:	6 21-in (533-mm) bow
Torpedoes:	
Radar:	Snoop Tray surface search
Sonar:	low-frequency active
	passive array
EW systems:	Brick Pulp
	Brick Split

The Victor was the first Soviet attack submarine considered by U.S. Navy officials to be developed primarily for the anti-submarine role; these were the first Soviet submarines to have low-frequency sonar.

Design: Double-hull configuration with a high-speed hull design. There are two small propeller pods or "spinners" on the horizontal stern control surfaces.

Names: One unit is named 50 LET SSR ("50 years of the USSR").

A Victor I sail with Snoop Tray radar, two periscopes, and a radio antenna raised; the retracted forward diving planes are covered over in this view. (Royal Navy)

The Victor I has a high-speed hull design with a small, streamlined sail structure. The forward diving planes retract into the hull when surfaced (just under the forward edge of the sail).

3 (?) ATTACK SUBMARINES: ECHO I CLASS (PROJECT 659)

Number	Builders	Completed
3 (?) units	Shipyard 199 (Komsomol'sk)	1960–1962

Displacement:	4,500 tons surfaced
	5,500 tons submerged
Length:	373 ft 11 in (114.0 m) overall
Beam:	29 ft 6 in (9.0 m)
Draft:	21 ft 4 in (6.5 m)
Propulsion:	2 steam turbines; 25,000 shp; 2 shafts (5-bladed propellers)
Reactors:	2 pressurized-water type
Speed:	20 knots surfaced
	25 knots submerged
Depth:	985 ft (300 m)
Complement:	approx. 75
Missiles:	removed
Torpedo tubes:	6 21-in (533-mm) M-57 bow
	4 15.75-in (400-mm) stern
Torpedoes:	
Radar:	Snoop Tray surface search
Sonar:	medium-frequency active passive array
EW systems:	radar warning

These are guided missile submarines developed specifically for the land attack role (similar to the abortive U.S. Regulus program). Because they lacked the Front Door/Front Piece radar for carrying anti-ship variants of the SS-N-3 Shaddock missile, they were converted to an attack submarine configuration.

As of 1989 only three of these submarines remained in service. Those were expected to be discarded in the early 1990s.

Conversion: Converted from an SSGN to attack submarine (SSN) configuration about 1970–1975.

Design: Double-hull configuration.

Operational: These submarines served their entire careers in the Pacific.

The Echo I SSNs as well as the November SSNs are being retired from naval service as part of the reduction in operating forces. The Echo I lacked the Front Door/Front Piece radar of the Echo II and Juliett classes. The radio mast visible here folds back into a recess in the deck.

5 (?) ATTACK SUBMARINES: CONVERTED HOTEL II CLASS (PROJ. 658)

Number	Builders	Completed
5 (?) units	Shipyard 402 (Severodvinsk)	1961–1962

Displacement:	5,000 tons surfaced
	6,000 tons submerged
Length:	377 ft 2 in (115 m) overall
Beam:	29 ft 6 in (9 m)
Draft:	23 ft (7 m)
Propulsion:	2 steam turbines; 30,000 shp
	2 shafts (6-bladed propellers)
Reactors:	2 pressurized-water type
Speed:	20 knots surfaced
	23–25 knots submerged
Depth:	
Complement:	approx. 80
Missiles:	removed
Torpedo tubes:	6 21-in (533-mm) M-57 bow
	2 15.75-in (400-mm) stern
Torpedoes:	
Radar:	Snoop Tray surface search
Sonar:	medium-frequency active
	passive array
Electronic warfare:	Stop Light

A Hotel II–class submarine in the SSBN configuration off the coast of Newfoundland. (1972, Ministry of Defence)

The Hotel was the world's first nuclear-propelled ballistic missile submarine (SSBN) to be constructed, slightly predating the U.S. Polaris submarines.

Only one unit remains in service as an SSBN, the single Hotel III missile test ship. All others have had their SLBM capability deleted under the U.S.-Soviet SALT agreement; of the latter, one serves as a communication ship with others employed in the torpedo-attack role (SSN). These SSNs were expected to be discarded in the early 1990s.

Class: All eight Hotel-class SSBNs completed between 1959 and 1962 were upgraded from the SS-N-4 SLBM capability (surface launch) to the SS-N-5 (underwater launch) missile. See Hotel III listing (above) for additional details.

Conversion: In the late 1980s one Hotel was extensively modified for research purposes, being fitted with a large number of hydrodynamic sensors and other devices on her forward deck and sail structure. A small pair of fixed planes were also mounted on the hull, beneath the sail.

Design: Double-hull configuration.

Names: One unit was named KRASNOGVARDETS.

A former Hotel II–class SSBN as converted to a hydrodynamic test platform in the late 1980s. Note the variety of sensors and other devices installed on deck forward of the bridge and the extensively modified sail structure; there are also sensor devices projecting from the sides of the sail (just above the fixed planes). (Royal Navy)

FEW ATTACK SUBMARINES: NOVEMBER CLASS (PROJECT 627)

Number	Builders	Completed
few units	Shipyard 402 (Severodvinsk)	1958–1963

Displacement:	4,500 tons surfaced
	5,300 tons submerged
Length:	358.59 ft (109.3 m) waterline
	359.9 ft (109.7 m) overall (see notes)
Beam:	29 ft 10 in (9.1 m)
Draft:	25 ft 3 in (7.7 m)
Propulsion:	2 steam turbines; 35,000 shp; 2 shafts (4- or 6-bladed propellers)
Reactors:	2 pressurized-water type
Speed:	16 knots surfaced
	30 knots submerged
Depth:	985 ft (300 m)
Complement:	approx. 80
Torpedo tubes:	8 21-in (533-mm) M-57 bow
Torpedoes:	24
Radar:	Snoop Tray surface search
Sonar:	medium-frequency active passive array
EW systems:	radar warning

This was the first Soviet nuclear-propelled submarine class, designed under the direction of Engineer-Captain 1st Rank V.N. Peregudov. Construction of the lead ship began in 1954; she was placed in commission on 8 April 1958.

As of 1989, one unit had been lost (see below) and at least one unit had been scrapped; all others were being stricken in the early 1990s.

Class: Some sources list 15 submarines of this class having been constructed (two units completed in 1964); however, 13 is the more likely number.

Design: Double-hull configuration with a highly streamlined hull and a small, streamlined sail structure. The design also has a distinctive upper rudder.

Western sources generally credit the November with four 15.75-inch (400-mm) stern torpedo tubes. They were not fitted according to Soviet sources.

Engineering: Some and possibly all November-class submarines underwent extensive modification to their propulsion plants after completion: their overall length was increased from 323¾ feet (98.7 m) to the length indicated above (i.e., an insert of about 36 feet/11 m).

Names: The lead ship was named LENINSKIY KOMSOMOL after her voyage to the geographic North Pole in July 1962. Another unit was named LENINETS.

Operational: These submarines have suffered a number of engineering casualties and fires.

One November sank in the Atlantic off Cape Finisterre (Spain) in April 1970, during exercise *Okean*. This first Soviet nuclear submarine loss came after the submarine suffered an engineering casualty; the submarine was able to surface and most if not all of the crew was removed before the craft sank.

The November-class SSN was the Soviet Navy's first nuclear-propelled submarine but was constructed almost simultaneously with the Hotel SSBN and Echo SSGN classes.

Sail structure of a November SSN; only a radome is raised. (1970)

November-class SSN showing bow and sail-mounted sonar "windows." (Soviet Navy)

Kilo-class submarine showing the elongated sail structure, which may house a surface-to-air missile system. (U.S. Navy)

ATTACK SUBMARINE: MIKE (PROJECT 845)

The single Mike-type submarine (named KOMSOMOLETS) was developed, according to Soviet reports, to test 12 advanced submarine technologies. However, she was considered a fully operational submarine, and after extensive trails undertook a "combat" deployment (see Operational notes). She was designed in the 1960s, but the date that construction began is not publicly known; she was launched in June 1983.

She was accidently lost at sea on 7 April 1989.

Design: Double-hull configuration with titanium pressure hull with seven compartments. Explosive charges were fitted to expel water from the ballast tanks in an emergency at deep depths.

The KOMSOMOLETS was fitted with a personnel rescue sphere, provided for the escape of the crew in the event the submarine was disabled. As she sank the commanding officer and four other crew members entered the sphere as the submarine plunged to the bottom; the sphere was released but was partially flooded and filled with toxic gas; only one man survived the rapid ascent and surfacing of the sphere before it sank.

The KOMSOMOLETS was highly automated with a crew of only 68 (in addition, a senior political officer was on board at the time of her loss; he survived).

Designation: The project number 690 has also been reported for this submarine.

Engineering: Before the submarine's loss, Western intelligence had estimated that the Mike had two liquid-metal/lead-bismuth reactors. She was fitted with a single pressurized-water reactor.

Operational: The single Mike SSN was lost following a fire that erupted in the aftermost compartment while the submarine was running submerged. The KOMSOMOLETS was able to surface and the fire was fought for several hours before the submarine began flooding and sank. She went down 112 n.miles (180 km) southeast of Bear Island, off the Norwegian coast, in water approximately 4,900 ft (1,500 m) deep. Of 69 men on board, four apparently died in the fire; four in the rescue chamber because of toxic gases and other problems; and another 34 died in the water of hypothermia, heart failure, or drowning—a total loss of 42 men.

She was on her first operational (combat) patrol after extensive trials and evaluation. The KOMSOMOLETS carried ten torpedoes at the time of her loss, two of which had nuclear warheads.

19+ SUBMARINES: KILO CLASS (PROJECT 877)

Number	Builders	Completed
1 unit	Shipyard 199 (Komsomol'sk)	Apr 1982
13+ units	Sudomekh/Admiralty (Leningrad) Krasnoye Sormovo (Gor'kiy) Shipyard 199 (Komsomol'sk)	1983—

Displacement:	2,300 tons surfaced
	2,900 tons submerged
Length:	229 ft 7 in (73.0 m) overall
Beam:	32 ft 6 in (9.9 m)
Draft:	21 ft 4 in (6.5 m)
Propulsion:	2 diesel engines
	2 electric motors
	1 shaft (6-bladed propeller)
Speed:	12 knots surfaced
	25 knots submerged
Range:	
Depth:	
Complement:	approx. 60
Missiles:	SAM in some units[8]
Torpedo tubes:	6 21-in (533-mm) bow
Torpedoes:	12
Radar:	Snoop Tray
Sonar:	low-frequency
EW systems:	Brick Pulp

These are advanced attack submarines being constructed simultaneously for Soviet use and for foreign transfer (the latter being built by Sudomekh and possibly Gor'kiy). The construction rate in the late 1980s was four units per year with three for transfer and one for Soviet service. Over 30 units were completed by early 1991 with four per year being built during the late 1980s for Soviet and foreign use.

The lead unit was launched in September 1980.

Class: Submarines of this class have been transferred upon completion to Algeria (2), India (8), Poland (1), and Romania (1).

Design: The Kilo has a more pronounced tear-drop hull form than previous Soviet conventional submarines. The design has a double-hull configuration with bow-mounted diving planes.

Engineering: The Kilo's diesel engines have a high degree of supercharging; other improvements, some of which are related to supercharging, include reducing the specific weight of the engines and notably reducing the specific fuel consumption in comparison with earlier Soviet diesel-electric submarines.

Missiles: Some units have been fitted with a short-range SAM system.

8. SAM = Surface-to-Air Missile.

The Kilo-class diesel-electric submarine is being constructed at three shipyards for Soviet and foreign service. Some of the Soviet units are reported to have an anti-aircraft missile system. (1989, JMSDF)

The Kilo-class attack submarine has a modified "tear-drop" hull design, somewhat similar to the U.S. Navy's last diesel-electric submarines of the BARBEL (SS 580) class.

APPROX. 15 LONG-RANGE SUBMARINES: TANGO CLASS

Number	Builders	Completed
approx. 15 units	Krasnoye Sormovo (Gor'kiy)	1972–1982

Displacement:	3,200 tons surfaced
	3,900 tons submerged
Length:	300 ft 10 in (91.7 m) waterline
	300 ft 2 in (91.5 m) overall
Beam:	29 ft 6 in (9.0 m)
Draft:	23 ft (7.0 m)
Propulsion:	3 diesel engines; 6,000 bhp
	3 electric motors; 6,000 shp
	3 shafts (5-blade propellers)
Speed:	20 knots surfaced
	18 knots submerged
Range:	
Depth:	1,310 ft (400 m)
Complement:	approx. 70
Missiles:	SAM fitted in some units
	SS-N-15 ASW
Torpedo tubes:	10 21-in (533-mm) 6 bow + 4 stern
Torpedoes:	
Radar:	Snoop Tray
Sonar:	low-frequency
EW systems:	

The Tango is a follow-on to the Foxtrot class, with improved underwater endurance through battery capacity. Several units were laid up or stricken in the late 1980s.

A Tango at sea with anechoic tiles missing from her after section. The production run of this submarine was small in comparison with its predecessor, the Foxtrot. No successor in this size category of diesel-electric submarines has evolved.

Class: The exact number built is not publicly known; the range of Western estimates is generally 21 or 22 units, completed from 1972 to 1982.

Design: Double-hull configuration.

Missiles: One or more units have been fitted with a short-range SA-N-14 SAM system.

Foxtrot with Quad Loop direction-finder and Snoop Tray radar antennas visible. The retracting radio mast is in the raised position, at the after end of the sail on the starboard side. (U.S. Navy)

The Tango's bow is much more "filled out" than that of the Foxtrot; also, the bow sonar domes of the Tango and Kilo are "dark" compared to the sonar "windows" of earlier Soviet submarines.

APPROX. 40 LONG-RANGE SUBMARINES: FOXTROT CLASS (PROJECT 641)

Number	Builders	Completed
approx. 40 units	Sudomekh (Leningrad)	1958–1973

Displacement:	1,950 tons surfaced
	2,400 tons submerged
Length:	295 ft 3 in (90.0 m) waterline
	300 ft 2 in (91.5 m) overall
Beam:	24 ft 7 in (7.5 m)
Draft:	20 ft (6.1 m)
Propulsion:	3 37D diesel engines in early units and 2D42 diesel
	engines in later units; 6,000 bhp
	3 electric motors; 5,300 shp
	3 shafts
Speed:	16 knots surfaced
	15.5 knots submerged
Range:	20,000 n.miles surfaced at economical speed
	11,000 n.miles on snorkel at 8 knots
	350 n.miles submerged at 2 knots
Depth:	985 ft (300 m)
Complement:	78 (8 officers + 70 enlisted)
Missiles:	none
Torpedo tubes:	10 21-in (533-mm) M-57: 6 bow + 4 stern in early units;
	later units have 4 15.75-in (400-mm) tubes in stern
Torpedoes:	22
Radar:	Snoop Tray
	Snoop Slab refitted in some units
Sonar:	Herkules medium-frequency
	Feniks passive
EW systems:	Stop Light

Foxtrot-class SS

These are long-range submarines, a much-improved successor to the Zulu class. This is the second largest class of conventional submarines built by any navy since World War II (the Whiskey class being the largest). As of early 1990 approximately 40 units remained in active Soviet service with others laid up or stricken.

Class: The Sudomekh yard in Leningrad is believed to have completed 45 units for Soviet service between 1958 and 1967 with the Severodvinsk yard completing three units in 1962; an additional 14 units were then completed at Sudomekh between 1971 and 1973.

Up to 17 additional Foxtrots were built specifically for foreign transfer, completed from 1969 to 1984 at Sudomekh: Cuba (3), India (8), and Libya (6). In some instances, older Soviet units may have been transferred with the new construction Foxtrots being placed in Soviet service.

Some sources list a total of 80 units being constructed. One or more Soviet units may have been lost operationally, but official data cannot be obtained.

Conversions: Several units have operated as hydrographic research submarines (see below).

Design: Double-hull design. The pressure hull diameter is approximately 13 ft 2 in (4 m). The class has several different limber-hole configurations.

Engineering: Fuel capacity is 360 tons. Note that submerged endurance (without snorkeling) is more than seven days at slow speed.

Names: Known Foxtrot-class names honor young Communist (*Komsomol*) groups.

CHELYABINSKIY KOMSOMOLETS
KOMSOMOLETS KAZAKHSTANA
KUIBISHEVSKIY KOMSOMOLETS
MAGNITOGORSKIY KOMSOMOLETS
UL'YANOVSKIY KOMSOMOLETS
VLADIMIRSKIY KOMSOMOLETS
YAROSLAVSKIY KOMSOMOLETS

Operational: Endurance is estimated at 70 days.

A Foxtrot-class SS in the Pacific; the extensive bow and sail-mounted sonar antennas are evident. (1989, JMSDF)

FEW MEDIUM-RANGE SUBMARINES: WHISKEY CLASS (PROJECT 613)

Number	Builders	Completed
few units	Krasnoye Sormovo (Gor'kiy) Marti (south) (Nikolayev) Shipyard 199 (Komsomol'sk) Baltic Shipyard (Leningrad)	1951–1956

Displacement:	1,055 tons surfaced 1,350 tons submerged
Length:	246 ft 9 in (75.2 m) waterline 249 ft 4 in (76.0 m) overall
Beam:	20 ft 8 in (6.3 m)
Draft:	16 ft 1 in (4.9 m)
Propulsion:	2 37D diesel engines; 4,000 bhp 2 electric motors; 2,500 shp 2 electric creeping motors; 100 shp 2 shafts (3- and 4-bladed propellers)
Speed:	17 knots surfaced 7 knots snorkeling 13.5 knots submerged
Range:	12,000–15,000 n.miles (22,080–27,600 km) surfaced at 10 knots 6,000 n.miles on snorkel at 5 knots
Depth:	656 ft (200 m)
Complement:	56
Missiles:	none
Torpedo tubes:	6 21-in (533-mm) 4 bow + 2 stern
Guns:	(see notes)
Radar:	Snoop Plate surface search
Sonar:	Tamir-5L medium-frequency Feniks passive
EW systems:	Stop Light

This was the largest submarine class to be built in peacetime by any nation—236 units were completed from 1950 to 1957; it was the largest submarine class in history except for the German Type VII of World War II. Sections and components for an additional 21 units were delivered to China for assembly in Chinese shipyards.

About 45 units remained in active Soviet service in early 1989 plus a large number of units in various stages of reserve; all surviving units were being discarded in 1989–1991. All of the specialized conversions of Whiskey-class submarines have been discarded.

The Krasnoye Sormovo in Gor'kiy served as the lead yard for the Whiskey project (building 146 units). After launching in 1950, the first unit was moved to Baku by transporter dock for fitting out. The Nosenko (Marti) yard in Nikolayev delivered its first unit in 1951 (65 built), the Amur River (No. 199) shipyard in Komsomol'sk in 1954 (11 built), and the Baltic shipyard in Leningrad in 1955 (14 built).

(This was the last Soviet submarine design to be constructed at more than two shipyards until the Kilo class of 1982.)

Class: Forty-three Whiskey-class submarines have been transferred to other navies, in addition to the components for 21 units transferred to China for assembly (see appendix C). The NATO code name Whiskey was given suffixes I through V to indicate variants.

The construction of Whiskey-class submarines was halted prematurely in the defense cutbacks of 1953; subsequent production apparently was based on components already produced.

Conversions: *Canvas Bag*—Five and possibly six submarines were converted from 1959 to 1963 to the Canvas Bag radar picket configuration and fitted with the Boat Sail air-search radar.

One of the last active Whiskey-class submarines. (1988, JMSDF)

Single-cylinder—One Whiskey was converted to single-cylinder guided missile configuration with a single SS-N-3 Shaddock missile canister/launcher fitted aft of the conning tower.

Twin cylinder—Five Whiskeys were fitted with a twin Shaddock canister/launcher aft of the conning tower.

Long Bin—This was the "ultimate" Shaddock configuration, with four missile tubes fitted into the forward end of an enlarged conning tower. The craft was awkward to handle while submerged. There were seven conversions with some sources indicating that up to 72 were planned. These submarines were lengthened to 272¼ ft (83 m).

Research—A number of Whiskey-class submarines have served as trial platforms for weapons and sonar equipment. Several units were fitted with various deck-mounted, large-diameter torpedo tubes and others with a variety of sonar devices.

Special operations—The Whiskey Va sub-type was fitted for carrying swimmers with hatch covering for lockout chamber fitted forward of the conning tower.

Fisheries research—Two units converted in 1950s for civilian research; armament deleted and refitted with oceanographic and fisheries research laboratories. Renamed SERVERYANKA and SLAV-YANKA; first oceanographic cruise in December 1958.

Design: The Whiskey design appears to date to 1944, having been conceived as a successor to the S class. Some captured German Type XXI technology was incorporated into the design after the war.

The conning tower of a Whiskey-class submarine: at right are a raised radio antenna; mast-mounted Stop Light ECM antenna; fixed Quad Loop direction-finding antenna; and the fixed snorkel exhaust. (1982)

Double-hull construction with seven compartments. The pressure hull diameter is 15 ft–15 ft 9 in (4.6–4.8 m).

Engineering: Fuel capacity is 120 tons. Snorkel installations were provided to most or all active Soviet units in the 1950s.

Guns: The earliest Whiskey-class units mounted a single 100-mm/51-cal deck gun abaft the conning tower. The Whiskey I units had only the twin 25-mm mount. In the later Whiskey II units a twin 57-mm deck gun was mounted in lieu of the 100-m weapon. Both variants had additionally a twin 25-mm AA gun installed forward of the conning tower. Toward the end of the 1950s all gun armament appears to have been removed from units retained by the Soviet Navy (Whiskey III). The Whiskey IV retained the 25-mm mount with a snorkel installation while the Whiskey V had no guns, with the gun step deleted from forward of the conning tower.

Names: One unit of this class was named PSKOVSKIY KOMSOM-OLETS.

Operational: Estimated endurance is 40–45 days.

Torpedoes: Torpedo armament was considerably less than in contemporary U.S. submarines as well as in the later war-built Soviet (K-class) submarines.

MEDIUM-RANGE SUBMARINES (SS): ROMEO CLASS (PROJECT 633)

Twenty medium-range submarines of the Romeo class, a much-improved successor to the Whiskey class, were completed from 1958 to 1962. The last Soviet units were taken out of active service in the late 1980s. Thirteen units were transferred to other navies after Soviet service; see appendix C. See 4th edition, page 154, for description.

Additional Romeo-class submarines were built in China; several of those units were transferred to Egypt and North Korea.

COASTAL SUBMARINES (SS): QUEBEC CLASS (PROJECT 615)

The 30 submarines of the Quebec class were completed from 1954 to 1957, apparently intended as successor to the M classes for operation in the Baltic and Black Seas. The design was intended to employ a closed-cycle propulsion. All units were stricken by the early 1980s. See 3rd edition, page 116, for characteristics.

SMALL SUBMARINES (SS): IMPROVED M CLASS

Ten or 11 small submarines of the M series of post-World War II design were completed from 1947 to 1950, probably all at the Sudomekh Shipyard in Leningrad. Characteristics of the submarines were not known in the West, but some or all were probably experimental types of various designs.

(A large number of M-class submarines were built in the 1930s and 1940s, the M indicating *Malyutka*, or "little one.")

SPECIAL-PURPOSE SUBMARINES

Golf SSQ
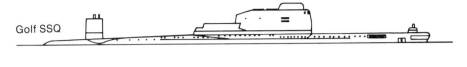

India class
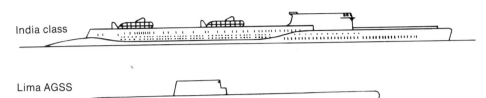

Lima AGSS

Bravo class

1 EXPERIMENTAL SUBMARINE: BELUGA (PROJECT 949)

Number	Builders	Completed
1 unit	Sudomekh/Admiralty (Leningrad)	1987–1988

Displacement:	2,000 tons surfaced
	2,500 tons submerged
Length:	213 ft 2 in (65.0 m) overall
Beam:	32 ft 10 in (10.0 m)
Draft:	19 ft 8 in (6.0 m)
Propulsion:	unknown
Speed:	
Range:	
Depth:	
Complement:	
Missiles:	
Torpedo tubes:	
Radar:	
Sonar:	
EW systems:	

The Beluga is a one-of-a-kind submarine with an advanced, non-nuclear propulsion system. Western intelligence estimates that the Beluga could have (1) a Stirling closed-cycle engine, (2) fuel cells, or (3) a diesel-electric system with a small nuclear reactor to keep a charge on the battery.

The Beluga may be a propulsion prototype for series production of non-nuclear submarines.

The above dimensions are approximate.

Design: The submarine has what appears to be a high-speed hull configuration, somewhat similar to the nuclear-propelled Alfa.

1 COMMUNICATIONS SUBMARINE: CONVERTED HOTEL CLASS

One Hotel II-class SSBN has been reconfigured as a communications submarine, similar to the three Golf-class conversions. See Hotel III (above) for characteristics.

A Golf-class SSQ conversion; the precise role of these submarines and the modified Hotel SSQN is not publicly known. The communications mast on the port side of the sail folds down into a deck recess; the after mast partially retracts. (1984, JMSDF)

3 COMMUNICATIONS SUBMARINES: CONVERTED GOLF CLASS

Three Golf I units were converted in the 1970s to serve as communications ships. Their missile tubes were deleted and they were fitted with extensive communications gear, including buoys and masts; conning tower structure enlarged and after torpedo tubes probably deleted. Pert Spring satellite communications antenna installed.

1 DEEP-DIVING RESEARCH SUBMARINE: XRAY

Number	Builders	Completed
1 unit	Sudomekh/Admiralty (Leningrad)	1983

Displacement:	approx. 450 tons submerged
Length:	144 ft 4 in (44.0 m) overall
Beam:	13 ft (4.0 m)
Draft:	14 ft 5 in (4.4 m)
Propulsion:	
Reactors:	1 pressurized-water type
Speed:	5 knots surfaced
	4 knots submerged

The single Xray is a deep-diving research submarine, in some respects similar to the U.S. Navy's nuclear-propelled submersible NR-1. She is probably unarmed.

The Golf SSQ sail structure has been cut down with the deletion of three tubes for the SS-N-5 ballistic missile; the stepped casing aft of the sail probably houses towed communications buoys. A raised "cockpit" is fitted atop the Golf's sail.

2 SPECIAL MISSION SUBMARINES: UNIFORM CLASS

Number	Builders	Completed
1 unit	Sudomekh/Admiralty (Leningrad)	1983–1984
1 unit	Sudomekh/Admiralty (Leningrad)	1989–1990

Displacement:	2,000 tons submerged
Length:	239 ft 5 in (73.0 m) overall
Beam:	23 ft (7.0 m)
Draft:	21 ft 3 in (6.5 m)
Propulsion:	probably steam turbines
Reactors:	2 pressurized-water type
Speed:	
Depth:	
Complement:	
Troops:	approx. 40
Torpedo tubes:	none

The Uniform is reported to be a special operations submarine. The first unit was launched in June 1982 and the second in 1987. One unit is assigned to the Northern Fleet and one to the Pacific Fleet.

Design: This is the first known Soviet nuclear-propelled submarine with a single-hull configuration. The craft are believed to have a deck shelter for one or more Swimmer Delivery Vehicles (SDV) and probably a swimmer lock-out chamber.

1 RESEARCH SUBMARINE (AGSS): LIMA

Number	Builders	Completed
1 unit	Sudomekh/Admiralty (Leningrad)	1978

Displacement:	2,000 tons surfaced
	2,400 tons submerged
Length:	282 ft 1 in (86.0 m) overall
Beam:	31 ft 2 in (9.5 m)
Draft:	24 ft 3 in (7.4 m)
Propulsion:	diesel engines
	electric motors
	1 shaft
Speed:	
Range:	
Depth:	
Complement:	
Missiles:	none
Torpedo tubes:	none
Radar:	
Sonar:	
EW systems:	

The Lima is a one-of-a-kind research submarine. Her exact function is not known. She operates in the Black Sea. All dimensions are approximations. The Lima is believed to not have any armament.

Design: Double-hull configuration. The Lima has an unusual hull form with a flat deck and sail structure set well amidships. There is a fixed radar mast.

A rare photo of the single Lima-type research submarine, which may be involved in acoustic research.

2 SALVAGE AND RESCUE SUBMARINES: INDIA CLASS

Number	Builders	Completed
1 unit	Shipyard 199 (Komsomol'sk)	1979
1 unit	Shipyard 199 (Komsomol'sk)	1980

Displacement:	3,900 tons surfaced
	4,800 tons submerged
Length:	347 ft 8 in (106.0 m) overall
Beam:	32 ft 10 in (10.0 m)
Draft:	
Propulsion:	diesel engines
	electric motors
	2 shafts
Speed:	15 knots surfaced
	15 knots submerged
Range:	
Depth:	
Complement:	
Missiles:	none
Torpedo tubes:	probably unarmed
Radar:	Snoop Tray surface search
Sonar:	Whale Tongue medium-frequency
EW systems:	Stop Light

Stern view of the Northern Fleet's India-class submarine showing the massive deck casing with two salvage and rescue submersibles on board. The diving planes are visible. (1982, U.S. Navy)

These submarines are specifically configured for salvage and rescue operations. They each carry two submersibles, which are carried semi-recessed, in tandem, on deck aft of the sail structure. The submersibles can be reached from within the submarine while submerged; they are launched and recovered underwater.

Design: Double-hull configuration. These are believed to be the only Soviet conventional submarines with sail-mounted (vice bow) diving planes.

Operational: One unit transited via the Northern Sea route to the Northern Fleet in 1980; the other unit remains in the Pacific.

The Pacific Fleet's India-class salvage and rescue submarine; note the bow sonar "window" and nested submersibles. These are the only Soviet diesel-electric submarines with sail-mounted diving planes. (1987, JMSDF)

4 TARGET SUBMARINES: BRAVO CLASS (PROJECT 600)

Number	Builders	Completed
1 unit	Shipyard 199 (Komsomol'sk)	1967
2 units	Shipyard 199 (Komsomol'sk)	1968
1 unit	Shipyard 199 (Komsomol'sk)	1970

Displacement:	2,400 tons surfaced
	2,900 tons submerged
Length:	219 ft 10 in (67.0 m) waterline
	230 ft (70.1 m) overall
Beam:	32 ft 2 in (9.8 m)
Draft:	24 ft 11 in (7.3 m)
Propulsion:	diesel engines
	electric motors
	1 shaft
Speed:	14 knots surfaced
	16 knots submerged
Range:	

Depth:	1,475 ft (450 m)
Complement:	approx. 65
Missiles:	none
Torpedo tubes:	6 21-in (533-mm) bow (see notes)
Torpedoes:	
Radar:	Snoop Tray
Sonar:	Trout Cheek (passive array)
EW systems:	Brick Pulp

These are ASW target-training submarines (SST), especially configured to take strikes by practice torpedoes. The submarines appear to have a secondary combat role, although the presence of torpedo tubes has not been officially confirmed by either Western or Soviet sources.

Design: Double-hull configuration.

Operational: Two units serve in the Black Sea and one each in the Northern and Pacific fleets.

The four Bravo-class target and training submarines appear to be targets for Soviet anti-submarine forces, possibly with the amidships section "padded" to take strikes by unarmed torpedoes. Western sources have not confirmed whether or not these craft have torpedo tubes. However, they do have a bow sonar array and there are sonar "windows" in the sail structure. (Royal Navy)

OCEANOGRAPHIC RESEARCH SUBMARINES: FOXTROT CLASS

Several Foxtrot-class submarines have been employed in the oceanographic research. When so employed they carry "star" names and have been observed with the names GLOBUS, SATURN, SIRIUS, and REGUL.

3 OCEANOGRAPHIC RESEARCH SUBMARINE: ZULU IV CLASS (PROJ. 611)

Number	Builders	Completed
3 units {	Sudomekh (Leningrad)	} 1952–1955
	Shipyard 402 (Molotovsk/Severodvinsk)	

Displacement:	1,900 tons surfaced
	2,350 tons submerged
Length:	295 ft 2 in (90.0 m) overall
Beam:	24 ft 7 in (7.5 m)
Draft:	10 ft 8 in (6.0 m)
Propulsion:	3 diesel engines (37D); 6,000 bhp
	3 electric motors; 5,300 shp
	3 shafts (4-blade propellers)
Speed:	18 knots surfaced
	16 knots submerged
Range:	20,000 n.miles surfaced at economical speed
	9,500 n.miles on snorkel at 8 knots
Depth:	656 ft (200 m)
Complement:	approx. 70
Missiles:	(see Conversion notes)
Torpedo tubes:	10 21-in (533-mm) 6 bow + 4 stern
Torpedoes:	22
Radar:	Snoop Plate surface search
Sonar:	Tamir-5L medium-frequency
EW systems:	

The Zulu was the first long-range Soviet submarine constructed after World War II. The design apparently was begun during the war (possibly in 1943), but benefited considerably from features of the German Type XXI design.

By the late 1980s only three Zulu IV submarines were believed to be in active service, probably employed for oceanographic research (see conversions). The above characteristics are for the attack-submarine configuration.

Class: Twenty-one Zulus were completed to a torpedo-attack configuration and five to a ballistic-missile configuration (Zulu V) from 1952–1955; the latter were the world's first ballistic missile submarines.

Conversions: *Ballistic missile*—The first Soviet submarine fitted to test launch an SLBM; designated Zulu IV½ by Western intelligence, the submarine had a single tube for launching a modified Army Scud missile. The first (surface) launching occurred in September 1955.

Five Zulu-class submarines were completed to the Zulu V missile configuration (SSB), each fitted with an enlarged sail containing launch tubes for two navalized Scud missiles and possible SS-N-4 surface-launch ballistic missiles.

Oceanographic research—Three or four submarines were converted to an oceanographic research role after service as attack submarines. Some if not all were fitted with thrusters for underwater maneuver and hover, and with diver lockout chambers. The names LIRA, MARS, VEGA, and possibly ORION have been identified with those submarines.

Design: Double-hull design. Sub-types I through III had deck guns; all were updated to the Zulu IV configuration with deck guns deleted and snorkel installed.

Engineering: The three-shaft arrangement has led to some speculation in the West that the design was originally intended to em-

A Foxtrot-class submarine employed in the research role with the name REGUL on her sail. (1984, JMSDF)

One of the few surviving Zulu IV submarines in the North Pacific, probably engaged in the research role. Some of her sister submarines served as the world's first ballistic missile submarines. (1987, JMSDF)

ploy a closed-cycle propulsion plant on the center shaft. A snorkel was fitted to all units when upgraded to the Zulu IV configuration or completed as Zulu V.

Operational: Endurance is estimated at 70 days.

RESEARCH SUBMARINES: WHISKEY CLASS

Several Whiskey-class submarines have been previously employed in research roles; see page 128. (Two Whiskey-class submarines were earlier converted to fisheries research configurations; they have been discarded.)

EXPERIMENTAL SUBMARINE: WHALE TYPE (PROJECT 617)

The Whale was an experimental submarine completed about 1956 and first sighted by Western observers late that year. There was some speculation in the West that this may have been a nuclear-propelled submarine. Rather, the Whale was a test platform for the Walter closed-cycle, High-Temperature Peroxide (HTP) turbine propulsion plant (as fitted in the German Type XXVI U-boat).

Whale was a code name assigned by Western intelligence. She was scrapped in the early 1960s.

MIDGET SUBMARINES AND SUBMERSIBLES

A large midget submarine—about 65 feet (20 m) long—was reported to be operating in the Baltic Sea in 1990–1991. This may be the first midget submarine as opposed to smaller submersibles to be operated by the Soviet Navy. The NATO name Losos is believed to be assigned to this craft.

The Soviet Navy operates several small submersibles, apparently for use by *Spetsnaz* special forces and for submarine rescue and salvage activities. The two India-class submarines are each configured to carry two of the latter craft. Other submarines, including a converted Echo II, may be modified for transporting submersibles.

Two types of submersibles have been identified with the India-class submarines: a 37-foot (11.3-m) craft and a 40-foot (12.2-m) craft. The submarine rescue ships of the EL'BRUS class can accommodate these craft plus a 45-foot (13.7-m) submersible. A 96-foot (29.3-m) midget submarine has also been identified in naval operations in Swedish reports.

A number of non-naval research craft have been identified, some of which support military programs. The most capable of these craft are the MIR-1 and MIR-2 ("Peace"), built by the Ramua-Repola shipyard in Finland for the Soviet Academy of Sciences. These craft have a 20,000-foot (6,100-m) operating depth, permitting them to reach 98 percent of the ocean floor. These craft are supported by the civilian research ship AKADEMIK MSTISLAV KELDYSH (see chapter 25).

The MIR-1 and MIR-2 were completed in 1987 and that December made successful dives to just below their rated depths.[9] In July 1989 the two MIRs—manned by joint U.S. and Soviet crews—undertook a 16-hour mission in the central Atlantic. Operating from the KELDYSH, they attempted (unsuccessfully) to link up at a depth of some 16,400 feet (5,000 m). On another mission, the MIRs were used to examine the wreckage of the Mike-class SSN that sank in April 1989.

Including the MIRs, the Institute of Oceanology of the Academy of Sciences operates six manned deep submersibles; the Ministry of Fish Production operates at least eight units.

---

9. The world's only other submarines capable of operating at that depth are the U.S. Navy's SEA CLIFF (DSV 4), the French NAUTILE, and the Japanese SHINKAI 6500.

(The three civilian hydrographic-meteorological research ships of the VITYAZ' class can carry submersibles as can the fishing industry's ODISSEY and IKHTIANDR.)

Soviet civilian submersibles that have been publicly identified are:

RESEARCH SUBMERSIBLES

Name	Builders	Completed*	Depth	Crew	Notes
ATLANT-2	USSR	1973	300 m	2	2 units built
ARGUS	USSR	1975	600 m	3	
BENTHOS-300	USSR		300 m		
MIR	Finland		6,100 m	3	2 units built
OSMOTR	USSR		300 m		diver lockout craft
PISCES VII	Canada	1975	2,000 m	3	
PISCES XI	Canada		2,000 m	3	
RIFT	USSR	(1992)	4,000 m		2 units being built; titanium hulls
SEVER-2	USSR	ca. 1969	2,000 m	3	2 units built
TINRO-2	USSR	1973	400 m		2 units built

* First unit of type in Soviet service

One of the Soviet Union's two 20,000-foot (6,100-m) MIR research submersibles operated by the Soviet Academy of Sciences. (Dr. Joe B. MacInnis)

The salvage and rescue submersibles carried by the India-class submarines are approximately 40 feet (12.2 m) long. They may be entered directly from the submarine while submerged, a capability that permits the rescue of crewmen from submarines disabled above their collapse depth.

CHAPTER 13

Aircraft Carriers

The development of aircraft carriers must be considered one of the most significant Soviet military developments of the post–World War II era. This is the ADMIRAL GORSHKOV (formerly BAKU) a combination missile cruiser and VSTOL carrier. The ADMIRAL KUZNETSOV and later carriers have enhanced aviation capabilities albeit with a reduced missile battery.

The first full-deck Soviet aircraft carrier, the ADMIRAL KUZNETSOV, is at sea. The largest warship constructed by any nation since World War II except for U.S. aircraft carriers, the KUZNETSOV went to sea in November of 1989, ''well ahead of our estimates,'' according to the U.S. Director of Naval Intelligence.[1] He speculated, ''The fact that flight operations were conducted so early in [the ship's] sea trials suggests the Soviet Navy felt the need to convince policymakers of the carrier's importance and viability during last fall's budget debate.''

As this edition of *Guide to the Soviet Navy* went to press the ADMIRAL KUZNETSOV (formerly named TBILISI) was en route to the Northern Fleet, and her sister ship, the VARYAG, was fitting out. A third, larger full-deck carrier, the UL'YANOVSK, was on the building ways and preparations were under way at the Nikolayev south shipyard (No. 444) for a fourth carrier.

1. Rear Adm. Thomas A. Brooks, USN, Director of Naval Intelligence, testimony before the House Armed Services Committee, 14 March 1990.

The magnitude of this carrier effort further demonstrates the national leadership's recognition of the importance of the use of the sea for political and military activities. By the year 2000 the Soviets could have at sea four carriers of the KUZNETSOV and later classes and the four VSTOL carriers of the KIEV class. (These are not full-deck ships, having their bow devoted to guns, missiles, and ASW weapons.)

Development of the KUZNETSOV design began in 1976. Admiral Chernavin has explained the rationale for the class:

> The VTOL [*sic*] deck-borne aircraft [in the KIEV] were attack aircraft, but now we needed to have fighters on our carriers—that is, aircraft to assume the defense role. Therefore, when people ask today whether the construction of aircraft-carrying ships contravenes our defensive doctrine, I reply: no. We see their main role as platforms for fighter aircraft able to provide long-range cover for our vessels when shore-based fighters are unable to help. This defensive function is enshrined in the new aircraft carrier. . . .[2]

The Soviets have encountered difficulties with the carrier, especially with the ship's elevators and with catapult development. The latter problem has led to the first ship of this class being fitted with a ski ramp forward, to facilitate—but limiting the ship to—VSTOL aircraft. However, the ski-ramp configuration can permit a heavier takeoff weight than possible with a straight-deck run by VSTOL aircraft.

The second and subsequent ships will likely have catapults forward. Several conventional aircraft are already being modified and

2. "Commentary by Fleet Admiral V.N. Chernavin, Commander in Chief of the Navy," *Pravda* (19 October 1989), p. 3.

tested for carrier use (see chapters 8 and 27). An improved VSTOL aircraft, the Yak-41, is in development.

The KUZNETSOV is being assigned to the Northern Fleet. The four KIEV-class VSTOL carriers are all at sea—two assigned to the Northern Fleet and two to the Pacific Fleet. The fourth ship, the ADMIRAL GORSHKOV, has significantly different weapons and electronics suites. The electronics appear to be similar to those in the KUZNETSOV.

Although the Soviet aviation ships have significantly less aircraft capability than U.S. aircraft carriers, especially the NIMITZ (CVN 68)-class ships, the Soviet KIEV and KUZNETSOV classes have aviation capabilities superior to most other Western carriers. In addition, the Soviet ships have massive missile, gun, and anti-submarine batteries.

Armament: Note that the carriers of the KUZNETSOV and KIEV classes carry much heavier defensive missile and gun armaments than are fitted in Western aircraft carriers. In addition, the KIEVs are fitted with heavy anti-ship missile batteries as well as anti-submarine weapons.

Names: Soviet aviation ships/aircraft carriers have been named for major cities. However, following the political unrest in certain Baltic and ethnic republics in the late 1980s, three ships were renamed in 1990: The BAKU and TBILISI were renamed for deceased commanders in chief of the Soviet Navy, while the RIGA was renamed VARYAG, a name at the time assigned to a Kynda-class missile cruiser (see chapter 14).

(2) AIRCRAFT CARRIERS: "UL'YANOVSK" CLASS

Name	Builder	Laid down	Launch	Complete	Status
UL'YANOVSK	Black Sea Shipyard, Nikolayev (south)	Dec 1988	(1991)	(1995–1996)	Building
. . . . . .	Black Sea Shipyard, Nikolayev (south)			(2000)	Planned

Displacement:	appox. 75,000 tons full load	Boilers:	4
Length:	approx. 1,049 ft 6 in (320 m) overall	Speed:	30+ knots
Propulsion:	CONAS: steam turbines; 250–300,000 shp; 4 shafts	Aircraft:	approx. 45–65
Reactors:	4 pressurized water		

The third full-deck carrier is expected to be some 10,000 tons larger than the first ships of the KUZNETSOV class. Soviet officials have stated that *at least* one more ship of this type will be constructed beyond the UL'YANOVSK.

Aircraft: The carrying capacity of these ships will depend upon whether all aircraft are stowed in the hangar deck, as in previous Soviet aviation ships. If accommodated as in U.S. carriers (on flight deck and hangar deck), some 75 aircraft could be operated.

Design: The UL'YANOVSK is believed to be generally similar to the previous ADMIRAL KUZNETSOV class except for being larger to

permit nuclear propulsion.

Engineering: The ship is expected to have a Combined Nuclear And Steam (CONAS) propulsion plant, essentially a double version of the plant provided in the KIROV-class battle cruisers (see chapter 14). The reactors are coupled to oil-fired boilers; assuming a double KIROV plant, the reactor "side" of the plant could generate up to 180,000 shp for a maximum speed of perhaps 25 knots, and the boilers up to 120,000 shp for the ship's maximum speed in excess of 30 knots.

Names: Ul'yanovsk was the birthplace of V.I. Lenin.

1 + 1 AIRCRAFT CARRIERS: "ADMIRAL KUZNETSOV" CLASS

Name	Builder	Laid down	Launched	Completed	Status
ADMIRAL KUZNETSOV (ex-TBILISI)	Black Sea Shipyard, Nikolayev (south)	Jan 1983	5 Dec 1985	1990	**Northern**
VARYAG (ex-RIGA)	Black Sea Shipyard, Nikolayev (south)	10 Dec 1985	4 Dec 1988	(1992–1993)	Building

Displacement:	approx. 65,000 tons full load	Missiles:	12 SS-N-19 anti-ship launchers
Length:	approx. 921 ft 8 in (281.0 m) waterline		24 SA-N-9 anti-air vertical launchers [192]
	approx. 1,000 ft (305.0 m) overall		8 combined 30-mm gun/SA-N-11 type anti-air launchers
Beam:	approx. 124 ft 8 in (38.0 m)		(CADS)
Extreme width:	239 ft 5 in (73.0 m)	Guns:	6 30-mm/65-cal close-in (multi-barrel)
Draft:	approx. 36 ft (11.0 m)	ASW weapons:	2 modified RBU-6000 rocket launchers
Propulsion:	4 steam turbines; 200,000 shp; 4 shafts	Torpedoes:	none
Boilers:	8 turbopressure type	Radars:	4 Cross Sword (fire control)
Speed:	30+ knots		3 Palm Frond (navigation)
Complement:			1 Plate Steer (3-D air search)
Aircraft:			4 Sky Watch (multi-purpose)
	approx. 30+ { MiG-29 Fulcum STOL		2 Strut Pair (air search)
	Su-25 Frogfoot STOL	Sonars:	low-frequency hull mounted
	Su-27 Flanker STOL	EW systems:	
	Ka-27 Helix helicopters		

These are the largest warships to be built by the Soviet Union and the largest constructed by any nation since World War II except for U.S. aircraft carriers.

Preparations for the construction of the first ship were initially observed by Western intelligence, apparently by U.S. reconnaissance satellites, late in 1979. This indicates a decision was taken to construct the ship in the five-year economic-defense plan begun in 1976.

The carriers are constructed in the same building dock as the KIEV-class carriers. The dock was enlarged after the fourth ship of the earlier class was started; the ADMIRAL KUZNETSOV was laid down shortly after the launching of the GORSHKOV. Completion of the lead ship coincided with the end of the 1986–1990 five-year economic plan.

The first ship was launched and the second unit was laid down in December 1985. The ceremonies may have been related to the retirement that month of Admiral Gorshkov as CinC of the Navy.

Aircraft: The ADMIRAL KUZNETSOV does not appear to have tie-down devices in her flight deck to permit the large-scale stowage of aircraft on deck (as in U.S. carriers). This indicates that the ship operates only that number of planes that can be fitted in the hangar, that is, some 30+ aircraft or one-half the number that would be embarked in a U.S. carrier of that size.

Classification: In an interview with *Pravda* on 19 October 1989, Admiral Chernavin continually referred to the warship as an "aircraft carrier"; on 22 October 1989 the newspaper *Pravda* reported that "through no fault of the author, the material contained a technical inaccuracy. [The ship] falls within the category of heavy aircraft-carrying cruisers and not within that of aircraft carriers, as said in the feature." The sensitivity on this subject appears to be caused by perceived restrictions on the passage of aircraft carriers through the Turkish Straits as put forward in the Montreaux Convention of 1936.

Design: The ships have an essentially conventional aircraft carrier design, differing from the previous KIEV class principally in the later ships' larger size and the lack of a fixed weapons battery on the bow for as in the KIEV class. The KUZNETSOV has an angled flight deck of about 5½° to the centerline with a ski ramp forward with an angle of about 12°; the subsequent ships are expected to be fitted with catapults for the operation of conventional fixed-wing aircraft.

Arresting gear is fitted with four cross-deck pendants.

Two deck-edge elevators are located on the starboard side, forward and aft of the island structure; one centerline elevator also appears to be fitted. The large island structure has a large funnel, indicating the combined-system propulsion plant; Sky Watch phased-array radar antennas are fitted on all sides of the structure, which is surmounted by a larger, circular TACAN (Tactical Aircraft Navigation) device known as Cake Stand (as in the ADMIRAL GORSHKOV).

Electronics: Big Ball satellite communication antennas are fitted as are Punch Bowl antennas associated targeting with anti-ship missiles.

Engineering: It was originally estimated by Western intelligence that these ships would have a Combined Nuclear And Steam (CONAS) propulsion plant. In late 1988, however, that estimate was changed to the ship having a conventional steam plant.

Missiles: The ship has 16 vertical-launch tubes for the SS-N-19 anti-ship missile recessed in the ski ramp. Large steel doors apparently open to permit missile launch and protect them from aircraft takeoffs. (The SS-N-19 is also carried in KIROV-class cruisers and Oscar-class submarines.)

The KUZNETSOV appears to be the second Soviet ship fitted with the Combined Air Defense System (CADS), the Western designation for a mount combining two 30-mm Gatling guns and launchers for eight SA-N-11 short-range missiles. The system was previously observed in the KIROV-class cruiser KALININ.

Names: In 1984 German sources predicted the lead ship would be named SOVETSKIY SOYUZ (Soviet Union); in 1985 some U.S. Navy sources predicted the name would be KREMLIN.

The lead ship was named LEONID BREZHNEV on 18 November 1982, eight days after the death of General Secretary Brezhnev, but was renamed TBILISI by the Soviet government to honor the capital of the Georgian SSR in November 1988. (A number of other posthumous honors awarded to Brezhnev were rescinded in late 1988.)

In 1990 the TBILISI was renamed ADMIRAL KUZNETSOV to honor the Commander in Chief of the Soviet Navy from 1939 to 1947, and again from 1951 to 1956.

Also in 1990, the second ship, named RIGA for the capital of the Latvian SSR, was renamed VARYAG ("norseman"), a traditional name of Russian and Soviet warships. At the time that name was carried by a Kynda-class cruiser.

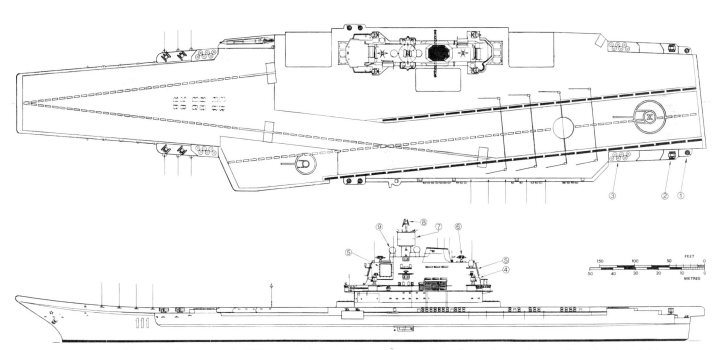

ADMIRAL KUZNETSOV: 1. 30-mm Gatling guns 2. RBU-series ASW rocket launchers 3. SA-N-9 launchers 4. Cross Sword radar 5. Sky Watch fixed-array radars 6. Strut Pair radar 7. Cake Stand housing 8. Plate Steer radar 9. Big Ball satellite communications antennas 10. SS-N-19 vertical launchers (under flight deck) (M.J. Dodgson)

1 AIRCRAFT CARRIER: MODIFIED "KIEV" CLASS

Name	Builder	Laid down	Launched	Completed	Status
ADMIRAL GORSHKOV (ex-BAKU)	Black Sea Shipyard, Nikolayev (south)	Dec 1978	17 Apr 1982	June 1988	**Northern**

Displacement:	38,000 tons standard	ASW weapons:	2 modified RBU-6000 rocket launchers
	45,000 tons full load (see Design notes)	Torpedoes:	none
Length:	818 ft 4 in (249.5 m) waterline	Radars:	4 Bass Tilt (fire control)
	895 ft 5 in (273.0 m) overall		4 Cross Sword (fire control)
Beam:	107 ft 3 in (32.7 m)		1 Kite Screech (fire control)
Extreme width:	173 ft 10 in (53.0 m)		3 Palm Frond (navigation)
Draft:	41 ft (12.5 m)		1 Plate Steer (3-D air search)
Propulsion:	4 steam turbines; 200,000 shp; 4 shafts		4 Sky Watch (multi-purpose)
Boilers:	8 turbopressure type		2 Strut Pair (air/surface search)
Speed:	32 knots		1 Trap Door-C (fire control)
Range:	4,000 n.miles at 30 knots	Sonars:	Horse Jaw low-frequency hull mounted (bistatic)
	13,500 n.miles at 18 knots		Horse Tail medium-frequency variable depth
Complement:	approx. 1,600 (including air group)	EW systems:	4 Bell series
Aircraft:	30 { 12 or 13 Yak-38 Forger VSTOL		4 Bell Thump
	{ 14 to 17 Ka-25 Hormone/Ka-27 Helix helicopters		2 Cage Pot
Missiles:	24 SA-N-9 anti-air vertical launchers [192]		8 Foot Ball
	12 SS-N-12 anti-ship launch tubes (1 quad, 1 octuple)		8 Wine Flask
	[no reloads]		
Guns:	2 100-mm/70-cal AA (2 single)		
	8 30-mm/65-cal close-in (8 multi-barrel)		

This fourth unit of the KIEV class was completed with an extensively modified armament and electronics configuration. Note the length of time between launch and completion required for her complex electronics suite.

The ship is assigned to the Northern Fleet.

Design: Similar to basic KIEV design with modified armament and island structure. There is no elevator or below-deck magazine for SS-N-12 missiles; this deletion probably provides more hangar space.

Electronics: Fitted with Sky Watch phased-array radar system and Cake Stand TACAN array. The ship also has twin Big Ball antennas for satellite targeting and two Punch Bowl communication domes. See KIEV class listing for additional data.

Missiles: Unlike the five previous Soviet aviation ships of the KIEV and MOSKVA classes, the GORSHKOV does not have conventional surface-to-air missile launchers (SA-N-1/3/4) or the SUW-N-1/ FRAS-1 ASW missile system.

The SA-N-9 launchers are arranged in four groups of six vertical launchers; there are two groups on the forecastle (ahead of the SS-N-12 launchers); the two other SA-N-9 groups are amidships: one on the starboard side aft of the island structure and the other to port.

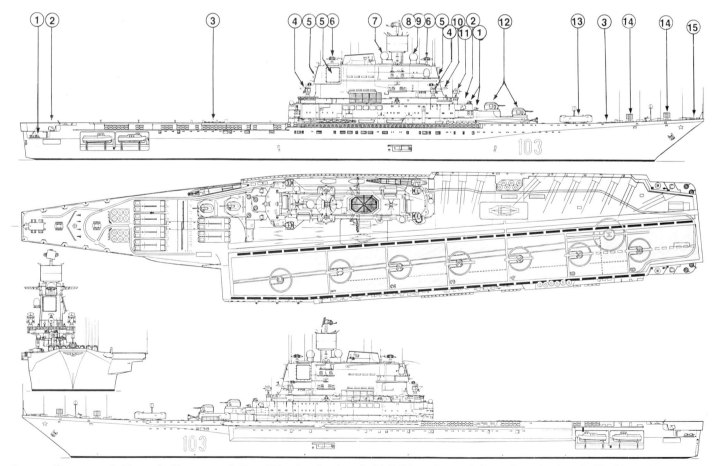

ADMIRAL GORSHKOV: 1. 30-mm Gatling guns   2. Bass Tilt radar director   3. SA-N-9 launchers   4. Cross Sword radar   5. Sky Watch fixed-array radars   6. Strut Pair radars   7. and 9. Big Ball satellite communications antennas   8. Top Plate/Top Steer radar   10. Palm Frond radar   11. Kite Screech radar   12. single 100-mm DP guns   13. SS-N-12 launchers   14. RBU-6000 (mod.) ASW rocket launchers   15. Trap Door Radar (M.J. Dodgson)

Names: This ship was originally thought by Western intelligence to be named for the city of Kharkov, but she went to sea with the name BAKU. In 1990 she was renamed ADMIRAL GORSHKOV, the Commander in Chief of the Soviet Navy from 1956 to 1985.

Operational: The ship entered the Mediterranean for the first time in June 1988. She deployed to the Northern Fleet in December 1988.

The ADMIRAL GORSHKOV has the same hull as the three previous KIEV-class carriers but with her flight deck extended some 40 feet (12.2 m), increased aviation support facilities, and an enlarged island structure to accommodate a more capable electronics suite. (1988, U.S. Navy, Lt. P.J. Azzolina)

The purpose of the "black plate" at the stern of the ADMIRAL GORSHKOV is to deflect the exhaust of VSTOL aircraft coming aboard; in the center of the stern are the doors over the variable depth sonar. Along the port deck edge (just abaft the aircraft) are six SS-N-9 missile launchers; another six are opposite on the starboard side, outboard of the elevator. (Royal Navy)

The ADMIRAL GORSHKOV has 12 SS-N-12 anti-ship missile canisters forward (with no reloads provided); forward of the canisters are two RBU-6000 ASW rocket launchers, a pair of saluting guns, and the cover for the retractable Trap Door guidance for the SS-N-12 missiles. The extension of the flight deck forced deletion of the 30-mm Gatling guns found at the forward end of the angled deck in the KIEV-class ships.

The bow of the ADMIRAL GORSHKOV shows an RBU-6000 ASW rocket launcher (left), covers for 12 SA-N-9 vertical-launch missile sets, and the forward edge of the bank of eight SS-N-12 missile tubes. (1990, Royal Navy)

3 AIRCRAFT CARRIERS: "KIEV" CLASS

Name	Builder	Laid down	Launched	Completed	Status
KIEV	Black Sea Shipyard, Nikolayev (south)	Sep 1970	31 Dec 1972	May 1975	**Northern**
MINSK	Black Sea Shipyard, Nikolayev (south)	Dec 1972	May 1975	Feb 1978	**Pacific**
NOVOROSSIYSK	Black Sea Shipyard, Nikolayev (south)	Oct 1975	Dec 1978	Sep 1982	**Pacific**

Displacement:	36,000 tons standard	ASW weapons:	1 twin SUW-N-1 missile launcher
	43,000 tons full load (see Design notes)		2 RBU-6000 rocket launchers
Length:	818 ft 4 in (249.5 m) waterline		torpedoes
	895 ft 5 in (273.0 m) overall	Torpedoes:	10 21-inch (533-mm) torpedo tubes (2 quin)

Radars sub-table:

Radars:	KIEV and MINSK	NOVOROSSIYSK
	4 Bass Tilt (fire control)	4 Bass Tilt (fire control)
	2 Don-2 (navigation)	3 Palm Frond (navigation)
	1 Don Kay (navigation)	
	2 Head Lights (fire control)	2 Head Lights (fire control)
	2 Owl Screech (fire control)	2 Owl Screech (fire control)
	2 Pop Group (fire control)	2 Strut Pair (air search)
	1 Trap Door (fire control)	1 Trap Door (fire control)
	1 Top Sail (3-D air search)	1 Top Sail (3-D air search)
	1 Top Steer (3-D air search)	1 Top Steer (3-D air search)

Beam: 107 ft 3 in (32.7 m)
Extreme width: 167 ft 3 in (51.0 m)
Draft: 41 ft (12.5 m)
Propulsion: 4 steam turbines; 200,000 shp; 4 shafts
Boilers: 8 turbopressure type
Speed: 32 knots
Range: 4,000 n.miles at 30 knots
13,500 n.miles at 18 knots
Complement: approx. 1,200 (including air group)
Aircraft: 30 { 12 or 13 Yak-38 Forger VSTOL
14 to 17 Ka-25 Hormone/Ka-27 Helix helicopters
Missiles: 2 twin SA-N-3 anti-air launchers [72]
2 twin SA-N-4 anti-air launchers [40];
not fitted in NOVOROSSIYSK
12 SA-N-9 anti-air vertical launchers [96] in NOVOROSSIYSK
8 SS-N-12 anti-ship launchers (4 twin) [16]
Guns: 4 76.2-mm/59-cal AA (2 twin)
8 30-mm/65-cal close-in (8 multi-barrel)

Sonars: low-frequency and medium frequency, hull mounted (bistatic)
medium-frequency, variable depth (see Sonar notes)
EW systems: 2 Bell Clout
4 Rum Tub
8 Side Globe (not fitted in NOVOROSSIYSK)
4 Top Hat-A
4 Top Hat-B

These ships were the first full-deck Soviet aircraft carriers to be built, having a full flight deck and a hull designed from the outset as a carrier. Two earlier Soviet carrier programs, of the late 1930s and early 1950s, were cancelled early on. Construction of this class was probably approved in the five-year economic plan that began in 1966.

A fourth ship of this design was completed with a significantly different electronics and weapons configuration and is listed separately.

The KIEV made her first operational deployment to the Mediterranean in July 1976. She transferred to the Northern Fleet that August, stayed with that fleet until late December 1977, then re-

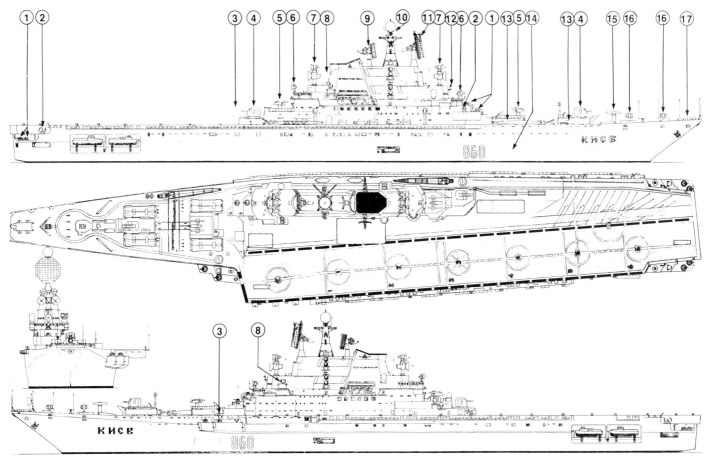

KIEV class: 1. 30-mm Gatling guns   2. Bass Tilt radar director   3. SA-N-4 launcher (retracted)   4. twin 76.2-mm AA guns   5. SA-N-3 launchers   6. Screech radar   7. Head lights radars   8. Pop Group radar   9. Top Steer radar   10. Top Knot radar   11. Top Sail radar   12. Don-2 radar   13. SS-N-12 launchers   14. 533-mm torpedo tubes (behind shutters)   15. SUW-N-1 ASW missile launcher   16. RBU-6000 ASW rocket launchers   17. Trap Door radar (M.J. Dodgson)

The Novorossiysk, one of two VSTOL carriers in the Pacific Fleet. Note the length of the island structure and large number of radar and other antennas, increased in later carriers. (1988, Japanese Maritime Self-Defense Force)

turned to the Mediterranean–Black Sea area. She is permanently based in the Murmansk area but returns to the Nikolayev yard for overhaul and upkeep. The MINSK transited to the Far East in 1979 and the NOVOROSSIYSK followed in 1984.

Aircraft: On her initial (1976) deployment into the Mediterranean the KIEV operated 25 aircraft—9 Yak-38 Forger-A and 1 Yak-38 Forger-B VSTOL aircraft plus 14 Ka-25 Hormone-A and 1 Ka-25 Hormone-B helicopters. All could be carried on the hangar deck. Maximum hangar capacity is estimated at 30 to 35 aircraft. (U.S. aircraft carriers stow less than one-half of their embarked aircraft in the hangar.) The two later ships embark Ka-27 Helix helicopters as well as Hormones.

Classification: The Soviet Navy originally classified the KIEV as a heavy anti-submarine cruiser (tyazholyi protivolodchyi kreyser) and then as a large (bolshoi) ASW cruiser. However, by the early 1980s, the ship was being referred to as a tactical aircraft-carrying cruiser (takticheskoye avianosnyy kreyser). Some senior Soviet naval officers refer to the ships as anti-submarine carriers or simply aircraft carriers.

Design: This class has a very large island structure on the starboard side and an angled flight deck, canted at about 4.5° to port from the centerline.

No catapults or arresting wires are fitted. Unlike U.S. aircraft carriers, the KIEV has a full missile cruiser's armament of anti-air,

This view of the MINSK shows the ship's paired SS-N-12 anti-ship missiles. Between the first pair is the forward 76.2-mm twin gun mount and between the second pair the forward SA-N-3 surface-to-air missile launcher; the reload elevator is shown between the missile groups. At lower right are a pair of 30-mm Gatling guns and a Bass Tilt gunfire control radar. (1979)

The KIEV at high speed with her flight deck empty. Soviet aircraft carriers can accommodate all aircraft in their hangars—some 30 in the KIEV class, 30+ in the KUZNETSOV class, and 14 helicopters in the MOSKVA class.

The MINSK at high speed. Her after elevator is lowered to the hangar deck; a second lift is alongside the island (behind the parked helicopters). The "black plate" on the port side of the stern counter is a blast defector for VSTOL aircraft landing aboard.

anti-ship, and anti-submarine weapons. Most of these are fitted forward, depriving the ship of significant forward flight-deck area. Portions of the flight deck are covered with blast-resistant (refractory) tile for VTOL aircraft operation.

There are two relatively small aircraft elevators, one alongside the island and one immediately abaft the island; these are approximately 63 ft × 34 ft (19.2 m × 10.37 m) and 60 ft 8 in × 15 ft 5 in (18.5 m × 4.7 m), respectively. There are also three or four weapon elevators that service the flight deck, one forward of the forward aircraft elevator, and two or three on the starboard side, aft of the island. (On some ships the two aftermost weapon elevators have been combined.) There is a dolly rail system on the flight deck connecting the weapon elevators.

The hull design features a large underwater bow "bulb"; boat stowage is cut into the after portion of the hull. Aft the ship has a freeboard of some 42 ft 6 in (13 m). The KIEV's stern counter has an opening for Variable Depth Sonar (VDS) and a reinforced panel to resist exhaust blast as aircraft hover immediately astern while transitioning from conventional to vertical landing flight configuration.

Active fin stabilizers are fitted.

The NOVOROSSIYSK has several minor differences including a wider flight deck with an enlarged aircraft parking area aft and a series of three plate fairings on the port side of the forecastle and a series of triangular shields aft, probably to reduce turbulence over the flight deck when steaming into the wind at high speed.

Electronics: The EW suite of the third ship differs from those of the other two. All have the large Top Knot spherical radome atop the superstructure; a smaller, spherical Bob Tail radiosextant antenna is immediately behind the funnel. Vee Bar long-range HF antennas and a pair of Punch Bowl satellite communication antennas are fitted.

Missiles: The KIEV and older Kynda cruiser classes are the only Soviet classes fitted with reloads for surface-to-surface missiles. The larger SS-N-12 missiles are stowed in a below-deck magazine and carried to the launch tubes by an athwartships elevator. Sixteen reloads are stowed in the magazine, giving the ship a total of 24 Sandbox missiles.

The NOVOROSSIYSK went to sea with plates over her SA-N-9 launchers and without the associated Cross Sword radar directors; the missiles and radars were fitted at a later date.

Names: These ships are named for major Soviet cities.

NATO assigned the code name Kurile to this class before the Soviet name KIEV became known. Subsequently the name KIEV was adopted for reporting purposes.

Sonar: The first two ships have the Moose Jaw LF and Bull Horn MF hull-mounted sonars and Mare Tail VDS; the NOVOROSSIYSK has only Horse Jaw LF hull-mounted sonar and the Horse Tail VDS.

Forward the KIEV-class carriers have eight SS-N-12 anti-ship missile canisters, with the first two pairs shown in the elevated (firing) position and the forward 76.2-mm twin gun mount trained to starboard in this view. There is a missile-loading rig on the starboard side, next to the SS-N-12 launchers. The cover for the retracting Trap Door radar is visible on the forecastle.

2 HELICOPTER CARRIERS: "MOSKVA" CLASS

Name	Builder	Laid down	Launched	Completed	Status
MOSKVA	Black Sea Shipyard, Nikolayev (south)	1962	1964	July 1967	**Black Sea**
LENINGRAD	Black Sea Shipyard, Nikolayev (south)	1964	1966	1968	**Black Sea**

Displacement:	15,500 tons standard		Guns:	4 57-mm/70-cal AA (2 twin)
	19,200 tons full load		ASW weapons:	1 twin SUW-N-1 missile launcher
Length:	587 ft 2 in (179.0 m) waterline			2 RBU-6000 rocket launchers
	623 ft 2 in (190.0 m) overall		Torpedoes:	removed
Beam:	85 ft 3 in (26.0 m)		Radars:	3 Don-2 (navigation)
Extreme width:	111 ft 10 in (34.1 m)			2 Head Lights (fire control)
Draft:	27 ft 11 in (8.5 m)			1 Head Net-C (3-D air search)
Propulsion:	2 steam turbines; 100,000 shp; 2 shafts			2 Muff Cob (fire control)
Boilers:	4 turbopressure type			1 Top Sail (3-D air search)
Speed:	30 knots		Sonars:	Moose Jaw low-frequency (hull mounted)
Range:	4,500 n.miles at 29 knots			Mare Tail medium-frequency (variable depth)
	14,000 n.miles at 12 knots		EW systems:	8 Bell series
Complement:	approx. 850 (including air group)			8 Side Globe
Helicopters:	14 Ka-25 Hormone helicopters			2 Top Hat
Missiles:	2 twin SA-N-3 anti-air launchers [44]			

These are combination helicopter carriers/missile cruisers. They were developed to counter Western strategic missile submarines, but the program was aborted after two ships because of the expanding capabilities of missile submarines. Both ships are based in the Black Sea and periodically deploy to the Mediterranean; they have also operated in the Atlantic and the LENINGRAD in the northwest Indian Ocean region.

The MOSKVA was trials ship for the Yak-38 Forger.

The ships have not undergone significant weapon or electronic upgrades.

Class: Additional ships of this class were probably planned; some Western analysts estimate that as many as 12 of the ships were proposed.

Classification: Soviet PKR type.

Design: The MOSKVA class was the first Soviet "carrier" design to be completed. These ships are missile cruisers forward; aft of the superstructure they have a clear, open flight deck. The superstructure is "stepped" forward to support missile launchers and radars, and has a smooth after face. A small hangar is located between the stack uptakes in the superstructure. Two elevators connect the flight deck to the hangar deck. The flight deck is approximately 282 ft × 112 ft (86 m × 34 m).

The stern is cut away for the VDS and boat stowage.

The MOSKVA class introduced the SA-N-3 missile system as well as Top Sail and Head Lights radars to Soviet warships.

Electronics: The hull-mounted sonar dome is retractable.

Names: These ships are named for the country's two traditional capital cities.

Operational: The MOSKVA's flight deck was modified in the early 1970s for flight tests of the Forger VSTOL aircraft (she has since reverted to her original configuration).

At sea the ships normally trim down by the bow about 3 ft (1 m); they have poor seakeeping qualities, possibly accounting for their having always been based in the Black Sea Fleet vice Northern or Pacific fleets.

Torpedoes: Two five-tube 21-inch rotating banks of torpedo tubes were fitted into the sides of the ships, located immediately aft of the accommodation ladders. They were deleted in the mid-1970s.

Stern aspect of the LENINGRAD; the variable depth sonar installation is visible under the fantail.

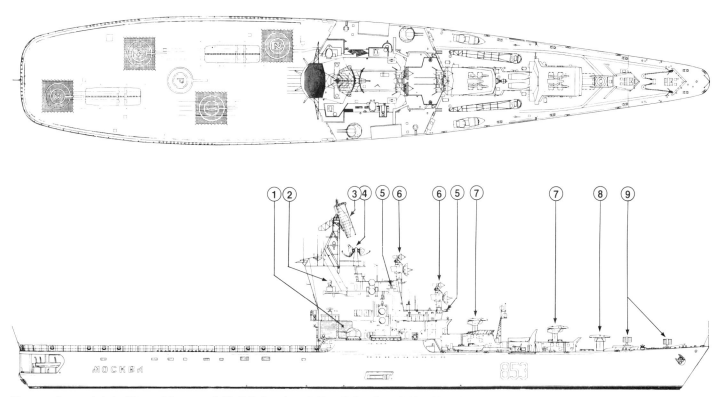

MOSKVA class: 1. twin 57-mm AA guns   2. Muff Cob radar   3. Top Sail radar   4. Head Net-C radar   5. Don-2 radar   6. Head Lights radars   7. SA-N-3 launchers   8. SUW-N-1 ASW missile launcher   9. RBU-6000 ASW rocket launcher (M.J. Dodgson)

The LENINGRAD under way in the eastern Atlantic. The LENINGRAD and MOSKVA initiated a series of innovative carrier designs for the Soviet Navy. No. 109 is at least the fifth pendant number carried by the LENINGRAD; the MOSKVA has also had at least five assigned. These ships have undergone minimal modernization during their careers. (1989, U.S. Navy)

The LENINGRAD with both flight deck elevators lowered and the two helicopter hangars within the superstructure opened; the flight deck control station is located above the hangars. Twin 57-mm gun mounts are fitted outboard of the superstructure, with missile and rocket launchers forward.

CHAPTER 14

Cruisers

The battle cruiser FRUNZE personifies the Soviet approach to constructing large warships with heavy weapon batteries and sensor arrays. The FRUNZE carries an estimated 284 missiles of various types (plus guns and rockets) and is fitted with eight different kinds of radar, two sonars, and several electronic warfare systems. (West German Navy)

The impressive Soviet cruiser construction program continues although the end of production of both the nuclear-propelled KIROV battle cruisers and SLAVA anti-ship missile cruisers is in sight. A fifth KIROV has been cancelled and there are reports that the plans for additional ships of the SLAVA class have been dropped.

The accelerated and belated retirement of all of the surviving SVERDLOV-class gun cruisers during the past few years may provide the Soviet naval command with a rationale for advocating additional cruiser construction. But a continued cruiser program must be balanced against the ongoing submarine, carrier, and destroyer programs. Further, in several respects the SOVREMENNYY and UDALOY destroyer designs have many features of earlier cruiser classes. Thus, the Soviet cruiser picture was far from clear when this volume went to press.

The Soviet Navy has constructed cruiser-type ships in all three of the postwar development phases. During the first phase, the 14 SVERDLOVS were built (completed in the years 1951–1954); they were refinements of the prewar CHAPAYEV design. And, several cruisers of the earlier program were completed. During the second phase, the Kynda, Kresta I/II, and Kara classes were built (completed in the years 1962–1980). The third phase has seen the development of the current KIROV and SLAVA programs.

The KIROVS are the largest surface warships except for aircraft carriers built by any nation since World War II. There will be four ships of this class, providing long-range platforms for the anti-air, anti-submarine, and anti-surface roles. (The U.S. Navy has nine significantly smaller nuclear-propelled cruisers; the last was completed in 1980. No additional U.S. nuclear surface ships are planned other than aircraft carriers.)

The SLAVA represents a major enigma in Soviet surface combatant construction. Configured primarily for an anti-ship role, the SLAVA has the heaviest surface-to-surface missile battery of any Soviet warship except for the KIROV and KIEV classes. The SLAVA has one-half the primary anti-aircraft system of the KIROV (SA-N-6 launchers/Top Dome radar) and minimal anti-submarine capabili-

ties. Note that many of the ship's weapons and sensors are from a previous generation, with the SA-N-6/Top Dome and 130-mm guns being the major contemporary weapons. One U.S. intelligence analyst said, "It was as if the Soviets simply took what systems were lying around the shipyard and put them into an old hull design." Still, the SLAVA could have a significant impact in many wartime situations.

The SLAVAS were constructed at the Nikolayev northern shipyard (No. 445), which had previously built the seven Kara-class cruisers (completed 1973–1980). The SLAVA could have been considered the successor for series production at that yard. A rate of one ship per year would have been feasible; instead, only four ships have been identified and are being completed at a very slow rate.

Names: Most Soviet cruisers are named for cities and Soviet political and military officials as well as a few tsarist-era naval officers. The SLAVA and CHERVONA UKRAINA are exceptions (see below).

Operational: Fleet assignments for cruisers are listed to the extent the data are available from Soviet and Western sources. However, ships regularly transit between the European fleet areas for exercises and overhauls.

3 + 1 NUCLEAR-PROPELLED BATTLE CRUISERS: "KIROV" CLASS

Name	Builder	Laid down	Launched	Completed	Status
KIROV	Baltic Shipyard, Leningrad	June 1973	26 Dec 1977	Sep 1980	**Northern**
FRUNZE	Baltic Shipyard, Leningrad	Jan 1978	23 May 1981	Aug 1984	**Pacific**
KALININ	Baltic Shipyard, Leningrad	May 1983	29 Apr 1986	Dec 1988	**Northern**
YURI ANDROPOV	Baltic Shipyard, Leningrad	24 Apr 1986	Apr 1989	(1991-1992)	Building

Displacement:	24,300 tons standard
	28,000 tons full load
Length:	754 ft 5 in (230.0 m) waterline
	813 ft 5 in (248.0 m) overall
Beam:	91 ft 10 in (28.0 m)
Draft:	34 ft 5 in (10.5 m)
Propulsion:	CONSAS: steam turbines; 150,000 shp; 2 shafts
Reactors:	2 pressurized-water type
Boilers:	2
Speed:	32 knots
Range:	virtually unlimited (see Engineering notes)
Complement:	approx. 800
Helicopters:	3 Ka-25 Hormone or Ka-27 Helix
Missiles:	2 twin SA-N-4 anti-air launchers [40]
	12 SA-N-6 anti-air vertical launchers [96]
	16 SA-N-9 anti-air vertical launchers [128] in FRUNZE and later units
	20 SS-N-19 anti-ship launchers
	6 combined 30-mm gun/SA-N-11 anti-air launchers in KALININ and YURI ANDROPOV (CADS)
Guns:	2 100-mm/70-cal DP (2 single) in KIROV
	2 130-mm/70-cal DP (1 twin) FRUNZE and YURI ANDROPOV
	8 30-mm/65-cal close-in (8 multi-barrel) in KIROV and FRUNZE
ASW weapons:	2 SS-N-14 launch tubes [8-12] in KIROV
	2 RBU-1000 rocket launchers
	1 RBU-6000 rocket launcher
	torpedoes
Torpedoes:	10 21-inch (533-mm) torpedo tubes (2 quin)
Radars:	4 Bass Tilt (fire control) in KIROV and FRUNZE
	2 Cross Sword (fire control) positions in FRUNZE and KALININ
	2 Eye Bowl (fire control) in KIROV
	1 Kite Screech (fire control)
	3 Palm Frond (navigation)
	2 Pop Group (fire control)
	2 Top Dome (fire control)
	1 Top Pair (3-D air search)
	1 Top Steer (3-D air search)
	2 Cross Sword (fire control) in FRUNZE and in later units
	. . . . . . (fire control) in KALININ and later unit
Sonars:	Horse Jaw low-frequency bow mounted
	Horse Tail low-frequency variable depth

EW systems:	KIROV	FRUNZE	KALININ
	10 Bell-series	10 Bell-series	4 Bell Bash
	8 Side Globe	8 Wine Flask	4 Bell Nip
	4 Rum Tub		4 Bell Push
			4 Bell Thumb
			8 Foot Ball

The stern aspect of the KALININ shows a larger number of electronic and weapon systems than are fitted in her three sister ships. The new CADS weapon mounts are just above the helicopter control position, fitted port and starboard. (1990, Royal Navy)

The Kirovs are the largest warships built by any nation since World War II except for aircraft carriers of various types (including the U.S. Navy LHA/LHD helicopter carriers). The Soviet ships have an elegant, streamlined design, reminiscent of earlier battle cruisers. They are significantly larger than their U.S. contemporaries (CGN types) as well as the U.S. strike cruiser (CSGN) proposed in the 1970s but never built. The only larger surface combatants in service with any navy today are the U.S. battleships of the Iowa (BB 61) class; the U.S. ships, however, are being deactivated during the next few years.

Reportedly, a fifth ship of this class was begun at the Baltic Shipyard in 1990 but was cancelled as part of the overall Soviet defense cutback.

Aircraft: The ships each carry three helicopters for ASW (Hormone-A in Kirov and Helix-A in Frunze) and for over-the-horizon targeting of the SS-N-19 missiles (Hormone-B). (See Design notes.)

Classification: Soviet RKR type. The NATO designation BAL-COM-1 (Baltic Combatant No. 1) was used before the lead ship appeared with the name Kirov.

The term *battle cruiser* has been widely used in the West for this class and seems appropriate in view of the ship's size, hull lines, and fire power.[1]

Design: The Kirovs present an impressive, powerful appearance. The design is credited with excellent seakeeping capabilities.

The design provides for a long forecastle, with the RBU-6000 and (in Kirov) SS-N-14 launchers visible and the large SA-N-6 and SS-N-19 batteries recessed below the main deck. The principal missile batteries are forward, leaving the after portion of the hull available for machinery and the helicopter hangar and large landing area. The ships have large superstructures with numerous radars, EW antennas, and weapons.

The Frunze has an enlarged deckhouse forward of the bridge and an after superstructure that has been extended farther aft. She has only a single, 130-mm gun mount. The two small deckhouses adjacent to the Kirov's helicopter deck (each with two CIWS) have been omitted in the Frunze. That ship's Gatling guns are farther forward, on the main superstructure.

---

1. The term *battle cruiser*, which evolved during the Dreadnought battleship era, denoted a ship with more firepower and speed than a battleship but less armor. The British Hood (completed in 1920) was the last battle cruiser completed by any nation; the Soviets twice began the construction of battle cruisers, the Kronshtadt and Stalingrad classes, but none was finished (see below). The U.S. Navy also never completed any battle cruisers, although the "large cruisers" Guam (CB 1) and Alaska (CB 2), both commissioned in 1944, were in some respects conceptually similar to battle cruisers.

The helicopters are lowered from the large landing deck to the hangar by an elevator, just forward of the landing area, which fits flush with the deck. The elevator opening is covered by a two-section hatch, with the sections opening upward. This arrangement allows a helicopter to be parked on the lift in the lowered position while the hangar is closed.

There is a hull-mounted sonar, and a large VDS is fitted in the stern.

Active fin stabilizers are provided.

Electronics: The EW antennas of the first two ships differ. Both of the Kirov's sonar systems are thought to be the first of their type installed in an operational ship.

These ships have extensive flagship facilities and communications equipment that includes two Punch Bowl satellite communications domes (also found in the Sverdlov and Don classes employed as flagships). The Kirov has a pair of distinctive Vee Tube-C antennas for HF radio communications, mounted on a frame at the forward end of the second radar mast. The Frunze does not have this antenna but instead has a pair of large Low Ball radomes for satellite communications provided abreast the bridge structure.

Fitted with the Round House TACAN (Tactical Aircraft Navigation) system.

Engineering: The Kirov class has a Combined Nuclear And Steam (CONAS) propulsion plant. The two reactors are coupled with oil-fired boilers. The reactors generate an estimated 90,000 shp for 24 or 25 knots. The boilers can provide an estimated 60,000 shp for a maximum speed of 32 knots.

Two arrangements have been suggested for the CONAS plant: the oil-fired boilers are used to boost the heat of the reactor-heated steam en route to the turbines, or, more likely, the boilers provide steam to a second set of turbines geared to the same propeller shafts as the nuclear-driven turbines. A 1981 U.S. Navy intelligence estimate noted, "Even if the fuel for the superheater were exhausted, ships of this class would still be able to make an estimated 29 knots using only the nuclear plant." Thus, the ships have a virtually unlimited cruising range.

Guns: The 130-mm DP guns in the Frunze are similar to those fitted in the cruisers of the Slava class and the destroyers of the Sovremennyy class.

Missiles: The Frunze has three surface-to-air missile systems, with the SA-N-9 vertical-launch system being provided, in part, at the expense of the SS-N-14 ASW missile system fitted in the Kirov. The SA-N-9 provides a short-range capability, primarily a defense against attacking anti-ship cruise missiles.

The SA-N-6 VLS has eight-round, rotating launchers. Unlike the system in the Slava class, the Kirov SA-N-6 system has large cover hatches (similar to the configuration in the Azov).

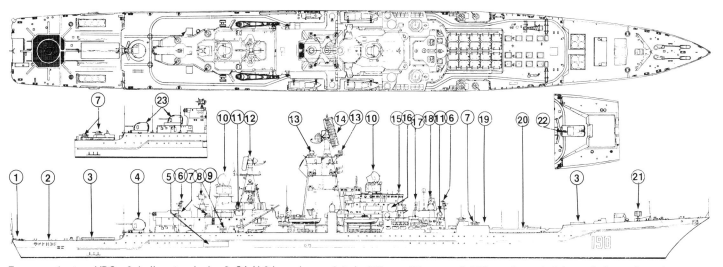

Frunze: 1. stern VDS 2. helicopter deck 3. SA-N-9 launchers 4. twin 130-mm DP guns 5. 533-mm torpedo tubes 6. Cross Sword radar 7. 30-mm Gatling guns 8. Kite Screech radar 9. RBU-1000 ASW rocket launchers 10. Top Dome radar 11. Bass Tilt radar 12. Top Steer radar 13. Round House TACAN 14. Top Pair radar 15. Palm Frond radar 16. Big Ball satellite communication antennas 17. SA-N-4 launchers (retracted) 18. Pop Group radar 19. SS-N-19 launchers 20. SA-N-6 launchers 21. RBU-6000 ASW rocket launchers Kirov inset: 22. SS-N-14 ASW launchers 23. single 100-mm DP guns (M.J. Dodgson)

The FRUNZE shows off the long, impressive lines of her design, somewhat reminiscent of the battle cruiser designs of World War II. She and the KALININ can be distinguished from the KIROV by the single, 130-mm twin turret amidships in place of the single 100-mm gun mounts in the lead ship. (West German Navy)

A CADS mount on the cruiser KALININ. There are two 30-mm rotary barrel Gatling guns, above which are launch positions for up to eight SA-N-11 short-range missiles. The KALININ is believed to be the first warship to have the system. (1990, Royal Navy)

The KALININ is believed the first warship to mount the Combined Air Defense System (CADS) consisting of two 30-mm Gatling guns co-mounted with launch rails for up to eight SA-N-11 short-range missiles.

The 20 SS-N-19 represent the heaviest anti-ship missile battery in the warship of any navy. The missiles are fitted in single, fixed launch tubes, angled forward at approximately 45°. These missiles require over-the-horizon targeting from a ship-based Hormone-B helicopter or off-board sensor systems. There are Punch Bowl antennas provided for satellite communications and data transmission. (The SS-N-19 is also fitted in the Oscar-class SSGNs.)

Only the KIROV has the SS-N-14 ASW system. This is the first reloadable launcher for the SS-N-14 in Soviet ships. An estimated 8 to 12 missiles are carried. The Eye Bowl radar is fitted to the KIROV for SS-N-14 guidance (other Soviet cruisers with that weapon have the Head Lights radar of the SA-N-3 system to guide the ASW weapon).

Names: The KIROV is named for S.M. Kirov (1888–1934), a leading Bolshevik revolutionary. The name was subsequently given to the lead ship of the only heavy cruiser class (7.1-inch-gun) built by the Soviets (completed 1938 and stricken in 1974).

M.V. Frunze (1885–1925) was a Bolshevik commander in the Russian Revolution and in 1925 served as People's Commissar for military and naval affairs. M.V. Kalinin (1875–1946), also a revolutionary, was president of the USSR from 1923 until his death.

Yuri Andropov (1914–1984) was head of the KGB for 15 years; he succeeded Leonid Brezhnev as head of the Communist party in November 1982 but died in February 1984 after a long illness.

Operational: The KIROV commenced sea trials in the Gulf of Finland on 23 May 1980; she first deployed to the Northern Fleet in September 1980. The FRUNZE began sea trials in November 1983; she deployed to the Northern Fleet in August 1984 and transited to the Far East via the Indian Ocean route in September–October 1985.

Torpedoes: The two banks of five torpedo tubes (not four as previously reported) are recessed in the hull amidships, behind sliding doors. They are located below the after Top Dome antenna.

The KALININ, the third ship of the KIROV class, differs from the first two ships with respect to her point-defense gun/missile system and electronics. The FRUNZE and KALININ have Big Ball satellite communication antennas alongside the bridge structure, and the KALININ has a Top Plate radar on the after pyramid in place of the Top Steer radar in the earlier ships. (1988, West German Navy)

The FRUNZE in the Baltic.

The FRUNZE with her 130-mm gun turret aimed at the camera. The door in the stern counter covers the variable depth sonar. (West German Navy)

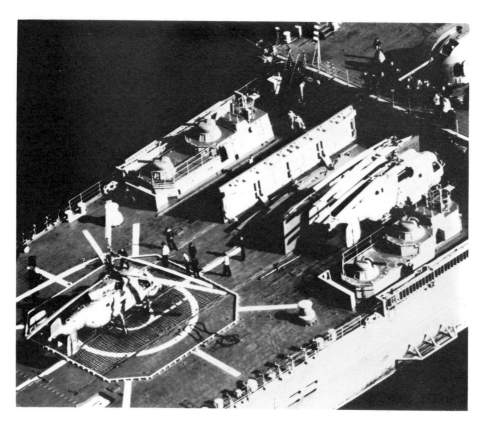

Details of the KIROV's fantail and elevator arrangement: Twin doors open to reveal the centerline lift; here a Ka-32 Helix is parked between the elevator and the starboard 30-mm Gatling guns; a Ka-25 Hormone is behind the elevator, resting on the net-like device used to prevent the helicopter from rolling until it is attached to the tracked traversing gear.

3 + 1 ANTI-SHIP GUIDED MISSILE CRUISERS: "SLAVA" CLASS

Name	Builders	Laid down	Launched	Completed	Status
SLAVA	61 Kommuna Shipyard, Nikolayev (north)	1976	1979	1982	**Black Sea**
MARSHAL USTINOV	61 Kommuna Shipyard, Nikolayev (north)	1978	1981	1986	**Northern**
CHERVONA UKRAINA	61 Kommuna Shipyard, Nikolayev (north)	1979	1983	1988	**Pacific**
ADMIRAL LOBOV	61 Kommuna Shipyard, Nikolayev (north)	1985	15 Aug 1990	(1992)	Building

Displacement:	10,000 tons standard
	12,500 tons full load
Length:	613 ft 4 in (187.0 m) overall
Beam:	68 ft 3 in (20.8 m)
Draft:	26 ft 3 in (8.0 m)
Propulsion:	4 gas turbines; 125,000 shp; 2 shafts
Speed:	34 knots
Range:	2,000 n.miles at 30 knots
	9,000 n.miles at 15 knots
Complement:	530 (85 officers + 445 enlisted)
Helicopters:	1 Ka-25 Hormone-B (see notes)
Missiles:	2 twin SA-N-4 anti-air launchers [40]
	8 rotary SA-N-6 anti-air launchers [64]
	16 SS-N-12 anti-ship tubes (8 twin)
Guns:	2 130-mm/70-cal DP (1 twin)
	6 30-mm/65-cal close-in (6 multi-barrel)
ASW weapons:	2 RBU-6000 rocket launchers
	torpedoes
Torpedoes:	10 21-inch (533-mm) torpedo tubes (2 quin)
Radars:	3 Bass Tilt (fire control)
	1 Front Door/Front Piece (fire control)
	1 Kite Screech (fire control)
	3 Palm Frond (navigation)
	2 Pop Group (fire control)
	1 Top Dome (fire control)
	1 Top Pair (3-D air search)
	1 Top Steer (3-D air search) except Top Plate in
	CHERNOVA UKRAINA and ADMIRAL LOBOV
Sonars:	low-frequency hull mounted
	medium-frequency variable depth
EW systems:	2 Bell series
	2 Bell Crown
	2 Bell Push
	4 Rum Tube

The SLAVAS are primarily anti-ship cruisers, armed with the same anti-ship missiles as the KIEV-class aircraft carriers and the modified Echo II SSGN and Juliett SSG classes. These ships were built simultaneously with the larger KIROV class.

Only four ships were built, over a relatively long period of time.

Classification: Soviet designation is RKR. The NATO designation was originally BLACK-COM-1 (Black Sea Combatant No. 1) and subsequently Krasina pending public knowledge of the lead ship's actual name.

Design: The basic hull form and machinery arrangement resemble those of the Kara class, the previous missile cruisers built at the 61 Kommuna Shipyard.

Launch tubes for the SS-N-12 missiles are paired to port and starboard, fitted at a fixed angle of about 15°, eight per side. There is a covered walkway between the missile ramps and the forward superstructure.

The SLAVA has a large, pyramidal mast structure forward with a smaller radar mast amidships, immediately ahead of the twin gas turbine exhaust stacks. The open space aft of twin, side-by-side funnels are for the SA-N-6 rotary-vertical missile launchers. The after deckhouse, topped by the Top Dome missile control radar, contains the helicopter hangar with the landing area aft. The hangar is a half deck below the flight deck and connected to it by a ramp.

Electronics: Two Punch Bowl satellite communications antennas are provided. The ship does not appear to have a bow sonar dome.

Engineering: These are the world's largest gas-turbine warships except for the British INVINCIBLE-class VSTOL carriers.

Helicopters: Officers on board the MARSHAL USTINOV have stated that the ship carries an ASW helicopter; however, a Hormone-B missile-targeting variant is more probable.

Missiles: This is the third class of surface combatants with a heavy battery of anti-ship missiles to be introduced in a three-year period by the Soviet Navy; the others are the KIROV and SOVREMENNYY classes. (All three classes also have a 130-mm gun battery.) A minimal ASW armament is fitted; this is the first Soviet cruiser or carrier design since the Kresta I that was not provided with either the SS-N-14 or FRAS-1 system.

The large SS-N-12 Sandbox missile tubes are an improved version of the SS-N-3 Shaddock.

Names: The name SLAVA is Russian for "glory"; the previous SLAVAS were a pre-dreadnought battleship completed in 1905, which saw major actions against German forces in World War I, and a heavy cruiser completed in 1941 as the MOLOTOV but renamed SLAVA in 1958.

Marshal of the Soviet Union Dmitri Ustinov (1908–1984), a civilian ordnance specialist and industrial administrator, was Min-ister of Defense from 1976 until his death. (He held the rank of engineer-colonel general before being appointed Minister of Defense.)

The previous CHERVONA UKRAINA was a cruiser launched in 1915 and originally named ADMIRAL NAKHIMOV.

Operational: The SLAVA transited from the Black Sea to the Mediterranean for the first time during September 1983. The MARSHAL USTINOV and the destroyer OTLICHNYY, accompanied by an oiler, visited Norfolk, Virginia, in July 1989. The SLAVA was to have been the Soviet host ship for the U.S.-Soviet summit meeting at Malta in December 1989; however, rough weather prevented Messrs. Bush and Gorbachev from meeting on the ship. The CHERVONA UKRAINA was transferred to the Pacific Fleet in late 1990.

Torpedoes: The torpedo tubes are fitted in the hull near the stern, five per side, covered by shutters. (They are installed below the Top Dome radar.)

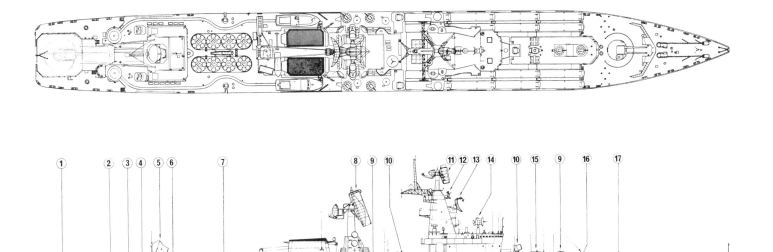

SLAVA class: 1. helicopter deck (VDS underneath) 2. SA-N-4 launcher (retracted) 3. helicopter hangar 4. Pop Group radar 5. Top Dome radar 6. 533-mm torpedo tubes (behind shutters) 7. SA-N-6 launchers 8. Top Pair radar 9. 30-mm Gatling guns 10. Bass Tilt radar 11. Top Steer radar 12. Palm Frond radar 13. Front Door radar 14. Kite Screech radar 15. RBU-6000 ASW rocket launchers 16. SS-N-12 launchers 17. twin 130-mm DP guns (M.J. Dodgson)

The MARSHAL USTINOV shows an unusual configuration. Two 30-mm Gatling guns and two RBU-6000 ASW rocket launchers are fitted in the "B" turret position, between the forward 130-mm gun mount and the bridge structure. Unlike the KIROVs, the SLAVAs have only one pyramid structure with the Top Sail radar mounted on a pylon mast.

This aerial view of the SLAVA at anchor in the Mediterranean shows the general arrangement of this class; the vertical, rotary launchers for the SA-N-6 surface-to-air missiles are amidships, between the twin funnels and the after deckhouse, topped by the Top Dome missile control radar. (1984, U.S. Navy)

The SLAVA showing off her 16 SS-N-12 anti-ship missile launchers. The SS-N-12 is a derivative of the SS-N-3 Shaddock missile, originally developed in the 1950s for the land-attack role. This is the heaviest missile battery found in any non-nuclear-propelled Soviet warship. (1990, Royal Navy)

7 ASW GUIDED MISSILE CRUISERS: KARA CLASS

Name	Builder	Laid down	Launched	Completed	Status
NIKOLAYEV	61 Kommuna Shipyard, Nikolayev (north)	1969	1971	1973	**Black Sea**
OCHAKOV	61 Kommuna Shipyard, Nikolayev (north)	1970	1972	1975	**Black Sea**
KERCH	61 Kommuna Shipyard, Nikolayev (north)	1971	1973	1976	**Black Sea**
AZOV	61 Kommuna Shipyard, Nikolayev (north)	1972	1974	1977	**Black Sea**
PETROPAVLOVSK	61 Kommuna Shipyard, Nikolayev (north)	1973	1975	1978	**Pacific**
TASHKENT	61 Kommuna Shipyard, Nikolayev (north)	1975	1976	1979	**Pacific**
TALLINN	61 Kommuna Shipyard, Nikolayev (north)	1976	1977	1980	**Pacific**

Displacement:	8,200 tons standard
	9,700 tons full load
Length:	567 ft 5 in (173.0 m) overall
Beam:	61 ft (18.6 m)
Draft:	22 ft (6.7 m)
Propulsion:	4 gas turbines; 120,000 shp; 2 shafts
Speed:	34 knots
Range:	3,000 n.miles at 32 knots
	6,000 n.miles at 15 knots
Complement:	approx. 520
Helicopters:	1 Ka-25 Hormone-A
Missiles:	2 twin SA-N-3 anti-air launchers [72] except 1 launcher in AZOV [36 missiles]
	2 twin SA-N-4 anti-air launchers [40]
	4 SA-N-6 anti-air vertical launchers [32] in AZOV
Guns:	4 76.2-mm/59-cal AA (2 twin)
	4 30-mm/65-cal close-in (4 multi-barrel)
ASW weapons:	8 SS-N-14 (2 quad)
	2 RBU-6000 rocket launchers
	2 RBU-1000 rocket launchers except none in PETROPAVLOVSK torpedoes
Torpedoes:	10 21-inch (533-mm) torpedo tubes (2 quin)
Radars:	2 Bass Tilt (fire control); none in AZOV
	1 Big Screen (3-D air search) in KERCH
	1 Don-2 or Palm Frond (navigation)
	2 Don-Kay (navigation)
	2 Head Lights-C (fire control); 1 in AZOV
	1 Head Net-C (3-D air search)
	2 Owl Screech (fire control)
	2 Pop Group (fire control)
	1 Top Dome (fire control) in AZOV
	1 Top Sail (3-D air search); none in KERCH
Sonars:	Bull Nose medium low-frequency bow mounted
	Mare Tail medium-frequency variable depth
EW systems:	2 Bell Clout
	2 Bell Slam
	2 Bell Tap, except 4 Rum Tub in KERCH and PETROPAVLOVSK
	8 Side Globe

These are large, graceful ships, a refinement of the Kresta II design with major anti-air and anti-submarine capabilities. The AZOV was an operational trials ship for the SA-N-6/Top Dome air defense system. From a schedule viewpoint they were built almost simultaneously with the Kresta II class constructed at the Zhdanov shipyard.

Classification: Soviet BPK class.

Design: These ships are significantly larger than the Kresta II class, have a heavier gun armament, are fitted with extensive command and control facilities, and are all gas-turbine propelled. Their superstructure is dominated by the large, square-topped gas-turbine funnel. The helicopter hangar, just forward of the landing area, is partially recessed below the flight deck. To stow the helicopter, the hangar's roof hatch and rear doors open and the helicopter is pushed in and then lowered by elevator to the hangar deck.

The PETROPAVLOVSK has a higher hangar structure with two Round House TACAN antennas fitted abreast the hangar (in place of RBU-1000 launchers).

Electronics: The KERCH was refitted with the new Big Screen 3-D radar in place of her Top Sail radar in 1988–1989; she was probably the first Soviet ship to have this system.

Engineering: When built these were the world's largest warships with all-gas turbine propulsion. They have subsequently been surpassed in size by the SLAVA and British INVINCIBLE classes.

Missiles: Although ostensibly armed with only AAW and ASW

The PETROPAVLOVSK with Round House TACAN antenna domes fitted alongside the hangar in place of the RBU-1000 ASW rocket launchers in the other ships of this class. The heavy torpedo battery—ten 21-inch (533-mm) tubes—is evident; Western ASW ships carry only 12.75-inch (324-mm) "short" tubes for lightweight ASW torpedoes. (1984, Japanese Maritime Self-Defense Force)

missiles, both the SA-N-3 and SS-N-14 have an anti-ship capability.

The AZOV was the trials ship for the SA-N-6 vertical-launch AAW system; an SA-N-6 launcher system replaced the after SA-N-3 system and the Top Dome missile control radar has been fitted in place of the after Head Lights.

Names: These ships are named for cities of the Soviet Union. All honor port cities except the TASHKENT, which is named for the capital of the Uzbek republic.

Operational: The PETROPAVLOVSK and TASHKENT transferred to the Pacific Fleet in 1979 (with the carrier MINSK); the TALLINN transferred shortly after her completion in 1981. (The ships deployed to the Far East with empty EW/ESM platforms; that equipment was installed at a later date.)

The AZOV did not deploy out of the Black Sea until January 1988. She and the three other ships in the Black Sea Fleet regularly operate in the Mediterranean.

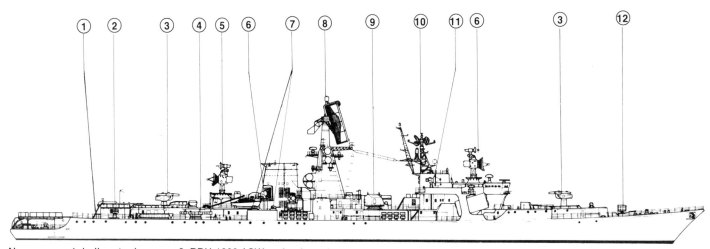

NIKOLAYEV: 1. helicopter hangar 2. RBU-1000 ASW rocket launchers 3. SA-N-3 launcher 4. 533-mm torpedo tubes 5. and 6. Head Lights-C radars 7. 30-mm Gatling guns 8. Top Sail radar 9. twin 76.2-mm AA guns 10. Head Net-C radar 11. Owl Screech radar 12. RBU-6000 ASW rocket launchers (L. Gassier)

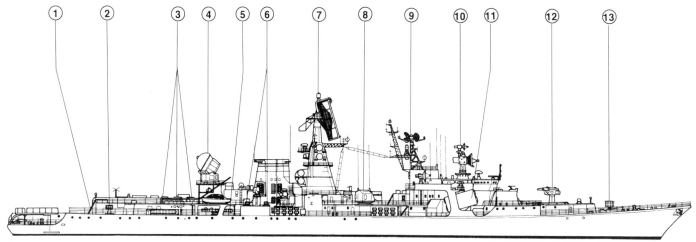

AZOV: 1. helicopter hangar 2. RBU-1000 ASW rocket launchers 3. SA-N-6 launchers 4. To Dome radar director 5. 533-mm torpedo tubes 6. 30-mm Gatling guns 7. Top Sail radar 8. twin 76.2-mm AA guns 9. Head Net-C radar 10. Head Lights-C radars 11. SS-N-14 ASW missile launchers 12. SA-N-3 launcher 13. RBU-6000 ASW rocket launchers (L. Gassier)

The cruiser Azov, photographed here in the Mediterranean, was trials ship for the SA-N-6/Top Dome anti-air system. The ship also differs in the torpedo tube arrangement (on the main deck, below the Top Dome radar). The six SA-N-6 vertical launch covers are different from those in the SLAVA and KIROV classes.

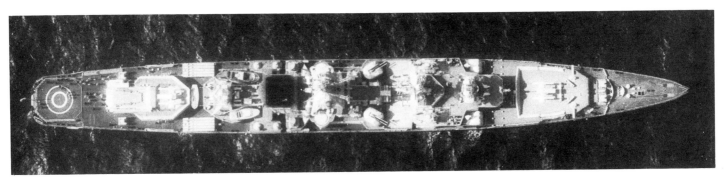

Kara-class ASW cruiser.

TALLINN in the Far East.

The KERCH at Sevastopol. She was the first warship to be identified
with the Big Screen air search radar, fitted in 1988–1989 (replaced
the Top Sail radar). The after Head Lights missile control radar is
also visible. (1989, Eric Grove)

10 ASW GUIDED MISSILE CRUISERS: KRESTA II CLASS

Name	Builder	Laid down	Launched	Completed	Status
KRONSHTADT	Zhdanov Shipyard, Leningrad	1966	1967	Dec 1969	**Northern**
ADMIRAL ISAKOV	Zhdanov Shipyard, Leningrad	1967	1968	Sep 1970	**Northern**
ADMIRAL NAKHIMOV	Zhdanov Shipyard, Leningrad	1968	1969	Aug 1971	**Baltic**
ADMIRAL MAKAROV	Zhdanov Shipyard, Leningrad	1969	1970	Aug 1972	**Northern**
MARSHAL VOROSHILOV	Zhdanov Shipyard, Leningrad	1969	1970	May 1973	**Pacific**
ADMIRAL OKTYABRSKIY	Zhdanov Shipyard, Leningrad	1970	1971	Nov 1973	**Pacific**
ADMIRAL ISACHENKOV	Zhdanov Shipyard, Leningrad	1971	1972	Sep 1974	**Baltic**
MARSHAL TIMOSHENKO	Zhdanov Shipyard, Leningrad	1972	1973	Sep 1975	**Northern**
VASILIY CHAPAYEV	Zhdanov Shipyard, Leningrad	1973	1975	Oct 1976	**Pacific**
ADMIRAL YUMASHEV	Zhdanov Shipyard, Leningrad	1974	1976	Jan 1978	**Northern**

Displacement:	6,200 tons standard	Torpedoes:	10 21-inch (533-mm) torpedo tubes (2 quin)
	7,700 tons full load	Radars:	2 Bass Tilt (fire control) in MARSHAL VOROSHILOV and
Length:	519 ft 11 in (158.5 m) overall		later ships
Beam:	56 ft 1 in (17.1 m)		1 Don-2 (navigation)
Draft:	20 ft 8 in (6.3 m)		2 Don-Kay (navigation)
Propulsion:	2 steam turbines; 100,000 shp; 2 shafts		2 Head Lights-C (fire control); earlier version in KRONSHTADT
Boilers:	4 turbopressure type		1 Head Net-C (3-D air search)
Speed:	34 knots		2 Muff Cob (fire control)
Range:	2,400 n.miles at 32 knots		1 Top Sail (3-D air search)
	10,500 n.miles at 14 knots	Sonars:	Bull Nose medium-frequency bow mounted
Complement:	approx. 380	EW systems:	1 Bell Clout
Helicopters:	1 Ka-25 Hormone-A		2 Bell Slam
Missiles:	2 twin SA-N-3 anti-air launchers [72]		2 Bell Tap
Guns:	4 57-mm/70-cal AA (2 twin)		8 Side Globe
	4 30-mm/65-cal close-in (4 multi-barrel)		
ASW weapons:	8 SS-N-14 Silex (2 quad)		
	2 RBU-6000 rocket launchers		
	2 RBU-1000 rocket launchers		
	torpedoes		

These are large ASW/AAW ships, similar to the Kresta I design but with improved surface-to-air missiles and electronics and the SS-N-14 anti-submarine system, which replaces the earlier ship's four SS-N-3 Shaddock anti-ship missiles.

Classification: Soviet BPK type.

Design: These ships have essentially the same hull and arrangement as the interim Kresta I design. Significant changes have been made in missiles and electronics; the most prominent features are the large Top Sail radar antenna surmounting the superstructure pyramid and the Head Lights fire control radars for the SA-N-3 missile systems. (The SA-N-3 has an anti-ship capability, as does

the SS-N-14.) The helicopter is hangared as in the Kara class.

The last three ships have an enlarged superstructure with a two-level deckhouse between the mast tower and funnel.

The ships are fitted with fin stabilizers.

Guns: The first four ships do not have the Bass Tilt fire control directors for the 30-mm Gatling guns. Those ships rely only on optical gun directors for those weapons.

Names: Most of these ships are named for Soviet military and naval commanders. V.I. Chapayev (1887–1919) was a Bolshevik military commander honored by the light cruiser CHAPAYEV (completed in 1949 and discarded in the late 1970s).

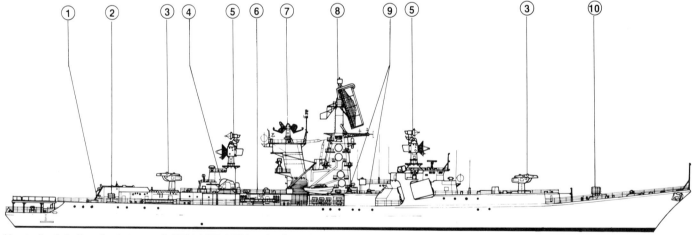

Kresta II 1. helicopter hangar 2. RBU-1000 ASW rocket launchers 3. SA-N-3 launchers 4. twin 57-mm AA guns 5. Head Lights-C radars 6. 533-mm torpedo tubes 7. Head Net-C radar 8. Top Sail radar 9. 30-mm Gatling guns 10. RBU-6000 ASW rocket launchers (L. Gassier)

The MARSHAL TIMOSHENKO, showing the quad SS-N-14 ASW missile launchers on either side of the bridge. The Head Lights radars in these ships can control the SS-N-14 missiles; smaller ships have the separate Eye Bowl guidance radars. (Royal Navy)

Stern aspect of a Kresta II. These ships have 57-mm guns abaft the torpedo tubes, which are also found in the Kresta I class. All other Soviet cruiser classes have heavier gun batteries. Although there is a raised helicopter platform, these ships do not have variable depth sonar. (1990, Royal Navy)

The MARSHAL VOROSHILOV, operating in the central Pacific (750 miles west of Midway) as part of a ten-ship task force. The forward Head Lights missile control radar is elevated. Note the funnel structure supporting the Head Net-C radar, between the forward pyramid structure carrying the Top Sail radar and the after Head Lights radar. (1985, U.S. Navy)

4 ANTI-SHIP GUIDED MISSILE CRUISERS: KRESTA I CLASS

Name	Shipyard	Laid down	Launched	Completed	Status
ADMIRAL ZOZULYA	Zhdanov Shipyard, Leningrad	Sep 1964	Oct 1965	Mar 1967	**Northern**
VLADIVOSTOK	Zhdanov Shipyard, Leningrad	1965	Aug 1966	Jan 1968	**Pacific**
VITSE ADMIRAL DROZD	Zhdanov Shipyard, Leningrad	1965	Jan 1967	Aug 1968	**Northern**
SEVASTOPOL	Zhdanov Shipyard, Leningrad	1966	June 1967	July 1969	**Pacific**

Displacement:	6,150 tons standard
	7,500 tons full load
Length:	487 ft (148.5 m) waterline
	510 ft (155.5 m) overall
Beam:	56 ft 1 in (17.1 m)
Draft:	22 ft (6.7 m)
Propulsion:	2 steam turbines; 100,000 shp; 2 shafts
Boilers:	4 turbopressure type
Speed:	34 knots
Range:	1,600 n.miles at 34 knots
	7,000 n.miles at 14 knots
Complement:	approx. 380
Helicopters:	1 Ka-25 Hormone-B
Missiles:	2 twin SA-N-1 anti-air launchers [44]
	4 SS-N-3b Shaddock anti-ship tubes (2 twin)
Guns:	4 57-mm/70-cal AA (2 twin)
	4 30-mm/65-cal close-in (4 multi-barrel) in
	VITSE ADMIRAL DROZD
ASW weapons:	2 RBU-6000 rocket launchers
	2 RBU-1000 rocket launchers
	torpedoes
Torpedoes:	10 21-inch (533-mm) torpedo tubes (2 quin)
Radars:	2 Base Tilt (fire control) in VITSE ADMIRAL DROZD
	1 Big Net (air search)
	1 or 2 Don-2 (navigation); none in ADMIRAL ZOZULYA
	1 Don-Kay (navigation) in ships with 1 Don-2 and
	ADMIRAL ZOZULYA
	2 Muff Cob (fire control)
	2 Palm Frond (navigation) in ADMIRAL ZOZULYA
	2 Peel Group (fire control)
	1 Scoop Pair (fire control)
Sonars:	Herkules medium-frequency hull mounted
EW systems:	1 Bell Clout
	2 Bell Slam
	2 Bell Strike
	2 Bell Tap
	2 Fig Jar
	8 Side Globe

These ships were an interim design, carrying the Shaddock anti-ship missiles but apparently intended for other weapon systems (see Kresta II listing). The lead ship began trials in the Gulf of Finland in February 1967. In 1990–1991 all four ships were being prepared for scrapping.

Aircraft: One Hormone-B is embarked to provide over-the-horizon targeting for the Shaddock missiles.

Classification: Originally designated BPK; changed to RKR in 1977–1978, reflecting the primary armament of anti-ship missiles.

Design: These ships are considerably larger than the previous Kynda series. They also have two surface-to-air missile systems and are the first Soviet surface combatants with a helicopter hangar. No mine rails are fitted, as in the previous post-war cruiser and destroyer classes.

Compared with the smaller Kynda-class rocket cruisers (RKR), the Kresta I design has only one-half the number of Shaddock launch tubes and one-fourth the total number of missiles. The Kresta missile tubes are mounted under cantilever bridge wings; they cannot be trained but are elevated to about 18° for firing.

Electronics: Fitted upon completion with two Plinth Net antennas for Shaddock data links.

Modifications: These ships have been modified during their service. The VITSE ADMIRAL DROZD in 1973–1975 was fitted with a two-deck structure installed between the bridge and radar pyramid, with four 30-mm close-in weapons (Gatling guns) fitted along with the associated Bass Tilt fire-control radars. The SEVASTOPOL received a similar deckhouse in 1980, but the Gatling guns and radars have not been observed. Plinth Net was installed in most ships in the 1980s.

Names: The names of these ships recall two Soviet flag officers and honor two major port cities.

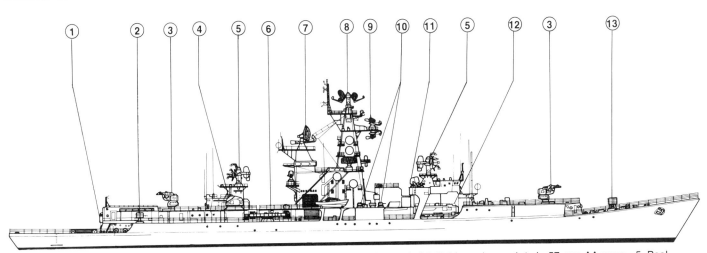

VITSE-ADMIRAL DROZD   1. helicopter hangar   2. RBU-1000 ASW rocket launchers   3. SA-N-1 launchers   4. twin 57-mm AA guns   5. Peel Group radars   6. 533-mm torpedo tubes   7. Big Net radar   8. Head Net-C radar   9. Scoop Pair radar   10. 30-mm Gatling guns   11. Bass Tilt radar director   12. SS-N-3b launchers   13. RBU-6000 ASW rocket launchers (L. Gassier)

The VLADIVOSTOK, one of the quartet of Kresta I cruisers, an interim design pending development of the definitive Kresta II and Kara ASW cruiser classes. The four SS-N-3b Shaddock missile tubes are alongside the bridge, in the position of SS-N-14 ASW missiles in the later ships. These ships are rarely observed at sea. (1987, JMSDF)

The Kresta I–class cruiser VITSE ADMIRAL DROZD. These were the first Soviet surface combatants to regularly embark a helicopter. These ships had the helicopter hangar on the same level as the landing platform, permitting the Ka-25 Hormone to be rolled directly into the hangar. The twin 57-mm gun mounts are aft of the torpedo tubes. (1986, U.S. Navy)

4 ANTI-SHIP GUIDED MISSILE CRUISERS: KYNDA CLASS

Name	Builder	Laid down		Launched		Completed		Status
GROZNYY	Zhdanov Shipyard, Leningrad	June	1959	Apr	1961	June	1962	**Baltic**
ADMIRAL FOKIN	Zhdanov Shipyard, Leningrad	Aug	1960	May	1962	Aug	1963	**Pacific**
ADMIRAL GOLOVKO	Zhdanov Shipyard, Leningrad	Dec	1960		1962	July	1964	**Black Sea**
VARYAG	Zhdanov Shipyard, Leningrad	Sep	1961	June	1963	Feb	1965	**Pacific**

Displacement:	4,600 tons standard
	5,700 tons full load
Length:	469 ft (143.0 m) overall
	442 ft 10 in (135.0) waterline
Beam:	51 ft 10 in (15.8 m)
Draft:	17 ft 5 in (5.3 m)
Propulsion:	steam turbines; 100,000 shp; 2 shafts
Boilers:	4 turbopressure type
Speed:	34 knots
Range:	2,000 n.miles at 32 knots
	7,000 n.miles at 14 knots
Complement:	approx. 375
Helicopters:	landing area only
Missiles:	1 twin SA-N-1 anti-air launcher [24]
	8 SS-N-3b Shaddock anti-ship tubes [8 + 8 reloads]
Guns:	4 76.2-mm/59-cal AA (2 twin)
	4 30-mm/65-cal close-in (4 multi-barrel) in GROZNYY and VARYAG
ASW weapons:	2 RBU-6000 rocket launchers
	torpedoes
Torpedoes:	6 21-inch (533-mm) torpedo tubes (2 triple)
Mines:	rails fitted
Radars:	2 Bass Tilt (fire control) in GROZNYY and VARYAG
	2 Don-2 (navigation)
	2 Head Net-A in ADMIRAL GOLOVKO and GROZNYY; 1 in ADMIRAL FOKIN
	2 Head Net-C in VARYAG; 1 in ADMIRAL FOKIN
	1 Owl Screech (fire control)
	1 Peel Group (fire control)
	2 Scoop Pair (fire control)
Sonars:	Herkules high-frequency hull mounted
EW systems:	1 Bell Clout
	1 Bell Slam
	1 Bell Tap
	2 Guard Dog
	4 Top Hat in ADMIRAL GOLOVKO

These were among the first of the modern Soviet warships resulting from the defense decisions made in the mid-1950s, after the death of Stalin. Additional ships of this design were probably planned but cancelled (as was a larger Shaddock-armed missile cruiser). The GROZNYY spent most of her career in the Black Sea, returning to the Baltic Fleet in 1982. In 1990–1991 all four ships were being prepared for scrapping.

Classification: Soviet RKR type. The U.S. Navy originally listed these ships and subsequent Soviet RKR/BPK ships as guided missile frigates (DLG) until the 1975 reclassification of U.S. frigates (DLG/DLGN) as destroyers or cruisers. At that time the Soviet RKR/BPK classes were changed to cruisers.

Design: The Kynda-class cruisers are only slightly longer than the Krupnyy and Kildin destroyer classes but have lines more akin to a cruiser hull and significantly more firepower. These ships introduced the imposing pyramid structure to Soviet ships to support radar and EW antennas. They are the only ships with pyramids and twin funnels.

No helicopter hangar or maintenance facilities are provided.

Electronics: Two Plinth Net antennas for Shaddock data links were apparently fitted in all except the VARYAG in the 1980s.

Missiles: The large Shaddock tubes are mounted in four-tube banks forward and amidships. The launchers swing outboard and elevate to fire. Eight reload missiles are in magazines in the superstructure, behind their respective launchers. Reloading the Shaddock tubes is a slow and awkward process.

Modifications: The GROZNYY was fitted with Gatling guns and Bass Tilt radars in 1980, and the VARYAG was similarly modified in 1981.

These ships were built with two Head Net-A radars; some ships were subsequently refitted with Head Net-C.

Names: Two ships remember Soviet flag officers: the GOLOVKO is named for Admiral A.G. Golovko, who commanded the Northern Fleet from 1940 to 1946 and the Baltic Fleet from 1952 to 1956; he was considered a leading candidate for head of the Navy when Admiral Gorshkov was appointed in 1956. GROZNYY and VARYAG are traditional Russian warship names (the first means "terrible" and refers to Ivan the Terrible; the second is a shortened form of "Varangian," or "Norseman").

The GROZNYY with her superstructure dominated by the two pyramid structures supporting a variety of radar and electronic warfare antennas. These were the first ships to have these pyramids to carry antennas. (1985, U.S. Navy)

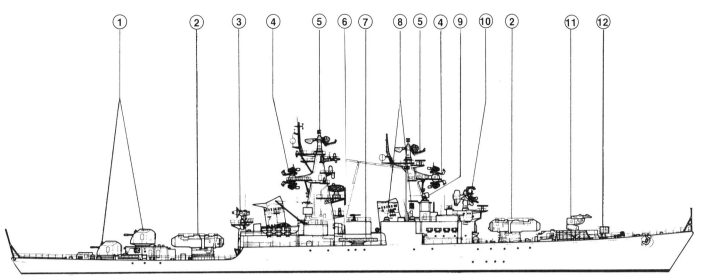

GROZNYY: 1. twin 76.2-mm AA guns 2. SS-N-3b launchers 3. Owl Screech radar 4. Scoop Pair radars 5. Head Net-A radars 6. Plinth Net data link antennas 7. 533-mm torpedo tubes 8. 30-mm Gatling guns 9. Bass Tilt radar director 10. Peel Group radar 11. SA-N-1 launcher 12. RBU-6000 ASW rocket launchers (L. Gassier)

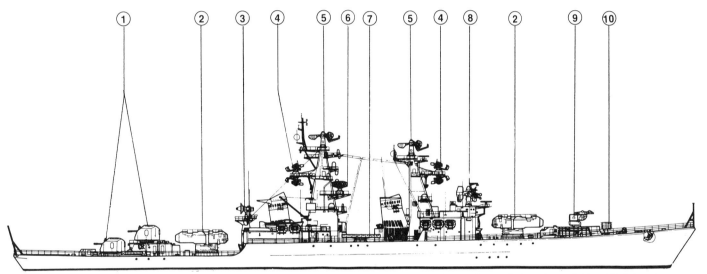

ADMIRAL GOLOVKO: 1. twin 76.2-mm AA guns 2. SS-N-3b launchers 3. Owl Screech radar 4. Scoop Pair radars 5. Head Net-A radars 6. Plinth Net data link antennas 7. 533-mm torpedo tubes 8. Peel Group radar 9. SA-N-1 launcher 10. RBU-6000 ASW rocket launchers (L. Gassier)

The VARYAG with a built-up amidships structure mounting two 30-mm Gatling guns on each side and Bass Tilt fire control radars behind the bridge. There is also a deckhouse added amidships, between the torpedo tubes. (1987, JMSDF)

GUIDED MISSILE CRUISERS: "SUPER" KYNDA

There is evidence that a ''super'' or enlarged Kynda design was planned, to be fitted with larger numbers of the SS-N-3 Shaddock missiles. There is no evidence that construction was begun before the shift to the Kresta design.

LIGHT AND COMMAND CRUISERS: "SVERDLOV" CLASS

The last of the 14 SVERDLOV-class cruisers armed with 6-inch (152-mm) guns are believed to have been withdrawn from active service in 1988–1989 and are in the process of being scrapped.

Twenty-four of these ships are believed to have been planned in the post–World War II construction program. Only 20 ships were laid down, with 14 completed between 1951 and 1955 as light cruisers; 3 additional hulls were launched but not finished. The completed ships are listed below. (See 4th edition, pages 190–193 for characteristics.)

ADMIRAL LAZAREV (completed 1952) operational until early 1980s.

ADMIRAL NAKHIMOV (1952) converted to a test ship for surface-to-surface missiles and operated in the Black Sea until scrapped in 1961.

ADMIRAL SENYAVIN (1954) converted to command ship in 1971–1972; operational into the late 1980s.

ADMIRAL USHAKOV (1953) operational into the mid-1980s; towed to Bangladesh for scrapping in November 1989.

ALEKSANDR NEVSKI (1952) operational into the late 1980s.

ALEKSANDR SUVOROV (1953) operational into the mid-1980s.

DMITRIY POZHARSKIY (1953) operational into the mid-1980s.

DZERZHINSKIY (1952) converted to guided-missile configuration with SA-N-2 Guideline system by 1961. She was not operationally successful. After operating in the Black Sea–Mediterranean area probably ceased to be operational in the late 1970s, although listed as in service by U.S. intelligence into the early 1980s; the DZERZHINSKIY's hulk was towed to Bangladesh for scrapping in November 1989.

MIKHAIL KUTUZOV (1955) operational into the 1980s.

MURMANSK (1955) operational into the late 1980s; the ship had a major upgrade of command facilities in the late 1980s and reportedly served as flagship for a major Northern Fleet exercise in 1989.

OKTYABRSKAYA REVOLUTSIYA (1954) originally named MOLOTOVSK; the ship was renamed in 1957 with the political demise of Foreign Minister V.M. Molotov. She was operational into the mid-1980s.

ORDZONIKIDZE (1951) transferred to Indonesia in October 1962 and renamed IRIAN. She was scrapped in Taiwan in 1972.

SVERDLOV (1951) operational into the early 1980s.

ZHDANOV (1952) converted to command ship in 1971–1972; operational into the late 1980s.

BATTLE CRUISERS: "STALINGRAD" CLASS

The Soviets began building the STALINGRAD-class battle cruisers after World War II. The information on these ships available in the West is limited and contradictory. The lead ship apparently was laid down at Nikolayev, but reports differ on whether this occurred in early 1949 or 1951. (The earlier date is considered more likely by the author; that ship was reported by the same sources as being about 60 percent complete and ready for launching in 1953 when she was cancelled shortly after Stalin's death.) A second ship, which may have been named MOSKVA, is reported to have been laid down at the Baltic Shipyard in Leningrad in October 1952, although the ship reported seen there may have been the remains of the earlier KRONSHTADT (see below); alternative reports are that the MOSKVA was to have been laid down at Nikolayev following the launching of the STALINGRAD. Again, reports vary on the fate of the hulls, some saying one and some saying both were broken up on the building ways; more likely, the STALINGRAD was floated and her hull expended in missile tests.

The STALINGRAD design was probably based on that of the prewar KRONSHTADT class. The older class (never completed) was

to have had a standard displacement of 35,240 tons with a full-load displacement of 38,360 tons and an overall length of 813 ft 8 in (248 m). Primary armament would have been nine 12-inch/56-cal guns in triple turrets. The STALINGRAD may have been slightly larger; that design was modified at some stage to launch the Kennel surface-to-surface missile (i.e., the initial version of the Kennel AS-1 missile) in place of one (or possibly two) of the triple 12-inch turrets.

LIGHT CRUISERS: "CHAPAYEV" CLASS

Seven CHAPAYEV-class light cruisers were laid down in 1938–1940. Full-load displacement was 15,000 tons with a main battery of 12 5.9-inch guns. All construction stopped when the Soviet Union entered the war in June 1941. Work resumed on five ships after the war; the CHAPAYEV, CHKALOV, and ZHELEZNIAKOV were completed in 1949, and the FRUNZE and KUIBISHEV in 1950. All were scrapped from 1962 onward.

HEAVY CRUISERS: "KIROV" CLASS

Six KIROV-class heavy cruisers were laid down in 1935–1939. Full-load displacement was 11,500 tons for the first two ships and 9,790 tons for the later four with a main battery of nine 7.1-inch guns. Four ships were completed in 1938–1941, before the outbreak of war: KIROV, MAKSIM GOR'KIY, MOLOTOV (later renamed SLAVA), and VOROSHILOV; two other ships were completed during the war, the KALININ in 1943 and the KAGANOVICH (later PETROPAVLOVSK) in 1944. The ships were broken up after 1956.

The MARSHAL USTINOV with a Ka-25 Hormone helicopter on deck. The net restricts movement of the helicopter in rough seas (also used on the MOSKVA-class helicopter cruisers). Note the narrow hangar with SA-N-4 launcher cylinders on either side; the Top Dome radar forward of the hangar; and twin funnels with a large boat crane between them. (West German Navy)

CHAPTER 15

Destroyers

The Vitse Admiral Kulakov reveals the heavily armed, compact design of the Udaloy-class ASW ships. The Soviet Navy now has two classes of destroyers in series production. The Kulakov—which transited to Cuba shortly after this photo was taken in the Mediterranean—has Strut Pair radars atop both lattice masts and no Cross Swords fire control radars. (1988, U.S. Navy, Lt. P.J. Azzolina)

The destroyer as a distinctive ship type from the cruiser is becoming a blurred issue in the Soviet Navy, as it has in the U.S. Navy. The new Udaloy-class anti-submarine destroyers are superior in ASW effectiveness to the Kresta II– and Kara cruiser classes (which the Soviets designate as ASW ships—BPK). Similarly, the Sovremennyy anti-ship destroyers are superior in some respects to the older *and smaller* Kresta I and Kynda missile cruisers (RKR).

The Soviet Navy continues a steady rate of construction of large destroyers of the Sovremennyy and Udaloy classes with both classes in series production at the rate of about one ship per year. They represent two distinct warship roles; their basic hull and propulsion systems are quite different, as are their armament and sensors. Two shipyards are engaged in building these two classes.

No new destroyers were completed in the Soviet Union between the last of the 20-ship Kashin class (1973) and the first units of the Sovremennyy and Udaloy classes (1981). That eight-year hiatus further indicates the lack of clarity between Soviet cruiser and destroyer classes as the Northern (formerly Zhdanov No. 190) Shipyard in Leningrad, which builds both the Udaloy and Sovremennyy classes, built the Kresta II–class cruisers during that period.

The 61 Kommuna shipyard in Nikolayev (north yard No. 445), which with the Zhdanov yard built the 20 destroyers of the Kashin class, built the Kara-class cruisers. Following completion of the last ship of that class in 1980, the yard began constructing the Slava-class cruisers and destroyer-type ships for India and modernizing older Soviet ship classes.

Udaloy construction is shared by the Zhdanov yard and the Yantar/Kaliningrad shipyard (No. 820 in the Lithuanian SSR). Thus, there is an increase in the warship building rate at Zhdanov while the Udaloy is the largest and most complex warship to have been built at the Kaliningrad yard. (The Yantar/Kaliningrad yard previously built Krivak-class frigates.) The construction rate for the Udaloy and Sovremennyy classes could probably be increased slightly at those two yards. And, of course, there is the possibility that the Nikolayev north shipyard, upon completing the Slava cruiser program, could be employed in producing one or both of these destroyer classes.

The total number of Soviet destroyers is declining rapidly as the older ships of the Kanin, Modified Kildin, SAM Kotlin, Kotlin, and SKORYY classes have been retired since 1987. In early 1990 only an estimated 14 pre-Kashin–class destroyers remained in active service; those survivors were expected to be scrapped in the early 1990s. (Additional destroyers are in reserve.)

Assuming a continuation of the current UDALOY and SO- VREMENNYY construction rates, by the mid-1990s the Soviet de- stroyer force could number some 45 to 50 ships:

approx. 16 UDALOY class
approx. 16 SOVREMENNYY class
approx. 15 Kashin class

This compares to about 65 destroyers in active service in the mid- 1980s; however, the mid-1990s force will be considerably more capable in both anti-submarine and anti-surface warfare. Although it could be argued the loss of Kanin and SAM Kotlin destroyers with their SA-N-1 missile system represents a loss in area anti-air coverage, the SOVREMENNYY's SA-N-7 missile and its supporting electronics are more effective, albeit having a slightly shorter range, while the UDALOY's SA-N-9 provides a more viable self- defense capability.

Again, the existing destroyer construction yards as well as the Nikolayev north could provide destroyers at a faster rate than the current two-per-year program.

In addition to their principal anti-air or anti-submarine weapons, both of the current construction classes have large torpedo tubes and mine rails; these features have long been deleted from U.S. destroyers (as well as from U.S. cruisers).

11+3 ASW GUIDED MISSILE DESTROYERS: "UDALOY" CLASS

Name	Builder	Laid down	Launched	Completed
UDALOY	Yantar, Kaliningrad	1978	1980	1981
VITSE ADMIRAL KULAKOV	Zhdanov Shipyard, Leningrad*	1978	1982	Apr 1982
MARSHAL VASIL'YEVSKIY	Zhdanov Shipyard, Leningrad	1979	1981	July 1983
ADMIRAL ZAKHAROV	Zhdanov Shipyard, Leningrad	1979	Feb 1982	1984
ADMIRAL SPIRIDONOV	Yantar, Kaliningrad	1981	1983	1985
ADMIRAL TRIBUTS	Zhdanov Shipyard, Leningrad	1982	1984	1986
MARSHAL SHAPOSHNIKOV	Yantar, Kaliningrad	1983	1985	1986
SIMFEROPOL	Yantar, Kaliningrad	1983	1986	1987
ADMIRAL LEVCHENKO	Zhdanov Shipyard, Leningrad	1984	1987	1988
ADMIRAL VINOGRADOV	Yantar, Kaliningrad	1984	1987	1988
ADMIRAL KHARLAMOV	Yantar, Kaliningrad	1984	1988	1989
3 units	Yantar, Kaliningrad			Building

* The Zhdanov shipyard (No. 190) was renamed Northern Shipyard in 1989.

Displacement:	6,700 tons standard
	8,100 tons full load
Length:	492 ft (150.0 m) waterline
	531 ft 4 in (162.0 m) overall
Beam:	63 ft 4 in (19.3 m)
Draft:	26 ft 3 in (8.0 m)
Propulsion:	4 gas turbines; 125,000 shp; 2 shafts
Speed:	35 knots
Range:	2,000 n.miles at 32 knots
	6,000 n.miles at 20 knots
Complement:	approx. 250
Helicopters:	2 Ka-27 Helix-A
Missiles:	8 SA-N-9 anti-air vertical launchers [64]
Guns:	2 100-mm/70-cal DP (2 single)
	4 30-mm/65-cal close-in (4 multi-barrel)
	8 12.7-mm machine guns (4 twin) in ADMIRAL VINOGRADOV and possibly others
ASW weapons:	8 SS-N-14 (2 quad)
	2 RBU-6000 rocket launchers
	torpedoes
Torpedoes:	8 21-inch (533-mm) torpedo tubes (2 quad)
Mines:	rails fitted
Radars:	2 Bass Tilt (fire control)
	up to 2 Cross Sword (fire control)
	2 Eye Bowl (fire control)
	1 Fly Screen (aircraft control)
	1 Kite Screech (fire control)
	3 Palm Frond (navigation)
	2 Strut Pair (surface search) in UDALOY and ADMIRAL KULAKOV; 1 in most later ships
	1 Top Plate (air search) in MARSHAL VASIL'YEVSKIY and later ships
Sonars:	Horse Jaw low-frequency bow mounted
	Horse Tail low-frequency variable depth
EW systems:	2 Bell Crown
	2 Bell Shroud
	2 Bell Squat
	4 Foot Ball in SIMFEROPOL

These are large anti-submarine destroyers, similar in concept to the U.S. SPRUANCE (DD 963) class. The UDALOY began trials in the Gulf of Finland in August 1980. Construction of the class continues with at least 14 units anticipated by Western intelligence.

As of early 1990, 3 ships were in the Northern Fleet, 4 in the Baltic, and 4 in the Pacific.

Classification: Soviet BPK type. Pending disclosure of the lead ship's name, this class was designated BAL-COM-3 (Baltic Com- batant No. 3) by NATO intelligence.

Design: These ships have a long, low superstructure with their quad SS-N-14 launchers under a cantilevered extension to the bridge structure, as in the Kresta II and Kara classes. The hangar has separate bays to accommodate two helicopters, which are low- ered into them by elevators (this is similar to the arrangement in the Kara and Kresta II classes). There is a control station between the hangar bays and a pair of Round House TACAN antennas. A variable-depth sonar, similar to that of the KIROV class, is fitted in the stern counter.

Electronics: The first two ships have Strut Pair air search radars atop their masts and hence have no height-finding capability. The SIMFEROPOL and later ships have a Strut Pair mounted on their forward mast with the Top Plate radar on the second mast.

The early ships were completed with empty positions for the Cross Sword radar directors (above the bridge and above the han- gars). The ADMIRAL ZAKHAROV was the first ship to have the full SA-N-9/Cross Sword system installed, with two Cross Sword radar directors provided in 1984 (with one later removed). As of late 1989 the first two ships still did not have an operational SA-N-9 system.

The SIMFEROPOL has four Foot Ball EW antennas on the after mast.

Guns: When the ADMIRAL VINOGRADOV deployed to the Far East in August 1989 the ship had four 12.7-mm twin machine gun mounts, two atop the bridge and two adjacent to the hangar.

Missiles: Between the second lattice mast and helicopter han- gar, are four vertical launchers for the SA-N-9, with another battery of four launchers on the forecastle, forward of the guns.

The SS-N-14 launchers are fixed in elevation and traverse.

Names: UDALOY, a traditional Soviet destroyer name, means "courageous" or "daring." The other ships are named for de- ceased senior officers of the Army and Navy. Earlier Soviet de- stroyers have adjective names.

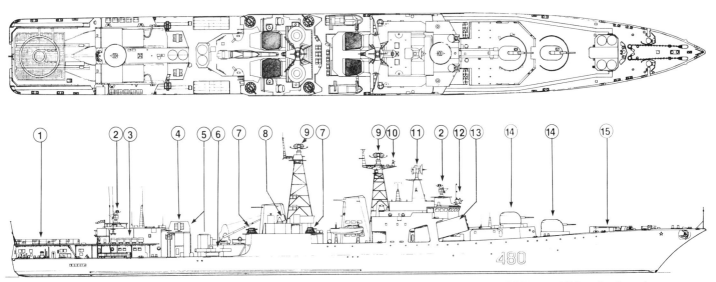

UDALOY class: 1. helicopter deck (above VDS)   2. Cross Sword radar   3. twin helicopter hangars   4. RBU-6000 ASW rocket launcher
5. SA-N-9 launchers   6. 533-mm torpedo tubes   7. 30-mm Gatling guns   8. Bass Tilt radar director   9. Strut Pair radar   10. Palm Frond
radar   11. Kite Screech radar   12. Eye Bowl radars   13. SS-N-14 ASW missile launchers   14. single 100-mm DP guns   15. SA-N-9
launchers (M.J. Dodgson)

The ADMIRAL ZAKHAROV in the Far East; this UDALOY-class destroyer has Cross Swords radars, no radar on the forward lattice mast, and a Top
Plate/Top Mesh atop the second, testimony to the variety of radar configurations found in these warships. (Japanese Maritime Self-Defense
Force, 1989)

The ADMIRAL TRIBUTS has a Cross Swords fire control radar between
the twin helicopter hangars with a Strut Pair radar atop the forward
lattice mast and a Top Plate/Top Mesh atop the second (flanked by
Round House TACAN antennas). The tracks in the flight deck for the
helicopter traversing system. (1988)

The unusual hangar configuration of the UDALOY class provides for
two ASW helicopters to be stowed in a relatively small space; twin
hangars with elevators to lower the helicopters several feet are fitted
on each side of the helicopter control station. The doors close and
roof hatches slide back. The platform between the hangars is for a
Cross Swords fire control director for the SA-N-9 missile.

The SS-N-14 ASW missiles of the VITSE ADMIRAL KULAKOV are located in quad launchers outboard of the bridge structure, similar to the arrangement of the smaller Kresta and larger Kara cruiser designs. The variable depth sonar is fitted below the raised helicopter platform.

12+8 ANTI-SHIP GUIDED MISSILE DESTROYERS: "SOVREMENNYY" CLASS

Name	Builder	Laid down	Launched	Completed
SOVREMENNYY	Zhdanov Shipyard, Leningrad*	1976	Nov 1978	1981
OTCHAYANNYY	Zhdanov Shipyard, Leningrad	1977	Aug 1980	1982
OTLICHNYY	Zhdanov Shipyard, Leningrad	1978	1981	1983
OSMOTRITEL'NYY	Zhdanov Shipyard, Leningrad	1979	June 1982	1984
BEZUPRECHNYY	Zhdanov Shipyard, Leningrad	1980	1983	July 1985
BOYEVOY	Zhdanov Shipyard, Leningrad	1981	1984	1986
STOYKIY	Zhdanov Shipyard, Leningrad	1982	1985	1987
OKRYLENNYY	Zhdanov Shipyard, Leningrad	1983	1986	1988
BURNYY	Zhdanov Shipyard, Leningrad	1983	1987	1989
GREMYASHCHIY	Zhdanov Shipyard, Leningrad	1984	1987	1989
BYSTRYY	Zhdanov Shipyard, Leningrad	1984	1987	1989
RASTOROPNYY	Zhdanov Shipyard, Leningrad	1985	1988	1990
. . . . . .	Zhdanov Shipyard, Leningrad	1985	1988	
. . . . . .	Zhdanov Shipyard, Leningrad	1986	1989	
6 units	Zhdanov Shipyard, Leningrad			

* The Zhdanov shipyard (No. 190) was renamed Northern Shipyard in 1989.

Displacement:	6,300 tons standard
	7,850 tons full load
Length:	475 ft 7 in (145.0 m) waterline
	511 ft 8 in (156.0 m) overall
Beam:	57 ft 5 in (17.5 m)
Draft:	23 ft (7.0 m)
Propulsion:	2 steam turbines; 100,000 shp; 2 shafts
Boilers:	4 turbopressure type
Speed:	34 knots
Range:	2,400 n.miles at 32 knots
	10,500 n.miles at 14 knots
Complement:	370 (37 officers + 333 enlisted)
Helicopters:	1 Ka-25 Hormone-B
Missiles:	2 SA-N-7 anti-air launchers [40]
	8 SS-N-22 anti-ship tubes (2 quad)
Guns:	4 130-mm/70-cal DP guns (2 twin)
	4 30-mm/65-cal close-in (4 multi-barrel)
ASW weapons:	2 RBU-1000 rocket launchers
	torpedoes
Torpedoes:	4 21-inch (533-mm) torpedo tubes (2 twin)
Mines:	rails fitted
Radars:	1 Band Stand (fire control)
	2 Bass Tilt (fire control)
	6 Front Dome (fire control)
	1 Kite Screech (fire control)
	3 Palm Frond (navigation)
	1 Plate Steer (3-D air search) in OSOMOTRITEL'NYY,
	BEZUPRECHNNY; Top Plate in BOYEVOY and later ships
Sonars:	medium-frequency hull mounted
EW systems:	2 Bell Shroud
	2 Bell Squat
	4 Foot Ball in most ships

This destroyer class is intended primarily for the anti-ship role. The ships have significant anti-air capability but minimal ASW weapons and sensors. The SOVREMENNYY began sea trials in the Gulf of Finland in August 1980. Construction continues with Western intelligence estimating a program of some 20 ships.

As of early 1990, there were 5 ships in the Northern Fleet, 2 in the Baltic Fleet (on trials), and 5 in the Pacific Fleet, with perhaps 20 to 24 units planned.

Classification: Soviet EM (destroyer) type. These ships were originally designated BAL-COM-2 by Western intelligence.

Design: These ships are similar in size to the UDALOY but with different hull form, propulsion, weapons, and sensors. The basic hull form and propulsion are similar to those of the Kresta II, built at the same shipyard. The quad surface-to-surface missile launchers are mounted slightly forward of the bridge structure; the main gun armament is divided fore and aft (the UDALOY has guns forward); pressure-fired steam propulsion is provided (vice the UDALOY's gas turbines); and there is a telescoping helicopter hangar adjacent to the landing areas to accommodate a single Ka-25 Hormone-B helicopter for over-the-horizon missile targeting. This is the first Soviet surface combatant with the landing area amidships instead of at the stern, and the first to use the telescoping hangar configuration.

Minimal ASW armament is fitted, and although the ship does have a bow sonar dome, it is smaller than that provided in the UDALOY and other recent BPK classes. However, like the UDALOY, these ships have mine rails.

Electronics: Two small, spherical radomes are located on platforms on both sides of the single stack. Their exact function is unknown, but they may be associated with over-the-horizon targeting for the SS-N-22 missiles.

The SOVREMENNYY has been refitted with four Foot Ball EW antennas; they were not fitted in the next four ships when this edition went to press, but are found in the BOYEVOY and later units.

Engineering: The use of steam propulsion in the SOVREMENNYY was somewhat surprising in view of the use of gas turbines in the previous Kara class and the contemporary UDALOY. The estimated ranges of the two destroyer classes is approximately the same.

Guns: The 130-mm guns are the same type fitted in the KIROV and SLAVA cruiser classes. They are the largest guns installed in any of the world's recent destroyers.

Missiles: The SS-N-22 anti-ship missiles are an improved version of the SS-N-9.

Names: These ships, like the Soviet destroyers of the past, have adjectival names; SOVREMENNYY, for example, means "modern."

Operational: The OTLICHNYY and the cruiser MARSHAL USTINOV, accompanied by an oiler, visited Norfolk, Virginia, in July 1989.

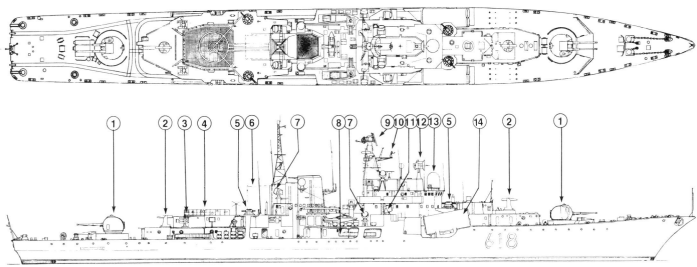

SOVREMENNYY class: 1. twin 130-mm DP guns 2. SA-N-7 launcher 3. RBU-1000 ASW rocket launchers 4. helicopter deck 5. 30-mm Gatling guns 6. telescoping hangar 7. Front Dome radars 8. 533-mm torpedo tubes 9. Plate Steer radar 10. Palm Frond radar 11. Bass Tilt radar directors 12. Kite Screech radar 13. Band Stand radar 14. SS-N-22 launchers (M.J. Dodgson)

The OTLICHNYY with the Top Steer radar found in the first four units of this class. With four 130-mm guns in twin mounts, these ships have the heaviest gun battery of any contemporary Soviet warship. (Royal Navy)

The stern aspect of the OTLICHNYY shows the after 130-mm gun mount and SA-N-7 missile launcher and the amidships helicopter deck and expanding hangar. The main deck mine rails roll over the stern. (Royal Navy)

Details of the destroyer OTLICHNYY. The superstructure is inundated with radomes and antennas. There are 30-mm Gatling guns forward of the bridge and amidships, controlled by the Bass Tilt radome directors. The new CADS-1 gun/missile system has radars fitted to the weapons mount. (1989, U.S. Navy)

The OSMORITEL'NYY ("Circumspect") with a missile on her SA-N-7 launcher and the combination Top Steer/Top Plate radar. An Electronic Intelligence (ELINT) collection van is parked on the flight deck. (West German Navy)

The OTLICHNYY ("Perfect") gained considerable attention in July 1989 when she visited Norfolk, Virginia. This photo, taken at about that time, clearly shows the position of the SS-N-22 missile tubes. Even though the arrangement is similar to the UDALOY class SS-N-14 missiles, the configuration is different. The torpedo tubes are on the main deck, just forward of the funnel.

1 GUIDED MISSILE TRIALS DESTROYER: CONVERTED KASHIN CLASS

Name	Completed	Converted
PROVORNYY	1965	1981

Builders:	61 Kommuna Shipyard, Nikolayev (north)
Displacement:	3,750 tons standard
	4,750 tons full load
Length:	472 ft 4 in (144.0 m) overall
Beam:	51 ft 2 in (15.8 m)
Draft:	15 ft 9 in (4.8 m)
Propulsion:	4 gas turbines; 96,000 shp; 2 shafts
Speed:	36 knots
Range:	1,000 n.miles at 35 knots
	4,500 n.miles at 18 knots
Complement:	approx. 300
Helicopters:	landing area aft
Missiles:	1 single SA-N-7 anti-air launcher [20] (see notes)
Guns:	4 76.2-mm/59-cal AA (2 twin)
ASW weapons:	2 RBU-6000 rocket launchers
	2 RBU-1000 rocket launchers
	torpedoes
Torpedoes:	5 21-inch (533-mm) torpedo tubes (1 quin)
Mines:	rails provided

Radars:	1 Don-2 (navigation)
	2 Don-Kay (navigation)
	8 Front Dome (fire control)
	1 Head Net-C (3-D air search)
	2 Owl Screech (fire control)
	1 Top Steer (air search)
Sonars:	Bull Nose medium-frequency hull mounted
EW systems:	deleted except for chaff launchers

The PROVORNYY was converted from a standard Kashin-class destroyer to a trials ship for the SA-N-7 missile system, its associated radars and fire control system. For additional details see the listing for the Kashin class.

Conversion: Converted in the 1970s, probably at the 61 Kommuna Shipyard in Nikolayev. The ship went to sea in her new configuration in late 1981. The two SA-N-1 missile systems were removed. An SA-N-7 launcher was installed aft; there are spaces for two additional SA-N-7 launchers forward, but they have not been installed, although by 1990 there were reports of an additional launcher being installed.

Like the cruiser AZOV, the trials ship for the SA-N-6/Top Dome system, the PROVORNYY retains major combat capabilities. However, note that the ship's electronic warfare capability has been reduced.

The weapons test ship PROVORNYY ("Ferocious"), converted from a Kashin-class destroyer for trials of the SA-N-7 missile and new fire control systems. There are empty SA-N-7 positions forward of the bridge and a single canvas-covered launcher aft. The Top Steer radar found in the SOVREMENNYY class is fitted to the after pyramid mast. (1982)

The PROVORNYY with canvas over the after SA-N-7 launcher. Several of the ship's eight Front Dome fire control radars can be seen in this view, which clearly shows the pyramid mast installed to carry the Top Steer radar.

4 GUIDED MISSILE DESTROYERS: MODIFIED KASHIN CLASS

Name	Builder	Completed		Converted	
SLAVNYY	Zhdanov	June	1966	Sep	1975
STROYNYY	61 Kommuna		1966		1980
SMYSHLENNYY	61 Kommuna		1968		1974
SDERZHANOYY	61 Kommuna		1973	(see notes)	

Builders:	61 Kommuna Shipyard, Nikolayev (north)
	Zhdanov Shipyard, Leningrad
Displacement:	3,950 tons standard
	4,950 tons full load
Length:	478 ft 11 in (146.0 m) overall
Beam:	51 ft 2 in (15.8 m)
Draft:	19 ft 8 in (6.0 m)
Propulsion:	4 gas turbines; 96,000 shp; 2 shafts
Speed:	36 knots
Range:	1,000 n.miles at 35 knots
	4,500 n.miles at 18 knots
Complement:	approx. 280
Helicopters:	landing area aft
Missiles:	2 twin SA-N-1 anti-air launchers [36]
	4 SS-N-2c Styx anti-ship tubes (4 single)
Guns:	4 76.2-mm/59-cal AA (2 twin)
	4 30-mm/65-cal close-in (4 multi-barrel)
ASW weapons:	2 RBU-6000 rocket launchers
	torpedoes
Torpedoes:	5 21-inch (533-mm) torpedo tubes (1 quin)

Mines:	rails removed
Radars:	2 Bass Tilt (fire control)
	1 Big Net (3-D air search)
	2 Don-Kay (navigation)
	1 Head Net-C (3-D air search)
	2 Owl Screech (fire control)
	2 Peel Group (fire control)
Sonars:	Bull Horn medium-frequency hull mounted
	Mare Tail medium-frequency variable depth
EW systems:	2 Bell Shroud
	2 Bell Squat

These are Kashin-class destroyers modified with improved electronics and four rear-firing improved Styx missiles. In addition to the SS-N-2c missiles, the SA-N-1 system has an anti-ship capability. See Kashin-class listing for additional details.

Class: Originally six ships were converted to this configuration. The SMEL'YY was transferred to Poland in December 1987 and the OGNEVOY was decommissioned in the late 1980s, probably for scrapping.

Classification: Soviet BPK type.

Conversion: The six conversions were completed between 1973 and 1980; the SDERZHANOYY was probably completed to this configuration. The hull was lengthened by approximately 6 ft 7 in (2 m) and a stern VDS was installed under the raised helicopter deck. Improved hull-mounted sonar was also fitted. Rapid-fire Gatling guns replaced the two RBU-1000 rocket launchers. The after 76.2-mm gun mount has a severely restricted field of fire.

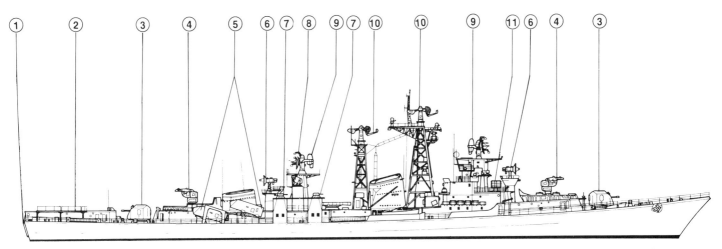

Modified Kashin class: 1. VDS housing 2. helicopter platform 3. twin 76.2-mm AA guns 4. SA-N-1 launchers 5. SS-N-2c launchers 6. Owl Screech radars 7. 30-mm Gatling guns 8. Bass Tilt radar director 9. Peel Group radars 10. Head Net-C radars (since updated) 11. RBU-6000 ASW rocket launchers (L. Gassier)

The Kashin-class destroyers have a balanced weapon and sensor arrangement. Most of the modified Kashins have a Head Net-C radar atop the first lattice mast and a Big Net radar atop the second; one or more retain two Head Net-A radars. (Royal Navy)

The SLAVNYY ("Glorious") under way. The aft-firing SS-N-2c Styx missile tubes are visible outboard of the after pair of funnels and SA-N-1 missile launcher. The after 76.2-mm twin gun mount has a restricted field of fire because of the helicopter platform, above and forward of the variable depth sonar. (Royal Navy)

12 GUIDED MISSILE DESTROYERS: KASHIN CLASS

Name	Builder	Completed
Komsomolets Ukrainyy	61 Kommuna	Feb 1962
Soobrazitel'nyy	61 Kommuna	Sep 1963
Obraztsovyy	Zhdanov	July 1965
Odarennyy	Zhdanov	Sep 1965
Steregushchiy	Zhdanov	Oct 1966
Krasnyy Kavkaz	61 Kommuna	1967
Reshitelnyy	61 Kommuna	Jan 1968
Strogiy	61 Kommuna	Aug 1968
Smetlivvy	61 Kommuna	Sep 1969
Krasnyy Krym	61 Kommuna	Sep 1970
Sposobnyy	61 Kommuna	Aug 1971
Skoryy	61 Kommuna	Aug 1972

Builders:	61 Kommuna Shipyard, Nikolayev (north)
	Zhdanov Shipyard, Leningrad
Displacement:	3,750 tons standard
	4,750 tons full load
Length:	472 ft 4 in (144.0 m) overall
Beam:	51 ft 2 in (15.8 m)
Draft:	19 ft 8 in (6.0 m)
Propulsion:	4 gas turbines; 96,000 shp; 2 shafts
Speed:	38 knots
Range:	1,000 n.miles at 35 knots
	4,500 n.miles at 18 knots
Complement:	approx. 280
Helicopters:	landing area aft
Missiles:	2 twin SA-N-1 anti-air launcher [36]
Guns:	4 76.2-mm/59-cal AA (2 twin)
ASW weapons:	2 RBU-6000 rocket launchers
	2 RBU-1000 rocket launchers
	torpedoes
Torpedoes:	5 21-inch (533-mm) torpedo tubes (1 quin)
Mines:	rails fitted
Radars:	2 or 3 Don-2 or 2 Don-Kay or 2 Palm Frond (navigation)
	1 Head Net-C and 1 Big Net, or 2 Big Net (3-D air search); see notes
	2 Owl Screech (fire control)
	2 Peel Group (fire control)
Sonars:	Bull Nose medium-frequency hull mounted
EW systems:	2 Watch Dog

The Kashins were the world's first major warships with all-gas turbine propulsion. They are multi-purpose destroyers. Of these ships, 1 is in the Northern Fleet, 1 in the Baltic, 8 in the Black Sea, and 2 in the Pacific.

Class: Twenty ships were built to this class for the Soviet Navy, and subsequently six modified ships (Kashin II) were built for the Indian Navy (completed from 1980 on). The Indian ships have four *forward-firing* SS-N-2c missile canisters; their after deck has a raised helicopter platform with the after 76.2-mm gun mount deleted in favor of a recessed hangar; 30-mm Gatling guns are fitted and they have Head Net-C and Big Net radars.

Six Soviet ships were extensively modified and are listed separately. The Provornyy was converted to a test ship for the SA-N-7 missile system.

Classification: Originally ordered as EM (destroyer) type, but completed as BRK (large missile ship) by the Soviets; changed to Soviet BPK in the early 1960s.

Design: These are large, graceful flush-deck destroyers, with a low superstructure topped by four large funnels for gas turbine exhaust, two radar-topped lattice masts, and four smaller radar towers. There is a helicopter landing area aft (with enclosed control station) but no hangar.

Electronics: The early ships were built with two Head Net-A radars, an outdated configuration retained in several units. The Head Net-C and Big Net radars were fitted in later units. The Odarennyy and Soobrazitel'nny have two Head Net-C radars; see photos.

Engineering: These ships became operational more than a decade before the first U.S. gas-turbine warships of the Spruance (DD 963) class.

Names: Most Kashin-class ships have adjective names. The exceptions are Komsomolets Ukrainyy (Ukrainian Young Communist), Krasnyy Kavkaz (Red Caucasus), and Krasnyy Krym (Red Crimea).

Operational: The Obraztsovyy made a port visit to Portsmouth, England, in May 1976, the first Soviet warship to visit Great Britain in two decades. (The previous visit had been by the Sverdlov-class cruiser Ordzhonikidze, carrying Soviet leaders Nikolai Bulganin and Nikita Khrushchev to Britain in April 1956.)

The Otvazhnyy was lost to an internal fire and explosion in the Black Sea on 31 August 1974. According to press reports, at least 200 crewmen were killed.

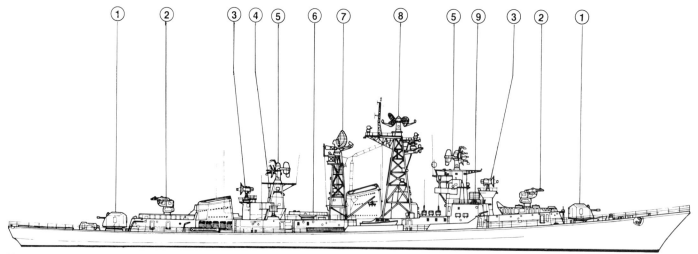

Kashin class: 1. twin 76.2-mm AA guns 2. SA-N-1 launchers 3. Owl Screech radars 4. Peel Group radars 5. RBU-1000 ASW rocket launchers 6. 533-mm torpedo tubes 7. Big Net radar 8. Head Net-C radar 9. RBU-6000 ASW rocket launchers (L. Gassier)

The KOMSOMOLETS UKRAINYY, the first of the Kashin-class destroyers. These were the world's first major warships with all gas-turbine propulsion. The KOMSOMOLETS UKRAINYY's after Owl Screech fire control radar and twin 76.2-mm gun mount are trained to starboard. Mine rails run across the helicopter landing area and over the stern. (1987, Royal Air Force)

The RESHITELNYY ("Decisive"), barely under way, has her forward Owl Screech radar and 76.2-mm gun mount trained to starboard. This ship has Head Net-C and Big Net radars; a few ships retain two Head Net-A radars. The latter ships will be retired before being refitted. (Royal Navy)

GUIDED MISSILE DESTROYERS: KANIN CLASS

The eight Kanin-class AAW/ASW destroyers converted from surface-to-surface missile ships were stricken in the late 1980s. The BOYKIY ran aground off Norway in November 1988 while being towed to Spain for scrapping.

These ships are converted Krupnyy-class missile destroyers (fitted with two SS-N-1 launchers), which in turn are modified Kotlin-class destroyers. In the Kanin configuration the forward SS-N-1 launcher was replaced by a second quad 57-mm mount and an RBU-6000; the after SS-N-1 launcher and quad 57-mm gun mount were deleted and the after section of the ship reconfigured for the SA-N-1 system and a larger helicopter deck.

The destroyers were completed between 1959 and 1961 as the Krupnyy class, and the conversions to the Kanin class were completed between 1968 and 1977.

See 4th edition, pages 208–209 for additional data.

(In May 1975 the now-stricken BOIKIY and ZHGUCHY visited the port of Boston, Massachusetts, to celebrate the 30th anniversary of the end of World War II. They were the first Soviet warships to visit the United States since the end of the war.)

GUIDED MISSILE DESTROYERS: MODIFIED KILDIN CLASS

The three modified Kildin-class ships were stricken in the late 1980s. They had their single SS-N-1 (aft) launcher replaced by twin 76.2-mm gun mounts and four SS-N-2c Styx anti-ship missiles.

Four ships were converted during construction to the Kildin configuration from Kotlin-class destroyers to the world's first missile destroyers; subsequently, three ships were modified with the installation of 76.2-mm guns and SS-N-2c missiles aft. The fourth Kildin, the NEUDERZHIMYY, was not converted.

See 4th edition, pages 210–211 for names and characteristics.

GUIDED MISSILE DESTROYERS: SAM KOTLIN CLASS

The eight Kotlin-class destroyers that had been reconfigured with an SA-N-1 missile launcher were stricken in the late 1980s; a ninth ship, the SPRAVEDLIVYY, had been transferred to Poland in 1970.

These ships were converted from standard Kotlin-class destroyers to this SAM configuration in 1969–1972. See 4th edition, pages 212–213 for names and characteristics.

DESTROYERS: KOTLIN CLASS

The Soviet Navy is scrapping the surviving all-gun destroyers of the Kotlin class. These were the world's last destroyers to be built to classic World War II–destroyer lines, mounting heavy DP and light AA gun batteries, with a large torpedo battery, high speed, and minimal ASW weapons and sensors.

Twenty-seven Kotlin-class ships of a planned 36 were completed between 1954 and 1961; nine of these ships were subsequently converted to the SAM Kotlin (SA-N-1) configuration. Four other of the Kotlin hulls were completed as Kildin (SS-N-1) missile destroyers, and eight new ships of this basic design were built as Krupnyy (SS-N-1) missile destroyers; the latter ships were later converted again, to the Kanin configuration (SA-N-1 system).

See 4th edition, pages 213–215.

DESTROYERS: "SKORYY" CLASS

The last of the all-gun destroyers of the SKORYY class are being scrapped. The surviving units had been laid up in reserve for the last few years. These were the first Soviet destroyers to be constructed after World War II, with 72 units completed from 1950 to 1953. After Soviet service, 6 units were transferred to Egypt, 7 to Indonesia, and 2 to Poland.

(The name of the lead ship—Russian for "speedy"—is now carried by a Kashin-class destroyer.)

See 4th edition, pages 216–217 for names and characteristics.

DESTROYER: TALLINN CLASS

The single destroyer of the Tallinn class, the NASTOYCHIVYY, later renamed NEUSTRASHIMY, was completed in 1955 and discarded in the 1970s. She was modeled after the Soviet destroyer TASHKENT, built in Italy before World War II. Additional ships of this class were apparently planned but not built.

See 4th edition, page 217 for characteristics.

The Kanin-class destroyer BOYKIY in Norwegian waters after breaking tow and running aground while en route to a breakers' yard in Spain. During the past few years the Soviets have scrapped scores of outdated surface warships and submarines. (1988)

CHAPTER 16

Frigates

A new frigate-type ship has been completed at the Yantar/Kaliningrad shipyard; however, for the remainder of this decade the Krivaks will be the primary ship of this type in the Soviet Navy. This is a Krivak II with two 100-mm guns aft. But the ship's main armament consists of ASW weapons.

The Soviet Navy employs frigate-type ships for conventional frigate roles—mainly anti-submarine warfare—as well as for coastal defense and patrol duties. The term frigate is used here in the contemporary Western context.

The ships in this chapter have the Soviet classification patrol ship (SKR—*Storozhevoy Korabl'*) or small ASW ship (MPK—*Malyy Protivolodochnyy Korabl'*); they are roughly equivalent in size and capability to Western small ASW frigates and corvettes; Western intelligence generally lists all but the Krivak, Koni, and Riga types as light frigates (i.e., FFL vice FF/FFG for the larger ships).

The employment of the Soviet SKR and MPK ship types, however, is quite different than those of Western frigates and corvettes, which are primarily escort ships. Rather, the Soviet patrol or ASW ships are intended to patrol or to guard a specific area. They can be employed as escort ships but lack the endurance and some capabilities (e.g., helicopters) to undertake escort operations in the Western sense of the role.

Four Riga-class frigates are the largest Soviet combatants assigned to the Caspian Sea Flotilla.

A large number of additional frigate-type ships are operated by the KGB Maritime Border Troops (see chapter 26).

A new frigate class is under construction at the Yantar/Kaliningrad yard (No. 820). In view of the large number of outdated Rigas still in service and the age of the Petya and Mirka classes, the continued construction of the Grisha class as well as a new frigate design can be expected.

The Soviet Navy's PARCHIM II–class ships are listed in this chapter because they are classified FFL by NATO intelligence. However, with a full load displacement of less than 1,000 tons they should be more properly considered corvettes.

When this edition went to press it appeared that the new German Navy would take over the PARCHIM I frigates/corvettes previously operated by the East German Navy (see chapter 34).

1+ ANTI-SUBMARINE FRIGATES: "NEUSTRASHIMYY" CLASS

Name	Builder	Completed
NEUSTRASHIMYY	Yantar Shipyard, Kaliningrad	1991
. . . . . .	Yantar Shipyard, Kaliningrad	

Displacement:	4,000+ tons full load
Length:	426 ft 5 in (130.0 m) overall
Beam:	50 ft 10 in (15.5 m)
Draft:	
Propulsion:	probably COGOG: 4 gas turbines; 2 shafts
Speed:	approx. 30 knots
Range:	
Complement:	
Helicopters:	1 Ka-27 Helix-A
Missiles:	4 SA-N-9 anti-air vertical launchers [32]
	2 combined 30-mm gun/SA-N-11 anti-air launchers (CADS)
Guns:	1 100-mm/70-cal DP
ASW weapons:	1 RBU-6000 rocket launcher
Torpedoes:	4 21-inch (533-mm) torpedo tubes (4 single)
Mines:	rails fitted
Radars:	1 Cross Sword (fire control)
	1 Kite Screech (fire control)
	2 Palm Frond (navigation)
	1 Top Plate (3-D air search)
Sonars:	medium-frequency hull mounted
	medium-frequency variable depth
EW systems:	several . . . . . .

This is a new anti-submarine frigate class. The lead ship was laid down in 1987 and launched in 1989; see Addenda for December 1990 trials photo.

The design—initially designated BAL-COM-8 by NATO—differs from previous Soviet frigates (except for the Krivak III) in having a helicopter capability. The ships are oriented primarily toward anti-submarine warfare with a self-defense capability against aircraft and anti-ship missiles.

Design: The NEUSTRASHIMYY has been designed with a reduced radar and infrared signatures, including unusually low gas turbine exhaust stacks.

Torpedoes: The fixed torpedo tubes are angled out from the after deckhouse, flanking the large helicopter hangar.

Names: The lead ship has a destroyer-type adjective name, meaning "redoubtable."

The forward portion of the NEUSTRASHIMYY showing the 100-mm gun, RBU-600, Kite Screech and Cross Swords radars, and forward turbine exhausts (level with bridge). Note square windows. (1990, West German Navy)

32 ANTI-SUBMARINE FRIGATES: KRIVAK I/II CLASSES

Name	Builder	Completed
(21 Krivak I)		
BDITEL'NYY	Kaliningrad	1970
BODRYY	Kaliningrad	1971
DOSTOYNYY	Kerch'	1971
SVIREPYY	Kaliningrad	1971
DOBLESTNYY	Kerch'	1972
SIL'NYY	Kaliningrad	1972
STOROZHEVOY	Kaliningrad	1972
RAZUMNYY	Kaliningrad	1973
RAZYASHCHIY	Kaliningrad	1973
DEYATEL'NYY	Kerch'	1975
DRUZHNYY	Zhdanov	1975
RETIVYY	Kaliningrad	1975
ZHARKYY	Kaliningrad	1975
LENINGRADSKIY KOMSOMOLETS	Zhdanov	1976
LETUCHIY	Zhdanov	1977
BEZZAVETNYY	Kerch'	1978
PYLKIY	Zhdanov	1979
ZADORNYY	Zhdanov	1979
BEZUKORIZNENNYY	Kerch'	1980
LADNYY	Kerch'	1980
PORYVISTYY	Kerch'	1982
(11 Krivak II)		
REZVYY	Kaliningrad	1975
REZKIY	Kaliningrad	1976
GROZYASHCHIY	Kaliningrad	1977
RAZITEL'NYY	Kaliningrad	1977
BESSMENNYY	Kaliningrad	1978
NEUKROTIMYY	Kaliningrad	1978
GORDELIVYY	Kaliningrad	1979
GROMKIY	Kaliningrad	1979
R'YANYY	Kaliningrad	1980
REVNOSTNYY	Kaliningrad	1980
PYTLIVYY	Kaliningrad	1982

Builders:	Kerch' = Kamysh-Burun Shipyard, Kerch'
	Kaliningrad = Yantar Shipyard, Kaliningrad
	Zhdanov = Zhdanov Shipyard, Leningrad
Displacement:	Krivak I 3,075 tons standard
	3,575 tons full load
	Krivak II 3,170 tons standard
	3,670 tons full load
Length:	383 ft 5 in (116.9 m) waterline
	405 ft 1 in (123.5 m) overall
Beam:	46 ft 3 in (14.1 m)
Draft:	Krivak I 14 ft 9 in (4.5 m)
	Krivak II 15 ft 1 in (4.6 m)
Propulsion:	COGOG: 2 gas turbines; 24,200 shp + 2 boost gas
	turbines; 24,400 shp = 48,600 shp; 2 shafts
Speed:	30.5 knots
Range:	700 n.miles at 30 knots
	3,900 n.miles at 20 knots
Complement:	approx. 200
Helicopters:	no facilities
Missiles:	2 twin SA-N-4 anti-air launchers [40]
Guns:	Krivak I 4 76.2-mm/59-cal AA (2 twin)
	Krivak II 2 100-mm/70-cal DP (2 single)
ASW weapons:	4 SS-N-14 (1 quad)
	2 RBU-6000 rocket launchers
	torpedoes
Torpedoes:	8 21-inch (533-mm) torpedo tubes (2 quad)
Mines:	rails for 20 mines

Radars:	Krivak I	Krivak II
	1 Don-2 or Spin Trough (navigation)	1 Don-Kay or Palm Frond (navigation)
	2 Eye Bowl (fire control)	2 Eye Bowl
	1 Head Net-C (3-D air search)	1 Head Net-C
	1 Kite Screech (fire control)	1 Owl Screech (fire control)
	2 Pop Group (fire control)	2 Pop Group (fire control)
Sonars:	Bull Nose medium-frequency bow mounted	
	Mare Tail medium-frequency variable depth	
EW systems:	2 Bell Shroud	
	2 Bell Squat	

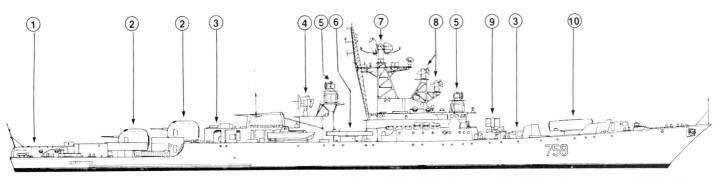

Krivak II: 1. VDS housing 2. 100-mm DP guns 3. SA-N-4 launchers (retracted) 4. Kite Screech radar 5. Pop Group radars 6. 533-mm torpedo tubes 7. Head Net-C radar 8. Eye Bowl radars 9. RBU-6000 ASW rocket launchers 10. SS-N-14 ASW missile launchers (M.J. Dodgson)

These low-lying, graceful ASW ships have a relatively short range and lack the helicopter capability of their Western contemporaries. The Krivak I and II classes are similar, the principal difference being their gun caliber. The later Krivak III has less ASW capability but embarks a utility helicopter.

Three shipyards participated in this program; the Krivak III is being built at the Kamish-Burun yard.

As of early 1990 there were 7 Krivaks assigned to the Northern Fleet, 8 to the Baltic Fleet, 6 to the Black Sea Fleet, and 11 to the Pacific Fleet.

Class: Construction continues of a modified Krivak for the KGB Maritime Border Troops; this class is designated Krivak III (see chapter 26).

The Krivaks represent the largest class of surface combatants (frigate and larger) built in the Soviet Union since the Stalin ship programs of the 1950s.

Classification: Soviet SKR, or patrol ship, type. Originally the Soviet designation was BPK, or large ASW ship; the classification changed to SKR in 1977–1978, probably a reflection of the ship's limited range.

Western intelligence originally classified these ships as destroyers, in part based on the estimate that the large missile launchers were for an SS-N-10 anti-ship weapon. In 1978 the Krivak was reclassified as a frigate in the West.

Design: These are among the most heavily armed frigates afloat. Their SA-N-4 systems, large torpedo battery, and gun battery make them relatively versatile ships; however, by Western standards the lack of helicopter facilities limits their ASW effectiveness.

The Krivak II has larger caliber guns and the improved Owl Screech gun radar/FCS. Also, the sonar housing is larger in the later ships (and the ZHARKYY of the Krivak I class).

Guns: These ships have no close-in defensive guns like those found in other Soviet frigates of recent construction.

Missiles: The quad SS-N-14 launcher rotates and elevates for firing. No reloads are provided.

Names: These ships have "adjective" or "trait" names; the name of the lead ship, BDITEL'NYY, means "vigilant."

A Krivak I with both of her SA-N-4 missile launchers in the raised position. The circular devices between the SA-N-4 launcher and the large SS-N-14 ASW missile launcher are for loading the ASW missiles. The aftermost 76.2-mm gun mount is elevated to clear the variable depth sonar housing.

The Krivak II-class frigate GROMKIY ("Thunderous") with her 100-mm guns at maximum elevation. Other than guns and radars, there is virtually no difference between the two naval variants of this large class of ASW ships.

The BEZUKORIZNENNYY ("Irreproachable") shows the low stern of the Krivak design to facilitate the handling of torpedo decoy devices as well as mines and the variable depth sonar.

1 ANTI-SUBMARINE FRIGATE: KONI CLASS

Name	Completed
DEL'FIN	1978

Builders:	Zelenodolsk
Displacement:	1,440 tons standard
	1,600 tons full load
Length:	316 ft 2 in (96.4 m) overall
Beam:	41 ft 2 in (12.55 m)
Draft:	16 ft 1 in (4.9 m)
Propulsion:	CODAG: 2 diesel engines; 15,000 bhp + 1 gas turbine;
	19,000 shp = 30,000 hp; 3 shafts
Speed:	27 knots
Range:	1,800 n.miles at 14 knots
Complement:	approx. 110
Helicopters:	no facilities
Missiles:	1 twin SA-N-4 anti-air launcher [20]
Guns:	4 76.2-mm/59-cal AA (2 twin)
	4 30-mm/65-cal close-in (2 twin)
ASW weapons:	2 RBU-6000 rocket launchers
	2 depth charge racks
Torpedoes:	none
Mines:	rails for 20 mines
Radars:	1 Don-2 (navigation)
	1 Drum Tilt (fire control)
	1 Hawk Screech (fire control)
	1 Pop Group (fire control)
	1 Strut Curve (air search)
Sonars:	medium-frequency hull mounted
EW systems:	2 Watch Dog

The Koni is a coastal ASW ship that is being constructed specifically for foreign transfer. Only the lead ship has been retained in Soviet service for demonstration and crew training. Construction continues for other navies.

The ASW sensors and weapons are both short range and intended for shallow depths (evident from a lack of variable-depth sonar and the presence of torpedo tubes that are unsuitable for shallow-water attacks); the ship is limited both in speed and range.

Class: Ships of this class have been transferred to Algeria (3), Cuba (2), East Germany (3), Libya (2), and Yugoslavia (2). The Koni is the largest surface warship ever to fly the Algerian and Cuban colors. The Libyan and Yugoslav ships are additionally armed with four SS-N-2c Styx missiles (arrangement differs); the Libyan ships are fitted with 15.75-inch (400-mm) torpedo tubes.

Classification: Soviet SKR type.

Design: The design follows Soviet small combatant lines, with the Koni having similar lines to the smaller Grisha. (The Grisha has only a two-step bridge structure and no gun mount forward.) The ship has a "split" superstructure; the space between possibly was intended for tubes in some roles (as mounted in the Grisha classes). There are two depth-charge racks aft as well as provisions for minelaying and minesweeping. A hull sonar dome is fitted as are fin stabilizers. The deckhouse arrangements differ in later ships.

Engineering: Combination Diesel And Gas turbine (CODAG) propulsion with a total horsepower output of 30,000 to the three shafts, with the diesel connected to the centerline shaft.

Names: The unit retained by the Soviet Navy is the DEL'FIN, not TIMOFEY UL'YANTSEV, as previously reported.

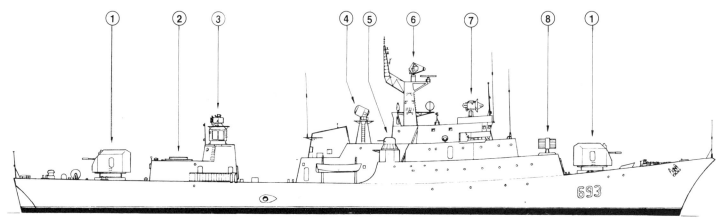

Koni class: 1. twin 76.2-mm AA guns   2. SA-N-4 launcher (retracted)   3. Pop Group radar   4. Drum Tilt radar director   5. twin 30-mm AA guns   6. Strut Curve radar   7. Hawk Screech radar   8. RBU-6000 ASW rocket launchers (M.J. Dodgson)

This East German Koni-class frigate shows the relative simplicity of the design. Some navies have "customized" their Konis by adding torpedo tubes and SS-N-2c Styx missile launchers. A single Koni is retained by the Soviet Navy. (1982, U.S. Navy)

12 LIGHT ANTI-SUBMARINE FRIGATES: "PARCHIM II" CLASS

Completed:	1986–1989
Builders:	Peenewerft, Wolgast (East Germany)
Displacement:	800 tons standard
	950 tons full load
Length:	237 ft 10 in (72.5 m) overall
Beam:	30 ft 10 in (9.4 m)
Draft:	13 ft 5½ in (4.1 m)
Propulsion:	3 diesel engines (M504); 14,250 bhp; 3 shafts
Speed:	28 knots
Range:	4,000 n.miles at 11 knots
Complement:	approx. 60
Helicopters:	no facilities
Missiles:	8 SA-N-5 or SA-N-8 anti-air launchers (2 quad)
Guns:	1 76.2-mm/59-cal AA
	1 30-mm/65-cal close-in (multi-barrel)
ASW weapons:	2 RBU-6000 rocket launchers
	2 depth charge racks [12]
Torpedoes:	4 21-inch (533-mm) (2 twin)
Mines:	rails fitted
Radars:	1 Bass Tilt (fire control)
	1 Positive-E (air/surface search)
	1 Spin Trough (navigation)
Sonars:	high-frequency hull mounted
	high-frequency dipping
EW systems:	2 Watch Dog

These light ASW frigates are built in East Germany, the first combatants to be built for the Soviet Navy in an Eastern Bloc nation. They are similar to the East German PARCHIM I class but with upgraded weapons and sensors. However, they are still inferior in capability to the contemporary units of the improved Grisha series being built in Soviet yards.

These ships were launched between 1985 and 1989.

Design: These ships bear some resemblance to the Soviet Grisha class in arrangement (the Soviet ships have combined gas turbine and diesel propulsion). The single Gatling gun is forward of the RBUs, on the 01 level; the Grishas have an SA-N-4 missile launcher forward (on the forecastle). The PARCHIM IIs can be easily distinguished from the Grishas by the half-spherical radome atop a squat lattice mast and the pyramid tower supporting the Bass Tilt gun director/radar; they can be distinguished from the PARCHIM I design by the after gun mount, the East German ships having a twin 57-mm mount aft.

The dipping sonar is lowered through a door on the starboard side of the superstructure.

Designation: These ships were originally given the NATO designation BAL-COM-4 when they were initially being constructed for East Germany.

The first PARCHIM II-class light frigate or corvette under way in the Baltic. These ships can be easily distinguished from the East German PARCHIMS by their large, hemispheric radome forward and the 76.2-mm gun mount aft (in place of the East German twin 57-mm mount); see chapter 34. (Royal Netherlands Navy)

The second PARCHIM II, before being fitted with the main radome. Note the 30-mm Gatling gun forward; the twin torpedo tubes amidships; and mine rails aft. (West German Navy)

13+ LIGHT ANTI-SUBMARINE FRIGATES: GRISHA V CLASS

Name	Completed
KIEVSKIY KOMSOMOLETS	
KOMSOMOLETS MOLDAVIY	1985—
. . . . . . (11+ units)	

Builders:	Kamysh Burun, Kerch
	Khabarovsk
	Leninskaya Kuznitsa, Kiev
	Zelenodolsk
Displacement:	910 tons standard
	1,200 tons full load
Length:	219 ft 5 in (66.9 m) waterline
	234 ft 10 in (71.6 m) overall
Beam:	32 ft 2 in (9.8 m)
Draft:	12 ft 1 in (3.7 m)
Propulsion:	CODAG: 2 twin diesels (M504); 20,000 bhp + 1 gas turbine;
	19,000 shp = 39,000 hp; 3 shafts
Speed:	31 knots
Range:	450 n.miles at 30 knots
	4,000 n.miles at 18 knots
Complement:	approx. 60
Helicopters:	no facilities
Missiles:	1 twin SA-N-4 anti-air launcher [20]
	2 SA-N-5 or SA-N-8 anti-air launchers (hand held)
Guns:	1 76.2-mm/59-cal DP
ASW weapons:	1 RBU-6000 rocket launcher
	torpedoes
	12 depth charges (or mines)
Torpedoes:	4 21-inch (533-mm) torpedo tubes (2 twin)
Mines:	rails provided
Radars:	1 Bass Tilt (fire control)
	1 Don-2 (navigation)
	1 Strut Pair (air search) or modified Top Plate (air search)
	1 Pop Group (fire control)
Sonars:	medium-frequency hull mounted
	high/medium-frequency dipping
EW systems:	2 Watch Dog

This is the latest and the current production version of the Grisha light ASW frigate. This design provides for a larger gun and improved air search radar at the cost of one ASW rocket launcher deleted; the Gatling gun of the Grisha III has also been beached.

Additional ships of this class are operated by the KGB.

Classification: These are Soviet MPK type. Western intelligence designates the Grishas and other Soviet light frigates as well as other small combatants with personal nicknames, with *Grisha* translating to "Greg."

Design: The Grishas have a heavy ASW armament coupled with a heavy self-defense armament. Racks for 12 depth charges can be fitted to the after end of the mine rails.

These ships have a layout similar to the larger Koni class but with only two "steps" forward on the superstructure. The Grishas also have a solid mast structure similar to the Koni, in contrast to the lattice masts of the earlier Mirkas and Petyas.

The dipping sonar is lowered through the hull from a position aft of the superstructure, between the centerline and starboard propeller shafts.

Missiles: There are positions for shoulder-fired SAM launchers at the break of the 01 level superstructure, just forward of the funnel.

Operational: The Grisha's variable depth sonar cannot be used while the ship is under way. Thus, Grishas normally perform ASW searches in pairs, alternating in the sprint and drift (sonar search) modes.

Torpedoes: The torpedo tubes are modified to launch wire-guided torpedoes.

This late production Grisha V has a modified Top Plate radar on her forward mast. Only a single RBU-6000 ASW rocket launcher is fitted, a second has been deleted to help compensate for the added weight of the radar and 76.2-mm gun mount. (Royal Navy)

A Grisha V fitted with the Strut Pair radar on the forward mast; these ships also have a small lattice mast amidships. The 533-mm torpedo tubes have an added section to provide for wire-guided torpedoes, enhancing the ship's ASW capability.

1 LIGHT ANTI-SUBMARINE FRIGATE: GRISHA IV

Builders:	
Displacement:	860 tons standard
	1,150 tons full load
Length:	219 ft 5 in (66.9 m) waterline
	234 ft 10 in (71.6 m) overall
Beam:	32 ft 2 in (9.8 m)
Draft:	11 ft 10 in (3.6 m)
Propulsion:	(unknown)
Speed:	31 knots
Range:	
Complement:	
Helicopters:	no facilities
Missiles:	3 SA-N-9 vertical anti-air launcher [24]
Guns:	1 30-mm/70-cal close-in (multi-barrel)
ASW weapons:	2 RBU-6000 rocket launchers
	torpedoes
	12 depth charges (or mines)
Torpedoes:	2 21-inch (533-mm) torpedo tubes (2 single)
Mines:	rails provided
Radars:	1 Bass Tilt (fire control)
	1 Cross Sword (fire control)
	1 . . . . . . (navigation)
Sonars:	Bull Nose medium-frequency hull mounted
	Elk Tail high/medium-frequency dipping
EW systems:	2 Watch Dog

The single Grisha IV is a modified Grisha III–class ship, refitted to serve as a test ship for the SA-N-9 anti-air missile system; apparently she retains a full ASW capability.

The ship is reported to also have a new propulsion system.

31 LIGHT ANTI-SUBMARINE FRIGATES: GRISHA III CLASS

Name	Completed
KOMSOMOLETS BASHKIRIY	
KOMSOMOLETS GRUZIN	
ORLOVSKIY KOMSOMOLETS	1975–1985
SMEL'YY	
27 units	

Builders:	Kamysh Burun, Kerch
	Kharbarovsk
	Leninskaya Kuznitsa, Kiev
	Zelenodolsk
Displacement:	860 tons standard
	1,150 tons full load
Length:	219 ft 5 in (66.9 m) waterline
	234 ft 10 in (71.6 m) overall
Beam:	32 ft 2 in (9.8 m)
Draft:	11 ft 10 in (3.6 m)
Propulsion:	CODAG: 2 twin diesels (M504); 20,000 bhp + 1 gas turbine; 19,000 shp = 39,000 hp; 3 shafts
Speed:	31 knots
Range:	450 n.miles at 30 knots
	4,000 n.miles at 18 knots
Complement:	approx. 60
Helicopters:	no facilities
Missiles:	1 twin SA-N-4 anti-air launcher [20]
Guns:	2 57-mm/80-cal AA (1 twin)
	1 30-mm/70-cal close-in (multi-barrel)
ASW weapons:	2 RBU-6000 rocket launchers
	torpedoes
	12 depth charges (or mines)
Torpedoes:	4 21-inch (533-mm) torpedo tubes (2 twin)
Mines:	rails provided
Radars:	1 Bass Tilt (fire control)
	1 Don-2 (navigation)
	1 Strut Curve (air search)
	1 Pop Group (fire control)
Sonars:	Bull Nose medium-frequency hull mounted
	Elk Tail high/medium-frequency dipping
EW systems:	2 Watch Dog

These are small ASW frigates. The principal differences from the Grisha I are the addition of a 30-mm Gatling gun with the associated Bass Tilt radar.

Classification: The Grisha I and III series are Soviet MPK type, having been briefly typed SPK when they first appeared.

A Grisha III in the Far East. Note that both gun mounts are aft. (1989, Japanese Maritime Self-Defense Force)

A Grisha III in the Far East with a tarpaulin spread forward of the bridge. The housing for the dipping sonar is in the after deckhouse (starboard side) and is lowered through a well between the propeller shafts. (1987, Japanese Maritime Self-Defense Force)

15 LIGHT ANTI-SUBMARINE FRIGATES: GRISHA I CLASS

Completed:	1968–1974
Builders:	Kamysh Burun, Kerch
	Khabarovsk
	Leninskaya Kuznitsa, Kiev
Displacement:	850 tons standard
	1,110 tons full load
Length:	219 ft 5 in (66.9 m) waterline
	234 ft 10 in (71.6 m) overall
Beam:	32 ft 2 in (9.8 m)
Draft:	11 ft 6 in (3.5 m)
Propulsion:	CODAG: 2 twin diesels (M503); 16,000 bhp + 1 gas turbine; 15,000 shp = 31,000 hp; 3 shafts
Speed:	30 knots
Range:	450 n.miles at 30 knots
	4,000 n.miles at 18 knots
Complement:	approx. 60
Helicopters:	no facilities
Missiles:	1 twin SA-N-4 anti-air launcher [20]
Guns:	2 57-mm/80-cal AA (1 twin)
ASW weapons:	2 RBU-6000 rocket launchers
	torpedoes
	12 depth charges (or mines)
Torpedoes:	4 21-inch (533-mm) torpedo tubes (2 twin)
Mines:	rails provided
Radars:	1 Don-2 (navigation)
	1 Muff Cob (fire control)
	1 Strut Curve (air search)
	1 Pop Group (fire control)
Sonars:	medium-frequency hull mounted
	high-frequency dipping
EW systems:	2 Watch Dog

These are small ASW frigates. The similar Grisha II serves in the KGB (see chapter 26); those units substitute a second 57-mm twin mount for the SA-N-4 system.

Classification: Soviet MPK type.

A Grisha I with a protective screen forward of the Muff Cob gunfire control radar to protect crewmen from radiation.

A Grisha I in the Barents Sea. (1982, U.S. Navy)

39 LIGHT ANTI-SUBMARINE FRIGATES: PETYA I/II/III CLASSES

Name		Completed
7 units	Petya I Class	⎫
11 units	Mod. Petya I class	⎬ 1961–1964
18 units	Petya II class	⎫
1 unit	Mod. Petya II class	⎬ 1964–1969
2 units	Petya III class	. . . . . .

Builders:	Khabarovsk (II)
	Komsomol'sk (I)
	Yantar/Kaliningrad (I/II)
Displacement:	950 tons standard
	1,150 tons full load
Length:	255 ft 10 in (78.0 m) waterline
	268 ft 4 in (81.8 m) overall
Beam:	30 ft 2 in (9.2 m)
Draft:	9 ft 2 in (2.8 m) hull
Propulsion:	CODAG: 1 diesel engine (Type 61V-3); 6,000 bhp + 2 gas turbines; 30,000 shp = 36,000 hp; 3 shafts
Speed:	30 knots
Range:	450 n.miles at 29 knots
	1,800 n.miles at 16 knots
Complement:	approx. 90
Helicopters:	no facilities
Guns:	4 76.2-mm/59-cal AA (2 twin) except reduced to 2 guns in a few modified ships
ASW weapons:	Petya I/III 4 RBU-2500 rocket launchers
	Petya II 2 RBU-6000 rocket launchers
	mod. ships 2 RBU-2500 rocket launchers
	2 depth charge racks; 1 in modified Petya I; removed from modified Petya II
	torpedoes
Torpedoes:	Petya I/mod. Petya II 5 15.75-inch (400-mm) torpedo tubes (1 quin)
	Petya II 10 15.75-inch (400-mm) torpedo tubes (2 quin)
	Petya III 3 21-inch (533-mm) torpedo tubes (1 triple)
Mines:	rails for 22 mines; removed from modified Petya I
Radars:	1 Don-2 (navigation)
	1 Hawk Screech (fire control)
	1 Slim Net (air search) or Strut Curve (air search) in Petya I; Strut Curve in Petya II/III
Sonars:	Herkules high-frequency hull mounted
	high-frequency dipping in modified Petya I
	medium-frequency variable depth in modified Petya I
EW systems:	2 Watch Dog

The Petya is a light ASW frigate that was produced in larger numbers than the contemporary Mirka class, indicating a more successful design. The Petyas have been built and modified into several different configurations; the principal difference in the several variants is the ASW weapons fit.

Class: Forty-five Petyas are believed to have been built for the Soviet Navy—18 of the Petya I type and 27 of the Petya II type. Of these, ex-Soviet Petya IIs were transferred to Ethiopia (2) and

Vietnam (3). The Petya III export versions were constructed for Ethiopia (2), India (10), Syria (2), and Vietnam (2). The Soviet Navy has retained two Petya IIIs. The Petya III ships intended for foreign transfer have larger torpedo tubes but few other differences.

Classification: Originally designated as the PLK type, these were the first Soviet ships to have the designation "anti-submarine ship." They were changed to "medium" ASW ship (SKR) in 1964. The NATO name *Petya* translates from Russian to "Peter."

Conversions: Several Petyas have been employed in experimental roles. About 1966 one was fitted with the SUW-N-1/FRAS-1 ASW rocket launcher in place of the forward 76.2-mm gun mount; from 1967 one ship tested the variable depth sonar for the Moskva-class helicopter ships; and another ship was modified by 1969 to test towed sonar arrays (a large deckhouse was installed aft).

Beginning in 1973, 11 of the Petya I type were modified with a large poop deck aft to carry variable depth sonar. The two after RBU-2500 launchers as well as mine rails were deleted, as was one depth-charge rack.

One Petya II was modified with a deckhouse aft, the purpose of which is not clear; that modification retains the mine rails.

Design: These ships have a large hull-mounted sonar, with a dome that projects almost four feet beneath the keel; the drag created by this structure reduces the ships' potential speed by approximately six knots.

Electronics: The dipping sonar is similar to that fitted in the Ka-25 Hormone-A helicopters.

Engineering: These were the first large Soviet warships to have gas-turbine propulsion. The diesel drives the centerline propeller.

Torpedoes: In the Petya II the second bank of ASW torpedo tubes was fitted on the stern in place of the two after RBU-2500s of the Petya I design.

A modified Petya I-class frigate with VDS gear deployed. Installation of the VDS housing required the removal of the mine rails. However, depth charge racks are retained (internal to the housing), with the starboard stern door visible next to the VDS opening. (1981)

Modified Petya I with a deck structure aft to house the variable depth sonar. The various Petyas can be distinguished from the Mirka classes by the Petya mast being "attached" to the bridge structure while that of the Mirka is "freestanding." (1985, JMSDF)

A Petya I in the Pacific, with crewmen gathered on the fantail near the after RBU-2500 ASW rocket launchers. Another pair of RBU-2500s is forward of the bridge. (1982, U.S. Navy)

A Petya II, with two banks of 400-mm torpedo tubes and only one pair of ASW rocket launchers (RBU-6000 series).

Modified Petya I with what is probably a variable depth sonar installation on the stern. The after 76.2-mm gun mount has been removed. The RBU-2500 ASW rocket launchers are forward of the bridge, the only ASW weapons carried in this particular ship.

A Petya refitted with three 533-mm torpedo tubes amidships. She retains the RBU-2500 ASW rocket launchers forward of the bridge and on the fantail, not having been refitted with RBU-6000s. (1979)

18 LIGHT ANTI-SUBMARINE FRIGATES: MIRKA I/II CLASSES

Name			Completed
9 units	Mirka	I	1964–1965
9 units	Mirka	II	1965–1966

Builders:	Yantar/Kaliningrad
Displacement:	950 tons standard
	1,150 tons full load
Length:	270 ft 3 in (82.4 m) overall
Beam:	30 ft 2 in (9.2 m)
Draft:	9 ft 6 in (2.9 m) hull
Propulsion:	CODAG: 2 diesel engines; 12,000 bhp + 2 gas turbines
	30,000 shp = 42,000 hp; 2 shafts
Speed:	34 knots
Range:	500 n.miles at 30 knots
	4,800 n.miles at 10 knots
Complement:	approx. 90
Helicopters:	no facilities
Guns:	4 76.2-mm/59-cal AA (2 twin)
ASW weapons:	Mirka I 4 RBU-6000 rocket launchers
	Mirka II 2 RBU-6000 rocket launchers
	Mirka I 1 depth charge rack
	torpedoes
Torpedoes:	Mirka I 5 15.75-inch (406-mm) torpedo tubes (1 quin)
	Mirka II 10 16-inch (406-mm) torpedo tubes (2 quin)
Mines:	no rails fitted
Radars:	1 or 2 Don-2 (navigation)
	1 Hawk Screech (fire control)
	1 Slim Net (air search) except Strut Curve in later Mirka II
	units
Sonars:	1 Herkules or Pegas high-frequency hull mounted
	1 high-frequency dipping in Mirka II
EW systems:	2 Watch Dog

A small number of these light ASW frigates were built simultaneous with the larger Petya program, being "sandwiched" between the Petya I and II series at the Kaliningrad yard. Nine ships are of the Mirka II configuration with a helicopter-type dipping sonar installed in a new stern structure. The ASW weapons are the principal differences in the Mirka I/II sub-types.

Some of these ships are probably in reserve.

Classification: Originally classified by the Soviet Navy as PLK; changed to SKR in 1964 (see notes under Petya class). The NATO name *Mirka* is the Russian nickname for Vladimir.

Design: These ships are generally similar to the Petya series but have a different propulsion arrangement (see Engineering below).

The two designs can be readily distinguished by the position of the mast: the Petya's mast is adjacent to the bridge structure and the Mirka's mast stands separate amidships. The Petya has a short, squat funnel amidships while the Mirka has large air intakes at the stern and exhaust ports in the stern transom. (The stern configuration necessary for the machinery arrangement prevents these ships from having mine rails.)

Electronics: The dipping sonar is similar to that in the Hormone-A helicopter.

Engineering: These ships have two shafts, each driven by a gas turbine and diesel compared to the triple-shaft Petya. In these ships the turbines were placed all the way aft, preventing the fitting of mine rails or VDS. The propellers are mounted in tunnels, with the gas turbines powering compressors that inject air into the tunnels to provide a pump-jet action.

The 4,800-n.mile range is accomplished with one diesel driving one shaft and the other shaft trailing.

Operational: All Mirkas are assigned to the Baltic and Black Sea fleets and apparently have not undertaken the long deployments that Petyas have made.

Mirka I with one bank of 400-mm torpedo tubes (between mast and after gun mount) and a second pair of RBU-6000 ASW rocket launchers aft. Watch Dog electronic warfare antennas are mounted halfway on the lattice mast. (Royal Navy)

Mirka II still in the water. The portside RBU-6000 ASW rocket launcher is in the vertical, reloading position. After firing, the rockets are automatically reloaded from magazines in the superstructure. The ship has two banks of 400-mm torpedo tubes. (Royal Navy)

28 (8) FRIGATES: RIGA CLASS

Name	Builder	Completed
10 units	various yards	1955–1956
ARKHANGEL'SKIY KOMSOMOLETS	Kaliningrad	1957
ASTRAKHAN'SKIY KOMSOMOLETS	Kaliningrad	1957
BARS	Kaliningrad	1957
BARSUK	Kaliningrad	1957
BOBR	Nikolayev (north)	1957
BUYVOL	Nikolayev (north)	1957
BYK	Nikolayev (north)	1957
GEPARD	Komsomol'sk	1957
GIENA	Kaliningrad	1958
KRASNOGARSKIY KOMSOMOLETS	Kaliningrad	1958
KUNITSA	Nikolayev (north)	1958
LEOPARD	Nikolayev (north)	1958
LEV	Nikolayev (north)	1958
LISA	Komsomol'sk	1958
LITVIY KOMSOMOLETS	Kaliningrad	1959
MEDVED	Kaliningrad	1959
PANTERA	Kaliningrad	1959
RYS	Kaliningrad	1959
ROSOMAKHA	Kaliningrad	1959
SHAKAL	Kaliningrad	1959
TIGR	Kaliningrad	1959
TUMAN	Nikolayev (north)	1959
VOLK	Nikolayev (north)	1959
VORON	Nikolayev (north)	1959
YAGUAR	Komsomol'sk	1959

Builders:	Komsomol'sk
	61 Kommuna, Nikolayev (north)
	Yantar/Kaliningrad
Displacement:	1,168 tons standard
	1,393 tons full load
Length:	288 ft 8 in (88.0 m) waterline
	300 ft 5 in (91.6 m) overall
Beam:	33 ft 6 in (10.2 m)
Draft:	14 ft 5 in (4.4 m)
Propulsion:	2 steam turbines; 20,000 shp; 2 shafts
Boilers	2

Speed:	28 knots
Range:	550 n.miles at 28 knots
	2,000 n.miles at 13 knots
Complement:	approx. 170
Helicopters:	no facilities
Guns:	3 100-mm/56-cal DP B-34 (3 single)
	4 37-mm/63-cal AA W-11-M (2 twin)
	4 25-mm/60-cal AA (2 twin) in most active ships
ASW weapons:	2 RBU-2500 rocket launchers; deleted in 1 ship (with Bell-series EW system)
	2 depth charge racks
	torpedoes
Torpedoes:	2 or 3 21-inch (533-mm) torpedo tubes (1 twin or triple)
Mines:	rails for 28 to 80 mines
Radars:	1 Don-2 or Neptune (navigation)
	1 Hawk Screech (fire control) in 1 ship
	1 Slim Net (air search)
	1 Sun Visor-B (fire control)
Sonars:	Herkules or Pegas-2M high-frequency hull mounted
EW systems:	2 Watch Dog
	2 Bell series in 1 ship

An estimated 66 Rigas were built—58 for the Soviet Navy plus 8 ships going directly to foreign navies. The lead ship of the class was completed in 1954.

Western intelligence estimated that 28 ships were in active service in early 1990; another eight units were thought to be laid up in reserve.

Class: Ships of this class have been transferred to Bulgaria (2), East Germany (5), Finland (2), and Indonesia (8). [1] Eight additional ships are believed to have been built specifically for foreign use; the other transfers are ex-Soviet ships for the class total of 66 units. A modified Riga design was constructed in China.

Classification: Soviet SKR type. Riga is a NATO code name.

Design: The Rigas are an improved and *smaller* development of the previous Kola class.

1. One of the East German ships was gutted by fire shortly after transfer and never entered operational service.

A Riga-class frigate under tow in the Northern Dvina River at Arkhangel'sk. The portside RBU-2500 ASW rocket launcher is visible adjacent to the No. 2 gun mount; there is a deck structure abaft the funnel (no torpedo tubes). (1985, Leo Van Ginderen collection)

A venerable Riga-class frigate. Few if any of these ships are expected to survive the fleet reductions of the early 1990s. The large Wasp Head gunfire control director with Sun Visor-B radar dominates bridge structure. (Royal Danish Navy)

Electronics: One ship has been modified with Bell Series EW system installed on a short mast fitted aft. Another ship has a Hawk Screech radar/director forward and the Sun Visor radar/director mounted aft.

Modernization: Most—but probably not all—surviving ships have had an ASW refit. Original ASW armament consisted of 1 MBU-600 hedgehog, 4 BMB-2 depth charge mortars, plus depth-charge racks, mines, and torpedoes. The original gun armament consisted of the 100-mm and 37-mm guns.

FRIGATES: KOLA CLASS

All earlier Kola-class frigates have been stricken. Eight ships were completed in 1951–1952, based partially on German designs of World War II. Each ship, displacing 1,500 tons full load, carried four 100-mm guns and three torpedo tubes, plus lesser guns and ASW weapons. All were stricken by the late 1970s.

The first Dergach-class surface effect corvette in the Black Sea. The ship introduces a new concept in surface combatants, a design long considered by the U.S. Navy but never pursued. (1990, Canadian Forces)

CHAPTER 17

Corvettes

This Tarantul II missile corvette is typical of the large numbers of corvettes and other small combatant craft employed by the Soviet Navy to control coastal waters. These ships and craft are configured for anti-surface and anti-submarine operations with construction of both types continuing. (Royal Navy)

The Soviet Navy operates approximately 150 corvette-type warships. These ships are employed mainly in the regional seas surrounding the Soviet Union and tend to be specialized for the anti-submarine or anti-ship role. The U.S. Navy does not operate corvette-type ships, although this type of ship is common in several European, Asian, and African navies. The U.S. Coast Guard cutters of the BEAR (WHEC 901) class are of corvette size but lack the combat capabilities (including speed) to effectively perform wartime tasks, especially in the anti-submarine role.

The PARCHIM II-class ships, classified as light frigates by NATO intelligence, should more properly be considered corvettes; they are described in chapter 16 of this edition.

Additional ships of this type are operated by the KGB Maritime Border Troops (see chapter 26).

1+? GUIDED MISSILE SURFACE EFFECT SHIPS: DERGACH CLASS

Completed:	1989–1990
Builders:	
Displacement:	approx. 760 tons full load
Length:	approx. 210 ft (64.0 m) overall
Beam:	
Draft:	
Propulsion:	CODAG: 2 or 3 gas turbines + 2 diesel engines; 2 propulsor systems (see notes)
Speed:	30+ knots
Range:	
Complement:	
Missiles:	8 SS-N-22 anti-ship (4 twin)
Guns:	1 76.2-mm/59-cal AA
	2 30-mm/65-cal close-in (2 multi-barrel)
ASW weapons:	none
Torpedoes:	none
Mines:	none
Radars:	1 Bandstand (fire control)
	1 Bass Tilt (fire control)
	1 Kivach-3 (surface search)
	1 Positive-E (air/surface search) (?)
Sonars:	none (?)
EW systems:	several systems

This is the world's first combat Surface Effect Ship (SES); the lead ship was seen in the Black Sea in 1989. This ship appears several years after the U.S. Navy had abandoned a program to develop a frigate-type SES of some 3,000 tons; the U.S. Navy does operate a 210-ton experimental SES (see *The Ships and Aircraft of the U.S. Fleet*, 14th ed., pp. 355–356, 572–574), while the Coast Guard operates three 110-ton SES in a patrol configuration for drug interdiction (see *Ships and Aircraft*, 14th ed., p. 542).

Design: The Dergach has rigid side hulls that penetrate the water with rubberized seals forward and aft to trap air as the ship rides on an ''air cushion.''

The ship has a massive superstructure ''block,'' with a large number of antenna domes. The 76.2-mm gun is forward with quad SS-N-22 missile launchers on either side of the superstructure. A 30-mm Gatling gun is mounted forward (between 76.2-mm gun and superstructure), and a second is fitted aft.

Propulsion: The ship appears to have Combined Diesel And Gas turbine (CODAG) propulsion; there are twin propulsor units at the stern, each consisting of a pod (apparently with pusher/puller propellers) that can be swung upward when the ship is not underway.

The world's first surface effect ship with a full combat systems suite is the Soviet Dergach. The corvette-size warship has a primary battery of SS-N-22 anti-ship missiles; she additionally has a 76.2-mm dual-purpose gun (forward) and 30-mm Gatling guns for close-in defense. A second unit has been reported. Note the large number of electronic antennas and domes. (1990)

38+ GUIDED MISSILE CORVETTES: TARANTUL I/II/III CLASSES

Name			Completed
2	units	Tarantul I	1979–1980
20+	units	Tarantul II	1981–1986
16+	units	Tarantul III	1987–

Builders:	Petrovskiy, Leningrad
	Srednyy Neva, Kolpino
	Ulis, Vladivostok
	Volodarskiy, Rybinsk (Tarantul I only)
Displacement:	480 tons standard
	540 tons full load
Length:	172 ft 2 in (52.5 m) waterline
	185 ft 4 in (56.5 m) overall
Beam:	34 ft 5 in (10.5 m)
Draft:	8 ft 3 in (2.5 m)
Propulsion:	Tarantul I/II
	COGOG: 2 gas turbines (NK-12M); 24,200 shp + 2 cruise gas turbines; approx. 6,000 shp = 24,200 hp; 2 shafts
	Tarantul III
	CODOG: 2 gas turbines (NK-12M); 24,200 shp + 1 diesel engine (M504); 5,000 bhp = 24,200 hp; 2 shafts

Speed:	36 knots
Range:	400 n.miles at 36 knots
	2,000 n.miles at 20 knots for Tarantul I (using diesel engines)
Complement:	approx. 40
Missiles:	Tarantul I/II 4 SS-N-2c Styx anti-ship (2 twin)
	Tarantul III 4 SS-N-22 anti-ship (2 twin)
	4 SA-N-5 or SA-N-8 anti-air launcher (1 quad) [16-20]
Guns:	1 76.2-mm/59-cal DP
	2 30-mm/65-cal close-in (2 multi-barrel)
ASW weapons:	none
Torpedoes:	none
Mines:	none
Radars:	1 Band Stand (fire control) in Tarantul II/III
	1 Bass Tilt (fire control)
	1 Kivach-3 (surface search)
	1 Plank Shave (targeting) in Tarantul I
Sonars:	none
EW systems:	4 . . . . . . (passive)

These missile corvettes are smaller and generally less capable than the previous Nanuchka design, except that the Tarantuls are several knots faster. They are more likely to be considered successors to the Osa missile craft, but because of the Tarantuls' larger size and more complex/capable weapons and sensors, it is unlikely that they can be built in sufficient numbers to constitute a significant replacement program for the Osas.

The Tarantul III continues in production for Soviet service.

Class: The two Tarantul I–class units that were retained in Soviet service were built at the Petrovskiy yard; the later units are being built at three yards. The Tarantul I units built for export were all constructed at the Volodarskiy shipyard in Rybinsk.

Tarantul I–class units have been provided to East Germany, Yemen, India, and Poland, with additional units being constructed in India. Transferred units do not have the Band Stand and certain other electronic equipment fitted in Soviet units.

Classification: Probably Soviet RK type.

Design: The Tarantul hull is similar to the Pauk-class ASW corvette but with a different propulsion system.

The Tarantul I and II/III designs differ primarily in propulsion; the Tarantul III has a more capable anti-ship missile.

Electronics: Fitted with Light Bulb missile data link for offboard targeting in the Tarantul II/III (spherical antenna atop mast).

The Tarantul III introduced the SS-N-22 anti-ship missile to Soviet corvettes. These ships have extensive electronic systems, as do other Soviet corvette classes. (West German Navy)

A Tarantul II being towed in Far Eastern waters. The Tarantul I/II classes have SS-N-2c Styx anti-ship missiles, supplemented by a 76.2-mm gun forward; self-defense is provided by two 30-mm Gatling guns aft. (1989, Japanese Maritime Self-Defense Force)

Two Tarantul I corvettes are retained by the Soviet Navy. Although armed with SS-N-2c Styx missiles, they lack the more capable electronics of the Tarantul II/III classes. (West German Navy)

33+ GUIDED MISSILE CORVETTES: NANUCHKA I/III CLASSES

Name	Name	Completed
(17 Nanuchka I)		
BURUN	SHTORM	
GRAD	TAYFUN	
MOLNIYA	TSIKLON	1969–1976
MUSSON	ZARNITSA	
RADUGA	ZUB'	
SHKVAL	6 units	
(16+ Nanuchka III)		
16+ units		1977–(?)

Builders:	Petrovskiy, Leningrad
	Ulis, Vladivostok
Displacement:	Nanuchka I 675 tons full load
	Nanuchka III 685 tons full load
Length:	165 ft (50.3 m) overall
Beam:	40 ft (12.2 m)
Draft:	10 ft 2 in (3.1 m)
Propulsion:	3 twin diesel engines (M517); 30,000 bhp (see notes);
	3 shafts
Speed:	32 knots
Range:	900 n.miles at 30 knots
	2,500 n.miles at 12 knots
Complement:	approx. 60
Missiles:	6 SS-N-9 anti-ship (2 triple) except 1 unit rearmed with 8
	SS-N-25 anti-ship (2 quad)
	1 SA-N-4 anti-air launcher [20]
Guns:	Nanuchka I 2 57-mm/80-cal AA (1 twin)
	Nanuchka III 1 76.2-mm/59-cal AA
	1 30-mm/65-cal close-in (multi-barrel)
ASW weapons:	none
Torpedoes:	none
Mines:	none
Radars:	1 Band Stand (fire control)
	1 Bass Tilt (fire control) in Nanuchka III
	1 Muff Cob (fire control) in Nanuchka I
	1 Peel Pair (air search)
	1 Pop Group (fire control) in Nanuchka I
Sonars:	none
EW systems:	4 . . . . . . (passive)

These are heavily armed coastal missile ships. They provide enhanced gun and anti-air defense capabilities in comparison with previous Soviet missile craft.

The Nanuchka II is an export version armed with the SS-N-2c Styx anti-ship missile in place of the SS-N-9 (see below). The Nanuchka differs from the Nanuchka I primarily in gun armament.

Construction of the first units began in 1967. Production of the Nanuchka III continues at a slow rate.

Class: The Nanuchka I and II classes were built at the Petrovskiy shipyard; the Nanuchka III at both Petrovskiy and Ulis.

The Nanuchka II, with the SS-N-2c missile, has the Square Tie search/fire-control radar within the Band Stand radome. Ships of this class have been transferred to Algeria (4), India (3), and Libya (4).

Classification: Soviet MRK type. The NATO designation *Nanuchka* is a child's name in Russian.

Design: These are broad-beam ships. They are cited as being poor sea boats.

The Nanuchka III, with a larger gun than the previous units plus the installation of a Gatling gun (also aft), has an enlarged, higher superstructure.

Engineering: Early units have M503 diesels with 24,000 bhp and a speed of 30 knots. The M504s are in three coupled pairs (designated M507 as pair). The 2,500-n.mile range is achieved by using a single diesel engine with two shafts trailing.

Missiles: At least one unit was fitted by 1987 with quad SS-N-25 missile tubes.

Names: The known names are Russian words for meteorological phenomena.

Nanuchka III at high speed. The ship has a large number of radars and electronic warfare systems. (Royal Navy)

One Nanuchka III has been rearmed with eight SS-N-25 anti-ship missiles in quad mountings on each side of the bridge structure. This photo shows the first such craft—sometimes dubbed Nanuchka IV—with coverings over the missile tubes. (1990, Royal Navy)

Nanuchka I with a twin 57-mm gun mount aft; no Gatling gun is provided. The Nanuchka II is an export version with SS-N-2c Styx missiles in place of the SS-N-9. The Nanuchka I/III bridge configurations differ. (1985, JMSDF)

With six SS-N-9 or eight SS-N-25 anti-ship missiles the Nanuchka is the most heavily armed missile corvette in service. The Nanuchka III has a 76.2-mm gun and a 30-mm Gatling gun aft, reflecting the increase in gun armament for corvettes and small combatants during the past few years. (1987, JMSDF)

30 + ANTI-SUBMARINE CORVETTES: PAUK CLASS

Completed:	1980–
Builders:	Ulis, Vladivostok
	Yavoslav
Displacement:	480 tons standard
	580 tons standard
Length:	172 ft 2½ in (52.5 m) waterline
	191 ft 11 in (58.5 m) overall
Beam:	32 ft 2 in (9.8 m)
Draft:	8 ft 2 in (2.5 m)
Propulsion:	2 diesel engines (M517); 20,000 bhp; 2 shafts
Speed:	32 knots
Range:	2,000 n.miles at 20 knots
Complement:	approx. 40
Missiles:	1 quad SA-N-5 or SA-N-8 anti-air launcher [16–20]
Guns:	1 76.2-mm/59-cal DP
	1 30-mm/65-cal close-in (multi-barrel)

ASW weapons:	2 RBU-1200 rocket launchers
	2 depth charge racks [12]
	torpedoes
Torpedoes:	4 15.75-inch (400-mm) (4 single)
Mines:	none
Radars:	1 Bass Tilt (fire control)
	1 Spin Trough (air search)
	1 Plank Shave (targeting)
Sonars:	medium-frequency hull mounted
	medium-frequency dipping
EW systems:	2 . . . . . . (passive)

These are coastal ASW ships. The lead unit is reported to have entered the Baltic for trials in early 1979. These ships are probably the successor to the Poti class. Some Pauk-class ships appear to be operated by the KGB (included in the above total). Several modi-

The ASW-configured Pauk has the same hull as the Tarantul missile corvette, but in addition to 76.2-mm and 30-mm Gatling guns, has 400-mm torpedo tubes and dipping sonar. The lattice mast is farther aft than in the Tarantuls. (West German Navy)

A Pauk under way, with the housing for the dipping sonar at the stern clearly visible. There are depth charge racks on either side of the housing. The ship's torpedo tubes and RBU-1200 ASW rocket launchers are covered with canvas. (West German Navy)

fied Pauks are being delivered to India.

Classification: Soviet MPK type; probably PSKR in KGB service.

Design: A circular housing for a dipping sonar is fitted in the stern. Some later units have the pilothouse one-half deck higher.

APPROX. 50 ANTI-SUBMARINE CORVETTES: POTI CLASS

Name	Completed
Approx. 50 units	1961–1967

Builders:	Zelendolosk
Displacement:	400 tons full load
Length:	194 ft 10 in (59.4 m) overall
Beam:	25 ft 11 in (7.9 m)
Draft:	6 ft 7 in (2.0 m) hull
Propulsion:	CODAG: 2 diesel engines (M503A); 8,000 bhp + 2 gas turbines; 40,000 shp; 2 shafts
Speed:	38 knots
Range:	500 n.miles at 37 knots
	4,500 n.miles at 10 knots
Complement:	approx. 40
Missiles:	none
Guns:	2 57-mm/80-cal AA (1 twin) (see notes)
ASW weapons:	2 RBU-6000 rocket launchers
	torpedoes
Torpedoes:	2 or 4 15.75-in (400-mm) torpedo tubes (2 or 4 single)
Mines:	none

Radars:	1 Don-2 (navigation)
	1 Muff Cob (fire control)
	1 Strut Curve (air search)
Sonars:	Herkules high-frequency hull mounted
	high-frequency dipping in some units
EW systems:	2 Watch Dog

About 70 of these ASW ships were built for the Soviet Navy; most remain in service. They are being succeeded by the Pauk-class ships.

Class: Three of these ships were transferred to Bulgaria and three to Romania; the Romanian ships had 21-in (533-mm) torpedo tubes and differed in other respects. See the following T-58 listing for additional class notes.

Classification: Soviet MPK type.

Design: The early ships were built with an open 57-mm/70-cal twin AA mount, two RBU-2500 rocket launchers, and two torpedo tubes. Most of those units were upgraded to the configuration shown above. The fixed torpedo tubes are angled out some 15° from the centerline.

The twin gas-turbine exhausts are in the stern.

Electronics: The dipping sonar, installed beginning in the mid-1970s, is the same as in the Ka-25 Hormone-A helicopter.

Engineering: These were the first large Soviet ships to have gas-turbine propulsion, giving them a relatively high speed.

The 4,500-n.mile range is accomplished with one diesel with one shaft trailing.

The 400-mm torpedo tubes on the Poti are amidships, outboard of the 57-mm gun mount. The large air intakes for the gas turbines fill most of the stern deck area with the gas turbine exhausts (closed) built into the stern counter. (West German Navy)

An early Poti with the open 57-mm twin mount amidships. This ship's No. 2 RBU-2500 ASW rocket launcher is in the near vertical position; these rocket launchers are manually reloaded. (Royal Navy)

3 RADAR PICKET SHIPS: Ex-T-58 CLASS MINESWEEPERS

Name	Completed	Converted
3 units	1957–1961	1979–1983

Builders:	(USSR)
Displacement:	760 tons standard
	880 tons full load
Length:	229 ft 6 in (70.0 m) overall
Beam:	29 ft 10 in (9.1 m)
Draft:	8 ft 2 in (2.5 m)
Propulsion:	2 diesel engines; 4,000 bhp; 2 shafts
Speed:	17 knots
Range:	2,500 n.miles at 13.5 knots
Complement:	approx. 100
Missiles:	2 quad SA-N-5 Grail anti-air launchers [16]
Guns:	2 57-mm/70-cal AA (1 twin)
	4 30-mm/65-cal close-in (2 twin)
ASW weapons:	2 depth-charge racks
Torpedoes:	none
Mines:	none

Radars:	1 Big Net (air search)
	1 Muff Cob (fire control)
	1 Spin Trough (air search)
	1 Strut Curve (air search)
Sonars:	high-frequency hull mounted
EW systems:	. . . . . . (passive)

These T-58 fleet minesweepers previously converted to the radar picket role have been further modified to carry the Big Net radar. The conversions were accomplished at the Izhora Shipyard in Leningrad.

The reference book *Combat Fleets* notes, "Considering the small number converted, the age of the hulls, and the pace of the program, these ships are probably intended for a specialized range security role, rather than as classical 'radar pickets.' "[1]

Designation: Probably Soviet KVN type.

1. Bernard Prézelin, English-language edition edited by A.D. Baker III, *Combat Fleets of the World 1990/1991* (Annapolis, Md.: Naval Institute Press, 1990), p. 621.

A T-58 radar picket fitted with a new deck structure aft and a Big Net radar antenna atop a squat lattice mast. The twin 57-mm guns are retained forward, two twin 30-mm rapid-fire gun mounts are installed aft. (1990, Royal Navy)

FEW PATROL CORVETTES: Ex-T-58 CLASS MINESWEEPERS

Completed:	1957–1961
Builders:	(USSR)
Displacement:	725 tons standard
	860 tons full load
Length:	229 ft 7 in (70.0 m) overall
Beam:	29 ft 10 in (9.1 m)
Draft:	8 ft 2 in (2.5 m)
Propulsion:	2 diesel engines; 4,000 bhp; 2 shafts
Speed:	18 knots
Range:	2,500 n.miles at 13.5 knots
Complement:	
Missiles:	none
Guns:	4 57-mm/70-cal AA (2 twin)
ASW weapons:	2 RBU-1200 rocket launchers
	2 depth charge racks
Torpedoes:	none
Mines:	rails for 18 mines

Radars:	1 Don-2 (navigation)
	1 Muff Cob (fire control)
	1 Spin Trough (air search)
Sonars:	high-frequency hull mounted
EW systems:	2 Watch Dog

These are former T-58 minesweepers reclassified in 1978 as patrol ships; some units are operated by the KGB Maritime Border Troops. Three were further modified to serve as radar picket ships (see above). Few of these ships remain in service as patrol ships; those remaining are being discarded.

Class: A total of 34 ships of this class were built as fleet minesweepers; none remain in that role with the Soviet Navy. One unit of this configuration has been transferred to Guinea and one to Yemen. Nineteen apparently were assigned to the patrol/corvette role; other T-58s serve in the auxiliary role in the Soviet and several other navies.

Classification: Soviet SKR type in naval service and PSKR in KGB service.

A T-58 employed as a patrol corvette. These steel-hull ships, built as fleet minesweepers, are employed in the patrol role by both the Navy and the KGB, and a few are operated by foreign navies. Few remain in Soviet naval service. (1978)

CHAPTER 18

Missile, Patrol, and Torpedo Craft

Coastal patrol craft—operated by the Navy and KGB—are important to the Soviet Union for coastal defense and to prevent illegal ingress and egress of individuals. On occasion, the naval craft operate far from their home ports, as this Osa I photographed in the Atlantic. (1983, U.S. Navy)

The Soviet Navy operates a large number of missile, torpedo, and patrol craft for coastal defense. When this edition of *Guide to the Soviet Navy* went to press there appeared to be no missile, torpedo, or patrol craft under construction for Soviet naval use except for the Mukha ASW hydrofoil. Construction of these craft does continue for the KGB Maritime Border Troops (see chapter 26).

The successors to the classes listed below are the larger, more capable corvettes and possibly the Wing-In-Ground (WIG) effect platforms (listed in chapters 17 and 22, respectively). The assignment of larger, more capable craft reflects the larger patrol areas of Soviet coastal defense forces.

In addition to the units listed here, a large number of patrol craft are operated by the KGB Maritime Border Troops. These include the Muravey, Stenka, and Zhuk classes, all of which may remain in production.

Large numbers of these missile, patrol, and torpedo craft have been transferred to other nations.

MISSILE CRAFT

16 GUIDED MISSILE BOATS: MATKA CLASS (SEMI-HYDROFOIL)

Completed:	1978–1981
Builders:	Izhora, Kalpino
Displacement:	225 tons standard
	260 tons full load
Length:	131 ft 2 in (40.0 m) overall
Beam:	24 ft 11 in (7.6 m) hull
	39 ft 4 in (12.0 m) over foils
Draft:	6 ft 11 in (2.1 m) hull-borne
	10 ft 6 in (3.2 m) foil-borne
Propulsion:	3 diesel engines (M504); 15,000 bhp; 3 shafts
Speed:	36 knots foil-borne
Range:	400 n.miles at 36 knots
	650 n.miles at 25 knots
Complement:	approx. 30
Missiles:	2 SS-N-2c Styx anti-ship (2 single)
Guns:	1 76.2-mm/59-cal DP
	1 30-mm/65-cal close-in (multi-barrel)
ASW weapons:	none
Torpedoes:	none
Mines:	none
Radars:	1 Bass Tilt (fire control)
	1 Cheese Cake (search)
	1 Plank Shave (targeting)
Sonars:	none

The Matka is a missile-armed version of the Turya-class hydrofoil torpedo boat, with a larger superstructure (to accommodate a more complex missile system) and different gun arrangement.

The termination of the program after only 16 craft indicates that it was not a successful program. The lead Matka was launched in 1976 and completed in 1978, although the search and targeting radars were not provided until 1980.

Classification: Soviet TKA type.

Design: This class is derived from the Osa, with the same hull and propulsion plant, with hydrofoils having been fitted forward only, technically making these *semi-hydrofoil* craft. At high speeds the craft's stern planes on the water surface.

The Matka is a small missile craft employing the same hull and propulsion plant as the Turya-class hydrofoil torpedo craft. The struts for the hydrofoil are visible just aft of the pendant No. 827. (Royal Danish Navy)

The SS-N-2c Styx missile tubes are visible in this view of a heavily armed Matka. There is a 76.2-mm gun mount forward and a 30-mm Gatling gun between the Styx missiles, evidence of the Soviet Navy's emphasis on guns. (West German Navy)

1 GUIDED MISSILE BOAT: SARANCHA CLASS (HYDROFOIL)

Completed:	1977
Builders:	Petrovskiy, Leningrad
Displacement:	320 tons full load
Length:	148 ft 3 in (45.2 m) hull
	175 ft 10 in (53.6 m) over foils
	166 ft (50.6 m) foil-borne
Beam:	36 ft 1 in (11.0 m) hull
	102 ft 8 in (31.3 m) over foils
Draft:	8 ft 6 in (2.6 m) hull-borne
	23 ft 11 in (7.3 m) foil-borne
Propulsion:	2 gas turbines; 30,000 shp; 2 shafts + 2 propeller pods on after foils
Speed:	58 knots
Range:	
Complement:	
Missiles:	4 SS-N-9 anti-ship (2 twin)
	1 twin SA-N-4 anti-air launcher [20]
Guns:	1 30-mm/65-cal close-in (multi-barrel)
ASW weapons:	none
Torpedoes:	none
Mines:	none
Radars:	1 Band Stand (fire control)
	1 Bass Tilt (fire control)
	1 Pop Group (fire control)
Sonars:	none

Only a single unit of this highly complex design has been constructed. Not considered to be successful.

Engineering: Two propellers are fitted to each of two pods mounted on the after foils.

The one-of-a-kind Sarancha at high speed on foils. The craft's hydroplane hull has a stepped bottom.

The Sarancha on foils; this stern aspect shows the craft's air intakes and twin exhausts for gas turbines.

APPROX. 25 GUIDED MISSILE BOATS: OSA II CLASS

Completed:	1966–1969
Builders:	Petrovskiy, Leningrad and other yards
Displacement:	215 tons standard
	245 tons full load
Length:	126 ft 7 in (38.6 m) overall
Beam:	25 ft (7.6 m)
Draft:	6 ft 7 in (2.0 m)
Propulsion:	3 diesel engines (M504); 15,000 bhp; 3 shafts
Speed:	35 knots
Range:	500 n.miles at 34 knots
	750 n.miles at 25 knots
Complement:	approx. 30
Missiles:	4 SS-N-2b/c Styx anti-ship (4 single)
	1 SA-N-5 or SA-N-8 anti-air launcher (hand held) in some units
Guns:	4 30-mm/65-cal close-in (2 twin)
ASW weapons:	none
Torpedoes:	none
Mines:	none
Radars:	1 Drum Tilt (fire control)
	1 Square Tie (search/targeting)
Sonars:	none

The Osa II is an improved version of the basic Osa I design, carrying the more capable SS-N-2c missile.

Class: About 115 units of this type were built; 92 boats have been transferred to Warsaw Pact and Third World navies—Algeria, Angola, Bulgaria, Cuba, Ethiopia, Finland, India, Iraq, Libya, Somalia, Syria, Vietnam, North Yemen, and South Yemen. Bulgaria is the only Warsaw Pact nation to operate this class, with one unit having been transferred in 1978 and one in 1982.

Classification: Soviet RKA type.

Design: These craft can be distinguished from the Osa I type by the later craft's circular missile tubes with rib-like rings and larger support structure for the Drum Tilt radar. At least one unit has been observed with a deckhouse between the bridge and Drum Tilt radar. See Osa I listing for additional notes.

Names: Soviet names believed to apply to this class are: AMURSKIY KOMSOMOLETS, BRESTSKIY KOMSOMOLETS, KALININGRADSKIY KOMSOMOLETS, KIROVSKIY KOMSOMOLETS, and TAMBOVSKIY KOMSOMOLETS.

Operational: Iraq has used Osa missile boats in combat against Iran during the 1980s Persian Gulf conflict, with at least four Iraqi Osa IIs being lost. (Also see Osa I notes.)

An Osa II posing for her portrait. This unit has a small, can-type navigation radar antenna above the Square Tie search/targeting radar common to all Osa variants. The Osa IIs have ribbed missile canisters. (1989, NATO Standing Naval Force Atlantic)

The Osa II showing the High Pole-B Interrogation Friend or Foe (IFF) protruding above the Square Tie radar on the mast and the twin antennas for the Square Head IFF system. Some units are fitted with SA-N-5/8 missiles aft.

Classification: Soviet RKA type. The NATO name *Osa* is Russian for "Wasp" "(*Komar* was "Mosquito").

Design: The Osa has an all-welded-steel hull with a superstructure of fabricated steel and aluminum alloy. A "citadel" control station is provided for operation in a NBC environment. These craft have four Styx missile launchers, twice the number in the preceding Komar class. The launchers are fixed, with the two after launchers elevated to approximately 15° firing over the forward launchers, elevated to about 12°. The mounting of the Drum Tilt gunfire control radar varies.

The Matka, Mol, Stenka, and Turya classes have the basic Osa hull and propulsion plant (the Mol being a torpedo boat developed for export).

Names: Soviet names associated with this class include KOMSOMOLETS TATARIY and KRONSHTADTSKIY KOMSOMOLETS.

Operational: Indian Osas sank a Pakistani destroyer as well as merchant ships in the war between those two nations in 1971. Egypt and Syria used Osa I missile craft against Israel in 1973 and sustained heavy losses while inflicting no damage on Israeli missile boats.

APPROX. 40 GUIDED MISSILE BOATS: OSA I CLASS

Completed:	1959–1966
Builders:	Petrovskiy, Leningrad and other yards
Displacement:	185 tons standard
	215 tons full load
Length:	126 ft 7 in (38.6 m) overall
Beam:	25 ft (7.6 m)
Draft:	5 ft 11 in (1.8 m)
Propulsion:	3 diesel engines (M503A); 12,000 bhp; 3 shafts
Speed:	36 knots
Range:	500 n.miles at 34 knots
	750 n.miles at 25 knots
Complement:	approx. 30
Missiles:	4 SS-N-2a/b Styx anti-ship (4 single)
	1 SA-N-5 or SA-N-8 anti-air launcher (hand held) in some units
Guns:	4 30-mm/65-cal/65-cal close-in (2 twin)
ASW weapons:	none
Torpedoes:	none
Mines:	none
Radars:	1 Drum Tilt (fire control)
	1 Square Tie (search/targeting)
Sonars:	none

An Osa I showing the large missile launch tubes for the early Styx missiles without folding fins. The later Osa II units have ribbed missile canisters. The gun and electronic systems in the two classes are similar. (1983, U.S. Navy)

These are steel-hull missile boats, developed to succeed the wood-hull Komar class that carried two Styx missiles. This class introduced the twin 30-mm rapid-fire, remote-control gun mountings now common to several Soviet ship classes.

Class: An estimated 175 units of this type were built in the Soviet Union plus up to 100 more being built in China. Ninety-three of the Soviet-built units have been transferred to Warsaw Pact and Third World navies—Algeria, Bulgaria, China, Cuba, Egypt, East Germany, India, Iraq, North Korea, Poland, Romania, Syria, and Yugoslavia. (China received four units about 1960, sans radars, for use as construction prototypes.)

Some of the earlier Osas have been discarded from Soviet service, with a number being converted to target craft.

GUIDED MISSILE BOATS: KOMAR CLASS

All wood-hull missile boats of the Komar class have been discarded from Soviet service. These were the world's first guided missile boats. About 100 units were completed from 1959 onward. They were built on the same hull as the P-6 torpedo boat with some 75 having been transferred to Third World navies. Another 40-plus units were built in China.

These boats each carried two SS-N-2 Styx missiles. Some units survive in target and other, auxiliary roles, and are still operational in other navies.

A pair of Egyptian missile boats sank the Israeli destroyer EILAT with three missile hits on 21 October 1967; the Egyptian boats were off Alexandria when they fired their missiles.

TORPEDO CRAFT

30 TORPEDO CRAFT: TURYA CLASS (SEMI-HYDROFOIL)

Completed:	1974–1979
Builders:	Srednyy Neva, Kolpino
	Ulis, Vladivostok
Displacement:	215 tons standard
	250 tons full load
Length:	127 ft 11 in (39.0 m) overall
Beam:	24 ft 11 in (7.6 m)
	41 ft (12.5 m) over foils
Draft:	6 ft 7 in (2.0 m) hull-borne
	13 ft 2 in (4.0 m) over foils
Propulsion:	3 diesel engines (M504); 15,000 bhp; 3 shafts
Speed:	40 knots
Range:	400 n.miles at 36 knots
	650 n.miles at 25 knots
Complement:	approx. 25
Missiles:	none
Guns:	2 57-mm/80-cal AA (1 twin)
	2 25-mm/60-cal AA (1 twin)
	several 12.7-mm or 14.5-mm machine guns fitted in some units
ASW weapons:	torpedoes
Torpedoes:	4 21-in (533-mm) torpedo tubes (4 single)
Mines:	none
Radars:	1 Muff Cob (fire control)
	1 Pot Drum (search/fire control)
Sonars:	high-frequency dipping

These are high-speed coastal ASW and torpedo attack craft.

Class: Nine units of this class have been transferred to Cuba (without dipping sonar); others have gone to Ethiopia, Kampuchea (Cambodia), the Seychelles, and Vietnam.

Classification: Soviet TK type.

Design: The Turya uses a modified Osa II hull and propulsion plant. The forward foils are fixed and at high speed the craft's stern

A Turya at high speed on her forward (and only) set of foils. She carries an over-under, open 25-mm gun mount forward with an enclosed, rapid-fire twin 57-mm mount aft. This is the only class of torpedo craft currently in Soviet service.

planes on the water. The stern is trimmed by an adjustable flap with twin supports protruding from the stern transom. Later units are reported to have semi-retractable foils to facilitate berthing.

Electronics: The Ka-25 Hormone-A helicopter dipping sonar is fitted on the starboard quarter.

TORPEDO BOATS

All older Soviet torpedo boats have been discarded. The last of the approximately 80 Shershen-class boats were transferred or otherwise disposed of in the early 1980s. They continue in service with several foreign navies and have been built in Yugoslavia under license.

The twin 57-mm mount dominates the Turya's silhouette. Other Soviet small craft have ASW torpedo tubes. (1988, Leo Van Ginderen collection)

PATROL CRAFT

1 PATROL BOAT: BABOCHKA TYPE (HYDROFOIL)

Completed:	1976
Builders:	(USSR)
Displacement:	400 tons full load
Length:	164 ft (50.0 m) overall
Beam:	27 ft 9 in (8.5 m) hull
	42 ft 8 in (13.0 m) over foils
Draft:	
Propulsion:	CODOG: 2 diesel engines + 3 gas turbines = approx. 30,000 shp; 3 shafts
Speed:	45+ knots
Range:	
Complement:	
Missiles:	none
Guns:	2 30-mm/65-cal close-in (2 multi-barrel)
ASW weapons:	torpedoes
Torpedoes:	8 15.75 in (400-mm) torpedo tubes (2 quad)
Mines:	none
Radars:	1 Bass Tilt (fire control)
	1 Don-2 (navigation)
	1 Peel Cone (search)
Sonars	none

This is a prototype-evaluation ASW patrol craft: only one unit has been built.

Design: There are fixed, fully submerged foils forward and aft. The torpedo tubes are stacked two above two, in two quad launchers on the bow, angled out to both sides.

The hydrofoil patrol craft given the NATO code name Babochka has not been series produced. Note the supports for the forward hydrofoils and the after gas turbine housing. One 30-mm Gatling gun mount and the 400-mm torpedo tubes are fitted on the forecastle; the second gun mount is aft of the mast.

1 PATROL GUNBOAT: SLEPEN TYPE

Completed:	~1969
Builders:	Petrovskiy, Leningrad
Displacement:	205 tons standard
	230 tons full load
Length:	126 ft 7 in (38.6 m) overall
Beam:	24 ft 11 in (7.6 m)
Draft:	6 ft 3 in (1.9 m)
Propulsion:	3 diesel engines (M504); 15,000 bhp; 3 shafts
Speed:	36 knots
Range:	500 n.miles at 34 knots
	750 n.miles at 25 knots
Complement:	approx. 30
Missiles:	none
Guns:	1 76.2-mm/59-cal DP
	1 30-mm/65-cal close-in (multi-barrel)
ASW weapons:	none
Torpedoes:	none
Mines:	none
Radars:	1 Bass Tilt (fire control)
	1 Don-2 (navigation)
Sonars:	none
EW systems:	2 . . . . . . (passive)

This is the Soviet Navy's only high-speed gunboat. The craft may be employed as a trials ship for small combatant systems.

Design: Similar to the Matka design but without either the hydrofoils or missiles.

Guns: As built, the ship had a twin 57-mm gun mount forward; replaced by the single 76.2 mm gun in 1975.

ANTI-SUBMARINE CRAFT

1+ ANTI-SUBMARINE CRAFT: MUKHA CLASS (HYDROFOIL)

Completed:	1986–
Builders:	(USSR)
Displacement:	
Length:	approx. 164 ft (50.0 m) overall
Beam:	
Draft:	
Propulsion:	
Speed:	
Range:	
Complement:	
Missiles:	none
Guns:	1 76.2-mm/59-cal AA
	1 30-mm/65-cal close-in (multi-barrel)
ASW weapons:	torpedoes
Torpedoes:	8 15.75-inch (400-mm) torpedo tubes (2 quad)
Mines:	none
Radars:	
Sonars:	

ANTI-SUBMARINE PATROL CRAFT: KRONSHTADT CLASS

Successors to the war-built Artillerist class, Soviets produced some 230 units of this class from 1946–1956. Numerous units were operated by the Soviet Navy and transferred to other navies; others served as the Libau-class communications craft in the Soviet Navy. All have been stricken.

RIVERINE CRAFT

The Soviet Navy operates riverine patrol craft on the Amur, Danube, and Ussuri rivers. Riverine craft perform routine peacetime patrols and in wartime would support ground operations (with their main guns and rocket launchers using army ammunition).

The large number of these craft and continuing construction indicates the Soviet concern for its river borders, especially with China.

1 RIVERINE FLAGSHIP: SSV-10

Completed:	
Builders:	(USSR)
Displacement:	360 tons full load
Length:	160 ft 9 in (49.0 m) overall
Beam:	
Draft:	
Propulsion:	diesel engines; 2 shafts
Speed:	
Range:	
Complement:	
Missiles:	none
Guns:	several machine guns
ASW weapons:	none
Torpedoes:	none
Mines:	none
Radars	. . . . . . (navigation)
Sonars:	none

This ship serves as flagship of the Danube riverine flotilla. Now designated SSV-10 (formerly PS-10); SSV indicates a communications vessel.

The Soviet Navy's Danube River flagship and accommodation ship SSV-10 in Vienna. She has a twin 25-mm over-under gun mount forward; the mast folds down to permit transit under bridges. (1985, Erwin Sieche)

FEW RIVERINE PATROL CRAFT: PIVYAKA CLASS

Displacement:	230 tons full load
Length:	126 ft 3 in (38.5 m) overall
Beam:	21 ft 4 in (6.5 m)
Draft:	
Propulsion:	diesels
Speed:	
Range:	
Complement:	
Missiles:	none
Guns:	
ASW weapons:	none
Torpedoes:	none
Mines:	
Radars:	. . . . . . (navigation)
Sonars:	none

These craft are intended for patrolling the Amur River border with China.

FEW RIVERINE MONITORS: VOSH CLASS

Completed:	1980–
Builders:	
Displacement:	180 tons standard
	250 tons full load
Length:	137 ft 9 in (42.0 m) overall
Beam:	23 ft (7.0 m)
Draft:	3 ft 3 in (1.0 m)
Propulsion:	2 diesels; 2 shafts
Speed:	18 knots
Range:	
Complement:	
Missiles:	none
Guns:	1 76.2-mm/48-cal
	6 14.5-mm machine guns (3 twin)
ASW weapons:	none
Torpedoes:	none
Mines:	
Radars:	. . . . . . (navigation)
Sonars:	none

Monitors intended for use on the Amur River.

20+ RIVERINE MONITORS: YAZ CLASS

Completed:	1981–
Builders:	Khabarovsk
Displacement:	400 tons full load
Length:	196 ft 11 in (60.0 m) overall
Beam:	
Draft:	
Propulsion:	2 diesel engines; 2 shafts
Speed:	15 knots
Range:	
Complement:	
Missiles:	none
Guns:	2 115-mm tank guns (2 single)
	2 30-mm/65-cal close-in (1 twin)
ASW weapons:	none
Torpedoes:	none
Mines:	none
Radars:	1 Bass Tilt (fire control)
	1 Kivach or Spin Trough (navigation)
Sonars:	none

These are riverine monitors employed on the Amur River in the Far East. World War II riverine gunboats built by the Soviets also had tank guns.

Guns: Some units may have 100-mm or 120-mm tank guns.

A Yaz-class river monitor with tank-turret guns fitted forward and aft.

APPROX. 80 RIVERINE GUNBOATS: SHMEL CLASS

Completed:	1967–1974
Builders:	(USSR)
Displacement:	60 tons full load
Length:	92 ft 10 in (28.3 m) overall
Beam:	15 ft 1 in (4.6 m)
Draft:	3 ft (0.9 m)
Propulsion:	2 diesel engines (M50F-4); 2,400 bhp; 2 shafts
Speed:	22 knots
Range:	240 n.miles at 20 knots
	600 n.miles at 10 knots
Complement:	approx. 15
Missiles:	1 18-tube 122-mm rocket launcher in some units
Guns:	1 76.2-mm/48-cal SP
	2 25-mm/60-cal AA machine guns (1 twin)
	5 7.62-mm machine guns (5 single; see notes)
ASW weapons:	none
Torpedoes:	none
Mines:	8 mines can be carried
Radars:	. . . . . . (navigation)
Sonars:	none

These are heavily armed river craft, similar in concept to the French and U.S. riverine monitors of the Indochina-Vietnam wars. The craft patrol the several Soviet rivers that border on foreign states. Many units are in reserve.

Class: Eighty-five units were built. Four units were transferred to Kampuchea (Cambodia) in 1984–1985.

Classification: Soviet AKA type.

Design: These are very shallow draft craft. They appear to have extensive NBC protection features for a small craft.

The 76.2-mm weapon is mounted in a PT-76 tank turret with one 7.62-mm MG coaxially mounted. The other 7.62-mm MGs are hand held and fired through ports in the open-top deckhouse. The rocket launcher—fitted between the deckhouse and the after 25-mm mounting—is deleted in some units.

A Shmel river patrol craft with a tank-turret 76.2-mm gun forward and a rocket launcher and over-under 25-mm gun mount aft. (1985, Erwin Sieche)

A Turya at rest; note the fittings for the hydrofoil and the over-under 25-mm gun mount forward.

CHAPTER 19

Mine Warfare Ships and Craft

The new minehunter Gorya, shown departing the Baltic in August 1989. She is the first all-new Soviet mine counter-measures ship since the early 1970s. She has the heaviest gun battery of a Soviet mine warfare ship, with a single 76.2-mm gun mount forward and a 30-mm Gatling gun amidships, plus two quad SA-N-8 missile launchers.

The Soviet Navy maintains the world's largest mine warfare forces, with a larger mine stockpile, a greater minelaying capability, and at least quantitatively a much more capable mine countermeasures capability than any other nation.

In addition to the three minelayers listed below, several Soviet surface combatant and small craft classes are configured to lay mines, as are Soviet bomber and maritime patrol aircraft. Essentially all Soviet combat submarines can also lay mines.

The large force of surface mine countermeasures craft—mine hunters and mine-sweepers—are supplemented by specialized minesweeping helicopters of the Mi-8 Hip and Mi-14 Haze types (see chapter 27). Note that most Soviet minesweepers have defensive guns and an ASW capability, permitting them to serve as escorts even with sweep gear installed.[1] Some can also carry a few mines, primarily for laying practice mines.

The Sonya-class coastal minesweepers and possibly the Ilyusha-class drone (unmanned) minesweepers are apparently the only minesweeper designs currently under construction for the Soviet Navy other than the new Gorya and Pelikan classes.

Several Polnocny-class landing ships are fitted for clearing mines and explosives from landing areas (see chapter 20).

---

1. In World War II the U.S. Navy built 58 submarine chaser sweepers (PCS), but these were 136-footers with their sweep gear removed and ASW weapons fitted in their place.

3 MINELAYERS: ALESHA CLASS

Name	Completed
PRIPET'	
VYCHEDGA	1967–1969
PECHORA	

Builders:	(USSR)
Displacement:	2,900 tons standard
	3,500 tons full load
Length:	318 ft 2 in (97.0 m) overall
Beam:	45 ft 11 in (14.0 m)
Draft:	17 ft 9 in (5.4 m)
Propulsion:	4 diesel engines; 8,000 bhp; 2 shafts
Speed:	17 knots
Range:	4,000 n.miles at 16 knots
	8,500 n.miles at 8 knots
Complement:	approx. 190
Helicopters:	no facilities
Guns:	4 57-mm/70-cal AA (1 quad)
ASW weapons:	none

Mines:	rails for approx. 300
Radars:	1 Don-2 (navigation)
	1 Muff Cob (fire control)
	1 Strut Curve (air search)
Sonars:	none

These are minelaying and support ships. They can lay mines, tend defensive anti-submarine nets, support minesweepers, and serve as command/control ships for mine clearance operations. They are believed to be the only specialized minelayers now in service with any major navy.

Classification: Soviet ZM type. NATO code names for Soviet mine warfare ships and craft are Russian names for children, as *Alesha*, *Natya*, and *Yurka* ("Georgie").

Design: Mine rails are fitted on two decks, with a stern ramp over which mines can be laid or large objects hauled aboard. The lead ship has a crane fitted forward and two booms amidships; the two others have a kingpost and booms forward.

The Pacific Fleet minelayer/support ship VYCHEGDA in the Tsushima Strait. The three Soviet ships of this class are the only specialized minelayers now serving in a major navy. Mine rails are visible on the after decks. Several Soviet surface ship classes and virtually all submarines can also lay mines as can bomber aircraft. (1985, Japanese Maritime Self-Defense Force)

2 + (?) AIR-CUSHION MINE COUNTERMEASURE CRAFT: PELIKAN CLASS

Completed:	1986–
Builders:	Yuznaya Tochka, Feodosiya
Displacement:	approx. 100 tons full load
Length:	98 ft 5 in (30.0 m) overall
Beam:	43 ft 7½ in (13.3 m)
Draft:	
Propulsion:	gas turbines
Speed:	
Range:	
Complement:	
Missiles:	
Guns:	
Radars:	. . . . . . (navigation)

At least two of these Air-Cushion Vehicles (ACV) have been produced at the Feodosiya facility with a mine countermeasures configuration. (See chapter 21 for other recent Feodosiya-produced ACVs.)

The use of ACV for mine countermeasures has been discussed by both the U.S. and Royal Navies, but no specialized mine-hunting-configured ACV has been developed.

1 + MINEHUNTERS: GORYA CLASS

Completed:	1989–
Builders:	Svedniy Neva, Kolpino
Displacement:	950 tons standard
	1,100 tons full load
Length:	216 ft 6 in (66.0 m) overall
Beam:	36 ft 1 in (11.0 m)
Draft:	9 ft 10 in (3.0 m)
Propulsion:	2 diesels; 5,000 bhp; 2 shafts
Speed:	16 knots
Range:	
Complement:	approx. 60
Missiles:	2 quad SA-N-14 anti-air launchers
Guns:	1 76.2-mm/59-cal DP
	1 30-mm/65-cal close-in (multibarrel)
ASW weapons:	(see notes)
Mines:	none
Radars:	1 Bass Tilt (fire control)
	1 Nayada (navigation)
	1 Palm Frond (navigation)
Sonars:	high-frequency minehunting
EW systems:	. . . . . . passive

This is a large minehunter design that was initially given the NATO designation BAL-COM-7; it was subsequently given the code name Gorya. The lead ship was launched in August 1987 and

MINE WARFARE SHIPS AND CRAFT

completed in 1989; it was transferred to the Black Sea in August of that year.

Additional units are probably under construction.

ASW weapons: Some sources cite possibly 2 RBU-1200 ASW rocket launchers being fitted aft (behind sliding doors in the side of the deckhouse). Alternatively, they may cover minesweeping gear.

Design: All-steel ships with a massive deck house. The small stern working area is crowded with sweep gear and twin handling davits.

Guns: The 76.2-mm gun is the largest weapon mounted on a Soviet mine warfare ship.

The Gorya has an elongated deckhouse, the after portion of which is a hangar for mine countermeasures devices. These can be lowered into the sea through doors on either side of the 01 level (under the 30-mm gun mount) and over the stern with the use of articulated handling gear. (1989, West German Navy)

35 FLEET MINESWEEPERS: NATYA I/II CLASSES

Name	Name	Completed
ADMIRAL PERSHIN	PULEMETCHIK	
ARTILLERIST	RADIST	
DIZELIST	RULEVOY	
DMITRIY LYSOV	SIGNAL'SHCHIK	
ELEKTRIK	SNAYPER	
KHARKOVSKIY KOMSOMOLETS	SVYAZIST	
KONTRA ADMIRAL HOROSHKIN	TURBINIST	1970–1982
KONTRA ADMIRAL PERSIN	VITSE ADMIRAL ZHUKOV	
KURSKIY KOMSOMOLETS	VSEVOLOD VISHNEVSKIY	
(ex-NOVODCHIK)	ZARYAD	
MASHINIST	ZENITCHIK	
MINER	12 units	
MOTORIST		

Builders:	Srednyy Neva, Kolpino and other yards
Displacement:	650 tons standard
	750 tons full load
Length:	188 ft 11 in (57.6 m) waterline
	200 ft 1 in (61.0 m) overall
Beam:	31 ft 6 in (9.6 m)
Draft:	9 ft 2 in (2.8 m)
Propulsion:	2 diesel engines: 5,000 bhp; 2 shafts
Speed:	17 knots
Range:	1,800 n.miles at 16 knots
	5,200 n.miles at 10 knots
Complement:	approx. 60
Missiles:	2 quad SA-N-5 or SA-N-8 anti-air launchers [16] in some units
Guns:	4 30-mm/65-cal close-in (2 twin)
	4 25-mm/60-cal AA (2 twin)
ASW weapons:	2 RBU-1200 rocket launchers
Mines:	can carry 10 mines
Radars:	1 or 2 Don-2 (navigation)
	1 Drum Tilt (fire control)
Sonars:	Tamir high-frequency minehunting

These are fleet minesweepers with a limited ASW capability and self-defense armament, permitting them to serve as anti-submarine escorts. One unit completed in 1982 is a modified minehunter (Natya II). That unit has an elongated deckhouse with the 25-mm guns and RBUs deleted. No additional units of this type have appeared.

Class: In addition to the above units, new construction ships have been built for India (12), Libya (8), and Syria (1); the last, transferred in 1985, is a training ship, without sweep gear.

Classification: Soviet MT type

Design: These ships have aluminum-alloy hulls. Early ships have fixed davits aft for handling sweeping gear; the davits are articulated in later units. There is a stern ramp to facilitate handling sweep gear. The twin 25-mm guns are "hidden" in the topside clutter, with one mount on the port side just forward of the funnel and the other on the starboard side, abaft the funnel and just behind the launch.

A Natya I under tow. The Drum Tilt fire control radar for the two 30-mm twin gun mounts is fitted atop the mast, which also carries the High Pole-B and Square Head IFF antennas, and the Don-2 search/navigation radar. (1988, Royal Netherlands Navy)

A Natya I transiting the Malacca Straits. These are the old-style davits for handing sweep gear. The stern ramp shown here facilitates handling such gear. (1982, U.S. Navy)

The single Natya II, which transferred to the Black Sea in 1985. Note the deckhouse aft, replacing sweep gear of the basic Natya configuration; there are SA-N-5/8 SAM launch positions aft of the lattice mast. As only one unit was procured, this is probably a trials ship for minehunting/minesweeping gear. (1985, U.S. Navy)

A Natya I-class fleet minesweeper with the new-style davits on her fantail to handle sweep gear. The starboard 25-mm mount (facing camera) is just aft of the funnel; the portside mount is between the deckhouse and funnel. These ships are well suited for coastal escort/patrol work. (1987, JMSDF)

41 FLEET MINESWEEPERS: YURKA CLASS

Name	Name	Completed
GAFEL'	YERGENIY MIKONOR	
KOMSOMOLETS BYELORUSSIY	37 units	1962–1969
SEMEN ROSHAL'		

Builders:	Izhora, Kalpino
	Kamyush-Burun, Kerch and other yards
Displacement:	400 tons standard
	460 tons full load
Length:	170 ft 7 in (52.0 m) overall
Beam:	30 ft 6 in (9.3 m)
Draft:	6 ft 7 in (2.0 m)
Propulsion:	2 diesel engines; 4,000 bhp; 2 shafts
Speed:	16 knots
Range:	2,000 n.miles at 14 knots
	3,200 n.miles at 10 knots
Complement:	approx. 45
Missiles:	2 quad SA-N-5 or SA-N-8 anti-air launchers [16] in some units
Guns:	4 30-mm/65-cal close-in (2 twin)
ASW weapons:	none
Mines:	can carry 20 mines
Radars:	1 or 2 Don-2 (navigation)
	1 Drum Tilt (fire control)
Sonars:	Tamir high-frequency minehunting

The Yurka is one of several large classes of fleet minesweepers in Soviet service. Two small, close-in navigation radar antennas are fitted on top of the bridge in addition to the larger Don-2 search/navigation radar. A Drum Tilt fire control radar tops the mast. (1985, JMSDF)

These are smaller than the later Natya-class minesweepers without the later ships' ASW weapons.

Class: Ships of this class have been transferred to Egypt (4) and Vietnam (1).

Classification: Soviet MT type.

Design: Aluminum-alloy hulls. This is a similar design to the Natya class but without the stern ramp. The Yurka's broad funnel indicates a side-by-side arrangement of the diesel engines. When viewed from the side, the classes are easily distinguished by the Natya's larger funnel.

The Yurka has an unusual funnel configuration but otherwise is typical of the large number of Soviet fleet minesweepers.

FLEET MINESWEEPERS: T-43 CLASS

The last of the T-43 class of fleet minesweepers were probably retired in the late 1980s. More than 200 ships of this class—the Soviet Navy's first post–World War II minesweeper design—were completed from 1949 to 1957. After serving as minesweepers, many units were modified for auxiliary roles as well as for radar picket ships; the KGB operates several as patrol ships (see chapter 26).

Ships of this class have been transferred to Albania, Algeria, Bulgaria, China, Egypt, Indonesia, Iraq, Poland, and Syria. (See *Guide to the Soviet Navy*, 4th ed. pp. 251–252, for characteristics.)

FLEET MINESWEEPERS: T-58 CLASS

None of the 58 fleet minesweepers of the T-58 class, completed between 1957 and 1961, remain in service as minesweepers. Nineteen were rerated as corvettes (both Navy and KGB operated) and others as auxiliary ships; several remain in service, including three radar picket ships (see chapter 17).

One T-58 has been transferred to Guinea and one to South Yemen.

60+ COASTAL MINESWEEPERS: SONYA CLASS

Name	Name	Completed
KHERSONSKIY KOMSOMOLETS	SEVASTOPOL'SKIY KOMSOMOLETS	
KOLOMENSKIY KOMSOMOLETS	(ex-KOMSOMOL'SKIY	1973—
KOMSOMOLETS KIRGIZIY	TELEGRAF)	
ORENBURGSKIY KOMSOMOLETS	55+ units	

Builders:	Ulis, Vladivostok and other yards
Displacement:	350 tons standard
	400 tons full load
Length:	159 ft 1 in (48.5 m) overall
Beam:	24 ft (7.3 m)
Draft:	6 ft 3 in (1.9 m)
Propulsion:	2 diesel engines; 2,400 bhp; 2 shafts
Speed:	15 knots
Range:	1,600 n.miles at 14 knots
	3,000 n.miles at 10 knots
Complement:	approx. 40
Missiles:	1 SA-N-5 or SA-N-8 anti-air launcher in some units [8]
Guns:	2 30-mm/65-cal close-in (1 twin)
	2 25-mm/60-cal AA (1 twin)
ASW weapons:	none
Mines:	none
Radars:	1 Spin Trough (search)
Sonars:	high-frequency minehunting

These are modern coastal minesweepers with wooden hulls sheathed in fiberglass.

Class: New-construction units have been transferred to Bulgaria (4), Cuba (4), Syria (1), and Vietnam (1).

Classification: Soviet BT type.

The Sonya-class coastal minesweepers are heavily armed, with a twin 30-mm gun mount forward (under canvas) and a twin 25-mm gun mount between the funnel and cable reel. (1987, JMSDF)

A Sonya under tow in the Far East. (1985, JMSDF)

2 COASTAL MINESWEEPERS: ZHENYA CLASS

Completed:	1967 and 1972
Builders:	(USSR)
Displacement:	220 tons standard
	300 tons full load
Length:	139 ft 1 in (42.4 m) overall
Beam:	25 ft 11 in (7.9 m)
Draft:	5 ft 11 in (1.8 m)
Propulsion:	2 diesel engines; 2,400 bhp; 2 shafts
Speed:	16 knots
Range:	1,400 n.miles at 14 knots
	2,400 n.miles at 10 knots
Complement:	approx. 40
Guns:	2 30-mm/65-cal close-in (1 twin)
ASW weapons:	none
Mines:	none
Radars:	1 Spin Trough (search)
Sonars:	

These were prototypes for an advanced coastal minesweeper but series construction was deferred, apparently in favor of the larger Sonya design.

Classification: Soviet BT type.

Design: Glass-reinforced plastic hulls.

Engineering: Some Western reports credit these ships with one diesel engine and a single shaft.

Zhenya-class coastal minesweeper.

APPROX. 65 COASTAL MINESWEEPERS: VANYA I/II CLASSES

Completed:	1961–1973
Builders:	Voldarskiy, Rybinsk and other yards
Displacement:	200 tons standard
	Vanya I 250 tons full load
	Vanya II 260 tons full load
Length:	Vanya I 130 ft 10 1/2 in (39.9 m) overall
	Vanya II 134 ft 2 in (40.9 m) overall
Beam:	25 ft 11 in (7.5 m)
Draft:	5 ft 11 in (1.8 m)
Propulsion:	2 diesel engines; 2,200 bhp; 2 shafts
Speed:	14 knots
Range:	1,400 n.miles at 14 knots
	2,400 n.miles at 10 knots
Complement:	approx. 30
Guns:	2 30-mm/65-cal close-in (1 twin) (see Modification notes)
ASW weapons:	none
Mines:	can carry 12 mines
Radars:	1 Don-2 (navigation) except Don-Kay in 1 unit
Sonars:	mine hunting

A large class of coastal minesweepers, at least one of which has been reconfigured as a minehunter (see below). The last three units (Vanya II) are one meter longer and have heavier stern davits.

One of the large number of Vanya-class coastal minesweepers in Soviet service.

Vanya-class coastal minesweeper.

Class: Ships of this class have transferred to Bulgaria (4), Syria (2), and Vietnam (1).

Classification: Soviet BT type.

Design: Wooden-hull ships. The three modified, or Vanya II, type are slightly larger, having a larger fantail work area; they can be identified by the larger diesel generator exhaust pipe amidships.

Engineering: Some Western reports credit these ships with one diesel and one shaft.

Modification: At least one unit was refitted (or possibly completed) as a mine hunter in 1974. That unit has two 25-mm guns (single mounts) in place of the 30-mm mount, a Don-Kay radar in place of the Don-2, a small mast fitted amidships, sweep gear removed, and other changes.

COASTAL MINESWEEPERS: SASHA CLASS

The last of this class of coastal sweepers was discarded in the early 1980s. The steel-hulled craft were also employed as patrol boats.

APPROX. 48 INSHORE MINESWEEPERS: YEVGENYA CLASS

Completed:	1970–1976
Builders:	Srednyy Neva, Kolpino
Displacement:	80 tons standard
	90 tons full load
Length:	85 ft 11 in (26.2 m) overall
Beam:	20 ft (6.1 m)
Draft:	4 ft 11 in (1.5 m)
Propulsion:	2 diesel engines; 600 bhp; 2 shafts
Speed:	11 knots
Range:	300 n.miles at 10 knots
Complement:	approx. 10
Guns:	2 14.5-mm machine guns (1 twin)
ASW weapons:	none
Mines:	none
Radars:	1 Spin Trough (search)
Sonars:	probably minehunting

These are fiberglass-hull craft, several of which have been transferred abroad.

Class: Units of this type have been transferred to Angola (2), Bulgaria (4), Cuba (9), India (6), Iraq (3), Mozambique (3), Nicaragua (4), Syria (4), Vietnam (3), and North Yemen (2). Some export versions have a twin 25-mm AA gun mount provided.

Classification: Soviet RT type.

Yevgenya-class inshore minesweeper. (West German Navy)

RIVER MINESWEEPERS: TR-40 CLASS

The approximately 25 wood-hull craft of this design are believed to have been striken.

APPROX. 25 MINESWEEPING BOATS: K-8 CLASS

Completed:	1954–1959
Builders:	Polnocny, Gdańsk (Poland)
Displacement:	19.4 tons standard
	26 tons full load
Length:	55 ft 5 in (16.9 m) overall
Beam:	10 ft 6 in (3.2 m)
Draft:	2 ft 7½ in (0.8 m)
Propulsion:	2 diesel engines (Type 3D6); 300 bhp; 2 shafts
Speed:	12 knots
Range:	300 n.miles at 9 knots
Complement:	6
Missiles:	none
Guns:	2 14.5-mm machine guns (1 twin)
ASW weapons:	none
Mines:	none
Radars:	none
Sonars:	none

These are outdated craft, most or all of which are laid up in reserve. Wooden construction; they tow minesweeping gear but cannot carry it on board.

Class: Minesweepers of this class have been transferred to Nicaragua (4) and Vietnam (5).

K-8–class minesweeping boat.

1 AUXILIARY MINESWEEPER: BALTIKA CLASS (former fishing boat)

Completed:	1978
Builders:	Leninskaya Kuznitsa, Kiev
Displacement:	210 tons full load
Length:	83 ft 8 in (25.5 m) overall
Beam:	22 ft 4 in (6.8 m)
Draft:	8 ft (2.45 m)
Propulsion:	1 diesel engine; 300 bhp; 1 shaft
Speed:	9.5 knots
Range:	1,350 n.miles at 9.5 knots
Complement:	approx. 10
Guns:	1 14.5-mm machine gun
ASW weapons:	none
Mines:	none
Radars:	. . . . . . (navigation)
Sonars:	

This is a stern-haul purse-seiner acquired about 1980–1981 and adapted for minesweeping to evaluate the feasibility of wartime conversion of fishing craft for this role.

During the Falklands War of 1982 the Royal Navy acquired five trawlers for mine countermeasures, although they were not used in that role. In the early 1980s the U.S. Navy initiated the Craft of Opportunity Program (COOP) to develop the methods and equipment for employing fishing craft and naval seamanship training craft (YP) in the mine countermeasure role.

2 SPECIAL MINESWEEPERS: ANDRYUSHA CLASS

Completed:	1975 and 1976
Builders:	(USSR)
Displacement:	320 tons standard
	360 tons full load
Length:	156 ft 9 in (47.8 m) overall
Beam:	27 ft 11 in (8.5 m)
Draft:	9 ft 11 in (3.0 m)
Propulsion:	2 diesel engines; 2,200 bhp; 2 shafts
Speed:	15 knots
Range:	
Complement:	approx. 40
Guns:	none
ASW weapons:	none
Mines:	none
Radars:	1 Spin Trough (search)
Sonars:	

These minesweepers have non-magnetic wooden or fiberglass hulls with large cable ducts along their sides, indicating a probable magnetic-sweep capability.

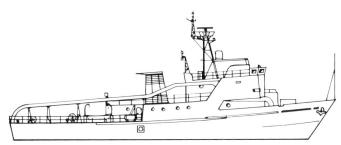

Andryusha-class special minesweeper.

Stern view of one of the Andryusha-class mine countermeasure ships with large cable ducts running along both sides. The large stack is a gas turbine exhaust for the ship's power generator; the ship's diesel propulsion plant exhausts through the sides of the hull (at the color change).

4 MINESWEEPING BOATS: OLYA CLASS

Completed:	1976
Builders:	(USSR)
Displacement:	44 tons standard
	50 tons full load
Length:	80 ft 8 in (24.6 m) overall
Beam:	13 ft 9 in (4.2 m)
Draft:	3 ft 3 in (1.0 m)
Propulsion:	2 diesel engines; 600 bhp; 2 shafts
Speed:	18 knots
Range:	500 n.miles at 10 knots
Complement:	approx. 15
Guns:	2 25-mm/60-cal AA (1 twin)
ASW weapons:	none
Mines:	none
Radars:	1 Spin Trough (search)
Sonars:	none

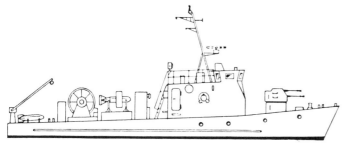

Olya-class minesweeping boat.

11 MINESWEEPING DRONES: ILYUSHA CLASS

Completed:	1970—
Builders:	(USSR)
Displacement:	80 tons standard
	85 tons full load
Length:	85 ft 11 in (26.2 m) overall
Beam:	19 ft (5.8 m)
Draft:	4 ft 11 in (1.5 m)
Propulsion:	1 diesel engine; 450 bhp; 1 shaft
Speed:	12 knots
Range:	
Complement:	10 (see notes)
Guns:	none
ASW weapons:	none
Mines:	none
Radars:	1 Spin Trough (search)
Sonars:	none

These are radio-controlled minesweeping craft, similar to the MSD type operated by the U.S. Navy in the Vietnam War. They can be manned for self-transit for short distances.

Ilyusha-class minesweeping drone.

FEW TOWED MINESWEEPING DRONES

Displacement:	approx. 25 tons
Length:	39 ft 4 in (12.0 m) overall
Beam:	13 ft 1½ in (4.0 m)
Draft:	4 ft 11 in (4.9 m)

These craft are towed by minesweepers or mine hunters; they have reels and winches to deploy magnetic sweep arrays or explosive line charges. They are transported on board ship. They are unmanned when employed in sweep activity.

A pair of minesweeping drones under tow. They can themselves tow a variety of sweep gear while they are being towed.

CHAPTER 20

Amphibious Warfare Ships

The IVAN ROGOV with her forward deck loaded with Naval Infantry vehicles. The ship can operate helicopters from either open deck, one of many flexible features of this design, the largest amphibious warfare class to be built in the Eastern Bloc. (1987, Japanese Maritime Self-Defense Force)

The number of amphibious ships in the Soviet Navy has been declining slightly. When this edition of *Guide to the Soviet Navy* went to press additional Repoucha-class landing ships—a design of the early 1970s—were being built in Poland for the Soviet Navy while the third large amphibious ship of the long-gestation IVAN ROGOV class has been completed at Kaliningrad. The political and economic events in Poland, however, make questionable if many more Repoucha LSTs or other major amphibious ships will be constructed in the near future.

Soviet amphibious capabilities for short-range operations are being increased considerably through the acquisition of large air-cushion landing craft and the Orlan-class Wing-In-Ground effect (WIG) vehicles (see chapters 21 and 22).

Except for the ROGOVs, all large Soviet amphibious ships (LST/LSM types) have been constructed in Poland.

Troop capacity: The troop capacity listed for amphibious ships is the number for which berths are provided; a larger number could be carried in all classes of amphibious ships for short transits.

3 HELICOPTER/DOCK LANDING SHIPS: "IVAN ROGOV" CLASS

Name	Launched	Completed
Ivan Rogov	1976	1978
Aleksandr Nikolayev		Nov 1982
Migrofan Moskalenko	1988	Dec 1989

Builders:	Yantar/Kaliningrad
Displacement:	11,000 tons standard
	13,000 tons full load
Length:	518 ft 3 in (158.0 m) overall
Beam:	78 ft 9 in (24.0 m)
Draft:	26 ft 11 in (8.2 m)
Propulsion:	2 gas turbines; 48,600 shp; 2 shafts
Speed:	23 knots
Range:	8,000 n.miles at 20 knots
	12,500 n.miles at 14 knots
Complement:	approx. 200
Troops:	approx. 525
Helicopters:	4 Ka-27 Helix-B
Missiles/rockets:	1 twin SA-N-4 anti-air launcher [20]
	2 quad SA-N-5 or SA-N-8 anti-air launchers [16–20]
	1 40-tube 122-mm barrage rocket launcher
Guns:	2 76.2-mm/59-cal DP (1 twin)
	4 30-mm close-in (4 multi-barrel)
Radars:	2 Bass Tilt (fire control)
	2 Don-Kay (navigation) in Rogov
	1 Head Net-C (air search) in Rogov and Nikolayev
	1 Owl Screech (fire control)
	2 Palm Frond (navigation) in Nikolayev and Moskalenko
	1 Pop Group (fire control)
	1 Top Plate in Moskalenko
EW systems:	2 Bell Shroud (3 in Nikolayev)
	2 Bell Squat

These are the largest and most versatile amphibious ships yet constructed for the Soviet Navy. Each ship can embark a Naval Infantry battalion, including its vehicles and equipment. They are also the only amphibious ships with a helicopter facility.

The first two ships are assigned to the Pacific Fleet. The third ship was in the Baltic when this edition went to press.

Class: The second ship was completed four years after the first unit; the third ship was delivered seven years after the second.

Classification: Soviet BDK type.

Design: These are multi-role amphibious ships, having bow vehicle ramps, a floodable docking well for landing craft and amphibious tractors, and a helicopter hangar with two landing decks (forward and abaft of the superstructure). The hangar can accommodate four Helix helicopters (formerly Ka-25 Hormone-C); they can be moved through the superstructure and down a ramp to the forward landing area. The funnel uptakes are split to provide the helicopter pass through. The float-in docking well can hold three Lebed air-cushion landing craft or six Ondatra conventional landing craft.

The ship has a flat bottom and large tank deck with bow doors to permit the unloading of amphibious vehicles into the water or across the beach. Ten light or medium tanks plus 30 armored personnel carriers can be transported.

The barrage rocket launcher is mounted atop a four-level structure offset to starboard, forward of the main superstructure. The four Gatling guns are mounted alongside the pylon mast. There is a four-level "stack" of canisters containing life rafts arranged outboard of the rocket-launcher structure.

Electronics: The Moskalenko has a Round House TACAN installation.

Names: Ivan Rogov was a political officer and Chief of the Main Political Directorate of the Soviet Navy during World War II; Aleksandr Nikolayev was the chief political officer of the Northern Fleet during World War II. Migrofan Moskalenko was logistics chief of the Baltic Fleet during World War II.

Operational: The lead ship, the Ivan Rogov, was transferred to the Pacific Fleet in 1979 (with the aircraft carrier Minsk); she returned to the Baltic in the fall of 1981 for the *Zapad* amphibious exercises. The Nikolayev transferred to the Pacific Fleet in late 1983 followed by the Rogov in late 1986.

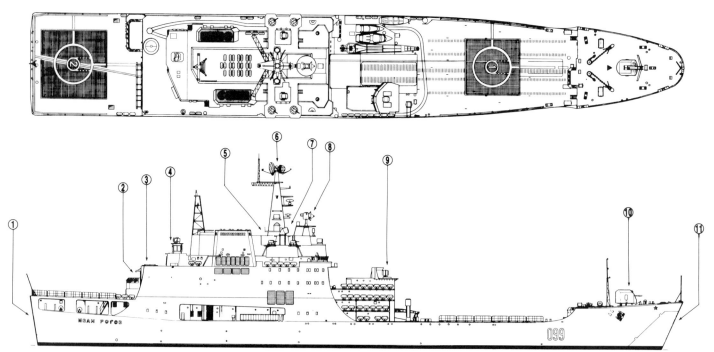

Ivan Rogov: 1. Stern gate   2. helicopter control station   3. SA-N-4 launcher (retracted)   4. Pop Group radar   5. 30-mm Gatling guns   6. Head Net-C radar   7. Bass Tilt radar director   8. Owl Screech radar   9. 122-mm barrage rocket launcher   10. twin 76.2-mm AA guns   11. bow doors (M.J. Dodgson)

The IVAN ROGOV with a Ka-25 Hormone-C on her flight deck and the doors open for access to her helicopter hangar/drive-through to the forward helicopter deck/parking area. The large stern gate opens into the docking well; the stern anchor is for retracting the ship after being beached. (1980, Royal Navy)

The IVAN ROGOV has bow doors faired into her hull and an internal ramp for unloading vehicles through the open doors. The four-level structure forward of the bridge mounts a 122-mm rocket launcher for shore bombardment during amphibious landings. Behind it is the passage through the ship's superstructure.

25+ TANK LANDING SHIPS: ROPUCHA CLASS

Name	Completed
ALEKSANDR SHABLIN	
BOBRUYSK	1975–1978
TSEZAR KUNIKOV	1982–1987
22 units	

Builders:	Stocznia Polnocny, Gdańsk (Poland)
Displacement:	2,600 tons standard
	3,600 tons full load
Length:	370 ft 8 in (113.0 m) overall
Beam:	45 ft 11 in (14.0 m)
Draft:	9 ft 6 in (2.9 m)
Propulsion:	2 diesel engines; 10,000 bhp; 2 shafts
Speed:	18 knots
Range:	3,500 n.miles at 16 knots
	6,000 n.miles at 12 knots
Complement:	approx. 70
Troops:	approx. 230
Helicopters:	no facilities
Missiles/rockets:	2 40-tube 122-mm barrage rocket launchers in some ships
	4 quad SA-N-5 or SA-N-8 anti-air launchers [32] in some ships
Guns:	4 57-mm/80-cal AA (2 twin)
Radars:	2 Don-2 (navigation)
	1 Muff Cob (fire control)
	1 Strut Curve (air search)

These ships are smaller than the previous, Soviet-built Alligator class. As of early 1990, 5 units were in the Northern Fleet, 10 in the Baltic, 3 in the Black Sea, and 7 in the Pacific Fleet.

Class: Eleven ships were completed from 1975 to 1978; the remainder from 1982 onward.

One ship of this class was transferred to South Yemen in 1979. No ships of this type are in Polish service. The East German Frosch class has some similarities although it is a significantly smaller design.

Classification: Soviet BDK type.

Design: The Ropucha class has traditional LST lines with the superstructure aft and both bow and stern ramps for unloading vehicles. Cargo capacity is 450 tons with a usable deck space of 600 m². Up to 25 armored personnel carriers can be embarked. The superstructure is big and boxy, with large, side-by-side funnels. The Ropucha class, as well as the Polnocny class, has a long sliding hatch cover above the bow section to permit vehicles and cargo to be lowered into the tank deck by dockside cranes.

Several ships have been fitted with Grail or Gremlin short-range missiles. There are provisions for two barrage rocket launchers on the forecastle, but they have only been installed in a few units.

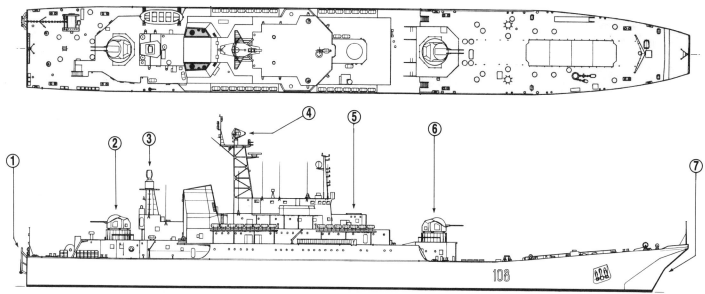

ROPUCHA: 1. stern gate   2. twin 57-mm AA guns   3. Muff Cobb radar director   4. Strut Curve radar   5. SA-N-4 launcher (retracted)   6. twin 57-mm AA guns   7. bow doors (M.J. Dodgson)

A Polish-built Ropucha-class LST in the Far East. The Polish Polnocny shipyard at Gdańsk has built most of the Soviet Navy's amphibious ships as well as many noncombatant ships for the Red fleet. The Polish Navy does not operate this class of landing ships. Life raft canisters are on the long forecastle deck (as well as along the superstructure). (1990, JMSDF)

This Ropucha-class tank landing ship is fitted with 122-mm rocket launchers on her main deck, forward of the deck structure and twin 57-mm gun mount.

Ropucha-class tank landing ship (1982, U.S. Navy)

14 TANK LANDING SHIPS: ALLIGATOR CLASS

Name	Name	Completed
ALEKSANDR TORTSEV	NIKOLAY VILKOV	
DONETSKIY SHAKHTER	NIKOLAY OBYEKOV	
ILYA AZAROV	PETR IL' ICHYEV	
KOMSOMOLETS KARELIYY	SERGEI LAZO	1964–1967
KRASNAYA PRESNYA	TOMSKIY KOMSOMOLETS	
KRYMSKIY KOMSOMOLETS	VORONEZHSKIY KOMSOMOLETS	
NIKOLAY FIL'CHENKOV	50 LET SHEFTSVA V.K.L.S.M.	

Builders:	Yantar/Kaliningrad
Displacement	3,400 tons standard
	4,700 tons full load
Length:	370 ft (112.8m) overall
Beam:	50 ft 2 in (15.3 m)
Draft:	14 ft 5 in (4.4 m)
Propulsion:	2 diesel engines; 8,000 bhp; 2 shafts
Speed:	18 knots
Range:	9,000 n.miles at 16 knots
	14,000 n.miles at 10 knots
Complement:	approx. 75
Troops:	approx. 300
Helicopters:	no facilities

Missiles/rockets:	1 40-tube 122-mm barrage rocket launcher in most ships
	3 quad SA-N-5 Grail anti-air launchers [24] in some ships
Guns:	2 57-mm/70-cal AA (1 twin)
	4 25-mm/60-cal AA (2 twin) in FIL'CHENKOV and VILKOV
Radars:	2 Don-2 (navigation) and/or Spin Trough (search)

Built on traditional LST lines, these ships are less attractive than the later Ropucha class but have a significantly larger cargo capacity. Two ships are assigned to the Northern Fleet, 2 to the Baltic Fleet, 5 to the Black Sea Fleet, and 5 to the Pacific Fleet.

Classification: Soviet BDK type.

Design: The Alligator class has a superstructure-aft configuration with bow and stern ramps for unloading vehicles. The arrangement of individual ships differs; early units have three cranes—one 15-ton capacity and two 5-ton capacity; later ships have one crane. There are two to four large hatches above the tank deck to permit vehicles and cargo to be lowered by shipboard or dockside cranes. Later ships have an enclosed bridge and a rocket launcher forward, and the last two ships have 25-mm guns aft.

About 25 to 30 tanks or armored personnel carriers, or 1,500 tons of cargo, can be carried; only about 600 tons can be carried for beaching operations.

The Alligator LSTs resemble small, superstructure-aft cargo ships. They have strengthened vehicle decks and bow doors and ramp. This Pacific Fleet unit has two positions just forward of the superstructure for SA-N-5/8 anti-aircraft missiles. The vehicles on her deck are BTR-60 armored personnel carriers. (1989, JMSDF)

An Alligator LST in the Baltic Fleet with a 122-mm rocket launcher for shore bombardment fitted on a small structure on the forecastle. (West German Navy)

9 MEDIUM LANDING SHIPS: POLNOCNY C CLASS

Completed:	1970–1973
Builders:	Stocznia Polnocny, Gdańsk (Poland)
Displacement:	1,150 tons full load
Length:	266 ft 8 in (81.3 m) overall
Beam:	33 ft 2 in (10.1 m)
Draft:	6 ft 11 in (2.1 m)
Propulsion:	2 diesel engines; 5,000 bhp; 2 shafts
Speed:	18 knots
Range:	1,800 n.miles at 18 knots
	3,000 n.miles at 14 knots
Complement:	approx. 40
Troops:	approx. 180
Helicopters:	no facilities
Missiles/rockets:	2 18-tube 140-mm barrage rocket launchers
	4 quad SA-N-5 or SA-N-8 anti-air launchers [32]
Guns:	4 30-mm/65-cal close-in (2 twin)
Radars:	1 Drum Tilt (fire control)
	1 Spin Trough (search)

The Polnocny design represents the largest series of landing ships in service with any navy. There are three distinct Polnocny sub-designs, identified by Western intelligence with suffix letters according to their NATO code names (derived from the yard where they were built).[1] Most of the Soviet units are of the B variant. The C variant, described above, has a longer hull and superstructure.

Western intelligence still lists four ships of the earlier MP-4 class in service as amphibious ships; the combined assignment of the 37 Polnocnys and four MP-4s is:

   5 Northern Fleet
 10 Baltic Fleet
  6 Black Sea Fleet
 15 Caspian Sea Flotilla
  5 Pacific Fleet

Class: Thirty-six ships of this class have been transferred to several nations since 1966:

	Polnocny A	Polnocny B	Polnocny C
Algeria	1		
Angola		3	
Cuba		2	
Egypt	3		
Ethiopia		2	
India	2		8
Iraq			3
Libya			3
Somalia		1	
Vietnam		3	
S. Yemen		4	

[1] Initially NATO designated the Polnocny classes with Roman numerals; subsequently the designations were changed to the A-B-C scheme.

Some of the C variant transfers have a platform for light helicopters installed immediately forward of the superstructure. Another 22 ships of this design—12 type A and 10 type B—were constructed at the Polnocny yard for the Polish Navy (completed 1964–1971). One Soviet B-type ship has been modified for use as a trials ship (see chapter 23). Thus, a total of 96 units of all variants have been completed.

Classification: Soviet SDK type.

Design: The Polnocnys have a conventional landing-ship appearance with bow doors. The A class has a convex bow form while the later series have a concave bow. Superstructure and mast details differ among classes and individual ships. Cargo capacity is about 180 tons in the A and B classes and 250 tons in the C class. The earlier ships can carry six to eight armored personnel carriers and the C class about eight. There are minor differences within the classes.

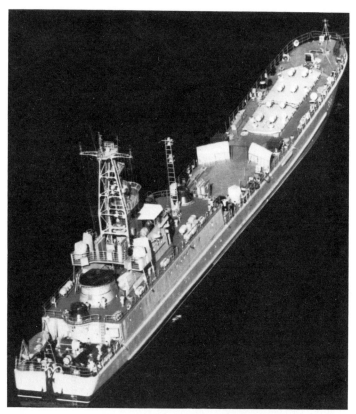

Polnocny C landing ship with lattice mast and superstructure extended forward. There are two rocket launchers on the forecastle ahead of blast deflectors. The Drum Tilt fire control radar is forward of the mast; twin 30-mm gun mounts are fitted forward and aft on the superstructure.

A Polish-built Polnocny C in the Soviet Navy. The Polnocny design is the largest series of landing ships built by any nation since World War II.

23 MEDIUM LANDING SHIPS: POLNOCNY B CLASS

Completed:	1968–1970
Builders:	Stocznia Polnocny, Gdańsk (Poland)
Displacement:	800 tons full load
Length:	242 ft 9 in (74.0 m) overall
Beam:	28 ft 2 in (8.6 m)
Draft:	6 ft 7 in (2.0 m)
Propulsion:	2 diesel engines; 5,000 bhp; 2 shafts
Speed:	18 knots
Range:	900 n.miles at 18 knots
	1,500 n.miles at 14 knots
Complement:	approx. 40
Troops:	approx. 100
Helicopters:	no facilities
Missiles/rockets:	2 18-tube 140-mm barrage rocket launchers
	4 quad SA-N-5 or SA-N-8 anti-air launchers [32]
Guns:	2 or 4 30-mm/65-cal close-in (1 or 2 twin)
Radars:	1 Drum Tilt (fire control)
	1 Spin Trough (search)

This design has a more streamlined superstructure and funnel. One unit was converted in the 1980s for service as a trials ship.

Polnocny B landing ship with tall, streamlined funnel; the other Soviet Polnocnys have short squat funnels. On the long forecastle are 140-mm rocket launchers and, farther forward, life raft canisters.

5 MEDIUM LANDING SHIPS: POLNOCNY A CLASS

Completed:	1963–1967(?)
Builders:	Stocznia Polnocny, Gdańsk (Poland)
Displacement:	770 tons full load
Length:	239 ft 5 in (73.0 m) overall
Beam:	28 ft 2 in (8.6 m)
Draft:	6 ft 3 in (1.9 m)
Propulsion:	2 diesel engines; 5,000 bhp; 2 shafts
Speed:	19 knots
Range:	900 n.miles at 18 knots
	1,500 n.miles at 14 knots
Complement:	approx. 35
Troops:	approx. 100
Helicopters:	no facilities
Missiles/rockets:	2 18-tube 140-mm barrage rocket launchers
	up to 4 quad SA-N-5 or SA-N-8 anti-air launchers [up to 32] in most ships
Guns:	2 30-mm/65-cal close-in (1 twin)
	or 2 14.5-mm machine guns (1 twin)
Radars:	1 Spin Trough (search)

Twin 18-tube 140-mm bombardment rocket launchers on a Polish Polnocny-class LSM. Forward of the rocket launchers are life-raft canisters. (1989, West German Navy)

This was the original Polnocny design.

Several Polnocny A and B ships have been modified to support mine countermeasure operations. These ships carry two radio-controlled boats that tow line-charge devices for clearing mines from the assault area. The ships have long troughs along the sides (see photo).

A Polnocny A–class ship fitted with SA-N-5/8 anti-aircraft rocket launchers just forward of the superstructure. The Drum Tilt radar is on a low platform forward of the mast. (1987, JMSDF)

A Polnocny A refitted to serve as a minesweeper support ship; she carries a pair of unmanned vehicles on chutes on the fantail with explosive-charge cables fitted along the sides of the ship. (1984, JMSDF)

4 MEDIUM LANDING SHIPS: MP-4 CLASS

Completed:	late 1950s
Builders:	(USSR)
Displacement:	780 tons full load
Length:	183 ft 8 in (56.0 m) overall
Beam:	29 ft 6 in (9.0 m)
Draft:	8 ft 10 in (2.7 m)
Propulsion:	2 diesel engines; 1,200 bhp; 2 shafts
Speed:	10 knots
Range:	5,500 n. miles at 12 knots
Complement:	approx. 50
Helicopters:	no facilities
Missiles:	none
Guns:	4 25-mm AA (2 twin)
Radars:	

These are the survivors of 25 MP-4 class cargo ships built for Soviet service; one other unit was built in Egypt. They are probably laid up in reserve and their condition is doubtful.

Classification: MP is a NATO designation. The original NATO code name for this class was Uzka.

LANDING SHIPS: MP-8 CLASS

Sixteen of these ships were completed from 1961. Full load displacement was 1,200 tons. All have been stricken.

LANDING SHIPS: MP-6 CLASS

These ten medium landing ships were converted from BIRA-class freighters from 1958 to 1961. Subsequently, their bow doors were welded shut and they were employed as freighters. The surviving ships have been reconfigured as auxiliaries; see chapter 23.

16 UTILITY LANDING SHIPS: VYDRA CLASS

Completed:	1967–1969
Builders:	(USSR)
Displacement:	425 tons standard
	600 tons full load
Length:	180 ft 1 in (54.9 m) overall
Beam:	24 ft 1 in (7.6 m)
Draft:	6 ft 7 in (2.0 m)
Propulsion:	2 diesel engines; 800 bhp; 2 shafts
Speed:	12 knots
Range:	1,900 n.miles at 12 knots
	2,700 n.miles at 10 knots
Complement:	approx. 20
Troops:	approx. 100
Helicopters:	no facilities
Missiles/rockets:	none
Guns:	none
Radars:	1 Spin Trough (search)

These are utility landing ships with an open tank deck; similar to Western LCU/LCT types but larger. Cargo capacity is approximately 250 tons.

Class: An estimated 56 of these ships were built. Units of this type have been transferred to Bulgaria (10) and Egypt (10).

Classification: Soviet DK type.

Vydra-class utility landing ship. (Royal Danish Navy)

CHAPTER 21

Landing Craft and Vehicles

A Pomornik-class air cushion landing craft on a Black Sea beach. Her bow ramp is lowered to permit the unloading of vehicles. This craft is fitted with a pair of shore bombardment rocket launchers in addition to 30-mm Gatling guns. (1989, U.S. Navy)

The following landing craft and vehicles support Soviet Naval Infantry operations. More than 80 air-cushion landing craft of various sizes are in Soviet naval service.

An air-cushion vehicle known as Pelikan has been reported, completed about 1986 (see chapter 19).

The Soviet Union also operates the world's largest fleet of commercial air-cushion vehicles.

3+ AIR-CUSHION LANDING CRAFT: POMORNIK CLASS

Completed:	1986—
Builders:	Dekabristov, Leningrad
	Yuznaya Tochka, Feodosiya
Displacement:	360 tons full load
Length:	193 ft 6 in (59.0 m) overall
Beam:	68 ft 11 in (21.0 m)
Draft:	
Propulsion:	2 gas turbines (NK-12) for lift fans; 24,200 shp
	3 gas turbines (NK-12) for propulsion (3 aircraft propellers); 36,300 shp
Speed:	approx. 55 knots on air cushion
Range:	
Complement:	approx. 40
Troops:	approx. 220

Missiles/rockets:	1 40-tube 122-mm barrage rocket launcher
	2 quad SA-N-5 or SA-N-8 anti-air launchers [16]
Guns:	2 30-mm/65-cal close-in (multi-barrel)
Radars:	1 Bass Tilt (fire control) in second and later units
	1 Positive-E (air/surface search) in first unit
	1 . . . . . . (navigation)

The Pomornik is the largest Soviet air-cushion vehicle. Note the distinctive superstructure. The Dekabristov facility was the lead yard for this craft.

Cargo capacity is rated at four PT-76 amphibious tanks, or three medium tanks plus 80 to 100 troops, or some 220 troops, unloaded over bow and stern ramps.

Electronics: The Pomornik has a radome similar to the Band Stand, but slightly larger in diameter and about 20 percent shorter.

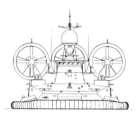

Pomornik-class air-cushion landing craft. The craft has bow and stern ramps for loading/unloading vehicles and troops. (M.J. Dodgson)

The Pomornik is the world's largest air cushion craft, part of the Soviet Navy's extensive capability for amphibious assault operations in the seas surrounding the USSR. There are bow and stern ramps in the craft; in addition to the three propulsion gas turbines at the stern, there are four lift engines. (West German Navy)

4+ AIR-CUSHION LANDING CRAFT: TSAPLYA CLASS

Completed:	1982—
Builders:	Yuznaya Tochka, Feodosiya
	Ussuri, Khabarovsk
Displacement:	115 tons full load
Length:	98 ft 5 in (30.0 m) overall
Beam:	42 ft 8 in (13.0 m)
Draft:	
Propulsion:	2 gas turbines; 8,000 shp
Speed:	

Range:	
Complement:	6
Troops:	approx. 160
Missiles:	
Guns:	
Radars:	

This class can reportedly carry one PT-76 amphibious tank plus 80 troops, or 160 troops, or 45 tons of cargo.

2+ AIR-CUSHION LANDING CRAFT: UTENOK CLASS

Completed: 1982—
Builders: Yuznaya Tochka, Feodosiya
Displacement: 70 tons full load
Length: 86 ft 3 in (26.3 m) overall
Beam: 42 ft 8 in (13.0 m)
Draft:
Propulsion: 1 gas turbine; 2 propellers
Speed: 65 knots on air cushion
Range:
Complement:
Troops:
Missiles:
Guns: 4 30-mm close-in (2 twin)
Radars:

This landing-craft class can carry one main battle tank plus 80 troops.

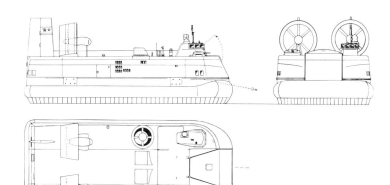

Lebed-class air-cushion landing craft.
(Siegfried Breyer)

20 AIR-CUSHION LANDING CRAFT: LEBED CLASS

Completed: 1976—
Builders: (USSR)
Displacement: 85 tons full load
Length: 81 ft 4 in (24.8 m) overall
Beam: 35 ft 5 in (10.8 m)
Draft:
Propulsion: 1 gas turbine for lift
2 gas turbines for propulsion (2 aircraft propellers)
Speed: 70 knots on air cushion
Range: 100 n.miles at 65 knots
Complement: 250 n.miles at 60 knots
Troops: approx. 120
Missiles: none
Guns: 1 30-mm/65-cal close-in (multibarrel)
Radars:

These landing craft are the type seen being carried by the amphibious ship IVAN ROGOV. The Lebeds can carry two PT-76 amphibious tanks, or 120 troops, or some 45 tons of cargo.

Design: The control cabin is offset to port with the Gatling gun mounted to starboard.

20 AIR-CUSHION LANDING CRAFT: AIST CLASS

Completed: 1971–1986
Builders: Dekabristov, Leningrad
Displacement: 220 tons full load
Length: 156 ft 9 in (47.8 m) overall
Beam: 57 ft 5 in (17.5 m)
Draft: 1 ft (0.3 m)
Propulsion: 2 gas turbines (NK-12MV) for 2 lift fans + 4 propellers (2 pusher/2 tractor)
Speed: 45 knots on air cushion
Range: 100 n.miles at 45 knots
200 n.miles at 40 knots
Complement:
Troops: approx. 220
Missiles: 2 quad SA-N-5 or SA-N-8 anti-air launchers in later units
Guns: 4 30-mm/65-cal close-in (2 twin)
Radars: 1 Drum Tilt (fire control)
1 Spin Trough (search)

These are the world's second largest military air-cushion vehicles. They can carry four PT-76 amphibious tanks, or two main battle tanks plus 220 troops or cargo. Bow and stern ramps are fitted for the "drive-through" cargo space.

Both 30-mm gun mounts are forward (only one mount was provided on the prototype).

The Soviet Union has led in the development of air cushion landing craft, such as this large Lebed moving at high speed in the Baltic Sea. There is a 30-mm Gatling gun forward on the starboard side with the control cabin/cockpit on the port side. The (closed) bow ramp is visible as are the large shrouded propellers and rudders. (Royal Danish Navy)

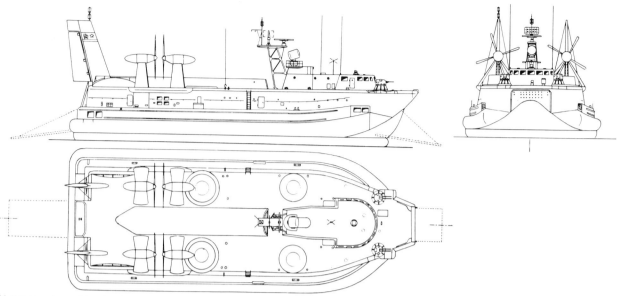

Aist-class air-cushion landing craft. (Siegfried Breyer)

An Aist air-cushion landing craft in the Baltic Sea showing the unusual arrangement of two tractor and two pusher propeller pods mounted forward of the twin rudders; the vertical propeller wells are visible amidships. Two 30-mm twin gun mounts are forward. (1988, West German Navy)

A PT-76 amphibious tank rolls ashore from an Aist air-cushion landing craft. These landing craft permit vehicles and troops to be unloaded on dry land. The 30-mm guns are at maximum elevation. (The U.S. Navy's smaller air-cushion landing craft are unarmed.)

30 AIR-CUSHION LANDING CRAFT: GUS CLASS

Completed:	1970–1974
Builders:	Dekabristov, Leningrad
Displacement:	27 tons full load
Length:	69 ft 10 in (21.3 m) overall
Beam:	23 ft 3 in (7.1 m)
Draft:	8 in (0.2 m)
Propulsion:	1 gas turbine for lift fan
	2 gas turbines for propulsion (2 aircraft propellers)
Speed:	60 knots on air cushion
Range:	185 n.miles at 50 knots
	200 n.miles at 43 knots
Complement:	
Troops:	approx. 25
Missiles:	none
Guns:	none
Radars:	1 . . . . . . (navigation)

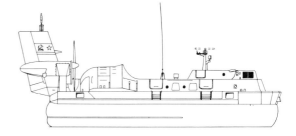

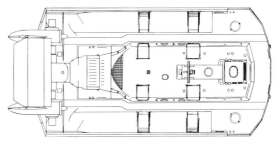

These were the first naval air-cushion vehicles to be produced in significant numbers. They cannot carry vehicles. There is a training version with two control cabins.

The Gus is a naval version of the civilian Skate air-cushion vehicle.

Gus-class air cushion landing craft. (Siegfried Breyer)

A Gus air-cushion landing craft in the Baltic Sea. This was the first air-cushion landing craft to be series produced for the Soviet Navy, with just over 30 units being built. (1985, Sovfoto)

A Gus air-cushion landing craft at high speed in the Caspian Sea. These craft carry only troops, not vehicles. (1987, Sovfoto)

16 LANDING CRAFT: ONDATRA CLASS

Completed:	1978–1979
Builders:	(USSR)
Displacement:	90 tons standard
	140 tons full load
Length:	79 ft 5 in (24.2 m) overall
Beam:	16 ft 5 in (5.0 m)
Draft:	4 ft 11 in (1.5 m)
Propulsion:	2 diesel engines; 600 bhp; 2 shafts
Speed:	10 knots
Range:	500 n.miles at 5 knots
Complement:	4
Troops:	
Guns:	none

These personnel/vehicle landing craft have a bow ramp. One is normally embarked in the IVAN ROGOV-class amphibious ships for use as a tug for the Lebed-class air-cushion vehicles. A ROGOV's docking well could accommodate six of these craft.

Class: Two units have been transferred to North Yemen.

LANDING CRAFT: T-4 CLASS

All of the T-4 landing craft are believed to have been discarded. These were small, bow-ramp landing craft that could carry a PT-76 amphibious tank.

The T-4 has been built in large numbers, with units transferred to several other navies.

CHAPTER 22

Wing-In-Ground Effect Vehicles

An artist's concept of the Utka anti-ship WIG vehicle. The vehicle has six fuselage-mounted SS-N-22 anti-ship missiles. Its eight engines are forward of the stub wing. (U.S. Department of Defense)

The Soviet Union has an active air vehicle program popularly known as the Wing-In-Ground (WIG) effect vehicles.[1] At least two combat-configured WIGs have been developed—an amphibious assault variant given the NATO code name Orlan and an anti-ship missile variant given the code name Utka.

The WIG vehicles generally resemble flying boats in configuration and normally fly in "ground effect" over water. These craft can come down on water, ice, or land (e.g., beaches). The configuration used by the Soviets is known as an *ekranoplan,* which means an aircraft that flies near the "screen," or surface. These are pure wing-in-ground effect vehicles that can fly out-of-ground effect if required.

The Soviets apparently began a major WIG development program in the mid-1950s and pursued several different design approaches to achieve an optimal solution. Several small WIG vehicles were probably flown and a large prototype referred to in the West as the "Caspian sea monster" (CAP-A). This was a vehicle in excess of 500 tons with a wing span of 120 feet (36.6 m) and length of 300 feet (91.5 m), powered by ten turbofan engines. A small craft some 200 feet (61 m) long was also flown (designated CAP-B).

One WIG vehicle carried Aeroflot livery and bore the registration CCCP-10687. That vehicle, now in the Soviet Air Forces Museum in Monino, was designated VVS-15 by the Soviets. It was built to evaluate the WIG concepts of designer Roberto Bartini, who apparently directed a WIG design bureau (OKB) at Taganorog, on the Sea of Azov, in the post–World War II period. (Taganorog was also the site of the G.M. Beriev design bureau responsible for the Be-42 Albatross flying boat; see chapter 27. There may well be a direct relationship between the WIG and advanced flying boat projects.)

---

1. See Floyd C. Painter, "Soviet Surface Effect Vehicles May Challenge Western Forces," *Defense Electronics* (June 1987), pp. 133–148; also, Geoffrey S. Sommer, "Ekranoplan: The Soviet Sea Monster," U.S. Naval Institute *Proceedings* (October 1988), pp. 144–145.

The Caspian Sea monsters and subsequent WIGs have the Power-Augmented-Ram (PAR) configuration with two sets of power plants, one for the generation of forward thrust and one for PAR. When the PAR engines are in operation the thrust output of the turbofan engines is directed downward under the main wing by thrust deflectors to generate an air cushion during transition flight. During flight operations the WIG vehicle initially acts like a displacement hull, moving through the water or over sand or ice like a conventional seaplane. Large main wing flaps are brought into play to increase the ram air lift under the wings. This causes the hull to unload and transit from the displacement to the planing mode. Further transition to flight is achieved by using thrust deflection until the horizontal stabilizer becomes effective.

Throughout the transition phase, forward motion is provided by the craft's main power plant and the dynamic lift generated by the wings replaces the static lift provided by the PAR as the craft becomes airborne and attains the optimum cushion balance. When the horizontal stabilizer becomes effective it is used for trim balance.

When the proper balance is achieved, some or all of the augmenting power can be secured, and the vehicle can be operated economically in ground effect on its main power plant. Power augmentation can be employed to increase the speed of flight or to help the WIG clear obstacles.

These craft generally have a limited ability to fly as aircraft, but longitudinal stability during flight out of ground effect is critical and maneuverability would be very restricted. Also, the significant power required for full flight would counter the fuel economy feature of the WIG concept.

The WIG's low-altitude, high-speed flight characteristics require automated flight control systems.

The Orlan WIG is an amphibious assault vehicle; several units have been produced. The Orlan has a bow ramp for unloading troops and light vehicles onto the beach or onto ice. (U.S. DoD)

1 + (?) ANTI-SHIP MISSILE VEHICLES: UTKA CLASS

Crew:	
Engines:	8 turbofan
Weights:	
Dimensions:	
Speed:	
Ceiling:	
Range:	
Armament:	6 SS-N-22 anti-ship launchers (3 twin)
Radar:	1 . . . . . . (targeting)
	1 . . . . . . (navigation)

The Utka is an anti-ship WIG vehicle armed with six SS-N-22 anti-ship missiles. At least one vehicle had been built by the late 1980s.

The Utka resembles a flying boat with eight turbofan engines mounted in pods fitted horizontally, four to each side, just aft of the aircraft-type cockpit. Farther aft is a broad, low-aspect-ratio wing with fixed wingtip floats. The flying boat hull ends with a T-tail featuring a large vertical stabilizer and immense, slightly swept horizontal tailplane.

The six SS-N-22 missiles are fitted in launchers mounted in pairs atop the fuselage. The launchers are fixed in elevation. A thimble-shaped radome is fitted in the nose and a second, search radar may be fitted just below the horizontal tailplane.

3 + AMPHIBIOUS ASSAULT VEHICLES: ORLAN CLASS

Crew:		
Troops:	approx. 400	
Engines:	2 Soloviev D-30KP turbofan; 26,500 lbst (12,020 kg) each	
	1 Kuznetsov NK-12M turboprop; 15,000 shp	
Weights:	empty	approx. 200,000 lb (90,719 kg)
	maximum	400,000+ lb (181,437+ kg)
Dimensions:	span	100 ft (30.5 m)
	length	200 ft (61.0 m)
Speed:	cruise	180 mph (290 km/h)
	maximum	350 mph (563 km/h)
Ceiling:	cruise IGE 40 ft (12.2 m)	
	maximum	2,000 ft (610 m)
Range:	approx. 4,342 nm (8,050 km) with full payload	
Armament:		
Radar:	. . . . . . (navigation)	
	. . . . . . (search)	

The Orlan is an amphibious assault vehicle, configured to carry troops and light vehicles that can be unloaded through a bow-opening.

The Orlan has stub wings with fixed wingtip floats, and a T-tail with a single, large turboprop engine fitted atop the horizontal stabilizer. The Kuznetsov turboprop has twin, contrarotating propellers. Nozzles fitted to both sides of the forward fuselage direct the exhaust from twin turbofan engines downward, creating the PAR effect. The bow opens for unloading troops and light combat vehicles.

(The U.S. Navy's R3Y Tradewind flying boat of the 1950s had a similar unloading configuration; that aircraft was referred to as a "flying LST.")

The aircraft has a thimble-like nose radome and a second radar antenna atop the fuselage.

CHAPTER 23

Naval Auxiliaries

Soviet auxiliary ships come in all shapes and sizes. Here the naval Goryn-class oceangoing tug SB-524 (left) and cargo ship TURGAY of the YUNIY PARTIZAN support a Foxtrot-class submarine. The use of a variety of naval auxiliaries and merchant ships to support submarines has reduced the Navy's requirement for specialized submarine tenders.

Most of the ships described in this chapter are manned by naval personnel. Many cargo ships, oilers, and tug-type ships, however, are civilian manned as are the Ob'-class hospital ships. The hospital ships have civilian crews but carry naval medical personnel.

The icebreakers, supply ships, and armed tugs operated by the KGB Maritime Border Troops are listed in chapter 26.

Auxiliary ships in this chapter are listed in the following order:

Submarine Support Ships
Repair Ships
Salvage and Rescue Ships
Mooring Tenders/Lift Ships
Heavy Lift Ships
Cable Ships
Missile Transports
Oilers and Tankers
Special-Purpose Tankers
Water Tankers
Cargo and Supply Ships
Hospital Ships
Training Ships
Experimental and Trials Ships
Generator Ships
Degaussing and Deperming Ships
Noise Measurement Ships
Icebreakers
Fleet Tugs
Service Craft and Target Craft

Western intelligence in 1989 credited the Soviet Navy with operating some 810 auxiliary ships in the following categories:

40	tankers (point-to-point carriers)
21	oilers (underway replenishment)
28*	other replenishment (store ships, water carriers)
70	tenders and support ships (including munition carriers)
150*	tug, salvage, and submarine rescue ships
500*	other auxiliaries (including AGIs, research, surveying, cargo, and miscellaneous ships)

*Includes units operated by the KGB Maritime Border Troops.

SUBMARINE SUPPORT SHIPS

These ships are similar to Western submarine tenders and depot ships. They provide specialized services to submarines in Soviet base areas and, on occasion, in remote areas. In addition, the Ugra and Don classes provide extensive command and control facilities for fleet or task force commanders.

The large submarine salvage and rescue ships of the EL'BRUS class may also have some submarine support capabilities (see pages 236–237).

7 SUBMARINE SUPPORT SHIPS: UGRA CLASS

Name	Name	Completed
IVAN KOLYSHKIN	TOBOL	
IVAN KUCHERENKO	VOLGA	} 1963–1972
IVAN VAKHRAMEEV	2 units	

Builders:	Black Sea Shipyard, Nikolayev (south)
Displacement:	6,750 tons standard
	9,600 tons full load
Length:	475 ft 7 in (145.0 m) overall
Beam:	58 ft (17.7 m)
Draft:	21 ft (6.4 m)
Propulsion:	4 diesel engines; 8,000 bhp; 2 shafts
Speed:	17 knots
Range:	21,000 n.miles at 10 knots
Complement:	approx. 450
Helicopters:	landing deck; hangar facilities for 1 Ka-25 Hormone-C in IVAN KOLYSHKIN
Missiles:	2 quad SA-N-5 or SA-N-8 anti-air launchers [16]
Guns:	8 57-mm/80-cal AA (4 twin)
Radars:	1 to 3 Don-2 (navigation)
	2 Muff Cob (fire control)
	1 Strut Curve (air search)
EW systems:	4 Watch Dog

These are enlarged versions of the previous Don-class submarine support ships. All have some flagship capabilities (see Design notes).

Class: Two additional ships of this design are employed as training ships and are listed separately (see page 265). One Ugra-class submarine tender was transferred to India upon completion, in December 1968; her armament and radars were different than the Soviet Navy suite, possibly to simplify maintenance by the Indian Navy.

Classification: Soviet PB type.

Design: These ships are larger than the previous Don class, with a larger forward superstructure and a shorter funnel. The ships have extensive workshops and can provide submarines with food, diesel fuel, fresh water, and torpedoes. They are fitted with one 10-ton-capacity and two 6-ton-capacity cranes. Extensive modifications have changed the appearance of these ships from their original configuration and from each other.

The IVAN KOLYSHKIN has been fitted with a helicopter hangar; she retains the after twin 57-mm gun mounts outboard of the hangar. The others have had the after superstructure built up; the IVAN KUCHERENKO and VOLGA have large lattice masts aft mounting Vee Cone communications antennas.

6 SUBMARINE SUPPORT SHIPS: DON CLASS

Name	Name	Completed
DMITRIY GALKIN	MAGOMED GADZIEV	
FYODOR VIDYAEV	MAGADANSKIY KOMSOMOLETS	} 1958–1961
KAMCHATSKIY KOMSOMOLETS	VIKTOR KOTEL'NIKOV	

Builders:	Black Sea Shipyard, Nikolayev (south)
Displacement:	6,730 tons standard
	9,000 tons full load
Length:	459 ft 2 in (140.0 m) overall
Beam:	58 ft (17.7 m)
Draft:	21 ft (6.4 m)
Propulsion:	4 diesel engines; 8,000 bhp; 2 shafts
Speed:	17 knots
Range:	21,000 n.miles at 10 knots
Complement:	approx. 450
Helicopters:	landing deck in MAGADANSKIY KOMSOMOLETS and VIKTOR KOTEL'NIKOV
Guns:	4 100-mm/56-cal DP (4 single) except 2 guns in KOTEL'NIKOV; none in MAGADANSKIY KOMSOMOLETS
	8 57-mm/70-cal AA (4 twin)
	8 25-mm/60-cal AA (4 twin) in VIDYAEV
Radars:	1 or 2 Don-2 (navigation)
	2 Hawk Screech (fire control) except removed from DMITRIY GALKIN and FYODOR VIDYAEV
	1 Slim Net (air search)
	1 Sun Visor-B (fire control) except none in MAGADANSKIY KOMSOMOLETS
EW systems:	2 Watch Dog

The Don-class ships were the Soviet Navy's first submarine tenders comparable to their Western counterparts.

Class: An additional ship of this class was transferred to Indonesia in 1962.

Classification: Soviet PB type.

Design: These are large submarine support ships and flagships. Details differ. Most ships retain the Wasp Head fire control director (with Sun Visor radar) atop the forward superstructure. The MAGADANSKIY KOMSOMOLETS was completed with a helicopter platform and without 100-mm guns. The VIKTOR KOTEL'NIKOV had her two after 100-mm gun mounts replaced by a helicopter platform.

At least two ships, the DMITRIY GALKIN and FYODOR VIDYAEV, have had Vee Cone antennas fitted to their after lattice masts, while the VIKTOR KOTEL'NIKOV has a pair of Big Ball satellite communication antennas (no Vee Cone). The ships with the Vee Cone have their Slim Net antenna on a lattice mast adjacent to the bridge structure.

The ships have a bow hook with a 100-ton lift capacity plus one 10-ton, two 5-ton, and two 1-ton cranes.

The Ivan Kolyshkin is probably the only Ugra-class submarine tender fitted with a helicopter hangar, which is topped with a Muff Cob fire control radar; twin 57-mm gun mounts are outboard of the hangar. The configurations of the Ugra and Don submarine tenders vary. Two other Ugras serve as naval training ships.

The Ivan Kucherenko is one of two Ugra-class ships with Vee Cone HF communications antennas atop the after lattice mast. The Volga is similarly fitted. The Kolyshkin has a larger helicopter deck than the other ships, extending farther aft. (1989, Japanese Maritime Self-Defense Force)

The Don-class submarine tender Viktor Kotel'nikov with the Big Ball SATCOM antennas abreast the lattice mast; note also the small control tower between the twin 57-mm mounts and the helicopter deck. A Wasp Head fire control director fitted with the Sun Visor-B radar tops the bridge structure.

The Dmitriy Galkin (above) and the Fyodor Vidyaev have Vee Cone HF antennas on the after lattice mast with the forward lattice mast carrying the Slim Net air search radar. Only two of the six Don-class ships have helicopter platforms.

The MAGADANSKIY KOMSOMOLETS is the only Don-class ship to have completely beached her 100-mm guns and associated Wasp Head fire control director. She retains the four 57-mm twin mounts, which are canvas covered in this view. Her helicopter platform differs from that of the VIKTOR KOTEL'NIKOV. (1986, JMSDF)

SUBMARINE SUPPORT SHIPS: "ATREK" CLASS

The six submarine support ships of this class, completed from 1955 to 1957, have been scrapped or reduced to hulks (some possibly used as accommodation ships).

See 4th edition, page 277.

REPAIR SHIPS

2 REPAIR SHIPS: MALINA CLASS

Name	Completed
PM-63	1984
PM-74	1985

Builders:	Black Sea Shipyard, Nikolayev (south)
Displacement:	12,000 tons full load
Length:	459 ft 1 in (140.0 m) overall
Beam:	72 ft 2 in (22.0 m)
Draft:	16 ft 5 in (5.0 m)
Propulsion:	4 gas turbines; 5,880 shp; 2 shafts
Speed:	17 knots
Range:	10,000 n.miles at 14 knots
Complement:	approx. 380
Helicopters:	no facilities
Guns:	none
Radars:	2 Palm Frond (navigation)

These are significantly larger than the previous Soviet naval repair ships. They have facilities for suppporting nuclear-propelled surface ships and submarines.

Classification: Soviet PM type.

Design: Fitted with two large, specialized 25-ton-capacity cranes for alongside recoring of nuclear submarines.

The Malina-class repair ships are the largest of this type in Soviet naval service. Their large open space forward belies their size. The Malinas have special facilities for nuclear support activities. There are two large cranes forward and twin booms amidships. (Royal Netherlands Navy)

29 REPAIR SHIPS: AMUR CLASS

Name	Name	Name	Completed
PM-5	PM-59	PM-97	
PM-9	PM-64	PM-129	
PM-10	PM-69	PM-138	
PM-15	PM-73	PM-139	1969–1978
PM-34	PM-75	PM-140	1981–1983
PM-37	PM-81	PM-156	1987–1988
PM-40	PM-82	PM-161	
PM-49	PM-86	PM-163	
PM-52	PM-92	PM-164	
PM-56	PM-94		

Builders:	Adolf Warski, Szczecin (Poland)
Displacement:	4,000 tons standard
	5,490 tons full load
Length:	399 ft 2 in (121.7 m) overall
Beam:	55 ft 9 in (17.0 m)
Draft:	16 ft 9 in (5.1 m)
Propulsion:	2 diesel engines; 4,000 bhp; 1 shaft
Speed:	12 knots
Range:	13,200 n.miles at 8 knots
Complement:	approx. 210
Helicopters:	no facilities
Guns:	none
Radars:	1 Don-2 (navigation)

These are enlarged Oskol-class repair ships. The PM-5 was the first ship of the second series (completed 1981–1983) and the PM-59 was the first of the third series (completed 1987); additional ships are likely.

Classification: Soviet PM type.

Design: These ships perform maintenance and repairs on surface ships and submarines. They have workshops and stock spare parts. Three cranes are fitted including two 5-ton-capacity cranes. Accommodations are provided for 200 crewmen of ships under repair.

The PM-5 and later ships have an elongated deckhouse on the forecastle (with mast protruding).

The repair ship PM-129 shows the clean lines of the Amur-class design. There are two light cranes forward and one aft on these relatively small ships. Note the mast-funnel configuration. No armament is fitted.

12 REPAIR SHIPS: OSKOL CLASS

Name	Name	Name	Completed
PM-2	PM-26	PM-68	
PM-20	PM-28	PM-146	1964–1967
PM-21	PM-51	PM-148	
PM-24	PM-62	PM-477	

Builders:	Adolf Warski, Szczecin (Poland)
Displacement:	2,500 tons standard
	3,000 tons full load
Length:	299 ft 9 in (91.4 m) overall
Beam:	40 ft (12.2 m)
Draft:	13 ft 1 in (4.0 m)
Propulsion:	2 diesel engines; 4,000 bhp; 1 shaft
Speed:	12 knots
Range:	9,000 n.miles at 8 knots
Complement:	approx. 60
Helicopters:	no facilities
Guns:	4 25-mm/60-cal AA (2 twin) in PM-24
	2 12.7-mm machine guns (1 twin) in some ships
Radars:	1 or 2 Don-2 (navigation)

These are small repair ships with limited capabilities. Each ship has one or two 3.4-ton-capacity cranes.

Classification: Soviet PM type.

Design: Details differ; the last three ships are flushdecked with higher bridges and are known as Oskol III type. The Oskols differ in basic configuration from the Amurs by a deck structure forward and the absence of a crane aft.

Guns: Only a few are armed; the PM-24 had a twin 57-mm gun mount removed from the bow in the early 1980s (no fire-control radar); she is known as Oskol II type.

The PM-26 shows the similarity between the Oskol and the larger Amur classes. There are twin cranes forward of the bridge and a small deckhouse on the forecastle.

The Oskol-class repair ship PM-24 with a Tango-class submarine moored alongside. The Oskol's twin 25-mm gun mounts are aft, behind the ship's boats. Soviet repair ships service both surface ships and submarines.

5 REPAIR SHIPS: DNEPR CLASS

Name	Name	Name	Completed
PM-17	PM-30	PM-135	1960–1964
PM-22	PM-130		

Builders:	Black Sea Shipyard, Nikolayev (south)
Displacement:	4,500 tons standard
	5,300 tons full load
Length:	371 ft 8 in (113.3 m) overall
Beam:	54 ft 2 in (16.5 m)
Draft:	14 ft 5 in (4.4 m)
Propulsion:	1 diesel engine; 2,000 bhp; 1 shaft
Speed:	11 knots
Range:	6,000 n.miles at 8 knots
Complement:	approx. 420
Helicopters:	no facilities
Guns:	none
Radars:	1 Don or Don-2 (navigation)

These repair ships have a distinctive, 150-ton-capacity bow hoist in addition to smaller cranes. They are primarily intended to support submarines.

Classification: Soviet PM type.

Design: Details and equipment vary. The last two ships are flush-decked (Dnepr II type).

Guns: These ships are designed to be armed with a 57-mm AA twin gun mount. It was installed on some ships when completed; subsequently removed.

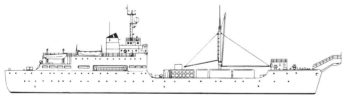

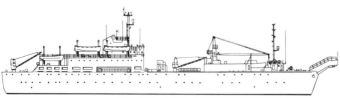

Drawings of the rarely photographed Dnepr I (top) and Dnepr II repair ships. The principal differences in the two types are the flush deck of the Dnepr II and their crane arrangements. (Siegfried Breyer)

SALVAGE AND RESCUE SHIPS

In addition to the salvage ships listed below, the Navy operates a number of buoy and mooring tenders and lift ships that can be used for salvage operations.

Smaller salvage and firefighting tugs are listed later in this chapter, as are the Ingul and PAMIR classes, which are designated as rescue ships by the Soviet Navy.

2 SALVAGE AND RESCUE SHIPS: "EL'BRUS" CLASS

Name	Launched	Completed
EL'BRUS	1977	1981
ALAGEZ	1984	1988

Builders:	61 Kommuna, Nikolayev (north)
Displacement:	20,000 tons full load
Length:	574 ft (175.0 m) overall
Beam:	82 ft (25.0 m)
Draft:	24 ft 7 in (7.5 m)
Propulsion:	4 diesel engines; 2 shafts
Speed:	17 knots
Range:	
Complement:	approx. 420
Helicopters:	1 Ka-25 Hormone-C
Guns:	see notes
Radars:	1 Don-2 (navigation)
	2 Don-Kay (navigation)

The EL'BRUS-class ships are the world's largest submarine salvage and rescue ships, almost five times the displacement of the U.S. Navy's largest ships of this type, the PIGEON (ASR 21) and ORTOLAN (ASR 22).

The EL'BRUS began her first deployment from the Black Sea into the Mediterranean in late December 1981. The second ship is in the Pacific.

Classification: Soviet SS type.

Design: The EL'BRUS has a massive superstructure and a helicopter platform aft. A hangar is provided, the "drawbridge" door forming a ramp down to the platform. There is a gantry-crane arrangement amidships for lowering submersibles over the side. The ships have extensive mooring, diving, and fire-fighting equipment and are capable of sustained operations in remote areas.

At least two and possibly four rescue submersibles are carried, similar to the same type carried on board the India-class submarines. In the EL'BRUS the submersibles are carried in a hangar abaft the funnel, with rails provided for moving them forward to where extending gantry cranes (port and starboard) can lower them to the water.

Guns: The ship has provisions for mounting four 30-mm guns of either the twin-barrel or multi-barrel (Gatling) type.

Names: EL'BRUS is named for the highest peak in Europe, in the Caucasus Mountains.

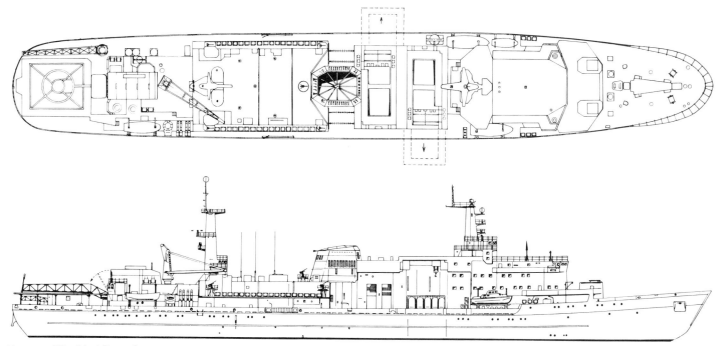

EL'BRUS. (Siegfried Breyer)

The large salvage and rescue ship EL'BRUS has no contemporaries in Western navies. There are twin traveling gantry cranes amidships as well as large cranes aft. In this view a diving chamber is located beneath the port-side gantry crane. (An overhead view of the EL'BRUS appears in the 4th edition, page 281.)

The ALAGEZ in the Pacific. (1990, Courtesy *Ships of the World*)

3 SALVAGE AND RESCUE SHIPS: "PIONEER MOSKVYY" CLASS

Name	Conversion Completed
MIKHAIL RUDNITSKIY	1979
GIORGIY KOZMIN	1980
GIORGIY TITOV	1983

Builders:	Vyborg
Displacement:	10,700 tons full load
Length:	430 ft (130.3 m) overall
Beam:	57 ft 1 in (17.3 m)
Draft:	22 ft 8 in (6.9 m)
Propulsion:	1 diesel engine (B&W 5DKRN 62/140-3); 6,100 bhp; 1 shaft
Speed:	15.5 knots
Range:	12,000 n.miles at 15.5 knots
Complement:	approx. 120
Helicopters:	no facilities
Guns:	none
Radars:	2 Don-2 (navigation)

These are cargo ships converted for salvage operations. A salvage submersible can be carried (stowed in the No. 2 hold).

Class: From 1973 onward, 27 ships of this class were delivered for Soviet merchant and naval use, plus two ships for the East German merchant service. The class is a variation of the SE-STRORETSK-class cellular container ships.

A fourth Navy ship, the SAYANIY, is an experimental ship (see page 267).

Design: These are large, superstructure-aft ships, with two large kingposts and two 40-ton-capacity and two 20-ton-capacity booms. Four holds are provided. For the salvage role, deckhouses have been built over the aftermost hold and over the forward hold in some ships; details differ. Bow and stern thrusters have been fitted and deep mooring gear is provided.

Names: These ships are named for pioneers in submersible development. (All of the Soviet merchant ships of this class have "pioneer" names.)

The GIORGIY KOZMIN is one of three large salvage ships converted while under construction as merchant ships. This ship participated in the search near Sakhalin Island for the Korean Air Lines flight 007 shot down by a Soviet fighter aircraft in 1983. (1983, U.S. Navy)

1 SUBMARINE RESCUE SHIP: NEPA CLASS

Name	Completed
KARPATY	1970

Builders:	Black Sea Shipyard, Nikolayev (south)
Displacement:	9,800 tons full load
Length:	424 ft 9 in (129.5 m) overall
Beam:	63 ft (19.2 m)
Draft:	21 ft (6.4 m)
Propulsion:	4 diesel engines; 8,000 bhp; 2 shafts
Speed:	16 knots
Range:	8,000 n.miles at 14 knots
Complement:	approx. 270
Helicopters:	no facilities
Guns:	none
Radars:	2 Don-2 (navigation)

The KARPATY is a large, one-of-a-kind submarine rescue ship. She has a 600-ton lift device mounted on her stern plus submarine rescue, fire-fighting, diving, and salvage equipment. Submarine rescue chambers are carried.

Classification: Soviet SS type.

The one-of-a-kind submarine rescue ship KARPATY has a large stern lifting device. There are submarine rescue chambers held by davits on both sides, immediately aft of the funnel. There is a stern anchor beneath the lifting device. (1988, Royal Netherlands Navy)

8 SUBMARINE RESCUE SHIPS: PRUT CLASS

Name	Name	Completed
ALTAY	SS-21	
BESHTAU	SS-23	1961–1968
VLADIMIR TREFOLEV	SS-26	
ZHIGULI	SS-83	

Builders:	61 Kommuna, Nikolayev (north)
Displacement:	2,800 tons standard
	3,300 tons full load
Length:	295 ft 10 in (90.2 m) overall
Beam:	46 ft 11 in (14.3 m)
Draft:	18 ft (5.5 m)
Propulsion:	4 diesel engines; 8,000 bhp; 2 shafts
Speed:	20 knots
Range:	10,000 n.miles at 16 knots
Complement:	approx. 120
Helicopters:	no facilities
Guns:	see notes
Radars:	1 or 2 Don or Don-2 (navigation)

These are large tug-type ships fitted for submarine rescue and diving operations. The mast arrangement and other details differ.

Class: The SS-44 of this class was lost in the 1970s.

Classification: Soviet SS type.

Guns: These ships have provisions for a single 57-mm AA quad mounting and Muff Cob radar; one ship was armed in this manner.

A Prut-class rescue ship at anchor with the crew mustered on the fantail. These ships are rigged for towing and salvage.

The Prut-class submarine rescue ship SS-26, one of a large class of ships that are similar to the smaller U.S. Navy ASRs of World War II construction. A diving bell and submarine rescue chamber are fitted on the port side; mooring buoys are behind the after mast. (1979, Royal Navy)

11 SUBMARINE RESCUE SHIPS: T-58 CLASS (EX-MINESWEEPERS)

Name	Name	Name	Completed
KAZBEK	ZANGEZUR	SS-47	
KHIBINY	SS-30	SS-50	late 1950s
VALDAY	SS-35	SS-51	
POLKOVO	SS-40		

Builders:	(USSR)
Displacement:	815 tons standard
	930 tons full load
Length:	235 ft 2 in (71.7 m) overall
Beam:	31 ft 6 in (9.6 m)
Draft:	8 ft 10 in (2.7 m)
Propulsion:	2 diesel engines; 4,000 bhp; 2 shafts
Speed:	17 knots
Range:	2,500 n.miles at 12 knots
Complement:	approx. 60
Helicopters:	no facilities
Guns:	(see notes)
Radars:	1 or 2 Don-2 (navigation)
	1 Spin Trough (search) in some units
Sonars:	Tamir high-frequency hull mounted

These ships were modified while under construction as minesweepers and were completed as submarine rescue ships. A rescue chamber is carried; fitted with diving equipment.

Class: One ship of this type was transferred to India in 1971.

Several Soviet ships have been stricken, including the GIDROLOG, which also operated in the intelligence collection role. Other ships of this class formerly served as patrol/corvette units, but only three remain as radar pickets (see chapter 17); no T-58s remain in the minesweeping role.

Classification: Soviet SS type.

Guns: In the minesweeping configuration two 57-mm AA twin mounts could be fitted as well as associated Ball End or Muff Cob radars. The rescue ships are not believed to have ever carried armament.

The submarine rescue chamber on a modified T-58 rescue ship. The device is similar to the U.S. Navy's McCann rescue chamber.

A former T-58 minesweeper reconfigured as a submarine rescue ship with a rescue chamber on the port side and lifting gear aft. (The U.S. Navy's first submarine rescue ships were converted World War I–built Bird-class minesweepers.) (1987, West German Navy)

MOORING TENDERS/LIFT SHIPS

These ships plant and maintain navigation buoys and undertake salvage tasks. They can also transport air cushion vehicles and small craft. The Soviet Navy's hydrographic ships, listed in chapter 24, also plant and maintain buoys.

8 MOORING TENDERS/LIFT SHIPS: KASHTAN CLASS

Name	Completed	Name	Completed
KIL-143	1989	KIL-927	1988
KIL-158	1989	KIL-. . .	1990
KIL-164	1989	KIL-. . .	1990
KIL-926	1988	KIL-. . .	1990

Builders:	Neptun, Rostock (East Germany)
Displacement:	4,600 tons full load
Length:	321 ft 5 in (98.0 m) waterline
	334 ft 7 in (102.0 m) overall
Beam:	65 ft 7 in (20.0 m)
Draft:	19 ft 8 in (6.0 m)
Propulsion:	diesel-electric: 5 diesel generator sets with electric drive; 2,900 shp; 2 shafts
Speed:	12 knots
Range:	
Complement:	approx. 80
Helicopters:	no facilities
Guns:	none
Radars:	1 Don-2 (navigation)
	1 Mius (navigation)

New class of heavy lift ships, apparently replacements for the Neptun class.

Design: These ships have a large working area amidships with a heavy-lift, 100-ton-capacity gantry at the stern, a 12-ton electro-hydraulic crane to starboard, and a 60-ton boom amidships.

Classification: Soviet KIL type.

The new mooring tender/lift ship KIL-927 is fitted with twin cranes amidships and heavy lift gear at the stern; the ship has a docking well amidships for stowing buoys and other gear. (1989, JMSDF)

The KIL-164 under way at high speed. This view shows the large superstructure block and ice-breaking prow of the Kashtan class. This unit is based at Murmansk. (1990, Royal Navy)

10 MOORING TENDERS/LIFT SHIPS: SURA CLASS

Name	Name	Name	Completed
KIL-1	KIL-23	KIL-32	
KIL-2	KIL-27	KIL-33	1965–1972
KIL-21	KIL-29	KIL-31	1976–1978
KIL-22	KIL-31		

Builders:	Neptun, Rostock (East Germany)
Displacement:	2,370 tons standard
	3,150 tons full load
Tonnage:	904 DWT
Length:	223 ft (68.0 m) waterline (see notes)
	285 ft 4 in (87.0 m) overall
Beam:	48 ft 6 in (14.8 m)
Draft:	16 ft 5 in (5.0 m)
Propulsion:	diesel-electric: 4 diesel engines (Karl Liebknecht); 2,240 hp;
	4 generators connected to 2 electric motors; 2 shafts
Speed:	13 knots
Range:	4,000 n.miles at 10 knots
Complement:	
Helicopters:	no facilities
Guns:	none
Radars:	2 Don-2 (navigation)

These are heavy lift ships used for handling buoys and other lift functions. The lifting rig projects over the stern and has a 60-ton capacity, accounting for the large difference in waterline and overall lengths. A smaller crane and lifting boom are fitted amidships. The ships have a cargo hold that can accommodate 890 tons, in addition to buoys or other material stowed on deck. The ships also have a very large fuel capacity for transfer to other ships.

Additional ships of this type are operated by the Soviet merchant marine.

Classification: Soviet KIL type.

Engineering: The propulsion machinery is forward in these ships, hence the use of the diesel-electric plant to alleviate the need for very long propeller shafts. A bow thruster is fitted for station keeping during lift operations.

MOORING TENDERS/LIFT SHIPS: NEPTUN CLASS

The ten Neptun-class ships, completed in 1957–1960, were probably stricken in the late 1980s; their replacement is the Kashtan class. See 4th edition, page 290.

The Sura-class heavy lift ship KIL-32 with a submersible on deck. These ships are employed in a variety of support roles. A Kashin-class destroyer is behind this ship during operations in the Sea of Japan. (1983, U.S. Navy)

The Sura-class KIL-2 showing the "tunnel" in the after superstructure and the complex stern lifting gear. These ships have a large, open working deck for handling buoys and submersibles. (1982, L. Van Ginderen)

HEAVY LIFT SHIPS

1 HEAVY LIFT SHIP: "ANADYR" TYPE

Name	Launched	Completed
ANADYR	Oct 1988	1990

Builders:	Wartsila, Helsinki (Finland)
Tonnage:	12,765 DWT
	34,151 gross
Length:	741 ft (226.1 m) waterline
Beam:	98 ft 5 in (30 m)
Draft:	21 ft 4 in (6.5 m)
Propulsion:	4 diesel engines (Wartsila/Vasa); 32,600 bhp; 2 shafts
Speed:	20 knots
Complement:	70
Helicopters:	2 utility
Missiles:	none
Guns:	none
Radars:	

This is a heavy lift ship intended to transport submarines and other naval craft. The ship was constructed in Finland but several problems prevented her from entering service until additional work was performed at a Swedish shipyard. Upon completion the ship was transferred to the Pacific.

Design: The ANADYR is an enlarged version of the Finnish-built BORIS POLEVOY-class barge carriers (two completed for the Soviet merchant fleet in 1984).

The superstructure is forward, with a double helicopter hangar built into the after end of the deck structure. There is a 120-ton-capacity traveling crane; a removable superdeck over the docking well can accommodate 868 standard freight containers. The ship floods down and the stern gate swings down to permit barges or naval craft to float in and out. The docking well is 419 ft 10 in (128 m) long and 59 ft (13 m) wide, with a floodable depth of 18 ft (5.5 m).

Bow and stern thrusters are fitted for maneuvering and station keeping while loading the docking well.

The ANADYR is one of the Soviet Navy's largest auxiliary ships; she was designed to carry small submarines and surface craft as well as other large objects. Additional heavy-lift ships of this general type are operated by the Soviet merchant marine. (1990, U.S. Navy)

The ANADYR under way in the Pacific. (1990, U.S. Navy)

CABLE SHIPS

Cable ships lay and tend underwater cables for communications purposes and support sea floor hydrophone arrays. They are supplemented in these roles by several civilian-operated cable ships (see chapter 25).

2 CABLE SHIPS: "BIRYUSA" CLASS

Name	Completed
BIRYUSA	4 Jul 1986
KEM'	23 Oct 1986

Builders:	Wartsila, Turku (Finland)
Displacement:	2,370 tons full load
Length:	258 ft 2 in (78.7 m) waterline
	282 ft 5 in (86.1 m) overall
Beam:	41 ft 4 in (12.6 m)
Draft:	10 ft 2 in (3.1 m)
Propulsion:	diesel electric: 2 diesels (Wartsila Vasa 8R22); 1,700 bhp; 2 shafts (shrouded propellers)
Speed:	11.8 knots
Range:	
Complement:	
Helicopters:	no facilities
Guns:	none
Radars:	1 . . . . . (navigation)

Improved cable ships based on the EMBA design. Capable of carrying 600 tons of cable. Both ships are in the Pacific.

Both launched on 29 November 1985.

Classification: Soviet KS type.

Design: Cable sheave and lift devices overhang the bow.

Engineering: Fitted with two shrouded Schottel-design propellers that swivel through 360° for precise maneuvering and station keeping; also fitted with bow thruster.

3 CABLE SHIPS: "EMBA" CLASS

Name	Completed
EMBA	1980
NEPRYADVA	1981
SETUN	1981

Builders:	Wartsila, Turku (Finland)
Displacement:	2,050 tons full load
Length:	224 ft 8 in (68.5 m) waterline
	248 ft 11 in (75.9 m) overall
Beam:	41 ft 4 in (12.6 m)
Draft:	10 ft 2 in (3.1 m)
Propulsion:	diesel-electric: 2 diesel engines (Wartsila Vasa 6R22); 1,360 bhp; 2 shafts (shrouded propellers)
Speed:	11 knots
Range:	
Complement:	approx. 40
Helicopters:	no facilities
Guns:	none
Radars:	1 . . . . . . (navigation)

These are coastal cable ships. Cable sheave and lift devices overhang the bow and there is a crane forward. Cargo capacity is 300 tons of cable.

Classification: Soviet KS type.

Engineering: Fitted with two shrouded Schottel-design propellers that swivel through 360° for precise maneuvering and station keeping. Also fitted with bow thruster.

The KEM' is a modified EMBA-class cable ship. Her bow cable sheaves differ from the EMBA; twin cranes are located on the forecastle. These ships are employed to lay and maintain seafloor communications cables and acoustic detection arrays. (1988)

The SETUN and her sister ships are much smaller than U.S. Navy cable ships. Like several other classes of Soviet naval auxiliaries, these ships were built in Finland. (1981, Wärtsila)

8 CABLE SHIPS: KLAZMA CLASS

Name	Completed
DONETS	1969
INGUL	1962
INGURI	1978
KATYN	1973
TAVDA	1977
TSNA	1968
YANA	1963
ZEYA	1970

Builders:	Wartsila, Turku (Finland)
Displacement:	6,920 tons full load except INGUL and YANA 6,810 tons; KATYN 7,885 tons
Tonnage:	3,750 DWT
Length:	393 ft 7 in (120.0 m) waterline (see notes)
	427 ft 9 in (130.4 m) overall
Beam:	52 ft 6 in (16.0 m)
Draft:	18 ft 10 in (5.75 m)
Propulsion:	diesel-electric: 5 diesel engines (Wartsila 624TS); 5,000 bhp; 5 generators connected to 2 electric motors (see notes); 2 shafts
Speed:	14 knots
Range:	12,000 n.miles at 14 knots
Complement	approx. 110
Helicopters:	no facilities
Guns:	none
Radars:	1 . . . . . . (navigation)

These are large cable ships, fitted with British-built cable equipment. Cable sheaves and handing gear project over both bow and stern. Details vary.

Classification: Soviet KS type.

Engineering: The first two ships completed, INGUL and YANA, have four 2,436-hp diesels; they have a longer forecastle. A 550-hp active rudder and 650-hp bow thruster are fitted to these ships for precise station keeping while handling cables.

CABLE SHIP: "TELNOVSK" CLASS

The KS-7, a Hungarian-built cable ship converted from a TELNOVSK-class cargo ship, is believed to have been stricken in the late 1980s. See *Guide to the Soviet Navy,* 4th edition, page 292 for data.

The cable ship INGURI of the Klazma class has both bow and stern cable sheaves. The eight Klazma-class ships are the largest of this type in Soviet service. (Royal Danish Navy)

MISSILE TRANSPORTS

1 LARGE MISSILE TRANSPORT: "ALEKSANDR BRYKIN"

Name	Completed
ALEKSANDR BRYKIN	1987

Builders:	United Admiralty, Leningrad
Displacement:	17,000 tons full load
Length:	482 ft 2 in (147.0 m) waterline
	524 ft 10 in (160.0 m) overall
Beam:	78 ft 9 in (24.0 m)
Draft:	28 ft 10 in (8.8 m)
Propulsion:	diesel-electric: 2 diesels; 1 shaft
Speed:	16 knots
Range:	
Complement:	approx. 140
Helicopters:	no facilities
Missiles:	2 quad SA-N-8 anti-air launches [16]
Guns:	4 30-mm/65-cal close-in (multi-barrel)
Radars:	2 Bass Tilt (fire control)
	1 Half Plate (navigation)
	1 Nayada (navigation)
EN systems:	2 Bell Shroud
	2 Bell Squat

The ALEKSANDR BRYKIN is designed specifically to rearm Typhoon-class SSBNs with the SS-N-20 missile; the ship may also be capable of carrying the SS-N-23 missile for the Delta IV SSBN.

The ship was launched in 1985; assigned to the Northern Fleet. No additional construction of this class has been reported.

Design: There is a vertical amidships magazine for 16 SS-N-20 ballistic missiles. These are served by a 75-ton-capacity crane; there are also two smaller cranes amidships.

Engineering: A bow thruster is fitted.

The amidships missile section of the ALEKSANDR BRYKIN has vertical cells for 16 large ballistic missiles. The massive crane can load/unload missiles for submarines moored to either side. (1987)

The ALEKSANDR BRYKIN is the world's largest ship configured specifically to carry missiles/munitions (some combination oiler-ammunition ships are larger). The ship can carry 16 large submarine-launched ballistic missiles; she may also provide other support services to submarines. (1987)

1 MISSILE TRANSPORT: CONVERTED "YUNYY PARTIZAN" CLASS

Name	Completed	Converted
VITSE ADMIRAL FOMIN (ex-PINEGA)	1976	1986

Builders:	Santierul Naval Shipyard, Turnu-Severin (Romania)
Displacement:	3,800 tons full load
Tonnage:	2,146 DWT
Length:	291 ft 1 in (88.75 m) overall
Beam:	42 ft (12.8 m)
Draft:	15 ft 1 in (4.6 m)
Propulsion:	1 diesel engine (Cegielski/Sulzer 8 cyl TAD 36); 2,080 bhp; 1 shaft
Speed:	12.75 knots
Range:	4,000 n.miles at 12 knots
Complement:	
Helicopters:	no facilities
Guns:	4 14.5-mm machine guns (2 twin)
Radars:	1 Don-2 (navigation)

This is a former naval cargo ship, one of 24 Romanian-built cargo-container ships of the YUNYY PARTIZAN class built for the Soviet Union. Twenty were merchant ships; the PINEGA and three others were Navy-manned cargo ships; see page 259 for additional data.

3 MISSILE TRANSPORTS: "AMGA" CLASS

Name	Completed
AMGA	1973
VETLUGA	1976
DAUGAVA	1981

Builders:	Krasnoye Sormovo, Gor'kiy	
Displacement:	4,500 tons standard	
	5,500 tons full load except DAUGAVA 6,200 tons	
Length:	AMGA	339 ft 10 in (103.6 m) overall
	VETLUGA	359 ft 6 in (109.6 m) overall
	DAUGAVA	371 ft (113.1 m) overall
Beam:	58 ft 5 in (17.7 m)	
Draft:	14 ft 6 in (4.4 m)	
Propulsion:	2 diesel engines; 4,000 bhp; 2 shafts	
Speed:	12 knots	
Range:	4,500 n.miles at 12 knots	
Complement:	approx. 200	
Helicopters:	none	
Guns:	4 25-mm/60-cal AA (2 twin)	
Radars:	1 Don-2 (navigation)	

These ships transport ballistic missiles for SSBNs.

Design: Improved versions of the previous Lama class, this design provides for lighter armament. Propulsion machinery, accommodations, and controls are aft with missile stowage forward. Their hulls are ice-strengthened. A 55-ton-capacity crane is fitted.

The AMGA shows the unusual configuration of these Soviet missile transports. These ships stow submarine-launched ballistic missiles in the horizontal position (unlike U.S. ships carrying SSBN missiles).

2 MISSILE TENDERS 5 MISSILE TRANSPORTS/TENDERS	} LAMA CLASS	
Name	Name	Completed
GENERAL RIYABAKOV	PM-131	
VORONEZH (PM-872)	PM-150	1963–1979
PM-44	PB-625	
PM-93		

Builders:	Black Sea Shipyard, Nikolayev (south)
Displacement:	4,500 tons full load
Length:	370 ft (112.8 m) overall
Beam:	48 ft 10 in (14.9 m)
Draft:	14 ft 5 in (4.4 m)
Propulsion:	2 diesel engines; 4,000 bhp; 2 shafts
Speed:	14 knots
Range:	6,000 n.miles at 10 knots
Complement:	approx. 250
Helicopters:	no facilities
Missiles:	2 or 4 quad SA-N-5 or SA-N-8 anti-air launchers [16 or 32]

Guns:	4 or 8 57-mm/70-cal AA (1 quad or 2 or 4 twin) except VORONEZH 2 57-mm/80-cal AA (1 twin)
	4 25-mm/60-cal AA guns (2 twin) in VORONEZH and 1 other unit
Radars:	1 Don-2 (navigation)
	1 Slim Net or Strut Curve (air search)
	1 or 2 Hawk Screech or 2 Muff Cob (fire control) except none in VORONEZH and 1 other unit

These ships carry cruise missiles for surface ships and submarines. Details with respect to weapons and radars differ for all ships. The VORONEZH and one other unit are modified to rearm and support missile corvettes and missile boats; they have larger magazines with smaller cranes.

Classification: Soviet PM type except GENERAL RIYABAKOV and PB 625 are designated PB.

Design: The design provides for machinery, accommodations, and controls aft with missile stowage forward. Five ships have 20-ton-capacity cranes and the VORONEZH and one other unit have two 10-ton-capacity cranes.

The GENERAL RIYABAKOV, a small superstructure missile transport of the Lama class with a rapid-fire 57-mm twin gun mount fitted on the forecastle. The ship also has four SA-N-5/8 missile launchers.

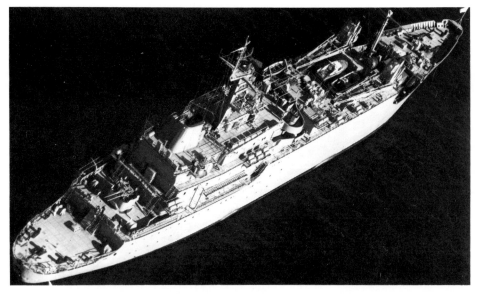

A Lama-class missile transport (pendant 877). This ship may be the VORONEZH, having an open 57-mm twin mount aft of the funnel plus 25-mm twin gun mounts atop the bridge. There are large cranes forward with small boats above the missile holds. (1986, U.S. Navy)

2 MISSILE TRANSPORTS }
3 CARGO SHIPS } **MODIFIED "ANDIZHAN" CLASS**

Name	(Type)	Completed
ONDA	(Cargo)	
POSET	(Cargo)	
YEMETSK	(Cargo)	1958–1960
VENTA (ex-LAKHTA)	(Missile)	
VILYUY (ex-POSYET)	(Missile)	

Builders:	Neptun, Rostock (East Germany)
Displacement:	4,500 tons standard
	6,740 tons full load
Tonnage:	4,375 DWT
Length:	341 ft 2 in (104.0 m) overall
Beam:	47 ft 3 in (14.4 m)
Draft:	21 ft 8 in (6.6 m)
Propulsion:	1 diesel engine (MAN); 3,250 bhp; 1 shaft
Speed:	13.5 knots
Range:	6,000 n.miles at 13.5 knots

Complement:	approx. 100
Helicopters:	landing platform in some ships
Guns:	none
Radars:	2 Don-2 (navigation)

These ships are former merchant ships converted in the 1970s, two to transport missiles and three to naval cargo ships.

Class: These are former ANDIZHAN/KOVEL-class dry cargo ships, almost 50 of which were built by the Neptun yard, most for Soviet merchant service, including three as merchant training ships. Three other ships were completed as naval oceanographic ships (see POLYUS class, chapter 24).

Classification: The missile transports are Soviet VTR type.

Design: In the missile transports a single heavy-lift crane is fitted forward and a pole mast aft in place of the original A-frame cranes. Their forward holds can carry ten SS-N-9 missiles and 20 SA-N-1 or SA-N-3 missiles. Cargo capacity is 3,950 tons.

The modified ANDIZHAN-class cargo ship VENTA, one of two ships of this design employed as a missile transport. There are four missile holds forward, serviced by a large crane. These missile ships are unarmed. (1988, JMSDF)

The ONDA retains the basic configuration of the ANDIZHAN class, with cargo-handling booms fitted to A-frame masts forward and aft. The position of the mast atop the bridge varies in these ships.

2 MISSILE TRANSPORTS }
3 CARGO SHIPS } **MP-6 CLASS (FORMER LANDING SHIPS)**

Name	(Type)	Completed
BIRA	(Cargo)	
BUREYA	(Missile)	
IRGIZ	(Cargo)	1958–1960
KHOPER	(Missile)	
VOLOGDYA	(Cargo)	

Builders:	(Hungary)
Displacement:	2,100 ton full load
Length:	245 ft (74.7 m) overall
Beam:	37 ft (11.3 m)
Draft:	14 ft 5 in (4.4 m)
Propulsion:	2 diesel engines (Buchau-Wolff 6 NVD48); 800 bhp; 1 shaft
Speed:	10.5 knots
Range:	3,300 n.miles at 9 knots
Complement:	approx. 40
Helicopters:	no facilities
Guns:	see notes
Radars:	1 Don-2 (navigation)

These are former MP-6 landing ships, two of which have been modified to transport missiles and three to naval cargo ships. They resemble small coastal freighters with their superstructure aft. They were not successful in the landing ship role.

The missile transports carried SS-N-5 ballistic missiles for Golf-class SSBs and Hotel SSBNs; they have a large crane. The KHOPER is in the Northern Fleet and the BUREYA in the Pacific Fleet.

Class: About ten landing ships of this design were built. They are generally similar to the large ELVA class of Hungarian-built merchant ships, most of which were operated by the Soviet merchant fleet.

Classification: All are believed to be Soviet VTR type. The MP-6 is a NATO designation.

Guns: No armament is fitted; there are provisions for six 37-mm/60-cal AA guns (3 twin mounts).

Modification: Their bow doors were welded shut and bow ramps removed about 1960 to permit use as cargo ships.

The BUREYA is one of the former landing ships of the MP-6 class employed as a missile transport. The ship retains an A-frame mast forward with a large crane amidships for handling missiles. Note the small radar mast atop the bridge. (1988, JMSDF)

The BIRA has the twin A-frame masts and booms of the cargo variant of the former MP-6 landing ships.

2 MISSILE TRANSPORTS: CONVERTED MELITOPOL CLASS

Name	Completed
INDIRKA FORT SHEVERENKO	} mid-1950s

Builders:	(USSR)
Displacement:	1,200 tons full load
Length:	188 ft 11 in (57.6 m) overall
Beam:	29 ft 6 in (9.0 m)
Draft:	14 ft 1 in (4.3 m)
Propulsion:	1 diesel engine (6DR 30/40); 600 bhp; 1 shaft
Speed:	11 knots
Range:	2,500 n.miles at 10.5 knots
Complement:	
Helicopters:	no facilities
Guns:	none
Radars:	1 Don-2 (navigation)

These are small, superstructure-aft cargo ships of the Melitopol class that were converted in the late 1970s to carry missiles. Cargo booms have been deleted.

Three sister ships serve as naval hydrographic survey ships (see chapter 24).

10 MISSILE AND TORPEDO TRANSPORTS: MUNA CLASS

Name	Name	Name	Completed
VTR-81	VTR-85	VTR-93	
VTR-82	VTR-91	VTR-94	} 1960s
VTR-83	VTR-92	VTR-148	
VTR-84			

Builders:	Nakhodka
Displacement:	680 tons full load
Length:	167 ft 3 in (51.0 m) overall

Beam:	27 ft 11 in (8.5 m)
Draft:	8 ft 10 in (2.7 m)
Propulsion:	1 diesel engine; 600 bhp; 1 shaft
Speed:	11 knots
Range:	
Complement:	approx. 40
Helicopters:	no facilities
Guns:	none
Radars:	1 or 2 Spin Trough (search)

These are small, superstructure-aft torpedo and missile transports. Cargo arrangements differ for specialized weapon-carrying roles.

Classification: They have the designation MBSS—*Morskaya Barzha Samokhodnaya Sukhogruznaya* (seagoing self-propelled dry-cargo lighters) when in Soviet home waters, and VTR when deployed.

Muna-class torpedo transport.

OILERS AND TANKERS

All of these ships are employed to carry fuels for Soviet naval forces. The terms "oiler" and "tanker" in the Western vernacular refer to ships that perform at-sea replenishment and point-to-point fuel transport, respectively. The ships listed here have the Soviet designations of military tanker (VT), except for the one-of-a-kind BEREZINA, which is a military transport (VTR). The latter designation is used for a number of naval dry-cargo ships as well as other auxiliaries.

The Soviet Navy has long used merchant tankers for at-sea replenishment and continues to do so on a large scale. Until the mid-1960s even naval fuel ships refueled warships while dead in the water or over-the-bow while being towed. Subsequently, several new classes were acquired in the 1960s and 1970s with an alongside Underway Replenishment (UNREP) capability, while older ships were refitted with a limited alongside capability.

The relatively high acquisition rate of naval fueling ships in the 1960s and 1970s abruptly halted in early 1979 when the last of four DUBNA-class ships was acquired. Only one ship of the large BEREZINA-class UNREP ship has been built. (She is the only Soviet ship comparable to the U.S. Navy's large AOE/AOR ships.) Subsequently, two oilers under construction in Finland were acquired from the merchant construction program in 1983.

(The acquisition of civilian tankers for the Soviet merchant and fishing fleets continues at a high rate.)

2 REPLENISHMENT OILERS: "KALININGRAD" CLASS

Name	Completed
ARGUN (ex-KALLARERE)	Nov 1982
VYAZ'MA (ex-KATUN)	Dec 1982

Builders:	Rauma-Repola, Repola (Finland)
Displacement:	8,700 tons full load
Tonnage:	5,873 DWT
Length:	378 ft 10 in (115.5 m) overall
Beam:	55 ft 9 in (17.0 m)
Draft:	21 ft 4 in (6.5 m)
Propulsion:	1 diesel engine (Bryansk/Burmeister & Wain 5 DKRP 50/110-2); 3,500 bhp; 1 shaft
Speed:	14 knots
Range:	5,000 n.miles at 14 knots
Complement:	approx. 30
Helicopters:	no facilities
Guns:	none
Radars:	2 Okean-A/B (navigation)

These ships were acquired for naval use shortly after completion as merchant tankers in 1982 (merchant names are shown in parentheses); placed in naval service in mid-1983.

Class: These were the last of 25 tankers of this design that were launched through 1983 by the Rauma-Repola shipyard for the Soviet fishing fleet.

Design: They carry 5,350 tons of fuels plus some dry cargo. They can replenish from either side and astern.

The VYAZ'MA is one of the two trim-looking KALINGRAD-class oilers in Soviet naval service. These small ships have tall, squared-off bridge structures and distinctive, square funnels. They can conduct underway refuelings alongside or over the bow or stern. (1988, Royal Netherlands Navy)

1 REPLENISHMENT OILER: "BEREZINA"

Name	Completed
BEREZINA	1978

Builders:	61 Kommuna, Nikolayev (north)
Displacement:	36,000 tons full load
Length:	695 ft 4 in (212.0 m) overall
Beam:	85 ft 3 in (26.0 m)
Draft:	32 ft 10 in (10.0 m)
Propulsion:	2 diesel engines; 54,000 bhp; 2 shafts
Speed:	22 knots
Range:	12,000 n.miles at 18 knots
Complement:	approx. 600
Helicopters:	2 Ka-25 Hormone-C
Missiles:	1 twin SA-N-4 anti-air launcher [20]
Guns:	4 57-mm/80-cal AA (2 twin)
	4 30-mm close-in (4 multi-barrel)
ASW weapons:	2 RBU-1000 rocket launchers

Radars:	2 Bass Tilt (fire control)
	1 Don-2 (navigation)
	2 Don-Kay (navigation)
	1 Muff Cob (fire control)
	1 Pop Group (fire control)
	1 Strut Curve (air search)
Sonars:	. . . . . . hull mounted
EW systems:	2 Bell Shroud
	2 Bell Squat

This is the Soviet Navy's largest and most capable underway replenishment ship. Only one unit has been built. The BEREZINA made her first operational deployment from the Black Sea into the Mediterranean in December 1978. She operates mainly in the Black Sea.

Classification: Soviet VTR type.

Design: BEREZINA was designed from the outset for the underway replenishment of petroleum, munitions, and stores. The ship

The BEREZINA is the Soviet Navy's only large combination oiler-ammunition ship that is comparable to Western AOE-type naval replenishment ships. The massive kingposts are for the transfer of missiles; there is a small helicopter deck aft with a hangar for two Ka-25 Hormone-C utility helicopters.

can carry an estimated 16,000 tons of fuels, 500 tons of fresh water, and 2,000 to 3,000 tons of munitions and provisions. The ship can transfer fuel stores to ships on either side and fuel over the stern. Special provisions are provided for replenishing submarines. There are four 10-ton-capacity cranes for loading stores and servicing ships alongside.

Of special significance is the ship's heavy armament, which includes ASW weapons. She is currently the only armed Soviet replenishment ship. Note that the ship has sonar fitted (as well as ASW weapons), probably the only naval auxiliary of any nation with this capability except for training ships. Two chaff launchers are also provided.

Names: Berezina is a major river in Belorussia and the scene of a major battle during Napoleon's retreat from Moscow in 1812.

The BEREZINA (right) at anchor in the Mediterranean with the water carrier MANYCH alongside. The BEREZINA has twin 30-mm Gatling guns outboard of the hangar; there are 57-mm guns and Gatling guns forward, plus ASW rocket launchers. The BEREZINA is the only auxiliary ship of any navy with anti-submarine weapons, except for training ships. One helicopter is in the hangar and a second is on the flight deck. (The MANYCH is unarmed.)

4 REPLENISHMENT OILERS: "DUBNA" CLASS

Name	Completed
DUBNA	1974
IKRUT	1975
PECHENGA	1978
SVENTA	1979

Builders:	Rauma-Repola, Rauma (Finland)
Displacement:	4,300 tons light
	11,100 tons full load
Tonnage:	6,500 DWT
Length:	426 ft 9 in (130.1 m) overall
Beam:	65 ft 7 in (20.0 m)
Draft:	23 ft 8 in (7.2 m)
Propulsion:	1 diesel engine (Russkiy 8DRPH 23/230); 6,000 bhp; 1 shaft
Speed:	16 knots

Range:	8,000 n.miles at 15 knots
Complement:	approx. 60
Helicopters:	no facilities
Guns:	none
Radars:	2 Don-2 (navigation)

These are small replenishment tankers with at least the first two units, the DUBNA and IKRUT, having initially been employed to support the Soviet fishing fleet as well as naval forces.

Class: Only these four units were built to this specific design.

Classification: Soviet VT type.

Design: These ships can transfer fuel and dry stores to ships on either side and over the stern.

Electronics: The commercial Okean radars originally fitted were replaced in the early 1980s by naval sets.

The DUBNA-class replenishment oiler PCHENGA. (1988, JMSDF)

6 REPLENISHMENT OILERS: "BORIS CHILIKIN" CLASS

Name	Name	Completed
BORIS BUTOMA	GENRIKH GASANOV	
BORIS CHILIKIN	IVAN BUBNOV	1971–1978
DNESTR	VLADIMIR KOLYACHITSKIY	

Builders:	Baltic, Leningrad
Displacement:	8,750 tons light
	24,500 tons full load
Tonnage:	16,300 DWT
Length:	532 ft 4 in (162.3 m) overall
Beam:	70 ft 2 in (21.4 m)
Draft:	37 ft 9 in (11.5 m)
Propulsion:	1 diesel engine (Bryansk/Burmeister & Wain or Cegielski/Sulzer); 9,600 bhp; 1 shaft
Speed:	17 knots
Range:	10,000 n.miles at 16.5 knots
Complement:	75
Helicopters:	no facilities
Guns:	removed
Radars:	2 Don-Kay (navigation)

These are naval versions of the VELIKIY OKTYABR-class merchant tankers.

Class: Twelve ships of this class were built for Soviet merchant service.

Classification: Soviet VT type.

Design: Cargo capacity is 13,500 tons of fuels and fresh water, 400 tons of munitions, and 800 tons of stores and provisions. There are provisions in these ships for transferring fuels to ships on either side and astern; the early units could transfer provisions on both sides, but the later ships only to starboard.

Guns: Four ships were completed with four 57-mm/80-cal AA guns in twin mounts forward as well as Muff Cob fire-control radar and Strut Curve air-search radar; subsequently removed. The IVAN BUBNOV and GENRIKH GASANOV were completed in merchant configuration without guns or naval radars.

The Boris Chilikin-class replenishment oiler Genrikh Gasanov was in the Soviet task group that visited Norfolk, Virginia, in 1989. Most of the other ships of this class were built with a gun armament, subsequently removed. The ship is manned by civilian crewmen, an arrangement similar to the U.S. Military Sealift Command and the British Royal Fleet Auxiliary.

5 REPLENISHMENT OILERS: "ALTAY" CLASS

Name	Name	Completed
ILIM	YEGORLIK	
IZHORA	YEL'NYA	1969–1973
KOLA		

Builders:	Rauma-Repola, Rauma (Finland)
Displacement:	approx. 2,200 tons light
	7,230 tons full load
Tonnage:	5,045 DWT
Length:	347 ft 8 in (106.0 m) overall
Beam:	49 ft 2½ in (15.0 m)
Draft:	22 ft (6.7 m)
Propulsion:	1 diesel engine (Bryansk/Burmeister & Wain BM-550 VTBN-110); 2,900 bhp; 1 shaft
Speed:	14 knots

Range:	5,000 n.miles at 13 knots
	8,600 n.miles at 12 knots
Complement:	approx. 60
Helicopters:	no facilities
Guns:	none
Radars:	2 Don-2 (navigation)

Converted merchant tankers fitted for underway replenishment.

Class: Some 60 ships of this type have been built, primarily for service with the Soviet fishing and merchant fleets, with most deliveries between 1968 and 1973; at least four are wine/vegetable oil carriers.

Classification: Soviet VT type.

Design: These ships can refuel one ship at a time from either side plus astern refueling. Their masts and details differ.

The Altay-class replenishment oiler Ilim in the central Pacific with a Soviet carrier task force. She is typical of the small replenishment ships employed by the Soviets. Numerous ships of this class serve with the Soviet merchant and fishing fleets. (1985, U.S. Navy)

3 TANKERS: "OLEKHMA" AND "PEVEK" CLASSES

Name	Completed
ZOLOTOI ROG	1960
OLEKHMA	1964
IMAN	1966

Builders:	Rauma-Repola, Rauma (Finland)
Displacement:	ROG 7,280 tons full load
	others 7,380 tons full load
Tonnage:	ROG 4,320 DWT
	others 4,400 DWT
Length:	ROG 344 ft 5 in (105.0 m) overall
	others 345 ft 9 in (105.4 m) overall
Beam:	48 ft 6 in (14.8 m)
Draft:	22 ft 4 in (6.8 m)
Propulsion:	1 diesel engine (Burmeister & Wain); 2,900 bhp; 1 shaft
Speed:	13.5 knots
Range:	10,000 n.miles at 13.5 knots
Complement:	approx. 40

Helicopters:	no facilities
Guns:	none
Radars:	1 Don-2 (navigation)

Fifty tankers of this basic design were built for the Soviet Union, two in Sweden and the remainder in Finland. The ZOLOTOI ROG belongs to the LOKBATAN or PEVEK series (delivered 1956–1960) and the other two ships to the AKSAY or OLEKHMA series (1961–1967).

Class: Most ships of these series remain in Soviet merchant service; two ex-Soviet ships were transferred to China and one to Indonesia.

Classification: Soviet VT type.

Design: The design has a traditional three-island superstructure arrangement (all later Soviet naval fuel ships of merchant design have a structure-aft configuration). The OLEKHMA was modernized in 1978 and has an A-frame abaft the bridge to permit fueling of a ship alongside; all can refuel over the stern while under way.

The OLEKHMA is one of a large series of tankers built for the Soviet Union, several of which were adopted for naval service. They have the traditional tanker configuration with a bridge amidships and machinery/funnel aft. An A-frame replenishment mast is fitted abaft the bridge.

1 TANKER: "SOFIA" CLASS

Name	Completed
AKHTUBA (ex-HANOI)	1963

Builders:	Admiralty, Leningrad
Displacement:	62,600 tons full load
Tonnage:	49,385 DWT
Length:	756 ft (230.5 m) overall
Beam:	101 ft 8 in (31.0 m)
Draft:	38 ft 8 in (11.8 m)
Propulsion:	2 steam turbines (Kirov); 19,000 shp; 1 shaft
Boilers:	2
Speed:	17 knots
Range:	21,000 n.miles at 17 knots
Complement:	approx. 70

Helicopters:	no facilities
Guns:	none
Radars:	

The AKHTUBA is the largest ship in service with the Soviet Navy except for aircraft carriers. She is in the Pacific.

Class: Twenty-two SOFIA-class tankers were delivered between 1963 and 1970, with one ship entering naval service in 1969.

Classification: Soviet VT type.

Design: This is the third largest merchant tanker design built in the Soviet Union (the KRYM class at 150,500 DWT and POBYEDA class at 67,980 DWT are larger). The AKHTUBA's cargo capacity is 44,500 tons of fuels. She can refuel only over the stern and is used mainly to transfer fuel to oilers and tankers.

In terms of displacement the large and long-serving naval tanker AKHTUBA is larger than any Soviet naval unit except for the TBILISI-class aircraft carriers. The ship operates in the Pacific. (1987, JMSDF)

6 TANKERS: UDA CLASS

Name	Name	Completed
DUNAY	SHEKSNA	
KOIDA	TEREK	} 1962–1964
LENA	VISHERA	

Builders:	Vyborg
Displacement:	7,100 tons full load
Length:	400 ft 2 in (122.0 m) overall
Beam:	51 ft 10 in (15.8 m)
Draft:	20 ft 8 in (6.3 m)
Propulsion:	2 diesel engines; 8,000 bhp; 2 shafts
Speed:	17 knots
Range:	4,000 n.miles at 17 knots

Complement:	approx. 85
Helicopters:	no facilities
Guns:	(see notes)
Radars:	1 or 2 Don or Don-2 (navigation)

These are small tankers built specifically for naval service.

Class: Three ships of this type were transferred to Indonesia.

Classification: Soviet VT type.

Design: There are provisions in each ship for fitting eight 57-mm/70-cal AA guns in quad mounts (plus one Strut Curve and two Muff Cob radars). At least one ship was observed in the Baltic in 1962 with armament, possibly for evaluation.

The LENA and VISHERA have a second A-frame, providing two amidships refueling positions.

The Uda-class tanker SHEKSNA, with a single amidships replenishment mast; some ships have two such masts, while the OIDA has none. (1983)

4 TANKERS: "KONDA" CLASS

Name	Name	Completed
KONDA	SOYANA	
ROSSOCH'	YAKHROMA	} 1954–1965

Builders:	Turku (Sweden)
Displacement:	1,980 tons full load
Tonnage:	1,265 DWT
Length:	226 ft 4 in (69.0 m) overall
Beam:	32 ft 10 in (10.0 m)
Draft:	14 ft 1 in (4.3 m)
Propulsion:	1 diesel engine; 1,600 bhp; 1 shaft

Speed:	12 knots
Range:	2,500 n.miles at 10 knots
Complement:	approx. 25
Helicopters:	no facilities
Guns:	none
Radars:	1 or 2 Don-2 (navigation) and/or Spin Trough (search)

These are small naval tankers, originally known as the ISKARA class.

Classification: Their naval designation is VT.

Design: Cargo capacity is approximately 1,100 tons of fuel. They refuel over the stern.

The KONDA-class tanker YAKHROMA. (1982, U.S. Navy)

13 TANKERS: "KHOBI" CLASS

Name	Name	Completed
CHEREMSHAN	SEIMA	
ORSHA	SHELON'	
INDIGA	SOS'VA	
KHOBI	SYSOLA	1950s
LOVAT'	TARTU	
METAN	TUNGUSKA	
SASHA		

Builders:	Zhdanov, Leningrad
Displacement:	1,525 tons full load
Tonnage:	834–915 DWT
Length:	203 ft 4 in (62.0 m) overall
Beam:	32 ft 10 in (10.0 m)
Draft:	14 ft 5 in (4.4 m)
Propulsion:	2 diesel engines; 1,600 bhp; 2 shafts
Speed:	12 knots
Range:	
Complement:	approx. 30
Helicopters:	no facilities
Guns:	none
Radars:	1 Don-2 (navigation)
	1 Spin Trough (search)

These are small tankers, similar to U.S. Navy gasoline tankers (AOG). They will probably be discarded in the near future.

Class: Ships of this type have been transferred to Albania and Indonesia. At least four other units have already been stricken from Soviet naval service—the ALAZAN, BAYMAK, GORYN, and TITAN.

Classification: Soviet VT type.

Design: Cargo capacity is approximately 1,500 tons of fuel. They generally refuel naval units over the bow while being towed at slow speed by the receiving ship.

The KHOBI-class tanker TARTU. (1982, Leo Van Ginderen)

3 TANKERS: "NERCHA" CLASS

Name	Name	Completed
KLYAZ'MA	NERCHA	1952–1955
NARVA		

Builders:	Crichton-Vulcan or Valmet, Abo (Finland)
Displacement:	1,800 tons full load
Tonnage:	1,300 DWT
Length:	208 ft 3 in (63.5 m) overall
Beam:	32 ft 10 in (10.0 m)
Draft:	14 ft 9 in (4.5 m)
Propulsion:	1 diesel engine; 1,000 bhp; 1 shaft
Speed:	11 knots
Range:	2,000 n.miles at 10 knots
Complement:	approx. 25
Helicopters:	no facilities
Guns:	none
Radars:	1 Don series (navigation)

Small tankers. Several similar ships are in Soviet merchant service. They refuel over the stern.

Classification: Soviet naval designation is VT.

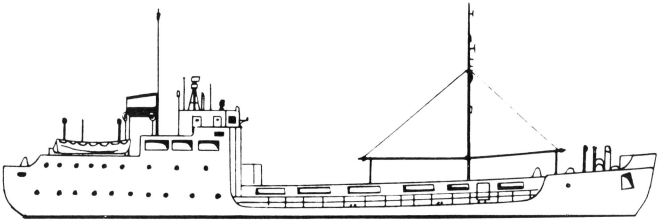

NERCHA-class tanker. (Siegfried Breyer)

3 TANKERS: "KAZBEK" CLASS

Name	Name	Name	Completed
ALATYR'	DESNA	VOLKHOV	early 1950s

Builders:	Kherson
Displacement:	16,250 tons full load
Tonnage:	11,800 DWT
Length:	477 ft 3 in (145.5 m) overall
Beam:	63 ft (19.2 m)
Draft:	27 ft 11 in (8.5 m)
Propulsion:	2 diesel engines (Russkiy); 4,000 bhp; 2 shafts
Speed:	14 knots
Range:	18,000 n.miles at 14 knots

Complement:	approx. 45
Helicopters:	no facilities
Guns:	none
Radars:	2 Don-2 (navigation)

About 50 of these tankers were built at Kherson and the Admiralty yard in Leningrad between 1951 and 1958; known as the LENINGRAD class. Many remain in merchant service and are used periodically to refuel naval ships.

Classification: Soviet VTR type.

Design: These ships are similar in design to the United States T-2 type of the late 1930s. Kingposts and an A-frame are fitted to the naval units to carry refueling hoses. They carry 11,600 tons of fuel.

A KAZBEK-class tanker refueling over the stern. The replenishment mast and cargo booms are forward of the bridge structure.

1 TANKER: "POLYARNIK" TYPE

Name	Completed
POLYARNIK (ex-KARNTEN, ex-TANKBOOT I)	1942

Builders:	C. av den Giessen, Krimpen (Netherlands)
Displacement:	12,500 tons full load
Tonnage:	6,640 DWT
Length:	433 ft 3 in (132.1 m) overall
Beam:	53 ft 1 in (16.2 m)
Draft:	24 ft 11 in (7.6 m)
Propulsion:	2 diesel engines (Werkspoor); 7,000 bhp; 2 shafts
Speed:	17 knots
Range:	

Complement:	approx. 55
Helicopters:	no facilities
Guns:	none
Radars:	

This ship was laid down for the Dutch Navy in December 1939 and taken over by German troops while still under construction in 1941; she was launched on 3 May 1941 and commissioned by the German Navy on 27 December 1941. The ship was taken over by the Soviets in December 1945. Still in active service, the POLYARNIK serves in the Pacific.

Classification: Soviet VT type.

Design: Cargo capacity is 5,600 tons of fuels; she also carries dry stores and provisions.

The POLYARNIK is the oldest naval tanker in Soviet service and one with a most unusual career.

SPECIAL-PURPOSE TANKERS

2 + RADIOACTIVE WASTE TANKERS: BELYANKA CLASS

Name	Completed
AMUR	1987
PINEGA	1988
. . . units (?)	

Builders:	Karamaki, Vyborg
Displacement:	approx. 10,000 tons full load
Length:	390 ft 4 in (119.0 m) waterline
	427 ft 5 in (130.3 m) overall
Beam:	56 ft 9 in (17.3 m)
Draft:	22 ft 9 in (6.9 m)
Propulsion:	1 diesel engine (Russkiy 5DKRN 62/140-3); 6,100 bhp; 1 shaft
Speed:	15.4 knots
Range:	
Complement:	
Helicopters:	no facilities
Guns:	none
Radars:	2 Kivach (navigation)

This is a new class of tankers to handle radioactive waste from nuclear-propelled surface ships and submarines.

Design: Modified PIONEER MOSKVYY-class merchant ship design which, in turn, is a variation of the SESTRORETSK-class cellular container ships.

1 RADIOACTIVE WASTE TANKER: "URAL" TYPE

Name	Completed
URAL	1969

Builders:	Dalzavod, Vladivostok
Displacement:	2,600 tons full load
Length:	295 ft 2 in (90.0 m) overall
Beam:	32 ft 10 in (10.0 m)
Draft:	12 ft 2 in (3.7 m)
Propulsion:	2 diesel engines; 1,200 bhp; 1 shaft
Speed:	12 knots
Range:	3,000 n.miles at 9 knots
Complement:	
Helicopters:	no facilities
Guns:	none
Radars:	1 Spin Trough (search)

The URAL is a small, superstructure-aft tanker employed to carry nuclear waste. Note high freeboard and travelling crane.

Classification: Soviet TNT type.

Special-purpose tanker URAL.

6 SPECIAL CARGO TANKERS: LUZA CLASS

Name	Name	Completed
ALAMBAY	DON	
ARAGUVY	KANA	1960s
BARGUZIN	SELENGA	

Builders:	Srrednyy Neva, Kolpino
Displacement:	1,900 tons full load
Length:	205 ft (62.5 m) overall
Beam:	35 ft 1 in (10.7 m)
Draft:	14 ft 1 in (4.3 m)
Propulsion:	1 diesel engine; 1,000 bhp; 1 shaft
Speed:	12 knots
Range:	2,000 n.miles at 11 knots
Complement:	
Helicopters:	no facilities
Guns:	(see notes)
Radars:	1 Don-2 (navigation)

These small tankers are used to transport volatile liquids such as radiological liquids and fuels for Soviet SLBMs. Some units have a 12.7-mm MG twin mount.

Class: Three ships were apparently stricken from naval service in the early 1980s—OKA, SASIMA, and YENISEY.

Classification: Soviet TNT type.

The special-purpose tanker BARGUZIN of the LUZA class. (1982)

5 RADIOACTIVE WASTE TANKERS: VALA CLASS

Name	Name	Name	Completed
TNT-11	TNT-19	1 unit	} early 1960s
TNT-12	TNT-29		

Builders:	
Displacement:	3,100 tons full load
Length:	250 ft (76.2 m) overall
Beam:	41 ft (12.5 m)
Draft:	16 ft 5 in (5.0 m)
Propulsion:	1 diesel engine; 1,000 bhp; 1 shaft
Speed:	14 knots
Range:	2,000 n.miles at 11 knots
Complement:	
Helicopters:	no facilities
Guns:	none
Radars:	1 . . . . . . (navigation)

This class of small tankers carries radioactive waste.
Classification: Soviet TNT type.

WATER TANKERS

Soviet water tankers provide water to submarines and surface ships
for crew consumption and (in surface ships) for use in boilers.

2 WATER TANKERS: "MANYCH" CLASS

Name	Completed
MANYCH	1971
TAYGIL	1977

Builders:	Vyborg
Displacement:	7,800 tons full load
Length:	379 ft 10 in (115.8 m) overall
Beam:	51 ft 10 in (15.8 m)
Draft:	22 ft (6.7 m)
Propulsion:	2 diesel engines; 9,000 bhp; 2 shafts
Speed:	18 knots
Range:	7,500 n.miles at 16 knots
	11,500 n.miles at 12 knots
Complement:	approx. 90
Helicopters:	no facilities
Guns:	see notes
Radars:	2 Don-Kay (navigation)
	2 Muff Cob (fire control) in MANYCH

These ships were built to serve as naval replenishment ships to
provide diesel fuel and stores to submarines. However, the design
was not operationally successful and they became water carriers.
Classification: Soviet MVT type.

Guns: The MANYCH was completed as an oiler with four 57-mm
AA guns in twin mounts supported by two Muff Cob radars. The
guns were removed in 1975 but the Muff Cob directors/radar were
retained. The TAYGIL was completed without armament.

14 WATER TANKERS: VODA CLASS

Name	Name	Name	Completed
ABAKAN	MVT-16	MVT-24	
SURA	MVT-17	MVT-134	
MVT-6	MVT-18	MVT-138	} 1950s
MVT-9	MVT-20	MVT-428	
MVT-10	MVT-21		

Builders:	
Displacement:	2,100 tons standard
	3,100 tons full load
Length:	267 ft 4 in (81.5 m) overall
Beam:	37 ft 9 in (11.5 m)
Draft:	14 ft 1 in (4.3 m)
Propulsion:	2 diesel engines; 1,600 bhp; 2 shafts
Speed:	12 knots
Range:	3,000 n.miles at 10 knots
Complement:	approx. 40
Helicopters:	no facilities
Guns:	none
Radars:	1 Don-2 (navigation)

These ships are water-distilling and -carrying ships.
Classification: Soviet MVT type.

The MANYCH-class water tanker TAYGIL.

TRANSPORTS

The Soviet merchant fleet operates the world's largest fleet of passenger ships, which would become available for naval service in wartime.

1 NAVAL TRANSPORT: "MIKHAIL KALININ" CLASS

Name	Completed
KUBAN (ex-NADEZHDA KRUPSKAYA)	1963

Builders:	Mathias Thesen, Wismar (East Germany)
Displacement:	6,400 tons full load
Length:	400 ft 10 in (122.2 m) overall
Beam:	52 ft 6 in (16.0 m)
Draft:	16 ft 9 in (5.1 m)

Propulsion:	2 diesel engines (DMR/MAN); 8,000 bhp; 2 shafts
Speed:	18 knots
Range:	8,100 n.miles at 17 knots
Complement:	
Passengers:	340
Helicopters:	no facilities
Guns:	none
Radars:	2 Don-2 (navigation)
	1 Spin Trough (search)

This former passenger cruise liner is employed to transport naval personnel in the Mediterranean.

Class: Nineteen ships of this class were delivered to the Soviet merchant fleet between 1958 and 1964, with the above ship being taken into naval service in 1976.

Design: The ship carries 1,000 tons of cargo, with cranes installed forward and aft.

The MIKHAIL KALININ-class transport KUBAN is the only ship of this type in Soviet naval service. She operates in the Black Sea and Mediterranean.

CARGO AND SUPPLY SHIPS

In addition to the cargo ships listed here, several are included above in the missile transport listings.

2 CARGO SHIPS: "NEON ANTONOV" CLASS

Name	Name
IRBIT	DVINA

Builders:	(USSR)
Displacement:	5,200 tons full load
Length:	311 ft 11 in (95.1 m) overall
Beam:	48 ft 3 in (14.7 m)
Draft:	21 ft 4 in (6.5 m)
Propulsion:	1 diesel engine; 1 shaft
Speed:	16 knots
Range:	
Complement:	
Helicopters:	no facilities
Guns:	see notes
Radars:	2 Palm Frond (navigation)

The IRBIT and DVINA the only Navy-operated ship of the class; the remaining units are operated by the KGB Maritime Border Troops (see chapter 26). The 11-ship class was completed from 1978 through 1987.

Guns: There are positions in the KGB ships for a twin 30-mm gun mount, two 14.5-mm twin machine-gun mounts, and two SA-N-5/SA-7 Grail missile launchers.

3 CARGO SHIPS: "YUNYY PARTIZAN" CLASS

Name	Completed
TURGAY	1975
PECHORA	1976
UFA	1978

Builders:	Santierul Naval Shipyard, Turnu-Severin (Romania)
Displacement:	3,947 tons full load
Tonnage:	2,150 DWT
Length:	291 ft 1 in (88.75 m) overall
Beam:	42 ft (12.8 m)
Draft:	17 ft 1 in (5.2 m)
Propulsion:	1 diesel engine (Cegielski/Sulzer TAD 36); 2,080 bhp; 1 shaft
Speed:	12.75 knots
Range:	4,000 n.miles at 12 knots
Complement:	approx. 25
Helicopters:	no facilities
Guns:	none
Radars:	1 Don-2 (navigation)

These are small coastal container ships.

Class: Twenty ships of this design were built for the Soviet merchant service plus several units for Cuba and Romania. Four naval units were delivered; one, the PINEGA, has been converted to a missile transport (see page 245).

Design: Cargo capacity in merchant service is 58 standard freight containers. These are superstructure-aft ships with three 10-ton-capacity cranes, one of which can be rigged to lift up to 28 tons.

The small naval cargo ship TURGAY of the YUNIY PARTIZAN class provides support to a Foxtrot-class submarine. Beyond the TURGAY is the large oceangoing tug SB-524 of the GORYN class. As indicated elsewhere in this volume, a variety of naval auxiliaries and—at times—merchant ships provide support for Soviet undersea craft.

1 CARGO SHIP: "AMGUEMA" CLASS

Name	Completed
YAUZA	1975

Builders:	(USSR)
Displacement:	15,100 tons full load
Tonnage:	9,045 DWT
Length:	436 ft 7 in (133.1 m) overall
Beam:	62 ft (18.9 m)
Draft:	29 ft 10 in (9.1 m)
Propulsion:	diesel-electric: 4 diesel engines with 4 electric generators; 7,200 bhp; 1 shaft
Speed:	15 knots

Range:	approx. 10,000 n.miles at 15 knots
Complement:	
Helicopters:	no facilities
Guns:	none
Radars:	2 Don-2 (navigation)

One of a class of about 15 cargo ships built for polar operations; others were delivered to the merchant fleet between 1962 and 1972. One ship, the MIKHAIL SOMOV, is a research and supply ship (see chapter 25).

Design: Cargo capacity is 6,600 tons. The ship has a limited icebreaking capability, recessed anchors, and other features for ice/cold-weather operations.

The AMGUEMA-class cargo ship YAUZA; note her icebreaking prow and the cargo booms stowed in the vertical position.

8 SUPPLY SHIPS: MAYAK CLASS

Name	Name	Name	Name	Conversion Completed
BULZULUK	LAMA	NEMAN	ULMA VYTEGRA	1971–1976
ISHIM	MIUS	RIONI		

Builders:	Dnepr, Kiev
Displacement:	1,050 tons full load
Tonnage:	690 GRT
Length:	178 ft 1 in (54.3 m) overall
Beam:	30 ft 8 in (9.3 m)
Draft:	11 ft 11 in (3.6 m)
Propulsion:	1 diesel engine; 800 bhp; 1 shaft
Speed:	11 knots
Range:	9,400 n.miles at 11 knots
Complement:	approx. 30
Helicopters:	no facilities
Guns:	none
Radars:	1 Spin Trough (search)

These are converted Mayak-class side trawlers. They have been modified to carry provisions for naval ships. A large number of these craft were completed from 1962 onward, with several others having been converted to naval intelligence ships (AGI); see chapter 24.

Classification: Soviet VTR type.

Design: Small, superstructure-aft ships, built to trawl over the starboard side and fitted with freezer holds.

One of the ubiquitous Mayak-class trawlers, shown here in the supply-ship configuration. This ship is the NEMAN. (1983)

8 SUPPLY SHIPS: "VYTEGRALES" CLASS

Name	Name	Completed
APSHERON (ex-TOSNALES)	DONBASS (ex-KIRISHI)	1963–1966
BASKUNCHAK (ex-VOSTOK–4)	SEVAN (ex-VYBORGLES)	
DAURIYA (ex-SUZDAL)	TAMAN' (ex-VOSTOK–3)	
DIKSON (ex-VAGALES)	YAMAL (ex-SVIRLES)	

Builders:	Zhdanov, Leningrad
Displacement:	9,650 tons full load
Length:	399 ft 10 in (121.9 m) overall
Beam:	54 ft 9 in (16.7 m)
Draft:	24 ft (7.3 m)
Propulsion:	1 diesel engine (Burmeister & Wain 950 VTBF 110); 5,200 bhp; 1 shaft
Speed:	16 knots
Range:	7,400 n.miles at 14.5 knots
Complement:	approx. 90
Helicopters:	landing platform
Guns:	none
Radars:	2 Don-2 (navigation) 1 Big Net (air search) in DONBASS

These are converted merchant timber carriers. They were originally converted to an SESS configuration with the addition of special communications and radar equipment plus a helicopter platform aft. They have subsequently been employed as fleet supply ships although they have been reported to continue to support space-related activities.

Class: About 20 additional ships of this class remain in merchant service, some of which have been modified to carry containers.

Another seven ships of this type were converted to civilian satellite tracking ships (under the aegis of the Soviet Academy of Sciences); see chapter 25.

Classification: Soviet VTR type.

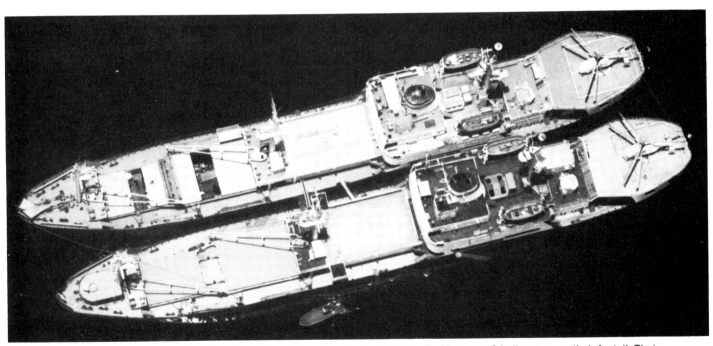

A pair of VYTEGRALES-class cargo ships, almost as alike as two peas in a pod, even to the Hormone-C helicopters on their fantail. Their configuration provides for cargo holds forward, served by two sets of cranes, with bridge, machinery, and living spaces aft.

The VYTEGRALES-class naval cargo ship DAURIYA with a Ka-25 Hormone-C helicopter on her fantail. The mast arrangements in these ships vary; some still carry tracking and electronic antennas making them multi-purpose auxiliaries. (1988, U.S. Navy)

9 CARGO SHIPS: "KEYLA" CLASS

Name	Name	Completed
MEZEN'	TULOMA	
ONEGA	UNZHA	
PONOY	USSURI	1960–1966
RITSA	YERUSLAN	
TERIBERKA		

Builders:	Angyalfold, Budapest (Hungary)
Displacement:	2,042 tons full load
Tonnage:	1,280 DWT
Length:	257 ft 6 in (78.5 m) overall
Beam:	34 ft 6 in (10.5 m)
Draft:	15 ft 1 in (4.6 m)
Propulsion:	1 diesel engine (Lang); 1,000 bhp; 1 shaft
Speed:	11.75 knots

Range:	4,000 n.miles at 11 knots
Complement:	approx. 25
Helicopters:	no facilities
Guns:	none
Radars:	1 Don-2 (navigation) or Spin Trough (search)

Small cargo ships. The RITSA has special communications equipment installed (deckhouse fitted over after hatch).

Class: Approximately 55 ships of this class were built in Hungary, most for the Soviet merchant fleet with several being transferred to Angola, Indonesia, Norway, and North Vietnam; six were retained by Hungary. Ten of the Soviet ships were provided to the Navy; one has been stricken, the TVERTSA.

Classification: Soviet VTR type.

Design: Cargo capacity is 1,100 tons.

KEYLA-class cargo ship.

The KEYLA-class cargo ship RITSA has been modified, primarily with a deckhouse erected forward of the bridge, a small deckhouse fitted at the base of the forward mast, and the installation of electronic antennas on the forward mast. Thus configured she may have a limited intelligence collection role.

1 CARGO SHIP: "LENINSKIY KOMSOMOL" CLASS

Name	Completed
SAMARA	1960s

Builders:	Kherson
Displacement:	approx. 22,000 tons full load
Tonnage:	16,220 DWT
Length:	557 ft 3 in (169.9 m) overall
Beam:	71 ft 10 in (21.9 m)
Draft:	31 ft 10 in (9.7 m)
Propulsion:	2 steam turbines (Kirov); 13,000 shp; 1 shaft
Boilers:	2
Speed:	19 knots
Range:	
Complement:	
Helicopters:	no facilities
Guns:	none
Radars:	2 . . . . . . (navigation)

The SAMARA is one of two ships of a class of 25 cargo ships that were taken into naval service in the early 1980s. The other naval unit, the KOLKHIDA, was sold for scrap in December 1989.

Class: The 25 ships of this class were completed in 1959–1966; only two of these ships remain in merchant service, one of which has been fitted with gas turbine propulsion. The previous merchant names of the two naval units are not known.

Classification: Soviet VTR type.

CARGO SHIPS: "CHULYM" CLASS

The four naval ships of this class—the INSAR, KAMCHATKA, and LENINSK-KUZNETSKIY, and SEVERODONETSK—were discarded in the 1980s. These ships were among 41 of this design built in Poland. None remain in Soviet merchant service. See 4th edition, page 311.

CARGO SHIP: "DONBASS" CLASS

The SVIR was the only ship of this large class to serve in the Soviet Navy. She was discarded in the 1980s. The DONBASS-class ships, built in the 1950s, were designed as colliers, with many serving as general (tramp) cargo ships in the Soviet merchant marine and several foreign merchant fleets; some served the Soviet fishing industry as fish carriers. None remain in Soviet service. See 4th edition, page 311.

CARGO SHIPS: "KOLOMNA" CLASS

Two naval cargo ships of the KOLOMNA class were discarded in the early 1980s, the KRASNOARMEYSK and MEGRA. The SVANETIYA was converted to an experimental ship; it was also discarded.

Six KOLOMNA-class cargo ships completed as submarine tenders (ATREK class) have been stricken; the MIKHAIL LOMONOSOV of this design serves as a civilian research ship (see chapter 25).

CARGO SHIPS: "TELNOVSK" CLASS

The three naval cargo ships of the TELNOVSK class have probably been retired—the BUREVESTNIK, LAG, and MANOMETER. See 3rd edition, page 256, for details.

The KS-7 of this class is a cable ship and is listed earlier in this chapter; several other units that served the Soviet Navy as survey ships have been discarded (see chapter 24).

HOSPITAL SHIPS

4 HOSPITAL SHIPS: "OB'" CLASS

Name	Completed	Name	Completed
OB'	1980	SVIR	1989
YENISEY	1981	IRTYSH	1990

Builders:	Adolf Warski, Szczecin (Poland)
Displacement:	11,000 tons full load
Length:	505 ft 2 in (154.0 m) overall
Beam:	67 ft 3 in (20.5 m)
Draft:	17 ft 1 in (5.2 m)
Propulsion:	2 diesel engines; 2 shafts
Speed:	20 knots
Range:	
Complement:	approx. 80 (civilian)
Medical staff:	approx. 200
Helicopters:	1 Ka-25 Hormone-C or Ka-32 Helix-D
Guns:	none
Radars:	3 Don-2 (navigation)

These are purpose-built hospital ships. The ships are civilian-manned but carry naval medical staffs. The commanding officers are believed to be Navy captains 3rd rank, with the medical staffs commanded by lieutenant colonels of the Naval Medical Service.

The OB' is assigned to the Pacific Fleet and the YENISEY to the Black Sea Fleet.

Design: The ships have seven operating rooms and 100 beds. A hangar is provided for a single helicopter for casualty evacuation.

Engineering: A bow thruster is provided.

The OB'-class hospital ship YENESEY under way at high speed. Both the U.S. and Soviet navies added hospital ships to their fleets in the 1980s; the much larger U.S. ships are converted tankers and were in reserve until the Desert Shield buildup in the Middle East that began in late 1990. Both Soviet ships appear to be in active service.

This stern aspect of the YENISEY shows her helicopter deck and open hangar for a Hormone-C employed for casualty evacuation.

TRAINING SHIPS

These ships serve primarily the Navy's higher naval schools (i.e., naval academies). The armament of the SMOL'NYY class permits those ships to be employed in limited combat roles in wartime.

The several Soviet sail training ships are operated under the aegis of the merchant and fishing fleets; see chapter 25.

3 ARMED TRAINING SHIPS: "SMOL'NYY" CLASS

Name	Name	Completed
KHASAN	SMOL'NYY	
PEREKOP		} 1976–1978

Builders:	Adolf Warski, Szczecin (Poland)
Displacement:	8,500 tons full load
Length:	452 ft 8 in (138.0 m) overall
Beam:	59 ft (18.0 m)
Draft:	20 ft 4 in (6.2 m)

Propulsion:	4 diesel engines; 16,000 bhp; 2 shafts
Speed:	20 knots
Range:	12,000 n.miles at 15 knots
Complement:	approx. 210 + 275 cadets
Helicopters:	no facilities
Guns:	4 76.2-mm/59-cal DP (2 twin)
	4 30-mm/65-cal close-in (2 twin)
ASW weapons:	2 RBU-2500 rocket launchers
Radars:	2 Don-2 (navigation) except 3 in PEREKOP
	1 Don-Kay in PEREKOP
	1 Drum Tilt (fire control)
	1 Head Net-C (air search)
	1 Owl Screech (fire control)
Sonars:	medium-frequency hull mounted
EW systems:	2 Watch Dog

These are large, graceful training ships, of a type not employed by Western navies.

Classification: Soviet US type.

The PEREKOP is one of the SMOL'NYY-class training ships that provide at-sea training for naval personnel and in wartime could serve as escort ships.

The SMOL'NYY, showing the ship's forward battery of 76.2-mm twin AA gun mounts and the RBU-2500 ASW rocket launchers. Western navies do not have training ships of this type.

2 TRAINING SHIPS: "WODNIK" CLASS

Name	Name	Completed
LUGA	OKA	1977

Builders:	Polnocny, Gdańsk (Poland)
Displacement:	1,500 tons standard
	1,800 tons full load
Length:	236 ft 2 in (72.0 m) overall
Beam:	39 ft 4 in (12.0 m)
Draft:	13 ft 9 in (4.2 m)
Propulsion:	2 diesel engines (Zgoda-Sulzer 6TD48); 3,600 bhp; 2 shafts
Speed:	16.5 knots
Range:	7,500 n.miles at 11 knots
Complement:	approx. 60 + 90 cadets
Helicopters:	no facilities
Guns:	none
Radars:	3 Don-2 (navigation)

Navigation training ships. Two similar ships serve in the Polish Navy and one served in the East German Navy. Both Soviet units are in the Baltic Fleet.

Classification: Soviet US type.

Design: The WODNIK design is based on the Moma class.

The OKA is one of two Polish-built training ships used by the Soviet Navy. The Soviet Navy is far more oriented to early shipboard training than is the U.S. Navy. (1977)

2 TRAINING SHIPS: UGRA CLASS

Name	Completed
BORODINO	1970
GANGUT	1971

Builders:	Black Sea, Nikolayev (south)
Displacement:	6,900 tons standard
	9,650 tons full load
Length:	475 ft 7 in (145.0 m) overall
Beam:	58 ft 1 in (17.7 m)
Draft:	21 ft (6.4 m)
Propulsion:	4 diesel engines; 8,000 bhp; 2 shafts
Speed:	17 knots
Range:	21,000 n.miles at 10 knots
Complement:	approx. 300 + 400 cadets
Helicopters:	no facilities
Guns:	8 57-mm/80-cal AA (4 twin)
Radars:	4 Don-2 (navigation)
	2 Muff Cob (fire control)
	1 Strut Curve (air search)
EW systems:	4 Watch Dog

These ships were built with classrooms and training facilities in place of the workshops and storerooms of the Ugra-class submarine tenders.

Classification: Soviet US type.

Design: The ships' superstructures have been built up aft in comparison with the submarine tenders. They retain cranes forward and amidships.

The GANGUT is one of two Ugra-class training ships; they have an appearance similar to the submarine tenders of this class but with a large "school house" amidships; no helicopter platform is fitted.

2+ ASW TRAINING SHIPS: MAYAK CLASS

Builders:	(USSR)
Displacement:	1,050 tons full load
Length:	177 ft 9 in (54.2 m) overall
Beam:	30 ft 6 in (9.3 m)
Draft:	11 ft 10 in (3.6 m)
Propulsion:	1 diesel engine (Karl Liebnecht 8NVD48); 800 bhp; 1 shaft
Speed:	11 knots
Range:	9,400 n.miles at 11 knots
Complement:	approx. 60 (including cadets)
Helicopters:	no facilities
Guns:	2 25-mm AA (1 twin)
ASW weapons:	4 RBU-1200 rocket launchers
	4 15.75-inch (400-mm) torpedo tubes (4 single)
	2 depth charge racks [12]
Radars:	1 Spin Trough (search)
Sonars:	high-frequency hull mounted

These Mayak-class trawlers were modified with ASW weapons and sensors for specialized training. Converted in the 1980s. Additional conversions may be forthcoming. They may also be employed for long-range ASW patrol in "low-threat" areas.

Classification: Soviet US type.

A Mayak-class trawler configured for ASW training. The ship's twin 25-mm gun mount (over-under arrangement) and RBU-1200 rocket launchers are visible ahead of the forward mast.

EXPERIMENTAL AND TRIALS SHIPS

The shipbuilding research ship IZUMRUD, constructed specifically for the Ministry of Shipbuilding to test ship structures and materials as well as other ship components, is listed under civilian auxiliary ships (see chapter 25).

1 TRIALS SHIP: MODIFIED SORUM CLASS

Name	Completed
OS-572	1987

Builders:	Yaroslavl (USSR)
Displacement:	1,250 tons standard
	1,696 tons full load
Length:	193 ft 10 in (59.1 m) overall
Beam:	41 ft 4 in (12.6 m)
Draft:	15 ft 1 in (4.6 m)
Propulsion:	diesel-electric: 2 diesel engines (5-2D42); 1,500 bhp; 1 shaft
Speed:	14 knots
Range:	6,700 n. miles at 13 knots
Complement:	approx. 60
Guns:	none
Radars:	2 Don-2 (navigation)
Sonars:	towed array

This is a modified Sorum-class tug completed as a trials platform for towed-array sonars.

Class: Additional tugs of this class are operated by the Navy and by the KGB Maritime Border Troops, the latter as armed patrol tugs (see chapter 26). Similar ships are operated as salvage tugs by the Ministry of Fisheries and merchant fleet (PURGA class); others have been transferred to Bulgaria and Poland.

Design: Modified from the standard Sorum design by the forecastle deck being extended to the stern, a raised fantail (poop) area, and support structure for towed array that projects beyond the original stern.

A Sorum-class oceangoing tug as modified to a trials ship for towed-array sonar. (1988, Royal Navy)

1 TRIALS SHIP: CONVERTED POLNOCNY B CLASS

Name
OS-246

Builders:	Polnocny, Gdańsk (Poland)
Displacement:	800 tons full load
Length:	242 ft 9 in (74.0 m) overall
Beam:	28 ft 2 in (8.6 m)
Draft:	6 ft 7 in (2.0 m)
Propulsion:	2 diesel engines; 5,000 bhp; 2 shafts
Speed:	18 knots
Range:	900 n.miles at 18 knots
	1,500 n.miles at 14 knots
Complement:	
Helicopters:	no facilities
Missiles/rockets:	removed
Guns:	removed
Radars:	1 Don-2 (navigation)

This is a former LSM of the Polnocny B class (completed 1968–1970); see chapter 20 for additional data. Converted to the trials role in the 1980s.

The OS-246 is a former Polnocny B–class LSM extensively modified for experimental activities. A number of masts and antennas have been added, leading some U.S. Navy sources to list her as an AGI; however, the major modifications indicate an experimental role.

5 TORPEDO TRIALS SHIPS: POTOK CLASS

Name	Name	Name	Completed
OS-100	OS-145	OS- . . .	
OS-138	OS-225		1978—

Builders:	
Displacement:	750 tons standard
	860 tons full load
Length:	232 ft 11 in (71.0 m) overall
Beam:	29 ft 10 in (9.1 m)
Draft:	8 ft 2 in (2.5 m)
Propulsion:	2 diesel engines; 4,000 bhp; 2 shafts
Speed:	18 knots
Range:	5,000 n.miles at 12 knots
Complement:	approx. 40
Helicopters:	no facilities
Guns:	none
ASW weapons:	1 21-inch (533-mm) torpedo tube
	1 15.75-inch (400-mm) torpedo tube
Radars:	1 Don-2 (navigation)

These are torpedo trials and recovery ships. They are probably replacements for the modified T-43 minesweepers previously employed in this role. A crane is provided aft for torpedo recovery.

Classification: Soviet OS type.

1 EXPERIMENTAL SHIP: "PIONEER MOSKVYY" CLASS

Name	Conversion Completed
Sayaniy	1984

Builders:	Vyborg
Displacement:	10,700 tons full load
Length:	430 ft (130.3 m) overall
Beam:	57 ft 1 in (17.3 m)
Draft:	24 ft 1 in (7.3 m)
Propulsion:	1 diesel engine (B&W 5DKRN 62/140-3); 6,100 bhp; 1 shaft
Speed:	15.5 knots
Range:	12,000 n.miles at 15.5 knots
Complement:	approx. 120
Helicopters:	no facilities
Guns:	none
Radars:	2 Don-2 (navigation)

The Sayaniy is a converted cargo ship. Three sister ships were converted to submarine rescue and salvage ships (see page 238).

The Sayaniy is a large experimental ship with deckhouses erected over most of her cargo spaces. She operates in the Pacific. (1984, JMSDF)

1+ TRIALS SHIPS: AL'PINIST CLASS

Name
OS-104

Builders:	Yaroslavl
Displacement:	1,200 tons full load
Length:	176 ft 2 in (53.7 m) overall
Beam:	34 ft 5 in (10.5 m)
Draft:	14 ft 1 in (4.3 m)
Propulsion:	1 diesel engine (8NVD48-2U); 1,320 bhp; 1 shaft
Speed:	13 knots
Range:	7,600 n.miles at 13 knots
Complement:	
Helicopters:	no facilities
Guns:	none
Radars:	1 Don-2 (navigation)
	1 . . . . . . (navigation)

This unit is a modified stern trawler; there is a two-level deckhouse built on the starboard side, aft of the bridge.

The OS-104 has been identified in the Pacific. Additional units are believed being converted. Additional units of this type serve in the AGI role (see chapter 24).

Al'pinist-class stem-haul trawler as configured to a trials ship, the OS-104. This class has been employed in several naval and civilian roles. (1985, JMSDF)

1 OR 2 TRIALS SHIPS: DALDYN CLASS

Builders:	
Displacement:	360 tons full load
Length:	104 ft (31.7 m) overall
Beam:	23 ft 7 in (7.2 m)
Draft:	9 ft 2 in (2.8 m)
Propulsion:	1 diesel engine (8NVD 36U); 300 bhp; 1 shaft
Speed:	9 knots
Range:	
Complement:	approx. 15
Helicopters:	no facilities
Guns:	none
Radars:	1 Spin Trough (search)

Modified seiners of the Kareliya class, used for experimental work.

EXPERIMENTAL SHIPS: T-43 CLASS

The former minesweepers of the T-43 class employed in various experimental roles with the OS classification have apparently been stricken.

ELECTRIC GENERATOR SHIPS

4 ELECTRIC GENERATOR SHIPS: TOMBA CLASS

Name	Name	Name	Completed
ENS-244	ENS-348	ENS-357	} 1974–1976
ENS-254			

Builders:	Adolf Warski, Szczecin (Poland)
Displacement:	4,400 tons standard
	5,800 tons full load
Length:	351 ft (107.0 m) overall
Beam:	55 ft 9 in (17.0 m)
Draft:	16 ft 5 in (5.0 m)
Propulsion:	1 diesel engine; 4,500 bhp; 1 shaft
Speed:	12 knots
Range:	7,000 n.miles at 12 knots
Complement:	approx. 50
Helicopters:	no facilities
Guns:	none
Radars:	1 Don-2 (navigation)

These ships provide electric power for naval activities in remote areas.

Classification: Soviet ENS type.

The Tomba-class power generator ship ENS-254. The ENS-244 and ENS-357 have a third mast faired into the leading edge of the second funnel. These ships provide electric power in remote areas. (1988, Royal Netherlands Navy)

DEGAUSSING/DEPERMING SHIPS

14 + DEPERMING SHIPS: BEREZA CLASS

Name	Name	Name	Completed
SR-23	SR-137	SR-560	
SR-28	SR-478	SR-569	
SR-59	SR-479	SR-570	1985–
SR-74	SR-541	SR-939	
SR-120	SR-548	SR-. . .	

Builders:	Stocznia Polnocny, Gdańsk (Poland)
Displacement:	2,700 tons full load
Length:	275 ft 6 in (84.0 m) overall
Beam:	44 ft 3 in (13.5 m)

Draft:	13 ft 1½ in (4.0 m)
Propulsion:	2 diesel engines (Zgoda/Sulzer 8TD48); 4,400 bhp; 2 shafts
Speed:	15 knots
Range:	
Complement:	approx. 60
Helicopters:	no facilities
Guns:	none
Radars:	1 Kivach (navigation)

These are built-for-the-purpose degaussing/deperming ships. Classification: Soviet SR type.

Design: These ships appear to be modifications of the Yug-class oceanographic ships. A large crane is fitted aft for handling deperming cables.

The Bereza-class degaussing/deperming ships are the largest ships of this type in any navy; they are intended to mitigate the magnetic signature of naval ships to reduce their vulnerability to magnetic mines.

20 + DEPERMING SHIPS: PELYM CLASS

Name	Name	Name	Completed
SR-77	SR-222	SR-409	
SR-111	SR-233	SR-455	
SR-179	SR-241	SR-. . .	
SR-180	SR-276	SR-. . .	1971–
SR-191	SR-280	SR-. . .	
SR-203	SR-281	SR-. . .	
SR-218	SR-407	SR-. . .	

Builders:	Khabarovsk
Displacement:	1,300 tons full load
Length:	214 ft 10 in (65.5 m) overall
Beam:	38 ft (11.6 m)
Draft:	11 ft 2 in (3.4 m)
Propulsion:	2 diesel engines; 2 shafts
Speed:	16 knots
Range:	4,500 n.miles at 12 knots
Complement:	approx. 40
Helicopters:	no facilities
Guns:	none
Radars:	1 Don-2 (navigation)

These are built-for-the-purpose degaussing/deperming ships.

Class: One unit was transferred to Cuba in 1982.

Classification: Soviet SR type.

Design: There are several variations to the design; later units have a tripod mast aft (SR-191, etc.), while others have the forecastle deck extended to the stern with a kingpost aft for handling deperming cables.

The modified Pelym-class deperming ship SR-233; she differs from earlier units by the extended forecastle deck and the fitting of a kingpost and cable-handling boom aft. (1987, JMSDF)

The Pelym-class deperming ship SR-222 shows the basic configuration of these ships. Some ships have a second mast aft (as in SR-191 and SR-241; see 4th edition, pages 317–318). (1987, JMSDF)

DEPERMING SHIPS: KHABAROV CLASS

These converted steel-hulled cargo ships, built in the 1950s, have been stricken. See 4th edition, page 318.

DEPERMING SHIPS: SEKSTAN AND KORALL CLASSES

These older, wood-hull ships have been stricken. See 4th edition, page 319.

NOISE MEASUREMENT SHIPS

10+ NOISE MEASUREMENT SHIPS: ONEGA CLASS

Name	Name	Name	Completed
GKS-52	GKS-286	SFP-340	
GKS-83	SFP-95	SFP-511	1973—
GKS-224	SFP-283	2+ units	

Builders:	(USSR)
Displacement:	1,925 tons full load
Length:	265 ft 8 in (81.0 m) overall
Beam:	36 ft 1 in (11.0 m)
Draft:	13 ft 9 in (4.2 m)
Propulsion:	2 diesel engines; 8,000 bhp; 2 shafts
Speed:	20 knots
Range:	
Complement:	approx. 120
Helicopters:	landing area
Guns:	none
Radars:	1 Don-2 (navigation)

These ships provide noise-measurement data on surface ships and submarines. Details differ with the GKS type having pylon masts and the SFP lattice masts.

Classification: Four ships are known to be Soviet GKS type and four SFP.

The Onega-class noise-measurement ship SFP-340.

17 NOISE MEASUREMENT SHIPS: T-43 CLASS

Name	Name	Name	Completed
GKS-11	GKS-17	GKS-23	
GKS-12	GKS-18	GKS-24	
GKS-13	GKS-19	GKS-26	
GKS-14	GKS-20	GKS-42	1950s
GKS-15	GKS-21	GKS-45	
GKS-16	GKS-22		

Builders:	(USSR)
Displacement:	500 tons standard
	570 tons full load
Length:	190 ft 3 in (58.0 m) overall
Beam:	28 ft 2 in (8.6 m)
Draft:	7 ft 6 in (2.3 m)
Propulsion:	2 diesel engines (Type 9D); 2,200 bhp; 2 shafts
Speed:	14 knots
Range:	
Complement:	approx. 75
Helicopters:	no facilities
Guns:	see notes
Radars:	1 Neptune (navigation) or Spin Trough (search)

These are former minesweepers, modified to lay bottom-mounted hydrophones to monitor surface ship and submarine noises.

Class: At least two units have been stricken, the GKS-25 and GKS-46. Others are expected to be replaced in the near future by the Onega-class ships.

Classification: Soviet GKS type.

Guns: Designed to mount a single 37-mm AA gun on the forecastle.

The converted T-43 minesweeper GKS-14 configured as a noise-measurement ship.

ICEBREAKERS

These are Navy-manned icebreakers. None is armed.

2 SUPPORT ICEBREAKERS: "IVAN SUSANIN" CLASS

Name	Completed
IVAN SUSANIN	1974
RUSLAN	1981

Builders:	Admiralty, Leningrad
Displacement:	3,400 tons full load
Length:	229 ft 7 in (70.0 m) overall
Beam:	60 ft (18.3 m)
Draft:	21 ft 4 in (6.5 m)
Propulsion:	diesel-electric: 3 diesel generators (13D100); 4,800 bhp; connected to 2 electric motors; 2 shafts
Speed:	14.5 knots
Range:	5,500 n.miles at 12.5 knots
	13,000 n.miles at 9.5 knots
Complement:	approx. 140
Helicopters:	landing area
Guns:	removed
Radars:	2 Don-Kay (navigation)

These are former KGB icebreakers; they are of the same basic design as the naval and civilian DOBRYNYA NIKITICH class. They were transferred to the Navy in the 1980s.

Class: Thirty-one ships of this general design are believed to have been built for the USSR: six are operated by the KGB Maritime Border Troops as patrol icebreakers (see chapter 26), nine by the Navy (including these two ships) as support icebreakers, one Navy-manned unit is employed as a research ship (see chapter 24), and the remaining are civilian manned—14 as icebreakers and one as a polar research ship (see chapter 25). One additional ship was built at the Admiralty yard for East Germany (delivered in 1968).

Classification: Soviet LDK type.

Design: These ships differ from the Navy units primarily because of their helicopter platform (no hangar) and enlarged superstructure. As KGB ships they were armed; see KGB listing in chapter 26 for details.

The former KGB patrol icebreaker IVAN SUSANIN, unarmed, in naval service. (1983)

7 SUPPORT ICEBREAKERS: "DOBRYNYA NIKITICH" CLASS

Name	Name	Completed
BURAN	PURGA	
DOBRYNYA NIKITICH	SADKO	1959–1974
IL'YA MUROMETS	VYUGA	
PERESVET		

Builders:	Admiralty, Leningrad
Displacement:	2,940 tons full load
Length:	222 ft 1 in (67.7 m) overall
Beam:	60 ft (18.3 m)
Draft:	20 ft (6.1 m)
Propulsion:	diesel-electric: 3 diesel generators (13D100); 4,800 bhp; connected to 2 electric motors; 3 shafts (1 bow + 2 stern; see notes)
Speed:	14.5 knots
Range:	5,500 n.miles at 12 knots
	13,000 n.miles at 9.5 knots
Complement:	approx. 80
Helicopters:	no facilities
Guns:	removed
Radars:	1 or 2 Don-2 (navigation)

These are Navy-manned icebreakers. None is armed. They differ from the IVAN SUSANIN class in having a smaller superstructure and an open stern to facilitate towing operations.

Class: See previous IVAN SUSANIN listing for class notes.

Classification: Soviet LDK type.

Design: These are small, efficient icebreakers. They are fitted for ocean towing. Later units do not have a bow propeller but retain the same horsepower rating.

Guns: Four ships were armed while in naval service, carryinig two 57-mm/70-cal AA guns (1 twin) and two 25-mm/60-cal AA guns (1 twin)—the PERESVET, PURGA, SADKO, and VYUGA; guns were removed in the 1980s.

Names: Il'ya Muromets (Russian Knight) was a Russian folk hero and the name given by Igor Sikorsky to the world's first four-engine aircraft, which he built in Russia in 1914. The name PURGA is also assigned to a civilian tug and was formerly assigned to a KGB patrol icebreaker.

The naval icebreaker SADKO, one of the numerous DOBRYNYA NIKITICH-class ships. The similar ships operated by the KGB are armed.

FLEET, SALVAGE, AND FIREFIGHTING TUGS

This section lists Soviet naval MB, SB, and PZHS types of tugs. The larger tug-type ships especially fitted for salvage and rescue operations are listed earlier in this chapter. The large SB-series tugs can support divers. Several armed tugs are operated in the patrol role by the KGB Maritime Border Troops (see chapter 26).

2 LARGE SALVAGE TUGS: "NIKOLAY CHIKER" CLASS

Name	Completed
SB-131 NIKOLAY CHIKER	Apr 1989
SB-135	June 1989

Builders:	Hollming, Rauma (Finland)
Displacement:	approx. 8,000 tons full load
Length:	321 ft 5 in (98.0 m) overall
Beam:	64 ft (19.5 m)
Draft:	23 ft 3 in (7.1 m)
Propulsion:	4 diesel engines; 24,480 bhp; 2 shafts
Speed:	18 knots
Range:	
Complement:	approx. 50
Passengers:	20
Helicopters:	landing area
Guns:	none
Radars:	

These are the world's most powerful salvage tugs. Fitted with two 8-ton cranes and one 3-ton crane. The helicopter landing deck is *forward* in these ships.

Engineering: A bow-thruster is fitted.

The NIKOLAY CHIKER under way, clearly showing the ship's helicopter platform forward of the bridge, an unusual position; however, this arrangement leaves the stern area clear for towing and salvage gear. (1990, Royal Navy)

4 SALVAGE TUGS: SLIVA CLASS

Name	Completed
SB-406	Feb 1984
SB-408	June 1984
SB-921	July 1985
SB-922	Dec 1985

Builders:	Rauma-Repola, Rauma (Finland)
Displacement:	3,400 tons full load
Tonnage:	810 DWT
Length:	227 ft (69.2 m) overall
Beam:	50 ft 6 in (15.4 m)
Draft:	16 ft 9 in (5.1 m)
Propulsion:	2 diesel engines (Russkiy/SEMT-Pielstick 6 PC 2.5 L 400); 7,800 bhp; 2 shafts
Speed:	16 knots
Range:	
Complement:	approx. 45 + 10 salvage crew
Guns:	none
Radars:	2 . . . . . (navigation)

These are ice-strengthened salvage tugs. The type is operated only by the Soviet Navy. They have accommodations for ten salvage specialists in addition to crew. Five-ton-capacity crane is fitted.

Classification: Soviet SB type.

Engineering: A bow thruster is provided for precise maneuvering and station keeping.

The Sliva-class salvage tug SB-921; there are three water cannon grouped atop the bridge, ahead of the twin, bar-antenna navigation radars. There is a heavy lift crane immediately aft of the twin funnels. (Royal Netherlands Navy)

1 TUG/SUPPLY SHIP: "NEFTEGAZ" CLASS

Name	Completed
ILGA	Nov 1983

Builders:	Adolf Warski, Szczecin (Poland)
Displacement:	2,800 tons full load
Tonnage:	1,396 DWT
Length:	211 ft 3 in (64.4 m) overall
Beam:	45 ft 3 in (45.0 m)
Draft:	17 ft 8 in (5.4 m)
Propulsion:	2 diesel engines (Cegielski/Sulzer); 8,700 bhp; 2 shafts
Speed:	14 knots
Range:	
Complement:	approx. 25
Guns:	none
Radars:	2 . . . . . (navigation)

This is a large oilfield tug/supply tug. She was among 60-plus units ordered by the USSR (the lead ship was transferred to Vietnam in 1987). The others are employed in civilian activity.

The ship has a large telemetry tracking radar aft and operates in the Northern Fleet.

Design: Polish B-92/B-922 design. Up to 600 tons of cargo can be carried on the after deck. They are fitted for firefighting (as are most Soviet naval tugs). According to the reference book *Combat Fleets,* their configuration "would permit the ship[s] to be rapidly adapted for minelaying."[1]

Engineering: A bow thruster is fitted.

1. Bernard Prézelin, English-language edition edited by A.D. Baker III, *Combat Fleets of the World 1990/91* (Annapolis, Md.: Naval Institute Press, 1990), p. 648.

The ILGA is the single Neftegaz-class tug/offshore supply ship acquired by the Soviet Navy. Large numbers of these ships were built in Poland for the Soviet Union. The unusual stern transom and twin funnels characterize these ships.

13 OCEANGOING TUGS: GORYN CLASS

Name	Name	Completed
MB-18 (ex-BEREZINSK)	MB-61	
MB-30	MB-105 (ex-BAYKALSK)	
MB-31	MB-119 (ex-BILBINO)	
MB-32	SB-365 (ex-MB-29)	1977–1978
MB-35	SB-522 (ex-MB-62)	1982–1983
MB-36	SB-523 (ex-MB-64)	
MB-38	SB-524 (ex-MB-108)	

Builders:	Rauma-Repola, Rauma (Finland)
Displacement:	2,240 tons standard
	2,600 tons full load
Tonnage:	681–775 DWT
Length:	208 ft 3 in (63.5 m) overall
Beam:	46 ft 11 in (14.3 m)
Draft:	16 ft 9 in (5.1 m)
Propulsion:	2 diesel engines (Russkiy 67N); 3,500 bhp; 1 shaft
Speed:	13.5 knots
Range:	
Complement:	approx. 40
Guns:	none
Radars:	2 Don-2 (navigation)

These are oceangoing tugs with a salvage and fire-fighting capability. The MB-15, 18, 105, and 119 were built in the first group (1977–1978); ten others were in the second (1982–1983).

Class: All ships of this class are believed to have been built for naval service although several have merchant colors. The BOLSHEVETSK was lost off Japan in February 1979.

An additional unit was completed in 1987 as a trials ship for towed-array sonar; she is designated OS-572 and is listed separately in this chapter.

The large Goryn-class oceangoing tugs have a four-level super-structure, as shown here on the MB-18. The squared-off funnel makes this class easy to identify. (1987, JMSDF)

Classification: Soviet MB type except for four units rated as SB (salvage tugs).

Engineering: A bow thruster is fitted.

Names: Three MB types were formally assigned names.

Many of the larger Soviet oceangoing tugs, such as this unit of the Goryn class, have a diving and salvage capability. The ship has two large, covered rescue boats on davits.

13 + OCEANGOING TUGS: SORUM CLASS

Name	Name	Name	Completed
MB-6	MB-99	MB-236	
MB-25	MB-112	MB-304	
MB-26	MB-115	MB-307	1974–
MB-28	MB-119		
MB-58	MB-148		

Builders:	Yaroslavl (USSR)
Displacement:	1,210 tons standard
	1,655 tons full load
Tonnage:	440 DWT
Length:	191 ft 3 in (58.3 m) overall
Beam:	41 ft 4 in (12.6 m)
Draft:	15 ft 1 in (4.6 m)
Propulsion:	diesel-electric: 2 diesel engines (5-2D42); 1,500 bhp; 1 shaft
Speed:	13.25 knots
Range:	6,700 n.miles at 13 knots
Complement:	approx. 35
Guns:	see notes
Radars:	2 Don-2 (navigation)

Additional tugs of this class are operated by the KGB Maritime Border Troops as armed patrol tugs (see chapter 26). About 35 similar ships are operated as salvage tugs by the Ministry of Fisheries and merchant fleet (PURGA class), and others have been transferred to Bulgaria and Poland.

Classification: Naval units are designated MB.

Guns: These ships are designed to carry two 30-mm close-in twin gun mountings.

The Sorum-class oceangoing tug MB-99. Note the complex mast arrangement; there is a water cannon atop the bridge and another plus two Don-2 radars on mast platforms. (1988, JMSDF)

3 SALVAGE AND RESCUE TUGS: INGUL CLASS

Name	Completed
MASHUK	1972
PAMIR	1975
ALATAU	1984

Builders:	Admiralty, Leningrad
Displacement:	3,200 tons standard
	4,050 tons full load
Length:	304 ft 5 in (92.8 m) overall
Beam:	50 ft 6 in (15.4 m)
Draft:	19 ft (5.8 m)
Propulsion:	2 diesel engines (Russki 58D-4R); 9,000 bhp; 2 shafts
Speed:	20 knots
Range:	9,000 n.miles at 19 knots
Complement:	approx. 120
Helicopters:	no facilities
Guns:	see notes
Radars:	2 Don-2 (navigation)

These are powerful salvage tugs, fitted with submarine rescue, diving, salvage, and fire-fighting equipment. They should not be confused with two (smaller) intelligence collection ships of the PAMIR class or the tugs of that class name (see below).

Class: Two similar units are in merchant service (YAGUAR class).

Classification: Soviet SS type.

Design: The hull has a bulbous bow.

Guns: These ships have provisions for mounting one 57-mm AA twin gun mount and two 25-mm AA twin gun mounts.

Engineering: A bow thruster is fitted for precise maneuvering. Note the high horsepower of these ships.

Names: Confusion with the INGUL cable ship should be avoided.

The Ingul-class salvage and rescue tug ALATAU is fitted for a variety of rescue and salvage functions. (1986, U.S. Navy)

11 SEAGOING FIRE-FIGHTING TUGS: KATUN CLASS

Name	Name	Name	Completed
PZHS-64	PZHS-123	PZHS-282	
PZHS-96	PZHS-124	4 units	1970–1981
PZHS-98	PZHS-209		

Builders:	(USSR)
Displacement:	1,016 tons full load
Length:	Katun I 205 ft 4 in (62.6 m) overall
	Katun II 215 ft 2 in (65.6 m) overall
Beam:	33 ft 6 in (10.2 m)
Draft:	11 ft 10 in (3.6 m)
Propulsion:	2 diesel engines (40DM); 4,000 bhp; 2 shafts
Speed:	17 knots
Range:	2,200 n.miles at 16 knots
Complement:	approx. 30
Guns:	none
Radars:	1 Don-2 (navigation)

These ships are ocean-going fire-fighting and decontamination tugs. The Admiralty yard has built additional ships of this type for civilian use.

Classification: Original Soviet PDS type (fire-fighting and decontamination ship); subsequently changed to PZHS (fire-fighting ship).

Design: The later ships are slightly longer and have an additional bridge level; they are designated Katun II.

2 SALVAGE TUGS: PAMIR CLASS

Name	Completed
AGATAN	1958
ALDAN	1958

Builders:	Gavle (Sweden)
Displacement:	1,445 tons standard
	2,240 tons full load
Length:	255 ft 10 in (78.0 m) overall
Beam:	42 ft (12.8 m)
Draft:	13 ft 2 in (4.0 m)
Propulsion:	2 diesel engines (MAN G10V); 4,200 bhp; 2 shafts
Speed:	17.5 knots
Range:	15,200 n.miles at 17.5 knots
	21,800 n.miles at 12 knots
Complement:	
Helicopters:	no facilities
Guns:	none
Radars:	2 Don-2 (navigation)

These are salvage tugs fitted for diving, salvage, and fire fighting. Two sister ships serve in the Soviet Navy as intelligence collectors (AGI).

Classification: Soviet SS type.

One of the two Pamir-class salvage tugs under way; these ships should not be confused with the larger salvage tug with the name Pamir (Ingul class).

APPROX. 40 OCEANGOING TUGS: OKHTENSKIY CLASS

Name	Completed
MB-173	
MB-175	
SB-5	1958–early 1960s
SB-28	
approx. 36 units	

Builders:	Petrozavod, Leningrad
Displacement:	700 tons standard
	925 tons full load
Length:	155 ft 2 in (47.3 m) overall
Beam:	33 ft 9 in (10.3 m)
Draft:	18 ft (5.5 m)
Propulsion:	2 diesel engines; 1,500 bhp; 1 shaft
Speed:	13 knots
Range:	5,800 n.miles at 13 knots
	7,800 n.miles at 7 knots
Complement:	approx. 40
Guns:	none
Radars:	1 or 2 Don-2 (navigation) or Spin Trough (search)

Several additional tugs of this type are armed and employed as patrol craft by the KGB Maritime Border Troops.

Class: Sixty-three tugs of this class were built. A few were operated as civilian tugs; none is believed to be in service.

Classification: All are MB or SB, the latter with an additional boat and other salvage gear.

Okhtenskiy-class oceangoing tug SB-5. The ships of this class are easily identified by their two tripod masts. The two units illustrated here have different antennas. (U.S. Navy)

The Okhtenskiy-class oceangoing tug SB-28. She was towing a Sonya-class minesweeper when this photo was taken in the Far East. The naval units of this class have numbers (SB or MB prefix); the civilian tugs have names. (1985, JMSDF)

2 SALVAGE TUGS: "OREL" CLASS

Name	Name	Completed
SB-38	SB-43	late 1950s

Builders:	Valmet, Tarku (Finland)
Displacement:	1,200 tons standard
	1,760 tons full load
Length:	201 ft (61.3 m) overall
Beam:	39 ft (11.9 m)
Draft:	14 ft 9 in (4.5 m)
Propulsion:	1 diesel engine (MAN G5Z52/70); 1,700 bhp; 1 shaft
Speed:	15 knots
Range:	13,000 n.miles at 13.5 knots
Complement:	approx. 35
Guns:	none
Radars:	1 Don-2 or Don (navigation)

The Orel-class salvage tug SB-43 and her single sister ship in naval service (SB-38) can be identified by their pole mast forward of the bridge and low-lying superstructure. Note the pendant "43" without the prefix SB. (1987, JMSDF)

The OREL class consisted of about 25 large tugs built in Tarku for the Soviet Navy and fishing fleet. Several naval units have been discarded. They are fitted for salvage.

Classification: Soviet SB type.

10 OCEANGOING TUGS: ROSLAVL CLASS

Name	Name	Name	Completed
MB-69	MB-143	MB-147	
MB-94	MB-145	SB-46	1950s
MB-134	MB-146	2 units	

Builders:	(USSR)
Displacement:	750 tons full load
Length:	147 ft (44.5 m) overall
Beam:	31 ft 2 in (9.5 m)
Draft:	11 ft 6 in (3.5 m)
Propulsion:	diesel-electric: 2 diesels; 1,200 hp; 2 shafts
Speed:	11 knots
Range:	6,000 n.miles at 11 knots
Complement:	approx. 30
Guns:	none
Radars:	1 Don-2 (navigation)

Small tug types, slowly being discarded.

Classification: Soviet MB type except that one unit is listed as salvage tug (SB).

Roslavl-class oceangoing tug MB-94 (1987, L. Van Ginderen)

YACHT

1 NAVAL YACHT: EX-GERMAN

Name	Launched	Completed
ANGARA (ex-HELA)	28 Dec 1939	16 Oct 1940

Displacement:	2,113 tons standard
	2,520 tons full load
Length:	327 ft 4 in (99.8 m) overall
Beam:	40 ft 4 in (12.3 m)
Draft:	13 ft 2 in (4.0 m)
Propulsion:	4 diesel engines (MAN W9Vu 40/46); 8,360 bhp; 2 shafts
Speed:	21 knots
Range:	2,000 n.miles at 15 knots
Complement:	approx. 225
Guns:	none
Radars:	1 . . . . . . (navigation)

Yacht assigned to the Commander in Chief of the Soviet Navy and CinC of the Black Sea Fleet. Built as yacht for the German Navy (rated as *Flottentender*); laid down in 1937. Acquired by the USSR in 1946 as war reparations.

Guns: In German naval service the ship carried two 4.1-inch (104-mm), one 37-mm, and two 20-mm guns; the 4.1-inch guns were in single mounts. She is unarmed in Soviet service.

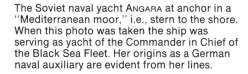

The Soviet naval yacht ANGARA at anchor in a "Mediterranean moor," i.e., stern to the shore. When this photo was taken the ship was serving as yacht of the Commander in Chief of the Black Sea Fleet. Her origins as a German naval auxiliary are evident from her lines.

SERVICE AND TARGET CRAFT

The Soviet Navy operates a large number of self-propelled and towed service craft. Only the larger, self-propelled units are listed here.

TORPEDO RETRIEVERS: SHELON CLASS

Completed:	1978—
Displacement:	270 tons full load
Length:	134 ft 6 in (41.0 m) overall
Beam:	19 ft 8 in (6.0 m)
Draft:	
Propulsion:	2 diesel engines (M504); 10,000 bhp; 2 shafts
Speed:	24 knots
Range:	
Complement:	approx. 40
Radars:	1 Spin Trough (search)
Sonars:	1 high-frequency dipping

These are torpedo recovery craft, with a boom aft and stern ramp. Fourteen or more are reported in service. They can be armed with a twin 25-mm or 30-mm AA mount forward for use in a patrol role.

Shelon-class torpedo retriever in the Baltic. The torpedo-handling space is partially covered. (1987)

Modified Shelon service craft with enlarged deckhouse and no after mast, torpedo recovery ramp, or dipping sonar. This was the first unit observed, shown here being towed by a civilian tug from the Black Sea to Vladivostok in 1983–1984. (1983)

Stern aspect of a Shelon-class torpedo retriever; the craft has a lattice mast forward and a tripod mast aft to support a torpedo recovery boom.

TORPEDO RETRIEVERS: POLUCHAT I CLASS

Displacement:	90 tons full load
Length:	97 ft 1 in (29.6 m) overall
Beam:	20 ft (6.1 m)
Draft:	6 ft 3 in (1.9 m)
Propulsion:	2 diesel engines (M50); 2,400 hp; 2 shafts
Speed:	18 knots
Range:	450 n.miles at 17 knots
	900 n.miles at 10 knots
Complement:	approx. 20
Radars:	1 Spin Trough (search)

A large number of these craft have been built, with up to 40 remaining in the Soviet Navy as torpedo recovery craft. Additional units were employed as patrol craft; all of these have been discarded from Soviet service although many are in foreign navies and coast guards.

Classification: Soviet TL type.

Poluchat I–class torpedo retriever. These craft are designed to be configured as patrol craft.

DIVING TENDERS: YELVA CLASS

Completed:	1973—
Displacement:	295 tons full load
Length:	134 ft 2 in (40.9 m) overall
Beam:	26 ft 3 in (8.0 m)
Draft:	6 ft 11 in (2.1 m)
Propulsion:	2 diesel engines (3D12A); 600 bhp; 2 shafts
Speed:	12.5 knots
Range:	
Complement:	approx. 30
Radars:	1 Spin Trough (search)

These ships can simultaneously support several divers working to depths of 200 feet (61 m). At least eight are in Soviet service and several units have gone to other countries.

A decompression chamber is fitted.

DIVING TENDERS: NYRYAT I CLASS

Completed:	late 1950s—mid-1960s
Displacement:	120 tons full load
Length:	95 ft 2 in (29.0 m) overall
Beam:	16 ft 5 in (5.0 m)
Draft:	5 ft 7 in (1.7 m)
Propulsion:	1 diesel engine; 450 bhp; 1 shaft
Speed:	12 knots
Range:	1,600 n.miles at 10 knots
Complement:	approx. 15
Radars:	1 Spin Trough (search)

Several of these craft are in service, built from the late 1950s. They were built after the tenders designated Nyryat II. Some have been transferred to other navies.

Classification: Soviet VM type.

Names: The Soviet name for this design is Krab-M.

DIVING TENDERS: NYRYAT II CLASS

Completed:	1950s
Displacement:	50 tons full load
Length:	69 ft (21.0 m) overall
Beam:	14 ft 9 in (4.5 m)
Draft:	
Propulsion:	1 diesel engine (3D6); 150 bhp; 1 shaft
Speed:	9 knots
Range:	
Complement:	approx. 10
Radars:	1 Spin Trough (search)

TARGET CONTROL BOATS: OSA CLASS

Several target control craft were built with the hulls and propulsion plants of the Osa missile boats. They carry the Square Tie radar, have large radio antenna arrays, and are used to direct various radio-controlled target craft.

Classification: Soviet KT type.

Osa-class hull employed as a missile target. The craft has been fitted with radar reflectors and actual radars, the latter to radiate energy for radar-homing missiles. (1990, Royal Navy)

A former Osa-class missile craft configured as a radio-controlled target. She is fitted with "furnaces" to produce infrared signatures and radar reflectors.

TARGET BARGES

A number of non-self-propelled (towed) barges are also employed for gun and missile-firing tests and training.

A rebuilt Osa missile craft employed as a target control craft. The Square Tie radar and High Pole IFF have been mounted atop the forward lattice mast.

HARBOR TUGS

Large numbers of harbor tugs are in Soviet service, of various designs. Several are especially rigged for the fire-fighting role.

TARGET CRAFT: MODIFIED OSA CLASS

Several Osa missile craft have been modified to serve as radio-controlled targets. They have radar reflectors fitted to large lattice masts, and heat generators with two large funnels are provided.

A few older Komar craft may also survive as target craft (with radar reflectors only).

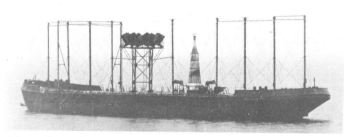

A target barge fitted for use as a target for infrared and radar homing missiles. (Royal Danish Navy)

ACCOMMODATION BARGES: BOLVA SERIES

Builders:	Valmet, Helsinki (Finland)
Completed:	1960–
Displacement:	6,500 tons full load
Length:	363 ft 9 in (110.9 m) overall
Beam:	45 ft 3 in (13.8 m)
Draft:	9 ft 2 in (2.8 m)
Accommodations:	375–400

These are large berthing barges, used by the Soviet Navy and civilian fleets for housing crews of ships undergoing repair and probably for submarines, whose crews do not always live on board when in port. They are non-self-propelled but have engineering plants to provide heat and electricity for "hotel" services. They have a hangar-like auditorium structure aft.

The barges may be able to provide submarines and small craft with provisions.

Class: About 40 of these large barges have been delivered for naval and civil use.

The Bolva-series accommodations barge BELOZERO under tow at Malta, where Soviet ships are often repaired. The hangar-like structure aft indicates she is one of the later series; note the funnel and only a few life-raft canisters visible on the upper deck. (Leo Van Ginderen)

ACCOMMODATION BARGES: VYN SERIES

Builders:	Rauma-Repola, Savonlinna (Finland)
Converted:	1960s
Displacement:	3,000 tons full load
Length:	301 ft 9 in (92.0 m) overall
Beam:	43 ft 11 in (13.4 m)
Draft:	15 ft 1 in (4.6 m)
Accommodations:	approx. 200

These are converted cargo barges built in the late 1940s–early 1950s. They may be used specifically to support submarines, since they are provided with torpedo loading hatches.

The Soviet Navy operates a large number of floating dry docks to supplement dry docks at various naval bases and shipyards. This 80,000-ton-capacity dock was built in Japan for use at Vladivostok to service aircraft carriers. In this view the PD-41 (for *Plavuchayashe,* or "floating dock") is under tow. Large cranes run on tracks along the dock walls; the warning signs on the side are "no mooring" and "slow speed."

FLOATING DRY DOCKS

The Soviet Navy as well as the merchant and fishing fleets make extensive use of floating dry docks at various bases and ports.

A Typhoon-class SSBN—the world's largest undersea craft—rests in a floating dry dock at Murmansk. Note the massive cranes on both walls of the dock. (© 1991, Kris Cole)

CHAPTER 24

Research and Intelligence Ships

Watching the watchers: A Moma-class intelligence collection ship watches a U.S. Air Force E-3A Sentry electronic surveillance aircraft land at Hickam Air Force Base on the island of Oahu, Hawaii. At far right is the nuclear-propelled submarine SAM HOUSTON (SSN 609), modified to support special operations, including covert surveillance activities. A Soviet AGI normally operates off the coast of Oahu to collect intelligence against U.S. headquarters on the island as well as Hickam field and the Pearl Harbor naval base. (1988, U.S. Navy)

The Soviet Union operates the world's largest fleets of research, space support, and intelligence collection ships. The ships of those categories manned by naval personnel or subordinate to naval commands are listed in this chapter.

The exact function of the huge SSV-33 is not definitely known on the basis of publicly available material; she carries the designation of an intelligence collection ship (AGI in Western terminology). To a lesser degree there is some question of the precise role of the Bambuk-class ships (Soviet KAMCHATKA/SSV-679). This ship is considered an AGI by Western intelligence but lacks the intercept antennas common to other ships of this type.

The ship types listed in this chapter are:
Intelligence Collection Ships
Oceanographic Research Ships
Hydrographic Survey Ships
Inshore Survey Ships and Craft
Missile Range Instrumentation Ships

INTELLIGENCE COLLECTION SHIPS

The Soviet Navy continues to design and produce new, specialized intelligence collection ships at a prodigious rate. The newer units, beginning probably with the PRIMOR'YE class, have an on-board intelligence-processing as well as collection capability.

Since the last edition of *Guide to the Soviet Navy* three new AGI classes have appeared, including the behemoth, nuclear-propelled SSV-33, while additional units of earlier classes have been constructed and another conversion has been added to the AGI list.

Most of the Soviet Navy's intelligence-collection ships (designated AGI by Western navies) are based on trawler designs, most likely because of the design's availability, good seakeeping qualities, long endurance, and insulated fish-storage holds that provide space for electronic equipment bays. The largest of the AGI classes—the Bal'zam class—appears to have been designed from the outset specifically for intelligence collection and processing.

In addition to the ships listed in this chapter, the modified KEYLA-class cargo ship RITSA is probably employed as an AGI; see page 262.

Classification: These ships generally have the Soviet classification of GS (hydrographic vessel) or SSV (communications vessel); see chapter 3.

Missiles: In addition to the weapons listed here, many AGIs have been observed with shoulder-fired SA-7 Grail anti-air missile launchers (the same missile fired from the SA-N-5 launcher); the SA-N-8 is an upgraded version of this weapon. SA-N-5/SA-N-8 launcher positions are noted; they are rarely seen installed.

1 SPACE SUPPORT/INTELLIGENCE COLLECTION SHIP: KAPUSTA TYPE

Number	Launched	Completed
SSV-33	May 1983	1987

Builders:	Baltic Shipyard, Leningrad
Displacement:	32,000 tons standard
	41,000 tons full load
Length:	829 ft ⅝ in (253.0 m) waterline
	869 ft (265.0 m) overall
Beam:	97 ft 1 in (29.6 m)
Draft:	29 ft 6 in (9.0 m)
Propulsion:	CONSAS: 4 steam turbines; 98.800 shp; 4 shafts
Reactors:	2 pressurized-water type
Boilers:	2 or 4
Speed:	27 knots
Range:	essentially unlimited
Complement:	approx. 950
Helicopters:	1 Ka-27 Helix-D
Missiles:	4 quad SA-N-10 anti-air launchers
Guns:	2 76.2-mm/59-cal DP (2 single)
	4 30-mm/65-cal close-in (4 multi-barrel)
	8 14.5-mm machine guns (4 twin)
ASW weapons:	none
Radars:	4 Mad Hack phased-array
	3 Palm Frond (navigation)
	1 Top Plate (3-D air search)
Sonar:	hull mounted
EW systems:	1 Cage Box
	1 Cake Tin
	. . . Football
	2 Soup Cup
	1 Trawl Net

The exact purposes of this ship are not publicly known. She carries the SSV-series designation common to most Soviet AGIs. However, her size and the space tracking antennas indicate that she is apparently intended for (1) tracking of Western missile launches, (2) monitoring/communications and control of Soviet spacecraft and satellites, and (3) military supporting research and development projects.

A senior U.S. naval intelligence officer has observed that a manned surveillance platform in space could provide the "ultimate force multiplier" for naval operations and that these ships could be the control/communications link for military-oriented manned space operations.[1]

In the AGI/space surveillance role or as space command/support ship the SSV-33 does not require the high sustained speed or endurance provided by her nuclear propulsion. The answer may lie in the very large amounts of electrical power available, which would facilitate the use of lasers for communications or even weapon purposes, although no laser systems have as yet been publicly identified with the ship.

The SSV-33 was laid down in May 1981; she began sea trials in the Baltic in 1987. She transited to the Far East in 1989. Her NATO codename Kapusta means "cabbage."

Classification: The Soviet designation for this nuclear-propelled missile/space support ship is SSV for *Sudno Svyazyy* ("communications vessel").

During construction the ship was given the designation BAL-AUX-2 (Baltic Auxiliary) by Western intelligence.

Design: This large ship has a massive superstructure topped by a massive radome and three mast structures. The center and after masts have exhaust on port and starboard.

Electronics: This behemoth has a large number of electronic arrays. In addition to the extensive tracking and communications antennas, the SSV-33 has three flat-faced, octagonal antennas that appear to be for a phased-array, three-dimensional tracking radar mounted on the second of three tall tower masts. There is a fourth, upward-looking array on the ship's 02 level, starboard side, just forward of the three ship's boats. (Other than AGIs the only Soviet ships publicly known to have phased-array radar with fixed antennas are the VSTOL carrier ADMIRAL GORSHKOV [ex-BAKU] and the aircraft carriers of the ADMIRAL KUZNETSOV [ex-TBILISI] class.)

Space communications/tracking/telemetry antennas in the SSV-33 include 2 Low Ball SATCOM, 6 Owl Perch tracking, 1 Punch Bowl, 1 Ship Bowl, and 1 Quad Leaf.

Round House TACAN antennas are fitted atop the center mast and a Fly Screen helicopter control radar is provided. A large array of electronic warfare/surveillance systems is installed.

Propulsion: The ship has a two-reactor, combined nuclear-oil propulsion plant similar to that of the KIROV-class battle cruisers, which are also built at the Baltic Shipyard. The Baltic yard also builds the ARKTIKA-class nuclear icebreakers. The nuclear plant is an indication of the wide application of nuclear propulsion to naval as well as merchant ships in the Soviet Union.

1. See Commo. (now Rear Adm.) Thomas A. Brooks, USN, "The Ultimate Force Multiplier," U.S. Naval Institute *Proceedings* (July 1985), pp. 137–139.

The stern of the SSV-33 showing the ship's third tower mast, helicopter hangar, and flight deck.

The precise role of the large, nuclear-propelled "communications ship" SSV-33 is not known publicly in the West. Although longer than the space support ship YURI GAGARIN, the SSV-33 has a lesser displacement. She has a variety of electronic antennas, including a set of four fixed, phased-array antennas (one is visible in the center superstructure). This photo shows the ship en route from the Black Sea to the Far East. (1989)

A port quarter view of the SSV-33. Note the variety of electronic antennas, single-barrel 76.2-mm gun mount aft, partially open helicopter hangar, and flight deck. There are 30-mm Gatling guns atop the hangar structure. (West German Navy)

1+ INTELLIGENCE COLLECTION SHIPS: "YUG" CLASS

Name	Completed	Converted
SSV-328 (ex-YUG)	1978	1988

Builders:	Stocznia Polnocny, Gdansk (Poland)
Displacement:	2,700 tons full load
Length:	270 ft 7 in (82.5 m) overall
Beam:	44 ft 3 in (13.5 m)
Draft:	13 ft 2 in (4.0 m)
Propulsion:	2 diesel engines (Zgoda/Sulzer STD48); 4,400 bhp; 2 shafts
Speed:	15.5 knots
Range:	9,000 n.miles at 12 knots
Complement:	approx. 80
Helicopters:	no facilities
Missiles:	2 quad SA-N-8 anti-air launchers [16]

Guns:	none
Radars:	2 Don-2 (navigation)
Sonars:	high-frequency dipping
EW systems:	2 Watch Dog

The SSV-328 is the converted oceanographic research ship YUG, one of 18 ships built to this design for naval service. She appears to be configured for handling a towed acoustic array, possibly similar to the U.S. Navy's Surveillance Towed Array Sonar System (SURTASS). Additional intelligence collection ships are expected to be converted or built to this design.

Conversion: The conversion included extending the ship's superstructure aft to provide more berthing and equipment spaces. A small radome structure has been fitted forward of the funnel. What appear to be positions for anti-air missile launchers have been

The SSV-328 is the former oceanographic research ship YUG, apparently converted to an AGI carrying a towed acoustic array, similar to the U.S. Navy's SURTASS/T-AGOS program. The ship has been extensively modified, although the twin-porthole arrangement, funnel position, and after kingpost reveal her origins. Additional conversions and/or new construction for this role can be expected.

fitted amidships, just aft of the kingpost mast, port and starboard. The original masts are retained.

Design: The ship was built with two 100-kilowatt electric motors for quiet, slow-speed operations and a 300-hp bow thruster for precise station keeping.

1+ INTELLIGENCE COLLECTION SHIPS: BAMBUK CLASS

Name	Completed
KAMCHATKA (SSV-679)	Dec 1987
1+ units	Building

Builders:	Admiralty, Leningrad
Displacement:	5,500 tons full load
Length:	351 ft (107.0 m) overall
Beam:	59 ft (18.0 m)
Draft:	19 ft 8 in (6.0 m)
Propulsion:	2 diesel engines; 1 shaft
Speed:	18 knots
Range:	
Complement:	approx. 180

Helicopters:	landing deck
Missiles:	2 quad SA-N-8 anti-air launchers
Guns:	2 30-mm/65-cal close-in (multi-barrel)
Radars:	3 Palm Frond (navigation)
Sonars:	hull mounted

The lead ship of this class is in the Pacific Fleet. Based on her designation, the ship is considered an AGI by Western intelligence; however, she lacks the array of intercept antennas seen on other AGIs. The Bambuk and Bal'zam classes are the largest specialized intelligence collection ships in Soviet naval service except for the nuclear-propelled SSV-33.

Design: The KAMCHATKA has an unusual design with a tall, flat-sided pylon mast aft of the bridge; sponsons on the mast support electronic intercept equipment; there is a smaller deckhouse amidships with a distinct separation between the two. A large helicopter deck is aft. There is also a small structure on the forecastle, topped by a pole mast.

Guns: Only optical directors are provided for the 30-mm Gatling guns.

The relatively large KAMCHATKA in the Pacific. Additional ships of this unusual configuration are believed to be under construction. The ship appears to be an acoustic test or surveillance platform, with the tower housing a large "dipping" sonar. When completed she had the designation SSV-391. (1990)

7+ INTELLIGENCE COLLECTION SHIPS: VISHNAYA CLASS

Number	Completed
SSV-520	1985
SSV-169	1987
SSV-175	1988
SSV-201	1987
SSV-208	1987
SSV-520	1985
SSV-535	1987
1+ units	building

Builders:	Stocznia Polnocny, Gdańsk (Poland)
Displacement:	2,500 tons full load
Length:	300 ft (91.5 m) overall
Beam:	47 ft 7 in (14.5 m)
Draft:	13 ft 2 in (4.0 m)
Propulsion:	2 diesel engines; 2 shafts
Speed:	18 knots
Range:	
Complement:	approx. 160
Helicopters:	no facilities
Missiles:	2 quad SA-N-5 or SA-N-8 anti-air launchers
Guns:	2 30-mm/65-cal close-in (multi-barrel)
Radars:	2 Nayada (navigation)
Sonars:	high-frequency dipping
EW systems:	4 Cage Flask
	1 Grid Wheel
	1 Prim Wheel
	1 Ring Web
	2 Sprat Star

A Vishnaya-class AGI in heavy weather. These ships are easily identified by their long bridge structure and twin lattice masts.

These are among the largest AGIs in Soviet service. This class has a hull that bears some resemblance to the similar-size Bal'zam class, but the mast, deck, and funnel arrangements differ considerably. The first unit, designated SSV-520, sailed on trials in the Baltic in July 1986. She subsequently observed the NATO exercise Northern Wedding later that year.

Electronics: The early ships began operation with empty mountings for two radomes atop the bridge structure; they are probably intended for satellite communications antennas. The SSV-201 (Black Sea) was one of the first ships to have the forward radome fitted (the second position remained vacant).

The Vishnaya radome positions are adjacent, with a light, lattice mast amidships (between the radome positions and the funnel) and a second lattice mast at the after end of the deck house; the Bal'zam class has a heavy mast structure between the two radomes. The SSV-535 has a small rectangular structure between the radome positions.

Guns: No radar/director is provided for the Gatling guns; optical sights only.

The SSV-201 was possibly the first Vishnaya-class AGI to be fitted with a radome atop the bridge, in the forward position. There are Krivak-class frigates tied up to starboard of the SSV-201. (1989, Eric Grove)

The Vishnaya-class SSV-520, clearly showing the two unoccupied radome positions atop the bridge. Also evident are the two 30-mm Gatling guns forward of the bridge, with positions for surface-to-air missile launchers (canvas covered) in the same position aft. These ships are being produced in large numbers.

4 INTELLIGENCE COLLECTION SHIPS: AL'PINIST CLASS

Name	Name	Name	Completed
GS-7	GS-19	GS-39	1981–1982
GS-8			

Builders:	Yaroslavl
Displacement:	1,200 tons full load
Tonnage:	322 DWT
Length:	176 ft 2 in (53.7 m) overall
Beam:	34 ft 5 in (10.5 m)
Draft:	14 ft 1 in (4.3 m)
Propulsion:	1 diesel engine (8NVD48-2U); 1,320 bhp; 1 shaft
Speed:	13 knots
Range:	7,600 n.miles at 13 knots
Complement:	approx. 50
Missiles:	2 quad SA-N-8 anti-air launchers [16] in GS-19, GS-39
Guns:	none
Radars:	1 Don-2 (navigation)

These are modified stern trawlers. Fitted with a bow thruster. The GS-39, first seen in February 1981, was rebuilt in 1986–1987, with forecastle extended to stern and new electronic intercept equipment installed.

Class: Several hundred stern trawlers of this type were built for the Soviet fishing fleet. Five units have been completed as civilian research ships for operation by the Ministry of Fisheries, and at least one serves as a naval trials ship (designated OS-104; see chapter 23).

The GS-39 of the Al'pinist class after being rebuilt with the forecastle extended to the stern and new electronic gear fitted. In the AGI role these ships retain the after kingpost of their trawling brethren. (1989, Hartmut Ehlers)

The GS-8 in Far Eastern waters shows the typical Al'pinist trawler lines. This is one of four ships of this class adopted for the AGI role; they are quite small compared to other recent Soviet AGIs. (1985, JMSDF)

The rebuilt GS-39 with her built up stern section. The port holes indicate more equipment and berthing spaces have probably been provided. The funnel is offset to port, alongside the mast. (Royal Netherlands Navy)

4 INTELLIGENCE COLLECTION SHIPS: BAL'ZAM CLASS

Name	Completed	Name	Completed
SSV-80	1983	SSV-516	} 1980
SSV-493	1982	SSV-571	} 1988

Builders:	Yantar/Kaliningrad
Displacement:	5,400 tons full load
Length:	346 ft (105.5 m) overall
Beam:	50 ft 10 in (15.5 m)
Draft:	19 ft (5.8 m)
Propulsion:	2 diesel engines; 9,000 bhp; 2 shafts
Speed:	22 knots
Range:	
Complement:	approx. 220
Missiles:	2 quad SA-N-5 or SA-N-8 anti-air launchers [16]
Guns:	1 30-mm close-in (multi-barrel)
Radars:	2 Don-Kay (navigation)

Sonars:	hull mounted
	high-frequency dipping
EW systems:	2 Cage Pot
	1 Cross Loop
	1 Fir Tree
	1 Log Maze
	1 Trawl Net
	1 Twin Wheel
	1 Wing Fold

These are among the largest and most capable AGIs in Soviet service. Additional units are believed to be under construction.

Previous reports of five ships of this class being in service were the result of the SSV-493 also being reported as the SSV-443.

Design: The Bal'zam class was the first Soviet ship type designed specifically for the intelligence collection role. There are significant at-sea replenishment facilities to permit them to provide

The SSV-493, showing the large superstructure common to the larger AGIs. (1987, U.S. Navy)

The SSV-493 of the Bal'zam class in the Far East. Like most modern Soviet AGIs, she is relatively large, carrying considerable electronics and having a long cruising range. A single 30-mm Gatling gun is fitted, forward of the bridge; there are also positions for SA-N-5/8 missiles. (1987, JMSDF)

supplies and fuel to other ships. The two large spherical radomes probably house satellite communications antennas.

Classification: Soviet SSV type.

Guns: No radar/director is provided for the Gatling gun; optical sight only.

6 INTELLIGENCE COLLECTION SHIPS: "PRIMOR'YE" CLASS

Name	Name	Completed
SSV-464 ZABAYKAL'YE	SSV-502 ZAKARPATYE	
SSV-465 PRIMOR'YE	SSV-590 KRYM	1969–1973
SSV-501 ZAPOROZH'YE	SSV-591 KAVKAZ	

Builders:	(USSR)
Displacement:	2,600 tons standard
	3,700 tons full load
Length:	277 ft 10 in (84.7 m) overall
Beam:	45 ft 11 in (14.0 m)
Draft:	18 ft (5.5 m)
Propulsion:	2 diesel engines (Russkiy); 2,000 bhp; 1 shaft
Speed:	13 knots
Range:	12,000 n.miles at 13 knots
	18,000 n.miles at 12 knots
Complement:	approx. 120
Missiles:	. . . SA-N-5 or SA-N-8 anti-air launchers (hand-held)
Guns:	none
Radars:	2 Don-Kay (navigation)

These AGIs have large, distinctive "box" deckhouses forward and aft on their superstructure to house electronic equipment.

Design: These ships are based on the highly successful, Soviet-built, MAYAKOVSKIY-class stern trawler-factory ships. More than 200 units of this design have been built, with several being modified to civilian research ships (see chapter 25).

In their AGI configuration the ships have distinctive superstructures with up to three antenna masts, while some ships retain the trawler kingpost aft (i.e., a total of four masts).

Electronics: The electronic configurations of these ships vary considerably. All except the SSV-464 and SSV-501 have large deckhouses for electronic equipment forward and aft of the funnel. The SSV-590's most recent configuration provides a large hemispheric antenna housing atop the forward deckhouse; the housing merges into the forward mast.

The SSV-464 carries what appears to be an electronics van in the after position; the SSV-501 has a large, three-face phased-array radar mounted on a small, tall deckhouse in the after position. That ship is employed to monitor U.S. missile tests (similar to the U.S. AN/SPQ-11 Cobra Judy radar project).

Names: Names were removed from the ships in 1979–1981.

The SSV-502 (former ZAKARPATIYE) has a five-mast configuration; the third mast is a "Christmas tree" laden with electronic intercept antennas.

The PRIMOR'YE-class AGIs have a variety of electronic configurations. The SSV-501 (formerly ZAPOROZH'YE) has been fitted with an after ''blockhouse'' probably containing fixed, phased-array Mad Hack radar faces of the type employed to monitor missile flight tests. The after kingpost reveals the fishing design origins of the class. (1988)

The SSV-591 (formerly KAVKAZ) has a large, inflated rubber radome above the bridge. She retains the standard light-colored electronics ''blockhouse'' amidships. This class of AGIs does not appear to be armed. (1989, U.S. Navy)

9 INTELLIGENCE COLLECTION SHIPS: MOMA CLASS

Name	Name	Completed
GS-117 IL'MEN	SSV-514 SELIGR	
SSV-501 VEGA	SSV- . . . EKVATOR	
SSV-506 NAKHODKA	SSV- . . . KIL'DIN	1968–1974
SSV-509 PELORUS	SSV- . . . YUPITER	
SSV-512 ARKHIPELAG		

Builders:	Stocznia Polnocny, Gdańsk (Poland)
Displacement:	1,260 tons standard
	1,540 tons full load
Length:	240 ft 5 in (73.3 m) overall
Beam:	35 ft 5 in (10.8 m)
Draft:	12 ft 6 in (3.8 m)
Propulsion:	2 diesel engines (Zgoda/Sulzer 6TD48); 3,600 bhp; 2 shafts
Speed:	17 knots
Range:	8,000 n.miles at 11 knots
Complement:	approx. 100
Missiles:	2 quad SA-N-5 or SA-N-8 anti-air launchers [16] in some ships
Guns:	none
Radars:	2 Don-2 (navigation)

These ships are converted survey ships/buoy tenders, with about 40 ships having been built to this design. The SELIGR was assigned to monitor the initial missile launch tests from the first U.S. Trident submarine, the OHIO (SSBN 726) off the Florida coast in January 1982.

Class: A number of these ships serve the Soviet Navy as hydrographic survey ships (see below).

Classification: Eight ships are designated SSV with the IL'MEN designated GS.

Design: The ships vary considerably in details. Some retain their buoy-handling cranes forward; others have a low deckhouse of varying length between the forward mast and superstructure; forward mast positions (in some ships) vary in height and configuration.

The YUPITER has been refitted with a large radome on her fantail. The others have a deck area aft of the funnel and boat davits for carrying vans with electronic equipment.

The Moma-class AGI YUPITER has a large, inflated rubber radome aft. The foremast has a number of platforms for antennas.

The SELIGER presents another variation of the Moma-class AGI, with a deckhouse forward and a tall antenna-bearing foremast. (1986, U.S. Navy)

The KIL'DIN retains the open working deck and crane forward, showing the configuration of these converted survey ships/buoy tenders. She has small structures aft for electronic gear.

8 INTELLIGENCE COLLECTION SHIPS: MAYAK CLASS

Name	Name	Completed
GS-239	KHERSONES	
GS-242	KURS	1967–1970
GS-536 GIRORULEVOY	KURSOGRAF	
ANEROYD	LADOGA	

Builders:	(USSR)
Displacement:	1,050 tons full load
Length:	177 ft 9 in (54.2 m) overall
Beam:	30 ft 6 in (9.3 m)
Draft:	11 ft 10 in (3.6 m)
Propulsion:	1 diesel engine (8NVD48); 800 bhp; 1 shaft
Speed:	11 knots
Range:	9,400 n.miles at 11 knots
	11,000 n.miles at 7.5 knots
Complement:	approx. 40
Missiles:	. . . SA-N-5 or SA-N-8 anti-air launchers (hand-held)
Guns:	4 14.5-mm machine guns (2 twin) in KURSOGRAF
Radars:	1 or 2 Don-2 (navigation) and/or Spin Trough (search)

Mayak-class AGI ANEROYD.

These ships are former side trawlers that have been converted to the AGI configuration.

Class: More than 100 Mayak-class ships were built in the 1960s; in addition to AGIs, several have been converted to naval supply ships and ASW training ships (see chapter 23).

Classification: Soviet naval GS type.

Design: Details vary; the GIRORULEVOY has a flat-topped radome fitted above the bridge, the KHERSONES has a wider main deckhouse; the LADOGA has a separate structure forward of the bridge and a third lattice mast; and the KURS has a tall deckhouse on the stern. The deckhouse forward of the bridge varies in length, and mast configurations vary. The KURSOGRAF was fitted two 14.5 mm MG twin mounts in 1980; they have been removed.

Name: Mayak is the NATO class name for this design. The Soviet ship named MAYAK is a naval hydrographic survey ship of the Melitopol class.

Mayak-class AGI GIRORULEVOY with lengthened deckhouse forward of the bridge and antenna housing atop the bridge. (1983, U.S. Navy)

Mayak-class AGI KHERSONES with a partial deckhouse forward of the bridge and a hemispheric radome atop the bridge.

The Mayak-class AGI KURS (left) has an extended deckhouse forward. All of these ships have two antenna masts and most have a deckhouse for electronic gear on the fantail.

4 INTELLIGENCE COLLECTION SHIP: MIRNYY CLASS

Name	Name	Name	Completed
BAKAN	VAL	VERTIKAL	1962–1964
LOTSMAN			

Builders:	61 Kommuna, Nikolayev (north)
Displacement:	850 tons standard
	1,300 tons full load
Length:	208 ft 7 in (63.6 m) overall
Beam:	31 ft 2 in (9.5 m)
Draft:	14 ft 9 in (4.5 m)
Propulsion:	diesel-electric: 4 diesel engines; 4,000 bhp; electric drive; 1 shaft
Speed:	17.5 knots
Range:	18,700 n.miles at 11 knots
Complement:	approx. 60
Missiles:	2 quad SA-N-5 or SA-N-8 anti-air launchers [16]
Guns:	none
Radars:	2 Don-2 (navigation)
	1 Spin Trough (search) in some ships

These ships are converted whale hunter/catcher ships, easily identified by their high, "notched" bow (for harpoon gun). All are assigned to the Black Sea Fleet.

Details vary. New deckhouses were fitted between the superstructure and forward mast in the early 1970s to provide additional intelligence equipment and working spaces.

Mirnyy-class AGI.

The Mirnyy-class AGI BAKAN retains the catwalk from bridge to forecastle and "notched" bow of her whale hunter/catcher design.

3 INTELLIGENCE COLLECTION SHIPS: "NIKOLAY ZUBOV" CLASS

Name	Name	Completed
SSV-468 GAVRIL SARYCHEV	SSV-503 KHARITON LAPTEV	1963–1968
SSV-469 SEMYEN CHELYUSHKIN		

Builders:	Adolf Warski, Szczecin (Poland)
Displacement:	2,200 tons standard
	3,100 tons full load
Length:	297 ft (90.0 m) overall
Beam:	42 ft 11 in (13.0 m)
Draft:	15 ft 6 in (4.7 m)
Propulsion:	2 diesel engines (Zgoda 8TD48); 4,800 bhp; 2 shafts
Speed:	16.5 knots
Range:	11,000 n.miles at 14 knots
Complement:	approx. 100
Helicopters:	small platform
Missiles:	3 quad SA-N-5 or SA-N-8 anti-air launchers [24]
Guns:	none
Radars:	2 Don-2 (navigation)

These are former oceanographic survey ships (completion dates above); subsequently converted to AGIs.

Class: Eight additional ships of this class serve as naval oceanographic research ships.

Design: The GAVRIL SARYCHEV has been extensively reconstructed with her forecastle deck extended to the stern and an additional level added to her superstructure. The others have a small raised platform aft, which is not a helicopter deck.

The NIKOLAY ZUBOV–class AGI KHARITON LAPTEV, with a tall pole mast fitted to the after A-frame mast. The forward A-frame mast is at the forward edge of the bridge structure. The ship has a deckhouse aft for electronic gear.

The NIKOLAY ZUBOV–class AGI GAVRIL SARYCHEV has beached the large dish antenna abaft of the funnel. These ships have enclosed crows nests and other features for Arctic operations.

15 INTELLIGENCE COLLECTION SHIP: OKEAN CLASS

Name	Name	Name	Completed
ALIDADA	EKHOLOT	REDUKTO	
AMPERMETR	GIDROFON	REPITER	
BAROGRAF	KRENOMETR	TEODOLIT	1962–1967
BAROMETR	LINZA	TRAVERS	
EFLEKTOR	LOTLIN' (GS-319)	ZOND	

Builders:	(East Germany)
Displacement:	700 tons full load
Length:	166 ft 8 in (50.8 m) overall
Beam:	29 ft 2 in (8.9 m)
Draft:	12 ft 2 in (3.7 m)
Propulsion:	1 diesel engine; 540 bhp; 1 shaft
Speed:	11 knots
Range:	7,900 n.miles at 11 knots
Complement:	approx. 60
Missiles:	2 quad SA-N-5 or SA-N-8 anti-air launchers [16]
Guns:	4 14.5-mm machine guns (2 twin) in BAROGRAF
Radars:	1 or 2 Don-2 (navigation)

This is the largest and hence probably most observed class of AGIs. They are converted side trawlers. Details differ. They retain their trawler arrangement of a tripod mast well forward and a pole mast well aft.

One ship has been fitted with machine guns.

Classification: Soviet GS type.

Names: Okean is the NATO class name. A Moma-class hydrographic survey ship carries the Soviet name OKEAN (listed in this chapter).

The Okean-class AGI LOTLIN', one of several ships with an extended deckhouse forward. The short funnel is immediately aft of the bridge.

An Okean-class AGI with Don-2 navigation radar on the forward mast.

2 INTELLIGENCE COLLECTION SHIPS: "PAMIR" CLASS

Name	Completed	Conversion Completed
SSV-477 PELENG (ex-PAMIR)	1958	
SSV-480 GIDROGRAF (ex-ARBAN)	1958	1967

Builders:	Gavle (Sweden)
Displacement:	1,443 tons standard
	2,300 tons full load
Length:	255 ft 10 in (78.0 m) overall
Beam:	42 ft (12.8 m)
Draft:	13 ft 2 in (4.0 m)
Propulsion:	2 diesel engines (MAN G10V 40/60); 4,200 bhp; 2 shafts
Speed:	17.5 knots
Range:	15,200 n.miles at 17.5 knots
	21,800 n.miles at 12 knots
Complement:	approx. 120
Missiles:	3 quad SA-N-5 or SA-N-8 anti-air launchers [24]
Guns:	none
Radars:	2 Don-2 (navigation)

These ships are converted salvage tugs (with two ships remaining in that role; see chapter 23). In the AGI configuration their superstructures have been enlarged and antennas fitted.

The PAMIR-class AGI GIDROGRAF, one of two large salvage tugs fitted for intelligence collection. There is a radome between the bridge and funnel.

INTELLIGENCE COLLECTION SHIPS: DNEPR CLASS

The Japanese-built AGIs IZERMETEL' and PROTRAKTOR (completed 1959) have apparently been stricken. See 4th edition, page 335.

INTELLIGENCE COLLECTION SHIPS: LENTRA CLASS

All AGIs of the Lentra class were retired by 1980.

OCEANOGRAPHIC RESEARCH SHIPS

The Soviet Navy operates more oceanographic and hydrographic research ships than the rest of the world's nations combined. In addition, there are a large number of civilian research ships (see chapter 25). Although these ships are Navy operated, they are mostly manned by civilian crews.

17 OCEANOGRAPHIC RESEARCH SHIPS: "YUG" CLASS

Name	Name	Completed
BRIZ	PERSEY	
DONUZLAY	PLUTON	
GALS	SENEZH	
GIDROLOG	STRELETS	
GORIZONT	STVOR	1978–1983
MANGYSHLAK	TAYGA	
MARSHAL GELOVANI	VIZIR	
NIKOLAY MATUSEVICH	ZODIAK	
PEGAS		

Builders:	Stocznia Polnocny, Gdańsk (Poland)
Displacement:	2,500 tons full load
Length:	270 ft 7 in (82.5 m) overall
Beam:	44 ft 3 in (13.5 m)
Draft:	13 ft 2 in (4.0 m)
Propulsion:	2 diesel engines (Zgoda/Sulzer 8D48); 4,400 bhp; 2 shafts
Speed:	15.5 knots
Range:	9,000 n.miles at 12 knots
Complement:	approx. 45 + 20 scientists
Helicopters:	no facilities
Missiles:	none
Guns:	see notes
Radars:	2 Don-2 (navigation)

These ships were built specifically for the oceanographic research role with facilities for hydrographic surveys. They have provisions for the installation of three 25-mm AA twin gun mounts.

Reportedly, one of the above ships has been renamed VITSE ADMIRAL VORONOV.

Class: Eighteen ships of this class were built. The lead ship, the YUG, completed in 1978, has been converted to an intelligence collection ship (SSV-328); see page 283.

Classification: Soviet EHOS type.

Design: These ships are fitted with two 100-kilowatt electric motors for quiet, slow-speed operations and a 300-hp bow thruster for precise station keeping. They have two 5-ton-capacity booms. Six laboratories. About 1985 the ZODIAK was fitted with a large gantry crane at the stern for handling towed objects.

The stern of the MANGYSHLAK has a stern ramp for handling oceanographic gear and cables. Note the control position fitted to the kingpost for handling gear with the boom and stern crane. (1986)

The YUG-class oceanographic research ship MANGYSHLAK shows the trim lines of this design. The lead ship has been extensively modified for her AGI-type role. The two Don-2 bar-type radar antennas were not yet fitted to the platforms on the forward mast when this photo was taken. (1986)

6 OCEANOGRAPHIC RESEARCH SHIPS: "AKADEMIK KRYLOV" CLASS

Name	Name	Completed
ADMIRAL VLADIMIRSKIY	LEONID DEMIN	
AKADEMIK KRYLOV	LEONID SOBELYEV	1974–1979
IVAN KRUZHENSTERN	MIKHAIL KRUSKIY	

Builders:	Adolf Warski, Szczecin (Poland)
Displacement:	6,600 tons standard
	9,100 tons full load
Length:	482 ft 2 in (147.0 m) overall except AKADEMIK KRYLOV and
	LEONID SOBELYEV 490 ft 4 in (149.5 m) overall
Beam:	61 ft (18.6 m)
Draft:	20 ft 8 in (6.3 m)
Propulsion:	4 diesel engines; 16,000 bhp; 2 shafts
Speed:	20.5 knots
Range:	23,000 n.miles at 15 knots
Complement:	approx. 90
Helicopters:	1 utility helicopter
Missiles:	none
Guns:	none
Radars:	3 Don-2 (navigation)
	2 Post Lamp (fire control) in ADMIRAL VLADIMIRSKIY

These ships are the largest oceanographic research ships in Soviet service.

Classification: Soviet EHOS type.

Design: This class has graceful, liner-like lines with a crane on the long forecastle. There are 20 to 26 laboratories in each ship. There is a helicopter hangar and flight deck aft. The AKADEMIK KRYLOV and LEONID SOBELYEV have pointed sterns, slightly increasing their length.

Endurance is rated at 90 days.

Electronics: The MIKHAIL KRUPSKIY has a large, spherical radome immediately aft of the bridge mast; the ADMIRAL KRYLOV has a smaller radome farther aft (ahead of the funnel).

The AKADEMIK KRYLOV–class ships are among the few ships of this type with a helicopter platform; note the offset hangar and centered control tower; this is the LEONID DEMIN (flat stern type).

The Ivan Kruzhenstern is one of the large, graceful Soviet research ships that operate on many of the world's seas. Like most of the Soviet research fleet, the Kruzhenstern was built in Poland. There is a heavy crane forward and twin booms aft (adjacent to the hangar).

1 OCEANOGRAPHIC RESEARCH SHIP: "DOBRYNYA NIKITICH" CLASS

Name	Completed
Vladimir Kavrayskiy	1973

Builders:	Admiralty, Leningrad
Displacement:	3,900 tons full load
Length:	229 ft 7 in (70.0 m) overall
Beam:	59 ft (18.0 m)
Draft:	21 ft (6.4 m)
Propulsion:	diesel-electric: 3 diesel generators (13D100); 4,800 bhp; connected to 2 electric motors; 2 shafts
Speed:	15.5 knots
Range:	5,500 n.miles at 12.5 knots
	13,000 n.miles at 9.5 knots
Complement:	
Helicopters:	landing deck
Missiles:	none
Guns:	none
Radars:	2 Don-2 (navigation)

One of the ubiquitous Dobrynaya Nikitich–class icebreakers, the Vladimir Kavrayskiy has been modified to serve as an Arctic research ship for the Navy; her near-sister, Otto Schmidt, serves in a similar role for the Academy of Sciences. The helicopter deck and control position are visible. (1974)

This ship is a Navy-manned icebreaker extensively modified for polar research. Sister ships serve with the KGB, Navy, and civilian agencies (see chapter 23 for class notes).

Design: The Vladimir Kavrayskiy has an enlarged superstructure compared to other ships of this class to provide additional accommodations and laboratory space.

The ship has a helicopter deck aft but no hangar; a helicopter control station is prominent at the after end of the superstructure. She is fitted with nine laboratories and has one 8-ton-capacity crane and two 3-ton booms.

Endurance is rated at 60 days.

The naval ships of the Akademik Kurchatov design have kingposts forward and aft, with a helicopter hangar and deck aft. In addition to booms, there is a stern crane at the stern. This is the Moldaviya.

4 OCEANOGRAPHIC RESEARCH SHIPS: "AKADEMIK KURCHATOV" CLASS

Name	Name	Completed
ABKHAZIYA	BASHKIRIYA	
ADZHARIYA	MOLDAVIYA	1971–1973

Builders:	Mathias Thesen, Wismar (East Germany)
Displacement:	5,460 tons standard
	7,500 tons full load
Length:	409 ft (124.7 m) overall
Beam:	55 ft 9 in (17.0 m)
Draft:	21 ft (6.4 m)
Propulsion:	2 diesel engines (Halberstadt-MAN K6Z 57/80); 8,000 bhp;
	2 shafts
Speed:	21 knots
Range:	20,000 n.miles at 16 knots
Complement:	approx. 85 + 80 technical staff

Helicopters:	1 utility helicopter
Missiles:	none
Guns:	none
Radars:	3 Don-2 (navigation)

These are Navy-manned research ships, similar to seven ships operated by the Academy of Science (see chapter 25).

Classification: Soviet EHOS type.

Design: Built with graceful, liner lines, these ships have a helicopter deck and telescoping hangar. There are 27 laboratories and extensive communications equipment (including Vee Cone antennas). Two 190-hp bow thrusters are fitted along with a 300-hp active rudder for precise station keeping; with the main engines stopped the active rudder can propel the ship at four knots for quiet operation.

Endurance is rated at 60 days.

The AKADEMIK KURCHATOV–class research ship ABKHAZIYA shows the passenger ship lines of this design. Vee Cone HF antennas are fitted to the amidships mast. (1988, Leo Van Ginderen)

8 OCEANOGRAPHIC RESEARCH SHIPS: "NIKOLAY ZUBOV" CLASS

Name	Name	Completed
ALEKSEY CHIRIKOV	FYDOR LITKE	
ANDREY VIL'KITSKIY	NIKOLAY ZUBOV	
BORIS DAVYDOV	SEMEN DEZHNEY	1963–1968
FADDEY BELLINGSGAUZEN	VASILIY GOLOVNIN	

Builders:	Adolf Warski, Szczecin (Poland)
Displacement:	2,200 tons standard
	3,020 tons full load
Length:	295 ft 2 in (90.0 m) overall
Beam:	42 ft 8 in (13.0 m)
Draft:	15 ft 5 in (4.7 m)
Propulsion:	2 diesel engines (Zgoda/Sulzer 8TD48); 4,800 bhp; 2 shafts
Speed:	16.5 knots
Range:	11,000 n.miles at 14 knots
Complement:	approx. 50
Helicopters:	small platform on some units

Missiles:	none
Guns:	none
Radars:	2 Don-2 (navigation)

These eight ships are configured for oceanographic research; three sister ships are AGIs, listed separately in this chapter. The lead ship, the NIKOLAY ZUBOV, was placed in commission on 1 April 1964.

Classification: Soviet EHOS type.

Design: These ships are designed for polar operations (e.g., ice-strengthened hulls and enclosed lookout positions). They have one 15-ton boom, two 7-ton, and two 5-ton booms; fitted with nine laboratories. Details of the ships vary. The ZUBOV and possibly others have more elaborate communications equipment, including Vee Cone antennas.

Endurance is rated at 60 days.

The FADDEY BELLINGSGAUZEN at Wellington shows the light helicopter platform fitted in some ships of this class. Cargo booms are fitted to the after A-frame mast. The BELLINGSGAUZEN has considerably more electronic gear than the CHIRIKOV. (1982, Leo Van Ginderen)

3 OCEANOGRAPHIC RESEARCH SHIPS: "POLYUS" CLASS

Name	Completed
POLYUS	1962
BALKHASH	1964
BAYKAL	1964

Builders:	Neptun, Rostock (East Germany)
Displacement:	4,560 tons standard
	6,900 tons full load
Length:	366 ft (111.6 m) overall
Beam:	47 ft 3 in (14.4 m)
Draft:	20 ft 8 in (6.3 m)
Propulsion:	diesel-electric: 4 diesel generators; 4,000 bhp; connected to 2 electric motors; 1 shaft
Speed:	13.5 knots
Range:	25,000 n.miles at 12 knots
Complement:	

Helicopters:	no facilities
Missiles:	none
Guns:	none
Radars:	2 Don-2 (navigation) except 2 Palm Frond in BALKHASH

These ships were built on ANDIZHAN/KOVEL cargo hulls for the oceanographic research role.

Class: About 50 ships of this class were built for merchant use, including these research ships and others converted to missile test support ships; three ships serve as merchant-cadet training ships.

Classification: Soviet EHOS type.

Design: Details and masts vary; the POLYUS has her bridge mast aft of the funnel, others are forward, and the POLYUS has a pole mast forward while the others have "goal posts." The ships have an active rudder and bow thruster for station keeping. There are 17 laboratories.

Endurance is rated at 75 days.

The BALKHASH is one of three virtually identical oceanographic research ships of the POLYUS class. She has a deckhouse forward (beneath twin cargo booms), a large deckhouse aft of the funnel, and another on the fantail. Other ships of this class serve as civilian auxiliary ships.

1 OCEANOGRAPHIC RESEARCH SHIP: "NEVEL'SKOY" TYPE

Name	Completed
NEVEL'SKOY	1961

Builders:	Nikolayev
Displacement:	2,350 tons full load
Length:	274 ft 10 in (83.8 m) overall
Beam:	49 ft 10 in (15.2 m)
Draft:	12 ft 6 in (3.8 m)
Propulsion:	2 diesel engines; 4,000 bhp; 2 shafts
Speed:	17 knots
Range:	10,000 n.miles at 11 knots
Complement:	approx. 45
Helicopters:	no facilities
Missiles:	none
Guns:	none
Radars:	2 Don-2 (navigation)

A one-of-a-kind ship, probably the prototype for the NIKOLAY ZUBOV class. The NEVEL'SKOY is one of the few Soviet oceanographic research ships built in the USSR (the ZUBOVs were built in Poland).

Classification: Soviet EHOS type.

The oceanographic research ship NEVEL'SKOY has the same basic arrangement as the NIKOLAY ZUBOV class but with a much smaller bridge structure.

HYDROGRAPHIC SURVEY SHIPS

These ships conduct hydrographic surveys and service the extensive Soviet coastal waterways—surveying and marking channels, planting and retrieving buoys, etc. These ships are operated by the Navy's Hydrographic Service. None are armed except for one unit believed to be employed in oceanographic research.

Classification: All Soviet GS type except inshore craft are GPB.

2 HYDROGRAPHIC SURVEY SHIPS: VINOGRAD CLASS

Name	Completed
GS-525	Nov 1985
GS-526	Dec 1985

Builders:	Rauma-Repola, Savonlinna (Finland)
Displacement:	450 tons full load
Length:	106 ft (32.3 m) overall
Beam:	31 ft 6 in (9.6 m)
Draft:	8 ft 6 in (2.6 m)
Propulsion:	2 diesel engines (Baykal 300); 600 bhp; 2 shafts
Speed:	10 knots
Range:	
Complement:	approx. 20
Helicopters:	no facilities
Missiles:	none
Guns:	none
Radars:	. . . . . . (navigation)

These are small coastal survey units.

The small survey ship GS-525. (1985, Rauma-Repola Shipyard)

24 HYDROGRAPHIC SURVEY SHIPS: FENIK CLASS

Name	Name	Name	Completed
GS-24	GS-278	GS-398	
GS-47	GS-280	GS-399	
GS-84	GS-296	GS-400	
GS-86	GS-297	GS-401	
GS-87	GS-301	GS-402	1979–1981
GS-260	GS-388	GS-403	
GS-270	GS-392	GS-404	
GS-272	GS-397	GS-405	

Builders:	Stocznia Polnocny, Gdańsk (Poland)
Displacement:	1,200 tons full load
Length:	201 ft 1 in (61.3 m) overall
Beam:	38 ft 8 in (11.8 m)
Draft:	10 ft 9 in (3.3 m)
Propulsion:	2 diesel engines (Cegielski/Sulzer); 1,920 bhp; 2 shafts (see notes)
Speed:	13 knots
Range:	3,000 n.miles at 13 knots
Complement:	approx. 30
Helicopters:	no facilities
Missiles:	none
Guns:	none
Radars:	2 Don-2 (navigation)

These ships are employed for hydrographic surveys as well as buoy tending.

Class: One ship of this type has been built for East Germany and four for Poland.

Design: A 7-ton-capacity crane is located forward, with a work area for handling buoys.

Engineering: The ships have two 75-kilowatt electric motors for quiet operation during surveys; they can reach six knots on these motors. A bow thruster is provided.

The Fenik-class hydrographic survey ship GS-397 is typical of the large number of ships of this type that are employed along the lengthy Soviet coast for surveys and to maintain marker buoys and other navigational aids. (1987, U.S. Navy)

A Fenik-class ship showing their basic arrangement, with a working area forward and large crane for handling buoys and other gear. (1984, JMSDF)

14 HYDROGRAPHIC SURVEY SHIPS: BIYA CLASS

Name	Name	Name	Completed
GS-182	GS-202	GS-214	
GS-192	GS-204	GS-269	
GS-193	GS-206	GS-271	1972–1976
GS-194	GS-208	GS-273	
GS-198	GS-210		

Builders:	Stocznia Polnocny, Gdańsk (Poland)
Displacement:	750 tons full load
Length:	180 ft 5 in (55.0 m) overall
Beam:	30 ft 2 in (9.2 m)
Draft:	8 ft 6 in (2.6 m)
Propulsion:	2 diesel engines; 1,200 bhp; 2 shafts
Speed:	13 knots
Range:	4,700 n.miles at 11 knots
Complement:	approx. 25
Helicopters:	no facilities
Missiles:	none
Guns:	none
Radars:	1 Don-2 (navigation)

Small hydrographic survey and buoy tending ships. Endurance is rated at 15 days.

Class: One ship was transferred to Cuba, one to Guinea-Bissau, and one to Cape Verde.

Design: Fitted with 5-ton-capacity crane.

11 HYDROGRAPHIC SURVEY SHIPS: KAMENKA CLASS

Name	Name	Name	Completed
GS-66	GS-103	GS-203	
GS-74	GS-107	GS-207	1968–1972
GS-78	GS-108 (ex-VERNIER)	GS-211	
GS-82	GS-113 (ex-BEL'BEK)		

Builders:	Stocznia Polnocny, Gdańsk (Poland)
Displacement:	703 tons full load
Length:	175 ft 6 in (53.5 m) overall
Beam:	29 ft 10 in (9.1 m)
Draft:	8 ft 6 in (2.6 m)
Propulsion:	2 diesel engines; 1,765 bhp; 2 shafts
Speed:	13.7 knots
Range:	4,000 n.miles at 10 knots
Complement:	approx. 40
Helicopters:	no facilities
Missiles:	none
Guns:	none
Radars:	1 Don-2 (navigation)

These ships are similar to the Biya class but have enhanced buoy-handling capability. Fitted with 5-ton-capacity crane.

Class: One ship of this class serves with the East German Navy.

Kamenka-class hydrographic survey ship.

19 HYDROGRAPHIC SURVEY SHIPS } MOMA CLASS
1 OCEANOGRAPHIC RESEARCH SHIP }

Name	Name	Name	Completed
AL'TAYR	BEREZAN	MORZHOVETS	
ANADYR'	CHELEKEN	OKEAN	
ANDROMEDA	EL'TON	RYBACHIY (ex-	
ANTARES	KOLGUEV	ODOGRAF)	1967–1974
ANTARTIKA	KRIL'ON	SEVER	
ARTIKA	LIMAN	TAYMRY	
ASKOL'D	MARS	ZAPOLAR'E	

Builders:	Stocznia Polnocny, Gdańsk (Poland)
Displacement:	1,260 tons standard
	1,540 tons full load
Length:	240 ft 5 in (73.3 m) overall
Beam:	35 ft 5 in (10.8 m)
Draft:	12 ft 6 in (3.8 m)
Propulsion:	2 diesel engines (Zgoda/Sulzer 6TD46); 3,600 bhp; 2 shafts
Speed:	17 knots
Range:	8,700 n.miles at 11 knots
Complement:	approx. 55
Helicopters:	no facilities
Missiles:	2 quad SA-N-5 or SA-N-8 anti-air launchers [32] in RYBACHIY
Guns:	4 12.7-mm machine guns (2 twin) in RYBACHIY
Radars:	2 Don-2 (navigation)

These are large hydrographic survey and research ships, which also tend buoys. The RYBACHIY is reported to be involved in oceanographic research.

Class: Nine ships of this class serve in the AGI role with the Soviet Navy. Others have been built at the Polnocny shipyard for the Bulgarian, Polish, and Yugoslav navies with some 40 having been built.

Design: There are large work areas forward and aft, with a 7-ton-capacity crane forward. Four laboratories are provided.

The RYBACHIY has a deckhouse forward (no crane) and has been armed.

Kamenka-class hydrographic survey ship GS-108.

The RYBACHIY of the Moma class has apparently been refitted for oceanographic research. She has a large deckhouse between the bridge and forecastle; positions for SA-N-5 quad missile launchers are located at the after end of her 01 deck level. (1985, JMSDF)

The classic Moma-class hydrographic survey ship.

15 HYDROGRAPHIC SURVEY SHIPS: SAMARA CLASS

Name	Name	Name	Completed
AZIMUT	GRADUS	TURA (ex-GLOBUS)	
DEVIATOR	KOMPAS	VAYGACH	
GIGROMETR	PAMYAT' MERKURIYA	VOSTOK	1962–1964
GLUBOMETR	RUMB (GS-118)	GS-275 (ex-YUG)	
GORIZONT	TROPIK	ZENIT	

Builders:	Stocznia Polnocny, Gdańsk (Poland)
Displacement:	1,050 tons standard
	1,276 tons full load
Length:	193 ft 6 in (59.0 m) overall
Beam:	34 ft 1 in (10.4 m)
Draft:	12 ft 6 in (3.8 m)
Propulsion:	2 diesel engines (Zgoda 5TD48); 3,000 bhp; 2 shafts
Speed:	15.5 knots
Range:	6,200 n.miles at 11 knots
Complement:	approx. 45
Helicopters:	no facilities
Missiles:	none
Guns:	none
Radars:	2 Don-2 (navigation)

Hydrographic research ships and buoy tenders. The TURA is employed in a training role. The DEVIATOR has served as an AGI.

The Soviets refer to these ships as the AZIMUT class.

Design: The ships are fitted with a 7-ton-capacity crane. The TURA has a large deckhouse forward (crane removed); she can accommodate a total of 120 men. Endurance is rated at 25 days.

The Samara-class hydrographic survey ship GLUBOMETR in Far Eastern waters. These ships can be readily identified by their mast configuration. (1987, JMSDF)

The VAYGACH has a deckhouse added forward of the bridge but retains her buoy-handling crane. (1982, U.S. Navy)

3 HYDROGRAPHIC SURVEY SHIPS: MELITOPOL CLASS

Name	Name	Name	Completed
MAYAK	NIVILER	PRIZMA	1952–1955

Builders:	(USSR)
Displacement:	1,200 tons full load
Tonnage:	776 DWT
Length:	188 ft 11 in (57.6 m) overall
Beam:	29 ft 6 in (9.0 m)
Draft:	14 ft 1 in (4.3 m)
Propulsion:	1 diesel engine (6DR 30/40); 600 bhp; 1 shaft
Speed:	11 knots
Range:	2,500 n.miles at 10.5 knots
Complement:	
Helicopters:	no facilities
Missiles:	none
Guns:	none
Radars:	1 Don (navigation)

These are the only Soviet-built ships employed as naval hydrographic survey ships. They were converted from small cargo ships.

Melitopol-class hydrographic survey ship.

HYDROGRAPHIC SURVEY SHIPS: "TELNOVSK" CLASS

The four ships of this class (AYTODOR, SIRENA, SVIYAGA, and ULYANA GROMOVA) have been discarded. See 3rd edition, page 305.

INSHORE SURVEY CRAFT

SEVERAL INSHORE SURVEY CRAFT: GPB-480 CLASS

Completed:	1960s
Builders:	(USSR)
Displacement:	120 tons full load
Length:	95 ft 2 in (29.0 m) overall
Beam:	16 ft 5 in (5.0 m)
Draft:	55 ft 9 in (1.7 m)
Propulsion:	1 diesel engine; 450 bhp; 1 shaft
Speed:	12 knots
Range:	1,600 n.miles at 10 knots
Complement:	approx. 15
Missiles:	none
Guns:	none
Radars:	1 Spin Trough (search)

These craft have the same hull and propulsion plant as the Nyryat I–class diving tenders. One 1-ton-boom and one 1½-ton boom are fitted. Endurance is rated at ten days.

Classification: Soviet GPB type.

SEVERAL INSHORE SURVEY BOATS: GPB-710 CLASS

Builders:	(USSR)
Displacement:	7 tons full load
Length:	36 ft 1 in (11.0 m) overall
Beam:	9 ft 10 in (3.0 m)
Draft:	2 ft 3 in (0.7 m)
Propulsion:	diesel engine
Speed:	10 knots
Range:	150 n.miles at 10 knots
Complement:	
Missiles:	none
Guns:	none
Radars:	1 . . . . . . (navigation)

These boats are carried on board larger oceanographic and hydrographic survey ships. They are rated as having a one-day operational endurance.

MISSILE RANGE INSTRUMENTATION SHIPS

These Navy-manned ships support the Soviet test firings of long-range ballistic missiles (ICBMs and SLBMs) and can additionally support military space activities. All of these ships are believed to operate in the Indian Ocean–Pacific area.

The civilian-manned Space Event Support Ships (SESS), described in chapter 25, do not normally provide range instrumentation for missile firings.

(The nuclear-propelled missile range instrumentation ship reported in the previous edition of *Guide to the Soviet Navy* is listed at the beginning of this chapter as the SSV-33.)

2 MISSILE RANGE INSTRUMENTATION SHIPS: "MARSHAL NEDELIN" CLASS

Name	Completed
MARSHAL NEDELIN	1984
MARSHAL KRYLOV	1989

Builders:	United Admiralty (Leningrad)
Displacement:	24,000 tons full load
Length:	698 ft 8 in (213.0 m) overall
Beam:	88 ft 11 in (27.1 m)
Draft:	25 ft 3 in (7.7 m)
Propulsion:	2 gas turbines; 54,000 shp; 2 shafts
Speed:	20 knots
Range:	
Complement:	approx. 200
Helicopters:	2 Ka-27 Helix-D
Missiles:	4 quad SA-N-5 or SA-N-8 anti-air launchers
Guns:	see notes

Radars:	1 End Tray (balloon tracking)
	1 Fly Screen (helicopter control)
	3 Palm Frond (navigation)
	1 Strut Pair (search) in NEDELIN
	1 Top Plate in KRYLOV

These are large missile range support ships, fitted with a large number of antenna arrays. The MARSHAL NEDELIN was transferred to the Far East in 1984.

Design: The ships have a radome some 65½ ft (20 m) in diameter immediately aft of the bridge structure. There is a large mast structure amidships, with several smaller masts and antenna supports.

Electronics: A pair of Round House TACAN antennas are mounted near the top of the larger (second) pylon mast and a large Ship Globe radome containing a tracking radar antenna is fitted aft of the first pylon mast. The ship's tracking radars include the Quad Leaf, Quad Rods, Quad Wedge, and Ship Globe. A pair of optical tracking devices are stepped on the forecastle.

Guns: These ships have foundations for the installation of six 30-mm Gatling guns and three associated Bass Tilt radar directors.

Names: Chief Marshal of Artillery M.I. Nedelin was the first commander in chief of the Soviet Strategic Rocket Forces, assuming that post on 19 December 1959. He was killed in October of the following year in the accidental explosion of an ICBM.

Chief Marshal of Artillery N. I. Krylov was a subsequent CinC of the SRF.

This stern aspect of the MARSHAL NEDELIN shows the helicopter deck and twin hangars and control station; the ship has two TACAN antennas on the after pylon mast. Just forward of the hangars is a Quad Spring communications antenna. (1984, Royal Netherlands Navy)

The MARSHAL NEDELIN is the Soviet Navy's largest dedicated missile range instrumentation ship. She has two theodolite tracking cameras stepped forward of the bridge; there is a massive array of antennas on the ship for missile tracking and communications. All of the Soviet range instrumentation ships operate in the Pacific–Indian Ocean areas. (1987, U.S. Navy)

2 MISSILE RANGE INSTRUMENTATION SHIPS: DESNA CLASS

Name	Completed
CHAZHMA (ex-DANGERA)	1963
CHUMIKAN (ex-DOLGESCHTCHEL'YE)	1963

Builders:	Warnow, Warnemunde (East Germany)
Displacement:	14,065 tons full load
Length:	458 ft 11 in (139.9 m) overall
Beam:	59 ft (18.0 m)
Draft:	25 ft 11 in (7.9 m)
Propulsion:	1 diesel engine (MAN); 5,400 bhp; 1 shaft
Speed:	15 knots
Range:	9,000 n.miles at 13 knots
Complement:	approx. 240
Helicopters:	1 Ka-25 Hormone-C
Missiles:	none
Guns:	none
Radars:	2 Don-2 (navigation)
	1 Head Net-C (air search)
EW systems:	2 Watch Dog

These are missile range instrumentation ships converted from DZHANKOY-class bulk ore/coal carriers. The NATO code name for the class is Desna.

Class: The Warnow yard delivered 15 merchant ships of the DZHANKOY design (9,750 DWT) to the Soviet merchant fleet between 1960 and 1962.

Classification: Soviet OS type.

Design: These ships have a distinctive arrangement, with two island superstructure groupings. The after structure consists of the funnel, with a faired-in mast mounting two Vee Cone communication antennas, and a helicopter hangar on each side of the funnel. There is a large helicopter landing area aft.

(The merchant ships of the DZHANKOY type are superstructure-aft ships.)

Electronics: Three large missile-tracking directors are mounted forward with the Ship Globe radome mounted above the forward island structure. These were the only ships fitted with the Head Net-B radar. Replaced by Head Net-C in both ships.

One of two East German–built Desna-class missile range instrumentation ships, the CHAZHMA was photographed in the mid-Pacific during Soviet ballistic missile tests. There are three tracking devices forward of the bridge and a large radar above the bridge encased in a radome, plus smaller tracking antennas. (1989, U.S. Navy)

One of the Desna-class ships. The short funnel is surmounted by a mast carrying twin Vee Cone HF antennas. The Navy-manned missile/space support ships have helicopter facilities; their civilian counterparts do not.

4 MISSILE RANGE INSTRUMENTATION SHIPS: "SIBIR'" CLASS

Name	Name	Completed
CHUKOTA	SIBIR'	
SAKHALIN	SPASSK (ex-SUCHAN)	} 1958

Builders:	Adolf Warski, Szczecin (Poland)
Displacement:	7,800 tons full load
Length:	354 ft 11 in (108.2 m) overall
Beam:	47 ft 11 in (14.6 m)
Draft:	23 ft 7 in (7.2 m)
Propulsion:	triple-expansion piston with low-pressure turbine; 2,300 shp; 1 shaft
Boilers:	2
Speed:	12 knots
Range:	11,800 n.miles at 12 knots
Complement:	approx. 240
Helicopters:	1 Ka-25 Hormone-C (no hangar)
Missiles:	none
Guns:	none
Radars:	1 Head Net-C (3-D air search) except Big Net (3-D air search) in CHUKOTA
	2 Don-2 (navigation)

These ships were converted during construction from DONBASS-class cargo ships. They were Polish built but completed in Leningrad; all converted about 1960 to the missile range instrumentation role.

Class: More than 40 DONBASS-class cargo ships (approx. 4,900 DWT) were delivered to the Soviet merchant fleet between 1952 and 1958, plus units delivered to other communist fleets.

Classification: Soviet OS type.

Design: The CHUKOTA is flush decked; the others have a well deck forward. They have an impressive appearance, with large antenna-bearing kingposts forward and aft of the central superstructure. Two or three missile-tracking directors are mounted forward of the bridge. A large helicopter platform is fitted aft. One utility helicopter is normally embarked, although the ships do not have a hangar.

Electronics: Fitted with Quad Rods tracking antennas in addition to the paired antennas forward of the bridge. All except the SIBIR' have an optical tracking device on the forecastle.

The SIBIR'-class missile range instrumentation ship SAKHALIN with a Head Net-C radar on her second kingpost; a kingpost mast abuts the bridge. There is a Ka-25 Hormone-C utility helicopter on the flight deck; these ships do not have hangars. (1987, U.S. Navy)

The CHUKOTA with a Big Net radar on her second kingpost mast. The hull lines and antenna arrays of the SIBIR'-class ships differ in detail.

CHAPTER 25

Civilian Auxiliary Ships

The Rossiya is one of the large, nuclear-propelled icebreakers of the Soviet merchant marine that have direct military support missions. Some if not all of the ships of the Arktika class, the world's largest icebreakers, carried out their sea trials with a gun armament and fire control radars. Note the electronic arrays of the Rossiya, surmounted by a Top Plate radar. (Royal Navy)

The Soviet Union's fleet of civilian research ships and specialized ships that could be of direct assistance to the Soviet Navy in time of war continues to expand. Of particular significance during the past few years has been the construction of additional oceanographic and hydrometrical research ships, and nuclear-propelled icebreakers. Also, construction of a new class of Space Event Support Ships (SESS) is under way. The previous deliveries of such ships, which were ten-year-old converted cargo ships, occurred in 1978.

Although some of the new construction ships are replacing older units, there is still a significant rate of growth in most of the categories covered in this chapter.

These ships are civilian-manned. None of them are armed although the nuclear-propelled icebreakers of the Arktika class were armed during sea trials.

SPACE EVENT SUPPORT SHIPS

These ships support civilian and military space activities as well as upper-atmosphere research and communications research programs. All operate under the direction of the Academy of Sciences. These ships are well suited to the collateral activities of intelligence collection and military communications relay.

(1) SPACE CONTROL-MONITORING SHIP: NEW CONSTRUCTION

Name	Launched	Completed
AKADEMIK NIKOLAY PILYUGIN		building

Builders:	United Admiralty (Leningrad)
Displacement:	24,000 tons full load
Length:	698 ft 8 in (213.0 m) overall
Beam:	88 ft 11 in (27.1 m)
Draft:	25 ft 3 in (7.7 m)
Propulsion:	2 gas turbines; 54,000 shp; 2 shafts
Speed:	20 knots
Range:	
Complement:	
Helicopters:	2 utility
Radars:	

The PILYUGIN is similar in design to the MARSHAL NEDELIN-class of missile range instrumentation ships, but outfitted for civilian space activities. The PILYUGIN may be a replacement for the KOSMONAUT VLADIMIR KOMAROV.

The ship was laid down on 15 April 1988.

Design: The ship's bridge structure is higher and mounted farther forward than in the NEDELIN class.

Electronics: The ship is expected to have Ship Bowl and Ship Shell communication antennas.

Names: N.A. Pilyugin was the Soviet Union's leading missile navigation and guidance expert from the mid-1940s.

4 SPACE CONTROL-MONITORING SHIPS: "KOSMONAUT PAVEL BELYAYEV"

Name	Completed	Conversion Completed
KOSMONAUT PAVEL BELYAYEV (ex-VYTEGRALES)	1963	1977
KOSMONAUT VLADILAV VOLKOV (ex-YENISEILES)	1964	1977
KOSMONAUT GEORGIY DOBROVOSLKIY (ex-SEMYON KOSINOV)	1968	1978
KOSMONAUT VIKTOR PATSAYEV (ex-NAZAR GUBIN)	1968	1978

Builders:	Zhdanov, Leningrad
Displacement:	9,000 tons full load
Tonnage:	2,010 DWT
Length:	399 ft 6 in (121.8 m) overall
Beam:	54 ft 11 in (16.75 m)
Draft:	23 ft 11 in (7.3 m)
Propulsion:	1 diesel engine (Bryansk/Burmeister & Wain 950 VTBF 110); 5,200 bhp; 1 shaft
Speed:	14.5 knots
Range:	
Complement:	approx. 90
Helicopters:	no facilities
Radars:	1 Don-2 (navigation)
	1 Kite Screech (tracking)
	1 Okean (navigation)

These ships were converted from VYTEGRALES-class cargo/timber carriers. Their conversion permitted two ships, the BEZHITSA and RISTNA, temporarily employed in this role, to return to merchant cargo service. All four of these ships are based in the Baltic.

Class: The Zhdanov yard produced 36 timber carriers of this type for the Soviet merchant fleet, of which eight were transferred to the Soviet Navy for conversion to auxiliary roles, and another

The space control-monitoring ship KOSMONAUT VIKTOR PATSAYEV is one of almost a dozen specialized merchant marine–operated ships used to support Soviet military and civilian space programs. The massive communications antenna pointed skyward between the deck structures is the Quad Spring.

eight were converted to the SESS role (BELYAYEV and BOROVICHI classes). A design derived from the VYTEGRALES class has been built at the Vyborg yard; the Navy's PIONEER MOSKVYY salvage ships are from the latter group.

Electronics: A Quad Spring communications antenna array is fitted amidships in addition to smaller satellite communications antennas.

Names: Civilian scientific ships are named for Soviet *kosmonauts* (astronauts) and scientists.

The KOSMONAUT GEORGIY DOBROVOLSKIY in Antwerp. There is a large structure supporting the Quad Spring antenna; the ship carries numerous other, smaller antennas. (1989, Leo Van Ginderen)

1 SPACE CONTROL-MONITORING SHIP: "KOSMONAUT YURI GAGARIN"

Name	Completed
KOSMONAUT YURI GAGARIN	Dec 1971

Builders:	Baltic, Leningrad
Displacement:	53,500 tons full load
Tonnage:	31,300 DWT
Length:	760 ft (231.7 m) overall
Beam:	102 ft (31.1 m)
Draft:	32 ft 10 in (10.0 m)
Propulsion:	turbo-electric: 2 steam turbines (Kirov) with electric drive; 19,000 shp; 1 shaft
Boilers:	2
Speed:	17.7 knots
Range:	24,000 n.miles at 17.7 knots
Complement:	approx. 160 + 180 scientists-technicians
Helicopters:	no facilities
Radars:	1 Don-Kay (navigation)
	1 Okean (navigation)

The GAGARIN is the world's largest ship fitted for scientific activities and the largest ship in service with turbo-electric propulsion. The ship was built specifically for scientific purposes with a SOFIYA-class tanker hull and propulsion plant. (The ship has a greater displacement than the longer naval SSV-33.) Based in the Black Sea (Odessa).

Class: Twenty-two tankers of the SOFIYA class were built at two Soviet yards; one serves as a naval tanker (AKHTUBA).

Design: The ship has a large bulbous bow and is fitted with bow and stern thrusters. Recreation facilities include three swimming pools and a theater seating 300 persons plus a sports hall.

Endurance is rated at 120 days.

Electronics: The ship's tracking-communications equipment includes Quad Ring, Ship Bowl, Ship Shell, and Vee Tube antennas. Two pair of the last—HF antennas—are rigged outboard of the ship's funnel.

Engineering: Fitted with bow and stern thrusters.

Names: Yuri Gagarin was the first man to fly in space; he was killed in an airplane crash in 1968.

Built two decades ago on the hull of a SOFIA-class tanker, the KOSMONAUT YURI GAGARIN was named for the first man in space. Two 90-foot (27.4-m)-diameter and two 41-foot (12.5-m)-diameter dish antennas used for communications with manned space vehicles dominate the ship's superstructure. Two pairs of Vee Cone HF antennas are fitted outboard of the stern funnel.

1 SPACE CONTROL-MONITORING SHIP: "AKADEMIK SERGEI KOROLEV"

Name	Completed
AKADEMIK SERGEI KOROLEV	Dec 1970

Builders:	Black Sea Shipyard, Nikolayev (south)
Displacement:	17.115 tons standard
	21,465 tons full load
Tonnage:	7,067 DWT
Length:	596 ft 8 in (181.9 m) overall
Beam:	82 ft (25.0 m)
Draft:	25 ft 11 in (7.9 m)
Propulsion:	1 diesel engine (Bryansk/Burmeister & Wain); 12,000 bhp; 1 shaft
Speed:	17.5 knots
Range:	22,500 n.miles at 17 knots
Complement:	approx. 190 + 170 scientists-technicians
Helicopters:	no facilities
Radars:	1 Don-2 (navigation)
	1 Okean (navigation)

Although smaller than the GAGARIN, this is still a large and imposing SESS. The KOROLEV was built from the keel up for this role.

Design: Fitted with 80 laboratories.

Electronics: Tracking and communications equipment includes Quad Ring, Ship Bowl, Ship Globe, and Vee Tube antennas (with the last, in pairs, angled out from the unusual twin-leg support mast forward of the funnel).

Names: Sergei Korolev was the foremost Soviet designer of guided and ballistic missiles and spacecraft; he died in 1966.

1 SPACE CONTROL-MONITORING SHIP: "KOSMONAUT V. KOMAROV"

Name	Completed	Conversion Completed
KOSMONAUT VLADIMIR KOMAROV (ex-GENICHESK)	1966	July 1967

Builders:	Kherson
Displacement:	11,090 tons standard
	17,500 tons full load
Tonnage:	7,065 DWT
Length:	510 ft 8 in (155.7) overall
Beam:	76 ft 5 in (23.3 m)
Draft:	28 ft 2 in (8.6 m)

Propulsion:	1 diesel engine (Bryansk/Burmeister & Wain); 9,000 bhp; 1 shaft
Speed:	17.5 knots
Range:	16,700 n.miles at 17.5 knots
Complement:	approx. 115 + 125 scientists-technicians
Helicopters:	no facilities
Radars:	2 Don-Kay (navigation)

The KOMAROV was converted during construction from a POLTAVA-class dry cargo ship, with her conversion being completed in Leningrad. Based in the Black Sea (Odessa).

Class: In addition to the KOMAROV, between 1962 and 1967 two Soviet yards produced 20 of the POLTAVA-class general cargo ships for the Soviet merchant fleet, plus another 31 ships for West Germany, Hungary, Iraq, India, Kuwait, and Pakistan.

Electronics: Tracking and communications antennas include Quad Ring, Ship Globe, and Ship Wheel, plus Vee Cone HF antennas at the masthead.

4 SPACE CONTROL-MONITORING SHIPS: "BOROVICHI" CLASS

Name	Completed	Name	Completed
BOROVICHI	1965	MORZHOVETS	1966
KEGOTROV	1966	NEVEL	1966

Builders:	Zhdanov, Leningrad
Displacement:	7,600 tons full load
Tonnage:	1,834 DWT
Length:	399 ft 11 in (121.9 m) overall
Beam:	54 ft 11 in (16.75 m)
Draft:	15 ft 5 in (4.7 m)
Propulsion:	1 diesel engine (Bryansk/Burmeister & Wain 950 VTBF 110); 5,200 bhp; 1 shaft
Speed:	15.5 knots
Range:	7,400 n.miles at 15 knots
Complement:	approx. 80
Helicopters:	no facilities
Radars:	2 Don-2 (navigation)

These ships were laid down as VYTEGRALES-type cargo ships but were completed to an SESS configuration. These ships differ significantly in configuration from the BELYAYEV class, which were converted after service as cargo ships (see above for class notes).

Electronics: Communications and tracking antennas include Quad Ring, Quint Ring, and Vee Cone HF; the last is mounted on a tall mast aft of the bridge and funnel.

The AKADEMIK SERGEI KOROLEV is a one-of-a-kind SESS, whose appearance belies the ship's medium size. The two pairs of Vee Cone HF antennas are mounted on a kingpost just forward of the funnel.

Two massive radomes dominate the superstructure of the KOSMONAUT VLADIMIR KOMAROV. There is a third, smaller radome, with the two sets of Vee Cone HF antennas mounted on separate masts. There are two Quad Rings and another communications antenna forward. (1984, Leo Van Ginderen)

Space event support ship KOSMONAUT VLADIMIR KOMAROV.

RESEARCH SHIPS

In addition to the civilian research ships listed here, there are more than 50 fisheries research ships in service under the aegis of the Ministry of Fisheries (see chapter 33).

(SEVERAL) HYDROGRAPHIC SURVEY SHIPS: NEW CONSTRUCTION

Builders:	Hollming, Rauma, and Turku (Finland)
Displacement:	1,570 tons full load
Length:	213 ft 2½ in (65.0 m) overall
Beam:	41 ft 7 in (12.7 m)
Draft:	11 ft 6 in (3.5 m)
Propulsion:	2 diesel engines; 3,500 bhp; 1 shaft
Speed:	17 knots
Range:	
Complement:	approx. 40
Helicopters:	no facilities
Radars:	. . . . . . (navigation)

At least three ships of this design were ordered in 1989 for hydrographic survey; when this edition went to press it was not clear if they would be civilian or naval subordinated.

(2) GEOLOGICAL RESEARCH SHIPS: "SIBIRYAKOV" CLASS

Name	Launched	Completed
SHIBIRYAKOV	May 1989	Building
. . . . . .		Building

Builders:	Adolf Warski, Szczecin (Poland)
Displacement:	2,700 tons
Length:	328 ft (100.0 m) overall
Beam:	55 ft 9 in (17.0 m)
Draft:	18 ft 8 in (5.7 m)
Propulsion:	diesel-electric: 2 diesel engines (Cegielski-Sulzer), 6,400 bhp; 2 electric motors, 5,100 shp; 4 propulsors
Speed:	16 knots
Range:	
Complement:	approx. 50 + 50 scientists-technicians
Helicopters:	no facilities
Radars:	. . . . . (navigation)

Mineral exploration ships. The first unit was laid down in Aug. 1988.

Design: These ships are of the Polish B-970 design. They can carry two subersibles. Provided with 14 laboratories.

Engineering: Fitted with two propulsors for precise maneuvering.

2 OCEANOGRAPHIC RESEARCH SHIPS: "AKADEMIK SERGEI VAVILOV"

Name	Launched	Completed
AKADEMIK SERGEI VAVILOV	16 Dec 1986	Feb 1988
AKADEMIK IOFFE	28 Aug 1987	Feb 1989

Builders:	Hollming, Rauma (Finland)
Displacement:	6,600 tons full load
Length:	384 ft 1 in (117.1 m) overall
Beam:	59 ft 8 in (18.2 m)
Draft:	19 ft 4 in (5.9 m)
Propulsion:	2 diesel engines (SEMT-Pielstick/Russkiy 6PC2.5 L400); 6,800 bhp; 2 shafts
Speed:	15 knots
Range:	20,000 n.miles at 15 knots
Complement:	approx. 75 + 50 scientists-technicians
Helicopters:	no facilities
Radars:	1 . . . . . . (navigation)
	1 Okean (navigation)

Large research ships configured for ocean-floor sampling and physical oceanographic research. They are operated by the Academy of Science.

Design: These ships are a modified version of the AKADEMIK MSTISLAV KELDYSH design. The IOFFE has a unique auxiliary propulsion system for quiet operation during research activities with two metal sails fitted between the bridge and lattice mast; the half-cylinder sails swing down when not in use.

Engineering: Bow and stern thrusters are fitted.

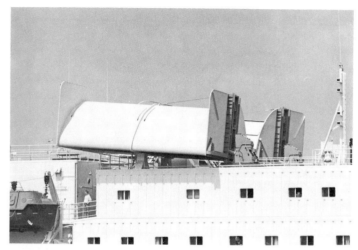

The "sails" of the AKADEMIK IOFFE in the down position; note the elevating equipment at the base of the devices. (1989, Leo Van Ginderen)

The large research ship AKADEMIK SERGEI VAVILOV has a large superstructure block and large, rectangular funnel near the stern. Note the position of the tall lattice mast. There are several survey boats embarked.

The AKADEMIK IOFFE, shown here at Antwerp, has two folding metal "sails" aft of the bridge, apparently intended for quiet operation of the ship while conducting acoustic experiments in which machinery noises could interfere. (1989, Leo Van Ginderen)

1 ANTARCTIC RESEARCH-SUPPORT SHIP: "AKADEMIK FEDOROV"

Name	Launched	Completed
AKADEMIK FEDOROV	27 Feb 1987	Aug 1987

Builders:	Rauma-Repola, Savonlinna (Finland)
Displacement:	16,200 tons full load
Tonnage:	7,600 DWT
Length:	463 ft 1½ in (141.2 m) overall
Beam:	77 ft 1 in (23.5 m)
Draft:	27 ft 11 in (8.5 m)
Propulsion:	diesel-electric: 2 diesel engines (Wartsila Vasa R32); 11,222 bhp; 1 shaft
Speed:	16 knots
Range:	20,000 n.miles at 16 knots
Complement:	approx. 90 + 160 scientists-technicians
Helicopters:	1 Mi-8 Hip
Radars:	2 . . . . . . (navigation)

This is a large research-support and supply ship intended specifically for Antarctic operations.

Design: The ship has a limited icebreaking capability. Fitted with two 50-ton-capacity and two 10-ton-capacity cranes.

The one-of-a-kind Arctic research/support ship AKADEMIK FEDOROV has a large helicopter deck amidships; the ship has a hangar and helicopter control position, one of the few Soviet civilian research ships with helicopter facilities. An Mi-8 Hip sits on deck. The ship is home ported at Leningrad. (1990, Leo Van Ginderen)

2 GEOTECHNICAL RESEARCH SHIPS: "BAVENIT" CLASS

Name	Launched	Completed
BAVENIT	1985	May 1986
BAKERIT	17 Jan 1986	Dec 1986

Builders:	Hollming, Rauma (Finland)
Displacement:	5,300 tons full load
Tonnage:	2,000 DWT
Length:	281 ft 5 in (85.8 m) overall
Beam:	55 ft 1 in (16.8 m)
Draft:	18 ft 4½ in (5.6 m)
Propulsion:	diesel-electric: 4 diesel generators (Russkiy EG-74/2), 1,700 bhp; electric motors, 6,000 shp; 2 rudder-propellers
Speed:	12.75 knots
Range:	8,000 n.miles at 12 knots
Complement:	approx. 65
Helicopters:	no facilities
Radars:	2 . . . . . (navigation)

The BAVENIT, one of the several unusual Soviet research ship designs; note the twin anchors forward and drilling derrick amidships. (1988, Royal Navy)

Designed for seafloor research and exploration under the aegis of the Ministry of Oil and Gas Industry, these ships are distinguished by their 114⅚-ft (35 m) derrick drill support amidships. They can drill through water 984 (300 m) deep.

Design: These ships have their funnel offset to starboard with the derrick structure over the centerline; there is a derrick control station at the after end of the bridge (see photo). The ships have four anchors for four-point mooring. The hull is strengthened for ice operations.

Engineering: The ships have ducted thrusters forward; Aquamaster shrouded rudder-propellers aft, which can rotate 360° for precision station keeping during drilling operation.

Stern aspect of the BAVENIT; the glazed control station at the after end of the bridge is evident as are twin anchors fitted against the stern counter. There is a modified A-frame at the stern. (1988, Royal Navy)

7 HYDROMETEOROLOGICAL RESEARCH SHIPS: "VADIM POPOV" CLASS

Name	Launched	Completed
VADIM POPOV	Mar 1986	Oct 1986
VIKTOR BUYNITSKIY	Apr 1986	Nov 1986
PAVEL GORDIENKO	June 1986	Feb 1987
VASILIY LOMINADZE	Oct 1986	May 1987
IGOR MAKSIMOV	Mar 1987	Oct 1987
IVAN PETROV	May 1987	Sep 1989
VLADIMIR PARSHIN	July 1987	1989

Builders:	Laivateollisuus, Turku (Finland)
Displacement:	960 tons full load
Tonnage:	294 DWT
Length:	163 ft 8 in (49.9 m) overall
Beam:	32 ft 10 in (10.0 m)
Draft:	11 ft 6 in (3.5 m)
Propulsion:	1 diesel engine (Wartsila Vasa 824-TS); 1,340 bhp; 1 shaft
Speed:	13 knots
Range:	
Complement:	approx. 35
Helicopters:	no facilities
Radars:	2 . . . . . . (navigation)

Small research ships configured for hydrometeorological reporting and for the supply of weather stations in the Far East. The ships have a 5-ton-capacity crane and carry a supply launch.

The ISKATEL' 2 catamaran research ship; this design facilitates the towing of a hydrophone array as well as a pneumatic pulsator array used for seismological/geophysical research in shallow, coastal waters. (1989, Skyphotos)

The PAVEL GORDIENKO is one of a large number of small research ships employed in hydrometeorological activities and for supplying weather stations. A small landing craft is usually carried forward, atop the cargo hold. (1987, Leo Van Ginderen)

The ISKATEL' 4 showing the low, aluminum deckhouse and twin funnel configuration of this Polish-designed research ship. (1989, Bernard Prézelin)

5 COASTAL RESEARCH SHIPS: "ISKATEL' " CLASS

Name	Launched	Completed
ISKATEL' 2	Dec 1985	Nov 1986
ISKATEL' 3	Dec 1986	Dec 1987
ISKATEL' 4		1988
ISKATEL' 5		
ISKATEL' 6		

Builders:	Stocznia Wisla, Gdańsk (Poland)
Displacement:	742 tons full load
Length:	161 ft 8½ in (49.3 m) overall
Beam:	59 ft 8½ in (18.2 m)
Draft:	4 ft 11 in (1.5 m)
Propulsion:	2 diesel engines (Cegielski/Sulzer 6 AL 20/24); 1,140 bhp; 2 Kort nozzles
Speed:	12 knots
Range:	
Complement:	approx. 15 + 10 scientists-technicians
Helicopters:	no facilities
Radars:	1 . . . . . . (navigation)

3 RESEARCH SHIPS: MODIFIED "AKADEMIK ALEKSEY KRYLOV" CLASS

Name	Completed
AKADEMIK NIKOLAY ANDREYEV	Oct 1986
AKADEMIK BORIS KONSTANTINOV	Mar 1989
GELENDZHIK	Dec 1989

Builders:	Okean, Oktyabr'skoye [Nikolayev]
Displacement:	11,600 tons full load
Tonnage:	2,060 DWT
Length:	468 ft (142.7 m) overall
Beam:	57 ft 5 in (17.5 m)
Draft:	23 ft 7 in (7.2 m)
Propulsion:	2 diesel engines (58-6R); 9,000 bhp; 2 shafts
Speed:	16 knots
Range:	15,000 n.miles at 15 knots
Complement:	approx. 120 + 30 scientists-technicians
Helicopters:	no facilities
Radars:	1 Palm Frond (navigation)
	1 Okean-A (navigation)
	1 Okean-B (navigation)

These are catamaran research ships based on the Polish NADEZHNYY-class trawlers. They are configured for seismological-geophysical research in shallow waters as part of the *Shel'f* program of offshore oil and gas exploration.

They are fitted with a towed hydrophone array.

These are large research ships based on the AKADEMIK ALEKSEY KRYLOV design. The two classes can be easily distinguished by the goalpost mast aft of the funnel in the newer units. The ANDREYEV is operated by the Institute of Acoustics.

Design: Facilities are provided for carrying submersibles.

The large Akademik Nikolay Andreyev now has a black hull, distinguishing the ship from the similar Akademik Aleksey Krylov. There are four masts forward with kingposts supporting a large cargo boom aft. The Krylov, with a different mast arrangement, does not have a kingpost. (Royal Norwegian Air Force)

9 + 2 GEOPHYSICAL RESEARCH SHIPS: "AKADEMIK FERSMAN" CLASS

Name	Launched	Completed
Akademik Fersman	24 Jan 1985	May 1986
Akademik Shatskiy	19 July 1985	1986
Akademik Selskiy	14 Dec 1985	1986
Akademik Lazarev	1986	1986
Akademik Gubin	24 Mar 1987	1988
Akademik Nalivkin	Apr 1987	1988
Akademik Nametkin	12 July 1987	1988
Akademik Kreps	Jan 1988	1989
Akademik Nemchinov	27 Feb 1988	1989
2 units		building

Builders:	Adolf Warski, Szczecin (Poland)
Displacement:	3,300 tons full load
Tonnage:	1,283 DWT
Length:	268 ft 6 in (81.85 m) overall
Beam:	48 ft 6½ in (14.8 m)
Draft:	16 ft 5 in (5.0 m)
Propulsion:	1 diesel (Zgoda/Sulzer 6 ZL 40/48; 4,200 bhp; 1 Kort nozzle
Speed:	14.5 knots
Range:	12,000 n.miles at 14.5 knots
Complement:	approx. 30 + 30 scientists-technicians
Helicopters:	no facilities
Radars:	2 . . . . . . (navigation)

These are mid-size research ships intended to support the *Shel'f* program of offshore oil and gas exploration. They have ice-strengthened hulls and stern ramps for towing a 3½-mile (6 km) seismic array.

Design: Polish B-13 design.

Engineering: Two auxiliary 630-kilowatt diesel generators provide power to the array. Fitted with bow thruster.

The Akademik Nalivkin is one of a class of medium-size ships for the support of offshore oil and gas exploration. They have a working area aft and a stern ramp for handling a variety of related research activities; the large superstructure houses several laboratories.

4 + 2 GEOPHYSICAL RESEARCH SHIPS: "AKADEMIK BORIS PETROV"

Name	Launched	Completed
Akademik Boris Petrov	7 July 1983	29 June 1984
Akademik M.A. Lavrent'yev	28 Oct 1983	12 Oct 1984
Akademik Nikolay Strakhov	3 Feb 1984	14 May 1985
Akademik Oparin	1 Feb 1985	29 Nov 1985
. . . . . .		building
. . . . . .		building

Builders:	Hollming, Rauma (Finland)
Displacement:	2,550 tons full load
Tonnage:	886 DWT
Length:	247 ft 6 in (75.45 m) overall
Beam:	48 ft 3 in (14.7 m)
Draft:	15 ft 5 in (4.7 m)
Propulsion:	2 diesel engines (SEMT-Pielstick/Russkiy 6PC 2.5 L400); 3,500 bhp; 1 shaft
Speed:	15.5 knots
Range:	15,000 n.miles at 14.75 knots
Complement:	approx. 75
Helicopters:	no facilities
Radars:	1 Okean (navigation)
	1 . . . . . . (navigation)

These ships are configured for geophysical and hydrophysical research. They are fitted with bow thrusters and cable reels at the stern for towing seismic cable.

The Oparin, configured for biological research, differs in detail from the others.

The AKADEMIK NIKOLAY STRAKHOV is configured for geophysical and hydrophysical research. Ships of this class have a bulbous underwater bow. There is a large cable reel and handling gear at the stern for a seismic recording "tail." (1986, Leo Van Ginderen)

The AKADEMIK OPARIN shows the open starboard side of the BORIS PETROV class to facilitate handing equipment over the side; the port side of these ships is plated in with portholes. (1986, Leo Van Ginderen)

The GEOLOG FERSMAN is one of eight PULKOVSKIY MERIDIAN—class stern trawler/ factory ships converted for geological research. Several others of this large class of twin-funnel, stern-chute ships serve in the fisheries research role. (1988, Leo Van Ginderen)

8 GEOLOGICAL RESEARCH SHIPS: "PULKOVSKIY MERIDIAN" CLASS

Name	Completed
XVII SYEZD PROFSOYUZOV	1982
MORSKOY GEOLOG	1983
AKADEMIK ALEKSANDR KARPINSKIY	1984
GEOLOG PYOTR ANTROPOV	1984
AKADEMIK ALEKSANDR SIDORENKO	1985
GEOLOG FERSMAN	1985
YUZHMORGEOLOGIYA	1985
SEVMORGEOLOGIYA	1989

Builders:	Black Sea Shipyard, Nikolayev (south)
Displacement:	5,620 tons full load
Tonnage:	1,959 DWT
Length:	340 ft (103.65 m) overall
Beam:	53 ft (16.15 m)
Draft:	20 ft (6.1 m)
Propulsion:	2 diesels (Skoda); 6,000 bhp; 1 shaft
Speed:	17 knots
Range:	7,000 n.miles at 14.5 knots
Complement:	approx. 90
Radars:	1 Don-2 (navigation)
	1 Okean (navigation)

The XVII SYEZD PROFSOYUZOV was converted from a PULKOVSKIY MERIDIAN-class stern trawler–factory ship; the other seven ships were constructed to that design specifically for the research role. All are operated by the Ministry of Geology.

Class: A total of 67 ships of this class were built as stern trawler–factory ships, completed 1978–1988. One ship was converted to a geological research role (above) and three were converted to fishery research ships (including the PULKOVSKIY MERIDIAN); the latter ships are not listed in *Guide to the Soviet Navy*.

Design: Fitted with a stern ramp, which facilitates handling research equipment. There are twin cargo booms forward and amidships, and a large A-frame hoist aft. These ships have a bulbous bow.

1 GEOLOGICAL RESEARCH SHIP: "GEOLOG PRIMOR'YE"

Name	Completed
GEOLOG PRIMOR'YE	Oct 1983

Builders:	Vladivostok
Displacement:	791 tons full load
Length:	281 ft 5 in (85.8 m) overall
Beam:	59 ft 8½ in (18.2 m)
Draft:	18 ft 4½ in (5.6 m)
Propulsion:	2 diesel engines; 2,300 bhp; 2 shafts
Speed:	9 knots
Range:	
Complement:	
Helicopters:	no facilities
Radars:	1 . . . . . . (navigation)

A catamaran ship for mineral resources research. Fitted for four-point mooring.

The geological research ship AKADEMIK ALEKSANDR KARPINSKIY is similar to the numerous stern-trawler factory ships of the PULKOVSKIY MERIDIAN class. Behind the bridge is a control station for supervising deck operations. Note the kingposts forward and aft, twin funnels amidships, and radars mounted on the pole mast above the bridge structure. (1984, Leo Van Ginderen)

7 + 2 HYDROMETEOROLOGICAL/SEISMIC RESEARCH SHIPS: MODIFIED "AKADEMIK SHULEYKIN" CLASS

Name	Completed
AKADEMIK GAMBURTSHEV	Dec 1983
AKADEMIK GOLITSYN	Feb 1984
PROFESSOR POLSHAOV	Apr 1984
GEOLOG DIMITRY NALYVKIN	Feb 1985
AKADEMIK ALEKSANDR SIDORENKO	June 1985
AR'NOLD VEYMER	1986
PROFESSOR GAGARINSKY	1989
2 units	building

Builders:	Laivateollisuus, Turku (Finland)
Displacement:	2,154 tons full load
Tonnage:	600 DWT
Length:	244 ft 4 in (74.5 m) overall
Beam:	48 ft 3 in (14.7 m)
Draft:	14 ft 9 in (4.5 m)
Propulsion:	2 diesel engines (SEMT-Pielstick 6PC2.5 L400); 3,500 bhp; 2 shafts
Speed:	14 knots
Range:	14,000 n.miles at 12 knots
Complement:	approx. 30-40 + 30-40 scientists-technicians
Helicopters:	no facilities
Radars:	1 Okean-B (navigation)
	1 Okean-M (navigation)

These are medium-size research ships built to an enlarged AKADEMIK SHULEYKIN design. The first five units are employed in seismic survey; the AR'NOLD VEYMER, launched on 14 February 1986, is configured for general oceanography; it is operated by the Estonian SSR Academy of Sciences.

Design: Funnel-aft design especially fitted for cold-weather operations. A 20-shp bow thruster is provided. They have 12 laboratories. The first five units have a cable-controlled unmanned submersible.

The GEOLOG DMITRIY NALYVKIN is one of the second series of hydrometeorological/seismic research ships of the AKADEMIK SHULEYKIN class. She has a stern deckhouse. (1986, Leo Van Ginderen)

The ARNOL'D VEYMER is one of the third series of the AKADEMIK SHULEYKIN class. Seen here at Antwerp, she has a pedestal-mounted radome amidships and the stepped navigation radars separate from the ship's masts. This series has heavy cranes forward and aft. (1989, Leo Van Ginderen)

5 HYDROMETEOROLOGICAL/SEISMIC RESEARCH SHIPS: "AKADEMIK SHULEYKIN" CLASS

Name	Completed
AKADEMIK SHULEYKIN	1982
PROFESSOR PAVEL MOLCHANOV	1982
AKADEMIK SHOKALSKIY	1982
PROFESSOR KHROMOV	1983
PROFESSOR MUL'TANOVSKIY	July 1983

Builders:	Laivateollisuus, Turku (Finland)
Displacement:	2,140 tons full load
Tonnage:	620 DWT
Length:	234 ft 10 in (71.6 m) overall
Beam:	42 ft (12.8 m)
Draft:	15 ft 9 in (4.85 m)
Propulsion:	2 diesel engines (Gor'kiy G-74); 3,120 bhp; 2 shafts
Speed:	14 knots
Range:	14,000 n.miles at 12 knots
Complement:	approx. 40 + 38 scientists-technicians
Helicopters:	no facilities
Radars:	1 Okean-B (navigation)
	1 Okean-M (navigation)

These are medium-sized research ships operated by the Academy of Sciences for hydrometeorological reporting.

Design: Funnel-aft design especially fitted for cold-weather operations. They have 12 laboratories.

Engineering: Bow thrusters are provided.

The PROFESSOR MUL'TANOVSKIY, one of the first series, showing the working space aft (only the third series has a heavy crane aft). These ships have davits for two boats on the port side, one to starboard.

1 RESEARCH SHIP: "AKADEMIK ALEKSEY KRYLOV"

Name	Completed
AKADEMIK ALEKSEY KRYLOV	1981

Builders:	Okean, Oktyabr'skoye [Nikolayev]
Displacement:	9,920 tons full load
Tonnage:	1,930 DWT
Length:	409 ft (124.7 m) overall
Beam:	57 ft 4 in (17.5 m)
Draft:	23 ft 9 in (7.2 m)
Propulsion:	2 diesel engines (58D-6R); 9,000 bhp; 2 shafts
Speed:	16 knots
Range:	10,000 n.miles at 16 knots
Complement:	approx. 120 + 32 scientists-technicians
Helicopters:	no facilities
Radars:	1 Don-2 (navigation)
	1 Okean (navigation)

This is a large scientific research ship. A research submersible is hangared on the port side, with an internal gantry crane for lowering and raising the craft. The ship operates in the Pacific.

Class: The AKADEMIK NIKOLAY ANDREYEV and subsequent units are a derivative of this design.

Engineering: Bow and stern thrusters are fitted for station keeping and precise maneuvering.

The AKADEMIK ALEKSEY KRYLOV is a large scientific research ship with facilities for carrying and handling a large submersible (with hangar opening on the port side). Note the stern anchor and opening in the transom, probably for towing scientific gear.

The AKADEMIK ALEKSANDR VINOGRADOV is one of three similar seabed research ships. They can carry an Argus submersible. They have the distinctive twin canted funnels of the Polish B-86 design. There are kingposts forward and aft for cargo booms (the forward mast without a crosspiece).

3 HYDROGRAPHIC-METEOROLOGICAL RESEARCH SHIPS: "VITYAZ'"

Name	Completed
VITYAZ'	1981
AKADEMIK ALEKSANDR NESMEYANOV	1982
AKADEMIK ALEKSANDR VINOGRADOV	1983

Builders:	Adolf Warski, Szczecin (Poland)
Displacement:	5,700 tons full load
Tonnage:	1,810 DWT
Length:	363 ft 9 in (110.9 m) overall
Beam:	54 ft 5 in (16.6 m)
Draft:	18 ft 8 in (5.7 m)
Propulsion:	2 diesel engines (Zgoda/Sulzer 6ZL140/48); 6,400 bhp; 2 shafts

Speed:	16 knots
Range:	16,000 n.miles at 16 knots
Complement:	approx. 60 + 65 scientists-technicians
Helicopters:	no facilities
Radars:	2 Don-2 (navigation)
	1 Okean (navigation)

Seabed research ships for exploring minerals; operated by the Academy of Sciences.

Design: These ships are of the Polish B-86 design. They are fitted with 20 to 26 laboratories and have provisions for deep-sea "saturation" diving to depths of 850 feet (259 m).

They each carry a manned research submersible of the Argus type and have diver support facilities.

Seabed research ship VITYAZ'. (1986, Luciano Grazioli)

1 OCEANOGRAPHIC RESEARCH SHIP: "AKADEMIK MSTISLAV KELDYSH"

Name	Completed
AKADEMIK MSTISLAV KELDYSH	Dec 1980

Builders:	Hollming, Rauma (Finland)
Displacement:	approx. 5,500 tons full load
Tonnage:	1,856 DWT
Length:	400 ft 10 in (122.2 m) overall
Beam:	58 ft 5 in (17.8 m)
Draft:	17 ft 9 in (5.4 m)
Propulsion:	4 diesel engines (Wärtsila Vasa 824TS); 5,820 bhp; 2 shafts
Speed:	16 knots
Range:	20,000 n.miles at 16 knots

Complement:	approx. 50 + 80 scientists-technicians
Helicopters:	no facilities
Radars:	

This is the world's largest oceanographic research ship. The ship is operated by the Academy of Sciences.

Design: There are 18 laboratories plus space for support vans. Two Pisces-type submersibles were carried in her original configuration. In the late 1980s the ships were modified to carry and support the deep-diving MIR-1 and MIR-2 submersibles (see chapter 12).

Engineering: Fitted with a bow thruster and a stern propulsor, the latter being capable of 360° operation.

The large oceanographic research ship AKADEMIK MSTISLAV KELDYSH has been refitted to carry the MIR submersibles, the deepest-diving craft in Soviet service. The starboard side of the ship is open for handling research gear; the port side is plated over.

Oceanographic research ship AKADEMIK MSTISLAV KELDYSH. (1989, Leo Van Ginderen)

1 RESEARCH ICEBREAKER: MODIFIED "DOBRYNYA NIKITICH" CLASS

Name	Completed
OTTO SCHMIDT	July 1979

Builders:	Admiralty, Leningrad
Displacement:	2,528 tons standard
	3,600 tons full load
Tonnage:	1,095 DWT
Length:	239 ft 5 in (73.0 m) overall
Beam:	59 ft (18.0 m)
Draft:	21 ft 8 in (6.6 m)
Propulsion:	diesel-electric: 3 diesel generators (13D100); 4,800 bhp; connected to 2 electric motors; 2 shafts
Speed:	14.5 knots
Range:	5,500 n.miles at 12 knots
	13,000 n.miles at 9.5 knots
Complement:	approx. 30 + 20 scientists-technicians
Helicopters:	no facilities
Radars:	1 Don-2 (navigation)
	1 Okean (navigation)

This ship is operated by the Arctic Research Institute of the Academy of Sciences. There are 14 laboratories. Based in the Arctic (Murmansk).

Class: Thirty-one units of this basic design have been built. See page 270 for class notes.

Design: Details vary from other ships of this class.

The OTTO SCHMIDT is a modified version of the ubiquitous DOBRYNYA NIKITICH–class icebreakers configured to support Arctic/Antarctic research. The ship has a built-up superstructure, 14 laboratories, and a kingpost aft.

1 SEAFLOOR RESEARCH SHIP: "SHEL'F 1"

Name	Completed
SHEL'F 1	1976

Builders:	(USSR)
Displacement:	
Tonnage:	193 DWT
Length:	205 ft 4 in (62.6 m) overall
Beam:	34 ft 5 in (10.5 m)
Draft:	10 ft 2 in (3.1 m)
Propulsion:	2 diesel engines; 2 shafts
Speed:	16.5 knots
Range:	
Complement:	
Helicopters:	no facilities
Radars:	

Specialized ship for developing seafloor mining techniques; capable of supporting operations to a depth of 325 feet (99 m).

1 POLAR RESEARCH AND LOGISTICS SHIP: "MIKHAIL SOMOV"

Name	Completed
MIKHAIL SOMOV	1975

Builders:	Kherson
Displacement:	5,000 tons standard
	14,000 tons full load
Tonnage:	8,445 DWT
Length:	436 ft 7 in (133.1 m) overall
Beam:	61 ft 8 in (18.8 m)
Draft:	30 ft 2 in (9.2 m)
Propulsion:	diesel-electric: 2 diesel engines; 7,150 bhp; driving generator connected to 1 electric motor; 7,150 hp; 2 shafts
Speed:	20 knots
Range:	10,000 n.miles at 16.5 knots
Complement:	approx. 100
Helicopters:	landing area (see notes)
Radars	2 Don-2 (navigation)

The Somov was converted from an Amguema-class cargo ship. The ship is operated by the Arctic and Antarctic Research Institute as a research and logistic support ship, primarily to support Soviet operations in the Antarctic. An Mi-8 Hip helicopter can be embarked in the ship (no hangar).

The Somov is being replaced by the Akademik Fedorov.

Design: The ship has an icebreaking bow and other features for cold-weather operations; a raised helicopter platform is provided at the stern. The ship has four cargo holds with four 10-ton and four 5-ton cranes.

The Antarctic research and supply ship Mikhail Somov carries a modified Mi-8 Hip helicopter aft (no hangar is provided). (1986, Leo Van Ginderen)

20+ HYDROGRAPHIC-METEOROLOGICAL RESEARCH SHIPS: "VALERIAN URYVAYEV" CLASS

Name	Completed	Name	Completed
Valerian Uryvayev*	1979	Lev Titov*	1980
Poisk	1974	Vektor	1980
Morskoy Geofizik	1974	Modul	1981
Vsevlod Berezkin*	1975	Chayvo	1982
Yakov Gakkel*	1975	Elm	1982
Vulkanolog	1975	Professor Fedynskiy	1982
Iskatel'	1976	Geofizikh	1983
Issledovatel'	1977	Impuls-I	1988
Rudolf Samoylovich*	1977	Resonans	1989
Dalniye Zelentsy*	1977	. . . units	building
Vyacheslav Frolov*	1978		

Builders:	Khabarovsk
Displacement:	1,050 tons full load
Tonnage:	350 DWT
Length:	179 ft 9 in (54.8 m) overall
Beam:	31 ft 2 in (9.5 m)
Draft:	13 ft 9 in (4.2 m)
Propulsion:	1 diesel engine (Karl Liebknecht); 880 bhp in early ships, 1,320 bhp in later ships; 1 shaft
Speed:	11.5 knots in early ships
	12.5 knots in later ships
Range:	10,000 n.miles at 11 knots
Complement:	approx. 40 + 12 scientists-technicians
Helicopters:	no facilities
Radars:	1 Don-2 (navigation)
	1 Okean (navigation)
	1 End Tray (tracking) in 7 ships*

These are small, funnel-aft research ships operated by various scientific and research agencies. Construction continues.

The End Tray radar is used for balloon tracking.

Design: Details of masts differ. Eight laboratories are provided.

Engineering: Fitted with a bow thruster for precision station keeping.

The research ship Vulkanolog of the Valerian Uryvayev class at Wellington. She has a kingpost at the stern. A few units have a kingpost abaft the funnel (and mast on forecastle). (1988, Leo Van Ginderen)

The research ship Morskoy Geofizik showing the non-kingpost configuration with a pole mast on the forecastle and a second fitted to the funnel. There is a platform above a stern winch. (1987, Leo Van Ginderen)

The LEV TITOV with a balloon-tracking radar fitted amidships and stern kingpost. (1983, Leo Van Ginderen)

The ERNST KRENKEL'; the ship has an End Tray balloon-tracking radar abaft the funnel. (1986, Leo Van Ginderen)

Hydrographic-meteorological research ship ERNST KRENKEL' at Antwerp. She has a crane forward and cargo booms aft. (1986, Leo Van Ginderen)

3 HYDROGRAPHIC-METEOROLOGICAL RESEARCH SHIPS: MODIFIED "PASSAT" CLASS

Name	Completed
ERNST KRENKEL' (ex-VIKHR)	1971
GEORGIY USHAKOV (ex-SCHKVAL)	1971
VIKTOR BUGAYEV (ex-PORYV)	1971

Builders:	Adolf Warski, Szczecin (Poland)
Displacement:	4,200 tons full load
Tonnage:	1,450 DWT
Length:	328 ft 4 in (100.1 m) overall
Beam:	48 ft 6 in (14.8 m)
Draft:	16 ft 9 in (5.1 m)
Propulsion:	2 diesel engines (Cegielski or Zgoda/Sulzer); 4,800 bhp; 2 shafts
Speed:	16 knots
Range:	15,000 n.miles at 16 knots
Complement:	approx. 110 + 60 scientists-technicians
Helicopters:	no facilities
Radars:	2 Don-2 (navigation)
	1 End Tray (tracking)

These are modified PASSAT-class ships; derived from the Polish B-88 design. All are based in the Black Sea (Odessa).

19 HYDROGRAPHIC RESEARCH SHIPS: "DMITRIY OVTSYN" CLASS

Name	Completed
10 Ships First Group	
DMITRIY LAPTEV	1970
DMITRIY OVTSYN	1970
DMITRIY STERLIGOV	1971
STEPAN MALYGIN	1971
EDUARD TOLL	1972
NIKOLAY KOLOMEYTSYEV	1972
VALERIAN ALBANOV	1972
VLADIMIR SUKHOTSKIY	1973
NIKOLAY YEVGENOV	1974
SERGEY KRAVKOV	1974

Name	Completed
9 Ships Second Group	
FEDOR MATISEN	1976
PROFESSOR BOGOROV	1976
PROFESSOR KURENTSOV	1976
PROFESSOR VODYANITSKIY	1976
GEORGIY MAKSIMOV	1977
IVAN KIREYEV	1977
PAVEL BASHMAKOV	1977
YAKOV SMIRNITSKIY	1977
PROFESSOR SHTOKMAN	1979

Builders:	Laivateollisuus, Abo and Turku (Finland)
Displacement:	1,600 tons full load
Tonnage:	561–639 DWT
Length:	225 ft 4 in (68.7 m) overall
Beam:	39 ft (11.9 m)
Draft:	13 ft 5 in (4.1 m)
Propulsion:	1 diesel engine (Humboldt-Klockner-Deutz); 2,200 bhp; 1 shaft
Speed:	13.75 knots
Range:	9,700 n.miles at 13.5 knots
Complement:	approx. 40
Helicopters:	no facilities
Radars:	1 or 2 Don, Don-2, or Okean (navigation)

Medium-size research ships with minor differences that lead to their consideration as two groups. Fourteen of the ships operate for the merchant fleet for hydrographic and seismic surveys; the others for the Academy of Sciences (ships with "professor" names plus one other).

Class: All built at Abo except BOGOROV at Turku.

Design: The class has a funnel-aft configuration. The first group has one cargo hold and an 8-ton-capacity crane; the second group has two cargo holds, two 3-ton-capacity cranes. Provided with ten laboratories.

The four ships with "professor" names have no crow's nest and no boats alongside the funnel.

Engineering: Bow thrusters are fitted.

The PROFESSOR KURENTSOV is one of the large DMITRIY OVTSYN-class of research ships. The basic configuration of the units is similar; the seismic research units—including this ship—have cable reels on their fantail. (1989, Leo Van Ginderen)

Research ship PROFESSOR BOGOROV. (1989, U.S. Navy)

23 COASTAL OCEANOGRAPHIC RESEARCH SHIPS: "AGAT" CLASS

Name	Name	Name	Completed
AGAT	ILMENIT	RUTIL	
AKVANAVT	KARTESH	SHELF	
BERILL	KVARTS	TANTAL	
BOREY	METAN	TOPAZ	1969–1979
BRIG	MONATSIT	TSIRKON	
GEOTERMIK	MORION	URAN	
GIDROLOG	PLUTON	YANTAR	
GRANAT	RADON		

Builders:	
Displacement:	350 tons full load
Tonnage:	35 DWT
Length:	111 ft 6 in (34.0 m) overall
Beam:	23 ft 3 in (7.1 m)
Draft:	8 ft 6 in (2.6 m)
Propulsion:	1 diesel engine (Karl Liebknecht); 300 bhp; 1 shaft
Speed:	9.5 knots
Range:	1,600 n.miles at 9 knots
Complement:	
Radars:	1 . . . . . . (navigation)

These are small oceanographic craft, converted from MANE-VRENNYY-class seiner fishing craft. These craft are operated by various agencies of the Academy of Sciences, including the Hydro-meteorological Institute and the Ministry of Geology.

The research ship SHELF at Gdynia. (1983, Leo Van Ginderen)

6 HYDROGRAPHIC-METEOROLOGICAL RESEARCH SHIPS: "PASSAT" CLASS

Name	Completed	Name	Completed
PASSAT	1968	OKEAN	1969
MUSSON	1968	PRIBOY	1969
VOLNA	1968	PRILIV	1970

Builders:	Adolf Warski, Szczecin (Poland)
Displacement:	4,145 tons full load
Tonnage:	998 DWT
Length:	317 ft 6 in (96.8 m) overall
Beam:	45 ft 3 in (13.8 m)
Draft:	17 ft (5.2 m)
Propulsion:	2 diesel engines (Cegielski or Zgoda/Sulzer 8TD48); 4,800 bhp; 2 shafts
Boilers:	1 auxiliary
Speed:	16 knots
Range:	15,000 n.miles at economical speed
Complement:	approx. 50–55 + 50–60 scientists-technicians
Helicopters:	no facilities
Radars:	2 Don-2 (navigation)
	1 End Tray (tracking)

These ships are of the Polish B-88 design. They are assigned to the Hydrometeorological Institute. The PASSAT was launched in February 1968.

Design: These ships are provided with 23 laboratories. Fitted with a 3-ton-capacity crane.

Endurance is rated at 90 days.

The Passat was the lead ship for two series of Soviet scientific research ships. Built to the Polish B-88 passenger ship design, the Passat is based at Odessa; all of the class are subordinated to the Hydrometeorological Institute of the Soviet Academy of Sciences.

The Volna is one of the Passat-class ships fitted with Vee Cone HF communications antennas; all ships have an End Tray radar amidships for tracking research balloons. The Volna is shown arriving at Antwerp. (1988, Leo Van Ginderen)

7 OCEANOGRAPHIC RESEARCH SHIPS: "AKADEMIK KURCHATOV" CLASS

Name	Completed	Name	Completed
AKADEMIK KURCHATOV	1966	PROFESSOR ZUBOV	1967
AKADEMIK KOROLOYOV	1967	DMITRIY MENDELEYEV	1968
AKADEMIK SHIRSHOV	1967	AKADEMIK VERNADSKIY	1968
PROFESSOR VIZE	1967		

Builders:	Mathias Thiesen, Wismar (East Germany)
Displacement:	6,986 tons full load
Tonnage:	2,000–2,059 DWT
Length:	407 ft 5 in (124.2 m) overall
Beam:	23 ft (17.0 m)
Draft:	20 ft (6.1 m)
Propulsion:	2 diesel engines (Halberstadt/MAN K6Z 57/80); 8,000 bhp; 2 shafts
Speed:	18.25 knots
Range:	20,000 n.miles at 16 knots
Complement:	approx. 85 + 80 scientists-technicians
Helicopters:	no facilities
Radars:	2 Don-2 (navigation except 1 Don-2 and 1 Okean in KOROLOYOV and MENDELEYEV)
	1 End Tray (tracking)

Large research ships, similar to four ships operated by the Soviet Navy (see chapter 24). The KURCHATOV, MENDELEYEV, and VERNADSKIY are assigned to the Institute of Oceanology; the four other ships are assigned to the Hydrometeorological Institute.

Design: This class has graceful, liner-like lines. There are 27 laboratories. The ships have a cargo hold with two 8-ton cranes and several of lesser capacity.

Electronics: Antenna configurations vary, with the SHIRSHOV having two domes for satellite communication antennas abaft the funnel. Vee Bar HF antennas are fitted to the masts of the weather (hydromet) ships.

Engineering: The ships are fitted with two 190-hp bow thrusters and an active 300-hp rudder for precise station keeping.

Operational: The KOROLEV, MENDELEYEV, and SHIRSHOV are based in the Far East (Vladivostok); the VERNADSKIY in the Black Sea; and others in the Baltic.

1 GEOLOGICAL RESEARCH SHIP: "SEVER"

Name	Completed
SEVER	1967

Builders:	Black Sea Shipyard, Nikolayev (south)
Displacement:	1,780 tons full load
Tonnage:	706 DWT
Length:	232 ft 11 in (71.0 m) overall
Beam:	43 ft (13.1 m)
Draft:	16 ft 5 in (5.0 m)
Propulsion:	diesel-electric: 3 diesel engines; 3,000 bhp; connected to electric motor; 1 shaft
Speed:	13.25 knots
Range:	11,000 n.miles at 13 knots
Complement:	approx. 50
Helicopters:	no facilities
Radars:	1 Don-2 (navigation)

The SEVER was built as the prototype for a stern trawler, but was an unsuccessful design. Operated by the Ministry of Geophysics in the research role in the Black Sea.

Design: The ship has four holds and two 3-ton-capacity booms.

The research ship PROFESSOR VIZE of the graceful AKADEMIK KURCHATOV class. Details of these ships differ: all except the MENDELEYEV and KURCHATOV have Vee Cone antennas on the tripod mast atop the bridge; the VIZE has a radome atop the bridge and another (different shape) amidships on the starboard side, with an End Tray radar opposite on the port side.

The AKADEMIK KURCHATOV at Rotterdam shows the massive stern crane found on several units; all have a kingpost of this type aft. The KURCHATOV has an End Tray radar amidships and an Okean radar on the tripod mast; the funnel cap is unique to the class. (1986, Leo Van Ginderen)

The AKADEMIK SHIRSKOV is one of two ships of the KURCHATOV class with large twin radomes amidships. This ship also has a large tracking radar aft. Three units have a mast on the forecastle (MENDELEYEV, KURCHATOV, VERNADSKIY). (1983, Leo Van Ginderen)

1 OCEANOGRAPHIC RESEARCH SHIP: "AKADEMIK PETROVSKIY"

Name	Completed
AKADEMIK PETROVSKIY (ex-MOSKOVSKIY UNIVERSITET)	1966

Builders:	Khabarovsk
Displacement:	922 tons full load
Tonnage:	277 DWT
Length:	177 ft 6 in (54.1 m) overall
Beam:	30 ft 6 in (9.3 m)
Draft:	12 ft 2 in (3.7 m)
Propulsion:	1 diesel engine; 780 bhp; 1 shaft
Speed:	11 knots
Range:	10,000 n.miles at 11 knots
Complement:	approx. 40 + 10 scientists
Helicopters:	no facilities
Radars:	1 Don-2 (navigation)
	1 Spin Trough (search)

Converted trawler operated by the Moscow State University on a variety of ocean study programs. Modernized and renamed in 1970.

Class: Several ships of this and the similar Mayak classes serve as fisheries research ships.

The single ship AKADEMIK PETROVSKIY is operated in a variety of ocean research roles by the Moscow State University. A large number of ships of this design serve as fisheries research ships. (Courtesy Flottes de Combat)

2 RESEARCH SHIPS: "TROPIK" CLASS

Name	Completed
PEGAS	1963
KALLISTO	1964

Builders:	Volks, Stralsund (East Germany)
Displacement:	approx. 3,000 tons full load
Tonnage:	988 DWT
Length:	261 ft 9 in (79.8 m) overall
Beam:	43 ft 4 in (13.2 m)
Draft:	16 ft 1 in (4.9 m)
Propulsion:	2 diesel engines (Karl Liebknecht); 1,660 bhp; 1 shaft
Speed:	11.75 knots
Range:	
Complement:	approx. 40 + 30 scientists-technicians
Helicopters:	no facilities
Radars:	2 Don-2 (navigation)

These are converted stern trawler–factory ships of the TROPIK class. The PEGAS operates for the Academy of Sciences and the KALLISTO for the Oceanographic Science Research Institute. (There is a Navy survey ship named TROPIK in the Samara Class.)

Class: About 90 ships of this class were built for the Soviet Union between 1962 and 1966, with several other units converted to the fishery research role. Several trawler–factory ships have been transferred to other nations (the prototype TROPIK went to Ghana).

The KALLISTO is one of several research ships converted from TROPIK-class stern trawler/factory ships; most operate under the auspices of the Ministry of Fisheries. She has kingposts forward and aft. (1983, Leo Van Ginderen)

3 RESEARCH SHIPS: "BOLOGUE" CLASS

Name	Completed
AKADEMIK ARCHANGELSKIY	1963
AKADEMIK A. KOVALEVSKIY	1963
YURIY GODIN	1963

Builders:	Leninskaya Kuznitsa, Kiev
Displacement:	580 tons full load
Tonnage:	142 DWT
Length:	143 ft (43.6 m) overall
Beam:	24 ft 11 in (7.6 m)
Draft:	9 ft 10 in (3.0 m)
Propulsion:	1 diesel engine (Karl Liebknecht); 450 bhp; 1 shaft
Speed:	10 knots
Range:	
Complement:	approx. 35 + 15 scientists-technicians
Helicopters:	no facilities
Radars:	1 Spin Trough (search)

These small research ships are converted BOLOGUE-class side trawlers, with the ARCHANGELSKIY operated by the Ministry of Geology and the GODIN by the Geophysics Institute. These ships operate in the Black Sea-Mediterranean areas.

The AKADEMIK A. KOVALEVSKIY is one of three small BOLOGUE-class side trawlers modified for research work, the KOVALEVSKIY for general oceanography. (1985, Leo Van Ginderen)

1 SEISMIC RESEARCH SHIP: "SHEL'F II"

Name	Completed	Converted
SHEL'F II (ex-LONGVA)	1962	1977

Builders:	A.M. Liasen, Alesund (Norway)
Displacement:	approx. 1,400 tons full load
Length:	206 ft 8 in (63.0 m) overall
Beam:	32 ft 10 in (10.0 m)
Draft:	13 ft 9 in (4.2 m)
Propulsion:	1 diesel engine (Humboldt-Klockner-Deutz); 1,500 bhp; 1 shaft
Speed:	13 knots
Range:	
Complement:	approx. 50
Helicopters:	no facilities
Radars:	3 . . . . . . (navigation)

This ship is especially configured for seismic research in support of oil exploration. The ship was purchased in 1977. Fitted with passive stabilization tanks and bow thruster.

4 RESEARCH SHIPS: "ALUPKA" CLASS

Name	Completed
AYU-DAG	1961
AY-PETRI	1962
PROFESSOR KOLESNIKOV (ex-AYTODOR)	1962
PITSUNDA	1963

Builders:	Georgi Dimitrov Shipyard, Varna (Bulgaria)
Displacement:	approx. 1,000 tons full load
Tonnage:	176 DWT
Length:	209 ft 3 in (63.8 m) overall
Beam:	30 ft 6 in (9.3 m)
Draft:	9 ft 10 in (3.0 m)
Propulsion:	2 diesel engines (Karl Liebknecht); 830 bhp; 2 shafts
Speed:	13 knots
Range:	
Complement:	
Helicopters:	no facilities
Radars:	

These ships were built as Black Sea passenger ferries; converted to environmental-geological research ships. They have a limited research capability. The PROFESSOR KOLESNIKOV has a different configuration from the others, with a larger deckhouse and different mast arrangement. Two other ships have been converted to merchant training ships.

The AYU-DAG is one of four passenger ferries that have undergone limited modification for oceanographic research. "Academy of Sciences of the Estonian SSR" is painted beneath the ship's bridge. (1983, Leo Van Ginderen)

1 HYDROMETEOROLOGICAL RESEARCH SHIP: "MAYAKOVSKIY" CLASS

Name	Completed
ALEXANDR IVANOVICH VOYEYKOV	1959

Builders:	Black Sea Shipyard, Nikolayev (south)
Displacement:	approx. 3,600 tons full load
Tonnage:	1,287 DWT
Length:	277 ft 11 in (84.7 m) overall
Beam:	45 ft 11 in (14.0 m)
Draft:	18 ft 8 in (5.7 m)
Propulsion:	2 diesel engines (Russkiy); 2,000 bhp; 1 shaft
Speed:	13 knots
Range:	18,000 n.miles at 12 knots
Complement:	approx. 55 + 35 scientists-technicians
Helicopters:	no facilities
Radars:	2 Don-2 (navigation)
	1 End Tray (tracking)

This is one of at least 15 ships of this class of stern trawler–factory ships that have been converted to research configurations. All of the others are fisheries research ships, subordinate to the Ministry of Fisheries (see chapter 33). This ship and the late YURI M. SHOKALSKIY carried out hydrographic and meteorological research.

Class: An estimated 227 ships of this class were built at two Soviet yards, including three completed for Bulgaria. They were delivered between 1958 and 1969.

The six purpose-built AGIs of the PRIMOR'YE class have the same hull and propulsion plant.

Design: The stern ramp has been plated over.

The research ship ALEXANDR IVANOVICH VOYEYKOV is one of several MAYAKOVSKIY-class stern trawler/factory ships converted to research roles; the others support the Ministry of Fisheries. There is an End Tray tracking radar on a pedestal amidships. (1987, Leo Van Ginderen)

1 OCEANOGRAPHIC RESEARCH SHIP: "MIKHAIL LOMONOSOV"

Name	Completed
MIKHAIL LOMONOSOV	1957

Builders:	Neptun, Rostock (East Germany)
Displacement:	5,960 tons full load
Tonnage:	2,452 DWT
Length:	335 ft 10 in (102.4 m) overall
Beam:	47 ft 3 in (14.4 m)
Draft:	19 ft 8 in (6.0 m)
Propulsion:	1 triple-expansion reciprocating engine (Karl Liebknecht) plus low-pressure turbine; 2,400 shp; 1 shaft
Boilers:	2
Speed:	13.5 knots
Range:	11,000 n.miles at 13.5 knots
Complement:	approx. 80 + 55 scientists-technicians
Helicopters:	no facilities
Radars:	2 Don-2 (navigation)

Converted during construction from a KOLOMNA-class cargo ship. Operated by the Ukraine Institute of Oceanology. Based in the Black Sea (Sevastopol).

Class: Some 30 ships of this class were built by the Neptun yard for the Soviet Union, several of which saw service as naval cargo ships. Six sister ships served as submarine tenders (ATREK class) and one is an experimental ship (see chapter 23).

Design: Fitted with 16 laboratories.

The MIKHAIL LOMONOSOV is one of the oldest Soviet scientific research ships still in service. She and other research ships of her age group are expected to be retired soon as the large construction program of research ships continues into the 1990s. (1986, Leo Van Ginderen)

2 NONMAGNETIC SAILING SCHOONERS: "KORALL" CLASS

Name	Completed
POLYARNYY ODISSEY	1950
ZARYA	1952

Builders:	Laivateollisuus, Turku (Finland)
Displacement:	approx. 600 tons full load
Tonnage:	78 DWT
Length:	139 ft 5 in (42.5 m) waterline
	172 ft 2 in (52.5 m) overall
Beam:	29 ft 6 in (9.0 m)
Draft:	10 ft 2 in (3.1 m)
Propulsion:	1 diesel engine (Halberstadt 6NVD36); 300 bhp; 1 shaft
Speed:	6.5 knots with sails
	8 knots with auxiliary engine
Complement:	approx. 35 + 10 scientists
Radars:	1 Spin Trough (search)

These are three-masted schooners with a wooden hull and minimum built-in iron and steel. Originally designed as sealing ships.

Brass and copper-bronze alloys are used where possible; metal masts were fitted in the early 1980s. The ZARYA is employed by the Institute of Terrestrial Magnetism, Academy of Sciences, and the ODISSEY by the northern branch of the Geological Society of the USSR in surveys of the earth's magnetic field and ocean currents.

In the early 1980s the ZARYA underwent an extensive modernization at the Zhdanov Shipyard in Leningrad.

Class: Two of a class of sailing schooners built by Finland as war reparations for the Soviet Union after World War II. Several served as naval deperming ships.

The long-serving research schooner ZARYA. Refitted in 1984–1985, she has a low magnetic signature to facilitate gravimetric research. (1987, Leo Van Ginderen)

2 HYDROACOUSTIC RESEARCH SHIPS: "PETR LEBEDEV" CLASS

Name	Completed	Converted
PETR LEBEDEV (ex-CHAPAYEV)	1957	1960
SERGEY VAVILOV (ex-FURMANOV)	1957	1960

Builders:	Crichton-Vulcan, Turku (Finland)
Displacement:	4,800 tons full load
Tonnage:	1,675 DWT
Length:	302 ft 5 in (92.2 m) overall
Beam:	45 ft 11 in (14.0 m)
Draft:	18 ft 8 in (5.7 m)
Propulsion:	1 diesel engine (Sulzer 6TD 56); 2,400 bhp; 1 shaft
Speed:	13.5 knots
Range:	6,000 n.miles at 13.5 knots
Complement:	approx. 75 + 25 scientists-technicians
Helicopters:	no facilities
Radars:	1 Don-2 (navigation)
	1 . . . . . . (navigation)

These are former cargo ships, rebuilt in 1960 as research ships. They are assigned to the Hydroacoustics Institute in support of Navy projects and operate together. They are based in Leningrad.

Class: These were the first two of 13 similar cargo ships of the FRYAZINO class delivered to the Soviet merchant fleet from 1957 through 1960.

The PETR LEBEDEV. (1988, Royal Navy)

The PETR LEBEDEV; note the small lattice radar mast on the starboard side of the forward funnel and the unusual configuration of the second funnel. (1988, Royal Navy)

1 SCIENTIFIC-RESEARCH AND SALVAGE SHIP: "KOMMUNA" TYPE

The long-serving Navy salvage ship VOLKHOV, launched in 1913 and completed in 1915, was renamed KOMMUNA after the 1917 Bolshevik Revolution. She remains in service in the USSR under civilian direction.

The ship was out of service after World War II until towed to the Netherlands in 1950 for refitting; she was towed back to the USSR for service in 1951. She was modified in the early 1970s for "scientific-research" activities; however, she appears to have retained her heavy lift capability.

The KOMMUNA is a catamaran ship. She was built with repair shops.

The venerable salvage ship KOMMUNA as she appeared after her refit in a Dutch shipyard in the early 1950s.

SEISMIC RESEARCH SHIP: CONVERTED TUG

The converted tug VLADIMIR OBRUCHEV, completed in 1959, was stricken in the 1980s. Built in Romania. See 4th edition, page 366.

EXPERIMENTAL AND TRIALS SHIPS

1 SHIPBUILDING RESEARCH SHIP: "IZUMRUD"

Name	Completed
IZUMRUD	1979

Builders:	Black Sea Shipyard, Nikolayev (south)
Displacement:	5,170 tons full load
	2,640 DWT
Length:	326 ft (99.4 m) overall
Beam:	45 ft 11 in (14.0 m)
Draft:	17 ft 9 in (5.4 m)
Propulsion:	diesel-electric; 4 diesel generators; 4,000 bhp connected to 4 electric motors; 1 shaft
Speed:	14 knots
Range:	
Complement:	approx. 110 (civilian) + 40 scientists-technicians
Helicopters:	no facilities
Radars:	1 Don-2 (navigation)
	1 Low Sieve (search)
	1 Okean (navigation)

The IZUMRUD was constructed specifically for the Ministry of Shipbuilding to test ship structures and materials as well as other ship components. The ship is civilian manned and operated by the Krylov Naval Institute of Shipbuilding in Leningrad; she operates in the Black Sea.

Design: The ship is based on the TAVRIYA-class passenger-cargo design. She has one cargo hold forward with a 3¼-ton crane.

Names: A Grisha II operated by the KGB Maritime Border Troops is also named IZUMRUD.

The IZUMRUD is a unique structures and materials test ship. She provides a useful platform for evaluating new ship concepts for naval and civilian use.

ICEBREAKERS

There are several river and inland icebreakers in service in addition to the ocean-going ships listed here. Other ocean-going icebreakers are operated by the Navy and by the KGB Maritime Border Troops (see chapters 23 and 26, respectively); the icebreaker OTTO SCHMIDT is listed in this chapter as a research ship (see page 316).

Most of these ships are fitted for ocean towing.

Operational: The ADMIRAL MAKAROV and VLADIMIR ARSENIEV entered ice-covered waters off Point Barrow, Alaska, in late October 1988 to help two stranded California gray whales escape to the open sea. Their mercy mission was part of a highly publicized effort on behalf of the trapped marine mammals.

2 NUCLEAR-PROPELLED ICEBREAKERS: NEW CONSTRUCTION

Name	Launched	Completed
TAYMYR	10 Apr 1987	18 Aug 1989
VAYGACH	26 Feb 1988	1990

Builders:	Wartsila, Helsinki (Finland)
Displacement:	20,480 tons standard
	23,460 tons full load
Length:	492 ft 8 in (150.2 m) overall
Beam:	95 ft 9 in (29.2)
Draft:	29 ft 6 in (9.0 m)
Propulsion:	nuclear/turbo-electric: 2 steam turbines with electric drive; 52,000 shp; 3 shafts
Reactors:	2 pressurized-water type
Speed:	20.5 knots
Range:	
Complement:	approx. 140 + helicopter detachment and transients
Helicopters:	1 Ka-32 Helix-D
Radars:	

These two nuclear-propelled polar icebreakers for use in the shallow estuaries of Siberian rivers were ordered from Wartsila in November 1984. The partially finished ships were towed to Leningrad for installation of their nuclear propulsion plants.

Design: Capable of breaking ice 5.8 feet (1.77 m) thick.

The TAYMYR en route to the Baltic Shipyard in Leningrad for installation of her nuclear plant. Her massive "apartment block" superstructure differs significantly from that of the ARKTIKA class of similar size. These ships, built in Finland, do not have provisions for weapons, as do the ARKTIKA-class nuclear icebreakers. (1989, Wartsila)

1 ICEBREAKER: MODIFIED "MUDYUG" CLASS

Name	Completed
MUDYUG	29 Oct 1982

Builders:	Wartsila, Helsinki (Finland)
Displacement:	7,775 tons full load
Length:	294 ft 6½ in (89.8 m) waterline
	365 ft 3 in (111.35 m) overall
Beam:	72 ft 10 in (22.2 m)
Draft:	21 ft 4 in (6.5 m)
Propulsion:	4 diesel engines (Wartsila Vasa 8R32; heavy-oil type); 12,400 bhp (9,500 bhp in ice); 2 shafts
Speed:	17.45 knots maximum
	16.5 knots sustained
Range:	
Complement:	approx. 35 + 9 transients
Helicopters:	landing deck in MUDYUG
Radars:	1 Don-2 (navigation)
	1 Okean (navigation)

The MUDYUG was extensively modified at Thyssen Nordseewerke, Emden (East Germany) from late July to late October 1986. She was fitted with a Thyssen-Waas flat-form bow and Jastran water hull lubrication system to enhance icebreaking capability with less power; her fuel capacity was also increased. A helicopter platform was subsequently removed.

Design: Fitted with air-bubble system. As rebuilt the MUDYUG is capable of breaking ice up to 6¼ feet (1.9 m) at slow speed and 4½ feet (1.4 m) at 6 knots.

The MUDYUG as rebuilt. Note the unusual ice pattern forward of the ship as she backs down before charging ahead during trials with her new bow configuration. A helicopter platform is temporarily fitted aft. (1987, Thyssen-Waas)

The modified MUDYUG. (1987, Thyssen-Waas)

2 ICEBREAKERS: "MUDYUG" CLASS

Name	Completed
MAGADAN	Dec 1982
DIKSON	Mar 1983

Builders:	Wartsila, Helsinki (Finland)
Displacement:	5,558 tons light
	6,210 tons full load
Tonnage:	1,257 DWT
Length:	290 ft 3 in (88.5 m) overall
Beam:	75 ft 2 in (22.9 m)
Draft:	21 ft 4 in (6.5 m)
Propulsion:	4 diesel engines (Wartsila Vasa 8R32; heavy-oil type); 12,400 bhp (9,500 bhp in ice); 2 shafts
Speed:	17.45 knots maximum
	16.5 knots sustained
Range:	
Complement:	approx. 35 + 9 transients
Helicopters:	no facilities
Radars:	

This class resembles a scaled-down SOROKIN icebreaker design (e.g., superstructure block is four levels plus bridge).

The MUDYUG was modified and is listed separately.

Design: Fitted with air-bubble system. Capable of breaking ice 1⅔ feet (0.5 m) thick.

The icebreaker DIKSON at sea. She has a large open stern area (with crane) for handling towing gear. (1990, Royal Navy)

The DIKSON. (1990, Royal Navy)

4 ICEBREAKERS: "KAPITAN SOROKIN" CLASS

Name	Completed	Name	Completed
KAPITAN SOROKIN	1977	KAPITAN DRANITSIN	1980
KAPITAN NIKOLAYEV	1978	KAPITAN KLEBNIKOV	1981

Builders: Wartsila, Helsinki (Finland)
Displacement: 10,440 tons standard
14,655 tons full load
Tonnage: 4,225 DWT
Length: 432 ft 8 in (131.9 m) overall
Beam: 86 ft 11 in (26.5 m)
Draft: 27 ft 11 in (8.5 m)
Propulsion: diesel-electric: 6 diesel engines (Wartsila/Sulzer 9ZL 40/48); 22,300 bhp; connected to 3 electric motors; 3 shafts
Speed: 18.75 knots maximum
16 knots sustained
Range: 10,700 n.miles at 16 knots
Complement: approx. 75
Helicopters: landing area
Radars:

These ships have a massive superstructure block; the first two units have five levels plus the bridge, the two later units have six levels plus the bridge. They are considered shallow-draft ocean-going icebreakers.

The KAPITAN SOROKIN is being modified with a Thyssen-Waas icebreaking bow (see MUDYUG listing).

Design: Fitted with an air-bubble system to keep lower hull ice free.

The large icebreaker KAPITAN NIKOLAYEV shows her "apartment house" superstructure. These and other icebreakers permit the Soviet naval and merchant fleets to operate essentially year round from their ice-blocked ports. (1990, Royal Navy)

5 + 1 NUCLEAR-PROPELLED ICEBREAKERS: "ARKTIKA" CLASS

Name	Launched	Completed
ARKTIKA (ex-LEONID BREZHNEV)	Oct 1973	1 May 1975
SIBIR'	23 Feb 1976	1977
ROSSIYA	2 Nov 1983	Nov 1985
SOVETSKIY SOYUZ (ex-LEONID BREZHNEV)	25 Sep 1986	1988
OKTYARSKAYA REVOLUTSIYA	4 Oct 1989	1991
URAL		(1994)

Builders: Baltic Shipyard, Leningrad
Displacement: 19,300 tons standard
ARKTIKA, SIBIR' 23,460 tons full load
ROSSIYA and later units 23,625 tons full load
Tonnage: 4,096 DWT
Length: 446 ft 1 in (136.0 m) waterline
ARKTIKA, SIBIR' 485 ft 5 in (148.0 m) overall
ROSSIYA and later units 492 ft (150.0 m) overall
Beam: 98 ft 5 in (30.0 m)
Draft: 36 ft 1 in (11.0 m)
Propulsion: turbo-electric: 2 steam turbines (Kirov); 75,000 shp; connected to 5 2,000-kilowatt primary generators; 3 shafts
Reactors: 2 pressurized-water type
Speed: 20.5 knots maximum
15 knots sustained
Complement: approx. 145 + 35 transients
Helicopters: 2 Ka-32 Helix-D or Mi-8 Hip
Radars: 1 Don-2 (navigation)
1 Head Net-C (search) in ARKTIKA and SIBIR'
1 Okean (navigation)
1 Top Plate (search) in ROSSIYA and later units

These are the world's largest and most powerful icebreakers. The ARKTIKA began sea trials on 3 November 1974, the SIBIR' began sea trials on 22 October 1977, and the ROSSIYA in 1984.

Armament: The ARKTIKA was armed during her initial sea trials, carrying 8 76.2-mm AA guns (4 twin) and 4 30-mm Gatling guns (4 multi-barrel), with 2 Hawk Screech and 2 Drum Tilt radar/GFCS plus an air search radar. All were removed before the ship departed the Baltic. Other ships of the class have carried guns and fire-control radars on trials. Thus, the ships are designed to be armed for wartime, when they would come under Navy operational control.

Design: The design provides for a large helicopter deck aft and helicopter hangar capable of accommodating two helicopters for ice reconnaissance. These ships are capable of continuous breaking of ice seven to eight feet (2.1–2.4 m) thick at three knots.

The ROSSIYA and later units have heated centerline strakes and improved, corrosion-resistant hulls.

The URAL may be an improved, larger design.

Engineering: The center shaft has 37,500 hp and the outboard shafts 18,750 hp each.

Names: The lead ship was originally named ARKTIKA. She was renamed LEONID BREZHNEV in 1982 but was again named ARKTIKA in 1986 when the fourth ship of the class was named for the late Soviet leader; however, in 1989 that ship was renamed SOVETSKIY SOYUZ (Soviet Union).

Operational: The ARKTIKA was the first surface ship in history to reach the geographic North Pole, doing so on 17 August 1977. The ARKTIKA spent 15 hours at the North Pole; her round trip from Murmansk took 13 days. The SIBIR' reached the North Pole in May 1987. (The U.S. Coast Guard icebreaker WESTWIND/WAGB 281 came within 375 n.miles/690 km of the North Pole in 1979.)

The Sibir' is one of the nuclear-propelled icebreakers of the Arktika class, the most powerful ships of their type ever constructed. There is a large helicopter deck and hangar aft. The Sibir' has a Head Net-C radar atop her forward mast; later ships have the Top Plate radar. (Royal Danish Navy)

3 ICEBREAKERS: "YERMAK" CLASS

Name	Completed
Yermak	Apr 1974
Admiral Makarov	June 1975
Krasin	Feb 1976

Builders:	Wärtsila, Helsinki (Finland)
Displacement:	13,280 tons standard
	20,241 tons full load
Tonnage:	7,560 DWT
Length:	445 ft 5 in (135.8 m) overall
Beam:	85 ft 3 in (26.0 m)
Draft:	36 ft 1 in (11.0 m)
Propulsion:	diesel-electric: 9 diesel engines (Wärtsila/Sulzer 12 ZH 40/48); 36,500 bhp; driving 9 generators connected to 3 electric motors; 3 shafts
Speed:	19.5 knots
Range:	29,300 n.miles at 14 knots
Complement:	approx. 145 + 28 transients
Helicopters:	1 utility helicopter
Radars:	

These ships are improved and enlarged versions of the Moskva class. They have a helicopter hangar and landing platform.

The Yermak bears some resemblance to the smaller but more powerful U.S. Coast Guard icebreakers of the Polar class. These ships—like other large icebreakers—have a helicopter deck and hangar to support helicopters that seek out passable ice. (U.S. Navy)

5 ICEBREAKERS: "MOSKVA" CLASS

Name	Completed	Name	Completed
Moskva	1960	Murmansk	1968
Leningrad	1962	Vladivostok	1969
Kiev	1966		

Builders:	Wartsila, Helsinki (Finland)
Displacement:	13,290 tons standard
	15,360 tons full load
Tonnage:	6,147 DWT
Length:	400 ft 6 in (122.1 m) overall
Beam:	80 ft 4 in (24.5 m)
Draft:	34 ft 5 in (10.5 m)
Propulsion:	diesel-electric: 8 diesel engines (Wartsila/Sulzer 9MH51); driving 8 generators connected to 4 electric motors; 26,300 hp; 3 shafts
Speed:	18.25 knots
Range:	20,000 n.miles at 14 knots
Complement:	approx. 115
Helicopters:	2 utility helicopters
Radars:	

These ships have a helicopter hangar and landing platform.

Icebreaker LENINGRAD. (1988, Japanese Maritime Self-Defense Force)

14 SUPPORT ICEBREAKERS: "DOBRYNYA NIKITICH" CLASS

Name	Completed	Name	Completed
VASILIY PRONCHISHCHEV	1961	SEMEN CHELYUSHKIN	1965
AFANASIY NIKITIN	1962	YURIY LISYANSKIY	1965
KHARITON LAPTEV	1962	PETR PAKHTUSOV	1966
VASILIY POYARKOV	1963	GEORGIY SEDOV	1967
YEROFEY KHABAROV	1963	FEODOR LITKE	1970
IVAN KRUZHENSHTERN	1964	IVAN MOSKVITIN	1971
VLADIMIR RUSANOV	1964	SEMYON DEZHNEV	1971

Builders:	Admiralty, Leningrad
Displacement:	2,675–2,940 tons full load
Length:	222 ft 1 in (67.7 m) overall
Beam:	60 ft (18.3 m)
Draft:	20 ft (6.1 m)
Propulsion:	diesel-electric: 3 diesel generators (13D100); 4,800 bhp; connected to 2 electric motors; 3 shafts (1 bow + 2 stern; see notes)
Speed:	14.5 knots
Range:	5,500 n.miles at 12 knots
	13,000 n.miles at 9.5 knots
Complement:	approx. 40
Helicopters:	no facilities
Radars:	1 or 2 Don-2 (navigation)

These are relatively small but highly useful icebreakers. Also employed as tugs. Several units have been disposed of beginning in 1988.

Class: There are 31 ships of this general design in Soviet service, also being operated in the research role and by the Navy and KGB Maritime Border Troops. See page 270 for class notes.

Guns: The KGB-operated units of this design—the IVAN SUSANIN class—are armed and have a helicopter landing platform.

Names: The early ships were originally named LEDOKIL ("icebreaker") with a numeral suffix.

The IVAN KRUZHENSHTERN. (1990, Leo Van Ginderen)

1 NUCLEAR-PROPELLED ICEBREAKER: "LENIN"

Name	Launched	Completed
LENIN	5 December 1957	September 1959

Builders:	Admiralty, Leningrad
Displacement:	15,940 tons standard
	19,240 tons full load
Tonnage:	3,849 DWT
Length:	439 ft 6 in (134.0 m) overall
Beam:	87 ft 11 in (26.8 m)
Draft:	34 ft 5 in (10.5 m)
Propulsion:	4 steam turbines (Kirov), 44,000 shp driving 4 generators connected to 3 electric motors (Elektrosila); 39,200 hp; 3 shafts
Reactors:	2 pressurized-water type
Speed:	19.7 knots maximum
	18 knots sustained
Complement:	approx. 150 + 70 transients
Helicopters:	1 utility helicopter
Radars:	

The LENIN was the world's first nuclear-propelled surface ship. The ship's keel was laid down on 25 August 1956; the ship left the Admiralty shipyard for the first time on 12 September 1959 and anchored in the Neva River until beginning sea trials on 15 September 1959.

She was decommissioned in 1989 and may be employed as a floating power station.

Design: A helicopter hangar and flight deck are provided.

Engineering: The ship was built with three reactors: two were sufficient to propel the ship at full speed and a third was available for maintenance and research.

The LENIN suffered a major nuclear radiation accident in 1966 or 1967, with some reports citing a "reactor meltdown." Up to 30 crewmen died as a result of radiation poisoning, and others suffered injuries. The ship lay abandoned for more than a year, after which she was towed to a Murmansk shipyard and rebuilt; a two-reactor plant was installed and the ship returned to service in 1972.

3 ICEBREAKERS: "KAPITAN BELOUSOV" CLASS

Name	Completed
KAPITAN BELOUSOV	1954
KAPITAN VORONIN	1955
KAPITAN MELEKHOV	1956

Builders:	Wartsila, Helsinki (Finland)
Displacement:	5,360 tons full load
Tonnage:	1,446 DWT
Length:	272 ft 11 in (83.2 m) overall
Beam:	63 ft 8 in (19.4 m)
Draft:	23 ft (7.0 m)
Propulsion:	diesel-electric: 6 diesel engines (Wartsila Polar); 10,500 bhp; driving 6 generators connected to electric motors; 4 shafts (2 bow + 2 stern)
Speed:	16.5 knots
Range:	10,000 n.miles at 14.8 knots
Complement:	approx. 120
Helicopters:	no facilities
Radars:	

These were the first icebreakers built for the Soviet Union after World War II. One additional icebreaker of this class was built for Sweden and one for Finland.

The KAPITAN MELEKHOV is one of the oldest icebreakers remaining in Soviet service; however, the ship is still effective in keeping Soviet sea routes open during the long Russian winter. (Royal Danish Navy)

TRAINING SHIPS

The following ships, with one exception, provide at-sea instruction for Soviet Merchant Marine personnel, mainly in engineering, seamanship, and cargo handling. Some of these ships have been identified with the training of naval personnel. There are also several smaller ships as well as a large number of fisheries training ships (see chapter 33). All Soviet large sail training ships are listed below.

The GIDROBIOLOG is employed to train students in physical and biological oceanography.

The sail training ships and probably other units also conduct oceanographic research.

1 TRAINING SHIP: "GIDROBIOLOG"

Name	Completed
GIDROBIOLOG	1985

Builders:	
Displacement:	168 tons full load
Length:	87 ft 7 in (26.7 m) overall
Beam:	20 ft (6.1 m)
Draft:	8 ft 10 in (2.7 m)
Propulsion:	1 diesel engine; 200 bhp; 1 shaft
Speed:	9 knots
Range:	
Complement:	
Helicopters:	no facilities
Radars:	

This is a small training ship for physical and biological oceanography; built for Moscow State University.

5 CADET TRAINING SHIPS: MODIFIED "BALTISKY" CLASS

Name	Completed	Name	Completed
PAVEL YABLOCHKOV	1980	VASILIY KALASHNIKOV	1981
ALEKSANDR POPOV	1981	IVAN POLZUNOV	1981
IVAN KULIBIN	1981		

Builders:	Laivateollisuus, Abo and Turku (Finland)
Displacement:	
Tonnage:	1,987 DWT
Length:	311 ft 7 in (95.0 m) overall
Beam:	43 ft 3 in (13.2 m)
Draft:	13 ft 1 in (4.0 m)
Propulsion:	2 diesel engines (Karl Liebknecht); 1,740 bhp; 2 shafts
Speed:	12.5 knots
Range:	
Complement:	
Helicopters:	no facilities
Radars:	

These ships have duplicated navigating bridges.

Class: Four additional ships of this type are sea-river cargo ships, placed in Soviet merchant service between 1978 and 1980.

Design: Small, superstructure-aft cargo ships.

The VASILIY KALASHNIKOV shows the superstructure-aft line of the BALTISKY-class cargo ships. Note the ship's unusual mast configuration. These ships carry small amounts of cargo on their training cruises. (1984, Leo Van Ginderen)

9 CADET TRAINING SHIPS: PROFESSOR CLASS

Name	Completed
PROFESSOR KUDREVICH	1970
PROFESSOR SHCHYOGOLEV	1970
PROFESSOR ANICHKOV	1971
PROFESSOR RYBALTOVSKIY	1971
PROFESSOR YUSHCHENKO	1971
PROFESSOR MINYAYEV	1972
PROFESSOR UKHOV	1972
PROFESSOR KHLYUSTIN	1973
PROFESSOR PAVLENKO	1973

Builders:	Stocznia, Szczecin (Poland)
Displacement:	
Tonnage:	5,385–5,457 DWT
Length:	403 ft 1 in (122.9 m) overall
Beam:	55 ft 9 in (17.0 m)
Draft:	23 ft 11 in (7.3 m)
Propulsion:	2 diesel engines (Cegielski/Burmeister & Wain); 4,900 bhp except KHLYUSTIN and PAVLENKO have Sulzer diesel engines of 5,500 bhp; 1 shaft
Speed:	15.25 knots except KHLYUSTIN and PAVLENKO 15.75 knots
Range:	
Complement:	
Helicopters:	no facilities
Radars:	

These are Polish-built ships of the B-80 design employed in cadet training. Details vary. A similar ship was built for Bulgaria, two for Poland, and one for Romania.

The PROFESSOR YUSHCHENKO is typical of the Polish-built cadet training ships of the B-80 design. They retain their forward cargo holds, kingpost, and booms and have a heavy crane aft. (1988, Leo Van Ginderen)

The PROFESSOR UKHOV was one of four ships of this class assigned to the Leningrad Higher Marine Engineering School when the ship was photographed at sea.

1 CADET TRAINING SHIP: "SAYMA" CLASS

Name	Completed
LAYNE (ex-YUNGA, ex-SULAK)	1969

Builders:	Baku
Displacement:	
Tonnage:	301 DWT
Length:	225 ft 4 in (68.7 m) overall
Beam:	31 ft 6 in (9.6 m)
Draft:	8 ft 6 in (2.6 m)
Propulsion:	2 diesel engines (Karl Liebknecht); 800 bhp; 1 shaft
Speed:	11.25 knots
Range:	
Complement:	
Helicopters:	no facilities
Radars:	

Converted from a small passenger ship to train cadets.

2 CADET TRAINING SHIPS: MODIFIED "KOVEL" CLASS

Name	Completed
GORIZONT	1961
MERIDIAN	1962

Builders:	Neptun, Rostock (East Germany)
Displacement:	
Tonnage:	3,083 DWT
Length:	344 ft 1 in (104.9 m) overall
Beam:	47 ft 3 in (14.4 m)
Draft:	20 ft 4 in (6.2 m)
Propulsion:	2 diesel engines (Gorlitzer); 3,250 bhp; 1 shaft
Speed:	13.5 knots
Range:	
Complement:	. . . . + 150 cadets
Helicopters:	no facilities
Radars:	

These ships were completed as cadet training ships, being converted during construction from KOVEL-class dry cargo ships. (Other ships of this class were civilian research ships.)

Class: The cadet training ship ZENIT of this class was broken up in 1987.

The GORIZONT was one of three ships completed specifically for the training of merchant marine cadets, the first Soviet ships of this type not converted from existing hulls. (1985, Leo Van Ginderen)

2 TRAINING SHIPS: "ALUPKA" CLASS

Name	Completed
ALUSHTA	1960
ALEKSANDR KUCHIN (ex-ALUPKA)	1960

Builders:	Georgi Dimitrov Shipyard, Varna (Bulgaria)
Displacement:	
Tonnage:	176 DWT
Length:	209 ft 3 in (63.8 m) overall
Beam:	30 ft 6 in (9.3 m)
Draft:	9 ft 10 in (3.0 m)
Propulsion:	1 diesel (Karl Liebknecht); 830 bhp; 1 shaft
Speed:	13 knots
Range:	
Complement:	
Helicopters:	no facilities
Radars:	

Both ships are former Black Sea ferries converted to a training role. Four others serve as civilian research ships (see page 322).

1 CADET TRAINING SHIP: "JAN KREUKS" CLASS

Name	Completed
VOLODYA DUBININ	1954

Builders:	Gheorghiu Dej, Budapest (Hungary)
Displacement:	
Tonnage:	294 DWT
Length:	230 ft 3 in (70.2 m) overall
Beam:	32 ft 10 in (10.0 m)
Draft:	12 ft 5 in (3.8 m)
Propulsion:	2 diesel engines (Ganz); 1,000 bhp; 2 shafts
Speed:	9.25 knots
Range:	
Complement:	
Helicopters:	no facilities
Radars:	

This ship apparently was a modified version of the JAN KREUKS class of small cargo ships.

Class: More than 100 general-cargo ships of this design were built for the Soviet Union between 1948 and 1959, with additional ships being built by Hungarian yards for other countries. Several remain in service with the Soviet merchant fleet.

4 SAIL TRAINING SHIPS: "MIR" CLASS

Name	Launched	Completed
MIR	30 Dec 1986	1987
DROUZJBA	31 Mar 1987	1987
KHERSONES		1989
PALLADA		1989

Builders:	Stocznia, Gdańsk (Poland)
Displacement:	
Tonnage:	607 DWT
Length:	260 ft 6 in (79.4 m) waterline
	345 ft 9 in (105.4 m) overall
Beam:	46 ft (14.0 m)

Draft:	19 ft 8 in (6.0 m)
Propulsion:	2 auxiliary diesel (Sulzer/Cegieski 20/24); 3,000 bhp; 1 shaft
Speed:	12 knots on diesel engines
Range:	
Complement:	
Radars:	

These are three-masted sail training ships of the Polish B-95 design. (They are not used by the Soviet Navy, as previously reported.)

Design: Based on the Polish DAR MLODZIEZY, delivered in 1982.

The sail-training bark MIR departing Antwerp. The acquisition of the MIR-class training ships demonstrates the continued importance placed on sail training by the Soviet merchant marine. (1990, Leo Van Ginderen)

1 SAIL TRAINING BARK: "TOVARISHCH"

Name	Completed
TOVARISHCH (ex-German GORCH FOCK)	1933

Builders:	Blohm & Voss, Hamburg (Germany)
Displacement:	1,350 tons standard
	1,500 tons full load
Length:	269 ft 6 in (81.7 m) overall
Beam:	39 ft 4 in (11.9 m)
Draft:	17 ft (5.2 m)
Propulsion:	1 auxiliary diesel engine; 520 bhp; 1 shaft
Speed:	8 knots on diesel engine
Range:	
Complement:	approx. 50 + 120 cadets
Radars:	

The ship was built as the training ship GORCH FOCK for the German Navy, one of four similar sail training vessels (the MIRCEA built for Romania and the HORST WESSEL and ALBERT LEO SCHLAGETER for Germany). The GORCH FOCK served as a naval

training ship until scuttled on 1 May 1945 near Stralsund. The ship was salvaged by Soviet forces in 1948 and placed in service in 1951 as the TOVARISHCH.[1]

She is home ported in Kherson as a training ship for the Soviet merchant marine.

Class: The HORST WESSEL now serves as the U.S. Coast Guard training bark EAGLE (WIX 327) and the ex-ALFRED LEO SCHLAGETER, after briefly being held by the U.S. Navy, serves in the Portuguese Navy.

Design: The ship carries approximately 17,220 ft^2 (1,600 m^2) of sail. Speed under sail is approximately 16 knots.

Operational: The TOVARISHCH and KRUZENSTERN (below) participated in Operation Sail during the American Bicentennial celebrations, visiting U.S. ports in July 1976.

---

1. Technically she was the TOVARISHCH II because an earlier TOVARISHCH was in commission, a four-masted bark formerly named LAURISTON.

The sail-training bark TOVARISHCH at New York. In the early 1980s, John Lehman, while Secretary of the Navy, attempted to acquire a sail-training ship for the U.S. Navy. The U.S. Coast Guard still operates the EAGLE in this role; she is a sister ship of the TOVARISHCH. (1990, U.S. Navy)

1 SAIL TRAINING BARK: "KRUZENSTERN"

Name	Completed
KRUZENSTERN (ex-German PADUA)	1926

Builders:	Tecklenborg, Wesermünde (Germany)
Displacement:	3,065 tons standard
	3,570 tons full load
Tonnage:	1,965 DWT
Length:	372 ft 11 in (113.7 m) overall
Beam:	45 ft 7 in (13.9 m)
Draft:	25 ft 5 in (7.75 m)
Propulsion:	2 auxiliary diesel engines; 1,600 bhp; 1 shaft
Speed:	15 knots on diesel engines
Range:	
Complement:	approx. 70 + 200 cadets

The KRUZENSTERN is the world's largest sailing ship.

The ship was the last cargo-carrying. four-masted bark to be built. Named PADUA, she sailed for the Hamburg firm of L. Laeisz until being laid up in 1932. She sailed again briefly before World War II and was taken over by the Soviet Union in 1945 and subsequently employed as a sail training ship.

She is home ported in Riga as a training ship for the fishing industry.

Design: The KRUZENSTERN carries approximately 43,000 ft^2 (4,000 m^2) of sail.

1 SAIL TRAINING BARK: "SEDOV"

Name	Completed
SEDOV (ex-German KOMMODORE JOHNSEN, ex-MAGDALENE VINNEN)	1922

Builders:	Germania, Kiel (Germany)
Displacement:	3,065 tons standard
	3,570 tons full load
Tonnage:	2,094 DWT
Length:	385 ft 1 in (117.4 m) overall
Beam:	47 ft 7 in (14.5 m)
Draft:	23 ft 11 in (7.3 m)
Propulsion:	2 auxiliary diesel engines; 1 shaft
Speed:	
Range:	
Complement:	. . . . + 130 cadets

This is a four-masted bark built as a training ship for the North German Lloyd line. She was acquired by the Soviet Union in 1945 and employed as a sail training ship. She was laid up from 1967 to January 1981; subsequently she was employed as a merchant marine and fisheries training ship. Home ported in Riga.

The sail-training bark KRUZENSTERN at Zeebrugge, Belgium. (1990, Leo Van Ginderen)

The Soviet merchant fleet operates old and new ships that have the potential for supporting naval activities. Almost 70 years separate the sail-training ship SEDOV, shown here at Zeebrugge, and the nuclear-propelled icebreaker VAYGACH (below), at Tallinn, Estonia. The U.S. merchant marine does not have sail-training ships nor does the country have nuclear icebreakers, although both have been recently proposed and debated. (1990, Leon Van Ginderen; 1990, Sovfoto, T. Veermae)

CHAPTER 26

KGB Maritime Border Troops

Sailors of the KGB Maritime Border Troops rush to their battle stations on the guided missile frigate MENZHINSKIY in the Far East. Most KGB ships are heavily armed and capable of carrying out combat missions; these are the ship's quad 21-inch torpedo tubes. (Sovfoto, S. Kozlov)

The Maritime Border Troops (*Morskaya Pogranichnaya Okhrama*—MPO) of the KGB are responsible for the coastal security of the Soviet Union—protecting that nation's maritime borders against penetration by foreign agents or paramilitary forces and preventing Soviet citizens from leaving by water without proper authorization.

The Border Troops have an army-style organization with Vice Admiral N.N. Dalmatov reported to hold the position of a deputy KGB commander for maritime forces. His staff maintains close liaison with naval headquarters, and there are obviously joint seamanship training and ship-procurement programs. Approximately 23,000 personnel are assigned to the Maritime Border Troops.

There are three higher border troops schools for training officers, which are at the level of Western military academies. Although none is specifically designated as a school for seagoing officers, some or all may educate MPO officers. These schools, all of which offer four-year periods of instruction, are:

Higher Border Military-Political Red Banner School Order of the October Revolution of the USSR KGB *imeni* K.Ye. Voroshilov (Moscow)

Higher Border Command Red Banner School Order of the October Revolution of the USSR KGB *imeni* F.E. Dzerzhinskiy (Alma-Ata)

Higher Border Command Red Banner School Order of the October Revolution of the USSR KGB *imeni* Mossoveta (Moscow)

The Maritime Border Troops have Navy-style uniforms, the officers having green shoulder boards bearing their insignia of rank, and enlisted men wearing green cap ribbons inscribed with the words "Naval Forces of the Border Troops."

SHIPS AND CRAFT

The KGB operates more than 200 frigates, patrol craft, and armed icebreakers plus several supply ships. In general, the KGB ships are similar to those of the Soviet Navy but with a reduction in anti-air and anti-submarine capabilities in favor of a heavier gun armament.

The exact numbers and types of ships and craft assigned to the Maritime Border Troops are not publicly known.

The KGB ships have a significant combat capability. In wartime they would undoubtedly be used to supplement naval forces in combat operations (much the same as the U.S. Coast Guard operates under U.S. Navy direction in wartime).

The classifications of KGB ships are listed in chapter 3.

AIRCRAFT

The KGB operates a large number of light fixed-wing aircraft and helicopters. Apparently several Ka-27 Helix and possibly Ka-25 Hormone-C utility helicopters are flown by the Maritime Border Troops and are based on board the Krivak III–class frigates and icebreakers.

COMBAT SHIPS

6+ PATROL FRIGATES: KRIVAK III CLASS

Name	Completed
MENZHINSKIY	Aug 1984
DZERZHINSKIY	Aug 1985
IMENI XXVII SYEZDA K.P.S.S.	Feb 1987
IMENI 70-LETTIYA VUK KGB	Apr 1988
IMENI 70-LETTIYA POGRANVOYSK	Apr 1989
KEDROV	1990

Builders:	Kamysh-Burun, Kerch
Displacement:	3,300 tons standard
	3,900 tons full load
Length:	383 ft 5 in (116.9 m) waterline
	410 ft (125.0 m) overall
Beam:	46 ft 3 in (14.1 m)
Draft:	16 ft 1 in (4.9 m)
Propulsion:	COGOG: 2 gas turbines; 24,200 shp + 2 boost gas turbines; 24,400 shp = 48,600 shp; 2 shafts
Speed:	30 knots
Range:	700 n.miles at 29 knots
	3,900 n.miles at 20 knots
Complement:	approx. 200
Helicopters:	1 Ka-27 Helix-C
Missiles:	1 twin SA-N-4 anti-air launcher [40]
Guns:	1 100-mm/70-cal DP
	2 30-mm close-in (2 multi-barrel)
ASW weapons:	2 RBU-6000 rocket launchers
	torpedoes
Torpedoes:	8 21-inch (533-mm) torpedo tubes (2 quad)
Mines:	rails for 20 mines

Radars:	1 Bass Tilt (fire control)
	1 Don-Kay (navigation)
	1 Head Net-C (3-D air search) in first two units; Top Plate (3-D air search) in later units
	1 Kite Screech (fire control)
	1 Palm Frond (navigation)
	1 Pop Group (fire control)
	Spin Trough (air search)
Sonars:	Bull Nose medium-frequency bow mounted
	Mare Tail medium-frequency variable depth
EW systems:	2 Bell Shroud
	2 Bell Squat

These are the largest combat ships to be operated by the KGB (and its predecessor NKVD) except for the icebreaker-gunboat PURGA (see below). They are an adaptation of the Krivak I/II-class ASW ships built for the Soviet Navy. Additional units may be under construction with some Western sources predicting a total class of perhaps 12 units.

The Krivak III is also the smallest Soviet combatant ship to regularly embark a helicopter. Even though both AAW and ASW armament have been reduced, these ships retain significant capabilities in both areas. No surface-to-surface weapons are fitted except for the single 100-mm gun forward, an adequate weapon for coastal guard and patrol duties.

Class: Naval construction of the Krivak I/II ceased after 32 units were built; see chapter 16. The Kamysh-Burun Shipyard built ships of the Krivak I class (with other naval Krivaks built at Kaliningrad and Leningrad).

Classification: Soviet classification is PSKR.

Design: The principal changes made to the basic Krivak design for the KGB service are a single-barrel 100-mm DP gun forward in place of the previous SS-N-14 ASW missile launcher and a raised helicopter platform aft in place of the second SA-N-4 missile launcher and after 76.2- or 100-mm gun mounts. Also, two 30-mm Gatling guns are mounted on top of the helicopter hangar (these weapons are not found in the Krivak I/II).

Two motor launches are carried compared to one in the Krivak I/II ships; they are fitted to port and starboard, abreast of the single funnel.

Electronics: The Spin Trough radar is employed for helicopter control; installed atop helicopter hangar.

Names: The lead ship is named for Viacheslav Rudolfovich Menzhinskiy, head of the OGPU (predecessor to the KGB) from 1926 until his death in 1934. Feliks Dzerzhinskiy organized and headed the Soviet *Cheka* or secret police from 1917 to 1921; this was the precursor of the OGPU. Previously a SVERDLOV-class cruiser carried his name as well as a T-58 class corvette operated by the KGB and a KGB higher command school.

The later ships are named, respectively, "in honor of the" 27th anniversary of the Communist Party of the Soviet Union, the 70th anniversary of the KGB, and the 70th anniversary of the border patrol.

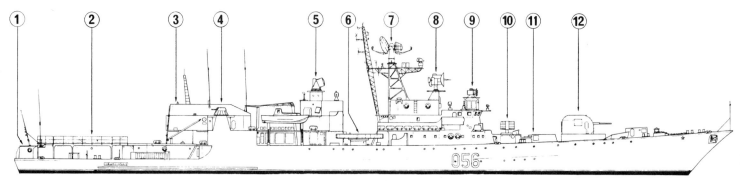

Krivak III: 1. Variable-depth sonar   2. helicopter deck   3. helicopter hangar   4. 30-mm Gatling guns (P/S)   5. Bass Tilt radar   6. 533-mm torpedo tubes (P/S)   7. Head Net-C radar   8. Kite Screech radar   9. Pop Group radar   10. RBU-6000 ASW rocket launchers (P/S)   11. SA-N-4 missile launcher (retracted)   12. 100-mm DP gun. Inset shows Top Plate radar. (M.J. Dodgson)

M. S. Kedrov was a particularly brutal secret police official (Cheka, OGPU, and NKVD). He and his son Igor, a secret police interrogator, were arrested in the Stalinist purges of the late 1930s; the son was executed in 1939 and the father in 1941.

Operational: All of these ships operate in the Far East, having transferred there shortly after completion. The MENZHINSKIY arrived at Nachodka on 22 October 1984.

The IMENI XXVII SYEZDA K.P.S.S. is one of the later Krivak III–class frigates, fitted with the Top Plate radar in place of the Head Net-C of the first two ships of this design. These are the first KGB ships other than icebreakers to have a helicopter capability. (1987, Japanese Maritime Self-Defense Force)

The latest Krivak III to go to sea is the KEDROV, shown here in the Far East. A photo of the MENZHINSKIY, fitted with the Head Net-C radar, appears in the 4th edition, page 379. (1990, JMSDF)

12 PATROL FRIGATES: GRISHA II CLASS

Name	Name	Completed
AMETIST	RUBIN	
BRILLIANT	SAFFIR	
IZUMRUD	ZHEMCHUG	1974—
PREDANYY	4+ units	
PROVORNYY		

Builders:	Zelenodolsk
Displacement:	850 tons standard
	1,100 tons full load
Length:	219 ft 5 in (66.9 m) waterline
	234 ft 10 in (71.6 m) overall
Beam:	32 ft 2 in (9.8 m)
Draft:	12 ft 2 in (3.7 m) hull
Propulsion:	CODAG: 4 diesel engines (twin M503 or M504);
	16,000 bhp + 1 gas turbine; 15,000 or 19,000 shp =
	31,000 or 39,000 shp; 3 shafts (see notes)
Speed:	30 or 31 knots
Range:	450 n.miles at 30 knots
	4,000 n.miles at 18 knots

Complement:	approx. 60
Helicopters:	no facilities
Missiles:	none
Guns:	4 57-mm/80-cal AA (2 twin)
ASW weapons:	2 RBU-6000 rocket launchers
	12 depth charges (see notes)
	torpedoes
Torpedoes:	4 21-inch (533-mm) torpedo tubes (2 twin)
Mines:	rails for 18 mines (see notes)
Radars:	1 Don-2 (navigation)
	1 Muff Cob (fire control)
	1 Strut Curve (air search)
Sonars:	Bull Nose medium-frequency hull mounted
	Elk Tail medium-frequency dipping
EW systems:	2 Watch Dog

These are small ASW frigates with minor differences in armament from the similar Grisha I/III/IV/V classes operated by the Navy. The Navy ships are similar except for an SA-N-4 launcher and associated Pop Group radar/FCS forward (in place of a twin 57-mm gun mount). See chapter 16 for additional details.

Armament: Racks for 12 depth charges can be fitted to the after end of the mine rails (in place of mines).

Classification: The Soviet classification is PSKR.

Engineering: The early ships have the lower horsepower gas turbine (with lower speed); later ships have same, higher rating plant as Grisha III class.

All of the Grisha II–class frigates are operated by the KGB. They have twin 57-mm rapid-fire AA gun mounts forward and aft; the Navy-manned Grishas have an SA-N-4 missile launcher forward. (Royal Navy)

The stern aspect of a Grisha II–class anti-submarine frigate. Mine rails are notched into the stern; depth charge racks can be attached, as shown here. (U.S. Navy)

2+ PATROL CORVETTES: SVETLAK CLASS

Completed:	1989—
Builders:	Dalzavod, Vladivostok
Displacement:	450 tons full load
Length:	approx. 164 ft (50.0 m) overall
Beam:	
Draft:	
Propulsion:	2 diesel engines (M517); 20,000 bhp; 2 shafts
Speed:	30+ knots
Range:	
Complement:	approx. 60
Missiles:	1 quad SA-N-8 anti-air launcher [16]
Guns:	1 76.2-mm/59-cal DP
	1 30-mm/65-cal close-in (multi-barrel)
ASW weapons:	torpedoes
	12 depth charges
Torpedoes:	2 15.75-inch (400-mm) torpedo tubes (2 single)
Mines:	none
Radars:	1 Bass Tilt (fire control)
	1 Peel Cone (air search)
	1 . . . . . . (navigation)
Sonars:	medium-frequency hull mounted

This is a modified Pauk-class patrol corvette, first sighted in 1989 in the Far East. The hull form resembles the Pauk, but the superstructure is quite different.

The NATO class name is Svetlak.

Classification: Also designated PAC-COM-1 (Pacific Combatant) by NATO intelligence.

A new KGB patrol corvette—the Svetlak class—as sighted for the first time in the Far East on 22 June 1989. (JMSDF courtesy *Ships of the World*)

FEW PATROL CORVETTES: PAUK CLASS

Completed:	1980—
Builders:	Yaroslavl
Displacement:	480 tons standard
	580 tons full load
Length:	191 ft 11 in (58.5 m) overall
Beam:	32 ft 2 in (9.8 m)
Draft:	8 ft 2 in (2.5 m) hull
Propulsion:	2 diesel engines (M517); 20,000 bhp; 2 shafts
Speed:	32 knots
Range:	2,000 n.miles at 20 knots
Complement:	approx. 40
Missiles:	1 quad SA-N-5 or SA-N-8 anti-air launcher [16—20]
Guns:	1 76.2-mm/59-cal DP
	1 30-mm/65-cal close-in (multi-barrel)
ASW weapons:	2 RBU-1200 rocket launchers
	12 depth charges
	torpedoes
Torpedoes:	4 15.75-in (400-mm) torpedo tubes (4 single)
Mines:	none
Radars:	1 Bass Tilt (fire control)
	1 Peel Cone (air search)
	1 Spin Trough (air search)
Sonars:	medium-frequency hull mounted
	medium- or high-frequency dipping

A few Pauk-class ASW corvettes are reported to be in service with the KGB Maritime Border Troops; most of the class serve with the Navy (see chapter 17).

Classification: Soviet PSKR type in KGB service.

Design: A circular housing for the dipping sonar is fitted in the stern on the starboard side. Some later units have the pilothouse one deck higher.

Pauk-class patrol corvette. (West German Navy)

FEW PATROL CORVETTES: T-58 CLASS (EX-MINESWEEPERS)

Completed:	1957–1961
Builders:	(USSR)
Displacement:	725 tons standard
	860 tons full load
Length:	229 ft 7 in (70.0 m) overall
Beam:	29 ft 10 in (9.1 m)
Draft:	8 ft 2 in (2.5 m)
Propulsion:	2 diesel engines; 4,000 bhp; 2 shafts
Speed:	18 knots
Range:	2,500 n.miles at 13.5 knots
Complement:	approx. 60
Missiles:	none
Guns:	4 57-mm/70-cal AA (2 twin)
ASW weapons:	2 RBU-1200 rocket launchers
	depth charges
Torpedoes:	none
Mines:	rails for 18 mines
Radars:	1 Don-2 (navigation)
	1 Muff Cob (fire control)
	1 Spin Trough (air search)
Sonars:	high-frequency hull mounted
EW systems:	2 Watch Dog

These are former T-58 minesweepers reclassified in 1978 as patrol ships; these and the former T-43 minesweepers are expected to be discarded by the KGB in the near future.

Classification: The KGB units are Soviet PSKR type.

T-58–class patrol corvette. (1978)

FEW PATROL CORVETTES: T-43 CLASS (EX-MINESWEEPERS)

Completed:	1947–1957
Builders:	(USSR)
Displacement:	500 tons standard
	590 tons full load
Length:	196 ft 10 in (60.0 m) overall
Beam:	28 ft 2 in (8.6 m)
Draft:	7 ft 7 in (2.3 m)
Propulsion:	2 diesel engines (Type 9D); 2,200 bhp; 2 shafts
Speed:	14 knots
Range:	2,000 n.miles at 14 knots
	3,200 n.miles at 10 knots
Complement:	approx. 65
Guns:	4 37-mm/60-cal AA (2 twin) or 2 45-mm/85-cal AA
	(2 single)
ASW weapons:	2 depth charge mortars
Mines:	rails for 16 mines
Radars:	1 Ball End (fire control)
	1 Don-2 (navigation) or Spin Trough (search)
Sonars:	Tamir-11 high-frequency hull mounted

These are former minesweepers, changed to patrol ships in the 1970s and transferred to the KGB. More than 200 of these units were built, several of which continue in naval service as minesweepers as well as in specialized auxiliary roles.

Classification: KGB designation is PSKR.

A T-43–class minesweeper with canvas covering the forward and after 37-mm gun mounts and various deck gear. Only a few of the once-numerous T-43s remain in Soviet service. (U.S. Navy)

14 + HYDROFOIL PATROL BOATS: MURAVEY CLASS

Completed:	1982—
Builders:	Feodosia
Displacement:	180 tons standard
	230 tons full load
Length:	131 ft 2 in (40.0 m) overall
Beam:	24 ft 11 in (7.6 m)
Draft:	6 ft 3 in (1.9 m)
Propulsion:	2 gas turbines; 24,200 shp; 2 shafts
Speed:	40+ knots
Range:	
Complement:	approx. 20
Missiles:	none
Guns:	1 76.2-mm/59-cal DP
	1 30-mm/65-cal close-in (multi-barrel)
ASW weapons:	torpedoes
	12 depth charges
Torpedoes:	2 15.75-inch (400-mm) torpedo tubes (2 single)
Mines:	none
Radars:	1 Bass Tilt (fire control)
	1 Peel Cone (air search)
	1 Spin Trough (search/navigation)
Sonars:	dipping sonar

This is a new patrol boat design. These craft are reported to be operated by the KGB in the Baltic and Black Sea areas.

Design: Fully submerged foil system. Some of these ships may operate without foils.

The Muravey-class patrol craft has a straightforward small combatant design except that this unit and most of those observed do not have the hydrofoils fitted. The ASW torpedo tubes are on the stern, flanking the 30-mm Gatling gun. Note the funnel arrangement. (1988, West German Navy)

60 + PATROL CRAFT: ZHUK CLASS

Completed:	1975—
Builders:	(USSR)
Displacement:	48 tons standard
	60 tons full load
Length:	78 ft 9 in (24.0 m) overall
Beam:	16 ft 5 in (5.0 m)
Draft:	5 ft 11 in (1.8 m)
Propulsion:	2 diesel engines (M50F-4); 2,400 bhp; 2 shafts
Speed:	34 knots
Range:	700 n.miles at 28 knots
	1,100 n.miles at 15 knots
Complement:	approx. 12
Missiles:	none
Guns:	2 or 4 14.5-mm machine guns (1 or 2 twin)
ASW weapons:	none
Torpedoes:	none
Mines:	none
Radars:	1 Spin Trough (search)
Sonars:	none

These patrol craft have been built in large numbers for Soviet and foreign use. Most and possibly all of the Soviet units are manned by KGB Border Troops. See appendix C for photo.

Class: Some 110 units of this class have been transferred to at least 17 other nations—Algeria, Angola, Benin, Bulgaria, Cape Verde Islands, Congo, Cuba, Ethiopia, Iraq, Mauritius, Mozambique, Nicaragua, Seychelles, Syria, Vietnam, and North and South Yemen.

Guns: One MG mount is fitted aft; units with two gun mounts have one forward of the bridge.

115 + PATROL CRAFT: STENKA CLASS

Completed:	1967—
Builders:	Petrovskiy, Leningrad
	and possibly other yards
Displacement:	170 tons standard
	210 tons full load
Length:	129 ft 7 in (39.5 m) overall
Beam:	24 ft 11 in (7.6 m)
Draft:	5 ft 11 in (1.8 m)
Propulsion:	3 diesel engines (M503A); 12,000 bhp; 3 shafts
Speed:	36 knots
Range:	550 n.miles at 34 knots
	750 n.miles at 25 knots
Complement:	approx. 20–25
Missiles:	none
Guns:	4 30-mm/65-cal close-in (2 twin)
ASW weapons:	12 depth charges
	torpedoes
Torpedoes:	4 15.75-inch (400-mm) torpedo tubes (4 single)
Mines:	none
Radars:	1 Pot Drum or Peel Cone (search)
	1 Drum Tilt (fire control)
Sonars:	high-frequency dipping sonar

These are graceful-looking patrol craft operated by the KGB Border Troops. This is the largest class in KGB service.

Class: The Stenka-class units have been transferred to Cuba. The modification of the Stenka for foreign use has been designated as the Mol class; these craft and "real" Stenkas have been transferred to Cambodia/Kampuchea, Cuba, Ethiopia, Iraq, Somalia, Sri Lanka, and South Yemen. Most of the transfer craft have had their torpedo tubes and dipping sonar deleted before transfer (see appendix C).

Classification: Soviet PSKR type.

Design: These are derivatives of the Osa design. The torpedo tubes are deleted in some units and a new search-navigation radar is fitted in recent units in place of the Pot Drum.

Electronics: Fitted with a Hormone-A helicopter dipping sonar.

A Stenka-class patrol boat at Malta; note the torpedo tubes and depth charge racks aft. (1983, Leo Van Ginderen)

Stenka-class patrol craft off Nakhodka. (Kohji Ishiwata)

PATROL CRAFT: PCHELA AND POLUCHAT I CLASSES

All units of these classes operated by the KGB have been discarded, the last in the early 1980s. See 3rd edition, pages 207 and 209.

Patrol craft of the Poluchat I class have been transferred to several other nations where many remain in service.

6 PATROL ICEBREAKERS: "IVAN SUSANIN" CLASS

Name	Completed
AYSBERG	
DUNAY	
IMENI XXV SYEZDA K.P.S.S.	1975–1981
IMENI XXVI SYEZDA K.P.S.S.	
NEVA	
VOLGA	

Builders:	Admiralty, Leningrad
Displacement:	3,400 tons full load
Length:	229 ft 7 in (70.0 m) overall
Beam:	60 ft (18.3 m)
Draft:	21 ft 4 in (6.5 m)
Propulsion:	diesel-electric: 3 diesel generators (13D100); 4,800 bhp; connected to 2 electric motors; 2 shafts
Speed:	14.5 knots
Range:	5,500 n.miles at 12 knots
	13,000 n.miles at 9.5 knots
Complement:	approx. 140
Helicopters:	landing area
Missiles:	see notes
Guns:	2 76.2-mm/59-cal DP (1 twin)
	2 30-mm/65-cal close-in (2 multi-barrel)
ASW weapons:	none
Torpedoes:	none
Mines:	none
Radars:	2 Don-Kay (navigation)
	1 Owl Screech (fire control)
	1 Strut Curve (search)

These are armed patrol icebreakers; they are of the same basic design as the naval and civilian DOBRYNYA NIKITICH class.

Class: Thirty-one ships of this general design are believed to have been built for the USSR; six of the IVAN SUSANIN class are operated by the KGB as patrol icebreakers. Two other ships of this class were transferred to the Navy in the 1980s (see chapter 23).

Classification: Soviet PSKR type in KGB service.

Design: These ships differ from the Navy units primarily with their helicopter platform (no hangar) and enlarged superstructure. Navy icebreakers are not armed. There are no Bass Tilt directors for the 30-mm Gatling guns, only optical sights.

The DUNAY and NEVA have been observed with positions for hand-held SA-N-5/SA-7 Grail missile launchers.

Operational: All of these ships are in the Pacific.

An armed IVAN SUSANIN–class icebreaker at sea. Of the large number of icebreakers of this general design in Soviet service, only the KGB units are armed. (1990, Royal Navy)

The VOLGA off the U.S. West Coast. The KGB patrol icebreaker visited San Francisco in May 1990 to take part in the U.S. Coast Guard's 200th anniversary celebration. Unlike larger icebreakers, these ships do not have helicopter hangars. (1990, U.S. Navy)

IVAN SUSANIN–class icebreaker showing the ship's raised helicopter platform, helicopter control station, and twin Gatling guns. (1990, Royal Navy)

1 PATROL ICEBREAKER-GUNBOAT: EX-"PURGA"

Name	Completed
. . . . . . (ex-PURGA)	1955

Builders:	Sudomekh, Leningrad
Displacement:	4,500 tons full load
Length:	319 ft 10 in (97.5 m) overall
Beam:	49 ft 10 in (15.2 m)
Draft:	21 ft (6.4 m)
Propulsion:	diesel-electric: 4 diesel engines with electric drive; 8,000 bhp; 2 shafts
Speed:	16 knots
Range:	
Complement:	approx. 250
Helicopters:	no facilities
Guns:	4 100-mm/56-cal DP (4 single)
ASW weapons:	removed
Torpedoes:	none
Mines:	rails for approx. 50–60 mines
Radars:	2 Don-2 (navigation)
	1 High Sieve (air search)
	1 Strut Curve (search)
	1 Sun Visor-B (fire control)
Sonars:	none
EW systems:	2 Watch Dog

The PURGA was laid down prior to World War II, probably in 1939, apparently as a combination icebreaker-gunboat in view of her heavy armament (see below). She was launched in 1951 or 1952. Only one ship of this design was built.

Reportedly, she was employed as a training ship as well as a patrol ship and icebreaker. She operates in the Pacific.

Armament: As completed, the PURGA additionally mounted eight 37-mm AA guns in twin mounts amidships; they were removed during a 1958–1960 overhaul. The ship was also built with four depth-charge projectors.

Like most Soviet naval ships completed in the 1950s, she has mine rails. A Wasp Head fire control director with the Sun Visor-B radar is fitted atop the bridge.

Name: The name PURGA is currently assigned to a civilian salvage tug.

Operational: The ship was apparently laid up during the 1970s.

The ex-PURGA in the Far East. Her current status is not known. (1983, U.S. Navy)

17 + PATROL TUGS: SORUM CLASS

Name	Name	Completed
AMUR	PRIMORSK	
BREST	PRIMOR'YE	
BUG	SAKHALIN	
CHUKOTA	URAL	
KALUGA	YAN BERZIN'	1974—
KAMCHATKA	YENISEY	
KAREZIYA	ZABAYKALYE	
LADOGA	ZAPOLYARE	
NEMAN		

Builders:	Yaroslavl
Displacement:	1,210 tons standard
	1,655 tons full load
Length:	191 ft 3 in (58.3 m) overall
Beam:	41 ft 4 in (12.6 m)
Draft:	15 ft 1 in (4.6 m)
Propulsion:	diesel-electric: 2 diesel engines (5-2D42) with electric drive; 1,500 bhp; 1 shaft
Speed:	14 knots
Range:	6,700 n. miles at 13 knots
Complement:	approx. 35
Guns:	4 30-mm/65 cal close-in (2 twin)
Radars:	2 Don-2 (navigation)

These are of the same class widely used by the Soviet Navy and civilian towing and salvage fleets. The KGB units have side-by-side 30-mm twin mounts installed forward of the bridge, atop the 01 level.

Classification: The KGB units are PSKR type.

A KGB-operated patrol tug of the Sorum class with 30-mm gun twin mounts forward of the bridge.

FEW ARMED TUGS: OKHTENSKIY CLASS

Completed:	1958–early 1960s
Builders:	Petrozavod, Leningrad
Displacement:	700 tons standard
	950 tons full load
Length:	155 ft 2 in (47.3 m) overall
Beam:	33 ft 9 in (10.3 m)
Draft:	
Propulsion:	2 diesel engines; 1,500 bhp; 1 shaft
Speed:	13 knots
Range:	7,800 n.miles at 7 knots
Complement:	approx. 40
Helicopters:	no facilities
Guns:	2 57-mm/70-cal AA (1 twin)
Radars:	1 or 2 Don-2 (navigation) or Spin Trough (search)

Standard Soviet tug design, with a few units armed and operated by the KGB. A total of 63 units were built for Soviet naval, civilian, and KGB service.

SUPPORT SHIPS

9 SUPPLY SHIPS: "NEON ANTONOV" CLASS

Name	Name	Completed
IVAN ASDNEV	NIKOLAY SIPYAGIN	
IVAN LEDNEV	NIKOLAY STARSHINKOV	
IVAN ODTEYEV	SERGEY SUDYESKIY	1978—
MIKHAIL KONOVALOV	VIKTOR DENISOV	
NEON ANTONOV		

Builders:	(USSR)
Displacement:	5,200 tons full load
Length:	311 ft 11 in (95.1 m) overall
Beam:	48 ft 3 in (14.7 m)
Draft:	21 ft 4 in (6.5 m)
Propulsion:	1 diesel engine; 1 shaft
Speed:	16 knots
Range:	
Complement:	approx. 40
Helicopters:	no facilities
Guns:	see notes
Radars:	2 Palm Frond (navigation)

These are specialized supply ships employed to support KGB Maritime Border Troops in remote locations. Two ships of this class are operated by the Navy, the IRBIT and DVINA (see chapter 23). One or two small landing craft are carried.

Guns: There are positions for two 14.5-mm twin machine gun mounts and two SA-N-5/SA-7 Grail missile launchers.

SUPPLY SHIPS: KHABAROVSK CLASS

Several small KGB supply ships of this class, built in the Soviet Union in the 1950s, have apparently been discarded as the ANTONOV class entered service. See 4th edition, page 386.

Supply ship Mikhail Konovalov. (1983)

KGB Maritime Border Troops board a ship intruding in Soviet territorial waters of the Barents Sea near the nuclear test area on Novaya Zemlya in October 1990. In the background is the Ivan Susanin-class patrol icebreaker Imeni Xxvi Sezda K.P.S.S. (Courtesy Greenpeace)

CHAPTER 27

Naval Aircraft

A navalized version of the Su-27 Flanker showing the folding outer wing panels for shipboard stowage. Shipboard variants of the MiG-29 Fulcrum also have folding wings. Note the height of the hangar deck of the carrier Admiral Kuznetsov (ex-Tbilisi). (Sovfoto)

This chapter describes the principal aircraft flown by Soviet Naval Aviation (SNA). Details on the strength, structure, and operations of SNA are found in chapter 8 of this volume. The aircraft described in this chapter are listed in table 27-1 in their respective order; aircraft are indicated below by type and date of SNA service entry.[1]

Designations. Soviet military aircraft are generally identified by three designations: a NATO code name that indicates the aircraft type and the specific aircraft, a Soviet design bureau designation, and a Soviet military designation. In addition, some aircraft have Soviet names.

The NATO scheme now in use was adopted in 1954, the name assignments being made by the Air Standards Coordinating Committee. The aircraft code names indicate the basic type; the following categories are applicable to SNA aircraft:

B = Bomber
C = Cargo
F = Fighter
H = Helicopter
M = Miscellaneous fixed-wing
        (including maritime patrol aircraft and airborne early warning)

One-syllable names are used for propeller aircraft and two-syllable names for jet aircraft. Suffix letters are appended to the NATO code names to indicate variants of a basic aircraft, as Bear-D; the use of *these* suffix letters with Soviet designations, as Tu-20D, is incorrect.

1. More detailed descriptions of contemporary Soviet aircraft will be found in the monthly journal *Air International*, the quarterly *World Air Power Journal*, and the annual *Jane's All the World's Aircraft*. The performance, dimensions, and weight data provided here are approximate, based on the best available public sources. Combat radius indicates the aircraft's radius, carrying weapons, with a majority of the flight to and from the target at optimum speed and altitude, with a low-level, high-speed "dash" to and from the target, except that missile-launching strike aircraft will release their weapons at a medium altitude (approximately 20,000 ft/6,100 m).

All drawings in this chapter were provided through the courtesy of Pilot Press, Bromley, Kent, England.

The shape of things to come: an Su-27 Flanker about to touch down on the deck of the aircraft carrier ADMIRAL KUZNETSOV (ex-TBILISI). In the foreground, parked abaft the island structure, is a Ka-27 Helix helicopter. During the ship's initial flight trials in late 1989 an Mi-8 Hip was also used as plane guard helicopter. (Sovfoto, A. Kremko)

Soviet design bureau and military designations applicable to naval aircraft are based on the following Soviet code scheme, derived from the names of the founders of the bureaus; the following are those currently used by naval aircraft:

An   = Antonov
Be   = Beriev
Il   = Ilyushin
Ka   = Kamov
Mi   = Mil'
MiG = Mikoyan and Gurevich
Su   = Sukhoi
Tu   = Tupolev
Yak = Yakovlev

This scheme was adopted by the Soviet government in 1940 (although aircraft designs supervised by Andrei N. Tupolev carried the bureau prefix ANT until 1947). The numbers used in conjunction with these bureau designations indicate the sequence of the aircraft, with two different numeral series in use for some aircraft; one indicates the bureau design and one the military designation (e.g., Tu-88 and Tu-16, respectively, for the Badger).

Suffix letters are used with these bureau designations. The most common ones for naval aircraft are *bis* for later variants, BT for *Buksirovshchik Tral* (minesweeper), M for *Modifikatsirovanny* (modification), MP for *Morskoy Pulubnyi* (maritime carrier-based), PL for *Protivolodchniy* (ASW), R for *Razvedchik* (reconnaissance), U for *Uchebny* (instructional—for trainer version), and UB for *Uchebny Boyevoi* (combat trainer).

Special abbreviations used in this chapter are AEW = Airborne Early Warning; IGE = In Ground Effect; IOC = Initial Operational Capability; MAD = Magnetic Anomaly Detection; OGE = Out of Ground Effect; st = static thrust; STOL = Short Take-Off and Landing; T/O = Take Off; and VSTOL = Vertical/Short Take-Off and Landing.

TABLE 27-1.   SOVIET NAVAL AIRCRAFT

Soviet Designations	NATO Name	Status[a]		Naval Roles
Bomber/Strike Aircraft				
Tu-22M	Backfire	SAF	SNA	bomber/missile strike
Tu-22	Blinder	SAF	SNA	bomber/photo reconnaissance
Tu-16	Badger	SAF	SNA	bomber/missile strike; ELINT; ECM; tanker; reconnaissance
Su-24	Fencer-E	SAF	SNA	reconnaissance/strike
Fighter/Attack Aircraft				
Yak-41[b]			SNA	fighter/attack[c]
Su-27	Flanker	SAF/ADF	SNA	fighter[c]
MiG-29	Fulcrum	SAF	SNA	fighter[c]
Su-25	Frogfoot	SAF	SNA	attack[c]
Yak-38MP	Forger		SNA	fighter/attack[c]
MiG-27	Flogger	SAF	SNA	attack
Su-17	Fitter	SAF	SNA	attack
Electronic/Reconnaissance Aircraft				
An-74	Madcap	SAF	SNA(?)	airborne early warning[d]
Tu-20	Bear-D		SNA	reconnaissance/missile targeting
Tu-142	Bear-J		SNA	communications relay
Maritime Patrol/Anti-Submarine Aircraft				
Be-42	(Albatross)		SNA	anti-submarine/search and rescue
Tu-142	Bear-F		SNA	anti-submarine
Il-38	May		SNA	anti-submarine
Be-12	Mail		SNA	anti-submarine
Cargo/Special Purpose Aircraft				
Il-20	Coot-A		SNA	ELINT/reconnaissance
An-22	Cub	SAF	SNA	cargo; ELINT; research
Helicopters				
Ka-27/Ka-29	Helix		SNA	anti-submarine; utility; transport[c]
Mi-14	Haze		SNA	anti-submarine; mine countermeasures; utility
Mi-8	Hip-C	SAF	SNA	transport; mine countermeasures
Ka-25	Hormone		SNA	anti-submarine; missile targeting; utility[c]

[a] SAF = Soviet Air Forces; ADF = Air Defense Forces; SNA = Soviet Naval Aviation.
[b] Expected to be operational in SNA in early 1990s.
[c] Ship/carrier based variants.
[d] Possibly carrier based variant.

BOMBER/STRIKE AIRCRAFT

Tu-160 Blackjack

The Blackjack is a new Soviet bomber-type aircraft that entered operational service in 1988 with the Soviet strategic air army at Dolon in Kazakhistan. It is the largest bomber aircraft now flown by any nation—some 20 percent larger than the U.S. B-1B strategic bomber.

When this edition of *Guide to the Soviet Navy* went to press there was no indication that the aircraft would be flown by SNA. Further, the entry of several new fighter-type aircraft and a new flying boat patrol/ASW aircraft into SNA service, plus the continued increases in the Backfire and Bear-F inventories, will probably account for all available SNA training and maintenance expansion for the foreseeable future.

(Note: Tu-160 is apparently the design bureau designation and not the military designation of the aircraft.)

Tu-22M Backfire

The Backfire is a long-range, high-performance bomber flown by Soviet strategic aviation and Soviet Naval Aviation. (In the former service the Backfire appears to be assigned to the theater strike role and is not intended for strategic attacks against the United States.) SNA employs the Backfire in the anti-ship missile role, replacing the long-serving Badger strike aircraft.

The Backfire is a variable-geometry aircraft. The outer wing sections extend for take-off, landing, and cruise flight and sweep back for high-speed flight. Two large turbofan engines are buried in the wing roots. The huge tail fin is fitted with fuel tanks and ECM equipment; a twin 23-mm, remote-control gun mount is provided in the tail. A fixed refueling probe can be installed in the nose. Offensive ordnance consists of one AS-4 or possibly AS-6 missile semi-recessed under the fuselage or two missiles carried on pylons under the forward portion of the very long engine housings. The aircraft also carries ECM pods and possibly decoys. An internal weapons bay is provided for carrying bombs but cannot be used when a missile is fitted in the semi-recessed configuration. In addition, detachable multiple weapon racks can be fitted under each engine nacelle; these racks, each some 18 ft 6 in (5.6 m) long, can carry nine bombs of probably 551-1b (250-kg) size. The twin turbofan engines are adopted from the now-abandoned Tu-144 Charger supersonic transport (developed concurrently with the Backfire).

The improved Backfire-C is now being delivered to SNA; it is believed to have an improved weapons delivery capability while radically different air intakes probably indicate higher-thrust engines than in the B model.

The prototype Backfire-A aircraft underwent extensive redesign to produce the definitive B version. In particular, the wings and landing gear were thoroughly changed, upgraded engines were provided, a tail gun position was added, and the pilot/copilot seating was changed from in-line to side-by-side.

Designation: The Soviet designation Tu-22M indicates that the Backfire may have evolved from an extensive modification of the Tu-22 Blinder (see below). The designation Tu-26 had been used for the Backfire in the Western press, while Tu-136 was apparently the design bureau designation.

Status: Flight tests began in 1969 with at least two prototypes. Up to 12 Backfire-A models were built and formed a transition/training unit. The Backfire-B entered SNA service in 1974, shortly after becoming operational with Soviet strategic aviation. Since the start of production, Backfires have been assigned to the two Soviet air services with more than 150 in SNA service by early 1990. Production for both services continued at the rate of some 30 per year during the 1980s.

BACKFIRE-B

Crew:	4 (pilot, copilot, navigator, electronics/weapons officer)
Engines:	2 Kuznetsov NK-144 derivative turbofan with afterburner; approx. 44,090 lbst (19,996 kgst) each
Weights:	empty 110,000 lbs (49,500 kg)
	maximum T/O 270,000 lbs (121,500 kg)
Dimensions:	span 113 ft (34.45 m) fully extended
	span 85 ft 11 in (26.2 m) fully swept
	length 139 ft 5 in (42.2 m)
	height 33 ft (10.06 m)
Speed:	cruise approx. 500 mph (800 km/h)
	maximum 1,250 mph (2,000 km/h) at 36,080 ft (11,000 m) Mach 1.8
	sea level 650 mph (1,050 km/h)
Ceiling:	service 55,760 ft (17,000 m)
Range:	radius 3,400 miles (5,500 km) unrefueled (range is extended in Backfire-C)
Armament:	2 AS-4 Kitchen air-to-surface missiles; also AS-9 anti-radar missile or 26,460 lbs (12,000 kg) of free-fall bombs or mines in weapons bay
	2 GSh-23 23-mm cannon (remote-control tail turret)
Radar:	Down Beat (bombnav)
	Box Tail (gunfire control)

Backfire-C.

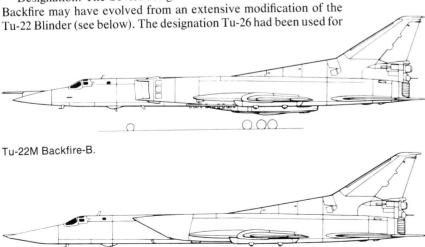

Tu-22M Backfire-B.

Tu-22M Backfire-C.

The Backfire-B with variable-geometry wings swept back for high-speed flight. The fixed, nose-mounted refueling probe has been removed in accord with Soviet-U.S. agreements to deter the use of Backfires as strategic bombers, although the probes can be installed in a matter of hours. Multiple weapon racks are visible under the fuselage.

Tu-22 Blinder

The Tu-22 Blinder was the first supersonic bomber to enter Soviet service. The twin-turbojet aircraft is in service with Soviet strategic aviation and SNA. However, it has been less than fully successful and did not enter large-scale production to replace the Badger, as once planned. The Blinder was the last bomber-type aircraft to be produced in the Soviet Union until the debut of the Tu-22M Backfire. In SNA service the Blinder is used to deliver free-fall bombs, with a few aircraft configured for reconnaissance and training.

The Blinder is a swept-wing aircraft with twin turbojet engines mounted in pods at the base of the tail fin. Most aircraft have a partially retractable in-flight refueling probe in the nose, a nose radome, and tandem seating for the crew of three. External fuel tanks are faired into the trailing edges of the wings. The Blinder-A carries bombs internally in two weapon bays; the Blinder-B (Air Forces) can carry an AS-4 Kitchen missile. Defensive armament consists of a remote-control single 23-mm tail gun. The Blinder-D trainer has a raised rear cockpit with dual controls for an instructor (replacing the radar observer's position). The aircraft has a supersonic dash capability.

Designation: The Tupolev design-bureau designation for the aircraft was Tu-105, with the military designation being Tu-22. The Blinder was apparently developed as a supersonic bomber to be competitive with the Myasishchev M-52 Bounder, which did not enter squadron service.

Status: First flight in 1959–1960. The Blinder entered service in 1962, with missile-armed aircraft being operational in the Soviet Air

Forces about 1967; fewer than 200 aircraft were built before production ended in 1969. Some 25 Blinder-A bombers remain in SNA service, plus a few Blinder-C reconnaissance and Blinder-D training aircraft. Blinders have been transferred to Iraq and Libya.

Naval variants:

Blinder-A	bomber aircraft carrying gravity bombs.
Blinder-C	photo-reconnaissance aircraft.
Blinder-D	trainer aircraft with modified cockpit (Tu-22U).

Crew:	3 (pilot, copilot, electronics/weapons officer)
Engines:	2 Kolesov RD-7 turbojet with afterburner; approx. 30,800 lbst (14,000 kgst) each
Weights:	empty 88,000 lbs (40,000 kg)
	maximum T/O 184,580 lbs (83,900 kg)
Dimensions:	span 89 ft 3 in (27.7 m)
	length 132 ft 11 in (40.53 m)
	height 35 ft (10.67 m)
Speed:	cruise 560 mph (900 km/h) at 36,080 ft (11,000 m) Mach 0.85
	maximum 920 mph (1,475 km/h) at 36,080 ft (11,000 m) Mach 1.5
Ceiling:	service 60,000 ft (18,300 m)
Range:	4,030 miles (6,500 km) all subsonic
	radius 1,800 miles (2,880 km) on hi-lo-hi mission
Armament:	1 NR-23 23-mm cannon
	17,600 lbs (8,000 kg) bombs
Radar:	Down Beat (bombnav)
	Bee Hind (gunfire control)

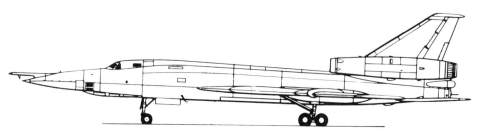

Tu-22 Blinder-A.

A Blinder-A showing the aircraft's sleek but unsuccessful design. Naval Blinders carry only free-fall bombs; those aircraft assigned to the Air Forces carry air-to-surface missiles. Few remain in naval service.

A Blinder-C reconnaissance aircraft with flaps and wheels lowered, coming in for a landing. The aircraft has photographic and probably electronic reconnaissance gear; a refueling probe is fitted. (U.S. Air Force)

Tu-16 Badger

The Tu-16 Badger is a turbojet-powered medium bomber that has been in wide use by the Soviet Union for three decades. It serves in the anti-ship missile, reconnaissance, ELINT, ECM, and tanker roles with SNA.

The Badger has a swept-wing configuration with two large turbojet engines housed in nacelles faired into the fuselage at the wing roots. The engines have been updated during the aircraft's long production run, culminating in the engines listed below. When employed in the tanker role, the Badger has fuel tanks fitted in the weapons bay and trails a drogue from the starboard wing-tip; the receiving probe is fitted in the port wing-tip of Badgers. The Badger-G strike aircraft carry air-to-surface missiles under the fuselage and on wing pylons. Most aircraft have two 23-mm cannon in dorsal, ventral, and tail mounts, and bombers not having a large radome can mount a seventh cannon fixed on the starboard side of the nose. Only two missiles are normally carried in exercises.

Designation: The Tupolev bureau's design designation for the Badger was Tu-88; the Tu-98 Backfin was a Badger airframe flown in 1955 in the research role; and the Tu-104 Camel was a civilian airliner derived from the Badger.

Status: First flight late 1952; production began the following year with squadron delivery to the Air Forces from 1954 to 1955 and deliveries to the Navy beginning in the late 1950s (with many Air Forces aircraft transferred to SNA).

Approximately 2,000 Badgers were built in the Soviet Union through the mid-1960s plus more than 80 produced in China, where production probably continues in Xian (aircraft designated H-6D). SNA currently flies some 145 Badgers in the missile-strike role; 45 Badger-A aircraft in the tanker role; and perhaps another 130 Badgers in the reconnaissance, ELINT, and ECM roles.

Badgers have been transferred to China, Egypt, Indonesia, Iraq, and Libya.

The naval variants are:

Badger-A   bomber, tanker, trainer; flown by SNA and strategic aviation; can carry 8,360 lbs (3,800 kg) bombs with 2,975 n.mile (4,800 km) radius; IOC 1954–1955. No longer in service except in the tanker role.

Badger-C   missile strike; 2 AS-2 Kipper or 2 AS-5 Kelt missiles; Puff Ball radar with AS-2; Short Horn radar with AS-5; IOC 1960. No longer in service.

Badger-D   electronic reconnaissance; Puff Ball and Short Horn radars.

Badger-E   photo reconnaissance; cameras in weapons bay.

Badger-F   electronic and photo reconnaissance.

Badger-G   missile strike; 3 AS-5 Kelt or 2 AS-6 Kingfish missiles; combat radius 1,985+ n.mile (3,200+ km); Short Horn radar; IOC 1965.

Badger-H   EW/strike escort.

Badger-J   EW/strike escort.

Badger-K   ELINT/electronic reconnaissance.

Crew:	6 (pilot, copilot, navigator, weapons systems officer, radio operator, gunner)
Engines:	2 Mikulin AM-3M turbojets; 20,950 lbst (9,425 kg) each in later aircraft
Weights:	empty 81,840 lbs (37,200 kg)
	maximum T/O 158,456 lbs (72,000 kg)
Dimensions:	span 108 ft (32.93 m)
	length 114 ft 2 in (34.8 m)
	height 35 ft 5 in (10.8 m)
Speed:	cruise 530 mph (850 km/h) Mach 0.8
	maximum 615 mph (990 km/h) Mach 0.9

Ceiling:	service 40,350 ft (12,300 m)
Range:	4,000 miles (6,400 km)
	radius 1,920 miles (3,100 km)
Armament:	19,800 lbs (9,000 kg) in weapons bay in Badger-A
	3 AS-5 Kelt or 2 AS-6 Kingfish missiles in Badger-G
	up to 7 23-mm cannon (nose + dorsal, ventral, tail turrets)
Radar:	See above for bombnav radars.
	Bee Hind (gunfire control)

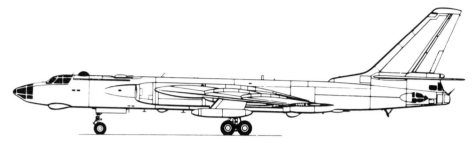

Tu-16 Badger-F electronic and photo reconnaissance variant with glazed nose and under-wing electronic pods.

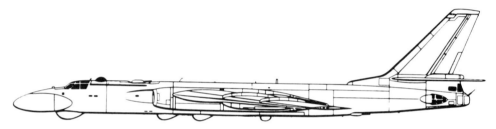

Tu-16 Badger-D electronic reconnaissance variant with Short Horn and Puff Ball radars in the nose.

Badger-D electronic reconnaissance aircraft with a large Short Horn radar in the nose and a Puff Ball radar in the chin position; two of the 23-mm twin turrets are visible; there is also a dorsal turret.

The Badger-E photo aircraft is fitted with cameras in the weapons bay. The dorsal and tail 23-mm gun positions are visible; another twin turret is in the ventral position. The Navy operates more Badgers than the Air Forces.

A Badger-C strike aircraft over the North Atlantic sans missiles. The three missile-carrying positions can be seen: two wing pylons (outboard of the landing-gear nacelles) and under the weapons bay. There is a small radome between the weapons bay and the nose gear doors. The Badger-G has a plexiglass nose. (U.S. Navy)

Su-24 Fencer

The Fencer is a high-speed, long-range strike and reconnaissance aircraft in service with Soviet strategic aviation. The naval air arm of the Baltic Fleet began flying the Fencer-E reconnaissance variant in early 1986; however, by the end of the decade dual-capable strike and reconnaissance variants were being transferred in large numbers from the Soviet Air Forces to the Navy. The Fencer has a night/poor-weather flight capability and in several respects is similar to the larger U.S. Air Force F-111 Aardvark.

The aircraft has a variable-sweep wing with three selectable sweep angles—16, 45, and 68 degrees. There is side-by-side seating for the two-man crew.

Armament consists of a six-barrel, 30-mm Gatling gun and eight pylons under the fuselage and wings for carrying a variety of conventional and nuclear weapons, including air-to-surface missiles. The missile-launch capability is retained in the naval variant. Up to four large (520–U.S.-gallon) drop tanks can be carried. The aircraft has a laser range-finder and target seeker.

Status: First flight in 1969–1970. Soviet Air Forces IOC in 1974. The Fencer-E entered SNA service with the Baltic Fleet in 1986. Believed to be in production. Fencers have been sold to Libya.

Badger-G naval strike aircraft with AS-5 Kelt missiles on wing pylons, outboard of the landing gear. Nose configurations vary; note the 23-mm cannon on the starboard side of the fuselage.

Crew:	2 (pilot, weapons systems operator)
Engines:	2 Lyulka AL-21F or Tumansky R-29 turbojet; approx. 24,250 lbst (11,000 kg) each with afterburner
Weights:	empty approx. 41,888 lbs (19,000 kg)
	maximum T/O approx. 90,390 lbs (41,000 kg)
Dimensions:	span 57 ft 5 in (17.5 m) extended
	span 34 ft 5 in (10.5 m) swept
	length 69 ft 10 in (21.29 m)
	height 19 ft 8 in (6.0 m)
Speed:	sea level 915 mph (1,470 km/h) Mach 1.2
	1,440 mph (2,317 km/h) Mach 2+ above 36,089 ft (11,000 m)
Ceiling:	54,134 ft (16,500 m)

Range:	radius 200+ miles (322 km) on lo-lo-lo mission
	radius 590 miles (950 km) on lo-lo-hi mission with 5,500 lbs (2,500 kg) weapons
	radius 800 miles (1,300 km) on hi-lo-lo-hi mission with 6,614 lbs (3,000 kg) weapons + 2 external fuel tanks (793 U.S. gal)
Armament:	1 six-barrel 30-mm cannon
	up to 24,250 lbs (11,000 kg) of bombs AS-7 Kerry or other air-to-surface missiles
Radar:	. . . . . . (fire control)
	. . . . . . (navigation Doppler)

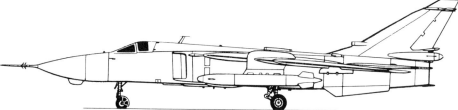

Su-24 Fencer-D.

A Fencer-D preparing to land. Note the twin ventral tail fins of this large aircraft. This is a strike version with weapon pylons under the wing and fuselage; the Soviet Navy initially flew the Fencer-E reconnaissance variant.

FIGHTER/ATTACK AIRCRAFT

The Soviets will employ the Su-27 Flanker and the MiG-29 Fulcrum in the fighter/attack role from the ADMIRAL KUZNETSOV and later aircraft carriers as well as the Su-25 Frogfoot. All three aircraft have been observed carrying out airfield tests of carrier operating techniques at Saki in the Crimea and, beginning in November 1989, they have all flown from the ADMIRAL KUZNETSOV (formerly TBILISI).

The Yak-38MP Forger flies from the KIEV-class VSTOL carriers with the Yak-41 expected to be the successor in the VSTOL fighter/attack role.

Yak-41

The Yak-41 is a VSTOL fighter/attack aircraft being developed as a replacement for the Yak-38 Forger on board the KIEV-class carriers. The Yak-41 has experienced development problems. Few details have been publicly revealed.

The aircraft bears a superficial resemblance to the larger MiG- and Su- series of fighter aircraft, with a high swept-back wing, large rectangular air intakes below the cockpit, and twin fins and rudders.

In August 1991 the Yak-41 project was cancelled; see Addenda.

A U.S. Department of Defense artist's view of the Yak-41 VSTOL aircraft on a Soviet carrier.

Su-27 Flanker

An air-intercept fighter assigned to the Soviet Air Defense Forces, the Flanker has a look-down/shoot-down capability and is capable of all-weather operation. It has been adopted for carrier STOL operation. The aircraft is highly maneuverable and believed to be comparable in capability to the U.S. F-15 Eagle. A ground-attack version is also being produced.

The Flanker is one of the world's most agile fighters and has established 27 time-to-altitude and sustained-altitude records. It is fitted with a multi-channel, fly-by-wire control system that automatically adjusts the full-span leading edge and half-span trailing edge flaps to maximize performance. There are small canards forward. Neither the Flanker nor Fulcrum is fitted for in-flight refueling.

The aircraft has the same track-while-scan radar as the MiG-29 Fulcrum with infrared search-and-track and laser range-finding systems. It is reported to carry up to eight AA-10 missiles in the fighter role or 13,200 lbs (6,000 kg) of other ordnance in the attack role.

There is a two-seat Su-27UB trainer variant (with radar retained, unlike the MiG-29UB).

Status: First flight (P-42 prototype) on 20 May 1977. The Flanker entered operational service in 1986 with the Soviet Air Forces. In production at Komsomol'sk.

Crew:	1 (2 in Su-27UB)
Engines:	2 Lyulka AL-31F turbojet; 27,588 lbst (12,500 kgst) each with afterburner
Weights:	empty 39,000 lbs (17,690 kg)
	normal T/O 48,400 lbs (22,000 kg)
	maximum T/O 66,139 lb (30,000 kg)
Dimensions:	span 48 ft 2 in (14.7 m)
	length 71 ft 10½ in (21.9 m)
	height 18 ft (5.5 m)
Speed:	maximum 1,553 mph (2,500 km/h) Mach 2.35
	1,320 mph (2,120 km/h) Mach 2 with 8 AAMs
Ceiling:	
Range:	radius 930 miles (1,500 km) with 8 AAMs
	maximum 2,485 miles (4,000 km)
Armament:	up to 13,200 lbs (6,000 kg) of external stores (AA-8 Aphid/ AA-10 Alamo/AA-11 Archer air-to-air missiles, rocket pods, bombs)
Radar:	Slot Back (multi-mode Doppler)

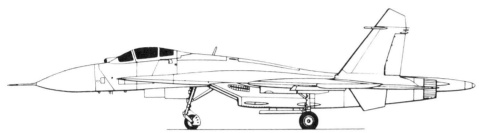

Su-27 Flanker.

The underside of a Flanker-B shown carrying five AA-10 Alamo missiles; the different missile configurations indicate infra-red and semi-active radar homing variants.

A Flanker-B shows the clean, advanced-design lines of this interceptor. There is a large dorsal air brake just behind the cockpit (folded); the projection between the engine exhausts houses the parachute brake.

MiG-29 Fulcrum

This is an advanced air-intercept fighter assigned to the Air Defense Forces; it is also being produced in a ground-attack configuration for the Air Forces. It has been modified for carrier STOL operation. The Fulcrum has been described by John W.R. Taylor, editor of *Jane's All the World's Aircraft,* as the "First of a completely new generation of Soviet fighters to enter service," while British aviation writer John Fricker observed: "There is no doubt that the appearance, handling and performance of the MiG-29 came as a great surprise" [to Western aviation experts at the 1988 Farnborough air show]. The Fulcrum is about the size of the U.S. F-16 Fighting Falcon.

In the air-intercept role the aircraft carries six air-to-air missiles; in the air-to-ground role the aircraft can deliver up to 8,800 lbs (3,960 kg) of ordnance carried on six wing pylons. It has a twin-barrel 23-mm cannon with a rate of fire of 3,000 rounds-per-minute. The pulse-Doppler radar can detect fighter-sized targets out to a range of 60 miles (100 km); it does not have a multi-target capability. Infrared search-and-track and laser range-finder systems are provided.

There is a two-seat trainer version, the MiG-29UB (Fulcrum-B); the length has been increased to 57 ft 2 in (17.42 m) but the radar has been deleted. The improved Fulcrum-C has an enlarged fuselage dorsal with increased fuel capacity. The Soviets revealed in 1989 that a fly-by-wire variant of the MiG-29 has been flown; in addition to a new control system, that aircraft has a modified tailplane and slight changes in the wing position and center of gravity.

Status: The aircraft entered squadron service with the Soviet Air Forces in 1984. The Fulcrum is also flown by the air forces of Czechoslovakia, East Germany, North Korea, India, Poland, Syria, and Yugoslavia.

Crew:	1 (2 in MiG-29UB)
Engines:	2 Tumansky R-33D turbofan; 11,110 lbst (5,040 kgst); 18,000 lbst (8,182 kgst) each with afterburner
Weights:	normal T/O 33,000 lbs (15,000 kg)
	maximum T/O 39,000 lbs (18,000 kg)
Dimensions:	span 37 ft 3½ in (11.36 m)
	length 56 ft 10 in (17.32 m)
	height 15 ft 6 in (4.73 m)
Speed:	Mach 2.3+
Ceiling:	service 55,775 ft (17,000 m)
Range:	strike radius 440 miles (710 km)
	maximum range 1,300 miles (2,100 km) with centerline tanks (390 U.S. gallons)
Armament:	1 30-mm cannon
	up to 8,800 lbs (3,960 kg) of external stores (AA-8 Aphid/AA-10 Alamo/AA-11 Archer air-to-air missiles, rocket pods, bombs)
Radar:	Slot Back (multi-mode Doppler)

This is a MiG-29UB two-seat combat trainer. The aircraft have up to six under-wing pylons for weapons; a fuel tank or weapons can also be carried under the fuselage. (Les Hart)

MiG-29 Fulcrum.

A Fulcrum climbing. Note the large rudders. Although the Fulcrum is smaller than the Flanker, the former's tail fins are proportionally larger. Visible above the rudders are tail-light fairings (top) and Sirena-3 electronic countermeasure antennas.

Su-25 Frogfoot

The Frogfoot is a subsonic ground-attack aircraft intended to attack tanks and defended ground positions. The aircraft has been adopted for STOL carrier operation. It is similar in concept to the U.S. A-10 Thunderbolt close-air-support aircraft (although its configuration is closer to the unsuccessful Northrop A-9 competitive prototype). The Frogfoot was used extensively in anti-guerrilla operations in Afghanistan during the 1980s. When this edition went to press, only the two-seat Su-25UB variant had flown from the carrier ADMIRAL KUZNETSOV.

An estimated 8,800 lbs (4,000 kg) of air-to-ground ordnance can be carried on eight wing pylons and two missile rails. Bombs and rockets are carried on eight wing pylons. Two small, outboard pylons can hold AA-2 Atoll or AA-8 Aphid air-to-air missiles for self-defense or for attacking helicopters. A twin-barrel 23-mm anti-tank cannon is fitted in the fuselage. The aircraft is armored with certain control surfaces designed to be highly survivable against light ground fire. It carries a large amount of deceptive chaff and flares to enhance survivability against ground fire. A laser range-finder and target marker are fitted.

The initial Frogfoot aircraft flew with Tumansky R-9 engines.

Status: First flight in 1975. The Frogfoot is believed to have become operational in 1981 with the Soviet Air Forces. It is also flown by several other nations.

Crew:	1 (2 in Su-25UB)
Engines:	2 Tumansky R13-300 turbojet; 9,340 lbst (4,237 kgst) each
Weights:	empty 20,950 lbs (9,500 kg)
	normal T/O 32,187 lbs (14,600 kg)
	maximum T/O 38,800 lbs (17,600 kg)
Dimensions:	span 46 ft 11 in (14.3 m)
	length 50 ft 6¾ in (15.4 m)
	height 15 ft 9 in (4.8 m)
Speed:	maximum 621 mph (1,000 km/h) Mach 0.82
Ceiling:	
Range:	radius 186 miles (300 km) with 4,450 lbs (2,000 kg) of weapons
Armament:	1 twin-barrel GSh-23 23-mm cannon [260 rounds]
	8 1,102-lb (500-kg) bombs
	or 16 16-round 57-mm rocket pods
	or AS-7 Kerry or AS-14 Kedge air-to-surface missiles
Radar:	none

A single-seat Frogfoot at the Paris Air Show. A two-seat Su-25UB aircraft was used for the initial flight trials aboard the ADMIRAL KUZNETSOV (then named TBILISI.) (John Fricker)

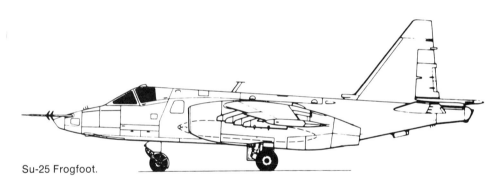

Su-25 Frogfoot.

The Frogfoot is a close-air support platform. The four weapon pylons under each wing are evident in this photo.

Yak-38MP Forger

The Forger is a VSTOL aircraft developed for operation from the KIEV-class aircraft carriers. The plane serves in the fighter/attack roles.

The Forger has a lift-plus-lift-cruise configuration using two forward lift engines that are mounted vertically and an aft-mounted, vectored-thrust engine for both vertical lift and propulsion. This configuration enhances VTOL payload compared to the British–U.S. Harrier VSTOL aircraft, with the Forger having a 64 percent VTOL payload advantage over the AV-8A model and 25 percent over the AV-8B. The Soviet plane initially was seen flying only in the VTOL mode but now operates as a VSTOL aircraft as well. The Forger has a swept-wing configuration with the outer panels folding upward for shipboard handling. The wing area is relatively small (approximately 199 ft^2/18.5 m^2). The single-seat A version is the standard, with one or two B versions normally embarked in carriers as an operational (combat) trainer. Four wing pylons can accommodate a variety of weapons or fuel tanks; in the interceptor role the aircraft generally carries two Aphid air-to-air missiles and two external fuel tanks.

(Steps in the Forger development included the MiG-21PFM Fishbed-G lift-engine test bed, a high-performance fighter with two lift engines buried in its fuselage, and the Yakovlev Yak-36 Freehand, a VSTOL technology demonstration aircraft having twin engines with vectorable nozzles. The Freehand, first seen publicly in 1967, flew VTOL sea trials from the helicopter carrier MOSKVA. The Yak-38 has also been flown from a container ship.)

Status: Forger first deployed on board the KIEV in 1976 and subsequently in the other ships of the class. Flown only by Soviet Naval Aviation with about 75 Forger-A variants in service plus a small number of Forger-B trainers.

Crew:	1 in Forger-A; 2 in Forger-B
Engines:	1 Tumansky R27V-300 turbojet cruise engine; approx. 15,000 lbst (6,800 kgst)
	2 Koliesov turbojet lift engines; approx. 7,875 lbst (3,500 kgst) each
Weights:	maximum T/O 25,740 lbs (11,700 kg)
Dimensions:	span 24 ft (7.32 m)
	Forger-A length 50 ft 10 in (15.5 m)
	Forger-B length 58 ft (17.68 m)
	height 14 ft 4 in (4.37 m)
Speed:	maximum 625 mph (1,010 km/h) at 36,000 ft (11,000 m) Mach 0.95
	sea level 610 mph (980 km/h) Mach 0.8
Ceiling:	39,360 ft (12,000 m)
Range:	radius as deck-launched interceptor 115 mi (185 km) with 75 minutes on station
	strike radius 150 mi (240 km) with approx. 6,600 lbs (3,000 kg) weapons (lo-lo-lo mission); 230 miles (370 km) with same payload (hi-lo-hi mission)
Armament:	approx. 6,600 lbs (2,970 kg) external stores (bombs, rockets, missiles, gun pods, including AA-8 Aphid air-to-air or SA-7 Kerry air-to-surface missiles)
Radar:	. . . . . . (small ranging radar)

A Forger-A with landing gear extended and air intake open for vertical-lift engines (behind cockpit). The Forger has been only a limited success. (West German Navy)

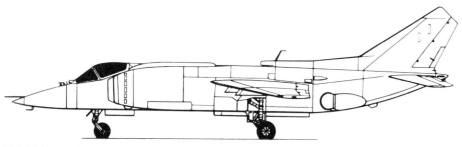

Yak-38 Forger-A.

A Forger-A approaching the carrier KIEV during flight operations in the Mediterranean. The naval ensign is on both sides of the fuselage, on the engine air intakes.

Forgers on the deck of a KIEV-class VSTOL carrier with wings folded. The air intakes are open for the vertical-lift engines, and AA-8 Aphid air-to-air missiles are visible under the wings of the aircraft.

A two-seat Forger-B is usually embarked in each of the KIEV-class VSTOL carriers. The aircraft is larger in most dimensions than the Forger-A. (Courtesy Pilot Press)

MiG-27 Flogger-D/K

The variable-sweep-wing Flogger was the first modern multi-role, fighter-type aircraft to enter Soviet service. Fighter-interceptor variants are designated MiG-23 while those configured for the ground attack role are designated MiG-27 (NATO code names Flogger-D/J/K). Soviet Naval Aviation began flying the MiG-27 Flogger about 1988 with small numbers being delivered for naval use from shore bases. In 1989–1990 some 40 MiG-27s were transferred to the Navy from the Soviet Air Forces to provide a strength of some 50 aircraft when this edition went to press.

The MiG-23 and MiG-27 broke with the MiG design tradition of nose-mounted engine air intakes and replaced the open-nose intakes with intakes on each side of the fuselage, forward of the wing root. The MiG-27 has fixed air intakes compared to variable-geometry intakes for the MiG-23 design, rough-field landing gear, bulged center fuselage, and a different gun. These changes have resulted in a reduction in maximum speeds. The wing angle can be changed from 72 to 16 degrees.

Ground-attack stores are carried on five wing and fuselage pylons and two fuselage bomb racks for 8,820 lbs (4,000 kg) of weapons. An internal, six-barrel 23-mm Gatling gun is fitted in the ventral position. (This was probably the first installation of a rotary-barrel cannon in a Soviet aircraft.) Fitted with laser range finder and target seeker for the use of laser-guided missiles.

The SNA Flogger-K is apparently configured as a strike-reconnaissance aircraft.

There is a MiG-23UB (Flogger-C) two-seat training version.

Status: Initial operational capability for MiG-23 in 1970; IOC for MiG-27 in 1975–1976. The MiG-27 Flogger is currently in production. It is also produced in India. (The MiG-23 is flown by several other nations.)

Crew:	1
Engines:	1 Tumansky R-29-300 turbojet; 17,635 lbst (7,999 kgst); 25,350 lbst (11,499 kgst) with afterburner
Weights:	empty 18,078 lb (8,200 kg)
	clean loaded T/O 34,170 lb (15,500 kg)
	maximum T/O 44,313 lb (20,100 kg)
Dimensions:	span 46 ft 9 in (14.25 m) extended
	span 27 ft 6 in (8.38 m) swept
	length 52 ft 6 in (16.0 m)
	height 18 ft (5.5 m)
Speed:	1,056 mph (1,700 km/h) above 36,090 ft (11,000 m) Mach 1.6 clean
	685 mph (1,102 km/h) at 1,000 ft (305 m) Mach 0.95
Ceiling:	52,493 ft (16,000 m)
Range:	radius 210 miles (390 km) with 4,410 lbs (2,000 kg) of bombs/missiles
	+2 AA-2 Atoll air-to-air missiles
	+centerline fuel tank (208 U.S. gal)
Armament:	1 six-barrel 23-mm cannon
	5 pylons + 2 bomb racks for up 8,820 lbs (4,000 kg) of external stores including AS-7 Kerry air-to-surface missiles
Radar:	High Lark (ranging radar)

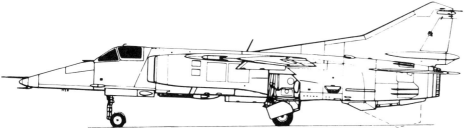

MiG-27 Flogger-D.

A Flogger-K in flight with a prominent pitot tube in the nose. Most ground-attack variants have a laser range finder in the extreme nose with a Swift Rod electronics antenna and the pitot head offset to starboard. The ventral tail fin retracts upward for landing and takeoff.

Su-17 Fitter-C/D

This is a ground-attack fighter with variable-sweep wings that evolved from the Su-7 fixed-wing strike fighter. The Fitter was the first land-based fighter aircraft to be flown by SNA since about 1960.

The Fitter-C is a variable-geometry aircraft, with a streamlined configuration based on a single, high-powered AL-21F engine. The outer wing sections, fitted with slats and trailing-edge flaps, are used primarily to aid STOL takeoff and landing. The aircraft suffers from limited internal fuel and is generally seen with two large drop tanks (294 U.S. gallons each) on twin fuselage pylons. The Fitter-C has an advanced weapon-aiming system with six or eight pylons for more than 7,000 lbs (3,150 kg) of weapons and drop tanks; two 30-mm cannon are fitted in the wing roots.

Designations: The Su-7/Fitter-A was a fixed-wing variant; the Su-7IG/Fitter-B was the test model for the variable-geometry aircraft; the Su-17/Fitter-C/D/H/K are single-seat variants; Su-22/Fitter-F/J are export models; and the Su-17/Fitter-E/G and Su-22/Fitter-G are two-seat trainers. Soviet-flown variants, including the Fitter-C, have sometimes been referred to as the Su-20; the exact correlation between the design bureau designations and NATO code names is not clear.

Status: A modified Su-7 served as a test bed for the variable-geometry aircraft and was first observed publicly in 1967. The definitive Su-27 Fitter-C was first seen in 1970. Fitters are flown by Soviet Air Forces and SNA as well as by several other nations.

About 70 Fitter-C aircraft were in SNA service in 1989; subsequently, some 100 Fitter-D and possibly Fitter-C aircraft were transferred to the Navy from the Soviet Air Forces in 1989–1990.

Crew:	1
Engines:	1 Lyulka AL-21F-3 turbojet; 24,200 lbst (11,000 kgst) with afterburner.
Weights:	empty 22,046 lbs (10,000 kg)
	normal T/O 30,865 lbs (14,000 kg)
	maximum T/O 38,940 lbs (17,700 kg)
Dimensions:	span 45 ft 3 in (13.8 m) fully extended
	span 34 ft 10 in (10.0 m) fully swept
	length 50 ft 6 in (15.4 m) fuselage
	length 61 ft 6 in (18.75 m) over nose probe
	height 15 ft 7 in (4.75 m)
Speed:	maximum 1,333 mph (2,133 km/h) at 36,000 ft (11,000 m) Mach 2.0
	sea level 790 mph (1,246 km/h) (clean) Mach 1.05
	sea level with external stores approx. 590 mph (685 km/h) Mach 0.8
Ceiling:	59,050 ft (18,000 m)
Range:	radius 390 miles (625 km) with 4,400 lbs (2,000 kg) external stores on hi-lo-hi mission; 225 miles (360 km) with same load on lo-lo-lo mission
Armament:	2 NR-30 30-mm cannon [140 rounds]
	7,000 lbs (3,150 kg) external stores (bombs, rockets, missiles, including AA-2 Atoll air-to-air missiles; AS-9 anti-radar missiles; and probably AS-7 Kerry air-to-surface missiles)
Radar:	High Fix (air intercept)

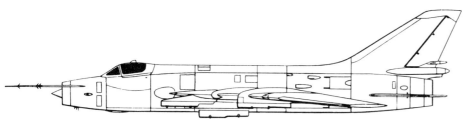

Su-17 Fitter-C.

A Fitter-C making a landing approach. These fighter-attack aircraft and the later Flogger-D/K aircraft provide a tactical strike capability to support naval and amphibious operations.

A Fitter fighter-attack aircraft with two drop tanks fitted under the wing and a pair of air-to-air missiles attached to the wing gloves. (U.S. Navy)

ELECTRONIC/RECONNAISSANCE AIRCRAFT

An-74 Madcap

The Madcap is an Airborne Early-Warning (AEW) version of the An-72/74 Coaler cargo aircraft. It is reported that this version may be flown from Soviet aircraft carriers of the UL'YANOVSK class. This is a highly maneuverable aircraft with STOL characteristics.

The An-72 has twin turbofan engines mounted on the upper surface of the wing and extending forward, close to the fuselage. This engine placement allows the jet exhaust to create what is known as the "Coanda effect" which significantly increases lift when the flaps are lowered. (This engine arrangement was also used in the U.S. YC-14 cargo aircraft.) Also contributing to STOL performance are the combination of double-slotted and triple-slotted flaps on the wing trailing edge and full-span leading edge slats.

The Madcap AEW variant has a large, flat rotodome mounted on the tailfin. The unusual location of the rotodome is due to the placement of the engines; a more conventional dorsal mounting would expose the rotodome to interference and damage from the engine exhaust.

If adapted for carrier operation, the Madcap would be the world's largest carrier-based aircraft following the U.S. Navy decision in 1988 to discontinue operating the A-3/A3D Skywarrior aboard ship.

Status: First flight of An-72 in 1977. The An-72/74 are in service with the Soviet Air Forces. Only a few An-74A Madcap variants have been produced.

COALER

Crew:	4 (pilot, copilot, navigator, flight engineer) + AEW mission crew
Engines:	2 Lotarev D-36 turbofan; 14,330 lbst (6,514 kgst)
Weights:	maximum T/O 76,060 lbs (34,500 kg)
Dimensions:	span 104 ft 7½ in (31.89 m)
	length 92 ft 1¼ in (28.07 m)
	height 28 ft 4½ in (8.65 m)
Speed:	normal cruise 342 mph (550 km/h)
	maximum cruise 438 mph (705 km/h)
Ceiling:	34,450 ft (10,500 m)
Range:	with payload of 16,534 lbs (7,500 kg) 2,796 miles (4,500 km)
Radar:	. . . . . . (air search) in AEW
	. . . . . . (navigation Doppler)

Then-Secretary of Defense Frank Carlucci and President Mikhail Gorbachev examine Soviet aircraft—at right is an An-72A Coaler transport; behind them is the tail of an An-74 Madcap AEW aircraft. (Courtesy John W.R. Taylor)

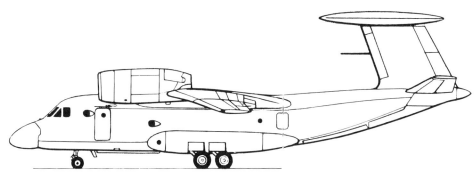

An-74 Madcap.

Tu-20 Bear-D

The Tu-20 Bear was developed as a strategic bomber and has been in Soviet service for over three decades. The Bear-F is an ASW aircraft (see below) while the Bear-D is configured for long-range reconnaissance and for targeting anti-ship missiles, especially the ship/submarine-launched SS-N-3 Shaddock and SS-N-12 Sandbox missiles. (Other Bear models are flown by Soviet strategic aviation in the missile strike and photo-reconnaissance roles.)

The only turboprop-propelled strategic bomber to achieve operational service with any air force, the Bear is a large, swept-wing aircraft with four turboprop engines turning contra-rotating, four-blade propellers. The plane's long range can be further extended through in-flight refueling; a fixed receiving probe fitted in the nose. Defensive armament consists of up to three 23-mm twin gun mounts (dorsal, ventral, and tail). The Bear-D carries no offensive weapons and is fitted with the Big Bulge surface-search radar and a Video Data Link (VDL), called Drambuie by Western intelligence, for transmitting target data to missile-launching ships.

The Bear's engines, wing, tail assembly, and other components were used for the Tu-114 *Rossiya* (NATO Cleat) civilian airliner,

the world's largest civil passenger aircraft before the Boeing 747. The Bear also was the basis for the Tu-114D Moss, a Soviet AWACS (Airborne Warning And Control System) aircraft.

Designation: Tu-95 is the Tupolev design bureau designation, which is sometimes used (incorrectly) in the West to indicate military versions of the aircraft, which the Soviets at least initially designated Tu-20.

Status: First flight 1954; the aircraft entered service with strategic aviation in 1955 with SNA receiving its first Bear-D in the mid-1960s. SNA flies some 45 Bear-D reconnaissance-targeting aircraft assigned to the Northern and Pacific fleets.

(Approximately 250 to 300 Bear bomber aircraft were built into the mid-1960s, with production of the D and then F models following. Subsequently, production of the Bear-H to carry the AS-15 strategic cruise missile began in the early 1980s, with older bombers converted to the Bear-G to carry the AS-4 variant. The aircraft remains in service with Soviet strategic aviation as a missile strike aircraft and possibly a few Bear-E aircraft in the photo-reconnaissance role.)

BEAR-D

Crew:	
Engines:	4 Kuznetsov NK-12MV turboprop; 12,000 shp each
Weights:	empty approx. 165,000 lbs (75,000 kg)
	maximum T/O 356,000 lbs (160,200 kg)
Dimensions:	span 159 ft 1 in (48.5 m)
	length 155 ft 10 in (47.5 m)
	height 38 ft 8½ in (11.8 m)
Speed:	cruise 465 mph (750 km/h)
	maximum 575 mph (925 km/h)

Ceiling:	service 41,000 ft (12,500 m)
Range:	7,750+ mi (12,500+ km)
Armament;	up to 6 NR-23 23-mm cannon (twin dorsal, ventral, tail turrets)
Radar:	Big Bulge-A (surface search)
	Box Tail (gunfire control)
	Short Horn (surface search-missile guidance?)

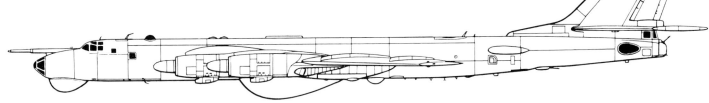

Tu-20 Bear-D.

The Bear is one of the most attractive aircraft flying today—a propeller-driven anachronism in the jet age. The contra-rotating propellers of this Bear-D are clearly visible in this view; a refueling probe protrudes from the nose. There are 23-mm dorsal, ventral turret, and turret gun turrets; the small chin radome is visible as are several electronic blisters. (U.S. Navy, Lt. Dana Barclay)

This view of a Bear-D shows discoloring under the wings from the exhaust of the aircraft's turboprop engines, the large Big Bulge-A radome, and the ventral and tail 23-mm gun turrets.

MARITIME PATROL/ASW AIRCRAFT

Be-40 Mermaid

The Be-42 Albatross—with the Beriev design bureau designation A-40—is the world's only turbojet/fan amphibian and the world's largest flying boat. The Navy has apparently not yet ordered the aircraft; however, a SAR variant designated Be-40 and a smaller, derivative commercial version designated Be-200 are being offered. Reportedly, *Aeroflot* plans to buy 100 of the latter. Albatross is the Soviet name; the NATO code name is Mermaid.

The new flying boat has a large, shoulder-mounted wing with moderate sweep, fitted with high-lift devices such as leading-edge slats or flaps, and slotted training-edge flaps. The engine nacelles are mounted on the fuselage "shoulders," in line with the wing trailing edges. There are fixed wingtip floats and a tall T-shaped tail with a Magnetic Anomaly Detection (MAD) "stinger" protruding (as in the Bear-F). A fixed refueling probe is fitted.

"The design of this aircraft began when the question of defending the Soviet Union from submarines was high on the agenda," admitted Alexander Batkov, head of the scientific directorate of the Ministry of Aircraft Industry, in an exclusive interview with the British magazine *Flight International*.[2] Batkov continued: "Now we would like to show the A-40 first as a technology demonstrator, secondly as a multipurpose aircraft and lastly as an example of [industrial] conversion."

The A-40 is apparently the long-awaited successor to two Soviet maritime patrol/ASW aircraft of questionable effectiveness—the Il-38 May and the Be-12 Mail. A new land-based ASW aircraft has been anticipated for some time. The surprise is that the aircraft is a flying boat. The last Soviet flying boat design known to have reached the flight test stage was the Be-10 Mallow, a multi-mission aircraft developed by the Beriev design bureau, formerly headed by G.M. Beriev, who died in 1979. The Be-10 was a swept-wing, twin-turbojet aircraft that was reported by the Soviets to be suitable for ASW, anti-ship, and minelaying operations. Setting a world flying-boat record of 566.7 mph (906.7 km/h) in 1961, the aircraft bore a superficial resemblance to the much larger U.S. Navy–Martin P6M Seamaster flying boat. (The cancelled U.S. aircraft was to have been employed primarily as an aerial minelayer although it

2. Boris Rybak, "Albatross by a Head," *Flight International*, 17 April 1991, p. 36.

may have eventually been employed as a nuclear strike aircraft.) Four preproduction Be-10 Mallow flying boats were publicly displayed in 1961. Although they were without any indication of carrying radar or MAD equipment, tail warning and a tail gun position were evident on the planes. No further Soviet production of the Be-10 was observed.

The Beriev design bureau produced the A-40. The designation TAG-D indicated the location where the prototype was observed, Taganorog, on the Sea of Azov.

The estimated characteristics of the A-40 are shown below. The power plant of two Lotarev D-18T turbofan engines, each with 51,588 pounds static thrust, is expected to produce a maximum speed of up to 600 mph (960 km/h) (Mach 0.9) with a mission profile of three hours on station at a range of some 1,500 miles (2,400 km) from base. Total mission endurance is expected to be ten hours. ASW torpedoes and depth bombs as well as mines are expected to be carried, with MAD, sonobuoys, radar, and electronic surveillance employed for submarine detection. Anti-ship missiles would also be carried.

The commercial derivative has the designation A-200 and is envisioned as a much lighter aircraft with a related reduction in performance. Potential commercial uses for the A-200 variant include search-and-rescue, fire-fighting, cargo, and passenger transport. In its military configuration the aircraft could accommodate up to 60 passengers; as a specialized transport about 100 passengers could be carried. A cargo variant would carry 37 passengers plus 6.5 metric tons of cargo with a range of 3,100 miles (5,000 km).

Crew:	
Engines:	2 Lotarev D-18T turbofan; 51,588 lbst (23,449 kgst) each
Weights:	empty approx. 176,370 lbs (80,168 kg)
	maximum T/O approx. 330,693 lbs (150,315 kg)
Dimensions:	span approx. 164 ft (50.0 m)
	length approx. 164 ft (50.0 m)
Speed:	
Ceiling:	
Range:	
Armament:	torpedoes, depth bombs
Radar:	

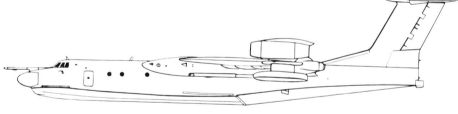

A-40 Albatross.

The Albatross was largely a surprise to the Western intelligence community as Soviet development of a new flying boat was unexpected. The large, graceful aircraft has two large turbofan engines mounted above the fuselage, aft of the swept wings. The aircraft has a stepped hull, fixed refueling probe, T-tail, and small rudder at the after end of the boat hull. (Sovfoto)

Tu-142 Bear-F/J

The Bear-F is the ASW derivative of the Tu-20/95 Bear aircraft (see below). The F variant is a larger, new production aircraft, configured specifically for long-range ASW; the Bear-J is a VLF communications relay aircraft, similar to the U.S. Navy's EC-130 Hercules and E-6 Hermes TACAMO aircraft.[3]

In comparison with the earlier Bear aircraft, the Bear-F incorporates several changes over previous models: it has been lengthened by a plug approximately 5 ft 9 in (1.75 m) inserted ahead of the wing, the tail fin enlarged, and the inboard engine nacelles enlarged (lengthened by 6 ft/1.8 m and widened). A redesigned wing incorporates double-slotted flaps in place of the plain flaps previously used, the wing fuel tankage has been slightly increased, and the crew rest and galley facilities improved.

The basic Bear-F was succeeded in production by the Mod I, which omitted the chin-mounted radar and returned to the smaller inboard engine nacelles; the Mod II has a revised flight deck with a related fuselage lengthening of 9 in (23 cm); the Mod III deleted the electronic sensors from the tailplane tips and added a Magnetic Anomaly Detector (MAD) boom projecting aft from the rudder top; and the Mod IV introduced a thimble radome in the nose as well as a chin-mounted multi-sensor radome, and an antenna group under the tail. All are fitted with a fixed in-flight refueling probe.

In addition to ECM, radar, and MAD, the Bear-F carries expendable sonobuoys for detecting submarines. These can be released through the after portion of the tandem weapons bays or from a smaller stores bay farther aft in the fuselage. The Bear-F can carry out ASW attacks with a large payload of homing torpedoes and depth bombs carried in the internal weapons bays (the other naval variants—the Bear-D/J—do not carry weapons). There is a 23-mm tail gun mount; a second, retractable dorsal mount may be fitted.

There is also a naval Bear-J aircraft employed as a VLF communications relay aircraft for strategic missile submarines (a role similar to the U.S. Navy's TACAMO program). This aircraft has a large antenna housing in the weapons bay position with blade antennas

3. TACAMO is an acronym for Take Charge And Move Out.

atop the fuselage; there is a shallow radome in the dorsal position, probably housing a satellite antenna and under-nose and tail sensor mountings are provided. The familiar side-viewing blisters in the tail are deleted in the Bear-F Mod IV as well as the Bear-J; only tail guns appear fitted in the F/J variants.

Designation: The Bear-F and Bear-J have the bureau designation Tu-142.

Status: The Bear-F entered SNA service in 1970 and the Bear-J in 1985. SNA flies some 60 Bear-F ASW aircraft, with production continuing at Kuibyshev. Only a small number of Bear-J aircraft have been produced. All of the Bear-F/J aircraft are assigned to the Northern and Pacific fleets.

India has purchased six Tu-142M Bear-F aircraft for the maritime patrol role with deliveries beginning in 1988; it is the only nation other than the USSR to fly the Bear.

BEAR-F

Crew:	
Engines:	4 Kuznetsov NK-12MV turboprop; 12,000 shp each
Weights:	empty approx. 165,000 lbs (75,000 kg)
	T/O 413,600 lbs (188,000 kg)
Dimensions:	span 167 ft 1 in (51.2 m)
	length 162 ft 4 in (49.5 m)
	height 39 ft 8 in (12.1 m)
Speed:	cruise 465 mph (750 km/h)
	maximum 575 mph (925 km/h)
Ceiling:	service 41,000 ft (12,500 m)
Range:	7,750+ mi (12,500+ km)
	radius 3,100 miles (5,000 km)
Armament:	2 NR-23 23-mm cannon (tail turret)
	17,600+ lbs (8,000+ kg) of torpedoes, depth bombs, mines
Radar:	Wet Eye (surface search)
	Box Tail (gunfire control)

Tu-142M Bear-F Mod IV.

A Bear-J variant of the Tu-142 configured as a communications link between the Soviet high command and strategic missile submarines at sea. What appears to be a MAD antenna is fitted atop the tail fin (in some Bear-J aircraft it faces forward); there is a ventral pod for the trailing-wire antenna beneath the fuselage, just aft of the large radome; there are two flat radomes forward (as in Bear-F); the 23-mm tail gun mount is retained.

A Bear-F with a MAD antenna atop the tail fin; on a few aircraft they point *forward*. These aircraft do not have a chin radome but have a navigation radar and a Wet Eye surface search radar in ventral domes. The ventral and dorsal 23-mm gun turrets are deleted. (U.S. Navy)

The Bear-F has a large weapons bay with twin doors immediately aft of the Wet Eye radar, and there is a third, smaller weapons bay farther aft. Depth bombs, torpedoes, and sonobuoys are normally carried, although mines could probably be delivered by these aircraft. (The naval Bear-D aircraft do not carry weapons.)

Il-38 May

Generally resembling the U.S. P-3 Orion patrol aircraft in appearance and role, the May is believed to be the first Soviet land-based aircraft designed from the outset for the maritime patrol/ASW mission. The aircraft was adopted from Il-18 Coot transport (much the same as the Orion was adapted from the commercial Lockheed Electra).

The May is a large, low-wing aircraft with four turboprop engines. The fuselage is lengthened from the original Il-18 design, and the wings have been strengthened and mounted farther forward. A radome is fitted under the forward fuselage, a MAD antenna boom extends from the tail, and there is an internal weapons bay for torpedoes, mines, and depth bombs. Expendable sonobuoys and non-acoustic sensors are also carried, and the plane has a computerized tactical evaluation system. No defensive armament is fitted.

(The Il-18 Coot ELINT aircraft are variants of the original passenger configuration and not of the Il-38 May.)

Status: The aircraft apparently flew in prototype form in 1967–1968 and entered squadron service in 1970. Several aircraft have been transferred to India. (Some Mays were flown with Egyptian markings until 1972 but were subsequently removed from Egypt.) About 45 remain in SNA service.

Crew:	12
Engines:	4 Ivchyenko AI-20M turboprop; 4,200 shp + 495 lbst (223 kgst) each
Weights:	empty 79,200 lbs (36,000 kg)
	maximum T/O 139,700 lbs (63,500 kg)
Dimensions:	span 122 ft 8 in (37.4 m)
	length 129 ft 10½ in (39.6 m) over MAD boom
	height 33 ft 4 in (10.16 m)
Speed:	cruise 250 mph (400 km/h)
	maximum 370 mph (600 km/h)
Ceiling:	
Range:	4,465 mi (7,200 km)
Endurance:	12 hours
Armament:	torpedoes, depth bombs, mines
Radar:	Wet Eye (surface search)

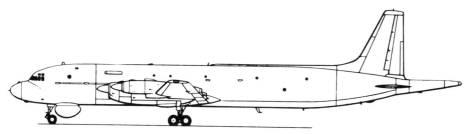

Il-38 May.

The May land-based patrol/anti-submarine aircraft was produced in relatively small numbers and has not enjoyed the wide use of its Western counterparts, especially the Lockheed P-3 Orion series. Note the four turboprop engines and the long MAD "stinger" in the tail. (U.S. Navy)

A May with its weapons bay open and the Wet Eye radar clearly visible. The aircraft was lengthened from the Il-18 Coot design to provide space for the weapons bay. (U.S. Navy)

Be-12 Mail

The Mail is one of the few flying boats remaining in first-line naval service. SNA flies some 90 of these amphibians for maritime patrol, ASW, and search-and-rescue operations. The Soviet designation for this aircraft is both Be-12 and M-12 and its popular Russian name is *Tchaika* ("seagull").

This is the last aircraft in a long line of Beriev flying boats produced in the Soviet Union. The Mail has distinctive gull-shaped wings, twin tail, and other features seen in the earlier, piston-engine Be-6 Madge. (China may continue to fly a few Be-6 flying boats.) The Mail has an elongated radome protruding from a glazed nose, and a MAD boom some 15 feet (4.6 m) protruding from the tail. The twin turboprop engines are mounted high on the wings. The main landing gear and tail wheel retract fully into the boat hull; the wingtip floats are non-retractable. Torpedoes, mines, and depth bombs can be carried on a pylon under each wing and in an internal weapons bay fitted in the after section of the hull. Expendable sonobuoys can also be carried. There are two small weapon pylons for rockets beneath each wing, outboard of the engines.

Status: First flight in February 1959; entered SNA service in 1964. Operational only in SNA although they were flown with Egyptian markings from 1968 to 1972 for surveillance of U.S. naval operations in the Mediterranean. More than 200 Be-12s were produced at Taganorog by the early 1970s with about 90 remaining in SNA service. Three aircraft were transferred to Vietnam in 1981, the only aircraft of this type to be flown by other nations.

Crew:	5 or 6
Engines:	2 Ivchyenko AL-20D turboprop; 4,190 shp each
Weights:	empty 47,850 lbs (21,700 kg)
	maximum T/O 64,790 lbs (29,450 kg)
Dimensions:	span 97 ft 5½ in (29.71 m)
	length 98 ft 11½ in (30.17 m)
	height 22 ft 11½ in (7.0 m) on undercarriage
Speed:	cruise 200 mph (320 km/h)
	maximum 380 mph (610 km/h)
Ceiling:	37,000 ft (11,280 m)
Range:	2,480 mi (4,000 km)
Endurance:	15 hours
Armament:	torpedoes, depth bombs, mines
Radar:	A304 (surface search)

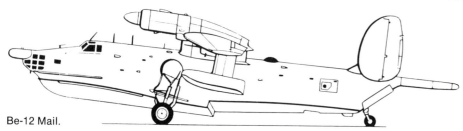

Be-12 Mail.

A Mail on the beach with its landing gear extended. There is an internal, fuselage weapons bay, and weapons can be carried on wing pylons.

Maintenance personnel check a Mail's turboprop engines before flight.

The Mail continues in Soviet service, providing a limited-endurance patrol/ASW/search-and-rescue platform. Some missions will be taken over by the Albatross, but only the outdated May and Mail now provide these capabilities for the Baltic and Black Sea–Mediterranean areas. (Royal Navy)

CARGO/SPECIAL PURPOSE AIRCRAFT

The aircraft listed below are those cargo-type aircraft known to be employed by SNA for ELINT, reconnaissance, and research purposes. Several other aircraft of this category are flown by SNA in the cargo and utility roles.

Il-20 Coot-A

The Coot-A is a naval ELINT aircraft derived from the basic Il-18, a turboprop-powered transport that was in wide use during the 1960s and early 1970s with *Aeroflot,* the Soviet national airline, on both domestic and international routes. In the late 1970s a modified version of the Coot was observed flying in the ELINT role, designated Coot-A by NATO.

The aircraft is a low-wing, four-turboprop aircraft of conventional design. The improved Il-18D civilian variant carries up to 122 passengers. Several aircraft have been configured for research projects with Il-18D aircraft configured for polar research operating in the Antarctic and from Arctic drift stations. The Coot-A ELINT version has a large, side-looking radar beneath the forward fuselage in a "canoe" housing estimated to be 10.25 m long and 1.15 m in diameter; other antennas are faired into the fuselage, including a large "hump" on the left forward side of the fuselage (approximately 4.4 m long and 0.88 m in diameter).

Status: In operational service as a civilian airliner and, in limited numbers, as a research and ELINT aircraft. The first flight took place in July 1957 with estimates of total production ranging from 600 to 900 aircraft. The ELINT versions are probably conversions of civilian or military passenger aircraft. The first Coot-A was observed in early 1978. Although being phased out of Aeroflot, it is still flown by several Eastern European nations as well as North Korea and Vietnam.

Il-18D/E (transport)

Crew:	5 + 122 passengers
Engines:	4 Ivchyenko AI-20M turboprop; 4,250 ehp each
Weights:	empty 77,000 lbs (35,000 kg)
	maximum T/O 140,800 lbs (64,000 kg)
Dimensions:	span 122 ft 9 in (37.4 m)
	length 117 ft 9 in (35.9 m)
	height 33 ft 4 in (10.17 m)
Speed:	cruise 390 mph (625 km/h)
	maximum cruise 420 mph (675 km/h)
Ceiling:	26,250–32,800 ft (8,000–10,000 m)
Range:	2,480 mi (4,000 km) with 29,700-lb (13,500 kg) payload; 4,030 mi (6,500 km) with 14,300 lbs (6,500 kg)
Armament:	none
Radar:	. . . . . . (navigation)

A Coot-A ELINT aircraft overflying a NATO exercise. Unlike the Il-38 May, the Coot-A is externally almost identical to the civilian Il-18 aircraft except for various antennas, including the large Side-Looking Aircraft Radar (SLAR) fitted in the under-fuselage "canoe." (Royal Navy)

An-22 Cub

The An-12 Cub is a cargo/transport aircraft, one of the most important aircraft of this category in Soviet military and civilian operation. Several planes have been configured for the ECM and ELINT roles and at least one Cub has been observed as an ASW systems test bed. The Soviet designation for the basic cargo/transport aircraft is An-12BP.

The Cub evolved as a militarized version of the An-10 Cat transport. The aircraft has a high-wing configuration to provide clear cargo space and has four turboprop engines. Similarly, the main landing gear is housed in pods on the fuselage to avoid cutting into floor space. The sharply upswept rear fuselage incorporates an underside rear-loading ramp. A tail-gun position for a twin 23-mm turret is provided in most aircraft (some with civilian markings), although there is no fire-control radar. In the cargo role up to 44,090 lbs (20,015 kg) of material can be lifted. A variety of military electronic configurations of the Cub have been observed since 1970. The Cub-B designation covers ECM aircraft, with antenna domes faired into the fuselage and tail (no tail turret); Cub-C is used for ELINT configurations, with ventral antenna housings and other features indicating the capability of "ferreting" electronic intelligence. In the early 1980s a Cub was identified in the ASW role, apparently as a systems test bed.

Status: First flight 1955; the first flight of the military An-12PB variant took place in 1958. About 850 aircraft produced. In the cargo/transport role the Cub is widely used by the Soviet Air Forces as well as those of other Warsaw Pact and Third World air arms. Some electronic aircraft—civilian and military—fly with *Aeroflot* markings, and some Cubs in an electronic configuration have been seen with Egyptian markings.

CUB-A (transport)

Crew:	6 (including tail gunner) + 100 troops
Engines:	4 Ivchyenko AI-20K turboprop; 4,000-shp each
Weights:	empty 61,600 lbs (28,000 kg)
	maximum T/O 134,200 lbs (61,000 kg)
Dimensions:	span 124 ft 8 in (38.0 m)
	length 108 ft 7 in (33.1 m)
	height 34 ft 6½ in (10.53 m)
Speed:	cruise 360 mph (580 km/h)
	maximum cruise 415 mph (670 km/h)
Ceiling:	33,450 ft (10,200 m)
Range:	2,230 mi (3,600 km) with 22,000 lbs (10,000 kg) payload
Armament:	2 23-mm NR-23 cannon in some aircraft (tail turret)
Radar:	Toad Stool (navigation)

This electronics-configured Cub has civilian (*Aeroflot*) markings; it is fitted with large electronic blisters in the cheek position, on the after-loading ramp, and under the tail-gun position (no guns fitted).

A Cub-B ELINT aircraft in naval markings; the aircraft has ventral radomes and a flat antenna in the dorsal position (behind the wing). Twin 23-mm guns are fitted in the tail position.

HELICOPTERS

The length is the overall length of fuselage, excluding main and tail rotor blades.

Ka-27/Ka-29 Helix

This Kamov-designed Helix is the successor to the Ka-25 Hormone as a ship-based ASW helicopter. The Ka-29 Helix-B variant is a troop transport employed by Soviet Naval Infantry and Helix-D is a search-and-rescue variant. A modified Helix with two large, box-like fairings on each side of the fuselage, observed on the ADMIRAL KUZNETSOV, may be an early-warning aircraft.

The Helix is similar in appearance to the Hormone, having the familiar contra-rotating rotors of Kamov helicopters of the past 40 years. The Helix is substantially larger and the empennage has a horizontal stabilizer with twin fins (the Hormone has three fins). The Helix-A anti-submarine systems include radar, dipping sonar, and sonobuoys, with an internal weapons bay for torpedoes and depth charges. Maximum endurance is 4½ hours.

The Helix-B has two pylons for weapons on either side and space for about 12 troops. The "chin" position pod carries various electronic sensors (no radar as fitted in the Helix-A/C); the Helix-B variant has various infrared jamming and electronic surveillance devices.

Designation: The civil version is designated Ka-32; a Ka-32S variant with more comprehensive avionics is intended for use on the larger civilian icebreakers. The export variants are designated Ka-28.

Status: The Helix-A became operational in 1980 and was first observed at sea on board the ASW destroyer UDALOY in September 1981. (Two helicopters were embarked, one in standard Soviet naval markings and one in *Aeroflot* colors.) The Helix-D was first observed in 1981. Eighteen Helix ASW helicopters have been or-

dered by the Indian Navy. About 75 Helix-A helicopters are in SNA service plus several of other variants.

The naval variants are:

Ka-27	Helix-A	anti-submarine variant.
Ka-27B	Helix-B	troop carrier variant (Ka-29).
Ka-27TB	Helix-B	assault/gunship variant (Ka-29).
Ka-27PS	Helix-D	search-and-rescue variant.

HELIX-A

Crew:	4 or 5
Engines:	2 Isotov TV3-117VK turboshaft; 2,200 shp each
Weights:	normal T/O 24,200 lbs (11,000 kg)
	maximum T/O 27,720 lbs (12,600 kg)
Dimensions:	length 36 ft 1 in (11.0 m)
	rotor diameter 54 ft 11 in (16.75 m)
Speed:	cruise 143 mph (230 km/h)
	maximum 161 mph (260 km/h)
Ceiling:	19,680 ft (6,000 m)
Range:	radius 185 mi (300 km)
Armament:	torpedoes, depth bombs
Radar:	. . . . . . (surface search)

HELIX-B

Crew:	2 + approx. 12 troops
Engines:	2 Isotov TV3-117VK turboshaft; 2,200 shp each
Weights:	maximum T/O 26,455 lbs (12,000 kg)
Dimensions:	length 36 ft 1 in (11.0 m)
	rotor diameter 54 ft 11 in (16.75 m)
Speed:	maximum 164.5 mph (265 km/h)
Ceiling:	11,483 ft (3,500 m)
Range:	310 mi (550 km)
Armament:	4 pylons for AT-6 Spiral anti-tank missiles or 57-mm or 80-mm rocket pods
Radar:	none

The Helix generally resembles its predecessor, the Hormone. The later helicopter is larger, has only two tail fins, and different equipment. The chin radome houses a search radar (and lateral searchlights in the Helix-A/C); the cases on the side of the fuselage house emergency flotation gear. (Royal Navy)

Rear view of a Helix ASW helicopter with the dipping sonar lowered. The quadracycle landing gear of the Hormone is retained. (Royal Navy)

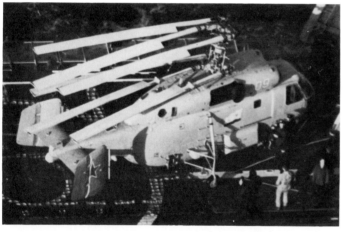

The twin rotors of the Helix fold for shipboard storage—here on board the destroyer UDALOY—while the lack of a tail rotor and supporting structure facilitates the handling of Kamov helicopters on board ship. A Helix with dipping sonar lowered is illustrated in chapter 29.

Mi-14 Haze

This is a land-based ASW and mine countermeasures helicopter, developed as a replacement for the less-capable and outdated ASW configuration of the Mi-4 Hound. It is the only amphibious helicopter flown by the Warsaw Pact. The Haze is too large for the elevators of the helicopter ships of the MOSKVA class or aircraft carriers of the KIEV class. Both the Haze and Hip helicopters have been observed taking on sweep gear from surface minesweepers.

The Haze is a derivative of the Mi-8 helicopter (see below), using the basic power plant and dynamic components of the Hip-C (early Mi-14s had TV2-117 engines). The two helicopters differ primarily in the fuselage configuration and installed equipment. The ASW configuration has an amphibious hull with stabilizing sponsons on each side that house the main wheels of the tricycle undercarriage. A surface-search radar is fitted in the "chin" position, with the dome projecting beneath the hull. The Haze-A has towed MAD gear, expendable sonobuoys, and a dipping sonar, and can carry ASW homing torpedoes. (The earlier versions had TV3-117A turboshaft engines each developing 1,900 shp.)

A mine countermeasures version that tows a "sled" is designated Haze-B; a search-and-rescue Haze-C version has a double-width sliding door (left side), retractable rescue hoist, searchlight on each side of fuselage, and enlarged floats.

Status: The first flight of the Haze occurred in September 1969; it entered service with SNA in 1975. About 100 Haze-A helicopters are in SNA service plus a number of the other variants with production continuing. These helicopters have also been transferred to Bulgaria, Cuba, Ethiopia, East Germany, North Korea, Libya, Poland, Romania, Syria, Vietnam, and Yugoslavia.

The naval variants of the Haze are:

Mi-14PL	Haze-A	anti-submarine variant.
Mi-14BT	Haze-B	mine countermeasures variant.
Mi-14PS	Haze-C	search and rescue variant.

Crew:	4 to 6
Engines:	2 Isotov TV3-117 turboshaft; 2,200 shp each
Weights:	empty 15,026 lb (6,816 kg)
	maximum T/O 30,865 lbs (14,000 kg)
Dimensions:	length 60 ft 34 in (18.31 m)
	rotor diameter 68 ft 10¾ in (21.29 m)
	height 22 ft 7¾ ft (6.9 m)
Speed:	cruise 140 mph (225 km/h)
	maximum 161 mph (260 km/h)
Ceiling:	service 14,760 ft (4,500 m)
	hover IGE 6,235 ft (1,900 m)
	hover OGE 2,625 ft (800 m)
Range:	radius 155 mi (250 km)
Armament:	torpedoes, depth bombs
Radar:	. . . . . . (surface search) fitted under nose
	. . . . . . (Doppler) under tail boom

The Soviet Navy operates a large number of land-based ASW helicopters of the Haze-A type. The Haze is derived from the Mi-8 Hip, configured with a boat hull; a radome is fitted in the chin position, a dipping sonar is lowered from the rear of the cabin, and a MAD detector is carried at the rear of the cabin. (U.S. Navy)

Haze-A ASW helicopter in flight, showing details of the fuselage, towed MAD head, and small, stabilizing float under the tail boom. The Haze—like the Helix and Hormone—has an internal weapons bay. (U.S. Navy)

Mi-8 Hip-C

The Hip is the primary transport helicopter of the Soviet armed forces and has been flown by about 30 other nations. The Navy has employed the Hip as a land-based transport and in the minesweeping role. The helicopter carrier LENINGRAD has operated the Hip in mine clearing operations; however, it is too large for the ship's elevators and remains on the flight deck when embarked.

The basic Hip design has a five-blade main rotor and a three-blade tail rotor driven by two turboshaft engines. A fixed tricycle landing gear is fitted. There are clamshell doors at the rear of the cabin. Up to 8,820 lbs (4,000 kg) of cargo can be carried internally. External fuel tanks can be fitted.

Status: The Hip-C is the production version, the A/B having been prototypes; the E/F models are assault helicopter/gunships fitted with anti-tank missiles. The first flight of the Mi-8 occurred in 1962, and it was introduced into Soviet military service in 1967.

HIP-C

Crew:	2 + 26 troops
Engines:	2 Isotov TV2-117A turboshaft; 1,700 shp each
Weights:	empty 15,972 lbs (7,260 kg)
	loaded 26,400 lbs (12,000 kg)
Dimensions:	length 59 ft 7 in (18.17 m)
	rotor diameter 69 ft 10 in (21.29 m)
Speed:	cruise 111.5 mph (180 km/h)
	maximum 155 mph (250 km/h)
Ceiling:	hover OGE 2,625 ft (800 m)
	hover IGE 6,232 ft (1,900 m)
	service 14,760 ft (4,500 m)
Range:	radius 185 miles (300 km)
Armament:	none
Radar:	none

The multi-purpose Hip helicopter is used by both the Soviet Navy and Naval Infantry. This helicopter has a flexible 12.7-mm machine gun in the nose and three pylons on each side of the cabin for rockets and anti-tank missiles. The Hip has been employed in the aerial minesweeping role from the MOSKVA-class helicopter carriers.

Ka-25 Hormone

The Hormone is the principal Soviet ship-based ASW and missile-targeting helicopter, being found on board the KIEV and MOSKVA carriers, as well as in various cruiser classes and auxiliary ships. There are two principal versions, the A for anti-submarine operations and the B for missile targeting. The C model is flown in the utility and rescue roles.

The Ka-20 Harp was the prototype for the Hormone, with the earlier aircraft being publicly seen for the first time in July 1961, flying at a Soviet aviation display with two dummy missiles fitted on its fuselage. The Hormone has a distinctive configuration with a compact fuselage, two contra-rotating rotors driven by twin turboshaft engines, a short tail boom supporting a multi-fin empennage, and a quadricycle landing gear. The rotor arrangement alleviates the need for a tail boom to facilitate shipboard handling; the main rotors also fold. Some helicopters have inflatable flotation bags attached to the landing gear in the event the helicopter has to come down at sea. The Hormone-B can partially retract its landing gear to avoid interference with operation of its search radar.

The Hormone-A ASW configuration has the Puff Ball surface search radar, expendable sonobuoys, dipping sonar that can be lowered while the helicopter is hovering, and an internal weapons bay for ASW homing torpedoes or depth bombs. An electro-optical sensor has been seen on some helicopters. The Hormone-B is fitted with the larger Big Bulge-B radar for surface surveillance radar and can transmit targeting data via VDL to surface ships and submarines armed with anti-ship missiles. The Hormone-C is a utility/passenger variant that can carry 12 passengers. None has been observed armed with air-to-surface missiles, as indicated they would be by the Ka-20 prototype.

(The helicopter is used as a civilian flying crane in the Ka-25K version; the following characteristics are primarily for the civil version.)

Status: The Hormone entered operational service in 1967, going to sea that year in the MOSKVA and Kresta II cruiser classes. Hormone-A helicopters have been transferred to India and Yugoslavia. About 100 Hormone-A helicopters are in SNA service plus lesser numbers of other variants.

Crew:	4 or 5
Engines:	2 Glushenkov GTD-3F turboshaft; 900 shp each
Weights:	empty 10,485 lbs (4,765 kg)
	loaded 16,500 lbs (7,500 kg)
Dimensions:	length 32 ft (9.75 m)
	rotor diameter 51 ft 6 in (15.7 m)
Speed:	cruise 120 mph (193 km/h)
	maximum 136 mph (220 km/h)
Ceiling:	service 11,480 ft (3,500 m)
Range:	radius 155 mi (250 km)
Armament:	torpedoes, depth bombs
Radar:	Puff Ball (surface search) in Hormone-A
	Big Bulge-B (surface search) in Hormone-B

A Hormone-A ASW variant that has been modified to carry larger torpedoes than can be accommodated in the helicopter's internal weapons bay; a wire reel is fitted on the port side, forward of the main cabin door (partially open); above the stubby tail boom is a cylindrical radome.

The over-the-horizon targeting variant of the Ka-25, the Hormone-B can be identified by the spherical Big Bulge-B radar under the nose, the lack of a weapons bay, and a cylindrical radome beneath the rear of the cabin. Hormones are often seen with auxiliary fuel tanks fitted to the sides of the fuselage.

A Hormone-A ASW helicopter landing on board the carrier MINSK. Sonobuoys are fitted; the paired turboshaft engines are mounted directly above the cabin. The Ka-25 has the four-wheel landing gear common to many Kamov helicopters.

The large VSTOL carrier MINSK moored at Vladivostok. The ship has seen little operational service in recent years, the result of the cutback in naval operations and—according to some reports—engineering problems. The MINSK has an extended port-side sponson to support twin 30-mm Gatling guns and their Bass Tilt fire control director. (1990, Greenpeace photo courtesy Messrs. William Arkin and Joshua Handler)

RBU-2500

Sixteen-barrel launcher arranged in two rows of eight; can be trained and elevated. Manual reloading. Formerly designated MBU-2500.

Maximum range:	2,730 yds (2,500 m)
Barrel length:	5 ft 3 in (1.6 m)
Projectile diameter:	
Projectile weight:	250 mm
Warhead weight:	46 lbs (21 kg)
IOC:	1957
Platforms:	*frigates* Riga, Petya I
	corvettes Poti
	auxilliary ships SMOL'NYY

Crewmen load an RBU-2500 ASW rocket launcher.

RBU-1200

Five barrels, with three mounted over two; the tubes elevate but do not train. Manual reloading. Formerly designated MBU-1800.

Maximum range:	1,310 yds (1,200 m)
Barrel length:	4 ft 7 in (1.4 m)
Projectile diameter:	250 mm
Projectile weight:	154 lbs (70 kg)
Warhead weight:	75 lbs (34 kg)
IOC:	1958
Platforms:	*corvettes* Pauk, T-58
	minesweepers Gorya (?), Natya
	auxiliary ships Mayak (ASW training units)

RBU-1000

Six barrels in two vertical rows of three that can be trained and elevated. Automatic reloading. Formerly designated MBU-4500.

Maximum range:	1,095 yds (1,000 m)
Barrel length:	5 ft 11 in (1.8 m)
Projectile diameter:	300 mm
Projectile weight:	198 lbs (90 kg)
Warhead weight:	121 lbs (55 kg)
IOC:	1962
Platforms:	*cruisers* Kara, Kresta I/II
	destroyers Kashin, SOVREMENNYY
	auxiliary ships BEREZINA

RBU-1000 ASW rocket launcher on the cruiser KERCH; a loading hatch is visible at the front of the launcher's base. (Eric Grove)

NAVAL GUNS

130-mm/70-caliber DP (twin)[2]

These are fully automatic guns of recent design. With the demise of the SVERDLOV-class light cruisers with 152-mm guns, these are the largest guns in the Soviet Navy. They have water cooling. The range of the gun exceeds that of the earlier 152-mm guns fitted in the SVERDLOV class (see 4th edition, page 412).

Muzzle velocity:	3,280 ft/sec (1,000 m/sec)
Rate of fire:	approx. 30 rounds per minute per mount
Maximum range:	30,620 yds (28,000 m)
Effective range:	
Elevation:	−15° to +85°
Projectile weight:	
Fire control radar:	Kite Screech
Platforms:	*cruisers* KIROV (later units), SLAVA
	destroyers SOVREMENNYY

2. Gun barrel length is determined by multiplying the inner diameter of the barrel by the caliber. Thus, the 130-mm/70 gun has a length of 9,100 mm, or approximately 30.3 feet.

The after 130-mm/70-cal twin gun mount on the SOVREMENNYY-class destroyer BOYEVOY. There are cooling hoses under the barrels of the rapid-fire guns. (West German Navy)

100-mm/70-caliber DP (single)

This is a rapid-fire, water-cooled gun fitted in Soviet warships from mid-1970s. Only the first unit of the KIROV-class battle cruisers has this weapon, with later units being fitted with 130-mm guns, as is the fourth KIEV-class carrier.

Muzzle velocity:	
Rate of fire:	80 rounds per minute
Maximum range:	16,400 yds (15,000 m)
Effective range:	8,750 yds (8,000 m)
Elevation:	
Projectile weight:	
Fire control radar:	Kite Screech

Platforms:		
	carriers	ADMIRAL GORSHKOV (ex-BAKU)
	cruisers	KIROV (1 unit)
	destroyers	UDALOY
	frigates	Krivak II/III, NEUSTRASHIMYY

Single-barrel 100-mm/70-cal gun mount on the destroyer UDALOY; note the cooling hose under the barrel.

100-mm/56-caliber SP (single)

This outdated dual-purpose gun is fitted in shields rather than fully enclosed mounts. Their limited elevation limits anti-aircraft effectiveness. They were developed in the 1930s and updated for installation from 1947 in postwar Soviet ships.

Muzzle velocity:	2,788 ft/sec (850 m/sec)
Rate of fire:	15 rounds per minute
Maximum range:	17,500 yds (16,000 m)
Effective range:	10,930 yds (10,000 m)
Elevation:	−5° to +40°
Projectile weight:	30 lbs (13.5 kg)
Fire control radar:	Wasp Head director with Sun Visor-B; Top Bow

Platforms:		
	frigates	Riga
	auxiliary ships	Don

Single-barrel 100-mm/56-cal gun mount on Riga-class frigate with Wasp Head/Sun Visor-B at right; these mounts have gun shields with the rear open. (U.S. Navy)

76.2-mm/59-caliber DP (twin)

These are rapid-fire gun mounts in Soviet surface warships and auxiliary ships. They have been fitted in ships completed from the early 1960s. Soviet designation is AK-276.

Muzzle velocity:	2,952 ft/sec (900 m/sec)
Rate of fire:	45 rounds per minute per barrel
Maximum range:	anti-air 10,930 yds (10,000 m)
Effective range:	anti-air 6,560–7,650 yds (6,000–7,000 m)
Elevation:	+80°
Projectile weight:	35 lbs (16 kg)
Fire control radar:	Hawk Screech or Owl Screech

Platforms:		
	carriers	KIEV
	cruisers	Kara, Kynda
	destroyers	Kashin
	frigates	Koni, Krivak I, Mirka, Petya
	auxiliary ships	IVAN SUSANIN, SMOL'NYY

Twin-barrel 76.2-mm/59-cal mount in a Kara-class cruiser. On the pyramid structure forward the Top Sail radar antenna and Side Globe EW domes are visible. (T. Matsumoto, © Asahishimbun AERA)

76.2-mm/59-caliber DP (single)

Fully automatic gun installed in corvettes and small combatants from the late 1970s onward. In these ships they have generally replaced 57-mm guns, providing an increase in weapon range and a considerable increase in warhead potency. Soviet designation is AK-176.

Muzzle velocity:	
Rate of fire:	120 rounds per minute per barrel
Maximum range:	anti-surface 15,300 yds (14,000 m)
	anti-air 10,930 yds (10,000 m)
Effective range:	anti-air 6,560–7,650 yds (6,000–7,000 m)
Elevation:	+85°
Projectile weight:	35 lbs (16 kg)

Fire control radar: Bass Tilt
Platforms: *frigates*   Grisha V, Parchim II
                       corvettes   Nanuchka III, Pauk, Svetlak,
                         Tarantul
                       small combatants Gorya, Matka, Mukha, Muravey,
                                          Slepen

The 76.2-mm/59-cal single mount is found on several Soviet corvette and small combatant classes—such as this Nanuchka III in the Far East—as part of the "upgunning" of smaller Soviet warships. There is a 30-mm Gatling gun forward of the 76.2-mm mount. (JMSDF)

57-mm/80-caliber AA (twin)

This is a fully automatic weapon installed in a variety of ships of various sizes. The barrels are water cooled. In service from the early 1960s.

Muzzle velocity: 3,281 ft/sec (1,000 m/sec)
Rate of fire: 110 t0 120 rounds per minute per barrel
Maximum range: anti-surface 13,120 yds (12,000 m)
                     anti-air 7,325 yds (6,700 m)
Effective range: anti-air 5,470–6,560 yds (5,000–6,000 m)
Elevation: +85°
Projectile weight: 6 lbs (2.8 kg)
Fire control radar: Bass Tilt or Muff Cob
Platforms: *carriers*   Moskva
                     cruisers   Kresta I/II
                     frigates   Grisha I/II
                     corvettes   Nanuchka I, Poti
                     small combatants Turya
                     amphibious   Ropucha
                     auxiliary ships Berezina, Boris Chilikin,
                                        Manych, Ugra

Sailors maintain the twin 57-mm/80-cal rapid-fire, anti-aircraft gun mounts on Parchim I–class corvettes. Note the water-cooling tubes and jackets. (Bredow courtesy Alfred Albusberger)

57-mm/70-caliber AA (single, twin, quad)

This is a widely used weapon, installed in a variety of ships since the 1950s.

Muzzle velocity: 2,953–3,281 ft/sec (900 to 1,000 m/sec)
Rate of fire: 120 rounds per minute per barrel
Maximum range: anti-surface 9,840 yds (9,000 m)
                     anti-air 6,560 yds (6,000 m)
Effective range: anti-surface 8,750 yds (8,000 m)
                     anti-air 4,920 yds (4,500 m)
Elevation: +90°
Projectile weight: 6 lbs (2.8 kg)
Fire control radar: Hawk Screech or Muff Cob
Platforms: *corvettes*   T-58
                     minelayers   Alesha
                     minesweepers   Sasha
                     amphibious   Alligator
                     auxiliary ships Don, Lama

This is a quad mounting of the 57-mm/70-cal gun found in several older Soviet ship classes. The destroyers armed with this weapon—a Kanin is shown here—are being retired. (*The Boston Globe*)

45-mm/85-caliber AA (single)

This is a semi-automatic weapon that was mounted principally in older destroyers in a quad mounting. Only the Sasha-class minesweepers now have mount. Operational in Soviet ships from about 1955.

Muzzle velocity:	2,952 ft/sec (900 m/sec)
Rate of fire:	75 rounds per minute per barrel
Maximum range:	anti-surface 9,840 yds (9,000 m)
	anti-air 7,650 yds (7,000 m)
Effective range:	anti-surface 4,375 yds (4,000 m)
	anti-air 4,150 yds (3,800 m)
Elevation:	+90°
Projectile weight:	4.8 lbs (2.2 kg)
Fire control radar:	Hawk Screech (in destroyers); none in minesweepers
Platforms:	*minesweepers* Sasha

37-mm/60-caliber AA (twin)

These semi-automatic anti-aircraft mounts are fitted in older surface combatants. Initial operational capability about 1949.

Muzzle velocity:	2,953 ft/sec (900 m/sec)
Rate of fire:	160 rounds per minute per barrel
Maximum range:	anti-surface 10,170 yds (9,300 m)
	anti-air 6,125 yds (5,600 m)
Effective range:	anti-surface 4,375 yds (4,000 m)
	anti-air 3,280 yds (3,000 m)
Elevation:	+80°
Projectile weight:	1.5 lbs (0.7 kg)
Fire control radar:	none
Platforms:	*destroyers* Skoryy
	frigates Riga
	minesweepers T-43

Twin 37-mm/60-cal gun mount. The gun crew wears Soviet-style steel helmets except for the telephone talker, who wears a "soft helmet" with earphones and holds a microphone.

30-mm/65-caliber close-in (multi-barrel)

This is a close-in weapon intended to defeat incoming anti-ship missiles. This gun was introduced in the late 1960s. The mounting has six 30-mm barrels within a larger, rotating cylinder—popularly referred to as a Gatling gun for the American machine gun inventor John Gatling. It is similar in concept to the U.S. Navy's 20-mm/76-caliber Mk 15 Phalanx Close-In Weapon System (CIWS). The Soviet weapon was originally reported to have a 23-mm barrel diameter. An optical backup director is provided in some ships; in a few units only the optical director is provided.

Paired 30-mm Gatling guns are provided in the new Combined Air Defense System (CADS-1), which has self-contained radars and can mount up to eight SA-N-11 short-range missiles (see below). The system first appeared on the third ship of the KIROV class, the KALININ, followed by the aircraft carrier ADMIRAL KUZNETSOV. It may also be fitted in the NEUSTRASHIMYY-class frigate. (All other ships listed below have the standard "single" multi-barrel gun mount.)

Designation: The Soviet designation is AK-630 and the NATO designation is ADMG-630.

Muzzle velocity:	3,280 ft/sec (1,000 m/sec)
Rate of fire:	3,000 rounds per minute per mount
Maximum range:	
Effective range:	547–656 yds (500–600 m)
Elevation:	+90°
Projectile weight:	
Fire control radar:	Base Tilt (see notes)
Platforms:	
carriers	ADMIRAL KUZNETSOV, KIEV
cruisers	KARA, KIROV, Kresta I/II, Kynda
destroyers	Kashin, SOVREMENNYY, UDALOY
frigates	Grisha III, NEUSTRASHIMYY
corvettes	Nanuchka III, PARCHIM II, Pauk, Tarantul
small combatants	Babochka, Matka, Sarancha, Slepen
amphibious	IVAN ROGOV
landing craft	Lebed
auxiliary ships	BAL'ZAM, BEREZINA, IVAN SUSANIN

The twin 30-mm multi-barrel guns of a CADS-1 system in the cruiser KALININ point skyward. There are canvas covers over the muzzles. The SA-N-11 short-range missiles are fitted above the gun housings; see page 381. (Royal Navy)

The Soviet 30-mm/65-cal multi-barrel gun mount was the world's first Gatling-type gun to be fitted on ships. Unlike the U.S. 20-mm Phalanx gun system, which has its fire control radar atop the gun housing, the Soviet weapon's radar and optical controls are separate.

30-mm/65-caliber close-in (twin)

These are fully automatic, close-in defense weapons introduced into the Soviet Navy about 1960. The theoretical rate of fire is reported to be 1,050 rounds per minute per barrel, but 200–240 rounds is the maximum realistic firing rate. The gun mount is belt-fed from a 1,000-round magazine. There is a backup optical director (designated Kolonka-I).

Designation: The Soviet designation is AK-230.

Velocity:	3,444 ft/sec (1,050 m/sec)
Rate of fire:	approx. 1,000 rounds per barrel per minute
Maximum range:	anti-surface 4,375 yds (4,000 m)
	anti-air 5,465 yds (5,000 m)
Effective range:	anti-surface 2,735 yds (2,500 m)
	anti-air 2,735–3,280 yds (2,500 to 3,000 m)
Elevation:	+85°
Projectile weight:	1.2 lbs (0.54 kg)
Fire control radar:	Drum Tilt (or optical director)
Platforms:	*destroyers* Kanin, SAM Kotlin
	frigates Koni
	small combatants Osa, Shershen, Stenka
	minesweepers various classes
	amphibious Polnocny
	landing craft Aist, Utenok
	auxiliary ships various classes

Twin 30-mm/65-cal twin gun mounts on board a SAM Kotlin-class destroyer; their Drum Tilt fire control radar is at left, one deck higher. (U.S. Navy)

25-mm/60-caliber AA (twin)

These weapons are fitted in open, shielded, and fully enclosed twin mounts. Operational from the early 1950s.

Muzzle velocity:	2,953 ft/sec (900 m/sec)
Rate of fire:	150–200 rounds per minute per barrel
Maximum range:	anti-surface 4,375 yds (4,000 m)
Effective range:	anti-surface 2,515 yds (2,300 m)
	anti-air 3,280 yds (3,000 m)
Elevation:	+85°
Projectile weight:	0.75 lbs (0.34 kg)
Fire control radar:	none
Platforms:	*frigates* Riga
	small combatants Smel, Turya, Natya, Sonya, T-43
	amphibious Alligator
	auxiliary ships Amga, Don, Mayak, Oskol

NAVAL MINES

The Soviet Navy is estimated to maintain a stockpile of between 250,000 and 425,000 naval mines, several times the number available to the U.S. Navy. Many of these mines date to World War II; however, most are newer weapons. Among the newer mines are several deep-water types, apparently capable of being planted in depths of at least 3,000 feet (915 m). These include "rising" mines that are fitted with passive acoustic detection and, like the U.S. Navy's Mk-60 CAPTOR mine, release an anti-submarine weapon that homes on submarine targets.

Analyses of Soviet literature indicate that the Soviet Navy has developed influence mines of all types—homing mines, rising mines, and remotely controlled mines. The most recent development is the Underwater Electrical Potential (UEP) mine, which uses the short-range electric potential of submarines to activate the mine.

Minelaying is exercised by naval aircraft, surface ships, and submarines. Many classes of cruisers, destroyers, and frigates as well as small combatants (including minesweepers) have mine rails, while most submarines can carry mines in place of torpedoes at the ratio of one or two mines per torpedo, depending upon the type of mine.

The relative distances at which the Soviets can sow mines was addressed by the NATO Supreme Allied Commander Atlantic:

> They pose distinct threats to our reinforcement and resupply of [Europe]. Their mining of the entrances to the Norwegian Sea, although the depth of water sometimes does not accommodate all of the mines that they are capable of laying, will pose threats to our naval combatants passing into the Norwegian Sea as they attempt to contain the Soviet northern fleet and the Warsaw Pact navies in that area of the world.[3]

The Soviets have provided relatively modern mines to other nations, as evidenced by the planting of Soviet mines in the Gulf of Suez and Red Sea during July 1985 by a Libyan merchant ship. Eighteen merchant ships of various flags were damaged between 9 July and 20 September. Following a multi-nation sweeping operation, a single, bottom-laid KMD-series mine of recent Soviet manufacture (1981) was recovered from a depth of 150 feet (46 m). The canister-shaped weapon was 10 feet (3 m) long and 21 inches (533 mm) in diameter and held only a fraction of its warhead capacity estimated at 1,500 pounds (675 kg) of high explosives. The reduced charge led British naval analysts to conclude that the effort was intended only to scare shippers and not sink ships.[4]

During the conflict between Iraq and Iran in the 1980s, the Iranians laid mines in the Persian Gulf. An Iranian ship was captured by U.S. forces in 1987 carrying M-08 mines of Russian design and North Korean manufacture.

The intense Soviet interest in mine warfare is also demonstrated by the Navy's large coastal and ocean-going mine countermeasures forces; see chapter 19.

The mines following have been publicly identified; they are arranged in alphabetical order by their Soviet designation with exceptions as noted.

AMG-1

Aircraft-laid moored contact mine. The mine is laid like a bomb, without a parachute, from low altitudes.

Weight:	1,080 lbs (486 kg) + 1,200-lb (540-lb) anchor
Warhead:	575 lbs (260 kg)
Depth:	minimum 30 ft (9 m)
	maximum 100 ft (330 m)
Platforms:	aircraft
IOC:	1939

3. Adm. Wesley L. McDonald, USN, Supreme Allied Commander Atlantic (NATO) and Commander in Chief U.S. Atlantic Command, testimony before Armed Services Committee, Senate, 27 February 1985.

4. For an analysis of the Libyan mining operation see Dr. Scott C. Truver, "Mines of August: An International Whodunit," U.S. Naval Institute *Proceedings*, May 1985, pp. 94–117.

AMD-500

The AMD-series mines are air-dropped versions of the MKD mine series. These are bottom influence mines; mods provide for magnetic, acoustic, pressure, and combination influence. (The suffix number refers to the weight of the mine.)

Weight:	1,100 lbs (495 kg)
Warhead:	660 lbs (300 kg)
Depth:	minimum 16 ft (5 m)
	maximum 230 ft (70 m)
Platforms:	aircraft
	surface ships
IOC:	

AMD-1000

Bottom influence mine similar to the AMD-500 but larger.

Weight:	2,205 lbs (1,000 kg)
Warhead:	1,540 lbs (700 kg)
Depth:	minimum 16 ft (5 m)
	maximum 655 ft (200 m)
Platforms:	aircraft
	surface ships
IOC:	

BPM-2

This is a small limpet mine for use by swimmers against hostile ships and underwater installations.

Weight:	
Warhead:	7 lbs (3 kg)
Depth:	limited by swimmer capability
Platforms:	swimmers
IOC:	

Cluster Bay

Moored rising mine with an influence (acoustic homing) warhead.

Weight:	
Warhead:	510 lbs (230 kg)
Depth:	minimum 265 ft (80 m)
	maximum 655 ft (200 m)
Platforms:	submarines
IOC:	

Cluster Gulf

Moored rising mine with an influence (acoustic homing) warhead.

Weight:	
Warhead:	510 lbs (230 kg)
Depth:	minimum 265 ft (80 m)
	maximum 6,560 ft (2,000 m)
Platforms:	submarines
IOC:	

KB-1

An improved version of the venerable M-08 series of moored contact mines. The KB-1 has a five-horn array and is intended specifically for Arctic use.

Weight:	
Warhead:	510 lbs (230 kg)
Depth:	minimum
	maximum 525 ft (160 m)
Platforms:	surface ships
IOC:	

KMD-500

The KMD is a bottom influence mine (mods for magnetic, acoustic, pressure, and combination influence). These mines may have been derived from German mine technology.

Weight:	1,100 lbs (500 kg)
Warhead:	660 lbs (300 kg)
Depth:	minimum 16 ft (5 m)
	maximum 230 ft (70 m)
Platforms:	surface ships
IOC:	late 1940s

KMD-1000

Enlarged version of the KMD-500.

Weight:	2,205 lbs (1,000 kg)
Warhead:	1,540 lbs (700 kg)
Depth:	minimum 16 ft (5 m)
	maximum 655 ft (200 m)
Platforms:	surface ships
IOC:	late 1940s

KRAB

This is a moored influence mine.

Weight:	
Warhead:	510 lbs (230 kg)
Depth:	minimum 60 ft (18 m)
	maximum 885 ft (270 m)
Platforms:	surface ships
IOC:	

M-08

Moored contact mine developed before World War I but still in use by several nations. Those used by Iran in the Persian Gulf were manufactured in North Korea.

Weight:	
Warhead:	varies; 265 lb (120 kg) maximum
Depth:	minimum 20 ft (6 m)
	maximum 360 ft (110 m)
Platforms:	surface ships
IOC:	1908

These are M-08 mines of Russian design and North Korean manufacture that are still in use. (Those shown here were captured by the U.S. Navy in the Persian Gulf in 1987.) This type of mine demonstrates the variety of mines available to Soviet forces—from these whose design dates from 1908(!) to modern, acoustic homing weapons. Note contact "horns" on these mines. (U.S. Navy, PH3 Henry Cleveland)

M-12
Moored contact mine.

Weight:	1,320 lbs (600 kg)
Warhead:	255 lbs (115 kg)
Depth:	minimum 20 ft (6 m)
	maximum 360 ft (110 m)
Platforms:	surface ships
IOC:	1912

M-26
Moored contact mine.

Weight:	
Warhead:	530 lbs (240 kg)
Depth:	minimum 20 ft (6 m)
	maximum 460 ft (140 m)
Platforms:	surface ships
IOC:	1926

M-31
Moored contact mine.

Weight:	
Warhead:	440 lbs (200 kg)
Depth:	
Platforms:	aircraft
IOC:	1931

MAG
Moored contact mine specifically for use against submarines. It could be used with or without horns fitted.

Weight:	980 lbs (445 kg) + 1,415-lb (640-kg) anchor
Warhead:	510 lbs (230 kg)
Depth:	minimum 262 ft (80 m)
	maximum 1,510 ft (460 m)
Platforms:	surface ships
IOC:	

MIRAB
Bottom influence (magnetic induction) mine. Designed for air launch, the mine's casing was too fragile; subsequently laid only by surface ships.

Weight:	616 lbs (277 kg)
Warhead:	145 lbs (65 kg)
Depth:	minimum 33 ft (10 m)
	maximum
Platforms:	surface ships
IOC:	1928

MKB
Moored contact or influence mine.

Weight:	980 lbs (445 kg) + 1,415-lb (640-kg) anchor
Warhead:	510 lbs (230 kg)
Depth:	minimum 30 ft (9 m)
	maximum 885 ft (270 m)
Platforms:	surface ships
IOC:	

(mobile influence mine)
This is a self-propelled mine launched from submarine torpedo tubes; acoustic influence. (The Soviet designation is not known.)

Weight:	
Warhead:	
Depth:	minimum 130 ft (40 m)
	maximum 230 ft (70 m)
Platforms:	submarines
IOC:	

MYaM
Small moored contact mine with three chemical horns. These mines were used in the Korean War (1950–1953) by North Korean forces.

Weight:	142 lbs (64 kg) + 243-lb (110-kg) anchor
Warhead:	45 lb (20 kg)
Depth:	minimum 10 ft (3 m)
	maximum 197 ft (60 m)
Platforms:	surface ships
IOC:	

PLT-3
Submarine-laid moored contact mine with four horns.

Weight:	2,220 lbs (1,000 kg)
Warhead:	220 lbs (100 kg)
Depth:	minimum 30 ft (9 m)
	maximum 420 ft (128 m)
Platforms:	submarines
IOC:	

PLT-150
Submarine-laid moored contact mine.

Weight:	
Warhead:	330 lbs (150 kg)
Depth:	
Platforms:	submarines
IOC:	1924

R
Small ship-laid, moored contact mine; intended for shallow water use. (R was the U.S. designation; Soviet designation unknown.)

Weight:	
Warhead:	22 lbs (10 kg)
Depth:	minimum 20 ft (6 m)
	maximum 115 ft (35 m)
Platforms:	surface ships
IOC:	

R-1
Similar in concept to R-type mine. (Soviet designation unknown.)

Weight:	235 lbs (105 kg) + 352-lb (158-kg) anchor
Warhead:	90 lbs (40 kg)
Depth:	minimum 10 ft (3 m)
	maximum 115 ft (35 m)
Platforms:	surface ships
IOC:	1940s

TURTLE
Swimmer-planted limpet mine. No details are publicly available. (Turtle is U.S. designation.)

UEP (underwater electrical potential) mine
Advanced anti-submarine mine; very difficult to counter.

Weight:	
Warhead:	500 lbs (227 kg)
Depth:	maximum 1,610 ft (490 m)
Platforms:	submarines
	surface ships
IOC:	1980s

VZD-1M
Swimmer-planted limpet mine. No details are publicly available.

YAM
Small, moored contact mine for use by surface ships and small craft; suitable for use in shallow water. This mine was employed by both Iraq and Iran in the Persian Gulf conflict of the 1970s. It was first reported to have been used in the Korean War.

Weight:	142 lbs (64 kg) + 243-lb (110-kg) anchor
Warhead:	44 lbs (20 kg)
Depth:	minimum 9 ft (2.75 m)
	maximum 167 ft (50 m)
Platforms:	surface ships
IOC:	

YARM
Small mine similar to the YAM.

Weight:	
Warhead:	7 lbs (3 kg)
Depth:	
Platforms:	surface ships
IOC:	

MISSILES

The missiles currently known to be in use with the Soviet Navy are described below. Some of the air-launched missiles are also used by Soviet strategic and tactical aviation. All weapons in the naval missile designation schemes—even those no longer in service—are listed to provide continuity.

Designations. Soviet missiles are given designations in two NATO schemes, one of which assigns an alpha-numeric serial and the other a code name. The serial number indicates the launch platform and target with the following primary designations:

AS   = Air-to-Surface
SA   = Surface-to-Air
SS   = Surface-to-Surface
            (also underwater-to-surface)
SSC   = Surface-to-Surface Coastal
SUW   = Surface-to-Underwater (Weapon)

The additional letter N is added to the designation of all missiles except air-launched weapons to indicate naval use; NX is used to indicate naval missiles that are under development.

The NATO code names, which are not assigned to all missiles, indicate the launch platform and target with the following initial letters:

G   = surface-to-air
K   = air-to-surface
S   = surface-to-surface (also underwater-to-surface and
           underwater-to-underwater)

Soviet strategic aviation also has the AS-4/5/15 and possibly AS-6 missiles, mainly for use against ground targets but with the AS-4 and possibly some others having a secondary capability against surface ships.

Details of Soviet missile designations are not publicly known. Known Soviet names and designations are provided; the suffix M indicates *Morskoy* (naval) or *Modifikatsirovanny* (modification).

Characteristics. The characteristics provided are approximate, based mainly on published U.S. Department of Defense and other Western estimates.

AIR-TO-SURFACE MISSILES

Beyond the missiles listed here, a stealth (low radar cross section), high speed (Mach 3+) air-to-surface missile is believed to be under development for Soviet Naval Aviation.

AS-12 Kegler
Anti-radiation missile; possibly developed from the AS-9 missile.

Weight:
Length:
Span:
Propulsion:
Range:
Guidance: anti-radar homing
Warhead: conventional
Platforms: Fencer
IOC: mid-1980s

AS-10 Karen
Advanced tactical air-to-surface missile with electro-optical guidance. Speed is about 0.9. A longer range variant of this missile has been reported with the designation AS-14.

Weight: 882 lbs (400 kg)
Length: 11 ft 6 in (3.5 m)
Span:
Diameter: 12 in (305 mm)
Propulsion: solid-fuel rocket
Range: 6 n.miles (9.5 km)
Guidance: electro-optical
Warhead: 220 lb (100 kg) conventional
Platforms: Fitter-D

AS-9 Kyle
High-speed, Mach 3 attack missile for use against radar installations.

Weight: 1,430 lbs (650 kg)
Length: approx. 19 ft 9 in (6.03 m)
Span:
Propulsion: turbojet
Range: 43–54 n.miles (80–100 km)
Guidance: anti-radar homing
Warhead: 330 lbs (150 kg) conventional
Platforms: Backfire
                   Badger
                   Fencer
                   Fitter-C/D
IOC: late 1970s

AS-7 Kerry
Tactical missile that can be carried by naval Fitter and Forger fighter-attack aircraft. Speed is approximately Mach 1. The Soviet name for the missile is *Grom*.

Weight: 882 lbs (400 kg)
Length: 11 ft 6 in (3.5 m)
Span: 3 ft 1 in (1.1 m)
Propulsion: solid-propellant rocket
Range: approx. 7 n.miles (13 km)
Guidance: radio command and radar homing
Warhead: 220 lbs (100 kg) conventional
Platforms: Fitter-C/D
                   Forger
IOC: late 1970s

AS-6 Kingfish
This is an advanced anti-ship missile, believed to have been developed for use from the Backfire bomber. However, up to press time of this edition the AS-6 has been observed only on Badger aircraft. A flight profile similar to the AS-4 is estimated with maximum speed of Mach 2.5 to 3.5. Range varies with flight (altitude) profile.

Weight: 10,780 lbs (4,900 kg)
Length: 34 ft 5½ in (10.5 m)
Span: 7 ft 10 in (2.4 m)
Propulsion: turbojet
Range: 350 n.miles (652 km); 150 n.miles (275 km) low altitude
Guidance: inertial and terminal (1) active radar or (2) anti-radar homing
Warhead: 350 KT nuclear or 2,200 lbs (1,000 kg) conventional
Platforms: Backfire-B/C (?)
                   Badger-G
IOC: early 1970s

AS-6 Kingfish anti-ship missile on the wing of a Badger-G strike aircraft. Badgers can carry up to three anti-ship missiles, one under each wing and one semi-recessed in the weapons bay.

AS-5 Kelt

Improved anti-ship missile that replaced the AS-1 Kennel in the anti-ship role. Speed is Mach 0.9 to 1.2. Range varies with flight (altitude) profile.

Weight:	10,340 lbs (4,700 kg)
Length:	27 ft 10 in (8.5 m)
Span:	15 ft 9 in (4.8 m)
Propulsion:	liquid-fuel rocket
Range:	175 n.miles (326 km); 90 n.miles (170 km) low altitude
Guidance:	inertial and terminal (1) active radar or (2) anti-radar homing
Warhead:	2,200 lbs (1,000 kg) conventional or nuclear
Platforms:	Badger-G
IOC:	1965–1966

AS-4 Kitchen

The AS-4 was developed as a stand-off, anti-ship missile for the Bear and Blinder bombers, first seen in 1961 on the Blinder-B of the strategic air forces. It has been subsequently adopted for the Backfire-B. (SNA Blinders and Bears do not carry missiles.) The ventral fin of the AS-4 folds to starboard while carried aboard the launching aircraft. After launch from medium altitude (approximately 20,000 ft/6,100 m), the missile climbs steeply to achieve a high cruise altitude and speeds estimated at between Mach 2.5 and 3.5, and then dives steeply at its target.

It is carried by SNA Backfire bombers and Soviet Air Forces Bear-G bombers; previously it was carried by Air Forces Blinder-B aircraft.

The Soviet name for the missile is *Burya*.

Weight:	14,300 lbs (6,500 kg)
Length:	37 ft 1 in (11.3 m)
Span:	11 ft (3.35 m)
Propulsion:	turbojet
Range:	148–250 n.miles (275–465 km); 150 n.miles (275 km) low altitude
Guidance:	inertial and terminal (1) active radar or (2) anti-radiation homing
Warhead:	nuclear or 2,200 lbs (1,000 kg) conventional
Platforms:	Backfire-B/C
	Bear-G
IOC:	1967

AS-4 Kitchen anti-ship missile under the fuselage of a Backfire-B strike aircraft.

AS-3 Kangaroo

This was a strategic-attack missile fitted with a nuclear warhead carried by the Bear-B/C bombers of Soviet strategic aviation. Range was estimated at more than 199 n.miles (370 km). The Bear-B/C aircraft have been reconfigured to the Bear-G variant to carry the AS-4 missile.

AS-2 Kipper

This anti-ship missile, carried by Badger-C/G strike aircraft, has probably been phased out of Soviet service in favor of the AS-5. The AS-2 became operational in 1961; it carried a 2,200-lb (1,000-kg) conventional or nuclear warhead and had active radar guidance. See 4th edition, page 420.

AS-1 Kennel

This was probably the first fully operational Soviet air-to-surface missile, designated Komet in Soviet service. Development started in 1946 or possibly earlier for launching from the Tu-4 Bull, the Soviet copy of the Boeing B-29 Superfortress, and subsequently the Tu-16 Badger. Admiral Gorshkov had implied that the missile was developed for use on surface ships, but limitations of the engine dictated that it be used only from aircraft.[5] The land-based SSC-2b Samlet coastal defense missile, which has been phased out of the Soviet armed forces, was a variant of this weapon.

SURFACE-TO-AIR MISSILES[6]

SA-N-( )

The Soviet Navy is believed to have developed at least two surface-to-air missile systems for use from submarines. Deployment on a limited basis began in the early 1980s in the Tango and Kilo classes. Subsequently, surface-to-air missiles have been reported in some later nuclear-propelled submarines. These weapons may be adaptations of the SA-N-5/SA-N-8 missiles.

The missile is probably launched from just below the surface or with the submarine's sail partially awash. (A fully submerged submarine can detect aircraft with a towed passive sonar array.)

Britain has developed a submarine anti-aircraft missile system with the Blowpipe missile, the launcher extending from the sail and out of the water for firing. The U.S. Navy has looked at several submarine-launched missile concepts, one dubbed "Subwinder" (based on the Sidewinder missile) and, more recently, the SIAM (Self-Initiating Anti-aircraft Missile); neither Britain nor the United States has plans to deploy such missiles.

SA-N-11

This is the missile component of the CADS-1 combined air defense system fitted in Soviet ships since 1989. The CADS-1 can accommodate up to eight SA-N-11 missiles (as well as two 30-mm Gatling guns). The entire mount trains and elevates, bringing all weapons to bear on the target. Unlike the previous close-in gun systems in Soviet ships, CADS-1 has autonomous search and track radars (similar to the U.S. Phalanx CIWS).

The SA-N-11 may be a navalized version of the ground-launched SA-19 missile. It is loaded and launched from a disposable canister.

The KIROV-class battle cruiser KALININ introduced the new weapon system in place of the standard "single" 30-mm Gatling guns; the KALININ installation was followed by the aircraft carrier ADMIRAL KUZNETSOV. It is also fitted in the new NEUSTRASHIMYY-class frigate.

There is a land-based version of the naval mount, the 2S6, which entered service with Soviet Ground Forces (army) in 1988; the system has the NATO code name M-1986, the missiles are designated SA-19, and the self-contained acquisition and fire control guidance radars are designated Hot Shot. The 2S6 also has an electro-optical system, and there are some indications that the missile may be laser guided.

The following data reflect the SA-19 missile.

Weight:		
Length:	6 ft 7 in (2.0 m)	
Span:		
Diameter:	6 in (150 mm)	
Propulsion:	two-stage solid-fuel rocket	
Range:		
Altitude:		
Guidance:	infrared; possibly laser	
Warhead:	conventional	
Platforms:	*carriers*	ADMIRAL KUZNETSOV (ex-TBILISI)
	cruisers	KIROV (2 ships)
	frigates	NEUSTRASHIMYY
IOC:	1989	

5. Admiral S.G. Gorshkov, *The Sea Power of the State* (Annapolis, Md.: Naval Institute Press, 1976), p. 204.

6. The best publicly available reference on this subject is Steven J. Zaloga, *Soviet Air Defence Missiles* (Coulsdon, Surrey: Jane's Information Group, 1989).

The new combination close-in gun (two barrels) and surface-to-air missile CADS-1 system (eight missiles) in the third KIROV-class battle cruiser, the KALININ. The mount has an integral radar, unlike previous Soviet CIWS, with a fire control director at right, one deck higher. At left are a Kite Screech gunfire control radar for the 130-mm guns and the Top Dome missile control radar for the SA-N-6. (West German Navy)

SA-N-9

Advanced vertical-launch, short-range missile capable of anti-aircraft and anti-missile defense. Reportedly the SA-N-9 was developed as a joint project for the Navy and Air Defense Forces.

The SA-N-9 system is fitted in the two later carriers of the KIEV class in place of the SA-N-4 launchers, and in the second and third battle cruisers of the KIROV class in place of the SS-N-14 ASW missile system (the SA-N-4 launchers are retained in the later KIROVS). In the KUZNETSOV-class carriers and UDALOY-class destroyers the SA-N-9 is the ships' principal SAM system. The ships have groups of circular vertical launchers, each with eight missiles fitted. The arrangement of four-launcher groups varies in the ships.

Although the UDALOY went to sea in 1981 and the NOVOROSSIYSK in 1982, neither ship had an operational SA-N-9 system. The first few UDALOYS did not have operational SA-N-9 systems (i.e., two Cross Swords fire control radars and operational launchers). The system probably became operational in 1983–1984.

Designation: The land-based SA-15 appears to be a derivative of the naval SA-N-9.

Weight:	440 lbs (200 kg)	
Length:	11 ft 6 in (3.5 m)	
Span:		
Diameter:	7 ft 11 in (2.0 m)	
Propulsion:	solid-propellant rocket	
Range:	8 n.miles (15 km)	
Altitude:	6.5 n.miles (12 km)	
Guidance:		
Warhead:	44 lbs (20 kg) conventional	
Platforms:	*carriers*	KIEV (2 ships), ADMIRAL KUZNETSOV
	cruisers	KIROV (2 ships)
	destroyers	UDALOY
	frigates	NEUSTRASHIMYY
IOC:	1983–1984	

SA-N-5 Grail/SA-N-8 Gremlin

These are the shipboard variants of the shoulder-launched SA-7 Grail and SA-14 Gremlin anti-air missiles. They are fitted in various small combatants and amphibious and auxiliary ships, being fired from fixed quad launchers or by their shoulder-held launch tubes. Similar to the well-known U.S. Redeye and Stinger missiles, the Soviet weapons first became operational in 1966 with the Soviet Ground Forces (army). The Navy appears to have begun using the SA-7/SA-N-5 missile in the 1970s with a quad mounting developed in the late 1970s. The SA-14 probably entered Soviet service in the

mid- to late-1970s. More than 200 Soviet and other ships now carry the missile.

The missile has a target acquisition time of one minute or less based on the launch tube's thermal battery; however, extra batteries are fitted and they can be quickly replaced. This battery provides power until target detection, when the missile's power supply cuts on. Target acquisition is signaled to the gunner by an audible tone from the launcher and a green light in his sight.

The SA-14 launcher can be easily distinguished from the earlier SA-7 by the larger, ball-shaped thermal battery fitted below the muzzle of the launcher (forward of the trigger/grip assembly).

Designation: The Soviet name for the SA-7 is *Strela*-2 ("Arrow") with an improved version designated 2M; the SA-14 is the *Strela*-3.

The following data is for the hand-held variants.

Missile weight:	SA-N-5	20.25 lbs (9.2 kg)
	SA-N-5 (2M)	22 lbs (9.97 kg)
	SA-N-8	21.75 lbs (9.9 kg)
Launcher weight:	SA-N-5	9.2 lbs (4.2 kg)
	SA-N-5 (2M)	10.35 lbs (4.7 kg)
	SA-N-8	13.4 lbs (6.1 kg)
Length:	SA-N-5	4 ft 8 in (1.4 m)
	SA-N-5 (2M)	4 ft 9 in (1.45 m)
	SA-N-8	4 ft 7 in (1.4 m)
Span:	(small canard stabilizing fins)	
Diameter:	2¾ in (70 mm)	
Propulsion:	two-stage solid-fuel rocket	
Range:	SA-N-5	3,900 yds (3.6 km)
	SA-N-5 (2M)	6,000 yds (5.5 km)
	SA-N-8	6,550 yds (6 km)
Altitude:	SA-N-5	3,825 yds (3.5 km)
	SA-N-5 (2M)	4,900 yds (4.5 km)
	SA-N-8	6,000 yds (5.5 km)
Guidance:	infrared homing	
Warhead:	5.5 lbs (2.5 kg) conventional	
Platforms:	*corvettes*	Pauk, Tarantul, T-58 radar pickets, Svetlak
	small combatants	Osa, Turya
	mine warfare	Natya, Yurka, Sonya, Gorya
	amphibious ships	Polnocny, Ropocha
	landing craft	Pomornik
	auxiliary ships	various AGIs
IOC:	SA-N-5 approx. 1974	SA-N-8 approx. 1986

These quad mounts for the normally shoulder-launched SA-N-5/SA-N-8 anti-aircraft missiles are found on large numbers of Soviet small combatants and auxiliary ships. They provide protection against terrorist-type air attacks as well as helicopters that are not armed with stand-off missiles. The missiles are loaded onto the launcher in the expendable canisters.

A quad SA-N-5/SA-N-8 missile launcher on a Yurka-class minesweeper. Note the simplicity of the mount and the open ring-type sights. (West German Navy)

An SA-7 Grail missile, shown here being demonstrated by an Afghan guerrilla. These weapons are carried in a number of Soviet ships, fired in this mode or by the quad launchers shown above.

SA-N-7 Gadfly

This missile went to sea in 1981 in the Kashin-class destroyer PROVORNYY and subsequently in the SOVREMENNYY-class destroyers. The PROVORNYY was extensively modified with eight Front Dome tracker/illuminators for the SA-N-7 but there is only one single-arm launcher, installed aft, in place of the original SA-N-1 launcher. There appear to be provisions forward for two more launchers (forward) and there were some reports of their installation in the late 1980s. Speed is Mach 3.

The system has a single-arm launcher (similar to the U.S. Navy Mk 13 for the Tartar/Standard missiles). The SOVREMENNYY-class ships have two launchers and six Front Dome directors. The number of control/engagement radars indicates a high rate of fire.

Designation: This is a shipboard version of the land-based SA-11 Gadfly missile.

Weight: 1,430 lbs (650 kg)
Length: 18 ft 4½ in (5.6 m)
Span: 3 ft 11 in (1.2 m)
Diameter: 15¾ in (400 mm)
Propulsion: solid-fuel rocket
Range: 16 n.miles (30 km)
Altitude: 8 n.miles (15 km)
Guidance: radio command with semi-active radar homing; fitted with infrared or electro-optical backup
Warhead: 176 lbs (80 kg) conventional
Platforms: destroyers Kashin (1 unit), SOVREMENNYY
IOC: 1981

The forward SA-N-7 single-rail launcher with a missile in the load position on board the SOVREMENNYY-class destroyer BOYEVOY. Except for the single Kashin-class trials ship, the SOVREMENNYYs are the only ships known to be fitted with this weapon. (West German Navy)

Close-up of an SA-N-7 launcher on the SOVREMENNYY-class destroyer BEZUPRECHNYY.

SA-N-6 Grumble

This is an advanced surface-to-air missile with anti-cruise missile capabilities. It is a large SAM system, developed to replace the conventional SA-N-1 and SA-N-3 launchers in major warships.

The SA-N-6 is vertically launched from a below-deck rotary magazine, with eight missiles per launcher. Guidance provides for track-via-missile with the in-flight missile providing radar data to the launching ship. Initially fitted in one Kara-class cruiser, the Azov, completed in late 1977 as a trials ship, and subsequently in cruisers of the KIROV and SLAVA classes. The SA-N-6 system employs the Top Pair and Top Steer acquisition radar and the distinctive Top Dome engagement radar. Missile speed is approximately Mach 6.

The AZOV has 4 rotary launchers with the KIROV-class ships having 12 and the SLAVA-class ships 8. The launcher hatches differ, with the AZOV and KIROVS having square hatch covers; the SLAVAS have circular drum housings. The AZOV and SLAVAS each have a single Top Dome radar while the KIROVS have two.

Some reports credit the SA-N-6 with a nuclear capability; it probably has an anti-ship capability.

Designation: The missile is adapted from the land-based SA-10 Grumble.

Weight:	3,300 lbs (1,500 kg)
Length:	23 ft (7 m)
Span:	
Diameter:	17¾ in (450 mm)
Propulsion:	solid-fuel rocket
Range:	54 n.miles (100 km)
Altitude:	16 n.miles (30.5 km)
Guidance:	command track-via-missile
Warhead:	198 lbs (90 kg) conventional; possibly nuclear
Platforms:	*cruisers* Kara (1 ship), KIROV, SLAVA
IOC:	1981

SA-N-4 Gecko

The SA-N-4 system serves as a point-defense weapon for large warships and as the primary anti-air system in small combatants. The launcher system is fitted into the vertical drum magazine; a two-panel upper hatch opens and the launcher slides upward for loading and firing. The first ship to be fitted with the SA-N-4 was the Grisha I ASW frigate, completed in 1968. (The KGB-operated Grisha II has a second 57-mm gun mount in place of the forward SA-N-4; the KGB's Krivak-class frigates retain one SA-N-4.) Only the first two KIEV-class carriers have the SA-N-4; the two later ships of the class have the SA-N-9 missile. The system was also fitted in the two SVERDLOV-class cruisers converted to command ships (ADMIRAL SENYAVIN and ZHDANOV) and is the only SAM system fitted in amphibious and auxiliary ships (not including shoulder-fired type missiles).

The SA-N-4 uses the Pop Group missile control radar, which is similar to the radar associated with the land-based SA-8 surface-to-air missile. A limited anti-ship capability is credited to the missile. Speed is about Mach 3.

Designation: The SA-N-4 is a navalized version of the SA-8 Gecko missile (which became operational *after* the naval version, about 1973). The Soviet code name for the naval missile is *Osa*-M (''Wasp''); the code name for the SA-8 is *Romb* (''Diamond'').

Weight:	286 lbs (130 kg)	
Length:	10 ft 2 in (3.1 m)	
Span:	2 ft 1 in (0.64 m)	
Diameter:	8¼ in (210 mm)	
Propulsion:	solid-fuel rocket	
Range:	6.5–8 n.miles (12–15 m)	
Altitude:	same as range	
Guidance:	command/semi-active homing	
Warhead:	39.5 lbs (18 kg) conventional	
Platforms:	*carriers*	KIEV (2 ships)
	cruisers	Kara, KIROV, SLAVA
	frigates	Krivak, Koni, Grisha I/III/V
	corvettes	Nanuchka, Grisha, Dergach
	small combatants	Sarancha
	amphibious ships	IVAN ROGOV
	auxiliary ships	BEREZINA
IOC:	1968	

An SA-N-4 missile launcher in the raised position on a Krivak I–class frigate. At left are RBU-6000 ASW rocket launchers. There are blast shields between the RBUs and behind the SA-N-4 launcher. A saluting gun is fitted on the main deck on both sides of the RBUs.

SA-N-3 Goblet

This SA-N-3 missile system went to sea in the second generation of warships developed during the Gorshkov regime, beginning with the MOSKVA-class helicopter carrier-cruisers and Kresta II cruisers. The missile is unique among Soviet missiles in that it was the first surface-to-air weapon developed specifically for naval use, although it is in part derived from the land-based SA-3 Goa system. (Initially the SA-N-3 was thought in the West to have been derived from the land-based SA-6 Gainful missile.)

The SA-N-3 is a low- to medium-altitude missile with improved capabilities over the SA-N-1, which it succeeds. The missile is also capable of use in the anti-ship role. Maximum speed is approximately Mach 2.5. It is employed with the Head Lights fire control radar. An improved version has been provided to the KIEV-class ships; reportedly it has considerably greater range.

Weight:	1,200 lbs (545 kg)	
Length:	20 ft (6.1 m)	
Span:	4 ft 7 in (1.4 m)	
Diameter:	23½ in (600 mm)	
Propulsion:	ramjet with solid-fuel booster	
Range:	29.5 n.miles (55 km)	
Altitude:	13.5 n.miles (25 km)	
Guidance:	semi-active homing	
Warhead:	176 lbs (80 kg) nuclear or conventional	
Platforms:	*carriers*	MOSKVA, KIEV
	cruisers	Kresta II, Kara
IOC:	1967	

An SA-N-3 twin-rail launcher on board the Kara-class cruiser KERCH. The huge Head Lights missile control radar is seen above the ship's bridge. (Eric Grove)

An SA-N-3 launcher on a Kresta II–class ASW cruiser. SA-N-1/SA-N-3 launchers are being superseded on modern large surface combatants by vertical-launch missile systems. (West German Navy)

SA-N-2 Guideline
The SA-N-2 was adapted from the widely used land-based SA-2 missile system and is considered a medium-altitude weapon.

Only one cruiser, the DZERZHINSKIY of the SVERDLOV class, was refitted from 1959 to 1962 with the sea-based version, indicating a lack of success in the naval version. The ship has been discarded (see page 164).

Designation: The Soviet naval designation was M-2.

SA-N-1 Goa
This was the first surface-to-air missile to be installed in Soviet warships and is considered effective at low-to-medium altitudes as well as in the surface-to-surface mode. The first ship to be fitted with the SA-N-1, the SAM Kotlin-class destroyer BRAVYY, began trials in June 1962.

The system has a twin-arm launcher fitted in destroyers and cruisers. The missiles load with the launcher at 90° elevation from a below-deck magazine. The four square-shaped tail fins are folded until the missile leaves the launcher. Maximum speed is approximately Mach 3.5. The Peel Group fire control radar is used with the SA-N-1.

All existing ships are fitted with two launchers, including the Kashin transferred to Poland and the several modified Kashin-class destroyers constructed for India.

Designation: The Soviet designation is M-1 with the name *Volga-M* assigned.

The missile system is derived from the land-based SA-3 system, which became operational in 1961.

Weight:	880 lbs (400 kg)
Length:	20 ft (6.1 m)
Span:	missile 3 ft 11 in (1.2 m)
	booster 7 ft 6½ in (2.3 m)
Diameter:	missile 14½ in (370 mm)
	booster 21⅔ in (550 mm)
Propulsion:	solid-fuel rocket with tandem solid-fuel boosters
Range:	15.6 n.miles (29 km)
Altitude:	
Guidance:	radio command
Warhead:	132 lbs (60 kg) conventional; some sources cite a possible nuclear warhead alternative
Platforms:	*cruisers* Kresta I, Kynda
	destroyers Kashin
IOC:	1961

The forward SA-N-1 missile launcher on a Kashin-class destroyer. The launcher is in the vertical reload position; the loading hatches beneath the launcher are visible beneath the twin rails. (West German Navy)

SA-N-1 anti-aircraft missile in flight.

SURFACE-TO-SURFACE COASTAL MISSILES

SSC-X-( )

A ground-launched variant of the SS-NX-24 submarine-launched missile is believed to be in development.

SSC-X-4

This is a ground-launched variant of the SS-N-21 and AS-15 cruise missiles, launched by attack submarines and Bear-H aircraft, respectively. The SSC-X-4 became operational in 1986–1987 but apparently was not deployed. The missile was banned by the December 1987 treaty on Intermediate-range Nuclear Force (INF) missiles between the United States and Soviet Union. The Soviets had 84 SSC-X-4 missiles in storage at Jelgava, south of Riga in the Latvian SSR, with six prototype launch vehicles. Each mobile launcher could carry six launch canisters. They have now been destroyed.

See SS-N-21 for data (page 388).

Designation: The Soviet designation for the missile was RK-55.

SSC-3 Styx

This is an adaptation of the SS-N-2 Styx anti-ship missile, fitted in twin launchers on eight-wheel MAZ vehicles with a self-contained fire control radar. The range is believed to be on the order of 43–48.5 n.miles (80–90 km). The system is in service with Yugoslav coastal defense forces; it was previously operated by East Germany.

SSC-2 Samlet

The Samlet was a ground-launched missile developed from the AS-1 air-launched cruise missile. It was previously used by Soviet, Bulgarian, East German, and Yugoslav coastal defense forces, with the SSC-2b variant believed still in use with Cuban, Polish, Romanian, and possibly Egyptian forces. Estimated range is 55–108 n.miles (100–200 km), the latter range when modified for midcourse guidance.

Designation. The Soviet designations were S-2 and 4K-87, the latter being the classified designation.

SSC-1 Sepal

Land-based, anti-ship missile in service with the Navy's Coastal Missile-Artillery Force. This is a land-launched version of the SS-N-3 Shaddock missile (see page 391 for description). The SSC-1b has a range of some 250 n.miles (350 km); it can carry a conventional and probably a nuclear warhead.

The launcher is fitted to an eight-wheel vehicle.

Designation: The Soviet designation is P-35.

SUBMARINE-LAUNCHED BALLISTIC MISSILES

The Soviet Navy has an estimated 940 SLBMs in 62 modern SSBNs; in addition, there are two diesel-electric Golf-class SSBNs in service, carrying six SLBMs for the theater strike role. One older Hotel-class SSBN is employed as a trials ship for the SS-N-8 SLBM. The estimated Soviet SLBM strength as of early 1991 is shown in table 28-1.

TABLE 28-1. SUBMARINE-LAUNCHED BALLISTIC MISSILES

Submarines*	Missiles	RVs	Notes
6 SSBN Typhoon	20 SS-N-20	6 to 9	
6 SSBN Delta IV	16 SS-N-23	10	submarine in production
14 SSBN Delta III	16 SS-N-18		
	Mod 1	3	
	Mod 2	1	
	Mod 3	7	
4 SSBN Delta II	16 SS-N-8	1	
18 SSBN Delta I	12 SS-N-8	1	
1 SSBN Yankee II	12 SS-N-17	1	
13 SSBN Yankee I	16 SS-N-6		submarines being phased out
	Mods 1/2	1	
	Mod 3	2	
1 SSBN Hotel III	6 SS-N-8	1	test platform
2 SSB Golf II	3 SS-N-5	1	submarines being phased out

* Active units.

All Soviet SLBMs have liquid-propellant rocket motors, except the SS-N-17 and SS-N-20, which have solid-propellant motors (as do all Western SLBMs).

SS-N-23 Skiff

Submarine-launched ballistic missile developed for the Delta IV–class submarines. This is a three-stage missile. The missile is believed to have more accuracy and throw weight than the SS-N-18. It may be backfitted in the Delta III–class SSBNs.

A modified SS-N-23 missile became operational in 1988. Western intelligence considers the SS-N-23 to be the most accurate Soviet SLBM in service, providing a hard-target-kill capability. CEP is publicly estimated at 540 yards (500 m).

Weight:	approx. 88,000 lbs (40,000 kg)
Length:	approx. 45 ft 11 in (14 m)
Span:	(ballistic)
Diameter:	71 in (1.8 m)
Propulsion:	liquid-fuel rocket
Range:	4,500 n.miles (8,300 km)
Guidance:	inertial
Warhead:	nuclear (10 MIRV)
Platforms:	*submarines* Delta IV
IOC:	1986

SS-N-20 Sturgeon

The largest Soviet SLBM yet produced, the three-stage SS-N-20 was developed for launch from the Typhoon-class SSBN. The missile is believed to have a greater payload and more accuracy than any previous Soviet SLBM and is the first solid-propellant SLBM to be produced in quantity. The missile was reported to have experienced significant development problems. The SS-N-20 is larger than the U.S. Navy's Trident II (D-5) missile.

A modified SS-N-20 missile is in development.

One Golf-class submarine was modified to serve as trials ship for the missile.

Weight:	132,000 lbs (60,000 kg)
Length:	approx. 48 ft 3 in (14.7 m)
Span:	(ballistic)
Diameter:	85½ in (2.2 m)
Propulsion:	solid-fuel rocket
Range:	4,500 n.miles (8,300 km)
Guidance:	inertial
Warhead:	nuclear (6–9 MIRV) 100+ KT
Platforms:	*submarines* Typhoon
IOC:	1983

SS-N-18 Stingray

One variant of the SS-N-18 is the first Soviet SLBM to have a MIRV warhead (initially two re-entry vehicles). This is a two-stage weapon. Flight testing began in 1975.

The missile's CEP has been estimated in the Western press as 0.76 n.miles for the MIRV version.

Designation. The Soviet designation for this missile is RSM-50.

Weight:	74,800 lbs (34,000 kg)
Length:	44 ft 7 in (13.6 m)
Span:	(ballistic)
Diameter:	67 in (1.7 m)
Propulsion:	liquid-fuel rocket
Range:	Mod 1 3,530 n.miles (6,500 km)
	Mod 2 4,350 n.miles (8,000 km)
	Mod 3 3,530 n.miles (6,500 km)
Guidance:	inertial
Warhead:	nuclear (approx. 450 KT for single warhead, approx. 200 KT for each multiple warhead; Mod 1 has 3 MIRV; Mod 2 has 1 RV; Mod 3 has 7 RV)
Platforms:	*submarines* Delta III
IOC:	1978

SS-N-17 Snipe

A single Yankee-class SSBN has been fitted with the SS-N-17 missile. This missile was the first Soviet solid-propellant SLBM and the first to employ a Post Boost Vehicle (PBV) or "bus" to aim the single re-entry vehicle. It is credited with greater accuracy than previous Soviet SLBMs but has not been deployed beyond replacing the SS-N-6 in a single submarine. Flight testing began in 1975.

(Note that the Yankee II carries 12 SS-N-17 missiles compared to 16 of the SS-N-6 missiles in the basic Yankee class.)

Weight:	49,040 lbs (20,290 kg)
Length:	34 ft 9 in (10.6 m)
Span:	(ballistic)
Diameter:	67 in (1.7 m)
Propulsion:	solid-fuel rocket
Range:	2,100+ n.miles (3,900+ km)
Guidance:	inertial
Warhead:	nuclear (1 RV 800 KT or 2 MRV 200 KT)
Platforms:	*submarines* Yankee II
IOC:	1977

SS-NX-13

This is a submarine-launched, tactical ballistic missile developed for the anti-carrier role. Development began in the early 1960s, with subsequent flight tests being conducted until November 1973. The missile was not deployed.

The SS-NX-13 was apparently developed for launching from the Yankee-class SSBNs, probably with satellite targeting at launch and a terminal radar-homing system. Range was approximately 600 n.miles (1,120 km) with a terminal maneuvering capability of some 30 n.miles (55 km). A nuclear warhead would have been employed.

Some Western analysts believe that the missile may also have been intended in a later version for the anti-SSBN role, had long-range targeting capabilities been available.

SS-N-8

This SLBM was developed for the Delta-class strategic-missile submarines. It is the first Soviet two-stage submarine missile, being significantly larger than the SS-N-6, used in the previous Yankee-class SSBNs, indicating that it was developed from the SS-N-4/5 SLBM series. One Golf-class SSB and one Hotel-class SSBN were modified as trials ships for the SS-N-8.

Some variants of this missile were given the NATO name Sawfly.

Weight:	66,000 lbs (30,000 kg)	
Length:	42 ft 8 in (13.0 m)	
Span:	(ballistic)	
Diameter:	65 in (1.65 m)	
Propulsion:	liquid-fuel rocket	
Range:	Mod 1	4,240 n.miles (7,800 km)
	Mod 2	4,950 n.miles (9,100 km)
Guidance:	inertial	
Warhead:	nuclear (1 RV 800 KT or 2 RV 500 KT)	
Platforms:	*submarines* Delta I/II, Hotel III	
IOC:	Mod 1	1973
	Mod 2	1977

SS-N-6

This strategic missile was deployed in the Yankee-class submarines, the first modern Soviet SSBN design. It is a single-stage, liquid-fuel, underwater-launch missile. All Yankee SSBNs originally carried the SS-N-6; one has subsequently been rearmed with the SS-N-17, and some have had their missile tube sections removed in accordance with the SALT I agreement. A single Golf-class SSB was fitted as trials ship for the SS-N-6. The SS-N-6 initially had a range of 1,300 n.miles (2,395 km).

Designed by the Chelomei design bureau.

Weight:	41,580 lbs (18,900 kg)	
Length:	32 ft 10 in (10 m)	
Span:	(ballistic)	
Diameter:	71 in (1.8 m)	
Propulsion:	liquid-fuel rocket	
Range:	Mod 1	1,300 n.miles (2,400 km)
	Mod 2	1,600 n.miles (2,950 km)
	Mod 3	1,600 n.miles (2,950 km)
Guidance:	inertial	
Warhead:	nuclear (approx. 1 MT; Mod 1 and 2 have 1 RV; Mod 3 has 2 MRV)	
Platforms:	*submarines* Yankee I	
IOC:	Mod 2/3	1972–1973

SS-N-5

The SS-N-5 was an improved SLBM, featuring underwater launch and a greater range compared to the previous SS-N-4. It replaced the SS-N-4 in 13 of the Golf class submarines and all eight of the Hotel-class SSBNs (3 missiles per submarine); all of the latter have been discarded or converted. The missile range is believed to have been increased during service life from approximately 700 n.miles (1,300 km) to the distance indicated below. The NATO name Serb was assigned to some variants of this missile.

With the expected disposal of the last of the Golf II missile submarines in 1990 this missile will have passed out of service.

Designed by the Yangel design bureau.

Designation: The Soviet designations are D-4 and R-21, the latter being the classified designation.

Weight:	36,300 lbs (16,500 kg)
Length:	42 ft 8 in (13 m)
Span:	(ballistic)
Diameter:	47½ in (1.2 m)
Propulsion:	liquid-fuel rocket
Range:	900 n.miles (1,650 km)
Guidance:	inertial
Warhead:	nuclear (1 RV approx. 800 KT)
Platforms:	*submarines* Golf II
IOC:	1963

SS-N-4

The SS-N-4 was the Soviet Navy's first operational SLBM, being a surface-launch weapon originally fitted in the Zulu V, Golf I, and Hotel I classes. The Zulu V craft (2 missiles) were discarded, while 13 of the Golf class and all 8 of the nuclear-powered Hotel class were converted to fire the SS-N-5 missile (3 missiles per submarine). Range was approx. 350 n.miles (650 km). The NATO name Sark was assigned to some variants of this missile.

SURFACE-TO-SURFACE MISSILES

These are cruise/guided missiles intended for land-attack, anti-ship, or anti-submarine use, the last being the SS-N-14/15/16. The latter weapons, however, can also be used against surface ships. The submarine-launched missiles can be fired while the submarine is submerged except for the SS-N-3 and its derivative SS-N-12, for which the Echo II SSGN or Juliett SSG must surface. When employed against surface targets the submarine must remain on the surface to relay target update information to the in-flight missile.

SS-N-25

This is a small, anti-ship missile similar to the U.S. Harpoon missile. It is a subsonic missile. The new Soviet weapon was first observed in 1988 fitted in quad canisters on the East German Navy's SASSNITZ guided missile patrol craft number 91 (completed in 1987–1988). Two quad launchers were fitted to the craft. Subsequently, the missile has been fitted in the Nanuchka IV–class corvettes (eight missiles).

The missile is expected to be fitted in future Soviet small combatants.

SS-NX-24 Scorpion

This is an advanced, submarine-launched, land-attack cruise missile of much larger dimensions than the SS-N-21. The missile has a supersonic speed, possibly in the region of Mach 2. It underwent launch trials from a former Yankee-class SSBN specifically converted for this role. Development continued in 1990. "at a slow pace," according to U.S. officials.

It is not clear if additional Yankee-class submarines will be converted to fire the missile. A new SSGN class may be under construction.

The missile carries a large nuclear warhead. Speed approximately Mach 2.

An air-launched version designated AS-X-19 is also in development and a ground-based version is reported in development for coastal defense.

The SS-NX-24 is estimated to have a speed of Mach 3.

Weight:	
Length:	approx. 41 ft (12.5 m)
Diameter:	approx. 4 ft (1.2 m)
Span:	approx. 18 ft (5.5 m)
Propulsion:	turbojet or turbofan
Range:	approx. 1,630 n.miles (3,000 km)
Guidance:	inertial with terminal homing
Warhead:	nuclear
Platforms:	*submarines* Yankee SSGN conversion
	new construction SSGN (?)
IOC:	1990–1991(?)

SS-N-22 Sunburn

This anti-ship missile is an improved version of the SS-N-9 anti-ship cruise missile. It is carried in quad launchers in the SOVREMENNYY class and in twin launchers in the Tarantul II class as well as in the Utka-class WIG vehicles and Dergach surface effects ship. Missile speed is estimated at Mach 2.5.

Weight:	
Length:	approx. 30 ft (9.15 m)
Span:	5 ft 3 in (1.6 m)
Propulsion:	solid-fuel rocket
Range:	approx. 50 n.miles (93 km)
Guidance:	mid-course guidance with active radar homing
Warhead:	conventional or nuclear (approx. 200 KT)
Platforms:	*destroyers* SOVREMENNYY
	corvettes Tarantul II, Dergrach
	WIG vehicles Utka
IOC:	1981

The portside quad SS-N-22 missile canisters on a SOVREMENNYY-class destroyer. Immediately above the missiles are a 30-mm Gatling gun and the Band Stand radome housing the guidance radar for the missiles. A variety of periscopes and laser rangefinders are also visible. (West German Navy)

SS-N-21 Sampson

This is an advanced land-attack cruise missile believed to be launched from standard Soviet submarine torpedo tubes, much like the U.S. Navy Tomahawk Land-Attack Missile (TLAM); the similarity of design to the U.S. weapon has led to the Soviet weapon being called "Tomahawkski" by Western intelligence. Speed is estimated at Mach 0.7.

Launch trials for the SS-NX-21 were conducted from a modified Victor III–class SSN; that submarine was distinguished by a long cylinder fitted on the deck immediately forward of the sail structure. The first two Akula SSNs subsequently carried out extensive SS-N-21 trials. A single Yankee SSBN has been converted to the Yankee Notch configuration to carry large numbers of SS-N-21s.

The air-launched version of this missile is the AS-15; a ground-launched version designated SSC-X-4 was developed but not deployed (see above).

Weight:	3,740 lbs (1,700 kg)
Length:	26 ft 6 in (8.1 m)
Span:	
Diameter:	approx. 19⅔ in (510 mm)
Propulsion:	turbofan
Range:	approx. 1,630 n.mi (3,000 km)
Guidance:	inertial; probably with Terrain Contour Matching (TERCOM) homing
Warhead:	nuclear (approx. 200–300 KT)
Platforms:	*submarines* Yankee Notch, various SSN classes
IOC:	1987–1988

SS-N-19 Shipwreck

This is an improved long-range, anti-ship cruise missile that evolved from the SS-N-3/12 designs. The high speed of the SS-N-19 (Mach 1+) alleviates the need for mid-course guidance because of the limited distance that the target ship could travel during the missile's time of flight. It is carried in the large KIROV-class nuclear cruisers and ADMIRAL KUZNETSOV–class carriers, and submerged-launched from the large Oscar-class SSGNs. Speed is Mach 2.5.

Weight:	approx. 11,000 lbs (5,000 kg)
Length:	35 ft 5 in (10.5 m)
Span:	5 ft 3 in (1.6 m)
Propulsion:	turbojet
Range:	300 n.miles (555 km)
Guidance:	inertial with anti-radar homing
Warhead:	conventional or nuclear (approx. 500 KT)
Platforms:	*carriers* ADMIRAL KUZNETSOV (ex-TBILISI)
	cruisers KIROV
	submarines Oscar
IOC:	1981

SS-N-16 Stallion

A further development of the SS-N-15, this missile carries an anti-submarine homing torpedo in lieu of the nuclear warhead. A parachute lowers the torpedo into the water, and a protective nosecap separates upon water entry; when the torpedo reaches a prescribed depth, a programmed search maneuver is begun, with the torpedo homing on any target detected during the search. The weapon is launched from the 25.5-in (650-mm) tubes.

The warhead is a 15.75-in (400-mm) or possibly 21-in (533-mm), ASW torpedo.

The now-cancelled conventional version of the U.S. Navy's Sea Lance missile was to be similar although carrying a smaller torpedo (the 324-mm Mk-50 torpedo).

Weight:	
Length:	
Span:	
Diameter:	25½ in (650 mm) (maximum)
Propulsion:	solid-fuel rocket
Range:	54 n.miles (100 km)
Guidance:	inertial to torpedo release point
Warhead:	ASW homing torpedo (conventional and possibly nuclear)
Platforms:	*submarines* Akula, Sierra, Oscar, Victor II/III
IOC:	1980

SS-N-15 Starfish

An ASW weapon similar to the now-discarded U.S. Navy SUBROC (Submarine Rocket), the SS-N-15 is fired from standard 21-in (533-mm) submarine torpedo tubes and carries a nuclear warhead. The weapon is fired with range and bearing probably derived from the launching submarine's active sonar.

Weight:	
Length:	approx. 21 ft (6.4 m)
Span:	
Diameter:	21 in (533 mm) (maximum)
Propulsion:	solid-fuel rocket
Range:	25 n.miles (46 km)
Guidance:	inertial
Warhead:	nuclear
Platforms:	*submarines* Akula, Alfa, Charlie I/II, Oscar, Papa, Sierra, Tango, Victor I/II/III, Yankee SSN
IOC:	1972

SS-N-14 Silex

This is a rocket-propelled anti-submarine weapon, carrying a homing torpedo out to the first sonar convergence zone. Speed is approximately Mach 0.95; water entry is slowed by a parachute. Minimum effective range is estimated at four n.miles (7.4 km). It can probably be employed against surface ships as well. The Head Lights or Eye Bowl radar is used for in-flight guidance.

Of the five warship classes armed with the missile, only the nuclear-powered KIROV has an on-board reload capability. A pair of quad launchers—two tubes above two—are fitted in cruisers and destroyers (eight missiles total); the Krivak-class frigate has a single, four-tube launcher of a different type. The KGB-operated Krivak III–class ships do not have the SS-N-14.

It may be possible to fit a nuclear warhead to this weapon.

The SS-N-14 was initially evaluated by Western intelligence as an anti-ship weapon and designated SS-N-10.

Weight:	
Length:	approx. 25 ft (7.6 m)
Span:	
Propulsion:	solid-fuel rocket
Range:	30 n.miles (55 km)
Guidance:	command radio and inertial
Warhead:	acoustic ASW homing torpedo (conventional); see notes
Platforms:	*cruisers* Kara, KIROV (1 ship), Kresta II
	destroyers UDALOY
	frigates Krivak I/II
IOC:	1969

Quad canister launchers for SS-N-14 ASW missiles on the destroyer UDALOY. Two Eye Bowl guidance radars are mounted above the bridge. In larger ships the Head Lights missile control radar provides guidance for the SS-N-14 as well as the SA-N-3.

SS-N-12 Sandbox

An advanced version of the SS-N-3 Shaddock anti-ship missile, capable of supersonic speed. It is fitted in surface ships and modified Echo II–class SSGNs, with one Juliett-class SSG also reported to have been upgraded to the SS-N-12. It is used with the Trap Door radar in the KIEV-class carriers and the Front Door/Piece radar of the Echo II, Juliett, and SLAVA classes. Speed is reported as Mach 2.5.

Weight:	10,560 lbs (4,800 kg)
Length:	35 ft 5 in (10.8 m)
Span:	5 ft 11 in (1.8 m)
Propulsion:	turbojet
Range:	300 n.miles (555 km)
Guidance:	radio command and (1) active radar or (2) anti-radar homing
Warhead:	nuclear (approx. 350 KT) or conventional (2,200 lbs/1,000 kg)
Platforms:	*carriers* KIEV
	cruisers SLAVA
	submarines mod. Echo II, mod. Juliett
IOC:	1973

The battle cruiser KIROV is the only ship fitted with a reloadable SS-N-14 ASW missile launcher (at left); reloads are stowed forward of the launcher. In the center are 12 hatches for the vertical-launch (rotary) SA-N-6 missile system and at right are hatches for the SS-N-19 missile.

The first three KIEV-class VSTOL carriers have eight launch tubes for the SS-N-12 anti-ship missile; there is a reloading device between the forward and after missile pairs, with reloads stowed below decks. Between the forward pairs of SS-N-12 tubes is a twin 76.2-mm gun mount and between the after pairs an SA-N-3 missile launcher; forward is an SUW-N-1 launcher and RBU-6000 ASW rocket launchers.

An SS-N-12 missile launcher on the cruiser SLAVA with the nuclear-tipped missile visible. The only surface ships that carry this missile are four missile cruisers and the four KIEV-class carriers—the same number of surface ships as the earlier SS-N-3 Shaddock. (Natural Resources Defense Council)

SS-N-11

This designation was initially assigned to an improved version of the Styx, which was subsequently redesignated SS-N-2c.

SS-N-10

The SS-N-14 anti-submarine missile was originally assigned this designation.

SS-N-9 Siren

This is a supersonic anti-ship missile, launched initially from surface ships and subsequently fitted in the Charlie II–class SSGNs for underwater launch. It is also reported by Western intelligence to be carried by the one-of-a-kind Papa SSGN. Maximum speed is approximately Mach 0.9. The Band Stand radar is used on surface ships for search and fire control. The Nanuchka-class missile corvettes transferred to other nations have the SS-N-2c missile in place of the SS-N-9.

Weight:	7,260 lbs (3,300 kg)
Length:	29 ft (8.84 m)
Span:	5 ft 3 in (1.6 m)
Propulsion:	solid-fuel rocket
Range:	60 n.miles (111 km)
Guidance:	inertial and (1) active radar or (2) anti-radar homing
Warhead:	nuclear (200 KT) or conventional (1,100 lbs/500 kg)
Platforms:	*small combatants* Nanuchka I/III, Sarancha
	submarines Charlie II, Papa (?)
IOC:	1969

SS-N-7 Starbright

The SS-N-7 was the world's first underwater-launched, anti-ship cruise missile. Maximum speed is approximately Mach 0.9. It has been succeeded in later, Charlie II–class SSGNs by the SS-N-9, which has about double the earlier missile's range. Some Western sources indicate that the missile carries only a conventional warhead.

SS-N-7 missiles were probably not provided to India in 1988 for the Charlie I SSGN transferred that year.

Weight:	6,380 lbs (2,900 kg)
Length:	22 ft 11½ in (7 m)
Span:	
Diameter:	
Propulsion:	solid-fuel rocket
Range:	35 n.miles (64 km)
Guidance:	(1) active radar or (2) anti-radar homing
Warhead:	nuclear (200 KT) or conventional (1,100 lbs/500 kg); see notes
Platforms:	*submarines* Charlie I
IOC:	1968

SS-N-3 Shaddock

The Shaddock is a large, air-breathing cruise missile originally developed for the strategic attack role in the SS-N-3c variant (a contemporary of the U.S. Regulus missile, which was operational from 1954, on a limited basis, to 1964). When submarine-launched it is fired from the surface. The land-launched SSC-1 Sepal missile is similar. The SS-N-3b was also assigned the NATO code name Sepal, but all ship-launched versions are generally referred to as Shaddock. The SS-N-12 has replaced the SS-N-3 in some Echo II submarines and at least one Juliett SSG. (The five Echo I SSGNs that originally carried the SS-N-3 have been converted to attack submarines, and the earlier Whiskey SSG conversions have been discarded.) The Scoop Pair radar is used for fire control in surface ships and the Front Door or Front Piece radar in submarines.

The missile requires mid-course guidance for over-the-horizon use. This is sent as a radar picture via Video Data Link (VDL) from the targeting ship or aircraft to the launching ship and then relayed—with target indicated—to the missile in flight. The launching submarine is thus required to remain on the surface after launch, possibly for as long as 25 minutes when firing against targets at a range of some 250 n.miles. The Plinth Net antennas in surface ships support the VDL system.

Designation: The Soviet designations for the SS-N-3c are P-6 and P-7.

Weight:	SS-N-3a/b 9,900 lbs (4,500 kg)
	SS-N-3c 11,880 lbs (5,400 kg)
Length:	SS-N-3c 38 ft 6 in (11.75 m)
	SS-N-3a/b 33 ft 6 in (10.2 m)
Span:	16 ft 5 in (5 m)
Diameter:	approx. 38½ in (975 mm)
Propulsion:	turboject + 2 solid-fuel boosters
Range:	SS-N-3c 400+ n.miles (740+ km)
	SS-N-3a/b 250 n.miles (463 km)
Guidance:	SS-N-3a/b inertial with mid-course command; active radar homing for terminal phase
	SS-N-3c inertial
Warhead:	nuclear (350 KT; possibly 800 KT in SS-N-3c) or conventional (2,200 lbs/1,000 kg)
Platforms:	SS-N-3a *submarines* Juliett, Echo II
	SS-N-3b *cruisers* Kynda, Kresta I
	SS-N-3c *submarines* Juliett, Echo II
IOC:	SS-N-3a 1962
	SS-N-3b 1962
	SS-N-3c 1960

The Kresta I has the lightest missile armament of any Soviet cruiser armed with anti-ship missiles—only four SS-N-3b Shaddock launchers. Here the starboard pair is fully elevated; no reloads are carried in these ships.

The after bank of SS-N-3b Shaddock launchers on the Kynda-class cruiser ADMIRAL GOLOVKO. The launchers (shown here in stowed position) are trained outboard and elevated for firing. Reloads are carried in the superstructure at left; reloading is awkward and is normally done at anchor or alongside a pier.

SS-N-2c Styx

This is an improved version of the Styx, having been initially designated SS-N-11 when first observed by Western intelligence. (The missile has also been fitted in Soviet-built Koni-class frigates transferred to Libya and Yugoslavia and provided to several other nations.) Speed is Mach 1.3.

There is no data link to the missile after launch.

Weight:	5,500 lbs (2,500 kg)
Length:	21 ft 4 in (6.5 m)
Span:	8 ft 2 in (2.5 m)
Diameter:	31½ in (800 mm)
Propulsion:	turbojet with solid-fuel booster
Range:	45 n.miles (83 km)
Guidance:	(1) active radar or (2) infrared homing
Warhead:	conventional (1,100 lbs/500 kg)
Platforms:	*destroyers* mod. Kashin
	small combatants Osa II, Matka, Tarantul; Nanuchkas for foreign transfer
IOC:	1967

SS-N-2a/b Styx

The Styx was developed to provide an anti-ship missile capability for small combat craft in the coastal defense role. It is a subsonic missile that has undergone several development stages. Soviet doctrine appears to call for launching the SS-N-2a/b versions at a range of some 10 to 13 n.miles (18 to 24 km), or about one-half of their maximum range. Maximum speed is approximately Mach 1.3. The Square Tie radar is used to detect targets. Once launched, there is no data link to the SS-N-2a/b version; the missile's terminal radar seeker is automatically switched on some five miles from the estimated target position; the missile will home on the largest target in a group of ships.

The SS-N-2a was first deployed on Soviet Komar-class missile boats and subsequently in the Osa I. The 2b version, which has folding wings, was initially used in the Osa II.

If Third World sales are included, the Styx was the world's most widely used anti-ship missile before the French Exocet became operational in 1973 and the U.S. Harpoon in 1977. The Styx gained international attention after Egyptian Komar boats, from just outside of Port Said harbor, sank the Israeli destroyer ELIAT steaming 13.5 n.miles (25 km) offshore on 21 October 1967. The weapon was subsequently used by the Indian Navy to sink a number of Pakistani ships in the 1971 Indo-Pakistani conflict, including the destroyer KHAIBER.

Designation: The Soviet designations are P-15 and 4K-40, the latter being the classified designation.

Weight:	approx. 5,060 lbs (2,300 kg)
Length:	21 ft 4 in (6.5 m)
Span:	8 ft 2 in (2.5 m)
Diameter:	31½ in (800 mm)
Propulsion:	turbojet with solid-fuel booster
Range:	SS-N-2a approx. 25 n.miles (46 km)
	SS-N-2b approx. 27 n.miles (50 km)
Guidance:	active radar homing
Warhead:	conventional (1,100 lbs/500 kg)
Platforms:	*small combatants* Osa
IOC:	SS-N-2a 1958
	SS-N-2b 1964

SS-N-1 Scrubber/Strela

The Scrubber was the first surface-to-surface missile to be deployed by the Soviet Navy, going to sea from 1959 in four destroyers of the Kildin class (1 launcher) and from 1960 in eight destroyers of the Krupnyy class (2 launchers). The missile had a maximum range of approximately 100 n.miles (185 km).

The SS-N-1 had several limitations and was awkward to handle on board ship (each combination launcher/magazine held six missiles). By the late 1960s the ships were being discarded or converted. Scrubber was the NATO code name, but U.S. intelligence agencies generally used the name Strela.

An SS-N-2a Styx being loaded in an Osa I–class missile craft. All four missile launchers are open. Later versions of the Styx have folding wings and are launched from circular canisters. Sailors surround the forward 30-mm gun mount on the East German JOSEPH SCHARES. (Michna courtesy Alfred Albusberger)

SURFACE-TO-UNDERWATER MISSILES

SUW-N-1

This is a short-range ASW missile system found on the two Soviet carrier classes, apparently in place of the SS-N-14 ASW guided missile found in other modern Soviet warships. The SUW-N-1 is a ballistic weapon with a shorter range and carries only a nuclear warhead. The projectile itself is designated FRAS-1 for Free Rocket Anti-Submarine. The SUW-N-1 is a twin-arm launcher similar in design to the SA-N-1/3 launchers. The rocket was developed from the FROG-7 artillery rocket (Free Rocket Over Ground) and is unguided after being launched on a ballistic trajectory.

The fourth carrier of the KIEV class, the ADMIRAL GORSHKOV (ex-BAKU), does not have the SUW-N-1.

Weight:	
Length:	
Span:	(ballistic)
Propulsion:	solid-fuel rocket
Range:	16 n.miles (29.6 km)
Guidance:	unguided (inertial)
Warhead:	nuclear
Platforms:	*carriers* KIEV, MOSKVA
IOC:	1967

A FRAS-1 missile on a twin-rail SUW-N-1 launcher of a MOSKVA-class helicopter ship. The reloading hatches are to the right of the launcher. Only the MOSKVA and KIEV classes have this ASW weapon, adopted from a ground-launched missile.

NUCLEAR WEAPONS

The Soviet Navy has a large number and large variety of nuclear weapons available. Such weapons have been in the Soviet Fleet since the 1950s, when nuclear torpedoes were deployed that were, according to Western intelligence sources, intended for "strategic" attacks against Western coastal cities.

Subsequently the Soviets have deployed nuclear weapons at sea and in naval aircraft for the anti-air, anti-submarine, anti-surface, and land-attack roles. The reported detection of torpedoes with nuclear warheads in the Whiskey-class submarine that ran aground in Swedish waters in October 1981 tends to indicate the proliferation of these weapons in the fleet. That Whiskey was at least 25 years old, operating in waters close to the Soviet Union, in a non-crisis period, and on an intelligence-collection mission against a neutral nation.

Although there have been periodic reports of Soviet naval mines with nuclear charges, there has been no official (Western) confirmation of such weapons. Further, from a tactical viewpoint such weapons are hardly practical.

Naval weapon systems indicated to have a nuclear capability are listed in table 28-2 with current U.S. nuclear-capable naval systems indicated for comparative purposes.

TORPEDOES

The Soviet Navy employs primarily torpedoes of 553-mm (21-inch) and 400-mm (15.75-inch) diameter. More recently, a torpedo with a diameter estimated at 650 mm (25.5 inches) has entered service.[7] A 450-mm (17.75-inch) diameter torpedo may also be employed, possibly from aircraft.

The Soviet designations for these torpedoes are based on their size (diameter), with the basic designations being Type 65 (650 mm), Type 53 (533 mm), Type 45 (450 mm), and Type 40 (400 m).

650-mm torpedoes

These anti-ship torpedoes are believed to have entered service in the early 1980s, carried by Soviet SSN/SSGN-type submarines. The torpedo is approximately 30 feet (9.1 m) long with an advanced, closed-cycle thermal propulsion system. Public estimates of performance are 50 knots for up to 27 n.miles (50 km) or 30 knots for up to

---

7. In this century the only torpedoes to enter service with a larger diameter than 533 mm were the German Type H-8 (23.6 in/600 mm) and British Mk I (24.5 in/622 mm) of World War I, and the famed Japanese Type-93 "Long Lance" (24 in/610 mm) of World War II.

TABLE 28-2. NAVAL NUCLEAR WEAPONS

Launch Platform	Weapon	Role	U.S. Naval System
Surface ships	SA-N-1	anti-aircraft/anti-ship	
	SA-N-3	anti-aircraft/anti-ship	
	SA-N-6 (?)	anti-aircraft/anti-ship	
	SS-N-3b	anti-ship	
	SS-N-9	anti-ship	
	SS-N-12	anti-ship	
	SS-N-19	anti-ship	
	SS-N-22	anti-ship	
	torpedoes (?)	anti-ship/ASW	
	SUW-N-1/FRAS-1	anti-submarine	
Attack/Guided Missile Submarines			
	torpedoes	anti-ship/ASW	
	SS-N-3	anti-ship/land-attack[a]	
	SS-N-7 (?)	anti-ship	
	SS-N-9	anti-ship	
	SS-N-12	anti-ship/land-attack	
	SS-N-15	anti-submarine	
	SS-N-21	land-attack	TLAM-N[b]
	SS-N-24	land-attack	
Strategic Missile Submarines			
	SS-N-5	theater strike[a]	
	SS-N-6	strategic-theater strike[a]	
	SS-N-8	strategic	Poseidon C-3[a]
	SS-N-17	strategic	
	SS-N-18	strategic	
	SS-N-20	strategic	
	SS-N-23	strategic	Trident C-4/D-5
Aircraft			
	bombs	anti-ship/land-attack	B-57
			B-61
	depth bomb	ASW	B-57
	AS-4	anti-ship	
	AS-5	anti-ship	
	AS-6	anti-ship	
Coastal Defense	SSC-1	anti-ship	

[a] Being phased out of service.
[b] TLAM = Tomahawk Land-Attack Missile-Nuclear.

54 n.miles (100 km). Warhead size is estimated at about 2,000–2,200 pounds (900–1,000 kg); guidance is wake homing.

Submarine classes that are believed to have 650-mm torpedo tubes are the Typhoon, Delta IV SSBN; Oscar SSGN; and the Akula, Sierra, and Victor II/III SSN types.

This is the world's largest torpedo, carrying the heaviest explosive charge of any torpedo in service, with the ability to be fitted with a nuclear warhead.

533-mm torpedoes

These torpedoes are launched from trainable tubes in surface warships and fixed tubes in submarines for use against surface and submarine targets. These torpedoes are up to 27 feet long (8.2 m), much longer than their Western counterparts. Propulsion is provided by steam or electric motors (batteries) with speeds from 28 up to approximately 45 knots and effective ranges from 2 miles (3.2 km) up to possibly 10 miles (16 km). Guidance is both pre-set (straight-running) and acoustic homing. The torpedo has several

warheads, the largest possibly a high-explosive warhead of 1,250 lbs (562.5 kg), while some export versions have 474 lbs (215 kg). Nuclear warheads are also fitted, submarine torpedoes having been the first Soviet naval weapon with a nuclear capability.[8]

400-mm torpedoes

These are anti-submarine weapons that are launched from small ASW ships and craft, and from stern tubes in older submarines. They are also dropped from ASW fixed-wing aircraft and helicopters with a parachute fitted to slow water entry. These torpedoes apparently have electric (battery) propulsion, acoustic homing guidance, and high-explosive warheads. They may be used as the warhead in the SS-N-14 and SS-N-16 ASW missile systems.

8. The U.S. Navy's only nuclear torpedo was the Mk-45 ASTOR (Anti-Submarine Torpedo), which was in service in attack and strategic missile submarines from 1958 to 1977.

Three 533-mm torpedoes are partially exposed in the starboard bank of torpedo tubes of this Krivak I–class ASW frigate. Frigates and larger Soviet warships have 533-mm torpedo tubes; contemporary U.S. and NATO surface ships have only "short" tubes for 324-mm Mk-44/46/50 ASW torpedoes. Soviet 533-mm torpedoes also appear to be longer than U.S. torpedoes of that size.

CHAPTER 29

Naval Electronics

Soviet warships appear to be inundated with electronic antennas, as this Kresta II–class ASW cruiser being looked over by a Royal Navy Lynx helicopter. Soviet electronic systems appear to be individually less capable than their Western counterparts. Compared to Western electronics, however, they seem to be more rugged, easier to maintain, and redundant. (Royal Navy)

This chapter describes those Soviet naval electronic systems that have been publicly identified by Soviet or Western sources.

Designations: Systems listed in this chapter are identified by their NATO code names. Most aircraft and all shipboard radars and Electronic Warfare (EW) systems are identified by two one-syllable words. The words generally indicate the physical characteristics of the radar, except that the term ''screech'' in fire control radars is believed to be derived from the distinctive, screech-like signal emitted by the radar. In turn, bird names are used to differentiate screech-series radars (i.e., Hawk, Kite, Owl).

The basic words used in radar and EW antenna designations are:

(1) Position: Front, head, high, side, tilt, and top.

(2) Shape: Ball, band stand, bar, bell, big, bowl, brick, bulge, cob, cone, dome, drum, eye, fan, globe, hat, head, high, house, light, mushroom (one word), palm frond, park lamp, peel (as orange peel), pole, pot, puff ball, round, rum tub, sail, scoop, short horn, shroud, slab, slim, spring, square, squat, stop light, tail, tee (shaped as the letter "T"), toadstool (one word), tray, and tube.

(3) Design: Cage, curve, mesh, net, plate, plinth, round, strut, and tilt.

(4) Multiple antennas: Group and pair.

(5) Size: Big.

There are several exceptions to this designation scheme. The radar names Neptun and *Okean* (ocean) are Soviet names, and not NATO. "Guard" names are used for some Electronic Surveillance Measures (ESM) systems, i.e., Guard Dog and Watch Dog.

Suffix letters are assigned to major variations, as Big Bulge-A/B and Head Net-A/B/C.

ELECTRONIC WARFARE

Soviet combat aircraft, surface ships, and submarines have electronic warfare equipment to (1) detect threats, (2) collect Electronic Intelligence (ELINT), (3) Identification Friend or Foe (IFF), and (4) detect and counter threats (ESM/ECM). Few details of these systems are available for publication.

The following are the identified EW systems fitted in Soviet surface ships and submarines. IFF sets are noted. (In addition, surface ships as well as some aircraft have chaff and decoy launchers.)

Surface Ships

Bell Bash	Dead Duck (IFF)	Side Globe
Bell Clout	Fir Tree	Sprat Star
Bell Nip	Foot Ball	Square Head
Bell Push	Guard Dog	Top Head
Bell Shroud	High Pole-A/B (IFF)	Trawl Net
Bell Slam	High Ring	Twin Wheel
Bell Squat	Log Maze	Watch Dog
Bell Tap	Long Head (IFF)	Watch Guard (IFF)
Bell Thumb	Park Plinth	Wing Fold
Cage Pot	Rum Tub	Wine Flask
Cross Loop	Salt Pot (IFF)	

Submarines

Brick Group	Park Lamp (DF)	Rim Hat
Brick Pulp	Quad Loop (DF)	Stop Light
Brick Split		

The High Pole and Square Head are considered to be a single IFF system by the Soviets, who call it the *Nikhram*. The High Pole is a direction finder while the Square Head is an emission receiver that can be used in both search and fire-control modes.

Park Lamp and Quad Loop are radio Direction Finders (DF).

An advanced Watch Dog EW antenna and a Square Head IFF antenna on a Grisha-class light frigate. Earlier Watch Dog installations had four tiers of microwave horns. (Royal Navy)

The massive pyramid structure of a Kresta II ASW cruiser mounts the large Side Globe EW domes. Side Globe is reported to be a broad-band electronic jamming system. There are generally four domes, mounted in pairs, on each side of the ship's superstructure in the several classes of cruisers and carriers that have the system. In newer ships the Side Globe is being replaced by the Foot Ball/Bell Thump systems in newer warships. (Royal Navy)

AIRCRAFT RADARS

Only aircraft of the types operated by the Soviet Navy are listed below.

Bee Hind
Tail warning radar generally to fitted bomber aircraft. I-band.

> *aircraft*   Badger
>   Bear-D
>   Blinder

Big Bulge
Surface-search and targeting radar; used with data link to transmit radar picture of target ships to missile-launching aircraft or submarines. Range against surface ships from medium altitudes is estimated at some 230 n.miles (423 km). I/J-band.

The Big Bulge-A is fitted in the large under-fuselage radome bulge on Bear-D aircraft and Big Bulge-B in a chin mounting on the Hormone-B helicopter.

> *aircraft*   Bear-D
>   Hormone-B

Box Tail
Tail warning radar in Tu-142 variants of the Bear. I-band.

> *aircraft*   Bear-F/J

Down Beat
Bombing/navigation radar for search and targeting with AS-4 and probably later air-to-surface missiles. Range is approximately 175 n.miles (322 km). I-band.

> *aircraft*   Backfire-B

The Box Tail warning radar is visible above the tail gun position on this Bear-D reconnaissance/targeting aircraft. Forward of the twin 23-mm gun position are observation blisters common to early Bears and naval aircraft until the Bear-F Mod IV. (U.S. Air Force)

Fan Tail
Gunfire-control radar for remote-controlled tail gun turret.

> *aircraft*   Backfire-B/C

High Fix
Range-only air-intercept radar in fighter-type aircraft. Range approximately 5 n.miles (9 km). I-band.

> *aircraft*   Fitter-C/D

Jay Bird
Range-only air intercept radar fitted in several fighter aircraft. Associated with AA-2/3/4/7/8 and AS-7 missiles. Relatively short range. I/J-band.

> *aircraft*   Fitter-C/D

Mushroom
Bombing/navigation (bomb/nav) radar used in several bomber and EW/ECM aircraft. Range is approximately 175 n.miles (322 km). Radome is located under forward fuselage. I-band.

> *aircraft*   Badger-A

Puff Ball
Bomb/nav radar used in Badger aircraft for targeting AS-2/5/6 missiles (although some carrying AS-5 missiles may have the Short Horn radar). Also fitted in Badger and Bison reconnaissance/EW aircraft, and employed as surface-search radar for Hormone-A ASW helicopter. Range is approximately 175 n.miles (322 km). I-band.

> *aircraft*   Badger-C and later models
>   Hormone-A

Short Horn
Bomb/nav radar used in earlier bomber-type aircraft and in some updated aircraft. Reportedly associated with AS-5/6 missiles. Range approximately 115 n.miles (212 km). J-band (14–15 GHz). Fitted in the ''chin'' radome of the Bear-D for missile guidance.

> *aircraft*   Badger-A/C/G
>   Bear-D
>   Blinder-A/D

Toadstool
Navigation radar. I-band.

> *aircraft*   Cub

Wet Eye
Surface-search radar, apparently with sufficient target definition for locating raised submarine periscopes and snorkel masts. Radomes differ. J-band.

> *aircraft*   Bear-F
>   May

Wet Eye radome beneath the nose of a May anti-submarine aircraft. (U.S. Navy)

SHIP AND SUBMARINE RADARS

The large radome at left, on the SOVREMENNYY-class destroyer OTLICHNYY, houses the Band Stand missile control radar for the SS-N-22 missiles. Above it is a Kite Screech gunfire control radar, Palm Frond radar, and (top) Top Steer radar. Four of the ship's six Front Dome SA-N-7 missile control radars are visible as is the Bass Tilt gunfire control radar. (French Navy)

Band Stand

Search and missile tracking and control radar and data link for over-the-horizon targeting for SS-N-9 and SS-N-22 anti-ship missiles. The radar is mounted in a large radome. The Nanuchka II–class missile corvettes transferred to Third World navies have the SS-N-2 Styx vice SS-N-9 missile, and their Band Stand radome contains a Square Tie radar. Range is 25–35 n.miles (46–64.5 km). G/H-band.

destroyers	SOVREMENNYY
corvettes	Nanuchka I/III, Tarantul II/III
small combatants	Sarancha

Bass Tilt

Primarily the fire-control radar for 30-mm close-in (multi-barrel) gun; in the smaller combat craft the Bass Tilt is also used to control 76.2-mm guns, and in the Grisha III, 57-mm guns. The Bass Tilt is similar to the Drum Tilt and Muff Cob fire-control radars. Range is 10–12 n.miles (18–22 km). H-band.

carriers	KIEV
cruisers	Kara, Kresta II, SLAVA
destroyers	UDALOY
frigates	Grisha III/V
corvettes	Nanuchka III, PARCHIM II, Svetlak, Tarantul, Dergach
small combatants	Babochka, Matka, Slepen, Gorya
amphibious ships	IVAN ROGOV
AGIs	SSV-33
auxiliary ships	various classes

Big Net

Long-range, three-dimensional air-surveillance radar, generally found in ships with the SA-N-1 missile (also fitted in the cruiser DZERZHINSKIY with the SA-N-2 system.) The antenna has an elliptical parabolic form with an offset-fed reflector providing a narrow-azimuth beam; the feed horn is curved and underslung, with twin balancing vanes. First seen at sea in the missile range ship SIBIR' in the early 1960s. The Big Net antenna is mounted back-to-back with the Top Sail to form the Top Pair. Capable of detecting aircraft at high altitudes out to some 200 n.miles (370 km) and medium-altitude targets at over 85 n.miles (156.5 km). L-band.

cruisers	Kresta I
destroyers	Kashin
radar pickets	T-58
auxiliary ships	SIBIR', Vytegrales (1 unit)

Big Screen

Advanced air-search radar, apparently first fitted in the Kara-class cruiser KERCH during her 1988–1989 refit; replaced the Top Sail antenna. The antenna is estimated to be about 29 ft^2 (8 m^2).

Cake Stand

Massive, cylindrical TACAN (Tactical Aircraft Navigation) array and aircraft control system mounted above the superstructure in newer Soviet aircraft carriers. The Cake Stand structure is 9-meters high.

carriers	ADMIRAL GORSHKOV (ex-BAKU), ADMIRAL KUZNETSOV (ex-TBILISI)

Cheese Cake

Missile targeting radar for SS-N-2c Styx missiles. Installed from late 1970s. Range is 17–25 n.miles (31–46 km). I-band.

small combatants	Matka, Dergach

Big Net has been fitted in a variety of Soviet naval ships as well as large merchant icebreakers. This installation is in a diminutive T-43 ex-minesweeper configured as a radar picket. Note the large balancing vane.

The Big Screen radar was first observed publicly on the Kara-class ASW cruiser KERCH. Between the KERCH's 76.2-mm gun barrels are Side Globe EW antennas. (Capt. G.A.S.C. Wilson, RN)

The Plank Shave search/targeting radar (left) and Cheese Cake antenna (right) support the SS-N-2c Styx missiles on the Matka missile craft. Between them is a Bass Tilt gunfire control radar for the craft's 76.2-mm gun forward and 30-mm Gatling gun aft. Note the angle of bridge roof.

Cross Sword missile control radar for the SA-N-9 is fitted in the new carrier and destroyer classes. There are back-to-back paraboloid antennas for air search fitted above the main tracking antenna. The radomes probably house a missile-tracking radar and data link antenna. (Royal Navy)

Cross Sword

Fire control radar for SA-N-9 surface-to-air missiles in new Soviet destroyers. Several of the early UDALOY-class ships deployed without the radar or with only one installation; two are standard for the ships, one atop the bridge and one between the twin helicopter hangars.

Apparently other radars perform the Cross Sword function in the later KIROV-class cruisers and KIEV-class aircraft carriers that have the SA-N-9 missile.

carriers	ADMIRAL KUZNETSOV (ex-TBILISI), ADMIRAL GORSHKOV (ex-BAKU)
destroyers	UDALOY
frigates	Grisha IV

Don series

These are primarily navigation radars but in combat ships and craft probably have a target-designation function as well. They are installed in a variety of naval ship types; the Palm Frond radar is being installed in their place in newer Soviet ships. The Don series are horizontally polarized I-band radars. Range is approximately 25 n.miles (46 km).

The series currently in service are the Don-2 (9,250–9,500 MHz) and the newer Don-Kay (9,350–9,500 MHz). A few ships have both types; e.g., the replenishment ship BEREZINA has one Don-2 and two Don-Kay installations.

Drum Tilt

Acquisition and tracking radar for twin 25-mm and 30-mm AA guns. First of the weapon-control radar antennas with drum shape. The distinctive plastic radome is tilted about 25°, enclosing a circular parabolic reflector. Range is approximately 22 n.miles (40.5 km). H/I bands.

frigates	Koni
small combatants	various classes
amphibious	Polnocny
landing craft	Aist
auxiliary ships	SMOL'NYY

The Drum Tilt gunfire control radar is found in a large number of Soviet and Eastern Bloc ships and small craft. This Drum Tilt, on a Soviet torpedo craft, is seen with the back-up optical director, a feature found in many Soviet ships. (Sovfoto)

Eye Bowl

Fire-control radar for the SS-N-14 ASW missile in ships without the larger Head Lights radar. Fitted in pairs. Only the lead ship of the KIROV-class battle cruisers has the SS-N-14. Range is 10–12 n.miles (18.5–22 km). F-band.

cruisers	KIROV (1 unit)
destroyers	UDALOY
frigates	Krivak I/II

A Krivak II–class ASW frigate showing, from left, the Head Net-C air search radar, Don-2 navigation radar, twin Eye Bowl SS-N-14 missile-control radars, and Pop Group gunfire-control radar. On ASW cruisers the Eye Bowl functions are performed by the Head Lights radar. (U.S. Navy)

Fly Screen
Helicopter-control radar fitted in noncarrier ships that operate multiple helicopters.

cruisers	KIROV
destroyers	UDALOY
AGIs	Bambuck, SSV-33
auxiliary ships	MARSHAL NEDELIN

Fly Trap
Aircraft control/landing aid radar.

carriers	ADMIRAL GORSHKOV (ex-BAKU)

Front Door/Front Piece
Front Door and Front Piece are submarine sail-mounted radars for mid-course guidance of the SS-N-3a Shaddock and SS-N-12 Sandbox anti-ship missiles. The forward edge of the submarine's sail structure swings open for radar operation. The SLAVA-class cruisers, with the SS-N-12 missile, have a Front Door/Front Piece radar mounted on their pyramid structure. F-band. Also see Trap Door.

submarines	Echo II, Juliett
cruisers	SLAVA

The Front Door/Front Piece of an Echo II–class SSGN is exposed in this view. The antenna to track the SS-N-3 Shaddock missile in flight and relay mid-course guidance instructions rotates 180 degrees to become the forward end of the conning tower when the submarine is submerged.

The Front Door/Front Piece radar in the stowed position on a Juliett-class SSG. The radar arrangement required fitting the "cockpit" in the center of the sail; aft of the conning station is a (retracted) Snoop Tray radar and (extended) snorkel intake mast and radio antenna.

The Front Door/Front Piece missile control radar antenna for the SS-N-12 missiles in the cruiser SLAVA. Variants of the Front Door/Front Piece radar are found in the submarines and (as the Trap Door) in aircraft carriers. (Royal Navy)

Front Dome
Multiple radome antenna system for target illumination and missile tracking of SA-N-7 system. The radomes resemble Bass Tilt gunfire control radars. The test ship PROVORNYY has eight domes and each of the SOVREMENNYY-class ships has six. H/I-band.

destroyers	Kashin (1 unit), SOVREMENNYY

Half Plate
One antenna of the Top Plate dual-antenna system, fitted in place of the Strut pair in later Grisha V–class frigates.

frigates	Grisha V (some units)

The Half Plate radar—one antenna of the Strut Pair radar—on a Grisha V–class frigate. An Identification Friend or Foe (IFF) bar antenna is fitted above the radar; there are stabilizing vanes at right. (Royal Navy)

Hawk Screech

Fire-control radar for 45-mm, 57-mm, 76.2-mm, and 100-mm anti-aircraft guns in smaller ships. The circular dish antenna with feed horn is supported by four legs with a large box housing for transmitter and receiver aft of the antenna. Associated with backup optical directors. Similar to the Owl Screech radar in newer ships. Range is 8–12 n.miles (15–22 km). I-band.

frigates	Koni, Mirka, Petya, Riga (1 ship)
auxiliary ships	various classes

The widely deployed Hawk Screech radar, here on a Petya-class frigate, is associated with a variety of gun systems. A radio direction-finding loop is fitted between the Hawk Screech and the ship's lattice mast.

Head Lights

Fire-control radar for the SA-N-3 missile system and SS-N-14 ASW missile. The antenna consists of two large (almost 4-meter diameter) dishes—somewhat resembling headlights—with two smaller dishes mounted above. The main dishes are balanced by vanes at their rear. The smaller dishes probably provide command signals to the missile and the larger antennas provide tracking. The entire array can elevate and rotate 360°.

Head Lights-A/C are fitted in carriers and the Head Lights-B in cruisers, in the latter ships for use with the SS-N-14 system as well as the SA-N-3. (The Novorossiysk may be the only Head Lights-C ship.) Range is 40 n.miles (74 km). G/H-bands.

carriers	Kiev, Moskva
cruisers	Kara, Kresta II

Head Net-A

Air-search radar with two identical sets mounted in some ships. Antennas consist of large, elliptical paraboloid reflectors of open construction, illuminated by a feed horn carried by a boom projecting from under the scanner's lower edge; fitted with large balancing vanes. The radar is also known as Strand. Maximum range is 120 n.miles (221 km); reportedly capable of detecting aircraft at medium altitudes out to 70 n.miles (129 km). C-band (500–1,000 MHz). Most, if not all, have been deleted from Kashin-class ships.

cruisers	Kynda (some ships)
destroyers	Kashin

The Head Lights fire control radar employed with the SA-N-3 missile system is found in 22 large Soviet warships. The four tracking dishes and several smaller antennas, including two apparently for data link transmission, are visible on the after Head Lights-C in the Kara-class ASW cruiser Kerch. (Eric Grove)

Head Net-A air search and Scoop Pair SS-N-3 Shaddock fire-control radar on the after pylon mast of a Kynda-class missile cruiser. A variety of small EW domes are also fitted; the forward mast also carries a Head Net-A and Scoop Pair. The Plinth Net antenna is normally fitted on the (empty) platform at the forward side of this mast.

Head Net-B

Air/surface search radar consisting of a back-to-back installation of two Head Net-A reflectors with one angled 15° in elevation to provide both high and low coverage. First seen on a Krupnyy-class destroyer in 1965; also found in two missile tracking ships of the Desna class, but replaced in the late 1980s by Head Net-C radar. E/F-band.

Head Net-C

Back-to-back installation of two Head Net-A antennas with one angled 30° in elevation for simultaneous use as air-search and height-finding radar. First observed in 1963, Head Net-C is widely used on missile-armed ships, in company with Top Sail on larger units. The back-to-back arrangement of the radar antennas provides the advantages of reducing structural interference to radar emissions, improving data rates, and possibly making track transfer from two- to three-dimensional radars faster and more accurate through common stabilization. Range is approximately 60–70 n.miles (111–129 km). E/F-band.

Soviet designation is MR-310.

carriers	MOSKVA
cruisers	Kara, Kresta I/II, Kynda (some ships)
destroyers	Kashin
frigates	Krivak
amphibious	IVAN ROGOV
auxiliary ships	several classes

Kite Screech

Fire-control radar for 100-mm and new 130-mm guns. Range is 10–12 n.miles (18–22 km). I/J-band.

carriers	ADMIRAL GORSHKOV (ex-BAKU)
cruisers	KIROV, SLAVA
destroyers	SOVREMENNYY, UDALOY
frigates	Krivak II/III

The Kite Screech radar (left) is used for controlling large-caliber guns in newer Soviet warships; at right are Palm Frond and (above) Strut Pair radars on the UDALOY-class ASW destroyer VITSE ADMIRAL KULAKOV. Later ships have the Top Plate air-search radar.

Kivach 3

Late-model navigation radar in corvettes and small combatants.

corvettes	Tarantul
riverine	Yaz

Light Bulb

Radome apparently containing a missile data-link antenna for use with the SS-N-22 anti-ship missile for smaller ships that do not have satellite communications terminals. Note that it is used in conjunction with the Band Stand system.

corvettes	Tarantul II/III

Mad Hack

Fixed-array air search radar fitted in two intelligence collection ships. The Mad Hack is a 12-sided antenna that differs significantly from the phased-array panels in aircraft carriers. The two AGIs have very different array arrangements: The SSV-33 (NATO name Kapusta) has a panel on each side of the massive center tower/mast structure, one panel on the same structure facing aft (into the third tower/mast), and a fourth panel on deck, to the starboard side of the second tower/mast, facing skyward; the SSV-501 (PRIMOR'YE class) has three panels on a large deckhouse amidships, with panels facing to each side and aft.

AGIs	SSV-33 (Kapusta)
	SSV-501 (PRIMOR'YE)

Muff Cob

Fire-control radar for twin 57-mm automatic gun mounts. Similar to Drum Tilt with improved stabilization. An electro-optical camera is generally fitted to the Muff Cob mounting. H-band.

carriers	MOSKVA
cruisers	Kresta I/II
frigates	Grisha I/II
corvettes	Nanuchka I, Poti, T-58
small combatants	various classes
amphibious	Ropucha
auxiliary ships	BEREZINA, Lama, Manych, Ugra

The Muff Cob radar used for the 57-mm twin gun mounts is found in numerous Soviet ship classes. This installation is in a Grisha I–class frigate. (Royal Navy)

Nayada

New navigation radar. First seen in 1985.

small combatants	Gorya
auxiliary ships	various classes

Neptun

Navigation radar found in older ships. Range is 20–25 n.miles (37–46 km). I-band.

frigates	Riga
auxiliary ships	various classes

Okean

Search and navigation radar in various auxiliary ships.

Owl Screech

Improved version of Hawk Screech fire-control radar for 76.2-mm guns. Range is 15–18 n.miles (27.5–33 km). I-band.

carriers	KIEV
cruisers	Kara, Kynda
destroyers	Kashin
frigates	Krivak I
amphibious	IVAN ROGOV
AGIs	SSV-33
auxiliary ships	IVAN SUSANIN, SMOLN'YY

The Owl Screech (used with the 76.2-mm gun system) and Peel Group (associated with the SA-N-1 missile system) on the Kashin-class missile destroyer Obraztsovy. The Peel Group is a very complex antenna system. (N. Polmar)

Palm Frond
Improved small search-navigation radar mounted in a variety of ship types and replacing the Don-series radars in older units. Range is 25 n.miles (46 km). A-band.

carriers	Kiev (some units)
cruisers	Kara, Kirov, Kresta I, Slava
destroyers	Kashin (some units), Sovremenny, Udaloy
frigates	Krivak II/III
amphibious	Ivan Rogov
auxiliary ships	various classes

Peel Cone
Small air/surface search radar that first appeared on the single Babochka patrol boat in 1978.

small combatants	Babochka, Muravey, Pauk, Stenka (some units)

Peel Group
Fire-control radar for SA-N-1 missile system. This is an awkward-looking grouping that consists of four radars with elliptical and solid reflectors; two large and two small antennas are mounted in the horizontal and vertical positions to provide tracking (I-band) and missile guidance (E-band). Range is 35–40 n.miles (64.5–74 km).

cruisers	Kresta I, Kynda
destroyers	Kashin

Peel Pair
Small surface search and navigation radar.

corvettes	Nanuchka I/III

Plank Shave
Missile targeting radar for smaller ships. Probably a successor to the Square Tie radar.

corvettes	Pauk, Tarantul I
small combatants	Matka

Plate Steer
Phased-array, three-dimensional air-search radar consisting of a Top Steer antenna mounted back-to-back with a Top Plate, the latter antenna inclined at an angle of about 15°. Fitted in the fourth and fifth ships of the Sovremennyy class (Osmotritelnyy and Bezuprechnyy) as well as the fourth ship of the Kiev class. The combination was initially referred to as Top Steer/Top Plate.

carriers	Admiral Kuznetsov (ex-Tbilisi), Admiral Gorshkov (ex-Baku)
destroyers	Sovremennyy (2 units)

A Top Steer antenna mounted back-to-back with a Top Plate to form a three-dimensional search radar. This is one of two Sovremennyy-class missile destroyers with the installation. Three Palm Frond navigation radars are mounted around the Top Plate/Top Steer; immediately below are two Front Dome missile-control radars. (West German Navy)

Plinth Net
Data link antenna associated with the SS-N-3b Shaddock missile system. The Kresta I cruisers were built with this link; refitted to most of the Kyndas in the early 1980s.

cruisers	Kresta I, Kynda

Pop Group
Fire-control radar for SA-N-4 low-altitude missile system. There are three co-located antennas, similar to the SA-8 Land Roll radar. The Pop Group may be a monopulse, frequency-hopping system that can be operated at different frequencies. Range is 35–40 n.miles (64.5–74 km). F/H/I-bands.

carriers	Kiev (3 units)
cruisers	Kara, Kirov, Slava
frigates	Grisha I/III/V, Koni, Krivak
corvettes	Nanuchka, Dergach
small combatants	Sarancha
amphibious	Ivan Rogov
auxiliary ships	Berezina

The Pop Group radar is fitted in the large number of ships with the short-range SA-N-4 missile system. The larger circular antenna is for target tracking, and the smaller one to the right for missile guidance; above it is a surveillance radar. The comparable land-based radar, given the NATO code name Land Roll, has two guidance antennas. (Royal Navy)

Rear aspect of a Pop Group fire control/radar system. (Royal Navy)

Positive-E

A radome-fitted air/surface search radar in the East German-built PARCHIM II–class frigates built for Soviet service and the large Pomornik-class air cushion landing craft. The PARCHIM I–class ships built for Germany have the Strut Curve radar in lieu of the Positive-E.

frigates	PARCHIM II
amphibious	Pomornik

Post Lamp

Now-discarded torpedo fire-control radar fitted in early post–World War II warships. Still fitted in the naval oceanographic research ship ADMIRAL VLADIMIRSKIY (two sets).

Pot Drum

Surface-search and torpedo fire-control radar for small combatants housed in drum-shaped radome with a diameter of about 1.5 meters. The radar is identical to the Square Tie in Osa missile boats but housed in a drum-like radome approximately 5 ft (1.5 m) in diameter. The Soviet designation for this radar is *Baklan*. Range is 18–20 n.miles (33–37 km). I-band.

(Pot Head is a similar, smaller radar that was in use on East German torpedo boats.)

small combatants	Stenka, Turya

Punch Bowl

Mast-mounted submarine radome.

Round House

Tactical Aircraft Navigation (TACAN)-type radar; for all-weather control and homing of aircraft. Fitted in ships with multi-helicopter capability.

cruisers	Kara (1 ship), KIROV
destroyers	UDALOY
AGIs	Bambuk

Scoop Pair

Fire-control radar for mid-course guidance of the SS-N-3b Shaddock missile in surface ships. The "pair" consists of top-and-bottom antennas, each with a double feed horn. Also see Front series.

cruisers	Kresta I, Kynda

Sheet Bend

Small navigation radar found on coastal and river craft.

Ship Globe

Large tracking radar for use with long-range missile tests and satellites. The parabolic reflector is about 52½ ft (16 m) in diameter. In use on missile range and space event support ships.

auxiliary ships	Desna, MARSHAL NEDELIN

Sky Watch

Phased-array radar with four "faces" fitted in the aircraft carriers ADMIRAL KUZNETSOV (ex-TBILISI) and ADMIRAL GORSHKOV (ex-BAKU), the fourth KIEV-class carrier. The antenna faces are approximately 19 ft 8 in × 24 ft 7 in (6 m × 7.5 m). There is a Watch Guard IFF antenna above each phased array. Also see Mad Hack.

carriers	ADMIRAL GORSHKOV (ex-BAKU), ADMIRAL KUZNETSOV (ex-TBILISI)

Slim Net

High-definition air- and surface-search radar. It replaced the Hair Net on early post–World War II cruisers and destroyers. Slim Net has a distinctive open, lattice-type antenna with multi-leg feed horn and two large balancing vanes. Maximum range over 175 n.miles (322 km), but realistic effective range against aircraft at medium altitude is 25–30 n.miles (46–64.5 km). E-band.

Soviet designation is FUT-N.

frigates	Petya I, Mirka I/II, Riga
auxiliary ships	various classes

Snoop series

Mast-mounted, surface/air-search radars found in various nuclear and conventional submarine classes. The identified types are Snoop Pair, Snoop Plate, Snoop Slab, and Snoop Tray. Range is estimated at 25 n.miles (46 km) against aircraft and 12 n.miles (22 km) against large surface ships. H/I-band.

The large Snoop Pair—found in the Typhoon SSBN and Oscar SSGN—has back-to-back reflectors with overhead feed horns of different sizes; the antenna assembly is mounted above a can-like structure that appears to be an ECM antenna.

Two of the four phased-array radar faces of the Sky Watch system on the VSTOL carrier ADMIRAL GORSHKOV (ex-BAKU). The ADMIRAL KUZNETSOV (ex-TBILISI) also has this radar. Above the island is the forward Big Ball SATCOM antenna, Cake Stand TACAN, and Plate Steer radar. (U.S. Navy, Lt. P.J. Azzolina)

A Slim Net search radar on a Petya I–class frigate. There are paired Watch Dog EW antennas hidden in the maze of waveguides and radio antennas; at left is a High Pole-B EW antenna.

The Snoop Pair radar of a Typhoon-class submarine shows the twin overhead feed horns and paraboloid antennas. The radar is fitted on a retractable mast. (Royal Navy)

Spin Trough

Search and navigation radar installed as alternative to Don-series radars, primarily in older surface ships and small craft. I-band.

frigates	Krivak I
corvettes	Pauk, T-58
small combatants	Zhuk, Yaz
mine warfare	Andryusha, Ilyusha, Olya, Sonya, T-43, Yevgenya, Zhenya
amphibious	Aist, Alligator, Polnocny, Vydra

Square Tie

Search and target designation radar in small combatants for the SS-N-2 Styx missile. Detection range for a destroyer up to 25 n.miles (46 km) and another missile boat at perhaps 10 n.miles (18.5 km). Also fitted in Nanuchka II–series missile corvettes for foreign transfer. I-band.

small combatants	Osa

The rear of a Snoop Tray radar on a Victor I SSN (left) and the front of the radar on a Victor II SSN (right). The feed is fitted in the rounded "head" of the radar mast. (Royal Navy)

Strand
See Head Net-A.

Strut Curve
Small air/surface-search radar fitted in smaller warships and auxiliary ships. Open, lattice-type elliptical parabolic reflector with horn feed from a boom projecting from the lower edge of the scanner. Maximum range is 150 n.miles (276 km) but realistically about 60 n.miles (111 km) against aircraft at medium altitudes. No balancing vanes are fitted. F-band (3,000–4,000 MHz).

frigates	Grisha, Koni, Mirka, Petya
corvettes	Poti, T-58
minelayers	Alesha
amphibious	Ropucha
auxiliary ships	BEREZINA, IVAN SUSANIN

Strut Pair
Air-search radar with antenna formed by two Strut Curve antennas mounted back-to-back. Fitted in aircraft carriers and smaller warships. F-band.

carriers	KIEV (2 units), ADMIRAL KUZNETSOV (ex-TBILISI)
destroyers	Kashin (1 unit), UDALOY (some units)
frigates	Grisha V (some units)

Sun Visor
Gunfire-control radar with solid parabolic antenna fitted to Wasp Head fire-control directors in older ships (completed from 1953 onward) for use with 130-mm and 100-mm guns. Sun Visor-B version fitted from 1956. Previously found in SVERDLOV-class cruisers and Kotlin-class destroyers. Range is 15 n.miles (27.5 km). H/I-band.

frigates	Riga
auxiliary ships	Don

The Sun Visor-B radar fitted to the Wasp Head gunfire control director of the now-discarded cruiser DZERZHINSKIY of the SVERDLOV class. This combination was found in several classes of warships from the late 1940s. There are twin 37-mm gun mounts in the foreground. (Sovfoto)

Top Dome
Missile guidance radar for SA-N-6 consisting of 4-meter hemispheric radome, fixed in elevation and mechanically steered in azimuth. It is installed with a series of smaller radomes, apparently for tracking multiple targets. The KIROV-class battle cruisers have two Top Dome antennas, the SLAVAS and SA-N-6 trials ship AZOV have one. Range is 40 n.miles (74 km). I/J-band.

cruisers	Kara (1 ship), KIROV, SLAVA

The after Top Dome missile control radar on a KIROV-class battle cruiser. The Top Dome/SA-N-6 system is found only in the KIROV and Kara cruiser classes. (Royal Navy)

Top Knot
Spherical Tactical Aircraft Navigation (TACAN) array. It was superseded in the fourth ship of the KIEV class by a large, cylindrical TACAN housing.

carriers	KIEV (3 units)

Top Pair
Long-range, three-dimensional surveillance radar. See Top Sail listing for details. C/F band.

cruisers	KIROV, SLAVA

Top Plate
Air/surface-search radar fitted to the UDALOY-class destroyers in place of one of the two Strut Pair radars beginning with the third ship of the class (the MARSHAL VASIL'YEVSKIY, completed in 1983). Also fitted in other ships back-to-back with the Top Steer to form the Plate Steer radar (see above). A modified, single-antenna Top Plate radar, mounted horizontally, is fitted in the Grisha V light frigate (see Half Plate).

The antenna has a flat ("solid") plate mounted in front of a "mesh" antenna plate.

destroyers	UDALOY (later units), SOVREMENNYY (later units)
icebreakers	ARKTIKA (some units)

The back-to-back Top Sail and Big Net radars form the Top Pair installation, shown here on a SLAVA-class cruiser. The combination is also found in KIROV-class ships. (Royal Navy).

Top Plate radar in a later UDALOY-class ASW destroyer with IFF interrogator antennas fixed above both of the asymmetrical antennas. Paired Round House TACAN antennas flank the radar; at right is a Salt Pot IFF antenna. (West German Navy)

The Top Plate radar on the UDALOY-class destroyer ADMIRAL SPIRIDOV shows an IFF interrogator atop both arrays. (Courtesy *Sea Power*)

Top Sail

Long-range, three-dimensional air-search and early-warning radar fitted in major warships. The antenna consists of a large lattice scanner that has a cylindrical cross section with the axis tilted back about 20° from the vertical. The reflector is illuminated by a linear radiating element located parallel to the cylindrical axis. It uses frequency scan in elevation. Two large balancing vanes are fitted. The Top Sail is used in conjunction with the Head Net-C search and Head Lights missile control radars. Top Sail is mounted back-to-back with Big Net to form the Top Pair radar. C-band. There are several variations.

carriers	KIEV (3 units), MOSKVA
cruisers	Kara, Kresta II, SLAVA

Top Steer

Medium-size, three-dimensional air-search radar, somewhat similar in appearance to the larger Top Sail. The larger antenna is fitted back-to-back with the Strut Pair radar antenna with a common feed. The Top Steer uses frequency scan in elevation. Range is 150 n.miles (276 km). F-Band.

carriers	KIEV (3 units)
destroyers	Kashin (1 unit), SOVREMENNYY

Tracking Radars

The large Soviet fleet of missile range instrumentation ships (Navy) and space event support ships (civilian) have a variety of tracking radars and telemetry/communications antennas. The following are NATO code names assigned to those systems:

End Tray	Quad Ring	Ship Globe (see above)
Owl Perch	Quad Spring	Ship Shell
Quad Leaf	Ship Bowl	

Trap Door

Radar for mid-course guidance of the SS-N-12 anti-ship missile. The Front-series radars in submarines and the cruiser SLAVA are similar. In the KIEV-class VSTOL carriers the antenna retracts into the forecastle when not in use. F-band.

carriers	KIEV

The KIEV-class VSTOL carrier MINSK, showing (from left) Top Steer, Top Knot, and Top Sail antennas. Both the Top Steer and Top Sail provided three-dimensional air search, reflecting the Soviet approach to redundancy in electronic capability. The Top Knot TACAN is found in only three of the KIEV-class ships.

SONARS

The Soviet Navy began major efforts in the early 1960s to put to sea high-performance sonars. The initial postwar surface ships had mostly the Tamir-5 series of high-frequency, hull-mounted sonars. They were succeeded by the Pegasus-2 series from the mid-1950s, and the Herkules series from the late 1950s. The contemporary submarines were fitted with the Tamir-5L sonar. Subsequently a variety of improved sonars were developed for the Soviet warships that began joining the fleet in the 1960s. Submarines were fitted with active-passive Herkules and passive Fenks sonars.

In particular, by the 1960s there was an effort to reduce frequencies, and during the past two decades they have been reduced from the 20–30 KHz range to about 2–15 KHz. Variable-Depth Sonars (VDS), dipping sonars (from helicopters and surface ships), and directional systems have been introduced.

Significantly, starting with the Victor III–class SSN, first introduced in 1978, the Soviets have deployed towed passive sonar arrays. Such systems appear to have narrow-band processors, greatly enhancing their capability. Other submarine classes have now been fitted with towed arrays.

The Soviet Navy is also testing a probable surveillance towed array sonar similar to the U.S. Navy's SURTASS (Surveillance Towed Array Sonar System). The SSV-328 (ex-YUG) is employed as a SURTASS ship; see chapter 24.

Soviet ASW fixed-wing aircraft and helicopters carry air-dropped, expendable sonobuoys.

The following table lists major Soviet sonars that have been identified. Herkules and Pegas are Soviet names; others are U.S./ NATO code names.

TABLE 29-1. SHIP AND SUBMARINE SONARS

Type*	Name	Ships/Submarines	
HF/keel-mounted	Herkules (Wolf Paw)	cruisers	Kynda, Kresta I
		corvettes	Poti
HF/keel-mounted	Herkules or Pegas	frigates	Mirka, Petya, Riga
MF/keel-mounted	Bull Horn	destroyers	SOVREMENNYY, mod. Kashin
MF/bow-mounted	Bull Nose	cruisers	Kara, Krivak II
		frigates	Krivak, Grisha
MF/VDS	Mare Tail	carriers	KIEV, MOSKVA
		destroyers	mod. Kashin, Kashin
		frigates	
LF/keel-mounted	Moose Jaw	carriers	KIEV, MOSKVA
LF/bow-mounted	Horse Jaw	cruisers	KIROV
		destroyers	UDALOY
LF/VDS	Horse Tail	destroyers	UDALOY
HF/dipping	Rat Tail	corvettes	several classes
		helicopters	Hormone-A
MF/dipping	Lamb Tail or Foal Tail	helicopters	Haze-A, Helix-A
MF/dipping	Elk Tail	frigates	Grisha II+
LF/dipping		frigates	Grisha I

* HF = High Frequency; MF = Medium Frequency; LF = Low Frequency; VDS = Variable-Depth Sonar.

A Helix-A ASW helicopter with its active dipping sonar being lowered. These helicopters are embarked in ASW surface combatants as well as aircraft carriers.

A helicopter-type dipping sonar fitted in a Mirka II–class frigate. Several classes of ASW surface ships and small craft are fitted with these sonars.

Variable-depth sonar "fish" being handled aboard a Krivak-class ASW frigate. The Soviet Navy has continued to pursue VDS systems after they have been largely superseded in the U.S. fleet by towed arrays.

A Charlie-class SSGN showing the sail structure with a large sonar installation forward, cockpit in the center, and various masts; the largest one is for the Brick Split/Brick Pulp EW antennas. The position of the targeting sonar facilitates its use when the boat is running at shallow depth tracking surface targets. The acoustically transparent paint over the sonar dome shows wear; some of the craft's anechoic tiles are missing.

Variable-depth sonar of the battle cruiser FRUNZE.

The bow sonar installation of a Foxtrot-class submarine: The "happy face" antenna around the bow is the Trout Cheek passive array; the larger dome has the Russian name *Feniks* and is a searchlight-type sonar; the upper antenna has the NATO code name Fez and is probably an underwater telephone. (U.S. Navy)

Towed array installation in a modified Petya I–class frigate; this variant is called a Type B by Western intelligence. The Type C has the sonar installation fully housed, with a transom door for lowering a VDS. The curved devices atop the towed array cable are stabilizers.

Seafloor Acoustic Systems

The Soviet Navy has employed limited seafloor acoustic systems to detect submarines since World War II, when hydrophones were planted near harbor entrances and across bays to detect German U-boats.

The Soviets have deployed a modern acoustic detection system with planar arrays in the Pacific near the Soviet land mass where broad-area surveillance is desired. This project is called Cluster Lance by NATO. The Soviets may also be deploying barrier arrays at points of ingress and egress from their SSBN operating areas in the Barents, Greenland, and Kara Seas, placed in or near trenches at choke points along the polar archipelago. These arrays would serve as choke-point "trip wires" to detect Western attack submarines and would not be for long-range surveillance (as is the U.S. SOSUS system). However, the lack of fixed, long-range acoustic systems have forced the Soviets to rely largely on ship and aircraft acoustic detection for open-ocean search.

Sonobuoys

Soviet ASW fixed-wing aircraft and helicopters carry expendable sonobuoys that can be dropped into the sea, deploy a hydrophone, and transmit underwater sounds to the aircraft. The first known Soviet sonobuoy was the RGB-56, which entered service in 1956. (The U.S. Navy introduced sonobuoys at the end of World War II.)

The RGB-56 was first seen by Western naval forces in 1959. It was released from an altitude of 500 to 1,000 feet (152 to 305 m) at a speed of 173 m.p.h. (277 km/h) or less. The sonobuoy was lowered to the water by parachute. Eighteen channels were available for aircraft monitoring of the buoys. Although the buoy had an estimated battery life of up to four or five days, the buoy was designed to scuttle within 24 hours. The RGB was approximately 48 inches (1.2 m) long and 8.75 inches (222.25 mm) in diameter and weighed 60 pounds (27.3 kg).

The subsequent RGB-64 was a smaller version of the RGB-56, both being omnidirectional. Later Soviet sonobuoys that have been identified publicly are the BM-1, which became operational in the late 1960s, and the Type 75, displayed by the U.S. Department of Defense in 1988. The BM-1 was 50.5 inches (1.28 m) long and 6 inches (152.4 mm) in diameter. The latter sonobuoy, according to Western officials, has an electronics package similar to the U.S. Navy's AN/SSQ-41B sonobuoy.

This unit is part of a fixed, bottom-moored submarine acoustic detection system given the Soviet designation MGS-407M (*Mashina Gidroakusticheskaya Svyaz'*—hydroacoustic communications machine). At right is the "pop-up" antenna that deploys to the surface at prescribed intervals to transmit data to a shore facility. These devices have been deployed off the U.S. coasts.

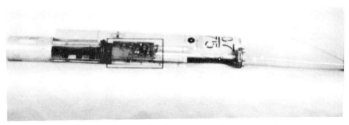

A Soviet Type 75 sonobuoy with the electronics compartment open. The partially extended data link antenna is seen at right. According to the U.S. Department of Defense, it has many features copied from the U.S. Navy's AN/SSQ-41B sonobuoy. (U.S. Department of Defense)

This is a Soviet RGAB (*Radio Gidroakusticheskaya Aviatsionnaya Buy*—radio hydroacoustic machine buoy). It has a ten-element hydrophone that detaches and is lowered from the buoy to a predetermined depth.

These are apparently sensors for a non-acoustic submarine detection system, shown here fitted on a Victor III–class SSN. This installation is installed in a fixed mounting to starboard of the submarine's cockpit. (Royal Navy)

Raised masts and periscopes of a Typhoon-class SSBN. From right are a Snoop Pair radar mounted on a Rim Hat electronic intercept (circular) antenna, general-purpose periscope, Park Lamp high-frequency direction-finder, attack periscope (small head), and Pert Spring satellite navigation antenna. The Park Lamp and Pert Spring masts have small plates fitted, probably to reduce flow turbulence when the masts are raised while underwater. (Royal Navy)

CHAPTER 30

Bases and Ports

Soviet warships, merchant ships, and a floating dry dock at the massive port complex of Vladivostok. In the center is the VSTOL carrier Novorossiysk and, beyond, a Sverdlov-class gun cruiser being stripped in preparation for scrapping. (Courtesy Abe Go)

The Soviet Union has a longer coastline than any other nation—half again as long as that of the United States:[1]

Region	length (n.miles)
Arctic	8,166
Baltic	988
Black Sea	867
Pacific	6,075
Total	16,096

Naval base facilities have been expanded during the past two decades, primarily to service the increasing number of nuclear-powered submarines and the larger surface warships of the Soviet fleet, especially the KIROV-class nuclear battle cruisers and the KIEV and later classes of aircraft carriers. In order to dry dock the latter ships in the Northern Fleet (Arctic) and Pacific Fleet (Far East) base areas, the Soviets have purchased large floating dry docks. A Swedish-built large floating dry dock was provided for the naval base at Murmansk and a Japanese-built floating dock for the base at Vladivostok, both capable of accommodating a KIEV-class aircraft carrier. A third large floating dry dock for carriers has been built in Yugoslavia and delivered to the Black Sea.

There is also an on-going expansion of commercial port capacity and increase in cargo-handling facilities. In an extensive containerization program, container ships have been constructed in large numbers (see chapter 32), ports have been built or refitted to handle containerized cargo, and a special rail service has been established to speed containers across the Soviet Union.

1. By comparison, the U.S. coastlines total 10,985 n.miles, of which 6,544 are in Alaska.

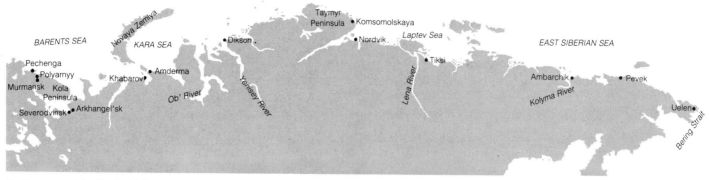

Arctic coast of the Soviet Union.

The Soviet port expansion has also included facilities for handling coal, ore, lumber, and petroleum products more rapidly. And since the Soviet Union has become a petroleum exporter (although most through pipelines to Eastern Europe), this includes provisions for handling large tankers.

The following are the major Soviet bases and ports, listed by geographic area.

ARCTIC COAST

The Northern Fleet is based almost entirely on the Kola Peninsula, with the largest complex of bases on the Kola inlet, which extends 32 miles (51 km) southward from the Barents Sea to the junction of the Tuloma and Kola rivers. On the eastern side of the inlet is the sprawling port of Murmansk and the large naval complex of Severomorsk, which is Northern Fleet headquarters, while on the eastern side of the inlet is Polyarnyy. There are also several smaller ports on the inlet.

Situated about 155 miles (250 km) east of the border with Norway, the inlet is free of ice year around, kept open by the warm waters of the Gulf Stream, which carries warm water northward from the Gulf of Mexico, a distance of 6,000 miles (9,600 km). Although there was interest in developing Murmansk as a port by Russian traders and whalers in the eighteenth century, there was little progress until World War I. The tsarist government wanted a port for sea access to the Allies, as the Baltic and Black Sea ports were vulnerable to German and Turkish interdiction.

By September 1916 a railroad to the port was complete and it was formally established to receive transports with military supplies for the Russian armies. American and British troops landed at Murmansk in the Russian Civil War, and it again became known to Americans in World War II because of the "Murmansk Run" for Allied merchant ships carrying war supplies to the Soviet Union. (Arkhangel'sk was also a key port for the convoys from Britain and the United States.)

Murmansk is some 125 miles (200 km) north of the Arctic Circle, the world's largest city north of the circle. Its current population is about 500,000 and Murmansk is experiencing a relatively rapid rate of growth. The port is the western terminus for the commercial Northern Sea Route. It has recently been modernized to handle freight containers and is a focal point of the fishing and fish-processing industries; it has two building yards for commercial ships and has maritime schools with intermediate and higher curricula.

The town of Severomorsk (formerly Vayenga), about ten miles (16 km) northeast of Murmansk, is headquarters for the Northern Fleet. The Severomorsk base complex has extensive support facilities for warships, including ammunition depots. (There was a disastrous explosion at a principal munitions depot in 1984 that destroyed a large portion of the Northern Fleet's missiles. The explosions were of a magnitude that led Western intelligence agencies to suspect initially that there had been a nuclear explosion.)

Polyarnyy (formerly Aleksandrovsk) is a major base for Northern Fleet surface ships and submarines. Although a small harbor, this was the principal base for the Northern Fleet during World War II. The harbor also suffers from poor holding ground and a large tidal range; however, it is generally free of ice.

Submarines are also believed to be based at the port of Gremikha (near Iokanga), some 125 miles (200 km) farther east than the Polyarnyy-Murmansk complex, and at the Litsa Guba-Bolshaya Litsa complex, about equal distance from the ports of Pechenga and Polyarnyy, and only some 35 miles (57 km) from the Norwegian border. There are four bases in Bolshaya Litsa: Litsa north is a submarine maintenance area, Litsa south is a base for nuclear attack submarines, and Litsa southeast is used for Typhoon and other SSBNs. These facilities are on the eastern side of the fjord; on the western side is another submarine support facility. Norwegian specialists, working from commercial satellite photography, estimate that there are a total of 67,570 feet (20,600 m) of piers in the fjord.[2]

At the Bolshaya Litsa complex—probably the southeast facility—are several large, underground tunnels for strategic missile submarines cut into the adjacent mountains. The tunnels, in which Northern Fleet SSBNs can be rearmed during a conflict, were initially completed in 1984. The tunnels are said to be large enough to accommodate Typhoon SSBNs, apparently providing protection from conventional and nuclear attack when they are undergoing maintenance or being rearmed.

Pechenga, formerly Finnish Petsamo, is both a naval and fishing port. It is northwest of Litsa Guba, only 18 miles (29 km) from the Norwegian border.

There are many other bases on the Kola Peninsula, which is estimated to have as many as 40 military airfields as well as bases for two army motorized rifle divisions and the Northern Fleet's Naval Infantry brigade.

Southeast of the Kola Peninsula, on the Gulf of Dvina, which opens onto the White Sea, is Arkhangel'sk (Archangel), the oldest seaport of the country. It is a major port, provincial capital, and the largest city on the Soviet Arctic coast. When Peter I became tsar in 1682 it was Russia's only outlet to the sea. Arkhangel'sk is blocked by ice for up to 190 days per year. The extensive use of icebreakers, however, keeps the port open to commercial shipping almost continuously. During the past few years the port's facilities—along 32 miles (51 km) of waterways—have been greatly enlarged, and container and fuel-handling facilities have been added. Arkhangel'sk can be reached by ship from Leningrad via the lake-canal route between Leningrad and the White Sea. The White Sea Canal (formerly the Stalin Canal) is iced over five or six months of the year, as is the White Sea itself. The canal is 140 miles (224 km) long and was built in just 20 months in the early 1930s as one of Stalin's first major slave-labor projects.[3] A 900-mile (1,440-km) rail line connects Murmansk with Leningrad, with goods being transferred at the port of Leningrad for the North Sea Route. From Murmansk, ships also sail westward, to Europe and the Americas, especially during the winter months when the eastern Baltic is partially blocked by ice.

2. Thomas Ries and Johnny Skorve, *Investigating Kola: A Study of Military Bases Using Satellite Photography* (London: Brassey's Defence Publishers, 1987), pp. 57–59.

3. Several hundred thousand slave laborers died in constructing the canal. A graphic description of their efforts and privations in building this inland waterway is given in Aleksandr I. Solzhenitsyn, *The Gulag Archipelago—Two* (New York: Harper & Row, 1975), pp. 86–100.

About 25 miles (40 km) west of Arkhangel'sk is the major shipyard complex of Severodvinsk, which was known as Molotovsk until 1957.[4] A railway line ties the two cities together and links them with the main rail systems to the south. Severodvinsk was founded in the late 1930s as Stalin sought to develop naval support facilities in the Arctic. Today Severodvinsk rivals Arkhangel'sk in size. It has a small port, but its principal importance is as a naval shipbuilding and industrial center.

There are a number of smaller but still significant commercial ports along the Arctic coast. Several are transshipment points for the intensive river traffic that plies the long Siberian rivers. South of the Novaya Zemlya islands in the Kara Sea are the ports of Khabarov and Amderma on the Yugorskiy peninsula. These ports are used to ship coal from mines on the mainland and have provided logistic support for the huge slave-labor camp established on Novaya Zemlya in the 1930s and later the early Soviet ICBM emplacements on those islands.

Farther east are the important ports of Dikson at the mouth of the Yenisey River, Komsomolskaya on Pravda island off the northern coast of the Taymyr Peninsula, Nordvik on Khatanga Bay, Tiksi at the delta of the Lena River, Ambarchik near the mouth of the Kolyma River, Pevek at Chaunskaya Bay, and Ulen on the Bering Strait, at the eastern tip of Siberia.

BALTIC SEA COAST

Leningrad is the second largest city of the Soviet Union (population over 4 million) and the shipping and shipbuilding center of the Soviet Baltic coast.[5] The city boasts five major shipyards, several lesser yards, and a large commercial port. Situated at the eastern end of the Gulf of Finland, the city is built on the delta of the Neva River and is laced with rivers and canals. The city is also the Baltic entrance to the lake-canal route to the White Sea.

4. See chapter 31 for descriptions of specific Soviet shipyards.

5. The city was founded as St. Petersburg by Tsar Peter the Great; it was changed to Petrograd in 1914 and renamed Leningrad upon Lenin's death in 1924. In 1991 the citizens of the city voted to change the name to St. Petersburg; it was changed on 6 September 1991.

The Gulf of Finland is iced over about one-half of the year, but here too the use of icebreakers significantly extends the shipping season and provides continuous access for naval units. Leningrad's large commercial port is on the southern side of the city. Although there are major naval shipyards and training activities in the city, the Baltic Fleet headquarters is not at Leningrad nor are many warships based there. However, there are always naval units there for trials, training, and overhaul.

Some 15 miles (24 km) west of Leningrad in the Gulf of Finland is Kotlin island. In its old port city of Kronshtadt are a commercial port, a naval base, and a major ship repair yard. Through World War II this was the principal base of the Baltic Fleet. Oranienbaum, south of Kronshtadt on the mainland, is believed to be a base for light naval forces.

The shipyards at Leningrad provide maintenance for diesel-electric submarines, which are based at Kronshtadt, Kaliningrad, Paldiski, and Liepaja.

Farther west, at the southern entrance to the gulf, is the port of Tallinn (formerly Revel), the capital of the Estonian Soviet Socialist Republic (SSR). Estonia, Latvia, and Lithuania comprise the Baltic states. They were Russian from the time of Peter I until World War I, then independent from 1918–1920 until 1939, when, at the outset of World War II, they were seized by Soviet troops and incorporated into the Soviet Union. (During World War II they were overrun by German forces.)

At Tallinn are naval and commercial ports that are ice-free most of the year, and numerous warships up to cruiser size are homeported there. Nearby are air bases amd army installations. There has been a recent addition of commercial port facilities at Tallinn, primarily for refrigerated goods and agricultural products. The first phase of construction was completed in the late 1980s with further expansion planned.

Almost directly south of Tallinn on the Gulf of Riga is the city of Riga, capital of the Latvian SSR and a major seaport. Riga's history as a port dates back more than one thousand years to when it was a crossroads for trade between Scandinavian tribes and Greece. Actually situated on the Daugava River, Riga has several shipyards

By 1990—when this photo was taken—the remains of hundreds of Soviet surface warships and submarines littered bays and coves along the Soviet coastline as older units were being discarded faster than they could be scrapped. This scene is near Murmansk in the Arctic. (Courtesy Messrs. William Arkin and Joshua Handler)

Riga—one of Europe's oldest ports—is typical of the older ports of the Soviet Union, having been expanded and modernized. The increase in Soviet merchant shipping has demanded the development of new ports as well as expanding older ones. (Sovfoto, Yuri Belinsky)

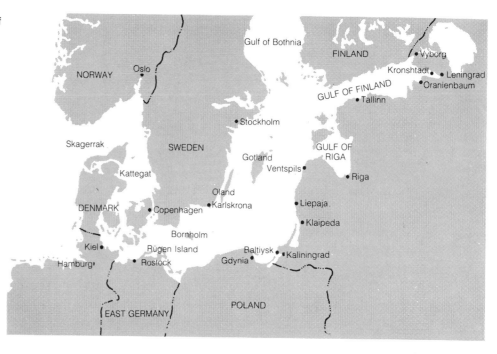

Baltic Sea.

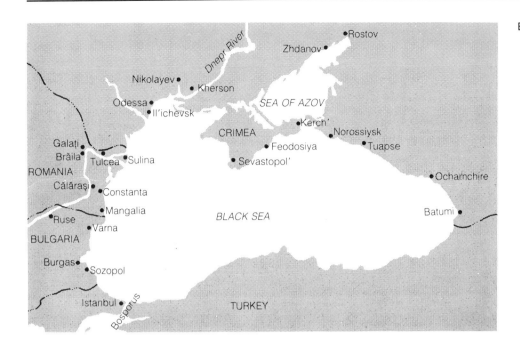

Black Sea.

and extensive container-handling facilities have been added. A Soviet naval base has been reported under development in the area.

West of Riga is the newer commercial port of Ventspils (formerly Windau), at the mouth of the Venta River. This port has several times the cargo-handling capacity of Riga, and an oil export facility can accommodate super tankers of more than 100,000 deadweight tons. American firms have assisted in the construction of a large loading complex for ammonia and other chemicals at the port. Although the Gulf of Riga is iced over for 80 to 90 days per year, Ventspils is almost always ice-free.

The next significant Baltic port is Liepaja (formerly Libau), on a narrow sandspit between the Baltic and Lake Libau. Protected naval and commercial harbors are located there. Klaipeda (formerly Memel) in the Lithuanian SSR at the mouth of the Memel River is the republic's capital city. It has long been a shipbuilding center, with commercial and naval harbors, and a petroleum-loading port.

The adjacent cities of Baltiysk (formerly Pillau) and Kaliningrad (Konigsberg) are of major importance to Soviet naval operations in the Baltic. Both are situated in what formerly was East Prussia, which, after being overrun by Soviet troops in World War II, was incorporated into the Soviet Union after the war. Baltiysk is headquarters for the Baltic Fleet and home port for many of the fleet's major warships. There is also a fishing port. And, being near the Polish border, it also hosts a flotilla of KGB Maritime Border Troops. Kaliningrad, on the Pregel River, is connected to Baltiysk by canal. It is a major commercial port and contains the large Yantar shipyard. A number of naval activities are located in the area, in part because these are the westernmost ports of the Soviet Union.

BLACK SEA COAST

The Black Sea is a major trading and shipbuilding region of the Soviet Union. The newest of the major ports is Ust'-Dunaysk at the western end of the sea, near Vilkovo, which lies at the northernmost mouth of the Danube River. The port was developed in the late 1970s to handle bulk cargo carriers and barge-carrying ships of the international association Interlikhter (whose members are Bulgaria, Czechoslovakia, Hungary, and the Soviet Union).

Odessa is probably the nation's largest port, handling over 20 million tons of cargo annually, almost twice the amount handled by Leningrad. Unlike most Soviet ports, Odessa is not located on a river but on the Black Sea coast, a few miles east of the mouth of the Dniester River. One of Russia's oldest cities, Odessa is also a major passenger/tourist terminal in an area of historical and cultural importance. Odessa's commercial port has more than five miles (eight km) of quays, with facilities for handling specialized cargoes

such as grain and sugar. Two large new ports are being built near Odessa because that port area is surrounded by the city proper and cannot be expanded. In addition, Odessa city officials fear that dust and air pollution from the ships and dry cargoes may discourage the tourist trade and damage historic structures. Odessa is also a naval base.

Twelve miles (19 km) southwest of Odessa is the commercial port of Il'ichevsk, whose construction began in the late 1950s. It has specialized facilities for handling containers and grain, as well as iron ore and coal. Nearby Yuzhnyy (South Port) is also being developed as a major port; the first ship to depart the port, the ammonia tanker BALDURY, sailed in August 1978. Pipelines running from a large mineral fertilizer plant in Odessa directly to the harbor permit the loading of ammonia into specialized tankers. Complexes for loading containers, lumber, coal, and ore have also been developed, with a goal of handling some 25 million tons of cargo per year. Eventually the Yuzhnyy port should be about as large as Odessa and Il'ichevsk combined.

These ports and others along this portion of the Black Sea coast are frozen for about three months of the year but are kept open for ship traffic by icebreakers.

The largest shipbuilding and industrial center and a major port of the Black Sea is Nikolayev. Located at the junction of the Bug and Ingul rivers, the city has two major and several lesser shipyards and ship repair facilities. The commercial port has more than two miles (3.2 km) of quays.

A short distance to the east is Kherson on the Dnepr River, about 20 miles (32 km) from where that long and important waterway enters the Black Sea. There are several maritime industries and a major shipyard in the city in addition to the large commercial port.

Historic Sevastopol on the Crimean peninsula is headquarters for the Black Sea Fleet and the main base area for naval units that operate in the Black Sea and Mediterranean. Small craft and submarines are based in Sevastopol and its southeastern suburb of Balaklava. Several small shipyards, as well as extensive naval storage and other support facilities, are located in and around Sevastopol. Also in the Crimea are the smaller ports of Balaklava and Feodosiya, which are used by submarines and escorts; Chernomorskoye; and Donuzlav. Most of the Black Sea Fleet's air bases are located in the Crimea including the naval aviation school and development center at Saki.

Northeast of the Crimea is the Sea of Azov, entered through the narrow Kerch Strait between the Kerch and Taman peninsulas. Most of the Sea of Azov is frozen from the end of November until mid-April. About 180 miles (288 km) northeast of the Kerch Strait and 30 miles (48 km) north of where the Don River enters the Sea of

Azov is the port of Rostov. Rostov is the meeting point for cargo from the Don and Volga rivers, which are connected by canal. Through these rivers and canals flow goods and materials from ports on the Black and Caspian seas as well as from the inland ports of European Russia.

After Rostov, Zhdanov (formerly Mariupol) on the western coast of the Sea of Azov, is the second major port of that sea. It is an industrial city, being a major steel center. Also shipped through Zhdanov's commercial port are grain, coal, and petroleum.

Novorossiysk, on the Black Sea to the east of the Kerch Strait, is another major industrial city with a commercial port and a naval harbor for light forces. There are repair yards in the area but no significant shipbuilding facility.

Lesser ports along the northern coast of the Black Sea include Kamysh-Burun and Tuapse, which are naval and commercial ports; Kerch, location of the major shipyard; Ochamchira, a small commercial port and possibly a submarine facility; Poti, at the mouth of the Rioni River, with both commercial and naval sections to its port, destroyers being based there; and Batumi, near the Turkish border and starting point of the Trans-Caucasian Railway. Batumi is also the coastal terminal for the oil pipeline from Baku and handles commercial and naval ships up to frigates.

PACIFIC COAST

Vladivostok—"Ruler of the East"—is the major Soviet port complex on the Pacific coast. Located at the southern end of the Muraiev peninsula, Vladivostok is at the head of Golden Horn Bay, an arm of Peter the Great Bay. Its hills and bays have led some visitors to call Vladivostok the "San Francisco of the Far East." The city was the original eastern port terminus of the Trans-Siberian Railway. Vladivostok is only ten miles (16 km) from the Chinese border, making it extremely vulnerable to an attack by China; it is less than 100 miles (160 km) from North Korea. (American and Japanese troops landed at Vladivostok in 1918, during the Russian Civil War; those troops were not withdrawn until 1922.) The waters off Vladivostok are covered by ice for about two months of the year with the inner part of the Golden Horn Bay frozen for almost three months. Again, icebreakers are able to keep shipping channels open.

Today Vladivostok is the largest city in the Soviet Far East, with a population of over 600,000. The city houses the headquarters of the Pacific Fleet and is home port for much of the fleet's surface and submarine forces, including two KIEV-class aircraft carriers. Naval installations include logistic and training centers for the fleet, some

located on adjacent Russian Island, which is connected to Vladivostok by several seafloor tunnels. A submarine school is also reported on Russian Island.

Adjacent to Vladivostok is Petrovka, which has a shipyard that completes the nuclear-propelled submarines built at Komsomol'sk, those craft being too large to transit the Amur River from Komsomol'sk to the sea after they are fitted out. Farther west is the Dunay/Strelok/Abrek naval base complex. Other military bases in the Peter the Great Bay include Novgoradsky, Possiet, Shkotovo, and Tynkin. Because of this vast array of military installations, Vladivostok is closed to most foreign ships. Westerners did obtain a look at the city in November 1974 when President Ford and Party Secretary Brezhnev held a summit meeting there with considerable press coverage.

In September 1990 the U.S. Aegis missile cruiser PRINCETON (CG 59) and ASW frigate REUBEN JAMES (FFG 57) visited Vladivostok in return for Soviet warship visits to the United States. It was the first visit by U.S. Navy ships to Vladivostok since 1937.

There is a major fishing base and fish-processing complex at Vladivostok as well as shipyards and repair facilities. A new fishing port at Troitsa, on Peter the Great Bay near Vladivostok, was begun in the late 1970s.

Sixty miles (96 km) east of Vladivostok lies Nakhodka on the Gulf of Amerika, formerly Wrangel Bay. This is the principal commercial port of Siberia, named "the find" because of its excellent location. During World War II this was the Pacific terminal for U.S. lend-lease supplies destined for the Russo-German front (the port probably being connected to the Trans-Siberian Railroad in the late 1930s). The port's development as a major shipping center began in 1960, and operation of the Soviet Union's first mechanized container-handling facility began there in late 1973. Within a few months it was handling 1,000 freight containers per day as the Siberian transfer point for the trans-Soviet express container run. Nakhodka is also being developed as a major passenger and fishing port. However, Nakhodka cannot handle the increasing volume of foreign and domestic trade. Thus, only nine miles (14 km) away, also on the Gulf of Amerika, Vostochnyy has been under development as a major port since 1970. It is called the "Japanese port" because of Japanese technical assistance and credits used in its development.

Vostochnyy was designed in conjunction with the new Siberian railway, the Baykal-Amur Mainline (BAM), which stretches from the Lena River to the Pacific coast. A local press report in 1984 declared that the port could handle more than 200,000 standard cargo containers per year. Soviet officials plan for Vostochnyy to

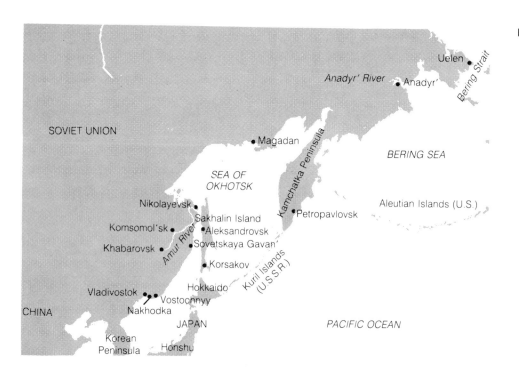

Pacific coast of the USSR.

have an eventual capacity of handling 30 to 40 million tons of cargo annually over its planned 66 wharves, making it the largest port in the Soviet Union.

Vostochnyy loads large amounts of Siberian timber, coal, oil, and fish for shipment to Japan. There is also a ferry service between Vostochnyy and Yokohama—which takes 52 hours—that brings thousands of Japanese tourists to the port every month. However, foreigners cannot remain overnight in Vostochnyy and immediately embark on a train to Khabarovsk, a 16-hour train connection.

Farther up the coast, on the Tartar Strait, is Sovetskaya Gavan (Soviet Bay), formerly Imperatorhafen, and above that the port of Nikolayevsk at the mouth of the Amur River, just below the Sea of Okhotsk. Sovetskaya Gavan is a commercial port, handling mostly timber, and is also one of the three most important naval bases of the Pacific Fleet (the others being the Vladivostok area and Petropavlovsk). A submarine base and school are reported to be located there, and the port serves as a base for warships up to destroyer size. In the past it was used to fit out ships constructed at Komsomol'sk. It is one of the best harbors in the Far East, although the harbor is frozen over from November until April, and during May, June, and July, thick fogs are almost continuous.

Nikolayevsk was opened as a port in 1916 to relieve pressure on the railway to Vladivostok to serve as a trans-shipment point for goods going up the Amur River. Although relatively shallow, the port was previously a naval base as well as commercial port. Today it is primarily a fishing center.

To the north, Anadyr, at the mouth of the river by that name, is important as a coal port and for Arctic shipping. Major improvements were made at the commercial port in the late 1970s. Light naval forces are believed to be based there. Neither Anadyr, Magadan on the Sea of Okhotsk, nor Petropavlovsk on Kamchatka Peninsula are connected to railway lines; rather, they are totally dependent upon sea and air transport. Located on Nagaevo Bay on the northern coast of the Sea of Okhotsk, Magadan is a base for submarines and light forces. This port is generally icebound from December until April or May but is kept open for naval and commercial ships by icebreakers. Fog, which is often heavy in the area, is usually light in the harbor.

Petropavlovsk on the southeastern coast of the Kamchatka peninsula is a domestic commercial shipping and fishing port, but it is also the principal base for submarines of the Pacific Fleet, with several small shipyards. Construction of a naval base began at Petropavlovsk in 1940. "Petro" has the advantage of direct access to the Pacific; ships or submarines leaving the port do not have to pass through narrow straits to get to the sea as is necessary with the other major Pacific Fleet bases. However, the naval and civilian populations of the peninsula (there are 220,000 inhabitants in the city), as well as the troops stationed in the area, must be supplied entirely by sea and air. The lack of overland communications has forced the Soviets to employ seafloor cables for communications between Kamchatka and the mainland. (The message traffic on these cables has been intercepted by U.S. submarines operating in the Sea of Okhotsk in a program known as Ivy Bells.[6])

The Pacific Fleet's Delta SSBNs and other submarines are based at Petropavlovsk, with a smaller, conventional submarine base reported some nine miles (15 km) north of Petropavlovsk, at the small port of Bitchivinka. The city of Petropavlovsk is located on the eastern side of Avachinskaya Bay. There are four berthing areas for naval and KGB patrol ships south of the city, three on Rakova Bay, and one across the Izemennyy Peninsula (with direct access to the entrance channel to Avachinskaya Bay). Only a few large warships are based at "Petro," but they include the fourth SLAVA-class missile cruiser and several Nanuchka-class missile craft. These, in consort with submarines and land-based aircraft, are intended to deter U.S. naval operations in the area.

The Lenin shipyard is located in Rakova Bay and apparently performs civilian and military work; the Freza yard at Petropavlovsk undertakes only commercial work with the city's commercial piers along the coast between the city and Rakova Bay handling both merchant and fishing ships.

Across the bay, southwest of Petropavlovsk, is the protected harbor of Bukhta Tar'ya, home port for nuclear-propelled submarines. The submarine piers and the Tar'ya refit/refueling facility are located between the towns of Primorsky and Primorskaya. The former is connected to Petropavlovsk by ferry, and there is a road around Avachinskaya Bay connecting the towns and port areas (with several airfields northwest of the bay also connected by roads). When other bays in the area are icebound Tar'ya is usually open because of the warm-water rivers and lakes that surround it, making year-round submarine operations possible.

Because of the number of Delta SSBNs in the Pacific Fleet, the remaining Yankee SSBNs have been displaced from Petropavlovsk, and are based along with other submarines at ports on Peter the Great Bay, near Vladivostok. The Kamchatka Peninsula and the Soviet-controlled Kuril Islands form a protective barrier for

---

6. The Soviets learned of this U.S. intercept operation from National Security Agency analyst-turned-traitor Ronald Pelton, probably as early as January 1980; Pelton was arrested in late 1985.

The commercial side of the port of Vladivostok, a city often compared to San Francisco. It is the largest city in the Far East, with several other commercial and naval ports nearby.

Another view of the naval port at Vladivostok. From left are the Krivak I–class frigate PORYVISTYY, the cruisers TALLINN and MARSHAL VOROSHILOV, the SOVREMENNYY-class destroyer STROYKIY, and the Krivak II–class frigate GORDELIVYY. Beyond this nest of warships are two floating dry docks and several merchant ships. Note the extensive use of "Mediterranean moorings." (Courtesy Abe Go)

the Sea of Okhotsk. The Soviets have sought through both legal arguments and practice to make the Sea of Okhotsk an "inland sea," forbidden to foreign military and commercial shipping.

On Sakhalin Island, held by Japan from 1905 to 1945 and taken over by the Soviets at the end of World War II, are the naval bases of Korsakov (formerly Otomari) and Aleksandorsk. Another port was developed at Kholmsk in the 1970s for handling cargo and supporting fish-factory ships, and Vostochnyy at the northern end of Sakhalin is a commercial port which began container operations in 1976.

Most Far Eastern ports are iced over for up to one-half of the year. At Vladivostok, the southernmost port, snow lies on the ground for more than three months of the year, and Peter the Great Bay is greatly hampered by ice during much of the winter. The entire Sea of Okhotsk is covered by thin ice from October to June. Again, the large fleet of Soviet coastal and oceangoing icebreakers keep the Far Eastern ports operating continuously.

To support the large military deployments in Siberia, and to counter possible American, Japanese, and Chinese assaults, the coastal areas also contain a large number of air and ground bases.

INLAND PORTS

Inland from the Pacific coast, on the Amur River, are the shipbuilding centers of Komsomol'sk and Khabarovsk. The latter, located at the confluence of the Amur and Ussuri rivers, is one of the largest cities in Siberia. Both have major military and commercial industries and are rail and river transportation crossroads. Their waterfronts are frozen over from November through June.

The Soviet Union has several major inland river and canal routes, some of which provide passage for small and some for medium-sized ships between the Arctic, Baltic, and Black Sea ports. In Siberia the long Lena, Ob', and Yenisey rivers all are navigable for more than 2,000 miles (3,200 km). They permit river craft to carry raw materials north to the Arctic coast, where they can be trans-shipped to seagoing cargo ships, and can also carry cargoes from European Russia down the rivers to Siberian cities and towns. Major ports along these rivers include Narym, Tomsk, Turukhansk, Verkholensk, Yakutsk, and Yeniseysk.

In European Russia the Volga River runs some 2,300 miles (3,680 km) and most of it, from north of Moscow south to the Caspian Sea, is navigable. The Volga-Don Canal, completed in 1952, links the Volga to the Don River and the Sea of Azov and hence to the Black Sea. There are numerous ports along this route. Among the more significant ones are Gor'kiy, with its submarine and rivercraft building yards; Kazan; Volgograd (formerly Stalingrad and before that Tsaritsyn); and Astrakhan, near the Volga's entrance into the Caspian Sea.

On the inland Caspian Sea, Baku is the largest city and chief port. It is headquarters for the Caspian Sea Flotilla and site of a higher naval school. Wharves line the coast of Baku Bay for several miles, with special facilities for tankers and offshore drilling support vessels. Smaller port facilities are found at Astrakhan, Guryev, and Krasnovodsk. These ports played a major role in the transshipment of U.S. lend-lease war materials sent to the Soviet Union through Iran during World War II.

In addition to coastal trade, the ports support offshore drilling in the Caspian Sea. The Soviet naval forces on the Caspian have a patrol and amphibious assault capability.

CHAPTER 31

Shipbuilding and Shipyards

An artist's sketch of two of the three submarine assembly halls at the Severodvinsk shipyard—the world's largest submarine construction facility. The taller structure at left constructs Typhoon SSBNs and Oscar SSGNs; the hall with two building-ways (at top right) is No. 42, which now constructs Delta IV–class SSBNs. The submarine sketched in the left foreground represents a Typhoon SSBN, the largest undersea craft yet built. (U.S. Department of Defense)

Shipbuilding is a major factor in the development and future capabilities of the Soviet Navy.[1] While shipbuilding in the West and Far East has suffered a severe depression during the 1980s, the shipyards of the Soviet Union continued to produce large numbers of modern naval and merchant ships, as well as smaller numbers of fishing and specialized research ships. Soviet yards also built a large number of ships for foreign merchant and fishing fleets as well as for foreign navies (see appendix C).

In many respects the Soviet shipbuilding industry is the world's largest. There are more than 20 major shipyards in the Soviet Union, a major yard being one that has more than 2,000 full-time employees.[2] The largest yards are used mainly for the construction of large ships, while hundreds of smaller yards build and maintain smaller ships of the naval, merchant, fishing, research, and river fleets. Of the major shipyards, four build only warships—Severodvinsk (submarines), Kaliningrad (destroyers), and Petrovskiy (small combatants), plus the Sudomekh portion of the Leningrad Admiralty Association (submarines—see below).

Collectively, these large and small yards compose the world's largest shipbuilding and repair industry, ably supported by an infrastructure of machinery and equipment firms, research institutes, and design bureaus. The Soviet shipbuilding capabilities were previously complemented by those of Eastern European nations, principally Finland, East Germany, and Poland. Their major yards provided up to 70 percent of their annual ship production to the Soviet Union. Those orders were especially important in view of the depression in shipbuilding outside of the Soviet bloc. (Polish and East German yards also built naval auxiliaries as well as trawlers and fishing support ships for the Soviet Union, with East Germany also building the Parchim II–class small frigates for the Soviet Navy.)

1. A history of Russian-Soviet shipbuilding and shipyards will be found in *Guide to the Soviet Navy*, 4th ed., pp. 463–467.
2. By this criterion the United States has 16 major shipyards—eight government-owned naval facilities and eight private yards. One of the government yards was scheduled for closing in the early 1990s.

The Soviet Union also buys a small number of merchant ships, generally of specialized designs, from Western nations. This practice, however, is limited because hard currencies are normally needed to procure products in the West.

In the late 1980s the economic crisis and restructuring in the Soviet Union began to affect the shipbuilding industry. Apparently some naval ship construction programs were halted (e.g., the KIROV-class battle cruisers), and there was a major effort initiated to convert some of the shipbuilding capacity (as well as other defense industries) to consumer-civil production.

All shipyards already produced such goods, primarily for the shipyard employees. For example, the Nikolayev Northern/61 Kommuna in 1990 was reported to produce some 40 consumer items, including a variety of furniture, metal garages, gas cylinders, and tents. In 1985 these goods were valued at 7 million rubles, in 1986 almost 7.5 million rubles, in 1987 10.3 million rubles, in 1988 11.3 million rubles, and in 1989 over 12 million rubles.

At the same time, some of the yards are increasing their production of commercial ships, especially fishing ships and craft. And, the radical political-economic changes in several Eastern European countries could lead Soviet shipyards to construct more of the research, oceanographic, and "hydromet" ships that the Soviets previously obtained from East Germany and Poland.

ORGANIZATION AND FACILITIES

The several hundred shipbuilding and ship-repair yards in the Soviet Union are under the cognizance of the Ministry of Ship Production and the four operating ministries—Navy (a component of the Ministry of Defense), Merchant Marine, Fishing Fleet, and River Fleet.

The Ministry of Ship Production directs the activities of more than 30 of the largest shipyards in the country. These yards construct primarily the naval ships and the large, complex merchant ships as well as various research ships. Created in 1939, the Ministry of Ship Production is one of the defense industry ministries.[3] The four ship-operating ministries—Navy, merchant, fishing, river—each operates additional yards that build, repair, and overhaul ships for their own use.

All of these yards participate in a centralized planning scheme with 5-, 10-, and 20-year programs. These long-term programs facilitate the procurement of large classes or series of ships with significant savings in labor, resources, and maintenance. Further, all yards employ uniform and mandatory procedures for calculating costs, with standardized practices and techniques used whenever possible.

Beyond shipyards, the Soviet shipbuilding industry also has an extensive array of design bureaus and research and design institutions. These, too, are subordinate to the various ministries. These institutions exist at several levels: at the highest level are the numerous institutes and laboratories of the Academy of Sciences, several of which specialize in ship-related fields such as Arctic studies, metallurgy, physics, fluid mechanics, nuclear technologies. Several of these institutes and laboratories operate specialized research ships.

At the next level are the central scientific and research institutes of the Ministry of Ship Production that specialize in various ship technologies, materials, standardization, and economics. The largest and most prestigious of these is the Krylov Institute in Leningrad, described by the U.S. Navy as the world's foremost shipbuilding research and development center.[4] The Krylov Institute operates several research ships, including the unique systems/materials research ship IZUMRUD. The institute is believed to have a staff of approximately 5,000 personnel, including 1,700 scientists and engineers.

The Merchant Marine, Fishing Fleet, and River Fleet ministries each has its own research institutes that specialize in such areas as ship maintenance and repair, transport automation, and fleet operations. Moreover, a number of the naval and maritime higher schools and academies have integral research centers that conduct similar research and study efforts; most of these centers tend to specialize in specific maritime areas. In all, there are an estimated 75 design bureaus and ship-related institutes and centers supporting the various "fleet" ministries.

As in other Soviet "hardware" industries, the leading technical institutes produce tables and codes that serve as baseline documents for all ship construction, naval and commercial. These also contribute to standardization in design and components and permit the rapid introduction of advanced designs and construction technologies.

Only a few of the yards still use inclined building ways. The larger ships are built in graving docks, the largest dock being at Nikolayev Black Sea (south) where the KIEV and ADMIRAL KUZNETSOV (ex-TBILISI) carrier classes were built. Production lines with horizontal assembly positions with indirect launching are used at most other Soviet yards. All of these practices increase efficiency and speed ship production. At the same time, the Soviets pursue the use of computer-driven cutting and fabrication equipment, laser metal cutting, and semi-automatic or automatic welding. The construction of the titanium-hulled Alfa, Mike, and Sierra SSNs demonstrates a capability to work this advanced metal in large sections, which does not now exist in the West. Another feature of Soviet shipyards is the extensive use of covered building halls, especially in the Arctic region, which permit year-round construction to take place. All submarine building ways are covered, a practice that provides a high degree of protection from U.S. reconnaissance satellites.

The quality of Soviet shipyard work can be gauged, in part, by the sales of naval units and merchant ships to other countries. Such traditional seafaring nations as Great Britain, Norway, and Sweden have been among the customers for Soviet-built merchant ships during the merchant fleet growth period of the 1970s. Reports concerning warships built for other navies have been mixed; some clients have liked their ships and others have been disappointed, complained to the Soviets, and in some instances have turned to the West after sampling Soviet products. (Soviet financial terms and weapons transfer policies in many instances compensate for questionable or poor quality of goods.) Some Soviet ships have had major problems that could be attributed to their construction. A large fish-factory ship built at the Admiralty yard in Leningrad required more than a year of additional work after her sea trials; the poor workmanship was cited in the Soviet press.

The following shipyard problems can also be cited:

> . . . a shortage of modern equipment in many areas of ship production, weak technologies discipline, and low quality of work. Being technically and financially unable to rapidly improve the overall technology level of the entire shipbuilding industry, the Soviets concentrate their efforts on certain important areas and have achieved significant results, especially in welding and cutting titanium and aluminum alloys, nonmetallic joining materials, and robotics.[5]

ENGINEERS, MANAGERS, AND WORKERS

There are more than 200,000 shipyard workers in the Soviet Union according to Western intelligence estimates (compared to just under 200,000 in the United States). Many Western sources, however, consider the estimate of the number of Soviet workers too low. The numbers do not include Soviet naval personnel who are assigned to ships and shipyards and participate in ship repair and maintenance. In addition, many thousands more men and women are employed in the associated ship design bureaus and research institutes.

---

3. The others are the Ministries of Defense, Aviation, Communications Equipment, Electronics, Radio, General Machine Building, Machine Building, and Medium Machine Building, the last a euphemism for nuclear weapons and power reactors.

4. Alexei H. Krylov was the principal designer of Russian battleships of the SEVASTOPOL and SOVIETSKIY SOYUZ classes of the Stalin period.

5. Dr. Boris S. Butman, "Soviet Shipbuilding and Ship Repair" (Arlington, Va.: Spectrum Associates, January 1986), p. 8-1.

"The Soviet shipbuilding industry has a corps of well-trained and efficient workers at all skill levels. Training continues after the worker joins a shipyard, as night school and correspondence school courses are offered in most disciplines," according to a U.S. Navy report.[6] The industry has a large and multi-layered, nation-wide infrastructure that hires, trains and educates, and pays employees of the shipyards and the related design bureaus and research institutes. One expert estimates that every year between 7,000 and 9,000 engineers with bachelor's or master's degrees enter ship-building and ship repair activities or the bureaus and institutes associated with them.

These men and women are educated at a reported 29 colleges and universities that offer 5- or 6-year engineering programs in ship-related fields, and at about 60 colleges and technical schools that offer a variety of related 2- to 4-year programs. This results in a very high educational level of the professional staff.

Compensation is based on nation-wide work rates and norms. The importance of the shipbuilding and ship repair, however, has led to a very high degree of flexibility within the industry. For example, there are extensive bonuses, overtime and regional incentive payments, and fixed long-term allowances for work in the Arctic and Far Eastern areas. The total bonuses can add 40 to 70 percent to a worker's takehome pay. Beyond ruble compensation, most shipyards provide housing and social amenities for their workers. The scope of this effort may be seen in the Nikolayev and Kherson shipyards (and possibly others), which have civil construction capabilities even greater than those of the government-owned construction companies.

The standards and norms existing throughout the shipbuilding and repair industry, the long-range planning processes, and the restrictions on labor mobility in the Soviet Union result in a high degree of employment stability, which, in turn, provides much less variance in labor requirements and hence costs of ship construction and repairs. And, this stability contributes to an increasingly competent shipyard work force.

There are, however, major problems in the work force. In some respects the worst problem in the shipbuilding industry—as in most of the Soviet society—is alcoholism. This is a particular problem in shipyards, where there are many spaces in which to drink unseen. A lesser problem at some yards is a shortage of housing, primarily for the newer workers.

ARCTIC SHIPYARDS

Severodvinsk (Shipyard No. 402)

The Severodvinsk yard is the world's only major shipbuilding facility above the Arctic circle and ranks as the world's largest submarine construction yard in terms of shipway capacity. Severodvinsk has built the world's largest submarines (i.e., the Typhoon-class SSBNs).

Location. The yard is situated in the delta of the Northern Dvina River, about 30 miles (48 km) across the delta from the city of Arkhangel'sk (to the east). The river opens onto the White Sea. The yard is connected to Leningrad by the White Sea–Baltic Canal system (completed in 1933) as well as by rail lines. After World War II a highway was constructed to permit road traffic between Severodvinsk-Arkhangel'sk and Moscow.

History. The yard was erected in the early 1930s to help make the Northern Fleet independent of the Baltic shipyards. Its location would reduce the vulnerability to enemy attack in time of war. An estimated 120,000 political and criminal prisoners were brought to the Severodvinsk area in the 1930s to construct the shipyard.

The yard, officially founded about 1938, was originally known as the Molotovsk yard for V.M. Molotov, a leading politician under Stalin; the name was changed in 1957 after Molotov fell from favor in the post-Stalin era.

Stalin envisioned the yard becoming the largest in the world, capable of building ships up to battleship size; the eventual work

Building hall No. 42 at Severodvinsk was erected on Stalin's orders to construct warships for the Northern Fleet. Shown here in June 1944, hall No. 42 was intended to simultaneously construct two battleships side-by-side. There are now three large building halls at Severodvinsk. (U.S. Navy)

force when the yard was completed was projected to be 35,000 to 40,000. The main building dock—now known as hall No. 50—was erected under cover to permit work to be carried on year round. This original building dock measures some 1,100 feet (335 m) in length and 452 feet (137 m) in width, having been intended to permit the side-by-side construction of two Sovietskiy Soyuz–class battleships.[7] One and possibly—albeit unlikely—two of these ships were laid down at Severodvinsk in 1939, but all work on capital ships in the Soviet Union ceased in October 1940. The components and materials for these ships were brought to the yard from shipyards and factories in Leningrad and Nikolayev.

During World War II the yard had a peak work force of about 5,000 men and women, and completed submarines of the L and S classes that had been built at Leningrad and Gor'kiy and brought to Severodvinsk through the canal-river system. Destroyers were begun at the Molotovsk yard during the war, but none was completed until after the war.

Subsequently, the yard began the construction of surface warships of the postwar programs—the Sverdlov-class light cruisers and the Skoryy-class destroyers. More significant, the Severodvinsk yard made preparations to construct advanced submarines and in 1953 completed the first of eight Zulu-class diesel attack submarines built at the yard. It then shifted to producing the Golf-class ballistic missile submarines (SSB). Three Foxtrot-class diesel submarines were also built at Severodvinsk (most of that large class being constructed at the Sudomekh yard in Leningrad. The yard did not participate in the massive Whiskey-class construction program).

The Severodvinsk yard built the first Soviet nuclear submarines of the November class, the lead unit being completed in August 1958. (Two years later the Komsomol'sk yard in the Far East completed its first nuclear submarine.) These were immediately followed by the nuclear-propelled Hotel (SSBN) and Echo II (SSGN) classes.

Subsequently the yard became the principal SSBN construction yard, building Yankee and Delta SSBN variants, and the large Typhoon SSBN. Also built at Severodvinsk were the Papa and Oscar SSGNs; three of the Alfa SSNs; and the one-of-a-kind Mike SSN. In addition to building nuclear submarines, the nuclear submarines built at Admiralty/Sudomekh in Leningrad and at Gor'kiy are moved on transporter docks through the inland waterway system to Severodvinsk for completion and sea trials. There appear to be separate fitting-out areas for the submarines produced by those yards.

The battleship-building hall begun in the early 1930s has been supplemented by two other large submarine construction halls. The original facility—building hall No. 50—built the November, Hotel, Yankee, and Delta submarines; hall No. 42, about 1,100 yards (1,000 m) north of the older hall, was used to construct the Golf SSBs and was then upgraded for the advanced-technology Alfa, Papa, and Mike programs and, most recently, the Akula class; the third building hall, adjacent to No. 50, produced the large Typhoon

6. Joel Bloom, "Technical Assessment of Current Soviet Shipbuilding Capabilities" (Suitland, Md.: Naval Intelligence Support Center, 24 February 1975), p. 14.

7. None of these battleships was completed; the one (or two) being built at Molotovsk, one at the Ordzhonikidze yard, and one at Marti (Nikolayev) were broken up still unfinished in the 1940s.

SSBNs and Oscar SSGNs. These halls are fully enclosed and heated for year-round work, and all permit horizontal construction. Hall No. 42 has special-atmosphere welding areas for working with titanium.

The submarine repair and overhaul portion of Severodvinsk is known as the Little Star shipyard, situated on the adjacent Zagry peninsula. This is where the major conversions of Yankee SSBNs to attack (SSN) and cruise missile (SSGN) configurations are undertaken.

(Some commercial work was done at the yard into the 1950s.)

The smaller Krasnaya Kuznitsa and Arkhangel'sk ship repair yards are located in Arkhangel'sk and perform commercial work. They have built small coastal and inland craft and floating dry docks, with the latter yard also building small air cushion vehicles. These are primarily repair yards.

At least through World War II there were two small shipyards at Murmansk on the Kola inlet, the Rosta naval dockyard to the north of the city and the Khaldeev Point yard to the south (adjacent to the port installations). Rosta, which was heavily damaged by the German bombing of Murmansk in World War II, was the only yard capable of making repairs to large ships at the Kola inlet (one graving dock was 350 feet/107 m and one 650 feet/198 m).

BALTIC SHIPYARDS

Admiralty (Shipyard No. 194)

The Admiralty yard, as part of the United Admiralty Association, is one of the four major shipyards in Leningrad, the shipbuilding center of the Soviet Union. In 1972 the Admiralty and the adjacent Sudomekh yard were consolidated into a single administrative entity known as the United Admiralty Association.

Recent programs at the Admiralty yard have consisted of merchant and fisheries support ships, naval auxiliaries, and nuclear-propelled submarines. Into the 1990s the Admiralty side of the yard constructed submarines of the Victor III SSN class.

Location. The Admiralty yard is located on Galerniy Island, at the intersection of the Neva River and Fontanka Canal. The Sudomekh yard is adjacent to the northeast, separated from Admiralty by the small Moika and Proshka rivers, and across the Neva from the Baltic shipyard on Vasilevski Island.

History. Tsar Paul I established the New Admiralty yard on the left bank of the Neva River at St. Petersburg (now Leningrad) in 1800 because the Main Admiralty yard (founded in 1704) was unsuitable for continued expansion because of the city growing up around it. Battleships were built at the New Admiralty from the early 1800s as the facility became one of the major Russian shipbuilding yards. The yard was extensively modernized in 1862–1863 and adapted to construct iron-hulled steam ships. From that time until the 1917 Revolution the Main Admiralty was the principal supplier of large warships to the Russian fleet.

In 1908 the New Admiralty yard was merged with the Galerniy Island yard, which had been building naval ships since 1713. After the merger the yard was called simply the Admiralty. Among the more famous ships built at the yard were the first Russian steamship, the ELIZAVETA, and the cruiser AVRORA. After the Revolution of 1917 the yard was renamed Marti, for the French sailor-revolutionary André Marti. From 1921 to 1926 the yard was administratively merged with the Baltic shipyard as the Soviets sought to rehabilitate the shipbuilding industry. The name subsequently was changed back to Admiralty.

Between the world wars SHCH-class submarines and then the large K class were built at the yard. Large surface warship construction began in 1938 with the keel laying of the light cruiser ZHELEZNIAKOV (not completed until 1949). The following year the keel was laid down for the lead ship of the KRONSHTADT-class battle cruisers (that were never finished).

Virtually all ship work halted at the Leningrad yards during World War II as the city was besieged by German forces for three

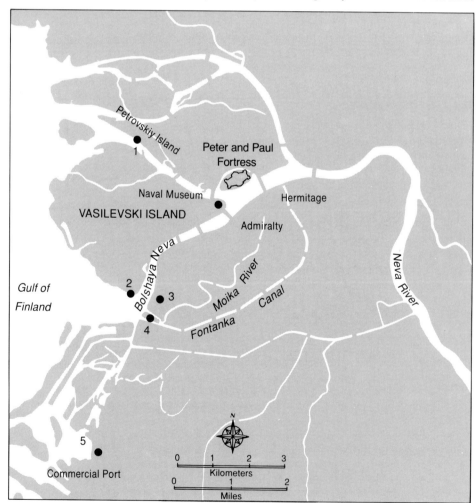

Leningrad-St. Petersburg
1 Petrovskiy Yard.   2 Baltic Yard.
3 Admiralty Yard.   4 Sudomekh Yard.
5 Northern Yard (formerly Zhdanov).

There are several shipyards in the Soviet Union that specialize in the construction of small combatants. This is the large Petrovskiy shipyard in Leningrad. Behind the crane is a large assembly hall. (N. Polmar)

years. After the war, in addition to completing the ZHELEZNIAKOV and other prewar ships, the yard geared up for participation in the SVERDLOV cruiser program. However, only three of these ships were completed before the yard ceased building surface warships. Similarly, some sources indicated that plans were under way to build STALINGRAD-class battle cruisers at the yard when that program was halted.

From the mid-1950s onward the Admiralty yard has specialized in non-naval construction—space support ships, merchant ships, icebreakers, large rescue and salvage ships, fish-factory ships, and floating dry docks. Several of these ships were completed for naval service.

The Admiralty yard built the nuclear icebreaker LENIN, which first got under way on nuclear power in September 1959, predating the first U.S. nuclear surface ships, the merchant ship SAVANNAH and the missile cruiser LONG BEACH (CGN 9).

Following the LENIN no additional nuclear ships were produced at Admiralty yard for a decade. (The subsequent Soviet nuclear icebreakers were built at the Baltic shipyard.) Rather, Admiralty became the fifth Soviet yard to produce nuclear submarines, with the first Victor SSN being launched in 1966. Construction of the Victor II/III classes followed. Nuclear submarines built at Admiralty are moved on transporter docks via the White Sea Canal to Severodvinsk for completion and sea trials.

Baltic (Shipyard No. 189)

The large Baltic or *Baltiyski* shipyard currently produces mainly merchant ships with the notable exception of nuclear-propelled surface ships. These are the ARKTIKA-class icebreakers, the KIROV-class battle cruisers, and the large space support/tracking ship SSV-33. The last, with a full load displacement of some 41,000 tons, is the largest naval ship yet built in the Leningrad area.

Location. The yard is at the lower end of Leningrad's large Vasilevski Island, near the mouth of the Neva River.

History. The yard was established in 1856 by the Scotsman M.L. MacPherson as a major ship construction facility to build merchant ships. It subsequently became the Carr and MacPherson yard. The Russian government directed that naval ships be built at the yard and in 1864 two monitors designed by Johann (John) Ericksson were launched. The yard continued to build merchant and naval ships.

However, the yard encountered financial difficulties and, in 1874, was sold to Prince Ochtomski. In 1877 the yard was reorganized as the Baltic Company for Railway, Vehicle, Ship and Machine Building and placed under the direction of a naval officer. In 1894 the yard became wholly owned by the government but continued to be managed as a private firm.

In 1892 the yard launched the famed armored cruiser RURIK; the yard also built several of the first Russian submarines and later produced early steel battleships. By the early 1900s the Baltic Works was the largest shipyard in St. Petersburg, employing almost 6,000 workers; by 1917 the work force had increased to almost 7,000. In 1912 the Baltic Works established a smaller subsidiary in Nikolayev to construct and assemble destroyers and submarines for the Black Sea Fleet.

After the 1917 Revolution and Civil War the yard was renamed Ordzhonikidze for an early Russian communist; subsequently it has been renamed the Baltic Shipyard.

The Baltic yard undertook the construction of two salvage vessels in 1923 and the first commercial ships built in Russia after the Revolution were four timber carriers, laid down at the Baltic yard in January 1925. Between 1936 and 1939 the yard was extensively modernized and began the construction of cruisers, destroyers, and several classes of submarines. Begun in 1935–1939 were the heavy cruisers KIROV and MAKSIM GOR'KIY, and the light cruisers CHAPAYEV and CHKALOV; the first two ships were completed in 1938–1940, the others after the war.

Submarine construction at the Ordzhonikidze/Baltic yard began with the first three units of the DEKABRIST or D class, the first Soviet-designed submarines, being laid down in 1927. These were followed by the construction of submarines of the L, SHCH, P, S, and K classes.

On the eve of World War II, in 1938 the yard began building the first of SOVIETSKIY SOYUZ–class battleships. Shipbuilding stopped during the siege of Leningrad and the yard was severely damaged by German bombing and artillery fire.

After the war the Baltic yard built six of the SVERDLOV-class cruisers and began series production of Whiskey-class submarines. The first Whiskeys built at the yard were completed in 1955. Only 14 of these submarines were built before the post-Stalin naval cutbacks and the yard was shifted primarily to merchant and special-purpose ships. A variety of merchant ships have been built at the Baltic yard since the late 1950s—tankers, refrigerated cargo ships, dry bulk cargo ships—as well as icebreakers and trawlers. Some of these ships have been for foreign customers. The yard has also built large space support ships.

The yard began constructing nuclear surface ships in the late 1960s, with the icebreaker ARKTIKA being launched in 1972, followed by several sister ships. Even more impressive, in 1973 the yard laid the keel for the nuclear-propelled KIROV, which would be the largest surface combatant built by any navy since World War II. The KIROV class was apparently to continue beyond four units but the program was terminated, probably in 1989, shortly after the fifth ship was begun. The yard also constructed the massive, nuclear-propelled SSV-33. Thus, the Baltic yard became the sixth Soviet yard with a nuclear capability, although it has not constructed nuclear-propelled submarines.

Baltiya/Klaipeda

Merchant ships are produced at this yard, which is also a former German shipyard, known as the Lindenau yard before the Soviet takeover of the Memel area at the end of World War II. Baltiya reached major shipyard status in the 1950s and since about 1960 has built only merchant ships. Recent production has included fish-factory ships, trawlers, and floating dry docks.

The yard is located at Klaipeda in Lithuania and was previously known as Memel. It is north of Kaliningrad on the Baltic coast.

Three additional yards at Klaipeda are involved mainly in repairs of merchant and fishing ships as well as small naval units.

Dekabristov

Specialized air cushion vehicle production facility on the Small Neva River, across from the Petrovskiy yard. Dekabristov has built a succession of ACVs, including the Gus, Aist, and Pomornik classes.

Izhora

The Izhora shipyard is located at Kolpino, southeast of Leningrad, where the Izhora River enters the Neva. The yard has previously constructed principally minesweepers and hydrofoil craft, including the T-43, T-58, Natya, and Yurka classes. Earlier the yard produced armor plating as well as constructing small warships.

The yard was previously named Ust-Izhora (mouth of Izhora) and is also called Simeoneva (Middle Neva) and has also been known as the Izhorski State Works.

Recently the yard has become a producer of fiberglass-reinforced plastic craft, among them the minesweepers and hunters of the Zhenya and Yevgenya classes. It also builds the Matka-class hydrofoil missile craft.

Kaliningrad (Shipyard No. 820)

The Yantar/Kaliningrad yard builds surface warships and amphibious ships. It is the former German Schichau shipyard.

Location. The yard is located at Kaliningrad, formerly the East Prussian city of Konigsberg. Situated near the large Soviet fleet base at Baltiysk (formerly Pillau), the yard is composed of almost 200 acres.

History. This yard became a major German shipbuilding facility in the 1880s constructing torpedo boats. After World War II the Soviets rebuilt the yard to produce small commercial and naval ships, among them frigates of the Kola, Riga, and Petya classes.

In the 1960s the Kaliningrad yard began producing the larger Krivak-class frigates and the Alligator-class landing ships. The complexity of the Krivak represented a considerable increase in the yard's capabilities. Subsequently, the yard has produced the UDALOY-class missile destroyers, at 8,200 tons the largest naval ships yet built at Kaliningrad except for the three IVAN ROGOV–class amphibious ships. In addition to the UDALOY class, the yard is building the NEUSTRASHIMYY-class (BAL-COM-8) frigates.

Further, the yard modernizes escort ships and performs overhaul and maintenance work for the Baltic Fleet. There has been only limited commercial construction at Kaliningrad since 1960 (e.g., ferries were built there in the 1970s).

Kronshtadt

The naval dockyard on Kronshtadt Island, near Leningrad, is a principal repair base for the Baltic Fleet. Historically this large facility has provided support for warships; no new construction is believed to have occurred in the twentieth century. Kronshtadt has some of the largest dry docks in the Soviet Union. At least through World War II the Kronshtadt base was also the site of the Leningrad submarine school.

Petrovskiy

This Leningrad yard constructs small combatants. It is located on Petrovskiy Island, in the Small Neva, north of Vasilevsky Island. The Petrovskiy yard became a major shipbuilding facility in the 1930s.

Various mine, patrol, torpedo, and missile boats have been built at Petrovskiy, including large numbers of the Osa missile boats. The largest ships built to date at the yard are Nanuchka and Tarantul classes of missile corvettes.

Srednyy Neva

This shipyard in Kolpino builds advanced small combatants. These have included the Tarantul II guided missile corvette, Turya hydrofoil torpedo craft, Natya minesweepers, and, most recently, the lead ship of the Gorya large mine countermeasures design.

Sudomekh (Shipyard No. 196)

The Sudomekh yard is a specialized submarine construction facility in Leningrad. It has built several advanced submarines as well as research and experimental undersea craft. The Sudomekh yard launched the first of the advanced Alfa-class nuclear submarines in April 1969, bringing to five the number of nuclear submarine construction yards in the Soviet Union.

Since 1972 the adjacent Admiralty and Sudomekh yards have been consolidated into a single administrative entity, the United Admiralty Association.

Location. Located in downtown Leningrad, Sudomekh is situated between the Neva and Moika rivers, separated by the latter from the Admiralty yard.

History. The yard became a major shipbuilding facility in the 1930s, at which time it built submarines of the SHCH and M classes. The yard was damaged extensively during the war but was rapidly rebuilt in the late 1940s for submarine construction. Equipment removed from German submarine yards was installed in Sudomekh and, with the help of German scientists and technicians, advanced submarine designs and propulsion systems were developed after the war, continuing closed-cycle propulsion work that had been started in the 1930s. Submarines of the SHCH and M classes were completed through 1952, as were the research submarine Whale and other experimental boats. The submarine dubbed Whale by Western naval intelligence had a Walter closed-cycle propulsion plant using a High-Temperature Peroxide (HTP) turbine.

Long-range Zulu-class diesel submarines were launched at Sudomekh from 1952 and smaller Quebec-class submarines were launched from 1954. Sudomekh built all 30 units of the Quebec class while sharing the Zulu program with Severodvinsk. From the late 1950s Sudomekh produced the long-range Foxtrot class, successor to the Zulu. Foxtrots were built at a steady rate of five or six units per year during the 1960s, with construction continuing into the 1980s for foreign transfer for a total of 76 of the estimated 79 Foxtrot-class submarines, the largest postwar class of diesel-electric submarines after the Whiskey class. (Severodvinsk built the three other Foxtrots.)

Sudomekh launched the first Alfa-class SSN in 1969, marking the debut of a submarine significantly faster and deeper diving than any previous combat submarine. After lengthy trials and extensive modification of that first unit, Sudomekh built another three Alfas (as did Severodvinsk). The Sudomekh yard also built the research-experimental submarines Uniform, Xray, Beluga, and Lima (Uniform and Xray are nuclear propelled). Nuclear submarines are transported through the inland waterway system to Severodvinsk for completion and trials.

The Admiralty-Sudomekh complex subsequently constructed the Kilo-class diesel attack submarines (for foreign transfer) while continuing SSN programs.

Vyborg

Vyborg is located in former Finnish territory, 75 miles (120 km) northwest of Leningrad.[8] Vyborg became a major shipyard in the 1960s and constructs almost exclusively dry cargo ships, including large container carriers, plus offshore oil rigs and rig support ships.

Zhdanov/Northern (Shipyard No. 190)

The large Zhdanov shipyard in Leningrad constructs both commercial and naval ships, the latter being missile destroyers of the UDALOY and SOVREMENNYY classes. On 2 August 1989 the yard was renamed the Northern Shipyard.

Location. The yard is located in the commercial port area, in the southern environs of Leningrad. The yard covers more than 200 acres.

History. From about 1855 the facility was an engine manufacturer, apparently known as the Putilov Marine Engine Works. The new Putilov works was rebuilt as a shipyard by the German firm of Blohm & Voss and began ship construction in 1912. Destroyers and light cruisers were begun before the 1917 Revolution. By 1917 it had some 4,200 workers. The yard was briefly known as the Northern Shipyard before being named for A.A. Zhdanov in 1935. (Zhdanov was a major communist figure of the period and politburo representative for naval matters.)

During the 1930s the yard constructed several submarines of the SHCH and M classes and prefabricated the components of the S class for assembly and fitting out at the Dalzavod yard at Vladivostok. The Zhdanov began building surface naval ships in 1936; ships up to destroyer size were laid down before World War II.

Extensively damaged during the war by the German siege of Leningrad, the yard was rehabilitated and became the leading

8. Russian troops of Peter the Great captured Vyborg in June 1710 and it remained under Russian control until 1918, when Finland gained independence from Russia. The city and port were ceded to the Soviet Union in 1940 after the Winter War, between Finland and the Soviet Union, but were occupied by Finnish and German forces from August 1941 to June 1944, when they were returned to Soviet control.

Kronshtadt is the large naval repair yard on Kotlin Island in the Gulf of Finland. Kronshtadt has not built ships in this century but is a principal repair facility with several dry docks. Here the cruiser OKTYARASKAYA REVOLUTSIYA is covered with scaffolding; a pair of Riga-class frigates are nearby. (Courtesy Hyman Grotkin)

Soviet producer of surface warships in the late 1940s. Initially destroyers were built at Zhdanov and then all missile cruisers of the Kynda and Kresta I/II classes; the yard also built Krivak I–class frigates.

The yard is currently constructing missile destroyers of the SOVREMENNYY and UDALOY classes as well as a variety of merchant ships, with about one-third of the yard currently allocated to commercial work. The latter includes the construction of roll-on/roll-off, dry cargo, and passenger ships. The yard has both open and covered building facilities.

The largest shipbuilding and repair yard of the River Fleet Ministry is located at Petrokrepost, on the southern shore of Lake Lagoda. This was a shipyard in the time of Peter I, and the adjacent canal contained huge berthing docks where sailing ships could be laid up during the winter months.

Smaller but significant Baltic-area yards include the Kanonerskiy and Petrozavodsk yards in Leningrad, and ship repair yards in Liepaja, Riga, and Tallinn.

BLACK SEA SHIPYARDS

Black Sea (Shipyard No. 444)

Known as the Chernomorskiy (Black Sea) as well as the Nikolayev south yard, and before that the Nosenko and Nikolayev-Marti yard, this is the largest shipyard on the Black Sea and one of the principal construction facilities in the Soviet Union. Aircraft carriers of the ADMIRAL KUZNETSOV (ex-TBILISI) and UL'YANOVSK classes are being constructed at the yard as well as commercial ships and naval auxiliaries. The carriers are the largest warships ever constructed outside of the United States. Submarine construction at the yard ended in the late 1950s.

Location. The yard is situated south of the city of Nikolayev, at the junction of the Ingul and Bug rivers, some 40 miles (64.5 km) from the mouth of the latter. The yard currently covers almost 500 acres.

History. The yard was built in 1895–1899 as a Belgian-owned enterprise known as the Nikolayev Shipbuilding, Mechanical, and Iron Works. It began building naval ships in 1901. In 1907 the firm was merged with the Company for Mechanized Production of South Russia and was known as the ''naval yard,'' after which it was further enlarged with support from the British firm Vickers. The

yard was able to engage in the massive pre–World War I shipbuilding program and by 1914 employed a reported 10,600 workers, making it one of the largest industrial establishments in Russia.

After the 1917 Revolution the yard was renamed for André Marti (Marti south). In the 1930s the construction of cruisers, destroyers, and submarines was initiated. The first included the heavy cruisers VOROSHILOV and MOLOTOV, and the light cruisers FRUNZE and ORDZHONIKIDZE. (The heavy cruisers were completed in 1940–1941, and one light cruiser in 1950; the other, unfinished, was scrapped after the war.) These were followed by the keel laying in 1938 of a battleship of the SOVIETSKIY SOYUZ class and the following year by the second ship of the KRONSHTADT class of battle cruisers, neither of which was completed. Because the water depth at the yard was limited, after launching, the battleship was to have been towed to Sevastopol for completion. (Work on the ship stopped in October 1940, but considerable progress had already been made.) Submarines of the S and M classes were built at the yard during the 1930s and into 1940–1941.

As German troops approached Nikolayev in 1941 several unfinished cruiser and destroyer hulls were towed from the Marti and 61 Kommuna yards to Black Sea ports farther east, but only one destroyer, launched in 1940 at the 61 Kommuna yard, was finished at Batum before the end of the war. A number of submarines were also towed to ports in the eastern Black Sea and Caspian Sea for completion. The Black Sea yard was occupied by German troops in August 1941 and was not recaptured by Soviet forces until March 1944. Extensive damage was inflicted on both Nikolayev yards in the close-in fighting and by German demolitions. The Marti (south) yard was rebuilt and was able to undertake the construction of surface ships and submarines in a relatively short period of time. Several M-class submarines were launched from 1947 to 1950, with the yard starting to launch Whiskey-class submarines beginning in 1951. Submarine construction continued only until the late 1950s, with an estimated 65 Whiskeys being built at the yard. No additional submarines have been built at the yard.

After the war the yard's surface warship programs included laying the keel for the first STALINGRAD-class battle cruiser in 1949. Work proceeded rapidly, and the ship is said to have been about 60 percent complete and ready for launching in early 1953 when Stalin died. All work on the project ceased and the hull was later launched and probably expended in weapon tests. (A second battle cruiser was to have been built on the ways vacated by the first hull.) The

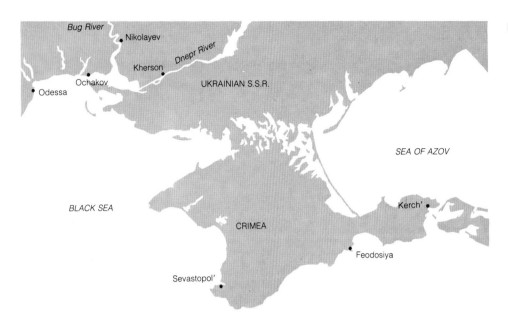

Northern Black Sea area.

yard also built three SVERDLOV-class light cruisers before the mid-1950s cutback in naval construction. The yard then concentrated on merchant construction for the remainder of the decade.

During this period the yard was known as the I.I. Nosenko Shipyard, or Nikolayev-Nosenko.[9]

Since the early 1960s the Black Sea shipyard has undertaken the construction of aviation ships for the Soviet Navy: the two MOSKVA-class helicopter cruisers, four KIEV-class VSTOL carriers, and the large carriers of the ADMIRAL KUZNETSOV (ex-TBILISI) class—the carriers being the largest naval ships to be built in the country. Naval auxiliaries are also constructed at the yard.

The Black Sea yard continues to produce large commercial ships, primarily dry cargo ships, fish factory ships, and trawlers. Recent construction includes the KHARITON GREKU series of bulk carriers with a 50,000 deadweight tonnage.

The yard has two shipbuilding areas, one for naval projects, with end-launch building ways and building docks, and the commercial area with a horizontal, dock-launching facility. The largest inclined way was approximately 850 feet (260 m). It has been extensively modified and enlarged to permit construction of aircraft carriers.

Kherson

The yard at Kherson builds merchant ships exclusively, mostly dry cargo ships, tankers, and floating dry docks (steel and concrete), some specifically for foreign transfer. The most impressive to date are the Arctic barge carriers of the ALEKSEY KOSYGIN class, with the lead ship delivered in 1983. These are 40,900-deadweight-ton ships.

The Kherson yard is located at the mouth of the Dnepr River. It achieved the status of a major shipyard in the 1950s.

Nikolayev Northern (Shipyard No. 445)

This yard has produced surface combatants, with the SLAVA-class cruisers recently constructed for the Soviet Navy and Kashin-class destroyers for the Indian Navy. It is also known as the 61 Kommuna yard.

Location. The yard is located at Nikolayev, at the junction of the Ingul and Bug rivers. It covers almost 200 acres.

History. The Nikolayev northern shipyard was begun as an admiralty shipyard in 1789, making use of shipwrights from the yards in St. Petersburg and Arkhangel'sk. The facility was intended as both a naval base and as a ship construction yard. It could be

ranked as a major shipbuilding facility from about 1800, but Nikolayev came to be less used as a naval base (with Sevastopol becoming the principal base for the Black Sea Fleet). The yard's viability decreased as iron and then steel warships came into service, and after more than a century of operation the yard was closed down in 1910 because the government considered it in a poor location and felt that its four shipways were too small to construct modern warships. Several major ships were built at the yard in this period, however, including the famed battleship POTEMKIN (completed in 1902).

In 1911 the yard reopened as a commercial venture, being leased by the French-owned Russian Shipbuilding Corporation (RUSSUD). However, pressure from Russian bankers forced the sale of stock to a Russian-controlled bank with ownership passing to a joint stock company, the Society of Nikolayevsk Shipyards. In 1915 both of the large Nikolayev yards were placed under a single administration by the stock owners. When World War I began in 1914 the RUSSUD yard employed almost 3,000 workers.

The RUSSUD yard built warships up to battleship size during the tsarist era. Submarine projects undertaken at the yard during World War I were the minelayer KRAB and BARS-class boats.

After the 1917 Revolution it was known as the Marti north yard and then as the 61 Kommuna yard. During the 1930s the yard built light cruisers, destroyers, and submarines of the SHCH class. Two light cruisers, the KUIBYSHEV and a sister ship, were laid down in 1939–1940, with the first not being completed until 1950 and the second broken up on the building ways. The yard was heavily damaged during the war.

After being rehabilitated, the yard produced a large number of destroyers and then the seven gas-turbine cruisers of the Kara class. The single large replenishment ship BEREZINA was also built at the yard. Nikolayev north was also the lead yard for the modernization of the Kashin and Kildin destroyer classes.

The yard is one of the few shipyards in the Soviet Union that has only inclined end-launch building ways and no covered construction halls. With completion of the fourth SLAVA-class cruiser there is no known Soviet naval construction at the yard.

Okean/Oktyabr'skoye

This yard constructs dry cargo and refrigerated cargo ships. It became a major shipbuilding center in the 1950s and has specialized in the construction of large merchant ships and trawlers, including the oil/ore carriers of the BORIS BUTOMA class (130,000 deadweight tons), and research ships.

The Okean shipyard is in Oktyabr'skoye near Nikolayev, the third major ship construction yard in the area.

---

9. Ivan Isidorovich Nosenko was director of the Ordzhonikidze/Baltic Shipyard, 1938–1939; the Peoples Commissar of Shipbuilding Production, 1940–1946; First Deputy Minister of Shipbuilding Production, 1952–1953, and Minister of Shipbuilding Production from 1954 until his death in 1956.

Ordzhonikidze/Sevastopol

The Ordzhonikidze naval yard is the main repair base of the Black Sea Fleet and additionally builds commercial ships and large floating cranes.

The yard is part of Sevastopol port—naval base complex on the bay of that name. It is one of the oldest Russian naval facilities on the Black Sea.

Zaliv/B.Ye. Butoma (Shipyard No. 532)

This yard constructs warships up to frigate size and large commercial ships, including the Soviet merchant fleet's supertankers.

Location. The yard is located at Kerch on the Crimean Peninsula near the entrance to the Sea of Azov. The yard occupies some 150 acres of land. It was named in 1981 for B.Ye. Butoma, longtime head of the ship production industry.

History. The yard became a major shipbuilding facility in the 1930s. In the postwar period the yard built small combatants as well as merchant ships. There was a major expansion of facilities beginning in the mid-1960s, at which time construction of frigates of the Krivak class was begun. Previously Poti-class corvettes were the largest combat ships built at Kerch. The merchant ships built at the yard range up to the KRYM-class supertankers, the largest such ships built in the Soviet Union. All eight ships of the class of 150,500 deadweight tons were built here.

The yard constructed the SEVMORPUT nuclear-propelled barge carrier for Arctic service. Thus, the yard has become the Soviet Union's seventh nuclear-capable shipyard.

It is also the only one of three Krivak building yards that is still producing these ships, in the Krivak III version for the KGB Maritime Border Troops.

Other construction yards in the Black Sea area are the Kamysh-Burun yard at Kerch, which built small combatants, including minesweepers, and more recently the surface effect ships of the Dergach class; and the Yuzhnaya Tochka shipyard at Feodosiya, on the Black Sea coast of the Crimea, a major construction facility for air cushion vehicles, including the Utenok, Tsaplya, and Pomornik ACV classes. Also, the Feodosiya shipyard, which constructs the Muravey-class hydrofoils as well as other small craft; Poti on the east coast of the Black Sea, which builds passenger hydrofoils; and the small commercial ship construction yards at Zhdanov and Rostov on the Sea of Azov.

There are large ship repair facilities at Il'ichevsk, near Odessa, which is the main repair base for Black Sea merchant ships and also builds small commercial ships. Near Sevastopol is a large repair yard that specializes in tankers.

Smaller repair yards are located at Batum, Kerch, Odessa, Sevastopol, and Tuapse.

FAR EAST SHIPYARDS

Dalzavod (Vladivostok) (Shipyard No. 202)

Vladivostok is a major maritime center with the Dalzavod shipyard constructing merchant and fishing ships and maintaining naval units as well.

Location. Vladivostok is situated on Peter the Great Bay, on the Sea of Japan.

History. During the 1930s this yard constructed destroyers and submarines of the L, S, and SHCH classes from components and sections manufactured in European Russia. No submarines have been built at Dalzavod in the postwar period.

In recent years the yard has constructed merchant and fishing ships.

There are several smaller shipyards in the Vladivostok area, some dedicated to the repair of merchant and fishing ships. The Ulis shipyard at Vladivostok has built minesweepers, the Turya hydrofoil torpedo craft, the Pauk-class corvettes, the Nanuchka II–class missile corvettes, and probably the new Svetlak-class KGB patrol corvette.

At nearby Nakhodka are two repair yards.

Khabarovsk

This yard, at the junction of the Amur and Ussuri rivers in the Far East, produces small combatants, merchant, and research ships. Khabarovsk is some 435 mi (695 km) south of the mouth of the Amur River where it enters the Tartar Strait.

The yard became a major shipbuilding facility in the 1950s. It produces patrol craft, small combatants, and minesweepers. The Tsaplya-class military air cushion vehicles are built at the yard. Some commercial ships are also built at the yard, including scientific research vessels.

Komsomol'sk (Shipyard No. 199)

This is a major submarine construction yard with some merchant work being undertaken. In the 1980s the yard built the Kilo-class diesel submarines and the Akula-class SSNs.

Location. The Komsomol'sk yard is about 280 miles (450 km) south of the mouth of the Amur River. The depth of water prevents the yard from completing larger ships and submarines, which must be fitted out at coastal shipyards after being launched at Komsomol'sk.

History. Construction of the Komsomol'sk yard began in 1932 at the site of the village of Permskoye to provide a major shipyard for the planned expansion of the Pacific Fleet. Its location was considered sufficiently far inland to preclude bombing by bombers based in Japan. Like Severodvinsk, the yard was to be capable of constructing two battleships in a covered hall (albeit with components sent from European factories and shipyards). However, a large iron and steel mill known as Amurstal was begun in 1935 about five miles (8 km) from the town. Other supporting industries were also built.

Destroyer construction began at Komsomol'sk in 1938 and in 1939 the keels were laid in the battleship hall at Komsomol'sk for the heavy cruisers KAGANOVICH and KALININ (completed in 1943–1944). Lesser naval ships and some merchant ships were also built at the yard. During the war, employment at the yard reached about 5,000, of whom one-half were women, with a total of six building ways located in two large covered halls—two large battleship ways in one and four smaller ways in the other (three of which could accommodate destroyers and one smaller ships).

In the postwar period the yard has been primarily engaged in submarine construction, although surface combatants up to destroyer size as well as merchant ships and icebreakers have been constructed. The first postwar submarines built at the yard were Whiskey-class diesel attack submarines (11 units) and subsequently Golf-class diesel ballistic missile craft (7 units plus one delivered in China).

Komsomol'sk became the second yard in the Soviet Union to construct nuclear-propelled submarines. The first of five Echo I–class SSGNs was completed in 1960, followed by 13 of the larger Echo II SSGNs. The yard subsequently converted the Echo I submarines to an SSN configuration. Kosomol'sk has since constructed ten of the Yankee and eight of the Delta I SSBNs, sharing these SSBN projects with Severodvinsk; later SSBN designs have been too large to be built at Komsomol'sk.

The yard has continued to develop advanced diesel-electric submarines. In the 1960s Komsomol'sk built four Bravo-class target and training submarines (SST), followed by the two India-class salvage and rescue craft (AGSS), and was the lead yard for the Kilo attack submarine (SS). The Victor III was the first nuclear torpedo-attack submarine to be constructed at Komsomol'sk, followed in 1984 by launching the first Akula-class SSN. Unable to construct large SSBNs, the yard has thus shifted to diesel and nuclear attack submarines.

The last significant surface warships built at Komsomol'sk were Petya I–class ASW frigates into the early 1960s; previously the yard had constructed surface combatants up to destroyer size (e.g., the Kotlin and Krupnyy classes).

Also on the Amur River is a yard at Blagoveschensk.

Petropavlovsk

There are two shipyards and a major submarine refit/refueling facility near the city of Petropavlovsk on Avachinskaya Bay on the southeastern coast of the Kamchatka Peninsula. On the eastern side of the bay, near the city, are the Lenin shipyard, which performs civilian and military work, and the Freza yard, which appears to undertake only commercial work. Across Avachinskaya Bay, southwest of Petropavlovsk, in the protected harbor of Bukhta Tar'ya is the Tar'ya nuclear submarine refit/refueling facility (see page 419).

INLAND SHIPYARDS

Krasnoye Sormovo (Shipyard No. 112)

Located at the large industrial city of Gor'kiy, this is one of four Soviet shipyards now building submarines. Current submarine programs are the titanium-hull Sierra SSN and the diesel-electric Kilo classes.

The nuclear-propelled submarines constructed at Gor'kiy are carried on transporter docks through the inland waterway system to Severodvinsk for completion and trials; diesel-electric submarines are taken down the Volga River to the Black Sea, most for subsequent assignment to other fleet areas.

In addition, river and inland craft are constructed, including hydrofoils and air cushion vehicles.

Location. This yard is located some 200 miles (320 km) east of Moscow on the Volga River at its confluence with the Oka River, just above the city of Gor'kiy.

History. Krasnoye Sormovo is credited with being the oldest significant shipbuilding site in the country. (Before 1932, Gor'kiy was known as Nizhny Novgorod, which was founded in the early 13th century and became a major trading center.)

The first "modern" shipbuilding effort was the Nizhegorodskaya Machine Plant, which started producing river boats and barges in 1849. Previously named Sormovski, the yard was renamed Krasnoye Sormovo in 1922.

The facility became one of the major shipyards of the Soviet Union in the early 1940s. At that time the yard built M-class submarines, which were fabricated in sections and then taken by train and barge to various coastal yards for assembly. The larger S-class submarines were also built at Gor'kiy and fitted out at Severodvinsk or Baltic shipyards.

After World War II, Gor'kiy became the principal yard producing Whiskey-class submarines. The yard completed 116 units from 1950 to 1957, with 40 submarines completed in the peak year of 1955. The yard then built the Romeo-class attack submarines and the 16 Juliett-class guided missile submarines (SSG).

Krasnoye Sormovo was the fourth Soviet shipyard to construct nuclear submarines, launching the first Charlie SSGN in 1966. While continuing Charlie I/II construction, in the 1970s, the yard also built three of the Victor II SSNs and initiated the Tango-class diesel attack submarine, partial successor to the Foxtrot class as a long-range diesel attack. In the early 1980s the yard began building the Sierra-class SSN and the Kilo-class diesel submarines. The titanium hull of the Sierra required special construction/welding facilities (with Severodvinsk and Sudomekh being the world's only other shipyards with this capability).

Large numbers of commercial inland and river craft are also built at Gor'kiy.

Leninskaya Kuznitsa

The Leninskaya Kuznitsa yard at Kiev builds large numbers of seagoing trawlers, self-propelled dredgers, and small naval units. The yard is noted for its highly developed machinery production facilities and fabricates ship components for other shipyards, especially those at Nikolayev and Kherson. The facility is sometimes referred to as the Dnepr yard.

The inland yard is some 500 miles (800 km) up the Dnepr River from the Black Sea.

Yaroslavl

The Yaroslavl shipyard produces the Pauk-class ASW corvettes.

This yard is located on the Volga River, some 160 miles (255 km) northeast of Moscow. Yaroslavl is a major industrial center (and one of the earliest manufacturing towns in Russia, having been founded ca. 1010 by Yaroslavl the Great).

Zelenodol'sk (Shipyard No. 340)

This yard produces mainly small combatants, trawlers, and hydrofoils. Among its naval products were the Kronshtadt, S.O.-1, Poti, and Grisha classes. In the mid-1970s construction began on the Koni-class frigates, the largest naval units to be built at the yard.

Zelenodol'sk is located 40 miles (65 km) west of Kazan', some 200 miles (320 km) east of Gor'kiy on the Vetluga River. The shipyard was established as a major shipyard during the war and employed some 5,000 workers during that period, with up to 75 percent of them being women. In addition to various repair shops, the complex included munitions plants. During the war the yard produced steel submarine chasers and motor torpedo boats.

There are numerous smaller inland yards on the many lakes and rivers of the Soviet Union. These include the Gorokhovets yard on the Klyazma River near Gor'kiy; the Kama yard at Perm' on the Kama River; three yards at Krasnoyarsk on the Yenisey River; the Limenda and Velikiy Ustyug yards on the Northern Dvina River; the Moryakovskiy building yard at Tomsk, on the Tom River near its junction with the Ob' River; the Oka yard at Navashino on the Oka River; the Omsk construction and repair yard on the Irtysk River; the newly expanded Osetrovo yard on the Lena River; the Tyumen' yard on the Tobol River, which builds large floating power stations; the Vympel Shipbuilding Association at Andropov (formerly Rybinsk) on the manmade Lake Rybinsk some 300 miles (480 km) north of Moscow; and the Volgagrad yard on the Volga River.

On the Caspian Sea, the Astrakhan Shipbuilding Association, at the mouth of the Volga River, builds tankers for the Caspian Sea trade as well as passenger ships and offshore oil drilling rigs. There are a total of four yards at Astrakhan and three at Baku.

CHAPTER 32

Merchant Marine

A tug tows the nuclear-propelled barge/container carrier SEVMORPUT into port. Like previous U.S. and West German efforts to operate nuclear merchant ships, the SEVMORPUT has encountered opposition from those concerned with potential environmental problems. (Sovfoto)

The Soviet Union continues to operate a large merchant fleet with more than 2,400 ships of all types—the world's second largest merchant fleet in number of ships and the seventh largest in carrying capacity (see table 32-1).[1]

Merchant fleets are invaluable to a nation's naval activities in wartime, as evidenced most recently in the British campaign in the Falklands in 1982 and the U.S. buildup and campaign in the Persian Gulf area (Desert Shield/Desert Storm).[2] Merchant fleets can also provide direct support to naval forces in peacetime—beyond their more obvious role of supporting a nation's political and economic goals. It thus becomes significant to any discussion of the Soviet Navy that the Soviet Union has one of the world's largest, most modern, and most flexible merchant fleets. According to a senior U.S. maritime analyst:

Soviet shipping is a major force in international maritime affairs. It is the product of a strong national policy dedicated to serving the Soviet Union's military, political, and economic interests. Some may question—with validity—the order of precedence between military and economic interests, considering the merchant navy's contribution of an estimated $2 billion in annual gross earnings to the Soviet Union's need for hard currencies. Nonetheless, the military aspects of the Soviet merchant and fishing fleets are of major strategic importance to the Soviet Navy.[3]

The 1980s were a period of international fleet decline, with very few new ships being added to Western merchant fleets. The Soviet merchant fleet has also declined during

1. See Maritime Administration, U.S. Department of Transportation, *Merchant Fleets of the World* (Washington, D.C.: 1991). Also see Lt. Cdr. D.M. Long, RN, *The Soviet Merchant Fleet—Its Growth, Strategy, Strength, and Weaknesses, 1920–1999* (London: Lloyd's of London Press, 1986).

2. During the Falklands War the British employed 45 merchant-type Ships Taken Up From Trade (STUFT) as aircraft transports and replenishment, hospital, cargo, and troop ships; five fishing trawlers were also taken on for use as minesweepers but were not used in that role.

3. Irwin M. Heine, "The Soviet Merchant Navy—A Two-Pronged Force," U.S. Naval Institute *Proceedings* (December 1984), p. 142. Mr. Heine was Chief Economist and Statistician of the U.S. Maritime Administration from 1953 to 1965, after which he was Chief for International Maritime Affairs until his retirement in 1970.

TABLE 32-1. WORLD MERCHANT FLEET RANKING, JANUARY 1990 (Tonnage in thousands)

	Number	Deadweight Tonnage		Gross Tonnage	
Panama	3,189	Liberia	88,275	Liberia	47,711
USSR	2,428	Panama	70,537	Panama	44,051
Liberia	1,409	Greece	36,537	Japan	23,285
China	1,281	Japan	36,237	Greece	19,799
Cyprus	1,054	Cyprus	29,729	USSR	18,917
Japan	1,007	Norway	28,800	Cyprus	16,580
Greece	914	USSR	25,735	Norway	15,991
Norway	587	Brit. dependent terr.	24,810	Brit. dependent terr.	14,046
Philippines	558	United States*	20,439	United States*	13,096
Brit. dependent terr.	545	Bahamas	19,719	China	12,747

SOURCE: U.S. Maritime Administration listing for ships of 1,000 gross tons and larger.

* The privately owned U.S. merchant fleet ships (with the international ranking of 12th) numbered 407 ships in January 1990; the U.S. government owned an additional 251 ships, with most of the latter laid up in reserve.

TABLE 32-2. SOVIET MERCHANT SHIPS, JANUARY 1990 (Tonnage in thousands)

	Number of Ships	Deadweight Tonnage	Gross Tonnage
General cargo ships	1,539	9,608	7,826
Container ships	92	690	655
Roll-on/roll-off ships	94	1,028	939
Barge carriers	7	217	201
Bulk carriers	244	7,060	4,395
Tankers	420	7,061	4,625
Passenger and combination ships	37*	84	327

SOURCE: U.S. Maritime Administration.
* In addition there are a large number of passenger ships and passenger/vehicle ferries sailing on coastal sea routes.

the past decade, albeit at a lesser rate than the world average. Further, as the other merchant fleets have declined, the ranking of the USSR has increased during the past decade, from ranking tenth in carry capacity to sixth.

Table 32-2 shows the composition of the Soviet merchant fleet with respect to freighters and tankers. Not included are the more than 50 passenger ships and such specialized ships as icebreakers and cable layers, or the merchant-type ships operated by the Merchant Fleet, Navy, and the KGB Maritime Border Troops.

The Soviet merchant marine has the world's largest number of passenger ships, break-bulk freighters, barge carriers, and Roll-On/Roll-Off (RO/RO) ships. The last are of particular value in military operations. The Soviet Union currently operates some 94 of these ships with additional units on order. Coupled with the Soviet Navy's amphibious ships, these RO/RO ships and certain other cargo ships provide a lift capacity for the entire Soviet Naval Infantry as well as several divisions of the Ground Forces. (The Soviets have exercised merchant ships in this role.)

During 1989, the last year for which complete data were available when this edition went to press, the Soviet merchant fleet added 26 ships of 327,119 Deadweight Tons (DWT).[4] Of these only five were delivered by Soviet shipyards; two were built by Bulgaria, four by Finland, one by West Germany, three by East Germany, two by Poland, one by Rumania, three by Yugoslavia, one by Malta, one by Greece, and three by Japan. As of March 1990, the Soviet Union had 39 merchant ships of 581,205 deadweight tons under construction. Although that was only a fraction over two percent of the number of ships being built world wide, only 13 nations had more ships on the building ways—three of them Eastern Bloc nations. (At the time only one merchant ship was under construction in the United States; she has since been delivered.)

Also during 1989, the Soviet merchant fleet scrapped 14 cargo ships of 98,022 DWT and six tankers of 106,864 DWT.

The Soviet Union experienced several major maritime disasters during the 1980s:

- 16 February 1986: The cruise ship MIKHAIL LERMONTOV (IVAN FRANKO class) sank after striking a rock off New Zealand. One person was lost.

- 31 August 1986: The passenger liner ADMIRAL NAKHIMOV collided with a Soviet freighter in the Black Sea, 45 minutes after sailing from the port of Novorossiysk. Both ships appear to have had radar and visual contact with the other before the cargo ship sliced into the liner. The ADMIRAL NAKHIMOV sank rapidly with the loss of 398 passengers and crew of 1,234 on board. Following the disaster, a Soviet merchant marine official declared, "The ships are not at fault. . . . The people are at fault." The NAKHIMOV was 61 years old at the time of her loss![5]

- May 1988: A fire on board the cruise ship PRIAMURYE while docked in Osaka, Japan, took the lives of 11 Soviet tourists.

- 30 June 1988: The cruise ship MAKSIM GOR'KIY with almost 575 passengers and 377 crew on board, struck an iceberg in the Greenland Sea, some 185 miles (296 km) east of Spitsbergen. All passengers were safely removed from the ship and, despite heavy flooding from two holes in her side, the ship survived.

History. After World War II the Soviet Union had little interest in a buildup of the merchant fleet, in part because of the priorities for rebuilding naval forces and because of the limited foreign trade. Further, a number of American-supplied merchant ships of recent construction were still held under the Soviet flag.

The Khrushchev period initiated a major expansion of the merchant fleet, initially to support overseas clients and then to help trade with other Third World nations. Khrushchev's interest in developing a strong Soviet merchant fleet was further reinforced by the Cuban missile crisis, which demonstrated the need for shipping to support long-range military operations. The ranking of the Soviet fleet rose from twenty-sixth place in the late 1950s to twelfth place in 1962, and to seventh place in 1964 (although since then it has periodically slipped to eighth place as there have been spurts in merchant fleet development). In the 1970s there was another phase of Soviet fleet expansion as merchant ships became a major earner of "hard" Western currencies.

Regular Soviet cargo service to the United States began in late 1970 after an absence of almost two decades. Soviet passenger

---

4. Deadweight Tons (DWT) are the carrying capacity of a ship measured in long tons (2,240 pounds).

5. The ADMIRAL NAKHIMOV was also the oldest ship of the Soviet passenger fleet, having been built in Germany in 1925 as the BERLIN. She was sunk in 1945 and was salvaged and rebuilt after the war. In Soviet service she was rated at 8,946 deadweight tons with 870 passenger berths.

ships began calling at New York and other U.S. cities in June 1973, initiating a service that would extend briefly to the Caribbean cruise route before ending a few years later. Soviet merchant ships increasingly called at almost 60 U.S. ports, reaching a peak of some 1,700 port arrivals per year. (Some of these were multiple U.S. port calls, because this figure includes the same ship calling at several ports). Soviet merchant service to U.S. ports was halted abruptly in 1979 when U.S. longshoremen protested the Soviet invasion of Afghanistan.

These economic-political goals of the merchant fleet were candidly linked by V. Kudryavtsev, a political observer for the Soviet newspaper *Izvestiya,* who wrote on 15 February 1972: "The Soviet Union does not conceal the fact that economic relations with the developing countries are an integral part of the struggle between two world systems, socialism and capitalism. These relations undermine the imperialist powers of economic and trade ties with the developing countries and force the capitalist states to make concessions."

The primary economic emphasis of the Soviet merchant fleet—beyond carrying cargo between Soviet ports—appears to be on earning "hard" Western currencies. Because Soviet ships are largely built in Soviet and Eastern Bloc shipyards with "soft" rubles—which have no exchange value outside of the country—and their operating costs and crews are paid for in rubles, the Western currency earned by the merchant fleet is a profit for the government. (Crew costs are estimated at less than 15 percent of the total cost of Soviet merchant fleet operations, much lower than comparable Western fleets.)

Today this merchant fleet carries cargo and passengers on more than 70 international trade routes, calling at ports in some 140 countries throughout the world. Soviet merchant ships compete effectively with Western shipping on virtually every major trade route throughout the world except those that call at U.S. ports. The Soviets practice rate cutting to ensure a share of those markets in which they have an interest. For example, when the Soviet Baltic Shipping Company began container service in 1974 to New York, Baltimore, and Philadelphia, the line announced that the service would be 10 percent below regular rates to ensure a certain amount of cargo would be carried. More recently, the Far East Shipping Company has been playing havoc in the Japan–Australia–Hong Kong cross trade by quoting rates as much as 40 percent below those of the Far Australia Conference. After extensive protests from members of the conference, the Soviet shippers agreed to charge no more than 10 percent below the conference rates.

Soviet shippers—with the world's largest fleet of passenger ships—have greatly encroached on cruise ship operations as well. When the British withdrew the passenger ships QUEEN ELIZABETH 2 and CANBERRA from the cruise trades in 1982 to carry troops to the Falklands, the Soviets seized the opportunity to increase their share of the British market from 10 percent in 1980 to more than 40 percent when this volume went to press. Criticizing the inroads made by Soviet ships in the British cruise-ship market, officials of British shipping lines estimated in late 1984 that they had lost £11.7 million during the two years following the Falklands conflict.

Soviet merchant ships have also supported Soviet military goals. This became evident to the West in the early 1960s when Soviet and Eastern Bloc merchant ships carried a variety of arms, including long-range missiles and strike aircraft to Cuba. Subsequently, during most of the Vietnam War an average of more than one Soviet ship per day entered North Vietnamese ports carrying equipment, food, building materials, and other supplies from the Soviet Union. (Most of the weapons and munitions from the Soviet Union apparently were transferred by rail through China, possibly because of the fear that the United States would blockade Vietnamese ports.)

Ships of the Soviet merchant marine have carried weapons and other supplies in support of Soviet political-economic-military goals to Third World nations throughout the world. In particular, the large amount of Soviet military assistance to the Middle East is carried largely in Soviet ships.

Finally, the merchant fleet continues to provide direct support to Soviet naval forces. They carry fuel, food, and munitions to ships at sea, and tankers regularly refuel warships on the high seas. Obviously, the merchant ships can also collect intelligence against targets of opportunity, an activity simplified by the fact that captains of most if not all large merchant ships are naval reserve officers. In wartime the merchant fleet would be pressed into service full time, as required, for amphibious and logistic duties. In addition to the above mentioned RO/RO ships, the many break-bulk cargo ships, and the large, barge-carrying ships are particularly well suited for supporting long-range military operations.

A final military-related aspect of Soviet merchant shipping is that several ships have been observed with such military features as CBR "washdown" systems to help clean off the effects of chemical, biological, and radiological (nuclear) weapons, and reinforced deck positions where weapons could apparently be mounted.

A merchant tanker of the 22,639-deadweight-ton RIYEKA class (center) refuels a UDALOY-class destroyer (left) and a Krivak-class frigate (right). The Soviet merchant fleet provides a variety of support to the Soviet Navy on a daily basis. In addition, the large merchant fleet helps to maintain the Soviet shipbuilding industry.

An instructor chats with cadets at the Murmansk merchant marine training school. These cadets will also spend time at sea in both powered and sail-training ships. (Sovfoto, Semyon Meistermann)

ORGANIZATION AND MANPOWER

Soviet merchant fleet activities are directed by the Ministry of Merchant Marine, which is headed by a civilian minister. Within the ministry there are regional organizations to administer each ocean area, with headquarters at Murmansk, Leningrad, Odessa, and Vladivostok. In Moscow and at each regional headquarters there is a computing center by which administrators can keep track of all shipping and help plan schedules, port calls, overhauls, and future operations.

Merchant ship operations on the intra-Soviet and international routes are under the jurisdiction of 16 shipping lines. Those that have operated most of the ships that called at U.S. ports in the 1970s have been the Baltic Shipping Company of Leningrad and the Far East Shipping Company (FESCO) of Vladivostok.[6]

The Ministry of Merchant Marine also operates ports, research institutes, ship repair yards, and schools. The ship repair yards provide maintenance and overhaul capabilities, while most new construction of the larger units is done at the building yards of the Ministry of Ship Production (see chapter 31). There are an estimated 20 merchant marine and fisheries colleges in the Soviet Union. The merchant schools train ship's officers and crewmen as well as certain specialists to operate shore equipment. Among the more noted merchant marine schools are the Admiral Makarov Higher Marine Engineering School in Leningrad and Odessa Higher Marine Engineering School, which educates merchant marine engineers. Students enter the maritime schools after completing high school, at age 17 or 18. The graduates of these schools, after 5½ years in the classroom and at sea, are awarded both academic degrees and officer (technical) certificates. Upon graduation they sail as third officers or (in passenger ships) as fourth officers.

A merchant marine officer is supposed to be given a month's leave for additional classes each year (in addition to personal leave). And, at intervals of at least five years, all officers take two months of refresher and advanced courses.

Several training ships are operated by these schools (see chapter 25). In addition to training hundreds of Soviet maritime students each year, their cadets include young men from more than 30 Eastern European and Third World nations.

History. The current merchant marine organizational structure dates to 25 August 1954 when the Ministries of Maritime and River Fleets and the Directorate of the Northern Sea Route were combined to form the Ministry of Merchant and River Fleets. The

organizational struggles within the government were reflected by a reversal to Independent River and Sea Ministries within nine months; however, in 1956 they were again reunited into the current Ministry of Merchant Fleet. The status of the ministry was upgraded in 1964 when the title became the All Union Ministry of Merchant Fleet.

MERCHANT SHIPS

Soviet merchant ships are smaller than the average ships operated by the major maritime nations. This is due in part to the many relatively small Soviet ports and the fact that a large percentage of the Soviet merchant fleet is assigned to intra-country routes. Also, these smaller ships are more suitable for serving on routes to Third World nations that have few ports that can accommodate the larger merchant ships built in the West and which have insufficient trade to make it profitable for Western shipping lines.

In an effort to reduce maintenance requirements, the Soviet merchant fleet has developed an extensive system of preplanned and preventive maintenance. Also, to reduce the expense of overseas repairs for merchant ships in foreign ports, under certain conditions repair teams are sent to sea to perform maintenance, or specialists are assigned to a crew to service new or difficult machinery.

New ships also have reduced manning requirements. More than 400 of the newer merchant ships operated by the Soviet Union have fully automated propulsion plants. And living conditions have been greatly improved; crew members in the newer ships have individual cabins, and some larger ships have gyms and swimming pools for the crew.

About one-half of the current Soviet merchant fleet has been built in the Soviet Union and almost one-half is from Eastern Europe—primarily from East German, Finnish, and Polish shipyards. The latter ships are purchased with rubles or obtained through various trade and aid agreements. A few merchant ships have been purchased from the Western nations, including Austria, Britain, France, Italy, and Norway. The Soviets appear to buy ships from the West primarily to obtain advanced designs and technologies.

It is beyond the scope of this volume to address specific characteristics of Soviet merchant ships.[7] The remainder of this chapter discusses some of the more significant categories and types of ships in the Soviet merchant fleet.

---

6. The other shipping companies are Azov, Black Sea, Caspian, Danube, Estonian, Georgian, Kamchatka, Latvian, Lithuanian, Murmansk, Northern, Novorossiysk, Primorsk, and Sakhalin.

7. Detailed characteristics of Soviet merchant ships are given in Ambrose Greenway, *Soviet Merchant Ships* (Emsworth, Hampshire: Kenneth Mason, 1989).

SEABEE/LASH Ships. These are merchant ships that carry large, fully loaded barges, or lighters, that can be floated or lifted on and off the ship. This scheme speeds up loading and unloading and allows cargo to be handled at ports where piers or wharves are unavailable. The two principal barge-carrying designs are known as LASH (Lighter Aboard Ship) and SEABEE (Sea Barge); the former use cranes to lift barges to the cargo decks and the latter employ elevators.

During the 1970s the Soviets purchased plans from a U.S. firm for the SEABEE design and contracted with the Finnish shipyard Valmet to construct two 37,830-DWT ships, larger than any barge carriers that had been built until that time. These ships, the JULIUS FUCIK (delivered in 1978) and TIBOR SZAMUELI (1979), are 876 feet (267 m) and can each carry 26 barges of 1,300 tons (loaded). They can offload up to 25,000 tons of cargo in 13 hours without the need of piers.

Obviously pleased with these ships, the Soviets have followed them up with a smaller class of "feeder" barge carriers of the BORIS POLEVOY class, also built by Valmet, and a pair of large ships built at the Kherson shipyard on the Black Sea. The latter ships, the ALEKSEY KOSYGIN class, were designed specifically for Arctic operation and at 40,881 deadweight tons, carry 82 barges or 1,480 standard freight containers, or various combinations of both. In 1985 the KOSYGIN was operating between Vladivostok and the mouth of the Yenisey River. (A later ship of this class has been named INDIRA GANDHI to honor the slain Indian leader.)

More impressive—although smaller—is the nuclear-propelled barge carrier SEVMORPUT, built at Kerch and completed in 1988. The ship, intended for Arctic operation, is 31,900 tons deadweight and can carry 73 barges of 500 tons or 1,300 freight containers. A single nuclear reactor driving both high- and low-pressure turbines will provide essentially unlimited endurance at 20.5 knots.[8]

The nuclear barge carrier is the world's first fully operational nuclear-propelled merchant ship, following one-of-a-kind demonstration ships built by the United States and West Germany. The nuclear barge ship significantly enhances cargo movement along the Arctic coast of the Soviet Union, where port facilities are limited and the river mouths are shallow. Further, supported by nuclear icebreakers, the ship greatly extends the shipping season in the Arctic region toward the Soviet long-term goal of year-round shipping between the Arctic and Far East.

Still, additional ships are not being built. The attitude of some Soviets toward nuclear ships is cautious. One Soviet journal reported:

> Everything seems to indicate that the Soviet people have learned well the sad lessons of the [nuclear accident at] Chernobyl. The welcome the first nuclear-powered lighter, SEVMORPUT, received in the port of Vladivostok was less than enthusiastic. The Executive Committee of the City Soviet had decided that the ship could not enter the port until a commission of experts checked out the dependability of the nuclear reactor protective systems. When the commission was satisfied, the city officials permitted the lighter to drop anchor on the inner roads and to begin unloading operations.[9]

General Cargo Ships. A major portion of the merchant fleets consists of general or break-bulk cargo ships. These ships are particularly suited for carrying military cargoes, and their generally small size permits them to call on relatively minor ports. During the past decade the Soviet Union has been the world's largest constructor of general cargo ships and should continue to build this type of ship, albeit at a slower rate, as a greater variety of merchant ship types are procured.

The most recent design built in the Soviet Union was the GEROI PANFILOVTSY class of 13,500 DWT, built at Kherson. These 15 ships, completed from 1973 to 1984, can carry 320 standard containers in holds plus 68 on deck, or palletized loads or bulk grain.

Container Ships. The Soviet merchant fleet has a large number of container and partial container ships, and combination

8. Their propulsion plants develop 40,000 shp; refuelings are scheduled at four-year intervals.

9. "The Port Is Closed," *Soviet Life*, July 1989, p. 8.

The TIBOR SZAMUELI is one of two American-designed, Finnish-built barge carriers in Soviet service. They provide highly flexible shipping capabilities.

container-RO/RO ships (see below). The largest all-container ships are the German-built modified MERCUR II type, delivered from 1982 to 1985. Built at Warnemunde in East Germany, these ships are 16,030 DWT ships that are 571 feet (174 m) long. They can carry 536 containers in holds plus 405 on deck. Twenty ships of this general design have been delivered, and the later ones are being lengthened to carry up to 1,254 containers.

Roll-On/Roll-Off Ships. The Soviets have more than 85 RO/RO ships in commercial service and more are being built. Again, these ships are particularly valuable for military operations. Although they require piers to unload their vehicles, their rapid unloading capability and large vehicle capacity are invaluable in military logistics.

Although most Soviet RO/ROs have a speed of 16–17 knots, the eight SKULPTOR KONENKOV–class ships (completed 1975–1982) are capable of 20.5 knots and the three KAPITAN SMIRNOV–class ships (1979–1980) are 25-knot, gas-turbine-propelled ships. The latter, at 20,175 DWT, can lift a significant number of vehicles or 1,246 containers. Additional RO/RO ships are being built for the Soviet merchant marine in Soviet and foreign shipyards, attesting to the importance of these ships to Soviet planners.

Ore–Bulk Oil Ships. The OBO ships transport large quantities of liquid fuel, grain, or ore. The first Soviet ship of this type, the MARSHAL BUDENNYY, was completed in 1975 at Gdynia, Poland. At 101,877 deadweight tons, the BUDENNYY is 804 feet (245.9 m)

The RO/RO-container ship KOMSOMOL'SK lowers her articulated, 118-foot (36-m) vehicle ramp at Bluff Harbour, New Zealand. The 21,000-deadweight-ton ship can carry 1,500 standard containers or a mix of containers and vehicles, unloading the latter through the stern. (Leo Van Ginderen)

The STAKHANOVETS YERMOLENKO departs Antwerp for Cuba with a heavy cargo. The three Finnish-built ships of this design are 5,717 deadweight tons. They have a modified LSD/LPD configuration with gantry cranes and traveling transporters to unload cargo over the stern without shore support. (Leo Van Ginderen)

The long Soviet coastline on the Arctic has led to the construction of specialized supply ship–icebreakers. The 10,690-deadweight-ton VITUS BERING, completed in 1986, is the first of a series of these ships that can carry and self-unload a variety of cargoes; there is a helicopter facility aft. Another ship is visible between the 12.5-ton-capacity cranes, which can be paired to lift 25 tons in tandem. (Leo Van Ginderen)

long and has nine large cargo holds. A total of 17 ships have been built in Poland, Norway, and the Okean yard in Nikolayev for the Soviet merchant fleet.

The Soviet Union has purchased 35 smaller bulk carriers from Western brokers. These are secondhand Western ships that have been laid up for lack of cargoes and were available at very low prices.

Tankers. The Soviet merchant fleet operates approximately 400 oil tankers, of which about 100 are subordinated to the Ministry of Fishing to support worldwide fishing activities. There are additionally a number of special-cargo tankers, especially liquified gas and ammonia gas carriers.

The Soviet Union lagged behind the Western maritime nations in the construction of supertankers (i.e., over 100,000 DWT). Be-

lately, the Soviets built one series of supertankers, the KRYM class of 150,500 DWT, with seven ships being completed at Kerch between 1975 and 1980. The ships are highly automated and can pump out a full cargo of 150,000 tons of oil in ten hours.

While the KRYM class was being built, the merchant-ship design bureau in Leningrad began plans for a tanker 1,135 feet (346 m) long with a capacity of some 300,000 to 370,000 tons. These larger ships were never built, however, because the world oil situation of the late 1970s reduced the need for them, and, in any case, there is little domestic use for these large tankers because of the limited size of Soviet ports.

The most recent large tankers acquired for the Soviet merchant fleet are the seven ships of the POBYEDA class, completed from 1981 to 1987. These 67,980-DWT ships are being built at Kerch. The

Another specialized merchant ship design used in significant numbers by the Soviet merchant fleet is the OBO (Ore-Bulk-Oil) ship. This is the 101,877-deadweight-ton MARSHAL ROKISSOVSKIY, seen here at Antwerp. (Leo Van Ginderen)

Much of the Soviet merchant fleet still consists of relatively small ships such as the Finnish-built timber carrier VORONEZH. This is a 3,930-deadweight-ton ship with four hatches. More than 40 timber carriers of about this size are currently in Soviet service. (Leo Van Ginderen)

The RO/RO-container AKADEMIK GORBUNOV shows the standard arrangement of this type of ship, found in large numbers in the Soviet merchant fleet. This class—the Polish-built B-481 design—is 18,462 deadweight tons and can accommodate 634 standard containers. (Leo Van Ginderen)

majority of the Soviet merchant tankers are smaller than the average in major Western merchant fleets, making them useful for naval and Third World operations in addition to being more suitable for Soviet ports. Recent acquisitions include ten ships built at the Rauma yard in Finland; these are the VENTSPILS-class ships, which are only 6,297 DWT and 371 feet (113 m) long. They are designed for Arctic operations (labeled the *Arktika* type by the Soviets). Also, the large OBO ships can transport petroleum.

Specialized Cargo Ships. There are a number of specialized cargo ships in Soviet service, among them heavy-lift ships that have important military support capabilities. The three heavy-lift ships of the STAKHANOVETS KOTOV class, completed in 1978–1979, at 5,717 DWT, can carry heavy, outsize loads, and have two 350-ton-capacity gantry cranes.

Another specialized cargo ship that should be of special interest to the Soviet Navy is the oil-drilling rig transport ship TRANSSHELF built at the Wartslia yard in Finland. This ship, delivered in 1987, can lift oil rigs and other floating equipment weighing up to 20,000 tons. The ship herself is 34,000 DWT, with an overall length of 567½ feet (173 m) and has a broad beam 131¼ feet (40 m), to provide stability. With a service speed of 14 knots, the ship can carry floating equipment that cannot be easily towed. To load cargo, the ship ballasts down and the rig or other equipment is floated on; the ship's ballast tanks are then emptied by compressed air. (The U.S. government has chartered ships of this type to carry military equipment.)

The Soviet merchant fleet makes extensive use of training simulators. This is a bridge simulator for a tanker, at Leningrad. (Sovfoto, Maxim Blokhin)

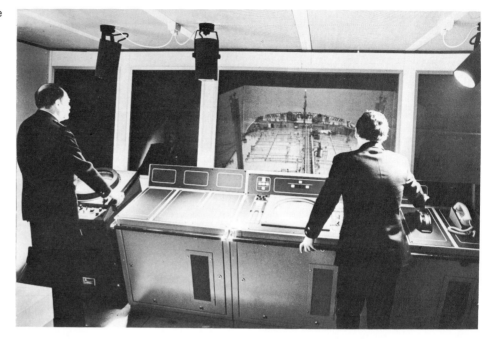

The Soviet merchant fleet contains numerous salvage tugs that support merchant and fishing operations. This is the Topaz of the Purga class; the Navy and KGB operate similar ships as the Sorum class. The Sorums have a lattice mast amidships, and the KGB units are armed. (Japanese Maritime Self-Defense Force)

The largest Soviet tankers are the seven ships of the Krym class at 150,500 deadweight tons; the Kavkaz is shown here in the Atlantic. These tankers, built at the Zaliv/B.Ye. Butoma yard in Kerch, sail under Soviet colors with petroleum carriers built in Britain, Bulgaria, Greece, Italy, Japan, Poland, Romania, Sweden, and Yugoslavia. (Leo Van Ginderen)

Passenger Ships. The Soviet Union has one of the world's largest fleets of passenger ships and currently operates about 50. The passenger ships sail on scheduled routes and in cruise service.

The largest of the Soviet passenger ships is the MAKSIM GOR'KIY, built in West Germany in 1968. The ship was operated by a German shipping line until 1974, when, found unprofitable to operate, it was purchased by the Soviet Union. The ship carries more than 600 passengers. Slightly smaller but with a larger passenger capacity are the British-built FEDOR SHALYAPIN (800 passengers) and the LEONID SOBINOV (930), both of which served 11 years under the British Red Ensign before being purchased by the Soviet Union in 1973. The four East German–built IVAN FRANKO–class ships, completed in 1964–1968, can carry 700–750 passengers.

Five smaller, 2,149-DWT combination RO/RO-passenger ships of the BYELORUSSIYA class have had part of their car deck space converted to additional cabins. This increased the number of passenger berths from 500 to 650. When employed as day ferries, these ships can accommodate another 500 passengers.

The passenger ships also earn hard currencies for the Soviet Union, help to capture trade routes, provide an opportunity for political influence, and offer the potential for moving large numbers of troops by sea.

Both cruise and liner service survive in the Soviet Union. This is the KAZAKHSTAN, one of five Finnish-built sister ships that have 650 passenger berths. Cars or containers can be carried internally, loaded through bow, stern, and side doors. (Leo Van Ginderen)

Soviet cruise ships increasingly tout modern, Western-style accommodations, such as this suite on the 550-berth ODESSA. These ships can earn hard currencies for the Soviet economy, at the same time "showing the flag." (International Cruise Center)

Western passengers relax on board the cruise ship ODESSA. She and other Soviet passenger ships operate on worldwide routes as the Soviet merchant fleet bids for all types of commercial service. (International Cruise Center)

Gas-Oil Industry Ships. A relatively new category of "merchant" ships are those developed specifically to support the offshore gas-oil industry. These ships include offshore drilling ships, exploration ships, and offshore supply and personnel ships to carry men and material to the offshore drilling and pumping facilities.

The Rauma-Repola yard in Finland has recently delivered three large, 7,425-DWT 490-foot (149-m) drilling ships of the VALENTIN SHASHIN type. Operated by the Ministry of Gas Industry, they are fitted with a dynamic positioning system of bow and stern thrusters so that they can hold precise positions while their drilling rig penetrates the ocean floor. Finnish yards have also delivered four large crane ships for offshore work, three of which are 3,343-DWT catamarans.

Training Ships. Several training ships support the merchant marine and fisheries training activities, the best-known being sail-training ships KRUZENSHTERN, SEDOV, and TOVARISHCH (see chapter 25). All German-built, they are the largest sailing vessels in the world, displacing more than 3,000 tons and carrying up to 200 cadets on their far-ranging cruises. These are now being supplemented by the MIR-class sail training ships built in Poland.

Icebreakers. The Soviet merchant marine operates a large number of icebreakers, including the large, nuclear-propelled ARKTIKA-class ships. These ships are vital for keeping the Arctic sea routes open for commercial as well as military sea traffic because almost 80 percent of the Soviet coastal shipping occurs between Soviet ports in the Arctic and the Far East. Icebreakers are also required for some Baltic and Pacific ports in winter. (Icebreakers are also operated by the Navy, KGB Maritime Border Troops, and Ministry of River Fleet.)

Additional shallow-water icebreakers with nuclear propulsion are under construction in Finland, which has constructed most of the icebreakers procured by the Soviet Union in the past few years. (The reactor plants for these ships are installed at the Baltic Shipyard in Leningrad.)

Soviet merchant ships suffered a number of major casualties during the 1980s. This is the 5,245-gross-ton cruise ship PRIAMURYE in flames while docked in Osaka, Japan, on 18 May 1988. The fire took the lives of 11 Soviet tourists. The ship was gutted and has been scrapped. (AP Wirephoto)

CHAPTER 33

Fishing Fleet

The PIONERSK-class fish factory/mother ship ALEKSEY POZDNYAKOV, shown departing Antwerp in late 1989, is typical of the larger ships of the Soviet fishing fleet. These 10,000-DWT/543-foot (165.5-m) ships can operate on remote fishing grounds for months, supporting smaller craft and processing their catch. (Leo Van Ginderen)

The Soviet Union operates the world's largest fishing fleet with more than 3,500 oceangoing fishing and support vessels that total 6.7 million deadweight tons. These include more than 2,600 fishing and factory ships, 150 support ships, and a large number of tugs. This fleet's annual catch is about 10 million tons, placing the Soviet Union second only to Japan in the size of the annual catch of marine life.

The fishing fleet also serves as an instrument of Soviet foreign policy and provides some military support capabilities. In support of foreign policy, the Soviets offer developing countries economic incentives in return for fishing rights within their territorial waters or economic zones. The Soviets then seek to use economic and political access to neutralize or weaken Western influence while, in some instances, attempting to subsequently gain naval and air access to ports and airfields.

In addition to seeking such access in less developed nations, there have been efforts to expand into other areas. For example, in 1979 the Soviets expressed a desire to construct a commercial repair base in the Australian state of Tasmania. Those plans, however, were aborted following the Soviet invasion of Afghanistan. The Soviets are pressing for fishing agreements to permit access to all Australian ports. Another current target for such agreements is the Philippines.

From a military viewpoint, in the past, fishing craft have performed intelligence collection and still have at least a secondary, overt role in this regard. Also, the support ships of the fishing fleet have in the past provided support to submarines. The Soviet fishing fleet includes a large number of research ships, training ships, tankers, and refrigerated fish carriers that could be pressed into naval service in wartime, all controlled through an extensive and centralized communications system. In discussing the relationship between the Soviet Navy and fishing fleets, the director of the U.S. Department of Defense's Office of Net Assessment has observed:

Looking the worse for wear, the GENERAL DADAYEV is one of 63 stern trawler/factory ships, three fisheries research ships, and eight geological research ships of the PULKOVSKIY MERIDIAN class, completed from 1978 to 1988. These graceful, Soviet-built ships are 2,529 DWT with a length of 352½ feet (107.5 m). (Leo Van Ginderen)

Among the smaller classes of Soviet stern trawler/factory ships are the five SPRUT-class ships, completed in Poland from 1978 to 1980 (design B-400). This is the lead ship of the class; she is 3,541 DWT with a length of 385 feet (117.5 m). (U.S. Navy)

Some years ago the fishing industry in collaboration with people in one of the Leningrad shipyards developed a plan for a tanker fleet to support the worldwide operations of the fishing fleet. This plan included the design of a tanker and specified the number of tankers in the proposed fleet. The plan was reviewed by the Navy, which proposed that three ship designs of varying tonnage and fueling capacity be included and that the total capacity of the tanker fleet be doubled. The fishing industry merely asked whether the Navy would support in the appropriate forums the allocation of resources and building space needed to carry out this program. When assured that the Navy would do so, the fishing industry forwarded the revised plan to the economic planners. The Navy gets to use these tankers for its current operations and has them available in future crises or war, but the expenditures show up in the fishing industry's budget.[1]

Finally, the fishing fleet's construction and repair yards contribute significantly to the viability and flexibility of the Soviet shipbuilding industry.

The Soviet Union exploits fishing grounds throughout the world's oceans with large flotillas of ships. Flotillas of up to 100 and 200 trawlers are not unusual and on occasion even larger formations have been observed. Some of the larger trawlers can handle up to 50 tons of fish per day and are equipped to filet, salt, and can or freeze the catch on board. Smaller trawlers transfer their catch directly to factory, or "mother," ships that process and can or freeze the fish. In many cases, while the trawlers and mother ships remain in the operating area, refrigerated fish carriers take off the catch and carry it to markets in the Soviet Union or other nations. Fishing flotillas in

remote areas are often supported by specialized repair ships, tugs, tankers, and fresh-water carriers, in addition to some 260 refrigerated fish carriers.

Most of the fish caught by these vessels—over 90 percent—is for human consumption, eaten by Soviets or given or sold to other nations. It is estimated that seafood accounts for 20 percent of Soviet protein consumption. The part of the catch not used as food is usually processed into fish meal or fertilizer. Fish oil is also produced. However, poor management, storage, and transportation facilities result in the loss of a significant fraction of the catch from the Arctic area.

Soviet fishing operations off U.S. territory have created confrontations between the United States and the Soviet Union. The establishment of a 200-mile economic zone around the United States in 1977 was, in part, an effort to restrict Soviet fishing activities, and the U.S. Coast Guard has occasionally arrested masters of Soviet fishing vessels for violating this zone. The Soviet fishing industry is being faced with protective policies in many areas of the world, thus restricting their fishing and forcing them to exploit new and more remote areas.

At the same time, the Soviet Union is providing technical assistance to the fishing industries of Third World countries. This not only makes for improved relations with those countries, but also allows the Soviets to share area catches and profits, and to export their fishing equipment including fishing vessels. Among the countries that have received Soviet assistance in this field have been Cuba, Egypt, Ghana, Guinea, India, Indonesia, Senegal, Sri Lanka, Sudan, Tanzania, Vietnam, and South Yemen. The fishing support facility that the Soviets built near Havana, Cuba encompasses 33 acres and includes repair ships, a floating dry dock, floating and gantry cranes, and other support equipment.

Straight commercial fishing agreements exist with some other countries. For example, a Soviet fishing flotilla operates in the rich fishing grounds off Peru through an agreement with the government in Lima. Their crews are rotated via *Aeroflot,* which operates through the Jorge Chavez Airport.

The Soviets, for both domestic and foreign economic reasons, need to increase their catch. With continued advances in technology and the modernization of its fishing fleet, the Soviet Union should in time become the leading harvester of the world's marine life.

ORGANIZATION AND PERSONNEL

As with other Soviet maritime fleets, the fishing industry is highly centralized, with a Ministry of Fish Production directing overall operations and fleet development. The ministry has a central computerized control center in Moscow that keeps track of the fleet's world-wide activities.

Under the ministry are specialized port facilities, ship repair yards, processing plants, the fishing fleet itself, fisheries research ships (and previously submarines!), and the various support ships. Personnel to man these ships are trained at several schools and on board special ships, and, as in the merchant fleet, many ship captains and masters are naval reserve officers.

Obviously, the fishing fleet—like the merchant fleet—can also provide intelligence for naval operations. In the past, the tankers supporting the fishing fleet, which is diesel-propelled, also provided fuel to diesel-electric submarines in remote areas.

TRAWLERS, SUPPORT SHIPS, AND AIRCRAFT

As with merchant and research-scientific ships, many Soviet fishing vessels are built abroad, mostly in Eastern Europe. During the 1960s a number of trawler-factory ships were built for the Soviet fleet in Danish, Dutch, French, and Japanese yards (and in the 1950s several were built in West Germany). The principal builders of trawlers are the Black Sea and Okean shipyards (Nikolayev), Baltic shipyard (Klaipeda), Mathias Thesen and Volkswerft in East Germany, and Gdańsk in Poland.

Trawlers. Soviet trawlers come in a variety of sizes and configurations. In numbers of ships, the largest classes of Soviet-built trawlers are the more than 225 ships of the MAYAKOVSKIY type (1,248–1,519 DWT) and the 150 ships of the KRONSHTADT class (1,182 DWT); these are stern-trawler/factory ships. Additional ships of these classes have been completed or converted to fisheries research ships while several have been transferred to other nations.

Two other large, and hence widely seen, classes are the ATLANTIC and ''Super'' ATLANTIC designs built in East German yards. There are more than 300 of these ships, whose deadweight tonnage varies from 1,116 for the earlier ships to 2,068 for the later ships.

The DALNERECHENSK is one of more than 200 Al'pinist-type small trawlers delivered from 1981 to 1987. Several of these Soviet-built craft have been converted to intelligence ships and others to the fisheries research role. They are 333 DWT and 176 feet (53.7 m) long. (Leo Van Ginderen)

The helicopter pad forward distinguishes the Polish-built RODINA-class tuna seiners (design B-406). These are ships of 1,756 DWT with a length of 279 feet (85.1 m). This is the IVAN BORZOV, one of ten ships completed between 1979 and 1981. (U.S. Navy)

Twenty additional ships of this design are employed for fisheries research and 12 more are fisheries training ships. More than 30 ''Super'' ATLANTIC factory trawlers have been delivered by East Germany.

The TURGENEV represents the large Soviet-built MAYAKOVSKIY-class stern trawler/factory ships, with some 200 ships built for the Soviet fishing industry, including 15 units converted to fisheries research ships. Completed from 1958 to 1969, these ships are 1,300 to 1,519 DWT and 278 feet (84.7 m) long.

Still another configuration of the ubiquitous Al'pinist class of stern trawlers is shown by the RIFT, one of five units converted to carry submersibles for the fisheries research role. Note the large gantry crane, large mast forward, and submersible control station abaft the bridge. The funnel is offset to port. (U.S. Navy)

The largest Soviet ships in the trawler category are three French-built ships of the NATALIA KOVHOVA class, delivered in 1965; these are 419-foot (127.5-m), 4,709-DWT ships that can both harvest and process fish.

The modified ATLANTICS of the MOONZUND series are still in production for the Soviet fishing fleet in the Volks yard in East Germany as are the stern-trawler/seine factory ships of the ORLYO-NOK class of 653–669 DWT.

Factory Ships. The most recent factory ship deliveries are three fish-crab cannery/mother ships built in Finland and delivered to the Soviet fishing fleet in 1988–1989. These SODRUZHESTVO-class ships are 10,200 DWT and are capable of producing 400,000 cans of fish or 50,000 cans of crabmeat per day. They are designed to remain at sea up to one year (with replenishments). They operate in the Far East.

The only other factory ships delivered in the 1980s were the last of the four ships of the 13,250-DWT 50 LET SSSR class (completed 1973–1980) and the last pair of the six 11,238-DWT KONSTITUTSIYA SSSR (1979-1981). They were built at the Admiralty (Leningrad) and Gdańsk yards, respectively.

The Soviet Union's largest fish factory ship remains the VOS-TOK, built at Leningrad's Admiralty yard and completed in 1971. The 22,110-DWT ship (43,000 displacement tons) suffered several delays in building and fitting out. She was intended to carry 14 fishing craft of 60 tons each plus helicopters and was designed to process more than 300 tons of fish daily. Even after completion the VOSTOK has not been fully successful, and instead of operating as a small-craft carrier and factory, she has been employed only in the latter role. No additional ships of the class have been built.

Approximately 115 smaller factory ships are in service (in addition to the trawler-factory vessels). These factory ships also provide logistic support, maintenance, and medical services to the trawlers in their working areas.

Support Ships. The Soviet fishing fleet operates a large number of refrigerated cargo ships, fuel tankers, water carriers, repair ships, and oceangoing tugs in support of the trawler fleet. There are some 100 tankers and over 500 refrigerated fish carriers (cargo ships) that support the fishing fleet. The two fish carrier classes now being built for the Soviet Union are the BUKHTA RUSSKAYA class, 4,900-DWT ships being constructed at the 61 Kommuna shipyard (Nikolayev), and the ALMANZNYY BEREG, 9,606-DWT ships being produced at the Mathias Thesen yard (Wismar, East Germany). There are eight of the former and more than 30 of the latter ships currently in service.[2]

Training Ships. There are several fisheries training ships in service, mostly trawlers modified for student accommodations and classrooms.

Research Ships and Submarines. The fishing industry has several trawlers modified to conduct research into fish hunting and catching techniques. There are some 65 fisheries research trawlers in service with at least two, the 1,070-DWT IKHTIANDR and ODISSEY, modified to carry research submersibles. Eight small submersibles are operated in support of fisheries activities, the largest number of deep-diving, manned submersibles operated under a single organization in any nation (see chapter 12).

(In the 1960s two diesel-electric submarines of the Whiskey class were converted to oceanographic-fisheries research submarines. Renamed SEVERYANKA and SLAVYANKA, their forward torpedo rooms were converted into laboratories, observation stations were installed to permit scientists to view the outside water, exterior lights were fitted, and provisions were made to recover seafloor samples. About six to eight scientists were assigned for these missions. The two undersea craft operated in the research role for several years before being discarded.)

Aircraft. Aircraft are employed periodically to support the fishing industry. Helicopters have been based on the larger ships to help track down schools of fish. In addition, land-based aircraft have been used, especially Il-14 Crate twin-engine aircraft and Il-18D Coot four-engine aircraft. The decision to use the longer-range Coot was made, in part, because of the farther-ranging fishing areas brought about by the 200-mile economic zones. The initial Coot flights in 1980–1981 were sponsored by the Polar Institute of Marine Fishing and Oceanography and the State Scientific Research Institute of Civil Aviation.

2. These ships are included in the totals given for the Soviet Merchant fleet; see chapter 33.

The ODISSEY is one of 15 fisheries research ships of the MAYAKOVSKIY class. The ODISSEY (left) and IKHTIANDR are configured to carry research submersibles in large, portside-opening hangars. The large fishing fleet and its shipyard infrastructure provide support to naval and research programs. (U.S. Navy)

CHAPTER 34

Warsaw Pact Navies

The Polish Navy's WARSZAWA, built as the Soviet Kashin-class destroyer SMEL'YY, was the largest warship in the Warsaw Pact outside of the USSR and Romania. The future status of this ship as well as other Warsaw Pact units is unclear in this period of rapid political change in Eastern Europe.

For 36 years—from 1955 until 1991—the Warsaw Pact military structure provided the Soviet Union with bases and logistic support in Eastern Europe for combat operations against the West. In some scenarios, Pact Forces could also be expected to participate in Soviet-directed military operations. In addition, Eastern Bloc nations provided surrogate military advisors for Soviet interests in Third World nations and provided intelligence collection against certain Western and Third World nations.

In concert with the dramatic political and economic changes in the Soviet Union and Eastern Europe, on 1 July 1991 the Warsaw Pact members abolished the organization. This chapter in *Guide to the Soviet Navy* describes the four non-Soviet Warsaw Pact navies at that time.

The members of the Warsaw Pact were the Soviet Union, Bulgaria, Czechoslovakia, East Germany, Hungary, Poland, and Romania. It was established in large part to counter the formation of the North Atlantic Treaty Organization (NATO) and to facilitate Soviet military operations against the West. Pact policy and doctrine as well as command was fully controlled by the Soviet Union with a Soviet officer serving as CinC of the Warsaw Treaty Organization with the additional title of First Deputy Minister of Defense. The military agencies of the Warsaw Pact were abolished as of 31 March 1991 and General of the Army P.G. Lushev was relieved as the CinC by decree of 26 April 1991.

The future of the former Warsaw Pact military services is unclear, although it has become obvious that the extensive naval modernization programs that several countries began in the 1980s are unlikely to be completed as originally envisioned. The Polish government, for example, as early as November 1989 made the decision to scale back its 412,000-strong military force, the largest of the Eastern Bloc forces. Defense Minister Florian Siwicki stated, "The basic goal is transformations in which the Army will be numerically smaller but showing high quality, mobility and ability to meet the demands of national security.[1] With respect to the Navy, financial problems probably led to the Polish decision to purchase two ex-Soviet Foxtrot-class submarines rather than new-construction Kilo-class units.

Major force reductions were announced by several Warsaw Pact nations during 1989, although the publicly stated numbers refer to "troops" as well as to tanks, artillery, armored personnel carriers, and aircraft. Details of specific naval reductions—if any—had not been revealed when this edition went to press. By 1990 the announced troop reductions, although generally a small percentage of Eastern Bloc armed forces on active duty, were still significant:

	Armed Forces Strength[2]	*Reductions*[3]
Bulgaria	117,900	10,000
Czechoslovakia	199,700	12,000
East Germany	173,100	10,000
Hungary	91,000	9,300
Poland	412,000	20,000+

Obviously, more reductions are in the offing, with the East German forces being disbanded.

Four of the Warsaw Pact nations have navies—Bulgaria, East Germany, Poland, and Romania, and two (East Germany and Poland) also possess small naval air arms. These nations had provided the Soviet military establishment with (1) a defensive buffer zone, (2) naval and air forces to help control the Baltic and Black seas, (3) amphibious forces to assist in coastal assaults and possible seizure of the Danish Straits and the Danish island of Bornholm, and (4) a major shipbuilding and repair capability.

East Germany and Poland have significant capabilities for combat in the Baltic.[4] In the mid-1980s these two navies began long-awaited modernization programs. Bulgaria and Romania have smaller naval forces in the Black Sea. Even though the latter have only marginal combat capabilities, the lack of an effective NATO threat in those waters makes their effectiveness a moot point. The Romanian fleet had been undergoing a major expansion before the 1989 revolution, but, according to one Western analyst, "The Romanian Navy remains an unbalanced force. . . . too large to defend coastal waters. . . . the coastal anti-submarine warfare capabilities are inadequate. . . . the mine countermeasures force is antiquated. . . . Amphibious lift capabilities are, for practical purposes, nonexistent."[5] Although the Romanian naval buildup was expensive, it appears to have been intended to satisfy the country's leadership and national prestige, not to enable the navy to carry out wartime tasks.

History. The Soviet Union and seven "satellite" nations in Eastern Europe signed the Treaty of Friendship and Mutual Assistance in Warsaw on 14 May 1955, taking the name of that city for the resulting military alliance. The treaty was in part a response to the

1. Quoted in "Poland to Cut Military, Defense Minister Says," *The Washington Post,* 4 January 1990.
2. International Institute for Strategic Studies, *The Military Balance, 1989–1990* (London, 1989).
3. Secretary of Defense, *Soviet Military Power 1989* (Washington, D.C., 1989).
4. This chapter is based in part on the extensive research of Milan Vego, a former Yugoslavian naval officer. From 1981 on he has written an annual essay on East European navies for the March issue of the Naval Institute *Proceedings,* which addresses international navies. Also see the biannual reference works *Flotte de Combat/Combat Fleets of the World* and *Weyer's Flotten Taschenbuch.*
5. Milan Vego, "The Romanian Navy," U.S. Naval Institute *Proceedings* (March 1989), p. 144.

establishment of the North Atlantic Treaty Organization (NATO) in 1949. The Warsaw Pact signatories were Albania, Bulgaria, Czechoslovakia, East Germany, Hungary, Poland, and Romania in addition to the Soviet Union. East Germany was only a "political" member of the Warsaw Pact until the existence of its armed forces was officially acknowledged in January 1956.

The Albanian government broke relations with the Soviet leadership for ideological reasons in 1961 and thus effectively withdrew from the Warsaw Pact. (This withdrawal was made official in 1968.) Albania's loss to the Soviet Union was significant from a naval perspective because the small country's coastline on the Adriatic Sea had provided the Soviets with Mediterranean bases. In 1960 a Soviet submarine tender and eight submarines had been sent to the Albanian island of Saseno (Sazan) in the Gulf of Valona. This base was abandoned by the Soviets in 1961, when Albania seized two Soviet Whiskey-class submarines, which it refused permission to leave at the time of the Soviet withdrawal. Two other Whiskey submarines had been transferred to Albania in 1960 to give Albania four submarines. By 1990 all were reported out of service with no replacements being acquired. (China has been the primary supplier of arms to Albania following the break with the USSR.)

Roles and Missions. The East German and Polish navies were intended primarily for operations in the Baltic and could not realistically be considered effective opponents for NATO forces beyond those restricted albeit important waters. Beginning in 1957 the Soviet, East German, and Polish navies conducted joint exercises in the Baltic on a regular basis. A joint command of these three Warsaw Pact navies in the Baltic was apparently established in May 1962, obviously under Soviet direction. Beginning in 1980 they have conducted exercises beyond the Danish Straits, in the North Sea. However, these operations appear to be primarily political and not military. At times these exercises have been under the tactical control of non-Soviet admirals.

During wartime the East German and Polish navies were to join Soviet naval forces to (1) provide support for Soviet ground operations along the southern Baltic coast, (2) deny use of the Baltic to NATO naval forces, and (3) seize control of the Danish straits. Amphibious landings would probably be carried out in support of these activities, including the capture of the Danish island of Bornholm, which lies north of Poland, and probably some of the Danish coastline along the straits. (Soviet troops had occupied Bornholm from 1945 to 1947.)

In the Black Sea the Bulgarian and Romanian navies have primarily coastal defense missions against Turkish naval forces that might seek to attack Warsaw Pact territory. Bulgaria, because of its proximity to the Turkish Straits, may have had strategic importance to Soviet military operations. The southern border of Bulgaria is about 50 miles (80 km) from Constantinople, and a Soviet attack on Turkey, presumably to seize the straits, would come through Bul-

TABLE 34-1. WARSAW PACT NAVIES

Ship type	Baltic Sea		Black Sea		Total
	East Germany	Poland	Bulgaria	Romania	
Submarines	—	4	4	1	9
Destroyers	—	1	—	1	2
Frigates	19a	1	3	3	26
Corvettes	5	4	3	3	15
Missile craft	13	12	10	6	41
Torpedo craft	10	—	6	35	51
Submarine chasers/ patrol craft	24b	62b	6	24b	116b
Landing ships	12	23	—	—	35
Landing craft	—	19	23	3	45
Minelayers	2	—	—	2	4
Minesweepers/ hunters	27	24	—	10	61
Coastal/inshore minesweepers	—	8	15	—	23
Auxiliary ships	38	21	3	12	74

a Includes PARCHIM I–class corvettes (classified as frigates by U.S. naval intelligence).
b Some or all operated by maritime border guards.

garia and by sea. The Bulgarian roads and bases could be most important for a thrust against Turkey or, less likely, against Greece or Yugoslavia. Bulgaria—which shares a border with NATO Turkey—has a large number of torpedo and patrol boats, plus two Romeo-class submarines. The Romanian Navy was undergoing a significant improvement at the time of the December 1989 revolution.

The Warsaw Pact's military activities were totally directed by the Soviet Union with a Soviet marshal in the post of commander in chief of the Pact military forces. Many other Soviet officers—some naval—are assigned to key staff positions with Admiral N.I. Khovrin, currently serving as the Deputy Commander in Chief for Naval Forces. It is not clear if Khovrin was to be the operational commander of the East German and Polish naval forces in wartime, or whether those forces would be placed under the command of the CinC of the Soviet Baltic Fleet.

In peacetime the Warsaw Pact high command directed the Groups of Soviet Forces in Czechoslovakia, East Germany, Hungary, and Poland, certain Soviet forces in the three western military districts of the Soviet Union, and all East German military forces. The military forces of the five smaller Warsaw Pact nations are subordinate to the Pact high command only during periods of external threat. (The Soviet Union attempted to establish standing Warsaw Pact armies in 1956–1957 and again in 1967–1968, but those efforts were rejected by the member nations.)

The air, ground, and naval forces of the non-Soviet nations use mainly Soviet-type equipment, training doctrine, and communications procedures, etc. There have been significant developments in equipment by East Germany and Poland, especially in the naval areas, but these are intended to fit into the Soviet "style" of warfare and often use Soviet components. (This commonality within the Warsaw Pact is in marked contrast to NATO nations, who for economic reasons tend to use significant amounts of some American equipment but have their own tactical doctrine as well as mostly their own equipment.)

Another major factor for the Soviet Navy is the shipbuilding capability of the Warsaw Pact nations. East Germany, Poland, and to a lesser extent Bulgaria and Romania, have been major suppliers of ships to the Soviet Union. Most of this East European shipbuilding effort for the Soviets consists of research, merchant, and fishing, ships; however, the East German and Polish yards have also provided the Soviet Navy with amphibious ships, intelligence collection ships, and research ships.

Table 34-1 provides a summary of the combat ships and craft of the four non-Soviet Warsaw Pact navies in 1990.

BULGARIA

Bulgaria borders on the Black Sea, between Romania to the north and the European portion of Turkey to the south. Bulgaria has a small outdated navy, consisting primarily of coastal forces plus river craft that serve on the Danube River.

Bulgaria has four Romeo-class submarines that were transferred from the Soviet Union, two in 1971–1972 (replacing two older Whiskey-class submarines) and the second pair in 1985–1986. The submarines can provide limited ASW training as well as serve in the coastal defense role.

The Navy's largest surface units are three Riga-class frigates. Two were acquired in 1957–1958 and extensively modernized in 1980–1981, with a third transferred from the USSR in 1985. The third Riga is fitted with a quad launcher for the short-range SA-N-5 missile, the only Riga known to be fitted with missiles. There are also ten Osa I/II missile craft and six Shershen torpedo boats. In addition to the Rigas, there is a limited ASW capability in three relatively modern Poti-class corvettes.

A minesweeping force also exists, with 32 small sweeps of various types. The Bulgarian Navy has a significant short-range amphibious lift capability consisting of 23 Soviet Vydra-class utility landing craft.

Significantly, the Bulgarian Navy has upgraded its replenishment force with the 3,500-ton DIMITRI A. DIMITROV, built in Bulgaria in 1980. There are also several small tankers in naval service.

The Danube River Flotilla has about a dozen small patrol craft.

TABLE 34-2. BULGARIAN NAVY

Number	Type	Class	Builder
4	submarines	Romeo	USSR
3	frigates	Riga	USSR
3	corvettes	Poti	USSR
4	missile craft	Osa I	USSR
6	missile craft	Osa II	USSR
6	torpedo craft	Shershen	USSR
6	patrol craft	Zhuk	USSR
4	minesweepers	Sonya	USSR
7	minesweepers	Vanya	USSR
4	inshore minesweepers	Yevgenya	USSR
23	landing craft	Vydra	USSR
1	replenishment ship	DIMITRI A. DIMITROV	Bulgaria
1	survey ship/tender	Moma	Poland
1	salvage tug	Type 700	East Germany

Naval aviation. Up to six Haze-A ASW helicopters have been acquired from the Soviet Union. More of these aircraft may be procured. The earlier Hoplite and Hound helicopters have apparently been discarded.

Special forces. No naval or ground troops specifically trained for amphibious landings have been identified. There is a coastal defense force with a battalion of SSC-2b Samlet missiles plus several gun batteries.

Command and personnel. Vice Admiral V.G. Yanakiev is CinC of the Navy. The Bulgarian Navy has some 8,800 uniformed personnel—of whom 2,100 are assigned to ships and craft, some 2,200 assigned to coastal defenses, 1,800 to training activities, 2,500 to shore support, and 200 to naval aviation. There are about 5,000 to 6,000 conscripts in the Navy on three years' obligated service.

Bases and ports. The principal bases and ports on the Black Sea are Sozopol; Varna, at the mouth of the Provadiya River with commercial and naval facilities; and Burgas, the nation's most important harbor and center of its fishing industry. The Danube flotilla has bases at Atiya, Balchik, and Vidin.

Shipyards. The major Bulgarian shipbuilding facilities are the George Dimitrov shipyard at Varna and yards at Burgas and Ruse (on the Danube, near the Romanian border). The principal customer of these yards has been the Soviet Union.

As of January 1989, Bulgaria ranked ninth in terms of nations with orders for major merchant ships. A reported 41 ships were under construction, of an estimated total of 519,000 DWT. Recent deliveries to the USSR include the 9,141-DWT cellular container ships of the SIMON BOLIVAR design and 24,354-DWT bulk carriers of the SOVIETSKIY KHUDOZHNIK class.

Merchant marine. In 1990, Bulgaria had 114 merchant ships of 1,898,000 DWT: 2 passenger ships, 46 general cargo ships, 2 container ships, 4 Roll-On/Roll-Off (RO/RO) ships, 46 bulk carriers, and 14 tankers. These ships are operated by the Bulgarian Maritime Shipping line.

CZECHOSLOVAKIA

Czechoslovakia has no coastline, but army personnel operate several armed motor launches on the Danube River. The government owns a large number of river craft.

Shipyards. There is a major shipyard—the Gabor Steiner yard—for building and maintaining river craft in Komarno as well as lesser facilities along the Danube. The Komarno yard has built more than 250 river and coastal ships for the Soviet Union since the late 1940s.

Merchant marine. The Czechoslovak International Maritime Company operates 21 ships totaling 311,000 DWT in 1990. There are 15 general cargo ships and 6 bulk/ore carriers.

EAST GERMANY

East Germany[6]—the German Democratic Republic—had been of considerable naval significance to the Soviet Union because of its

---

6. A recent, comprehensive work on the East German Navy is Hans Mehl, Knut Schafer, and Ulrich Israel, *Vom Küstenschutzboot zum Raketenschiff* (Berlin: Militärverlag der Deutschen Demokratischen Republik, 1989).

The East German Tarantul-class missile
corvette PAUL EISENSCHNEIDER under way. Her
twin 30-mm Gatling guns are visible at the
after end of the superstructure. Note the twin
gas turbine exhausts in the stern counter.
(Tessmer courtesy Alfred Albusberger)

The SASSNITZ (BAL-COM-10) is a new East
German attack craft. The first unit—completed
in 1987–1988—was initially armed with a
76.2-mm gun forward and two quad SS-N-25
missile launchers amidships for a Harpoon-
type missile. There is a 30-mm Gatling gun aft.
The missiles were removed before the craft
was transferred to the unified German Navy.
(West German Navy)

The NORDPERD is a modified East German
Frosch-class LSM. They have an 8-ton-capacity
crane forward for handling cargo but retain
bow ramp and other landing ship features. The
standard Frosch LSMs can carry 11 tanks and
a company of troops. These ships are being
scrapped. (West German Navy)

proximity to Denmark and the Danish Straits. The East German National Peoples Navy (*Nationale Volksmarine*), until the political upheaval of 1989–1990, ranked after the Polish Navy in size and was characterized by a large number of small combatants with considerable missile (SS-N-2 Styx), mine countermeasure, and amphibious capabilities. The missions of this force were apparently to help control the western Baltic and to conduct amphibious operations against the West German and Danish coasts.

During the 1980s the East German Navy began an extensive modernization program. Among the more recent acquisitions are three new Soviet-built frigates of the Koni class, two transferred in 1978–1979 and one in 1986 to replace two ineffective ships of the Riga class, and the first of a series of Soviet Tarantul I guided missile corvettes delivered in late 1984. The corvettes, which carry the SS-N-2c missile, have improved seakeeping and attack capabilities over the older Osa missile craft operated by the *Volksmarine*.

Also joining the German Navy since 1981 have been the 16 PARCHIM I-class, 950-ton anti-submarine frigates/corvettes.[7] These are German-built ships fitted with Soviet weapons and electronics. Production has apparently ended for Germany, although from 1986 the same yard that produced the PARCHIM (Peenewerft at Wolgast) has built the modified PARCHIM II for Soviet service (see page 181).

The most potent *Volksmarine* combat capability is found in the fast attack craft—five Tarantuls, about a dozen Osa I-class missile boats (each with four SS-N-2 Styx missiles), and perhaps a dozen remaining Shershen-class torpedo boats, all built in the Soviet Union. There are also some 20 smaller Libelle-class "light" torpedo boats that were built in Germany. The larger (540-ton), more heavily armed Tarantuls were replacing the Osas and probably Shershens but at a less than one-for-one rate because of the newer ships' cost.

A new East German–built missile craft SASSNITZ (designated BAL-COM-10 by NATO) was first observed in 1987–1988. This craft has two sets of four SS-N-25 missile tubes akin to the U.S. Harpoon missile launchers.

The East German mine countermeasure force is comprised of 27 large, 414-ton Kondor II sweeper/hunters. Three of these units serve as training ships for petty officers and as trials ships.

The Navy has a significant amphibious lift in 12 Frosch-class medium landing ships (LSM) of 1,950 tons displacement. These are similar to the Soviet Ropucha LST class but smaller and more heavily armed. Two slightly modified Frosch IIs are classified as

7. The PARCHIM design was initially given the NATO designation BAL-COM-4 when the first unit was being constructed.

An East German Shershen-class torpedo boat. These versatile craft—no longer in Soviet service—are highly effective in the torpedo, mine, and ASW roles in restricted seas. (West German Navy)

A pair of East German PARCHIM I-class corvettes at Goteborg, Sweden (note Swedish flags). These are effective coastal ASW ships; the East German–built improved PARCHIM II class has been provided to the Soviet Navy. (Courtesy Antonio Scrimali)

amphibious warfare support ships, retaining an over-the-beach landing capability. Both of the Frosch designs can also lay mines.

Another area of naval modernization in the 1980s had been the acquisition of six of the 2,300-ton DARSS class. These ships can support smaller units operating in the western Baltic or beyond the Danish Straits. The Navy also has several auxiliary tankers as well as harbor tankers; repair, survey, and salvage ships; icebreakers, and three intelligence collection ships (AGI). The AGIs consist of one modified DARSS and two Kondor I types that have been configured for the ELINT role.

The East German armed forces officially ceased to exist on 3 October 1990. By that time several older ships had been abandoned, in preparation for disposal, although construction of the SASSNITZ class was continuing. Subsequently, 30 former East German ships were transferred to the united Germany's Navy (*Bundesmarine*), all to be based at former East German ports. Those are:

2 frigates	Koni class
5 frigates/corvettes	PARCHIM I class
1 missile corvette	Tarantul I class
1 missile craft	SASSNITZ class
6 minesweepers	Kondor II class
6 tugs	
2 fuel lighters	
1 buoy tender	
6 barracks ships	

In addition, three SASSNITZ-class missile craft have been sold to Poland, without engines or weapons, and others are being sold on the open market.

Naval aviation. The *Volksmarine*'s air arm recently underwent a major expansion and now consists of 25 helicopters—Haze-A for ASW and Hip-C/F for amphibious assault. There are reports that a squadron of Su-22 Fitter aircraft was also formed for naval support.

Special forces. A limited amphibious assault force is provided by the Army's 29th Motorized Rifle Regiment (Ernst Moritz-Arndt), which is especially trained in amphibious operations. The regiment, numbering some 2,000 men, is based at Prora (Ruegen Island).

There is a Coastal Border Brigade that provides patrols and defenses along the Baltic coast. The brigade has some 4,100 men; it operates 18 Kondor I minesweepers plus about 50 small patrol craft. For coastal defense there are at least two missile battalions and five coastal gun batteries, the former having been rearmed about 1984–1985 with the SSC-3 anti-ship missile.

Command and personnel. The last East German naval commander was Vice Admiral Theodore Hoffman. He replaced the long-serving Vice Admiral Willi Ehm, who held the position of CinC of naval forces from August 1959 until 1989.

TABLE 34-3. EAST GERMAN NAVY

Number	Type	Class	Builder
3	frigates	Koni	USSR
16	frigates/corvettes	Parchim I	East Germany
5+	missile corvettes	Tarantul I	USSR
1+	missile craft	Sassnitz	East Germany
12	missile craft	Osa I	USSR
10	torpedo craft	Shershen	USSR
20	light torpedo craft	Libelle	East Germany
24[a]	patrol craft	(various)	East Germany
27	minesweeper/hunters	Kondor II	East Germany
12	landing ships	Frosch	East Germany
2	support ships/ minelayers	Frosch II	East Germany
6	support ships	Darss	East Germany
2	repair ships	Vogtland	East Germany
1	intelligence ship	mod. Darss	East Germany
2	intelligence ships	mod. Kondor I	East Germany
1	intelligence ship	Okean	East Germany
6	survey ships	(various)	Poland, East Germany
8	buoy tenders	(various)	East Germany
4	tankers	(various)	USSR-East Germany
1	training ship	Wodnik	Poland
1	salvage ship	Piast	Poland
6	experimental-research ships	(various)	East Germany

[a] Operated by the maritime border guards.

In 1989 the East German Navy had an estimated 16,300 personnel, including coastal defense personnel but not the 29th rifle regiment. Of these, an estimated 5,000 were assigned afloat, 4,100 to coastal defense, 2,000 to training activities, 4,200 to shore support, and about 1,000 to naval aviation. Some 8,000 of the men were conscripts with 18 months of required service in the Navy and the remainder officers (1,800) and long-term enlisted men.

Bases and ports. Rostock is the largest and most important port in East Germany, situated on the Warnow River near where it enters the Baltic Sea. Among the commercial and naval activities at Rostock are the Navy's headquarters (Rostock-Gehsdorf), a major oil terminal, and a large fishing center. The port has recently undergone a major expansion.

Warnemünde, the outer port of Rostock, is a seaside resort with naval and commercial facilities. Wismar, on the bay of that name, is mainly a commercial port; Stralsund, on the Strela Sund, is a naval base and commercial port, as is Sassnitz on the opposite side of Rügen Island; Wolgast, near the mouth of the Peene River, appears also to be a naval and commercial port; and nearby Peenemünde, former center for German wartime missile development, is a major naval facility.

The Navy's helicopters are based at Parow (near Stralsund) and Peenemünde. The Fitter squadron is believed to have been formed at Laage.

Shipyards. There are several shipyards in East Germany, most being employed to construct and repair fishing, coastal, and river

craft. There are five major shipyards: the Warnow yard at Warnemünde; the Matthias Thesen yard at Wismar; the Neptun yard at Rostock; the Volks yard at Stralsund; and the Peenewerft yard at Wolgast. All five yards build commercial ships; the Peenewerft yard also builds small combatants and the Frosch-class landing ships for the East German Navy, while Wolgast constructed the Parchim-class frigates for the Soviet and East German fleets.

Most of the merchant ships built in East German yards are for the Soviet Union. Since 1946 the Soviet Union has received more than 1,300 of the merchant and fishing ships built in East Germany. This represents more than 60 percent of the ships built in the country.

As of January 1989, East Germany ranked 13th in nations with orders for major merchant ships. A reported 28 ships were under construction, totaling an estimated 385,000 DWT.

Recent commercial shipbuilding programs undertaken in East German shipyards for the Soviet Union include more than a dozen of the 18,020-DWT RO/RO vehicle carrying ships of the Astrakhan class, the final eight units of the Kompozitor sea-river RO/RO ships of the 4,673-DWT Kompozitor Kara Karayev class, and the last of the ten ships of the 16,030-DWT cellular container ships of the Kapitan Gavrilov class. East German yards have also been a principal supplier of ships for the Soviet fishing industry, with recent deliveries including the new, 3,365-DWT Moonzund-class stern trawler/factory ships and the Kristal II–class fish carriers.

(The Moonzund class is the successor to the massive East German-built Atlantik and "Super" Atlantik program of stern trawler/factory ships completed from 1966 through 1983; see chapter 33.)

Merchant marine. In 1990 the East German merchant fleet had 147 ships of 1,692,000 DWT. These consist of 1 passenger ship, 106 general cargo ships, 10 container ships, 9 RO/RO ships, 17 bulk/ore carriers, and 4 tankers. The firm of VEB Deutfracht/Seereederei operated East Germany's merchant ships.

HUNGARY

Hungary, like Czechoslovakia, has no coastline but operates river patrol craft under army command on the Danube River. The army also has a few small landing craft. The smaller of these craft have been built at the minor shipyards along the Danube. Some of these yards have built large numbers of river tugs and other small craft for the Soviet Union. In particular, the Ganz shipyard and crane factory has delivered more than 1,200 small craft and about 2,000 gantry cranes to the Soviet Union since 1945.

Merchant marine. Fifteen ships totaling 109,000 DWT were registered to Hungary in 1990, all general cargo ships operated by the Mabart line.

POLAND

The Polish Navy is the largest of the non-Soviet Warsaw Pact forces in terms of ship size, ship tonnage, and number of naval personnel. The Navy (*Ludowa Marynarka Woyenna*) is reputed to

Poland has a long and proud submarine tradition. The Orzel is a traditional submarine name, now assigned to this Soviet-built Kilo. (West German Navy)

A Haze amphibious helicopter during exercises with Polish ships. Behind the tail boom is a PIAST-class salvage ship, a type found in the Polish and East German navies.

be the best trained and best maintained of the four satellite navies, based on a serious naval tradition.[8]

Like those of East Germany and Romania, the Polish fleet is currently being modernized with significant ship transfers from the Soviet Union as well as indigenous construction. Poland has one newly built Kilo-class submarine, but acquisition of these craft was terminated—probably for fiscal reasons—and the fleet has been supplemented by the acquisition of two former Soviet Foxtrot-class units. These replaced four Whiskey-class units in Polish service. One Kilo was transferred to Poland in 1986, followed by the second in 1987 and the two Foxtrots in 1988.

Poland had long been the only non-Soviet Warsaw Pact navy with a destroyer. In 1987 the Soviet Kashin-class destroyer SMEL'YY was acquired by Poland. Commissioned in the Polish Navy in November 1987 as the WARSZAWA, she is the largest warship operated by an Eastern Bloc navy except for Romania's destroyer. The WARSZAWA replaces a SAM Kotlin of that name that had been transferred to Poland in 1970 and stricken in 1986.

The Soviet replacement of the submarines and destroyer may have been delayed because of the political unrest in Poland during the early 1980s. The small combatant force is also being modernized, with the first Tarantul missile corvette acquired from the Soviet Union in December 1984. Up to eight are being provided to Poland. These ships—like those of the East German Navy—have the SS-N-2c Styx missile and not the longer-range SS-N-22 found in the current production Tarantuls for the Soviet Navy. These corvettes will replace 12 former Soviet Osa I–class missile boats, obviously on a less-than-one-for-one ratio.

Beyond the destroyer and missile corvettes, the Polish surface force is being modernized through the construction of frigates of the KASZUB class, the first of which was commissioned in 1987. Initially named BAL-COM-6 by NATO, these are 1,200-ton frigates armed with the SA-N-4 missile system and a single 57-mm twin AA mount, plus lighter weapons and an ASW armament. These are the first oceangoing warships to be built in Poland since before World War II. Obviously, the future of this program in the current Polish political context is uncertain.

A large number of patrol craft as well as several minesweepers are also in service. The Polish-built Notec class, 160-ton ships with glass-reinforced plastic hulls, are now entering service.

The Polish Navy has a significant amphibious lift capability in 23 Polnocny-class medium landing ships plus several smaller landing craft.

There are several auxiliary ships in naval service, including a large sail-training ship. One other noteworthy ship of recent con-

struction is the sail-driven oceanographic research ship OCEANIA, operated by the Polish Academy of Sciences. Completed in early 1986, this 550-ton ship has a hydraulic-operated sail system that can be operated by one man. (An auxiliary, 3,200-horsepower diesel is also fitted). The ship is manned by a crew of 15, plus 12 scientists.

Naval aviation. Poland has a large although outdated naval air arm, the only one among the Warsaw Pact navies with fixed-wing aircraft. There are an estimated six MiG-17 Fresco fighters flown in the reconnaissance role (the Il-28 Beagle reconnaissance aircraft have been discarded as have MiG-17s and MiG-19 Farmer fighters flying in the fighter-attack role). Also flown in the reconnaissance role are seven An-2 Colt transports.

The Navy has about 35 helicopters—Haze-A ASW helicopters and a few other Hazes configured for search-and-rescue, plus several older units employed for various duties.

A few training planes are also available. Again, all of the aircraft are overage and in need of replacement.

Special forces. The Polish Army's 7th Sea Landing Division regularly exercises with the Navy's amphibious ships. The division—with some 12,000 men—is based in the Gdańsk area.

There is a large coastal defense force with several battalions armed with the SSC-2b Samlet missile and a small number of gun batteries.

Command and personnel. Rear Admiral Piotr Kilodziejczyk commands the Polish Navy. There are a reported 19,300 men in the Polish navy: 5,200 afloat, 2,500 with the naval air arm, 4,100 assigned to coastal defense, 2,500 involved in training activities, and 5,000 in shore support assignments. Of this force, about 6,000 are conscripts, drafted for 18 months.

Bases and ports. Most Polish ports and naval bases are in territory that was German through World War II. All were heavily damaged during the war and then stripped by the Russians of their useful equipment and other material.[9]

The principal Polish commercial port and naval bases are at Gdynia, known as Gotenhafen from 1939 to 1945. It was a small fishing village until the mid-1920s when there was a period of rapid growth and development, making it a major port. It is now the main base of the Polish Navy, a large commercial port (especially for the shipment of coal from Upper Silesia), and a major shipbuilding center.

Just south of Gdynia, also on the Gulf of Danzig, is the city of Gdańsk, which is also a major commercial port and naval base, with a large shipyard.

There are smaller naval bases at Hel (formerly Hela) on the Polwysepottel Peninsula, and at Świnoujście (Swinemünde) on the Polish–East German border. Nearby Szczecin (Stettin), on the Oder River, is a commercial port. The naval aircraft and helicopters fly from fields at Elblag, Gdańsk, Koszalin, Sliepsk, and Szczecin.

---

8. A Polish Navy was established between the world wars. After the fall of Poland in 1939, a Polish-Navy-in-exile was organized with headquarters in England. At the end of the war the Polish Navy manned one light cruiser, six destroyers, six submarines, and several smaller craft; another cruiser, four destroyers, and two submarines were lost during the war. In the postwar period the Polish Navy was the first of the satellite navies to receive submarines (M class) in 1956, and the first to receive destroyers (SKORYY class) in 1957.

9. The Polish state that existed between the two world wars had Danzig (now Gdańsk) as the country's only port. It was connected to the rest of Poland by a narrow corridor separating East Prussia from the rest of Germany.

The Polish HYDROGRAF is a modified Moma-class ship configured as an AGI. The East German and Polish navies long had intelligence collectors that operated against NATO coastal activities and ships.

Shipyards. Poland has one of the world's most advanced ship-building industries with ship construction having long been the nation's largest "export" industry after coal. The Polish and former German shipyards, which were devastated in World War II, were totally rebuilt from the late 1940s onward with heavy Soviet assistance.

Since the first oceangoing ship was laid down in 1948, the Polish yards have produced more than 800 commercial ships for some two dozen nations. Most ships have gone to the Soviet Union, but other recent export customers have included Bulgaria, Czechoslovakia, France, West Germany, India, Mexico, the Netherlands, and Sweden.

Polish shipyards have also produced almost 100 landing ships of the Polnocny series and 11 of the Ropucha class as well as large numbers of intelligence collection ships, survey ships, and other naval units for the Soviet Union, with landing ships also being built for the Polish and several Third World navies. Although large naval ships are not built in Poland, the shipyards have built supertankers and large bulk carriers as well as relatively complex merchant ships.

There are five major shipyards and several smaller building and repair facilities. The principal shipbuilding facilities are the V.I. Lenin (ex-Schichau) and Stocznia Polnocny (ex-Danziger) in Gdańsk; the Paris Commune in Gdynia; and the Adolf Warski (ex-Vulcan) yard in Szczecin. Most recently a major yard was built at Ustka (formerly Stolpmünde). All five yards build commercial ships and some naval auxiliaries. The Polnocny yard produces amphibious ships while the Paris Commune yard concentrates on large merchant ships including tankers to carry petroleum and liquified gas.

As of January 1989, Poland ranked sixth in nations with orders for major merchant ships. A reported 41 ships were under construction, totaling an estimated 1,119,000 DWT. Recent construction programs for the Soviet Union, Poland's largest foreign customer, have included the RO/RO ships, fish factory/mother ships, refrigerated fish carriers, and research ships.

Major Polish shipyard deliveries to the USSR in the past few years include additional RO/RO ships of the 18,462-DWT SKULPTOR KONENKOV class, the 7,496-DWT KURSK-class refrigerated cargo ships (reefers), the first of the 7,578-DWT PAVLIN VINOGRADOV–class general cargo ships,[10] the 3,300-displacement ton research ships of the AKADEMIK FERSMAN class, and the numerous 2,800-displacement-ton tug/supply ships of the NEFTEGAZ design, used in Soviet commercial and naval service.

Polish shipyard workers have generally been among the leaders of political unrest in postwar Poland. The political crises of the early 1980s began in August 1980 when 17,000 workers at the Lenin

shipyard went on strike. The workers sought major labor and union reforms. But one of their key demands was for the construction of a monument to shipyard workers killed by police in 1970 in the riots that toppled the government of Wladyslaw Gomulka and brought to office the government in power when the 1980 unrest began. (The Solidarity political movement, which took power in Poland in 1989, was founded at the Lenin Shipyard during the 1980 strikes.)

Merchant marine. The Polish merchant marine in 1990 had a reported 245 ships of 4,258,000 DWT. These consist of 121 general cargo ships, 14 container ships, 8 RO/RO ships, 92 bulk/ore ships, 7 tankers, and 3 passenger ships. Poland is building additional RO/RO cargo ships and has also purchased ships from France and Spain.

Because of the political unrest in the country, the three shipping lines—the Polish Steamship Company, Polish Baltic Ship Company, and Polish Ocean Lines—have suffered a large number of crew desertions during the early 1980s, as has the large Polish fishing fleet.

There is also a joint shipping venture between China and Poland, Chinsko-Polskie Towarzystwo SA, which operates ships on liner services between the two nations. This liner fleet is equally divided between the two flags, with most ships having been acquired secondhand from other countries.

10. The PAVLIN VINOGRADOV design will be procured in large numbers to replace outdated general cargo and timber ships. This Polish design (B-352/B-749) is being constructed for the USSR simultaneously in Poland (at the Stocznia Polnocny yard in Gdańsk) and at yards in Malta and Spain. The lead ship was delivered (from Poland) in 1987.

TABLE 34-4. POLISH NAVY

Number	Type	Class	Builder
1	submarine	Kilo	USSR
2	submarines	Foxtrot	USSR
1	missile destroyer	mod. Kashin	USSR
1+	frigates	KASZUB	Poland
4+	missile corvettes	Tarantul I	USSR
12	missile craft	Osa I	USSR
8	patrol craft	mod. Obluze	Poland
5[a]	patrol craft	Obluze	Poland
9[a]	patrol craft	Gdańsk	Poland
40[a]	coastal patrol craft	(various)	Poland
12	minesweepers	KROGULEC	Poland
12	minesweepers	T-43	Poland
6+	coastal minesweepers	Notec (GOPLO)	Poland
2+	inshore minesweepers	Leniwka	Poland
23	landing ships	Polnocny-A/B/C	Poland
4	landing craft	Marabut	Poland
15	landing craft	Eichstaden	Poland
2	intelligence ships	Moma	Poland
1	intelligence ship	B-10 (trawler)	Poland
6	tankers	(various)	Poland
2	survey ships	Fenik	Poland
1	survey ship	Moma	Poland
2	salvage ships	PIAST	Poland
2	training ships	WODNIK	Poland
4	training ships	BRYZA	Poland
1	sail training ship	ISKARA II	Poland

[a] Operated by maritime border guards.

The V-33 is a Romanian Poti-class ASW corvette. She is shown here with Tetal-class frigates (left) and a Croitor-class tender (right) moored behind her.

ROMANIA

Romania lies on the western coast of the Black Sea, between Bulgaria and the Soviet Union. The 40-mile (64-km) canal between Cernavoda and the new port of Constanta-South connects the Danube River and the Black Sea, shortening the shipping route by some 300 miles (480 km). The canal gives Romania full control over all shipping entering and leaving the Danube River.

Although Romania has the smallest of the four non-Soviet Warsaw Pact naval forces, it was undergoing a major modernization and expansion at the time of the 1990 revolution.[11] The Navy (*Marina Militara Romana*) had consisted mainly of coastal torpedo and patrol boats until the commissioning in August 1985 of the 4,500-ton guided missile destroyer MUNTENIA, which some Romanian documents refer to as a "battle cruiser." She is armed with SA-N-4 and

SS-N-2c Styx missile systems and two 76.2-mm DP twin gun mounts with facilities for one or two Alouette III helicopters. A second ship of this class was apparently planned but her construction has not been publicly reported.

The Romanian Navy has also taken delivery since 1983 of four 1,800-ton Tetal-class light frigates. And, following rumors that the Navy was seeking submarines, the Soviets delivered a Kilo in December 1986.[12] No additional submarines had been acquired when this edition of *Guide to the Soviet Navy* went to press, although there were reports that at least one more Kilo was sought.

There are more than 70 small combat ships and craft in Romanian service, most outdated or of limited combat capability. These include six Osa I missile craft, 23 Huchuan hydrofoil torpedo craft, and 12 Epitrop-class torpedo craft. The Soviet-built Osas are outdated; the Huchuan-type torpedo boats were built in Romania

---

11. Also see Milan Vego, "The Romanian Navy," U.S. Naval Institute *Proceedings* (March 1989), pp. 144–147.

12. Early in World War II the Romanian Navy had two domestically built submarines and one Italian-built submarine.

Referred to as both a cruiser and destroyer, the Romanian MUTENIA also serves as a cadet training ship. The late President Ceausescu was present at her commissioning in Managalia in August 1985. Launchers— probably for the SS-N-2c Styx missile—are paired on both sides, forward and aft. (Agerpress)

TABLE 34-5.   ROMANIAN NAVY

Number	Type	Class	Builder
1	submarine	Kilo	USSR
1	missile destroyer	MUNTENIA	Romania
4	frigates	Tetal	Romania
3	corvettes	Poti	USSR
6	missile craft	Osa I	USSR
12+	torpedo craft	Epitrop	Romania
23[a]	torpedo craft	Huchuan	Romania
21[b]	patrol craft	Shanghai II	China-Romania
3	patrol craft	Kronshtadt	USSR
2	minelayers	Cosar	Romania
10	minesweepers	T-301	USSR
1	ocean research ship	mod. Cosar	Romania
2	support ships	CROITOR	Romania
3	coastal tankers	(various)	Romania
2	ocean tugs	Roslavl	USSR
2	headquarters ships	FRIPONNE	France (1916–1917)
1	survey ship	FRIPONNE	France (1916)
1	sail-training ship	MIRCEA	Germany (1938)

[a] 3 units were built in China and the remainder in Romania.
[b] Some operated by maritime border guards.

between 1973–1983 to a Chinese design; and the 200-ton Epitrop-class torpedo craft were built in Romania from 1980 onward. More of the last are being built. The remaining small combatants are mostly Shanghai II gunboats.

There are also a few minesweepers in service.

In addition to combat units, the Romanian naval modernization includes the recent construction of two 3,500-ton CROITOR-class support ships, which supplement three older coastal tankers.

For operations on the Danube River there is a flotilla of modern Brutar-class monitors plus some 40 patrol craft.

Naval aviation. The status of the Romanian naval air arm is questionable. Apparently a naval air arm was formed in 1983; it was last reported to comprise six Haze-A ASW helicopters and several French-produced Alouette III models.

Special forces. There is a coastal defense force that is believed to have a SSC-2 missile battalion plus several gun batteries.

There is no trained amphibious assault force.

Command and personnel. Rear Admiral Ioan Musat is commander of the Romanian Navy. The Navy has an estimated 7,500 personnel. Of these, some 3,400 are assigned to ships and craft, 700 to coastal defense, 400 to training activities, and 3,000 to shore support. The helicopters are apparently being flown by air force personnel, although this arrangement is not clear.

Naval conscripts are required to serve for two years on active duty.

Bases and ports. Romania, with the shortest coastline of those Warsaw Pact nations that border on seas, has two major seaports. Constanta, which handles most of the country's overseas trade, is the terminal point for the Ploesti oil pipeline and the country's major naval base. Constanta's port facilities are being expanded beyond the current capacity of handling 60 million tons of cargo per year. The expansion is to the south, toward Agigea, with a capacity goal of 250 million tons of cargo per year by 2000.

The port at Vilovo at the mouth of the Danube—called Ust'-Dunaysk—was opened in 1980 to handle bulk cargoes. Mangalia to the south has recently been enlarged to handle ships of up to 55,000 DWT.

Sulina at the central mouth of the Danube, and Tulcea and Braila on the Danube, have limited port facilities. A new port has been built during the past decade at Calarasi, an industrial center. It is connected with the Danube through a 3-mile (5-km) canal.

Shipyards. The country has four shipyards that build mostly coastal and small seagoing ships, as well as several minor facilities. The significant yards are at Braila, Constanta, Galati, Mangalia, and Sulina.

The Mangalia yard constructed the destroyer MUNTENIA and the Tetal-class light frigates as well as smaller naval craft. Constanta builds large bulk ore carriers. The Galati yard, located on the Danube, constructed two submarines at the beginning of World War II, but subsequent naval construction has been limited to smaller units.

The Soviet Union is a major customer for these yards while several merchant ships have also been built for Cuba during the past few years. Recent programs for the Soviets include the 7,410-DWT shallow-draft tankers of the SERGEY KIROV class, first delivered from 1983.

Merchant marine. Romania's rapidly increasing merchant fleet in 1990 had a reported 304 merchant ships of 5,789,000 DWT. These are 207 general cargo ships, 2 container ships, 11 RO/RO ships, 70 bulk/ore carriers, and 14 tankers flying the Romanian flag for the Navrom line.

Appendixes

APPENDIX A

Naval Leadership

The following is a listing of the known senior officers of the Soviet Navy at the time this edition of the *Guide to the Soviet Navy* went to press. Officers of the rank of captain known to be serving in billets normally assigned to flag officers are listed. (The abbreviations for ranks are listed at the end of this appendix.)

MINISTRY OF DEFENSE

Deputy Minister of Defense and Commander in Chief of Navy	Adm. Fleet	V.N. Chernavin
Main Directorate of Navigation and Oceanography Chief	Adm.	A.I. Rassokho
External Relations Directorate Deputy Chief	Rear Adm.	V.Z. Khuzhokov
Joint Armed Forces of the Warsaw Pact Deputy CinC for Naval Forces*	Adm.	N.I. Khorvin
General Inspectorate General Inspector	Adm. Fleet	G. Yegorov

NAVY HEADQUARTERS

Commander in Chief	Adm. Fleet	V.N. Chernavin
1st Deputy Commander in Chief	Adm. Fleet	I.M. Kapitanets
Deputy CinC for Naval Educational Institutions	Vice Adm.	E. Semenkov
Deputy	Engr. Rear Adm.	V.S. Yefremov
Deputy CinC for Combat Training	Vice Adm.	A.V. Kuz'min
1st Deputy	Vice Adm.	V.I. Zub
Deputy	Rear Adm.	I.F. Uskov
Chief of Ship Combat Training	Rear Adm.	V. Zatula
Deputy CinC for Rear Services	Vice Adm.	I.G. Makhonin
Deputy and Chief of Staff	Maj. Gen. Quartermaster	N.I. Kobelev
Chief Navy Finance Service	Maj. Gen. Quartermaster	V. Belov
Chief Navy Fuel Service	Engr. Col.	Ye. Stankevich
Chief Navy Medical Service	Maj. Gen. Medical Serv.	N. Potemkin
Chief Political Directorate	Vice Adm.	Yu.A. Kuznetsov
Deputy CinC for Shipbuilding and Armaments	Engr. Adm.	F.I. Novoselov
Deputy	Engr. Vice Adm.	I.I.Tynyankin
Deputy	Rear Adm.	L.L. Belyshev
Chief Main Directorate of Ship Repair Plants	Engr. Rear Adm.	A.M. Gevorkov
Deputy CinC/Chief Main Technical Directorate and Maintenance and Repair	Engr. Vice Adm.	V.V. Zaytsev
Deputy CinC	Engr. Adm.	V.G. Novikov

Main Naval Staff

Chief	Adm. Fleet	K.V. Makarov
1st Deputy Chief	Vice Adm.	D.M. Komarov
Chief Naval Personnel Directorate	Vice Adm.	Ye. Yermakov
Deputy	Rear Adm.	S.N. Kokotkin
Deputy Chief	Vice Adm.	Y.P. Kovel'
Deputy Chief	Vice Adm.	I.A. Sornev
Deputy Chief	Rear Adm.	O.M. Kalinin
Deputy Chief	Rear Adm.	V. Lyakin
Deputy Chief	Vice Adm.	Yu. Bystrov
Deputy Chief	Vice Adm.	N. Yasakov
Deputy Chief	Vice Adm.	G. Zolotukhin
Chief Observation Directorate	Rear Adm.	M.M. Krylov

Political Directorate

Chief	Adm.	V.I. Panin
1st Deputy Chief	Rear Adm.	A.A. Penkin
Deputy Chief	Rear Adm.	Ya. Grechko
Deputy Chief	Rear Adm.	A. Karlin
Deputy Chief for Agitation and	Rear Adm.	V.I. Zakhartsyev
Propaganda	Vice Adm.	V.N. Kharitonov
Chief of Staff		
Chief Organizational Party	Rear Adm.	S.M. Yefimov
Work Department	Rear Adm.	A. Kolchin
Party Commission Secretary		

Auxiliary Fleet

Chief	Vice Adm.	V.K. Chirvov

Salvage–Sea Rescue Service

Chief	Vice Adm.	R.L. Dymov

Medical Service

Chief	Maj. Gen. Med. Service	V.V. Zheglov

Inventions Bureau

Chief	Engr. Rear Adm.	N. Popov

Naval Air Defense

Chief	Rear Adm.	S.P. Teglev

Naval Aviation

Commander	Col. Gen. Aviation	V. Potapov
Deputy Commander	Col. Gen. Aviation	V.I. Voronov
Deputy Commander for		
Political Affairs	Maj. Gen. Aviation	M. Produkin
Chief of Staff	Lt. Gen. Aviation	V. Budeyev

Naval Infantry and Coastal Defense Forces

Commander	Maj. Gen.	I.S. Skuratov

NORTHERN FLEET

Commander in Chief	Adm.	F.N. Gromov
1st Deputy	Vice Adm.	I.V. Kasatonov
Deputy for Combat Training	Rear Adm.	V. Poroshin
Deputy for Rear Services	Rear Adm.	V.N. Dobushev
Chief of Staff	Rear Adm.	V. Denisov
Chief Finance Department	Maj. Gen. Quartermaster	I. Burnayev
Deputy Commander	Rear Adm.	A.V. Akatov
Deputy Commander for		
Construction	Maj. Gen. Engr.	V. Zakimatov
Deputy Commander for Civil	Rear Adm.	M. Povedenok
Defense		
Chief of Staff	Vice Adm.	V.K. Korobov
1st Deputy	Rear Adm.	M.D. Iskanderov
Chief Political Directorate	Rear Adm.	A.G. Selivanov
Deputy Chief	Rear Adm.	V. Chastukhin
Deputy Chief	Rear Adm.	V. Losikov
Commander Naval Aviation	Lt. Gen. Aviation	V. Deyneka
Chief Political Department	Maj. Gen. Aviation	V. Pupynin
Chief Military Procuracy	Maj. Gen. Justice	M. Guzeyev
Chief Military Tribunal	Maj. Gen. Justice	V. Bobkov

BALTIC FLEET

Commander in Chief	Adm.	V.P. Ivanov
1st Deputy	Vice Adm.	V. Yegorov
Deputy for Rear Services	Vice Adm.	P.P. Belous
Chief Political Department	Rear Adm.	V. Kabanov
Deputy for Operations &		
Training	Rear Adm.	Y. Chebanov
Deputy for Combat Training	Rear Adm.	M. Putintsev
Deputy for Construction	Lt. Gen. Engr.	O. Anikanov
Chief of Staff	Vice Adm.	V. Kolmagorov
Chief Personnel Directorate	Rear Adm.	A. Petrov
Chief Political Directorate	Vice Adm.	A.I. Korniyenko
1st Deputy	Rear Adm.	P.V. Kashauskas
Commander Naval Aviation	Lt. Gen. Aviation	P.I. Goncharov
Chief Political Department	Maj. Gen.	B.I. Grekov
Chief Military Procuracy	Col. Justice	S. Bernatskiy
Chief Military Tribunal	Maj. Gen. Justice	D. Zhdanov
Commander Tallinn Naval	Vice Adm.	Y.P. Belov
Garrison		

LENINGRAD NAVAL BASE

Commander	Vice Adm.	V.Y. Selivanov
1st Deputy	Rear Adm.	Ye.V. Butuzov
Deputy	Rear Adm.	V. Anokhin
Deputy	Rear Adm.	I.M. Kolchin
Deputy for Rear Services	Rear Adm.	V.N. Bashkin
Chief of Staff	Vice Adm.	A. Ushakov
Chief Political Department		
and Educational		
Institutions	Vice Adm.	A. Steblyanko
Deputy Chief	Rear Adm.	A.P. Prosvernitsyn

BLACK SEA FLEET

Commander in Chief	Adm.	M.N. Khronopulo
1st Deputy	Vice Adm.	V. Larionov
Deputy	Rear Adm.	P.T. Zenchenko
Deputy for Rear Services	Rear Adm.	V. Vasil'yev
Chief of Staff	Rear Adm.	L.Y. Dvidenko
Chief Political Department	Rear Adm.	A. Morozov
Deputy for Combat Training	Rear Adm.	F.T. Starozhilov
Deputy for Construction	Maj. Gen. Engr.	V. Shatokin
Chief of Staff	Vice Adm.	G.N. Gurinov
Chief Political Directorate	Vice Adm.	V.P. Nekrasov
1st Deputy	Rear Adm.	V.I. Popov
Deputy	Rear Adm.	S. Rybak
Commander Naval Aviation	. . . . . .	
Chief of Staff	Lt. Gen. Aviation	F.G. Nefedov
Chief Political Department	Maj. Gen. Aviation	Yu. Sinyakov
Chief of Communications	Rear Adm.	V. Averin
Chief Hydrographic		
Directorate	Rear Adm.	L.I. Mitin
Chief Military Procuracy	Maj. Gen. Justice	V.A. Krotenkov

CASPIAN FLOTILLA

Commander	Rear Adm.	V.B. Leshchenko
1st Deputy	Rear Adm.	V.Y. Zuyev
Deputy	Capt. 1st Rank	V.M. Zhuchkov
Deputy for Rear Services	Capt. 1st Rank	B.R. Knyazchyan
Chief of Staff	. . . . . .	
Chief Political Directorate	Rear Adm.	V.G. Kalinin

PACIFIC FLEET

Commander in Chief	Adm.	G.A. Khvatov
Assistant to the CinC	Rear Adm.	A. Makarenko
1st Deputy	Vice Adm.	E. Baltin
Deputy	Rear Adm.	A.N. Apollonov
Deputy for Rear Services	Rear Adm.	I. Makhonin
Chief Finance Service	Maj. Gen. Quartermaster	V. Novikov
Deputy for Maintenance and		
Repair	Rear Adm.	V.S. Topilin
Deputy for Construction	Maj. Gen. Engr.	V. Skuratov
Chief of Staff	Vice Adm.	V. Kalabin
Deputy Chief	Rear Adm.	V.N. Perelygin
Chief Observation &		
Communications		
Directorate	Rear Adm.	A. Morev
Chief Political Directorate	Vice Adm.	B.N. Pekedov
1st Deputy Chief	Capt. 1st Rank	E. Chukaryev
Deputy Chief	Rear Adm.	V.V. Abramov
Deputy Chief	Rear Adm.	V.G. Semiletenko
Chief Personnel Department	Rear Adm.	A. Shebanin
Commander Naval Aviation	Maj. Gen. Aviation	V.V. Akporisov
Deputy Commander	Maj. Gen. Aviation	P. Ryzhkov
Chief Auxiliary Fleet	Rear Adm.	A.E. Yakimchik
Commander Submarine Force	Vice Adm.	O. Faleyev
Chief Military Tribunal	Maj. Gen. Justice	V. Savin
Commander Sovgavan'sk		
Naval Garrison	Rear Adm.	V. Kuroyedov

NAVAL EDUCATIONAL INSTITUTIONS

Dzerzhinsky HNS (Engineering)	Vice Adm.	V. Kudryavtsev
Frunze HNS	Rear Adm.	A.S. Kovalchuk
Kuznetsov Naval Academy**	Vice Adm.	V.N. Ponikarovskiy
Deputy Chief for Scientific Work	Vice Adm.	V. Kalashnikov
Kaliningrad HNS	Vice Adm.	V. Buynov
Kiev HNS (Political)	Vice Adm.	N.S. Kaplunov
Kirov Caspian HNS	Vice Adm.	V.A. Arkhipov
Lenin HNS (Engineering)	Engr. Vice Adm.	B.A. Lapshin
Leninsky Komsomol HNS (Submarine Warfare)	Vice Adm.	G.L. Nevolin
Makarov Pacific HNS	Rear Adm.	I. Karmadonov
Nakhimov Black Sea HNS	Rear Adm.	V. Denisenkov
Popov HNS (Radio-Electronics)	Vice Adm.	A.A. Rulyuk
Sevastopol HNS (Engineering)	Engr. Vice Adm.	A.A. Sarkisov

MISCELLANEOUS ASSIGNMENTS

Chief Political Directorate, Institute of Military History	Vice Adm.	N.V. Usenko
Deputy Chief for Management, Institute of Military History	Rear Adm.	I. Petrov
Editor in Chief, *Morskoy Sbornik*	Rear Adm.	G.D. Agasonov
Military Attaché, Addis Ababa, Ethiopia	Rear Adm.	I.A. Bardeyev
Military Attaché, Havana, Cuba	Rear Adm.	G.A. Mikhaylov
Air Attaché, Paris, France	Rear Adm.	K.G. Lemzenko
Naval Attaché, Washington, D.C.	Capt. 1st Rank	V.A. Belyayev

Abbreviations of Ranks:

Adm. Fleet	= Admiral of the Fleet
Adm.	= Admiral
Vice Adm.	= Vice Admiral
Rear Adm.	= Rear Admiral
Col. Gen.	= Colonel General
Lt. Gen.	= Lieutenant General
Maj. Gen.	= Major General
Col.	= Colonel
Capt.	= Captain
Engr.	= Engineer

* Warsaw Pact military structure abolished on 1 April 1991.
** Naval Academy *imeni* Admiral of the Fleet of the Soviet Union N.G. Kuznetsov, formerly Grechko Naval Academy; name changed by order of 14 September 1990.

Naval Order of Battle, 1945—1990

	1945	1950	1955	1960	1965	1970	1975	1980	1985	1990–1991
Submarines—*nuclear*										
SSBN	—	—	—	1	9	31	60	70	63	63
SSGN	—	—	—	—	20	36	40	45	50	50
SSN	—	—	—	3	15	23	40	55	86	90
SSQN	—	—	—	—	—	—	—	—	—	1
AGSSN	—	—	—	—	—	—	—	1	3	4
Submarines—*conventional*										
SSB	—	—	—	13	29	25	23	17	15	2
SSG	—	—	—	1	25	33	25	25	16	14
SS/SSQ/SSR	—	—	117	285	259	208	143	155	143	78
SST/AGSS	—	—	—	—	—	4	4	few	15–20	10
pre-1950 classes	241	286	249	131	—	—	—	—	—	—
(Total submarines)	(241)	(286)	(366)	(434)	(357)	(360)	(335)	(372)	(395)	(310)
Aircraft carriers (KUZNETSOV)	—	—	—	—	—	—	—	—	—	1
VSTOL carriers (KIEV)	—	—	—	—	—	—	1	2	3	4
Helicopter carriers (MOSKVA)	—	—	—	—	—	2	2	2	2	2
Battleships	3	2	2	—	—	—	—	—	—	—
Battle cruisers (KIROV)	—	—	—	—	—	—	—	1	2	3
Guided missile cruisers	—	—	—	—	6	10	19	23	27	31
Heavy cruisers (180-mm guns)	7	7	7	5	2	2	—	—	—	—
Light cruisers (150–152-mm guns)	2	6	21	20	12	9	—	—	—	—
Guided missile destroyers	—	—	—	—	6	26	35	36	34	40
Guided missile destroyers (SSM only)	—	—	—	6	12	10	1	1	1	—
Destroyers	41	52	115	120	81	44	36	30	48	—
ASW frigates (Krivak/NEUSTRASHIMYY)	—	—	—	—	—	1	10	27	32	39[a]
Frigates/guard ships	19	29	67	88	56	45	} 106	} 135	} 160	} 168
Light frigates	—	—	—	—	34	64				

[a] Includes six Krivak III–class ships of Maritime Border Troops plus one NEUSTRASHIMYY (BAL-COM-8) class.

This appendix lists the major ships of the Soviet Navy estimated to be in active service at five-year intervals since the end of World War II. Sources vary as to the precise numbers because of differing methods of counting Soviet warships, different dates for data in the various categories, changes in counting dates, and other accounting problems.

Ships operated by the KGB Maritime Border Troops are not included except for the frigate classes indicated above.

Many of the submarines listed in the 1990–1991 are inactive and being prepared for disposal as were eight guided missile cruisers of the Kynda and Kresta I classes.

Naval Ship Transfers

The Soviets have constructed extensively modified Kashin-class missile destroyers for the Indian Navy. These ships—based on a late 1950s design—are more capable than the Soviet units. Today India is the recipient of the most advanced Soviet ships and aircraft being transferred to other nations. This is the Rajput; in the background is the Indian-built frigate Godavari, based on the British Leander design but with Soviet weapons and electronics. (Courtesy A. Prakash)

The Soviet Union continues to be a principal supplier of arms to the Third World, including surface ships and submarines. The current Soviet ship transfer policy has none of the constraints seen in Western arms policies. The Soviets provide weapons to nations that are allies, neutrals, or even historically aligned with the West; they provide new as well as used weapons; the recipient countries may or may not be capable of operating the weapons; and the terms of payment are highly flexible. A graphic example of this policy occurred in January 1988 when a Charlie I–class SSGN was transferred to India, the first time that a nuclear ship was transferred to a Third World nation.

From the Soviet viewpoint arms transfers have as many as five purposes: they can (1) earn hard foreign currency for ships that are built in Soviet or Eastern European shipyards for "soft" rubles; (2) provide the means for establishing a training-support infrastructure in the host country; (3) increase the receiving country's dependency upon the Soviet Union for spare parts and other logistics support; (4) provide a potential weapons reserve in the region for Soviet forces; and (5) create political-military problems for the West.

In many respects the last is the most significant, as evidenced by the cost to the United States of Soviet weapons supplied to North Vietnam during the 1962–1972 conflict, and the more recent arms transfers to such nations as Cuba, Grenada, and Nicaragua.

These arms transfers have not, however, been without problems for the Soviet Union. In some cases recipients have not been able to pay as promised or could not pay in hard currencies, causing a financial loss for the Soviets. By Western standards, the training and support personnel assigned to Third World countries have been of poor quality, while spare parts have been in short supply. The result has been dissatisfied customers and in some instances has strained relations between the Soviets and their clients.

This Soviet-built, Charlie I–class SSGN was the first nuclear-propelled ship to be operated by a Third World navy. Renamed CHAKRA, the submarine has served as a training and evaluation unit for the Indian Navy, which plans to procure additional nuclear submarines, probably through indigenous construction. This submarine was returned to the USSR early in 1991.

At the same time, by establishing major support and even production facilities overseas, as in India (for ships and aircraft) and Peru (for aircraft), the Soviets have made important political-military inroads in those countries. Also, such facilities and spare parts stores could be used under certain conditions by Soviet forces operating in the region.

The current Soviet arms transfer policy had its beginnings shortly after the death of Josef Stalin in 1953. Under the Stalinist regime Moscow viewed the world as bi-polar: a nation was either in the Soviet camp or was against it. Only China, North Korea, and allied Eastern European allies received ships as part of Soviet military assistance in the first decade after World War II.

Stalin's successors, led by Nikita Khrushchev, saw political and economic advantages by recognizing the so-called non-aligned nations. The first major Soviet arms transfer was announced in 1955, with the arms going to Egypt with Czechoslovakia as the intermediary. Previously the Egyptians had been dependent upon Britain for arms. This Soviet arms agreement—valued as high as $200 million by some sources—was thus significant for its size as well as for breaking a Western monopoly. The agreement was in essence a barter deal with the Egyptian government to pay for the arms with cotton and rice over a 12-year period. Thus, much of the major Egyptian crops for more than a decade was pledged for arms that were, in the view of some authorities, of poor quality. Moreover, most of the arms that were transferred in the first year were lost in the October 1956 conflict between Egypt and Israel and the ensuing Anglo-French invasion of Suez. After the 1956 war the Egyptians continued to rely on the Soviets for weapons.

Over the next 15 years a large fleet was provided to Egypt—initially a pair of small M-class submarines were transferred, which were soon followed by several submarines of the Whiskey and Romeo classes. Also transferred were SKORYY-class destroyers, Komar and then Osa missile boats, torpedo boats, and patrol craft. The Komars, each armed with two SS-N-2 Styx anti-ship missiles,

An Egyptian Shershen-class patrol craft—her torpedo tubes have been removed—patrols Alexandria harbor. Some Egyptian Shershens have twin 20-tube 122-mm artillery rocket launchers in place of torpedo tubes; most carry shoulder-held SA-7 Grail missiles.

made history on 21 October 1967 when, from a position just outside of Port Said harbor, they sank the Israeli destroyer ELIAT steaming 13.5 n.miles (25 km) offshore. That was the first sinking of a ship by guided missiles fired from another ship.[1] (Soviet-supplied Styx missiles were subsequently used by the Indian Navy to sink a number of Pakistani ships in the 1971 Indo-Pakistani conflict, including the destroyer KHAIBER.)

By the early 1970s the Egyptian Navy had 12 submarines plus the destroyers (albeit outdated) and missile and torpedo boats, providing a considerable naval capability—at least on paper. In addition, the Soviets transferred Tu-16 Badger strike aircraft armed with AS-1 Kennel missiles; Be-12 Mail and Il-38 May patrol/anti-submarine aircraft; and An-12 Cub electronic reconnaissance aircraft. The patrol and electronic aircraft flew with Soviet crews.

Soviet military assistance to Egypt ended in 1972, with Soviet advisors and air defense units being ordered out of the country. (The aircraft flown by Soviet crews returned to the Soviet Union at that time.) Although the Egyptians subsequently returned to the West as well as to China for arms, the Soviets continue to make most of their arms sales to the Middle East. By dollar volume more than one-third of the Soviet arms sales during 1979–1983 went to Middle East nations—estimated at $20 billion by the U.S. government. The primary Soviet customers in the Middle East are Iraq, Libya, and Syria. (U.S. transfers to the Middle East in that five-year period were $14 billion while those of other NATO nations totalled $18 billion.) The other major areas receiving Soviet arms are Africa (almost $14 billion in 1979–1983), Eastern Europe ($6.8 billion), East Asia ($6.5 billion), South Asia ($5.3 billion), and Latin America ($3.6 billion).

The only other nation to receive as large a Soviet fleet as the Egyptians was Indonesia. During the Sukarno regime, from the late 1950s ship transfers to Indonesia included a SVERDLOV-class cruiser (at 17,000 tons the largest warship ever transferred by the Soviet Navy), a dozen Whiskey-class submarines, several destroyers, and lesser craft. Again, the terms of the deal were simple with long repayment periods. Yet the capability of the receiving navy to operate the equipment was highly questionable; reportedly, some of the ships never left port under the Indonesian flag.

Some of the Soviet arms agreements had significant naval implications even if only minor naval craft were involved. For example, in the period 1968–1976 the Soviets provided Somalia with several torpedo boats and a Polnocny landing ship. In return, the airfield at Berbera was enlarged to handle strike aircraft, and a Soviet missile assembly facility was built. Because of Somalia's location at the southern entrance to the Red Sea and the Suez Canal, this Soviet

1. The first sinking of a major warship by guided missiles occurred in September 1943 when German aircraft launched guided bombs to sink the Italian battleship ROMA.

A Polish-built Polnocny-C LSM, the IBN AL FARAT, provided to Libya by the Soviet Union. Some ships of this class transferred to Third World navies have a light helicopter platform forward of the bridge.

presence had major strategic implications for the West. (Somalia going to war against Ethiopian-backed rebels in 1977 caused embarrassment to the Soviets because of Ethiopia's Marxist government; Soviet aid to Somalia ended and the estimated 1,500 Soviet and Cuban advisors were removed.)

Since the mid-1950s, 33 nations have received Soviet naval ships and submarines. Some, like Somalia, no longer have diplomatic relations with the Soviet Union. The ships transferred during those

The Soviet Union has transferred large numbers of Zhuk-class patrol craft to Third World navies. This is one of 27 transferred to Cuba (of which at least five were retransferred to Nicaragua). The craft's two 14.5-mm twin machine gun mounts are covered with canvas. (U.S. Navy)

A Cuban-operated Turya-class hydrofoil torpedo craft. The Soviets have provided Cuba with naval forces capable of interdicting U.S. merchant shipping in the Caribbean in time of war.

35 years are shown in the accompanying table. All of the landing ships transferred by the Soviet Union—one Ropucha LST and 31 Polnocny LSMs—were built in Poland.

Foreign-built ships of these types are among several sources of ships that the Soviets have available for transfer. The other sources are new construction specifically for foreign navies, new construction of the types of ships in production for the Soviet Navy, and units that have seen service under the Soviet naval ensign.

The most impressive of new construction ships to be built for transfer are the 4,950-ton modified Kashin–class missile destroyers that are going to India. The 61 Kommuna shipyard at Nikolayev has delivered six modified Kashins to the Indian Navy. Another batch of larger destroyer-type ships on order from the Soviet Union was cancelled in 1989.[2]

Also being built for foreign transfer is the 1,900-ton, Koni-class frigate or patrol ship. This ship, oriented toward anti-submarine warfare, may have initially been intended for Soviet service. Only the lead ship, however, was retained by the Soviet Navy, apparently for training foreign crews. The ten additional units built to date have been transferred to Algeria, Cuba, East Germany, Libya, and Yugoslavia. The Yugoslav and Libyan ships have additionally been fitted with four Styx anti-ship missiles.

Another new warship that may become a major foreign sale item is the Kilo-class submarine. This diesel-electric craft, with a submerged displacement of 3,000 tons, was introduced into the Soviet Navy in 1982. Production of this class is under way at three Soviet shipyards for both Soviet and foreign use. (Through the 1980s older submarines, including several built-for-transfer Foxtrots, were provided to other navies.)

A number of other ship classes that are being built for the Soviet Navy are also being transferred. In some instances there are significant modifications for foreign use. For example, Nanuchka-class missile corvettes being sold have the Styx missile in place of the more-capable SS-N-9 of Soviet units, and the Square Tie targeting radar instead of the Band Stand (although the lesser radar is housed in the same dome).

By the 1980s very few older used ships were being transferred by the Soviets. Rather, the Soviet government was committed to providing relatively modern and capable ships to its allies and to non-aligned nations. This policy will continue to cause problems for the West while garnering a number of benefits for the Soviet Union and the Soviet Navy.

2. Some sources believe that these ships were to be SOVREMENNYY-class destroyers; earlier reports predicted that they would be modified Kresta II–class cruisers.

The RANA is a modified Kashin-class destroyer built specifically for the Indian Navy. Note the helicopter deck and recessed hangar aft, twin Gatling gun mounts on each side amidships, and forward-firing SS-N-2c Styx missiles forward of the bridge.

The EL HANI, a Libyan Koni-class ASW frigate, modified with the addition of twin launchers forward, port and starboard, for the SS-N-2c Styx missile; ASW torpedoes are also fitted at the expense of one RBU-6000 ASW rocket launcher. (U.S. Navy)

TABLE C-1. SOVIET SHIP TRANSFERS

SUBMARINES

M VI-*bis* series	North Korea	2 (1950s)
M VI series	China	1 (1954)
M VI series	Romania	4 (1957)
S IX-*bis* series	China	3 (2 in 1954, 1 in 1955)
M XII-*bis* series	Bulgaria	3 (1954)
M XV series	China	2 (1954)
M XV series	Poland	6 (4 in 1954, 2 in 1955)
M XV series	China	2 (1955)
M XV series	Egypt	1 (1957)
Whiskey	China	5 (1956–1957) Note: 21 additional units built in China with Soviet-produced components; completed 1956 through 1964.
Whiskey	Egypt	7 (3 in 1957, 3 in 1958, 1 in 1962)
Whiskey	Bulgaria	2 (1958)
Whiskey	Indonesia	14 (1959–1962) Note: 2 units were purchased via Poland in 1959; the others were transferred directly from the USSR. At least 2 units procured only for spare parts.
Whiskey	Albania	4 (2 in 1960, 2 in 1961) Note: 2 units seized from USSR.
Whiskey	North Korea	4 (1960s)
Whiskey	Poland	4 (1 in 1962, 1 in 1964, 2 in 1969)
Whiskey	Cuba	1 (1979) Note: For use as battery-charging barge, non-operational.
Whiskey	Syria	1 (1986) Note: For use as battery-charging barge, non-operational.
Romeo	Egypt	6 (5 ih 1966, 1 in 1969) Note: 4 additional units built in China transferred in 1983–1984.
Romeo	Bulgaria	4 (2 in 1971–1972, 1 in 1985, 1 in 1986)
Romeo	Algeria	2 (1 in 1982, 1 in 1983)
Romeo	Syria	3 (2 in 1985, 1 in 1986)

Note: Additional Romeo-class submarines were built in China with several of those units being transferred to Egypt and North Korea.

Golf	China	1 Note: Assembled in China with Soviet components and technical assistance; launched in 1964.
Foxtrot	India	8 (1 in 1968, 1 in 1969, 2 in 1970, 2 in 1973, 2 in 1974)
Foxtrot	Libya	6 (1 in 1976, 3 in 1977–1978, 1 in 1981, 1 in 1982)
Foxtrot	Cuba	3 (1 in 1979, 1 in 1980, 1 in 1984)
Foxtrot	Poland	2
Kilo	Algeria	2 (1 in 1987, 1 in 1988)
Kilo	India	8 (1 in 1986, 1 in 1987, 2 in 1988, 2 in 1989, 1 in 1990)
Kilo	Poland	1 (1 in 1986, 1 in 1991)
Kilo	Romania	1 (1986)
Kilo	Syria	1? (1990)
Charlie I	India	1 (1988); returned to the USSR in early 1991.

CRUISERS

SVERDLOV	Indonesia	1 (1962 ex-Soviet ORDZHONIKIDZE)

GUIDED MISSILE DESTROYERS

SAM Kotlin	Poland	1 (1970)
Mod. Kashin	India	6 (1 in 1980, 1 in 1982, 1 in 1983, 1 in 1986, 1 in 1988) Note: Purpose built for India.
Mod. Kashin	Poland	1

DESTROYERS

GORDY	China	4 (1954–55)
SKORYY	Egypt	6 (2 in 1956, 2 in 1962, 2 in 1967)
SKORYY	Poland	2 (1957, 1958)
SKORYY	Indonesia	7 (1959–1964)

FRIGATES

Riga	China	4 (1954–1957) Note: 4 additional units built in China.
Riga	Bulgaria	3 (1 in 1957, 1 in 1958, 1 in 1985)
Riga	East Germany	5 (1957–1958)
Riga	Indonesia	6 (1962–1964)
Riga	Finland	2 (1964)
Petya II	Ethiopia	2 (1 in 1983, 1 in 1984)
Petya II	India	10 (1969–1975)
Petya II	Syria	2 (1975)
Petya II	Vietnam	5 (2 in 1978, 2 in 1983, 1 in 1984)
Koni	East Germany	3 (1 in 1978, 1 in 1979, 1 in 1986)
Koni	Algeria	3 (1980–1984)
Koni	Yugoslavia	2 (1 in 1980, 1 in 1983)
Koni	Cuba	2 (1 in 1981, 1 in 1984)
Koni	Libya	2 (1 in 1986, 1 in 1987)

CORVETTES

Poti	Bulgaria	3 (1975)
Poti	Poland	3 (1970)
Poti	Romania	3 (1970)
Nanuchka II	India	3+ (1 in 1976, 1 in 1977, 1 in 1978)
Nanuchka II	Algeria	4 (1980–1983)
Nanuchka II	Libya	4 (1981–1985)
Tarantul I	East Germany	5+ (1 in 1984, 2 in 1985, 2 in 1986)
Tarantul I	Poland	4 (1 in 1983, 1 in 1984, 1 in 1985, 1 in 1987)
Tarantul I	India	7+ (1987—) Note: Up to 24 units of this class may be on order for the Indian Navy, some to be built in India.
Tarantul I	Yemen	2 (1990)
Pauk	Cuba	1+ (1990–)
Pauk	India	2+ (1990–)

MISSILE CRAFT

Komar	Algeria	6 (1967)
Komar	China	7 or 8 (1960–1961) Note: Additional units built in China.
Komar	Cuba	18 (1962–1966)
Komar	Egypt	7 (1962–1967) Note: Additional units built in Egypt.
Komar	Indonesia	12 (1961–1965)
Komar	Iraq	3 (1972)
Komar	North Korea	10
Komar	Syria	9 (1963–1966)
Komar	North Vietnam	4 (1972)
Osa I	China	4 (1960s) Note: Additional units built in China.
Osa I	Romania	6 (1964)
Osa I	Yugoslavia	10 (1965–1969)
Osa I	Syria	8 (1966)
Osa I	Egypt	10 (1966)
Osa I	East Germany	15 (1966)
Osa I	Poland	13 (1966–1967)
Osa I	Algeria	3 (1967)
Osa I	North Korea	12 (1968–1973) Note: Additional units built in North Korea.
Osa I	Bulgaria	3 (1970–1971)
Osa I	India	8 (1971)
Osa I	Iraq	6 (2 in 1971–1972, 2 in 1973, 2 in 1974)
Osa I	Cuba	6 (2 in 1972, 2 in 1973, 2 in 1974)
Osa I	Benin	2 (1979)
Osa II	Iraq	10 (2 in 1974, 2 in 1975, 2 in 1976, 2 in 1977, 2 in 1984)
Osa II	Finland	4 (1975)
Osa II	Somalia	2 (1975)
Osa II	India	8 (1976)
Osa II	Libya	12 (1 in 1976, 4 in 1977, 1 in 1978, 3 in 1979, 3 in 1980)
Osa II	Algeria	9 (8 in 1976–1978, 1 in 1980)
Osa II	Cuba	13 (2 in 1977, 3 in 1978, 2 in 1979, 2 in 1981, 4 in 1982)
Osa II	Syria	12 (2 in 1978, 4 in 1979, 2 in 1982, 2 in 1984, 2 in 1985)
Osa II	Ethiopia	4 (1 in 1978, 1 in 1980, 1 in 1981, 1 in 1982)
Osa II	Bulgaria	6 (1978—)
Osa II	Vietnam	8 (2 in 1979, 4 in 1980, 2 in 1981)
Osa II	South Yemen	8 (1979–1983)
Osa II	North Yemen	2 (1982)
Osa II	Angola	6 (1982–1983)

TORPEDO CRAFT

Note: Some of the following units were delivered without torpedo tubes for use as patrol boats.

P-4	China	few (1950s) Note: Additional units built in China.
P-4	Romania	12
P-4	North Korea	12 (1952–1953)
P-4	Albania	6 (1956) Note: 6 additional units provided by China (1965).
P-4	Bulgaria	8 (1956)
P-4	East Germany	27 (1957–1958)
P-4	Syria	17 (1958–1960)
P-4	South Yemen	4 (1978)
P-4	North Yemen	4 (1 in 1960, 3 in 1970–1971)
P-4	North Vietnam	14 (1961–1964)
P-4	Cuba	12 (1962–1964)
P-4	Cyprus	6 (1964–1965)
P-4	Egypt	4 from Syria (1970)
P-4	Somalia	4 (1972)
P-4	Tanzania	4 (1972–1973)
P-4	Benin	2 (1979) Note: Transferred from North Korea.
P-4	Bangladesh	4 (1983) Note: Transferred from China.
P-4	Nicaragua	2 Note: Transferred from Bulgaria.
P-6	China	few Note: Additional units built in China.
P-6	Egypt	20 (1956–1968)
P-6	Poland	20 (1957–1958)
P-6	East Germany	27 (1957–1960)
P-6	North Korea	45 (1960s) Note: Additional units provided by China and built in North Korea.
P-6	Iraq	10 (1960–1962)
P-6	Indonesia	14 (1961–1962)
P-6	Cuba	12 (1962)
P-6	Algeria	10 (1963–1968)
P-6	Guinea	4 (1965–1967)
P-6	North Vietnam	3 (1967)
P-6	Somalia	4 (1968)
P-6	South Yemen	2 (1973)
P-6	Tanzania	3 from East Germany (1974–1975)
P-6	Guinea-Bissau	4 (1975–1976)
Shershen	Yugoslavia	4 (1965) Note: 10 additional units built in Yugoslavia.
Shershen	Egypt	6 (1967–1968)
Shershen	East Germany	18 (1968–1976)
Shershen	Bulgaria	6 (1970–1971)
Shershen	North Korea	4 (1973–1974)
Shershen	Angola	4 (1977–1979)
Shershen	Guinea	3 (1978–1979)
Shershen	Guinea-Bissau	1 (1978)
Shershen	Cape Verde Islands	2 (1979)
Shershen	Congo	1 (1979)
Shershen	Vietnam	16 (4 in 1979, 4 in 1980, 2 in 1981, 4 in 1983)
MOL	Ethiopia	2 (1978)
MOL	Somalia	4 (1976)
MOL	South Yemen	2 (1978)
MOL	Sri Lanka	1 (1975)
MOL (modified)	Iraq	2 (1990)(?)

Turya	Cuba	9 (2 in 1979, 2 in 1980, 2 in 1981, 3 in 1983)
Turya	Vietnam	5 (1984–1986)
Turya	Kampuchea	3 (1 in 1984, 2 in 1985)
Turya	Ethiopia	1 (1985)
Turya	Seychelles	1 (1986)

PATROL CRAFT

Artillerist	North Korea	1–2 (1950)
M.O. IV	North Korea	20 (1957–1960)
M.O. IV	Bulgaria	10
M.O. IV	Nigeria	3 (1967)
M.O. IV	Guinea	4 (?) (1972–1975)
S.O. 1	North Korea	6 (1957–1961) Note: 12 additional units built in North Korea.
S.O. 1	China	2 (1960)
S.O. 1	East Germany	16 (1960–1961)
S.O. 1	Iraq	3 (1962)
S.O. 1	Egypt	12 (1962–1967)
S.O. 1	Bulgaria	6 (1963–1964)
S.O. 1	Cuba	12 (6 in 1964, 6 in 1967)
S.O. 1	Algeria	6 (1965–1967)
S.O. 1	South Yemen	2 (1972)
S.O. 1	Mozambique	2 (1985)
S.O. 1	North Vietnam	8+ (1980–1983)
Kronshtadt	Romania	3 (1950)
Kronshtadt	Poland	6 (3 in 1950, 3 in 1956)
Kronshtadt	China	6 (1955)
Kronshtadt	Bulgaria	2 (1957)
Kronshtadt	Indonesia	14 (1958)
Kronshtadt	Albania	4 (1961)
Kronshtadt	Cuba	6 (1962)
Shmel	Kampuchea	4 (1984–1985)
Stenka	Cuba	4 (1985)
Zhuk	Cuba	27 (1972–1985)
Zhuk	Iraq	5 (1974–1975)
Zhuk	South Yemen	2 (1975)
Zhuk	Angola	2 (1977)
Zhuk	Vietnam	13 (3 in 1978, 3 in 1980, 1 in 1981, 1 in 1985, 3 in 1986, 2 in 1988)
Zhuk	North Yemen	9 (2 in 1978, 2 in 1980, 2 in 1984, 3 in 1987)
Zhuk	Mozambique	7 (1 in 1979, 2 in 1980, 2 in 1981, 2 in 1982)
Zhuk	Benin	4 (2 in 1979, 2 in 1980)
Zhuk	Mauritius	2 (1989)
Zhuk	Cape Verde Islands	3 (1980)
Zhuk	Bulgaria	7 (1980–1981)
Zhuk	Seychelles	2 (1 in 1981, 1 in 1982)
Zhuk	Syria	12 (1981–1985)
Zhuk	Algeria	1 (1981)
Zhuk	Congo	6 (3 in 1982, 3 in 1984)
Zhuk	Ethiopia	4 (2 in 1982, 2 in 1990)
Zhuk	Nicaragua	11 (1 in 1982, 1 in 1983, 1 in 1984, 5 in 1986–1987, 3 in 1989) Note: First unit transferred from Algeria; others from USSR and Cuba.
Bogomol	Guinea-Bissau	2 (1988)

AMPHIBIOUS SHIPS[3]

Ropucha	South Yemen	1 (1980)
Polnocny-A[4]	India	2 (1966)
Polnocny-A	Egypt	3 (1974)
Polnocny-A	Algeria	1 (1976)
Polnocny-A	Somalia	1 (1976)
Polnocny-B	South Yemen	4 (2 in 1973, 1 in 1977, 1 in 1979)
Polnocny-B	Angola	3 (1 in 1977, 1 in 1978, 1 in 1979)
Polnocny-B	Vietnam	3 (2 in 1979, 1 in 1980)
Polnocny-B	Ethiopia	2 (1 in 1981, 1 in 1983)
Polnocny-B	Cuba	2 (1982)
Polnocny-B	Syria	3 (1 in 1984, 2 in 1985)
Polnocny-C	India	8 (1 in 1975, 1 in 1976, 1 in 1984, 5 in 1985–1986)
Polnocny-C	Iraq	4 (2 in 1977, 1 in 1978, 1 in 1979)

Polnocny-C	Libya	3 (1 in 1977, 2 in 1979)
T-4	North Vietnam	15 (1967–1969)
T-4	Cuba	7 (1967–1974)
T-4	Somalia	4 (2 in 1968, 2 in 1979)
T-4	North Yemen	2 (1970)
T-4	South Yemen	5 (3 in 1970, 2 in 1982)
T-4	Guinea	4 (1974)
T-4	Guinea-Bissau	4 (2 in 1975, 2 in 1978)
T-4	Angola	5 (1976)
T-4	Ethiopia	6 (4 in 1977–1978, 2 in 1984)
T-4	Kampuchea	2 (1984 or 1985)
MP-6	Indonesia	1 (about 1962)
Vydra	Bulgaria	24 (1970–1979)
Vydra	Egypt	10 (1967–1969)
SMB-I	Egypt	4–5 (1965)

MINESWEEPERS

T-43	Poland	4 Note: 12 additional units built in Poland in 1955–1960
T-43	Bulgaria	2 (1953)
T-43	Egypt	6 (3 in 1956–1959, 3 in 1970s)
T-43	China	4 (1954–1955) Note: Approx. 20 additional units built in China.
T-43	Albania	2 (1960s)
T-43	Syria	2 (1962)
T-43	Indonesia	12 (1962–1964)
T-43	Algeria	2 (1968)
T-43	Iraq	2 (1969)
T-58	South Yemen	1 (1978)
T-58	Guinea	1 (1979)
T-301	Bulgaria	4 (1955)
T-301	Romania	14 (1956–1959)
T-301	Poland	8 (1957)
T-301	Albania	6 (1957–1960)
T-301	Indonesia	1 (about 1962)
T-301	Egypt	2 (1 in 1962, 1 in 1963)
Natya	India	8 (2 in 1978, 2 in 1979, 2 in 1980, 2 in 1986—)
Natya	Libya	8 (2 in 1981, 3 in 1983, 1 in 1984, 1 in 1985, 1 in 1986)
Yurka	Egypt	4 (1969)
Yurka	Vietnam	1 (1979)
Vanya	Bulgaria	4 (1970–1971)
Vanya	Syria	2 (1972)
Sonya	Cuba	4 (2 in 1980, 2 in 1985)
Sonya	Bulgaria	4 (1983—)
Sonya	Syria	1 (1986)
Sonya	Vietnam	1 (1987)
Yanya	Bulgaria	7 (1 in 1971, 1 in 1972; others in 1980s)
Yevgenya	Iraq	3 (1975)
Yevgenya	Syria	5 (1 in 1978. 1 in 1981, 2 in 1985, 1 in 1986)
Yevgenya	Cuba	11 (2 in 1978, 2 in 1979, 2 in 1980, 1 in 1982, 4 in 1984)
Yevgenya	North Yemen	2 (1982)
Yevgenya	India	6 (3 in 1983, 3 in 1984)
Yevgenya	Nicaragua	4 Note: 2 or more transferred from Cuba.
Yevgenya	Vietnam	2 (1984)
Yevgenya	Mozambique	2 (1985)
K-8[5]	Poland	22
K-8	Cuba	1 (1978)
K-8	Vietnam	5 (1980)
K-8	Nicaragua	4 (1984)

TORPEDO RECOVERY/PATROL CRAFT

Poluchat I[6]	Albania	4
Poluchat I	Egypt	2
Poluchat I	Vietnam	2 (1963)
Poluchat I	Iraq	2 (1966)
Poluchat I	Somalia	5 (1968–1969)
Poluchat I	Ghana	4 (1967)
Poluchat I	India	5 (1967–1969)
Poluchat I	North Yemen	4 (1970)

3. The Ropucha and Polnocny amphibious ships listed here were constructed in Poland.

4. Additional Polnocny LSMs built in Poland are operated by the Polish Navy.

5. All K-8 units were constructed in Poland.

6. Virtually all of these craft are employed in the role of patrol craft.

Poluchat I	South Yemen	1 (1970s)
Poluchat I	Tanzania	1 (1970s)
Poluchat I	Guinea	2 (1 in 1972, 1 in 1973)
Poluchat I	Bangladesh	1 (1973)
Poluchat I	Mozambique	1 (1977)
Poluchat I	Guinea-Bissau	2 (1978)
Poluchat I	Congo	2 (1 in 1978, 1 in 1979)
Poluchat I	Algeria	1 (1979)

Poluchat I	Angola	2 (1979)
Poluchat I	Ethiopia	1 (1982)
Poluchat I	Libya	1 (1985)
Poluchat I	Cuba	1+

AUXILIARY SHIPS

A large number of auxiliary ships built in the Soviet Union and Poland have been transferred to other Warsaw Pact as well as Third World nations.

The Soviet Navy has provided relatively few fixed-wing naval aircraft to other countries. This Indian Tu-142 Bear-F ASW aircraft personifies the special relationship of the Soviet Union and India: they are the only nations to fly the Bear.

Flags and Insignia

SOVIET MARITIME FLAGS

National Flag

Naval Ensign

Fleet Commander

Deputy Minister of Defense

Naval Auxiliary

Squadron Commander

Red Banner

Salvage & Rescue

Formation Commander

Guards (Honor)

Hydrographic Service

Formation Commander

KGB

Combat

Division Commander

Senior Commander

Jack

Commissioning Pennant
of an Auxiliary

COMBAT EFFICIENCY AWARDS

The Soviets conduct regular operational readiness inspections of their ships and those rated as outstanding are allowed to display the appropriate emblem. Below are depicted the various awards—these will usually be painted on the bridge, except the individual gun or combat action stations award which is printed on the winning station.

Outstanding Ship
of the Soviet Navy

Outstanding Ship
of a Fleet

Outstanding Ship

Stern Emblem
(Larger Ships)

Individual Guns or
Combat Stations

Artillery

Minelaying

Rockets (AAW) and
Radar

Torpedoes

Rockets (SSM)

Propulsion

Minesweeping

Air Defense/AAW

Rocket and Radar
Technology
(Gold border indicates
three or more awards)

ASW
(circles indicate
awarded by
Fleet Commander)

Artillery
(Gold circle indicates
awarded by CinC of
the Soviet Navy)

NAVAL RANK INSIGNIA
(SERVICE UNIFORMS AND DRESS OVERCOATS HAVE BLACK SHOULDER BOARDS VICE GOLD)

HIGHER OFFICERS

  *

Admiral of the Fleet
of the Soviet Union
(Admiral Flota
Sovetskogo Soyuza)

Admiral
(Admiral)

Vice Admiral
(Vitse-Admiral)

Rear Admiral
(Kontr-Admiral)

SENIOR OFFICERS

"Scrambled Eggs" and
Gold Chin Strap on Dress Service
Caps of Officers
and Service Caps
of Senior Officers

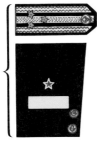

Captain, 1st Rank
(Kapitan Pervogo Ranga)

Captain, 2nd Rank
(Kapitan Vtorogo Ranga)

Captain, 3rd Rank
(Kapitan Tretyego Ranga)

JUNIOR OFFICERS

Captain-Lieutenant
(Kapitan-Leytenant)

Senior Lieutenant
(Starshiy-Leytenant)

Lieutenant
(Leytenant)

Junior Lieutenant
(Miadshiy-Leytenant)

Ornamentation on Collars of the
Full Dress and Dress Coats

Admiral
of the Fleet

Admirals
and Generals

Other Officers

Line Engineering Officers wear the same insignia but with the silver engineering device mounted on the shoulder boards.
* Admiral of the Fleet (not shown) insignia is similar to FASU except the shoulder board has only the large star and the sleeve has 31½ bars above the broad stripe.

ENLISTED SHOULDER BOARDS

AFLOAT

Senior
Chief
Petty Officer

Chief
Petty
Officer

Petty
Officer
1st Class
(Pacific Fleet)

Petty
Officer
2d Class
(Northern Fleet)

Senior
Seaman
(Black Sea Fleet)

Seaman
(Baltic Fleet)

SHORE-BASED UNITS AND NAVAL AVIATION

Master
Sergeant

Senior
Sergeant

Sergeant

Junior
Sergeant

Senior
Seaman

Seaman

NAVAL INFANTRY

Master
Sergeant

Senior
Sergeant

Sergeant

Junior
Sergeant

Corporal

Private

CAP DEVICES

Hat Ribbon
(With Name of Fleet)

On Winter Cap

On Service Cap

On Service Cap
of Naval Infantry

Unit Citation Hat Ribbon
Worn by Enlisted Personnel
Serving In Units or Vessels
Honored by "Guards" Designation

General Index

A-40. *See* Mermaid
Academies. *See* Higher naval schools and
    Naval Academy
Acoustic measuring ships, 270
Admiral Makarov Higher Marine Engineering
    School, 434
Admiral ranks, 71–72
Admiralty Shipyard. *See* Shipyards
AGI. *See* Intelligence collection ships
Air armies
    36th Air Army, 51
Airborne operations, 57, 58
Aircraft carriers
    data, 135–46
    development, 79, 83, 84, 85–86
Aircraft data, 345–70
Aircraft designations, 345–46
Air-cushion vehicles, 2, 57, 87, 215, 425, 429;
    data, 223–27
Air Independent Propulsion (AIP), 86, 93,
    426
Akhromeyev, Marshal SU S.F., 10, 34n
Aksenova, N.P., 65n
Albania, in Warsaw Pact, 446
Albatross, patrol/ASW aircraft, 361
Alexander, Arthur J., 87n
Amphibious warfare ships, 215–22
An-22 aircraft. *See* Cub
Andrews, Walter, 27n
Andropov, Yuri, 41, 150
Anechoic coatings, 92
Anti-air warfare, 30–31, 32
Anti-Satellite (ASAT), 3, 35
Anti-submarine aircraft, 52–53, 361–65
Anti-submarine warfare, 27–29, 32
Anti-submarine weapons, 371–73
Anti-surface warfare, 29–30
Arctic operations, 24
Aristov, Capt. 1st Rank A., 27n
Arkhipov, Gen. Army V., 11
Army
    18th Assault, 57
AS-series missiles, 380–81
ASAT. *See* Anti-Satellite
Aspin, Rep. Les, 28
ASTOR torpedo, 394n
Auxiliary ships, 231–80
Aviation. *See* Naval Aviation

Backfire aircraft, data, 347–48
Badger aircraft, data, 349–51
Baker, A.D., III, 197n, 272n
Baku Higher Combined Arms Command
    School, 61
Ball, Desmond, 33n
Ballistic missile development, 80–81
Baltic Fleet, 16–18
Band Stand radar, 398
Bases and ports
    Arctic coast, 414–15
    Baltic Sea coast, 415–17
    Black Sea coast, 417–18
    inland, 420
    naval, 413–20

    naval air, 50
    Pacific coast, 418–20
Bass Tilt radar, 398
"Bastion" concept, 25
Battle cruisers, 148–52
Battle for the first salvo, 26
Be-12 aircraft. *See* Mail
Be-42 aircraft. *See* Mermaid
Bear aircraft
    Bear-D, data, 359–60
    Bear-F/J, data, 362–63
Bee Hind radar, 397
Belli, Rear Adm. V.A., 25
Beriev, G.M., 229
Berkowitz, Marc J., 61n
Berlin, bombed by naval aircraft, 49n
"Better is the Enemy of Good Enough," 89
Big Bulge radar, 397
Big Net radar, 398–99
Big Screen radar, 398–99
Black Sea Fleet, 18–19
Blinder aircraft, data, 348–49
Bloom, Joel, 423n
Bomber/strike aircraft, 50–51, 347–52
Box Tail radar, 397
Boyd, Alexander, 87n
Brezhnev, Leonid, 37, 44, 74, 84, 86, 87, 88,
    97, 150
    carrier named for him, 137
    icebreaker named for him, 327
    in Great Patriotic War, 18, 56–57
Brigades
    1st Separate Naval Infantry, 56
    Kirkenesskiy, 58n
    63rd Red Banner, 58n
Brooks, Capt. Linton F., 31n
Brooks, Rear Adm. Thomas A., 2n, 27n, 33n,
    35n, 78, 87n, 135n, 282n, 371n
Buffardi, Lt. Col. Louis N., 58n
Bulganin, Marshal SU Nikolai A., 11–12, 38,
    174
Bulgaria
    merchant marine, 447
    navy, 447
    shipyards, 447
Bull Horn sonar, 409
Bull Nose sonar, 409
Burke, Adm. Arleigh A., 13n
Bush, George, 32n, 153
Butman, Dr. Boris, 422n
Butoma, B.Ye., 429
Bystrov, S., 75n

Cable, Sir James, 38, 43
Cable ships, 243–44
CADS-1. *See* Combined Air Defense System
Cake Stand TACAN, 398
Cam Ranh Bay, 8, 20, 43–44, 48, 50
Canvas Bag (radar picket submarines), 127
CAPTOR mine, 377
Cargo and supply ships, 259–63
Carlucci, Frank C., 87n, 359
Carnes, C.F., 33n
Caspian Sea Flotilla, 15, 19

"Caspian Sea Monsters," 87, 229
Castro, Fidel, 41, 42
CBR (Chemical-Biological-Radiological)
    defense, 31–32, 65, 66, 202, 205, 433
Ceausescu, Nicolae, 453
Chapayev, V.I., 158
Cheese Cake radar, 398–99
Chekov, Col. Gen. N.V., 11
Chemical warfare. *See* CBR defense
Cherkashin, Nikolay, 75n
Chernavin, Adm. Fleet V.N., 10, 11, 13–14,
    72, 457
    made CinC, 2
    quotations, 24, 25, 43, 136, 137
Chernenko, Konstantin, 12, 41
Chernov, Ye., 70n
Churikov, V., 68
Cigar, Norman, 45n
Cluster Lance acoustic system, 411
Coastal Missile-Artillery Force, 55, 60, 61, 386
Combined Air Defense System, described, 376
Committee for State Security. *See* KGB
Committee of Defense (GKO), 10
Communication submarines. *See* Hotel and
    Golf classes
Conquest, Dr. Robert, 2
Conscription, 64–65
Conventional Forces in Europe (CFE) treaty,
    48, 55
COOP minesweeper program (U.S.), 213
Coot aircraft, data, 365–66
Corvettes
    KGB, 338–40
    naval, 191–98
Crabb, Lionel, 38n
Craft Of Opportunity Program (COOP) (U.S.),
    213
Cromwell, Oliver, 25
Cross Sword radar, 399–400
Crowe, Adm. William, 3
Cruisers, 147–64
Cub aircraft, data, 366–67
Cuban missile crisis, 82, 432, 433
Czechoslovakia, 447

Dalmatov, Vice Adm. N.N., 335
Daniel, Donald C., 27n
Defense Council, 10
Degaussing/deperming ships, 269
Desert Shield/Desert Storm, U.S. operations,
    45, 263, 431
Destroyers, 165–76
Divisions
    Proletarian-Moscow-Minsk Guards
        Motorized Rifle, 38
    7th Sea Landing (Polish), 451
Djilas, Milovan, 39n
Don-series radar, 400
Dorozhinskiy, Lt. S.F., 48
DOSAAF, 12, 65–66
Down Beat radar, 397
Draft. *See* Conscription
Drum Tilt radar, 400
Dry docks, floating, 280

Ship Name and Ship Class Index

Ships operated by different Soviet agencies may have the same name (i.e., Navy, Maritime Border Troops, research institutes, fishing and merchant marine fleets).

Transliterations from the Russian Cyrillic alphabet are based on common usage, hence there may be differences in some spellings of the same names.

Hull numbers are provided for U.S. Navy ships; the following country abbreviations are used in this index.

Bulg. Bulgarian
Ger.   German
Pol.   Polish
Rom.   Romanian
U.S.   United States

* These ships are officially named ADMIRAL OF THE FLEET OF THE SOVIET UNION GORSHKOV and ADMIRAL OF THE FLEET OF THE SOVIET UNION KUZNETSOV, respectively.

Addenda

The lead frigate of the NEUSTRASHIMYY (BAL-COM-8) design on trials in the Baltic in December 1990. The ship carries anti-air/ship/submarine weapons and sensors. The superstructure is shaped to reduce radar and infrared signatures. However, the masts and the RBU anti-submarine rocket launcher in the "B" position could produce significant radar returns. (German Navy)

The abortive effort of a right-wing coup in the Soviet Union in August 1991 has greatly accelerated the rate of change taking place in Soviet institutions, including the armed forces. Based on his first speech after the coup, made on 21 August 1991, President Mikhail Gorbachev particularly cited the Soviet Navy as having done "nothing wrong" during the coup. However, there are reports that some components of the Baltic and Pacific Fleets did support the coup, although one Pacific submarine is reported to have gone to sea with the intention of not returning if the right-wing takeover was successful.

ORGANIZATION

Immediately following the anti-Gorbachev coup of 18–20 August 1991 it was announced that Marshal of the Soviet Union Dmitri Yazov had been replaced as Minister of Defense by Army General Mikhail Mosieyev, the Chief of the General Staff and Deputy Minister of Defense. Yazov was the only officer appointed to the rank of marshal during Gorbachev's tenure prior to the coup.

On 21 August, however, Mosieyev was implicated in the coup and he, in turn, was replaced as Minister of Defense by Colonel General of Aviation Ye.I. Shaposhnikov, who had become CinC of the Soviet Air Forces in 1990. A former fighter pilot with extensive service as a political worker, he is the first Air Forces officer to be appointed to the senior Soviet military post. Shaposhnikov, known as a reformer and strongly critical of the Air Forces' performance level, was promoted to the rank of Marshal of Aviation upon being named Minister of Defense.

Numerous senior military officers have been demoted or retired in the wake of the coup. Announced changes at the Ministry of Defense level include the following appointments:

First Deputy Minister of Defense: Lieutenant General P.S. Grachev, Commander in Chief of Airborne Forces

Chief of the General Staff: General of the Army Vladimir Lobov

CinC Ground Forces: Colonel General Vladimir Semenov

CinC Air Defense Forces: Colonel General of Aviation Viktor Prudnikov

CinC Air Forces: Colonel General of Aviation Petr Deynekin

Deputy Minister of Defense for Armaments: Lieutenant General V.P. Mironov

Chief of Civil Defense: Colonel General Boris Pyankov

Deputy Minister of Defense (USSR) and Chairman of the Defense Committee, Russian Republic: Lieutenant General Pavel Grachev[1]

Marshal of the Soviet Union Sergei Akhromeyev committed suicide, probably on 23 August 1991. He was appointed advisor to President Gorbachev in early 1989 after having served as Chief of the General Staff and Deputy Minister of Defense from 1984–1989.

On 28 August 1991 the Soviet prosecutor's office charged 13 men with leading the abortive coup, including former Minister of Defense Yazov and Deputy Minister Valentine Varennikov. (Also charged was the former head of the KGB, Vladimir Kryuchkov, and three senior KGB officials: Vladimir Grushko, deputy head of the KGB; Lieutenant General Yuri Plekhanov, head of the KGB guard at the Kremlin; and Vyacheslav Generalov, his deputy.)

When this edition went to press two senior naval officers had been relieved of duty (see below for pre-coup changes in naval leadership):

Admiral V.P. Ivanov, CinC of the Baltic Fleet since 1985; his forces had blockaded Riga during the abortive coup.

Vice Admiral V.Ye. Selivanov, who had recently taken command of the Leningrad naval base complex.

OPERATIONS AND EXERCISES

Admiral F.N. Gormov, CinC Northern Fleet, commanded the Soviet task force that visited Mayport, Florida, for a four-day visit in July 1991. His flagship was the cruiser MARSHAL USTINOV, which was accompanied by the guided missile destroyer SIMFEROPOL and the oiler DNESTR.

This was the third visit of Soviet warships to U.S. ports under the Gorbachev regime.

NAVAL AVIATION

Colonel General of Aviation V. Potapov has replaced G.A. Kuznetsov as commander of Soviet Naval Aviation.

Through mid-1991 an estimated 600 tactical aircraft have been transferred from the Soviet Air Forces to the Navy. These have been formed into nine new naval air regiments.

PERSONNEL

Shortly after becoming Minister of Defense, Marshal Shaposhnikov announced the abolition of party organs (i.e., the Communist Party) in the armed forces and his plan to develop an all-volunteer, "professional" armed forces.

Earlier the USSR Supreme Soviet had passed a decree for implementing the volunteer contract enlistment of seamen and petty officers for the period 1991–1994. The experiment will be conducted in surface ships, apparently centered on the Pacific Fleet, with ship commanding officers selecting men to be given the opportunity to volunteer.

The contract will be in force for a 30-month period for seamen after they have served at least six months of active compulsory duty. Upon completion of their contract service, seamen and petty officers will become eligible for further service at increased pay and allowances.

The Soviet Ministry of Defense on 1 October 1991 announced that the overall strength of the armed forces would be reduced by the mid-1990s to some 2 to 2½ million men and women.

The Naval Academy in St. Petersburg (Leningrad), named in 1976 for the late Marshal Grechko (formerly the Order of Lenin Naval Academy), has been renamed for the late Admiral of the Fleet of the Soviet Union N.G. Kuznetsov.

A State fact-finding commission announced in mid-1991 that non-combat deaths in the Soviet armed forces have averaged 8,000 per year for the past 15 years, with the rate increasing. One-half of the deaths were classified as suicide; 20 percent were due to beatings or other deliberately inflicted injuries; and 10 percent were attributed to accidents. A breakdown of death by military service was not made available.

NAVAL INFANTRY

A Coastal Defense Force has been officially established to absorb Naval Infantry and the Coastal Missile-Artillery Force. Within each fleet Coastal Defense Force there is a former motorized rifle division (four have been transferred from the Ground Forces to the Navy) as well as Naval Infantry and missile-artillery units.

The commander of the Coastal Defense Force is Lieutenant General Ivan Skuratov.

SUBMARINES

The Soviet SSBN strength has been reduced to 59 units: 6 Typhoon, 7 Delta IV, 14 Delta III, 4 Delta II, 18 Delta I, and 10 Yankee; the single Yankee II submarine is being dismantled. The 59 SSBNs carry 912 ballistic missiles.

TYPHOON CLASS

The early submarines of this class are reported to be undergoing modification to carry a new missile; it is not clear if it is a variant of the SS-N-20 or a later missile.

AKULA CLASS

A modification of the Akula-class SSN has been observed, apparently with a raised "hump" or other structure aft of her sail structure. The names PENTERA and PUMA have been identified with improved Akula-class submarines.

---

1. Ministers of Defense have been appointed for several of the republics that were formerly part of the USSR:

Russia	Army Gen. Konstantin Kobets
Azerbaijan	Lt. Gen. Valeg Barshatly
Georgia	Nodar Giorgadze
Uzbekistan	Maj. Gen. Rustam Akhmedov
Ukraine	Maj. Gen. of Aviation Konstantin Petrovich Morozov

TABLE 1. SOVIET SUBMARINE CONSTRUCTION, 1981–1990

Year	Nuclear-propelled		Diesel-electric
1981	1 SSBN	Delta III	1 SS Foxtrot (export)
	3 SSN	Victor III	2 SS Tango
	1 SSN	Alfa	1 SS Kilo
1982	1 SSBN	Typhoon	1 SS Foxtrot (export)
	1 SSBN	Delta III	2 SS Tango
	1 SSGN	Oscar I	1 SS Kilo
	3 SSN	Victor III	
1983	1 SSBN	Typhoon	1 SS Foxtrot (export)
	1 SSN	Mike	2 SS Kilo
	1 SSN	Sierra	
	2 SSN	Victor III	
1984	1 SSBN	Delta IV	3 SS Kilo (1 export)
	1 SSN	Akula	
	2 SSN	Victor III	
1985	1 SSBN	Typhoon	4 SS Kilo (2 export)
	1 SSBN	Delta IV	
	1 SSGN	Oscar II	
	1 SSN	Victor III	
1986	1 SSBN	Typhoon	4 SS Kilo (3 export)
	1 SSBN	Delta IV	
	1 SSGN	Oscar II	
	1 SSN	Akula	
	1 SSN	Sierra	
1987	1 SSBN	Delta IV	4 SS Kilo (2 export)
	1 SSGN	Oscar II	
	1 SSN	Akula	
	1 SSN	Victor III	
1988	1 SSBN	Delta IV	4 SS Kilo (2 export)
	1 SSGN	Oscar II	
	1 SSN	Akula	
	1 SSN	Victor III	
1989	1 SSBN	Typhoon	4 SS Kilo (1 export)
	1 SSBN	Delta IV	
	1 SSN	Akula	
	1 SSN	Sierra	
	1 SSN	Victor III	
1990	1 SSBN	Delta IV	4 SS Kilo (1 export)
	2 SSGN	Oscar II	
	2 SSN	Akula	
	1 SSN	Victor III	
1980–1990	1 AGSSN	Xray	1 AGSS Beluga
	2 AGSSN	Uniform	3 AGSS other types (see below)
Totals	51 nuclear-propelled submarines		41 non-nuclear submarines

Just prior to publication of this edition of *Guide to the Soviet Navy*, the U.S. Director of Naval Intelligence made available at the request of the author a detailed listing of Soviet submarine construction during the past decade. The launches in that period are shown in table 1.

Significantly, submarine production during Mr. Gorbachev's five full years in office (1986–1990) was higher than in the previous five years.

PROJECT 865

Two small submarines with the project number 865 are reported by the Swedish press, based on information said to be provided by the commanding officer of one of the craft. These submarines, also known as the MS 520 series, were constructed in the late 1980s at the Admiralty Shipyard in Leningrad. Although turned over to the fleet in 1988, according to the Soviet officer, the craft are not operational because of technical problems. They are assigned to the Baltic Fleet.

The craft are armed with torpedoes. The small crew size indicates a high degree of automation.

Displacement:	219 tons submerged
Propulsion:	diesel-electric
Speed:	6 knots submerged
Range:	520 n.miles (1,000 km) submerged
Endurance:	10 days
Depth:	656 feet (200 m)
Manning:	3 crew + divers

CRUISERS

"SLAVA" CLASS

The CHERVONA UKRAINA and ADMIRAL LOBOV have the Plate Steer 3-D radar mounted on the forward pyramid in place of the Top Steer in the first two ships of the class. With completion of the ADMIRAL LOBOV there will be no cruiser-type ships under construction in Soviet shipyards.

KARA CLASS

TALLINN renamed VLADIVOSTOK.

KRESTA II CLASS

MARSHAL VOROSHILOV renamed KHABAROVSK.

KYNDA and KRESTA I CLASSES

The four cruisers of the Kynda class and the four cruisers of the Kresta I class have been taken out of service and are being scrapped.

The CHERVONA UKRAINA, the third ship of the SLAVA class, at high speed while en route from the Black Sea to the Pacific Fleet. The four SLAVA-class cruisers are the last warships built at the 61 Kommuna Shipyard, Nikolayev (north). The CHERVONA UKRAINA and ADMIRAL LOBOV have the Plate Steer radar mounted on the forward pyramid in place of the Top Steer in the first two ships of the class.

DESTROYERS

"SOVREMENNYY" CLASS

The Navy accepted the thirteenth destroyer of this class in 1991; construction continues.

"UDALOY" CLASS

Construction of the UDALOY class ends with delivery of the twelfth ship to the fleet in 1991. A modified UDALOY design is under construction; that ship will have one 130-mm twin gun mount, at least two CADS-1 air defense systems, and improved sonar systems.

FRIGATES

KRIVAK CLASS

Several Krivak-class frigates are being upgraded with Half Plate air search radar (in place of Head Net-C) and with an enlarged variable-depth sonar installation; the ships may also be fitted with the quad SS-NX-25 anti-ship missile canisters seen on East German missile craft. The two RBU6000 anti-submarine rocket launchers are being removed to provide space and weight for the missiles.

WING-IN-GROUND EFFECT VEHICLES

ORLAN CLASS

The Soviets have revealed that four WIG projects are currently under way. The amphibious vehicle given the NATO code name Orlan is a joint project of the Sukhoi aircraft design bureau and the design staff at Nizhny Novgorod (formerly Gor'kiy) that has produced hydrofoil designs.

The Soviet designation for the Orlan is A.90.150. Both civilian and naval (amphibious) models have been produced, with passenger capacities rated at 100 to 150 with a single passenger deck, and up to 300 with two decks; the passenger compartment is 82 × 10⅝ × 9⅝ ft (25 × 3.3 × 3 m). A commercial variant could be ready for service by 1993.

The Orlan/A.90.150 characteristics are as follows:

Crew:	5
Troops:	300+ (high-density seating)
Lift engines:	2 NK-8 turbofan; 23,150 lbst (10,523 kgst) each
Flight engine:	1 Kuznetsov NK-12M turboprop; 14,795 ehp
Weights:	takeoff 110 tons
	maximum takeoff 125 tons
Dimensions:	span 103 ft 4 in (31.5 m)
	length 190 ft 3 in (58.0 m)
	height 52 ft 6 in (16.0 m)
Speed:	cruise 248 mph (400 km/h)
Range:	approx. 1,080 nm (2,000 km) with full payload
Armament:	2 23-mm cannon (1 twin)

AIRCRAFT

Su-27 Flanker

The carrier-based naval Flanker is designated Su-27K. This aircraft has *active* canards and a shortened tailcone in comparison with the standard Flanker (in addition to folding wings and tail hook). There is a two-seat naval variant of the Flanker, with side-by-side seating; the earlier, tandem cockpit configuration of the SU-27UB was apparently considered unacceptable for naval missions.

Both the Flanker and Fulcrum (below) are fitted with coherent pulse-doppler radar, which provides a look-down/shoot-down capability, infrared search-and-track system, and helmet-mounted sight.

MiG-29 Fulcrum

The carrier-based naval Fulcrum differs from the standard variants by deletion of the inlet foreign object damage system and the possible addition of more internal fuel.

Yak-41 Freestyle (design bureau designation Yak-141)

The Yak-41/141 is the world's only supersonic VSTOL aircraft and is intended for carrier operation. It is based on the earlier Yak-38 design but is significantly larger, faster, and otherwise more capable.

Although development and production of this advanced VSTOL aircraft was halted in August 1991, the Yakovlev design bureau began a new series of flight tests in September 1991. The design bureau will "bear the costs" of the flight tests, according to A.N. Dondukov, chairman and general designer of the bureau.

The aircraft is capable of both short-run and vertical takeoffs. It has a twin tail-boom configuration; wings fold for carrier stowage. It is fitted with a digital fly-by-wire system.

The first two flight test aircraft had flown about 200 flights, logging some 150 hours from their first flight in March 1989 through August 1991. Two additional aircraft serve as ground test and system integration vehicles. A two-seat trainer version is being built. Reportedly, the aircraft will be offered to India for carrier use; China is also said to have expressed interest in the aircraft.

The following are known aircraft characteristics:

Crew:	1 or 2
Engines:	1 Tumansky R-79 turbojet cruise engine; 34,170 lbst (15,500 kg) thrust on afterburner
	2 Rybinsk RD turbojet lift engines; 5,180 lbst (2,350 kg) thrust each
Weights:	maximum T/O 43,100 lb (19,500 kg) in STOL mode
	maxium T/O 30,150 lb (13,675 kg) in VTOL mode
Dimensions:	span 33 ft 1½ in (10.1 m)
	length 60 ft (18.3 m)
	height 16 ft 5 in (5.0 m)
Speed:	maximum 1,116 mph (1,800 km/h) at sea level (Mach 1.7)
Ceiling:	49,200+ ft (15,000+ m)
Armament:	1 30-mm cannon
	5,732 lbs (2,600 kg) of bombs, rockets, missiles
Radar:	multi-mode

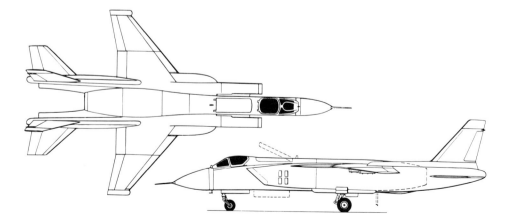

Yakovlev Yak-41/141 provisional drawing.
(Courtesy Pilot Press)

Be-42/Be-44 Mermaid

Designed and built by the Taganrog Scientific and Technical Complex *imeni* [named for] G. Beriev. The Be-42 is the search-and-rescue version and the Be-44 the ASW version.

Crew:	5 (flight crew)
Speed:	cruise 192–240 mph (320–400 km/h)
	maximum 420 mph (700 km/h)
Range:	3,300 miles (5,500 km) at 420 mph (700 km/h)

An-74 Madcap

This AEW aircraft will not be operated from the KUZNETSOV-class aircraft carriers, as first estimated by Western sources. Rather, it appears that an AEW variant of the Helix helicopter will be deployed on board Soviet carriers (including probably the KIEV/GORSHKOV class).

MiG Aircraft

The Soviet aerospace establishment has replaced the traditional MiG designation for aircraft with MIG (i.e., all capital letters). The Mikoyan-Gurevich design bureau (OKB) was formally redesignated as the Mikoyan OKB in 1971, although Mikoyan decided to retain the MiG abbreviation to honor his late collaborator.

MISSILES

The land-based counterpart of the naval SA-N-6 Grumble missile is the SA-10, given the Soviet designation S-300. That missile can intercept attack aircraft at altitudes from 82 feet (25 m) up to 82,000 feet (25,000 m). The system can simultaneously track and intercept six aerial targets, firing two missiles against each. The Soviets claim the same guidance precision as the U.S. Patriot missile system; the S-300 has a large warhead, thus increasing its probability of kill (pK).

NUCLEAR WEAPONS

The Soviet Navy was estimated to have some 7,400 nuclear weapons as of July 1991 (27 percent of the total Soviet nuclear arsenal).[2] These weapons are shown in table 2.

BASES AND PORTS

Stone Island is the location of the SSBN base in the Vladivostok area.

2. Data provided by William M. Arkin of Greenpeace and Robert S. Norris of the Natural Resources Defense Council; the data are based primarily on Western intelligence estimates.

TABLE 2.   SOVIET NAVAL NUCLEAR WEAPONS, 1991

	Launchers or weapons	Warheads
Submarine-launched ballistic missiles SS-N-6, SS-N-8, SS-N-18, SS-N-20, SS-N-23	912	4,000
Sea-launched cruise missiles SS-N-3, SS-N-7, SS-N-9, SS-N-12, SS-N-19, SS-N-21, SS-N-22, SS-N-24	600	600
Strike aircraft weapons AS-4, AS-5, AS-6, AS-11 missiles; bombs	600[a]	1,200
ASW aircraft weapons (depth bombs)	250[b]	300
ASW ship/submarine weapons SS-N-15, SS-N-16, FRAS-1 missiles; torpedoes	500+[c]	1,000
AAW missiles SA-N-1, SA-N-3, SA-N-6 missiles	47+[d]	200
Coastal defense missiles SSC-1	100	100

[a] Backfire, Badger, Blinder, Fencer, Flogger, Fitter aircraft.
[b] Bear-F, Haze, Helix-A, Hormone-A, May, Mail aircraft.
[c] Total number of surface ships and submarines that are nuclear capable.
[d] Cruisers, carriers, and destroyers armed with nuclear-capable missiles.

SHIPBUILDING

The Ministry of Shipbuilding was reported to have been abolished in early September 1991. It is being replaced by a consortium of shipbuilding enterprises.

The cruiser ADMIRAL LOBOV, the fourth cruiser of the SLAVA class, launched in September 1990, is the last naval unit built by the 61 Kommuna Shipyard, Nikolayev (north). The yard is now constructing floating hotels for commercial use.

NAVAL LEADERSHIP

New appointments:

Commander, Black Sea Fleet	Vice Adm. I.V. Kasatonov
Commander, Baltic Fleet	Vice Adm. V.G. Yegorov
Commander, Naval Aviation	Col. Gen. Aviation V. Potapov
Commander, Caspian Flotilla	Rear Adm. B.D. Zinin
Chief, Main Directorate of Navigation and Oceanography MOD	Vice Adm. Yu. Zheglov
Deputy Director, Severodvinsk Industrial complex	Vice Adm. N.P. Pakhomov
Chairman, Navy Committee for Science and Technology	Rear Adm. V. Beznosov

Stern aspect of the guided missile cruiser
MARSHAL USTINOV, showing the large boat
crane aft of the twin funnels (gas turbine
exhausts). The crew mans the rail as the
ship enters Mayport, Fla., on the third naval
visit to the United States under the
Gorbachev regime. (1991, Giorgio Arra)

The guided missile-ASW destroyer
SIMFEROPOL during the Soviet naval visit to
Mayport, Fla. Note the large lattice masts
carrying various electronic antennas,
somewhat reminiscent of the earlier Kashin-
class destroyers. (1991, Giorgio Arra)

The massive, forward pyramid structure of the MARSHAL USTINOV.
The radar antennas are, from right, Front Door missile
guidance, Palm Frond navigation, and Top Steer 3-D air search;
at left is another Palm Frond. (1991, Giorgio Arra)

NORMAN POLMAR is an internationally known analyst, author, and consultant. He has directed analytical and historical studies for the U.S. Navy, various offices of the Department of Defense, Army, Marine Corps, National Oceanic and Atmospheric Administration, and U.S. and foreign shipbuilding and aerospace firms. From 1982 to 1986 he was a member of the Secretary of the Navy's Research Advisory Committee (NRAC) and additionally served on the steering group for the Secretary's analysis of the Anglo-Argentine war in the Falklands. He was also an advisor to the Director of the Los Alamos National Laboratory.

Mr. Polmar has also consulted to three U.S. Senators and one member of the House of Representatives, and has served as a consultant or advisor to three Secretaries of the Navy and one Chief of Naval Operations.

From December 1986 until December 1988, he established the U.S. Naval Institute Military Database, providing an on-line computer database of military information.

Mr. Polmar is the author of twenty books on naval, strategic, and aviation subjects, including the Naval Institute's reference books *Guide to the Soviet Navy* and *The Ships and Aircraft of the U.S. Fleet,* both published at three-year intervals. Mr. Polmar is coauthor of the controversial biography *Rickover: Controversy and Genius,* the expose of Americans who have betrayed their country entitled *Merchants of Treason,* and the best-selling *CNN: War in the Gulf.*

His articles appear frequently in U.S. and foreign military journals and newspapers, and he writes a monthly column on the U.S. and Soviet navies in the Naval Institute *Proceedings.* These and other literary efforts have won him the Navy League's Alfred Thayer Mahan Award and the Naval Institute's award of merit as distinguished author.

Mr. Polmar has visited the Soviet Union and China as a guest of their respective governments, and has traveled extensively in Europe, the Middle East, and the Far East.

THE NAVAL INSTITUTE PRESS

THE NAVAL INSTITUTE GUIDE TO THE SOVIET NAVY
Fifth Edition

Set in Times Roman and Helvetica
by Bi-Comp, Inc.
York, Pennsylvania

Printed on 60-lb. Glatco Matte Smooth White
and bound in ICG Arrestox B
by The Maple-Vail Book Manufacturing Group
York, Pennsylvania